THE HEBREW BIBLE AND ITS MODERN INTERPRETERS

SOCIETY OF BIBLICAL LITERATURE

The Bible and Its Modern Interpreters

Douglas A. Knight, General Editor

1. *The Hebrew Bible and Its Modern Interpreters*
   Edited by Douglas A. Knight and Gene M. Tucker

2. *Early Judaism and Its Modern Interpreters*
   Edited by Robert A. Kraft and George W. E. Nickelsburg

3. *The New Testament and Its Modern Interpreters*
   Edited by Eldon Jay Epp and George W. MacRae

THE HEBREW BIBLE AND ITS MODERN INTERPRETERS

edited by

Douglas A. Knight
and
Gene M. Tucker

SCHOLARS PRESS
Chico, California

SOCIETY OF BIBLICAL LITERATURE

CENTENNIAL PUBLICATIONS

The Society of Biblical Literature gratefully acknowledges a grant from the National Endowment for the Humanities to underwrite certain editorial and research expenses of the Centennial Publications Series. Published results and interpretations do not necessarily represent the view of the Endowment.

Library of Congress Cataloging in Publication Data
Main entry under title:

The Hebrew Bible and its modern interpeters.

(The Bible and its modern interpreters; 1)
(Centennial publications/Society of Biblical Literature)
  Bibliography: p.
  Includes index.
  1. Bible. O.T.—Criticism, interpretation, etc.—History—20th century—Addresses, essays, lectures.
I. Knight, Douglas A. II. Tucker, Gene M. III. Series.
IV. Series: Centennial publications (Society of Biblical Literature)
BS1160.H43 1985   221.6'09'04   84-25936
ISBN 0-89130-784-2 (Scholars Press: pbk.)

Printed in the United States of America
on acid-free paper

CONTENTS

Editors and Contributors x

Preface to the Series xi

Editors' Preface xiii

Abbreviations xxiii

1. Israelite History
   J. Maxwell Miller 1
   I. Sources of Information 1
      The Biblical Texts 1
      Other Ancient Documents 2
      Artifacts 3
   II. Debated Issues 7
      The Point of Departure for Israelite History 7
      Israelite Occupation of the Land of Canaan 10
      The Roots of the Israelite Monarchy 12
      Chronological Data and Prophetical Narratives
      in Kings and Chronicles 14
      The Dates of Ezra and Nehemiah 17
   III. Trends in the Discussion 19
      "Altians" and "Albrightians" 19
      Current Trends 21

2. Syro-Palestinian and Biblical Archaeology
   William G. Dever 31
   I. Syro-Palestinian Archaeology, 1945–80:
      Retrospects and Prospects 32
      1945–55: The Postwar Era 32
      1950–60: A Revolution in Field Method
      and the Beginning of the National Schools 33
      1960–70: A Discipline Comes of Age 36
      1970–80: The "New Archaeology" 40
   II. "Biblical Archaeology," ca. 1945–80: A Critique 53
      The Foundations and the Principal Architects,
      1935–55 53
      The Heyday of Biblical Archaeology, 1955–70 55
      The Decline, 1970s and Beyond 59

III. New Vistas and New Relationships: 1980 and Beyond 61
      Prospects for Syro-Palestinian Archaeology 61
      What Syro-Palestinian Archaeology and Biblical Studies
      Can Contribute to Each Other 64

3. The Ancient Near Eastern Environment
   J. J. M. Roberts 75
     I. Collections of Texts 75
         Byblos, Alalakh, Nuzi 75
         Ugarit 77
         Mari 80
         Ebla 84
         Amarna 86
    II. Areas of Research 87
         Historiography 87
         Religion 89
         Law 92
         Covenant 93
         Wisdom 94
         Love Poetry 95
         Collections of Pictures and Texts in Translation 95
   III. Summary 96

4. Criticism of Literary Features, Form, Tradition,
   and Redaction
   Rolf Knierim 123
     I. Introduction: On Historical Exegesis 123
    II. The Individual Methods 128
         Literary Features 128
         Form 136
         Tradition 146
         Redaction 150
   III. The Unity of Historical Exegesis 153

5. Exploring New Directions
   Robert C. Culley 167
     I. Focus on Text: The Nature of Language 168
         Discourse Analysis 169
         Narrative Analysis 171
         Structural Analysis 173
         Symbol, Forms of Discourse, and Text 179
    II. Focus on Context: Society and Culture 180
         Folklore 180
         Anthropology and Sociology 184
   III. Final Comments 189

6. Israelite Religion

Patrick D. Miller 201

   I. The Decline and Rise of the History of Religions 201
   II. Methodological Issues 211
      Uniqueness versus Commonality 211
      Antiquity versus Late Retrojections 213
      Organizing the History of Israel's Religion 214
      The Nature of the Religion 215
   III. Some Further Aspects of Israel's Religion 218

7. Theology of the Hebrew Bible

George W. Coats 239

   I. The History of the Discipline 240
   II. Old Testament Theology as a Descriptive Discipline 241
   III. Old Testament Theology as a Kerygmatic Discipline 243
      A Cross-Section Method 244
      A Traditio-Historical Method 246
      Hermeneutical Implications 249
   IV. Old Testament Theology in the Context of the Canon 251
   V. A Moral Theology of the Old Testament 254
   VI. Conclusions 256

8. The Pentateuch

Douglas A. Knight 263

   I. A Synthesis and Its Dissolution 265
   II. History of the Pentateuchal Literature 272
      Preliterary Tradition 272
      Literary Development 275
      The Pentateuch as a Whole 286

9. The Historical Literature

Peter R. Ackroyd 297

   I. Textual Questions 297
   II. Joshua to Kings: The Deuteronomistic Work 300
      The Individual Books and Underlying Sources 301
      Stages in the Formation of the Books as a Whole 303
      The Final Form and Its Context 304
   III. Chronicles, Ezra, and Nehemiah 305
      Unity? 305
      The Sources and Their Use 308
      Theology and Purpose 309
   IV. Conclusion 311

10. Prophecy and the Prophetic Literature
Gene M. Tucker 325
   I. The Old and the New in the Prophets 326
      The Law and the Prophets 326
      Theological Traditions 331
   II. From Oral Tradition to Prophetic Books 335
      The Genres of Prophetic Speech and Literature 335
      The Growth and Composition of Prophetic Books 342
   III. The Backgrounds and Origins of Israelite Prophecy 345
      Prophecy in the Mari Texts 345
      The Origins of Prophecy 347
   IV. The Role and Social Location of the Prophet 348
      Cultic Prophecy 348
      Ecstatic Phenomena 350
      The Social Location of Prophecy 351
   V. True and False Prophecy 354

11. The Wisdom Literature
James L. Crenshaw 369
   I. The Elusive Quest 369
      Identification 369
      Appropriation by Modern Interpreters 373
   II. The Book of Proverbs 374
      Growth of Individual Collections 374
      Theological Analysis 376
   III. Qoheleth 377
      The Composition of the Book 377
      The Appropriation of Meaning 380
   IV. The Book of Job 382
      The Emergence of the Book 382
      Theological Mystification 384
      Non-Theological Interpretations 386
   V. The Wider Quest 388
   VI. Conclusion: The Unfinished Task 389
      Trends in Research 389
      Fruitful Avenues for Investigation 390

12. The Lyrical Literature
Erhard S. Gerstenberger 409
   I. Lyrics in the Hebrew Scriptures 409
   II. Text Criticism 410
   III. Lyrical/Poetic Language 412
   IV. Stylistic Features 419
   V. Opinions and Schools of Interpretation 424
   VI. Music, Instruments, and Ritual 426
   VII. Settings and Genres 427
   VIII. Parallels from Outside Israel 431

IX. Dating Lyrical Texts 432
X. Anthropology, Theology, and Influence 432

13. Legends of Wise Heroes and Heroines
Susan Niditch 445
    I. Esther 445
      Date: Maccabean, Hellenistic, Persian 445
      Historicity 446
      Genre: Historical Novel, Festal Legend, Midrash 446
      Sources, Redaction History 448
      Greek Versions 449
      Theology 449
      Style 450
      New Directions 450
    II. Ruth 451
      Date 451
      Language 451
      Legal Information 452
      Theology and Purpose 453
      Unity 454
      Redaction History 455
      Style and Genre 455
    III. Daniel 1–6 456

14. Apocalyptic Literature
Paul D. Hanson 465
    I. The Question of Definitions 466
    II. Time of Origin 472
    III. Sources of Apocalyptic 476
    IV. The Old Testament Apocalyptic Corpus 480
    V. Theological Significance 481
    VI. Concluding Observations 482

15. The Hebrew Bible and Modern Culture
Walter Harrelson 489
    I. The Postwar Years 489
      The Holocaust 489
      The Bible and Political Conservatism 490
      Desegregation and the Bible 492
      Sociological and Literary Studies 493
      The Bible and Women 494
      War and Peace 495
    II. The Ironies of the Bible's Influence 495
    III. Central Biblical Themes 496
      The Themes Stated 497
      The Cultural Impact of the Hebrew Bible 498

Maps 506

Index 509

Editors and Contributors

Peter R. Ackroyd, King's College, University of London, London, England

George W. Coats, Lexington Theological Seminary, Lexington, Kentucky

James L. Crenshaw, The Divinity School, Vanderbilt University, Nashville, Tennessee

Robert C. Culley, Faculty of Religious Studies, McGill University, Montreal, Quebec, Canada

William G. Dever, Department of Oriental Studies, University of Arizona, Tucson, Arizona

Erhard Gerstenberger, University of Giessen, Giessen, Federal Republic of Germany

Walter Harrelson, The Divinity School, Vanderbilt University, Nashville, Tennessee

Rolf Knierim, School of Theology at Claremont, Claremont, California

Douglas A. Knight, The Divinity School, Vanderbilt University, Nashville, Tennessee

J. Maxwell Miller, Candler School of Theology, Emory University, Atlanta, Georgia

Patrick D. Miller, Jr., Princeton Theological Seminary, Princeton, New Jersey

Susan Niditch, Amherst College, Amherst, Massachusetts

J. J. M. Roberts, Princeton Theological Seminary, Princeton, New Jersey

Gene M. Tucker, Candler School of Theology, Emory University, Atlanta, Georgia

Preface to the Series

The present volume is one part of a trilogy, The Bible and Its Modern Interpreters. Together with three other series—Biblical Scholarship in North America, Biblical Scholarship in Confessional Perspective, and The Bible in American Culture—it has been initiated by the Society of Biblical Literature to mark the 1980 centennial of its founding. As a whole, the Centennial Publications Program aims to scrutinize the history of biblical scholarship as well as the very diverse roles that the Bible has played in North American culture. Approximately 150 scholars are contributing to about forty volumes planned for these four series—graphic witness to the current vitality of biblical studies.

Whereas the other three series are devoted primarily to such North American phenomena as distinctive schools of thought, influential scholars, fields of special activity, various confessional contexts, and arenas of cultural impact, the three volumes that make up The Bible and Its Modern Interpreters focus on the full range of research on, respectively, the Hebrew Bible, Early Judaism, and the New Testament. Structured according to the usual subdisciplines and subject matter, each sets for itself the task of describing the course of international scholarship since ca. 1945. The essays are intended as critical reviews, appraising the current state of affairs in each area of study and calling attention to issues that scholars should face in the years ahead.

Deep appreciation goes to each person who has been involved in the planning and producing of this trilogy, most especially to the authors themselves, who have joined in this common effort to reflect on the developments in their fields. We also acknowledge gratefully the cooperation of the two publishers, Scholars Press and Fortress Press, as well as the generous support of the National Endowment for the Humanities.

DOUGLAS A. KNIGHT
Vanderbilt University

Editors' Preface

Biblical studies as a discipline has enjoyed considerable attention since the Age of Enlightenment. To be sure, during the preceding centuries there was also substantial scrutiny of these formative writings of the Jewish and Christian religions. Much of this had had a confessional motivation: the Masoretic efforts to establish a uniform, standard text; the patristic examination of the scriptures in order to develop and defend doctrine; the medieval commentators' exposition of the meaning of the text. However, with the rise of the historical-critical method in the seventeenth and eighteenth centuries decisive shifts in scholarly intent occurred. To complement and sometimes even to oppose the confessional inclinations of previous work, specialists began to emerge who were interested in investigating the Hebrew Bible, the New Testament, and other writings from Jewish and Christian antiquity—all in their own rights and not only as deposits of religious truths. As a result, these ancient documents were studied with the same methods and perspectives as any piece of literature might be, and that meant also that they were probed for all possible morsels of information about the culture, political history, society, intellectual history, and anything else pertaining to the people who stood behind that literature. As have other disciplines in the humanities, biblical studies has gone through a rich variety of methodological approaches, ideological styles, and fashionable emphases during these past three centuries.

It would be a mistake to argue that biblical studies has always developed along evolutionary lines, that is, to suggest that later scholarship is always more advanced, more refined, or more resilient than earlier work. The historian of research is all too familiar with the excesses, the extremist positions, the ideological oddities, the reactionary postures, and the partisan movements. Today, however, our fund of information concerning ancient realia is far greater than that which seventeenth-century scholars had at their disposal, primarily because of the archaeological work of the past century and a half. Moreover, because of the rise of the historical-critical and other methods, we have learned a great deal more than the pioneers in biblical criticism knew about the literature and its historical contexts. Still, even though we are in a very fortunate position because of the work of our predecessors, two matters are equally clear. First, not all moves in previous scholarship have proved to be useful or correct; and, second, almost as fast as puzzles concerning the Hebrew scriptures, ancient Israel, early Judaism, and early Christianity are solved, further mysteries present themselves.

The period since 1945 has seen extraordinary activity in biblical studies; it is this period which the present volume aims to assess. The end of the Second World War marked an important juncture in biblical scholarship in several notable ways. Beginning in 1945, Continental, British, Scandinavian, North American, and other scholars throughout the world could reestablish relationships that had been difficult to maintain during the previous decade. Universities found themselves in a better position to support the humanities, and the number of students and scholars increased accordingly. Gradually the level of publishing activity rose. Also in these postwar years archaeology became revitalized, and several discoveries of immeasurable worth—for example, Nag Hammadi in 1945 and Qumran in 1947—opened up new avenues for understanding antiquity.

Distinctive shifts in the sociology of scholarship itself have occurred since 1945, and these have profoundly influenced the methods, goals, and even subject matter of research. One such shift is demographic, with the growing number of women, minority group members, and persons of the Third World who have finally been able to become students and scholars in the biblical fields. These individuals and groups have prompted an increased concern with such matters as social justice and biblical ethics, and in so doing they have also raised fundamental hermeneutical questions about the dominant interpretational leanings of centuries of white, male, Western, upper-middle-class biblical scholars (see, e.g., the essays edited by P. Trible).

A second shift has occurred in terms of the religious orientation of research on the Hebrew Bible. One finds now a rather pronounced and widely shared support among scholars for a type of ecumenicity which can, at the same time, affirm the particularity of the respective religious traditions. Scholars from all faiths have learned to cooperate and to contribute to one another's research. This is evident in no less significant an undertaking than Bible translating, with committees often made up of adherents of different religious bodies. Especially since the Second Vatican Council, Roman Catholic scholars have begun to play an increasingly substantial role in critical studies, as can be seen in the current vitality of The Catholic Biblical Association of America, and elsewhere as well. Jewish researchers, based especially in North America and in Israel, have also been contributing significantly to international inquiry. Furthermore, evangelical scholars have often sought to make their work a part of the larger critical debate. Of course, within some contexts there is less chance for direct ecumenical cooperation, especially in some of the European countries which have less diversity of religious institutions than exists in North America.

A third shift is more limited to North America and England, namely, the development of many departments of religious studies in universities. Especially when this has occurred in American state universities after the Supreme Court decisions of 1948, 1952, and especially 1963, there has been a requisite absence of any confessional orientation which holds the Bible as authoritative for matters of theology and ethics (see Brueggemann and Knight; and various articles in Barr and Piediscalzi). The Bible could thus evoke considerable interest in these academic contexts, although primarily as a classic and a source of Western culture. More and more students have thereby become exposed to biblical studies, and more impetus has been given to the humanistic investigation of early Israel and its literature.

A fourth shift in the sociological shape of scholarship is the dramatic growth of scholarly societies, which have now become the primary context in which many researchers consult with one another and pursue common interests. While most such societies have grown and become international in membership, one can again take the Society of Biblical Literature, the sponsor of this volume, as an example of changes. In 1945 at the end of the war, the SBL had a total membership of 677; this itself marked a significant growth since the society was founded in 1880 with thirty-five members and eight in attendance at the first meeting. However, in 1980 at the centennial of the SBL there were 4,936 members altogether, and a total of 3,134 persons attended the joint meeting in Dallas of the SBL, the American Academy of Religion, and the American Schools of Oriental Research. There has been a parallel increase in the number of papers presented, and during these thirty-five years the society has also organized its meetings into a multitude of collaborative research groups. Moreover, during this time ten new regional organizations were formed in North America, each holding its own annual meeting as well. Add to this the establishment of a widely diverse publishing program and the formation of Scholars Press, and one can justly be astounded by the scholarly interest that the biblical literatures have come to enjoy (see the history of the SBL now completed by E. W. Saunders; also the discussion in Achtemeier and Tucker).

It is not easy to identify major trends in scholarship on the Hebrew Bible since 1945. Virtually every contributor to this volume remarks that there has been an acceleration of interest in the particular field in question. To be sure, the increase in the number of publications does not mean that the state of our understanding has been proportionately advanced, and the contributors have observed proper caution not to give a facile assessment of the present state of the art in each case. In looking at the whole, one can observe certain prominent features in the study of the Hebrew Bible since 1945:

(1) The 1950s and early 1960s witnessed a high interest in hermeneutical questions, but since that time the focus has shifted to methodological issues. Many exegetical manuals now exist, as well as numerous
theoretical studies of finer points of method. The so-called historical-
critical approach has come under fire from both sides—from those who
advocate other methods such as sociology, the "new" literary criticism, or
structuralism, on the one hand, and from those who call for a renewed
attention to the canonical shaping of the Hebrew Bible, on the other.
Nonetheless, interest in the more traditional methods of source criticism,
form criticism, tradition criticism, and redaction criticism has not
flagged, even if these methods need to be applied now with altered perspectives. We may well be on the way toward a paradigm shift—from
the historical to the linguistic—or at least toward a type of study that
attends to more facets of the texts and of Hebrew antiquity than earlier
scholarship considered.

(2) Text criticism has been revitalized by numerous new inscriptional and manuscript finds, from the discoveries in the Judean desert to
the recovery of the Aleppo Codex. One new critical edition of the
Hebrew Bible has already been completed (*Biblia Hebraica Stuttgarten-
sia*) and another started (*The Hebrew University Bible*). Work continues
on the Septuagint project in Göttingen, and critical editions of other
versions are newly in publication or in process. Similarly, there has been
extraordinary activity in the domain of translation, and numerous new
versions of the Bible are now available, most of which are based on careful scholarship.

(3) Archaeology has acquired new dimensions in several respects—
the sheer number of excavations, the expanded methods of the "new
archaeology," and its relative autonomy from the earlier conception of
"biblical archaeology." Digging has increased not only in Israel but also
in Jordan, Syria, and elsewhere. One of the most intriguing sites for
scholars of ancient Israel—even if its heyday seems to have occurred
nearly a millennium before the Israelites settled the Canaanite highlands—is Ebla, Tell Mardikh in Syria. Such interest, in fact, reflects two
continuing characteristics of Hebrew Bible studies, the alertness to phenomena in the wider world of the ancient Near East on the one hand
and the very unsettled question about the origin of Israel on the other. In
general, historians and sociologists have become more interested in the
everyday realia of Israel's social world, including life among the lower
classes, than was previously the case, and the "new archaeology" has
complied by sifting the dirt for more than simply the evidence of monumental architecture and wealthy culture. A variegated picture is emerging from this, yet also more questions and puzzles to investigate.

(4) The religious beliefs and practices of the ancient Israelites have
nearly always occupied a prominent position in scholarship, and several

general treatments have appeared since 1945. However, there has been less inquiry into the full range of issues than previous decades witnessed. Form-critical and traditio-historical work has indeed focused on specific festivals, sanctuaries, and cultic functionaries, but in such studies these phenomena are examined primarily with respect to the question of where and how certain literary traditions might have developed. Rather different from this, however, has been the investigation of the relationship between Israel-ite and "Canaanite" religion in light of the Ugaritic texts. Concerning theo-logical inquiry, much of the work during our period has also been affected by the study of the history of Israel's literature, ranging variously from the early stages of tradition development, to the composition of larger literary blocks on the basis of certain theological intentions, and on to the canonical level of this literary growth. The major alternative approach has been to examine the Israelite religious thought world in terms of overarching themes or problems, such as covenant, the salvific acts of God, or theodicy. In contrast, there has been remarkably little study of the ethics of ancient Israel, an area which will demand much more attention in the future on the basis of current sociological work as well as the traditional disciplines of philosophical and theological ethics.

(5) Philology has, as before, been a very active field of study, not the least because of the Ugaritic texts that have continued to emerge since 1929. Comparative Semitic philology has been able to draw on new studies in almost all of the known languages of the Fertile Crescent, including comprehensive lexical projects in several of them. Futhermore, especially since the early 1960s scholars have attended to the more theo-retical aspects of linguistics and philology so as to avoid some of the errors in earlier work. A new major critical dictionary of Hebrew has been published and is now undergoing a full revision, two large "theo-logical dictionaries" have been developed, and a few new grammars have also appeared. Considerably more work is yet to be done at both specific and general levels, but there seems to be no lack of willing and competent scholars who are trying to keep apace with the constant flow of new literary materials from the ancient Near East. The computer has become a valuable tool for, above all, fresh work in concordances and the study of various linguistic data.

(6) The publication of commentaries on biblical books is indicative of the increased activity in research. When the era began in 1945 there was relatively little interest in commentaries, either among scholars or among others—at least if publishers' lists can be considered an accurate indication. Virtually no scholarly series in English was in process, although various European languages were in a better position: Hand-buch zum Alten Testament (HAT), Züricher Bibelkommentare, La sainte Bible, Korte Verklaring der Heilige Schrift. In the United States in the early 1950s *The Interpreter's Bible* (*IB*) began to appear, its format and

aim reflecting the perspective of the so-called biblical theology approach of the time. Other commentary series initiated in that first decade after the war included the Soncino Books of the Bible, Das Alte Testament deutsch (ATD), the New International Commentary on the Old Testament (NICOT), and the Torch Bible Commentaries. In the production of critical scholarly commentaries thereafter, Germany led the way with the Biblischer Kommentar zum Alten Testament (BKAT) and the Kommentar zum Alten Testament (KAT; 2d series). The Old Testament Library series (OTL), begun in 1961 jointly in England and the United States, found it appropriate to draw on Das Alte Testament deutsch for most of its initial volumes. Other English-language series included the Cambridge Bible Commentary on the New English Bible, the Anchor Bible (AB), the New Century Bible (NCB), and the Layman's Bible Commentary. The situation has shifted dramatically with several new series in English commenced since 1970, such as Hermeneia, Interpretation, and The Forms of the Old Testament Literature, as well as others designed explicitly for ministers/priests/rabbis or for laity. Similar activity has occurred in other countries and languages. One must view this as a positive and encouraging development, reflecting increased interest in both the Bible and its critical interpretation.

Such scholarly activity and interest since 1945 constitute the subject matter scrutinized in the present volume. There are several notable predecessors that have reconstructed parts of the history of research on the Hebrew Bible. The classic study by Ludwig Diestel (1869) provided a detailed interpretation of scholarship conducted in the some eighteen centuries up to his time. More recently, Hans-Joachim Kraus (1956, revised 1969, 3d ed., 1982) and Emil G. Kraeling (1955) turned their attention to the period since the Reformation, following the line chronologically up to the present. Rather differently, Herbert F. Hahn (1954) organized his overview of the scholarship of the preceding century according to various methodological approaches or subdisciplines, such as anthropology, history of religion, form criticism, sociology, archaeology, and theology. Hahn's scheme of presentation is rather similar to that of the series of volumes issued by the Society for Old Testament Study: *The People and the Book*, edited by A. S Peake (1925); *Record and Revelation*, edited by H. Wheeler Robinson (1938); *The Old Testament and Modern Study*, edited by H. H. Rowley (1951); and most recently, *Tradition and Interpretation*, edited by George W. Anderson (1979). Each of these includes chapters written by various members of SOTS, and each volume focuses its attention on the immediately preceding generation of research. Together they provide a valuable survey of the discipline during much of this century. Augmenting the inclusive overviews such as these are many separate articles and monographs which retrace the history of scholarship in some specific subdiscipline (e.g., Semitic philology, Syro-Palestinian archaeology, or form criticism) or on a block of material (e.g., the ancestral literature, the Psalms, or Israelite religion). In addition, there exist a good number of studies on individual scholars who have made especially important contributions to our understanding of the Hebrew Bible; one thinks, for example, of the volumes devoted to the work of Richard Simon, Johann Gottfried Herder, Wilhelm Martin Leberecht de Wette, Julius Wellhausen, W. Robertson Smith, Hermann Gunkel, and Gerhard von Rad. The SBL Centennial Publications Program includes also a series entitled Biblical Scholarship in North America, which in its two parts is publishing monographs on disciplines and scholars especially prominent in the North American context.

Parallel to the other two volumes in this series, The Bible and Its Modern Interpreters, the present set of essays has established 1945 as the approximate terminus a quo for the scholarship assessed. However, this date is not a rigid boundary, for at many if not most points the status quo ante is crucial for the discussion. Furthermore, the assessments in each chapter do not intend to be regionally parochial, for the range of international scholarship deserves attention if one is to describe the course of biblical scholarship. Each chapter includes both review and critique of developments in the given field of inquiry. Under the rubric of review, authors attempt to describe the areas in which scholarly effort has concentrated and thereby to depict the state of the discipline by the beginning of the 1980s. Research directions, trends, and any attainment of consensus are noted, as is also any significant division of scholars into schools or camps. While each essay surveys an enormous number of publications, it does so with the purpose of interpreting the gains of scholarship rather than simply reviewing the published literature. The bibliography that concludes each chapter has been deliberately pruned to include only those titles to which specific reference is made in the discussion. The critical dimension of these reviews can also be seen at the many points where the contributors indicate that the discipline has taken wrong turns, has violated its own limitations, or has been avoiding important problems. In other words, these appraisals are not self-congratulatory, even though they do not hesitate to emphasize the clear gains that scholars have made. The authors have, in addition, attempted to draw attention to specific problems and areas which future scholarship needs to address.

One can readily observe that the volume has been organized according to traditional "subdisciplines" in the study of the Hebrew Bible. The chapters progress from history and archaeology to methods of interpretation, religion and theology, and on to the larger literary blocks, concluding with a discussion of the Hebrew Bible in the modern world.

The editors wish to express deep appreciation to all who had a part in bringing this project to a conclusion. The individual contributors have cooperated remarkably, especially in the face of delays in the publication of the volume. Several completed their essays in 1980 when they were first requested, and we have generally held this date as the terminus ad quem for all other discussions, with only minimal updating allowed throughout. We wish also to thank publicly several of our graduate students who have assisted in the editorial work: Andrew Dearman, Gail Preston, and Steven Reid at Emory University; and Joanne Kuemmerlin, Richard McLean, and Stephen Scott at Vanderbilt University. Paula McNutt of Vanderbilt has kindly drawn the two maps, which readers will find helpful for several of the chapters. Maurya Horgan and Paul Kobelski of Denver have made invaluable contributions in the final preparation of the entire manuscript for the press. Special gratitude goes also to Fortress Press, Philadelphia, for joining Scholars Press in this publishing venture. Finally, on behalf of the SBL we wish to express our appreciation to the National Endowment for the Humanities for supporting various editorial and research expenses of this volume and others in the SBL Centennial Publications Series. We hope that this work will contribute to the self-understanding and ongoing tasks of scholarship on the Hebrew Bible.

DOUGLAS A. KNIGHT
GENE M. TUCKER

WORKS CITED

Achtemeier, Paul J., and Gene M. Tucker
    1980   "Biblical Studies: The State of the Discipline." *BCSR* 11: 72–76.

Anderson, George W., ed.
    1979   *Tradition and Interpretation: Essays by Members of the Society for Old Testament Study.* Oxford: Clarendon.

Barr, David L., and Nicholas Piediscalzi, eds.
    1982   *The Bible in American Education: From Source Book to Textbook.* SBL The Bible in American Culture, 5. Philadelphia: Fortress Press; Chico, CA: Scholars Press.

Brueggemann, Walter, and Douglas A. Knight
    1980   "Why Study the Bible?" *BCSR* 11: 76–81.

Diestel, Ludwig
    1869   *Geschichte des Alten Testaments in der christlichen Kirche.* Jena: Mauke's Verlag.

Hahn, Herbert F.
    1954   *The Old Testament in Modern Research.* Philadelphia: Muhlenberg.

Kraeling, Emil G.
1955   *The Old Testament Since the Reformation.* London: Lutterworth.

Kraus, Hans-Joachim
1956   *Geschichte der historisch-kritischen Erforschung des Alten Testaments von der Reformation bis zur Gegenwart.* Neukirchen: Verlag der Buchhandlung des Erziehungsvereins. 2d ed., 1969. 3d ed., 1982.

Peake, Arthur S., ed.
1925   *The People and the Book.* Oxford: Clarendon.

Robinson, H. Wheeler, ed.
1938   *Record and Revelation: Essays on the Old Testament by Members of the Society for Old Testament Study.* Oxford: Clarendon.

Rowley, H. H., ed.
1951   *The Old Testament and Modern Study: A Generation of Discovery and Research.* London/Oxford/New York: Oxford University.

Saunders, Ernest W.
1982   *Searching the Scriptures: A History of the Society of Biblical Literature, 1880–1980.* SBL Biblical Scholarship in North America, 8. Chico, CA: Scholars Press.

Trible, Phyllis, ed.
1982   "The Effects of Women's Studies on Biblical Studies," with contributions by Dorothy C. Bass, Katherine Doob Sakenfeld, Mary K. Wakeman, Elizabeth Schüssler Fiorenza, Adela Yarbro Collins, Rosemary Radford Ruether, and Letty M. Russell. *JSOT* 22: 3–71.

Abbreviations

AASF	Annales academiae scientiarum fennicae
AB	Anchor Bible
ACOR	American Center for Oriental Research
AfO	*Archiv für Orientforschung*
AJA	*American Journal of Archaeology*
AnBib	Analecta biblica
ANET	*Ancient Near Eastern Texts*, ed. J. B. Pritchard
AnOr	Analecta orientalia
AOAT	Alter Orient und Altes Testament
AOATS	Alter Orient und Altes Testament, Sonderreihe
AOS	American Oriental Series
ARM	*Archives royale de Mari*
AS	Assyriological Studies
ASOR	American Schools of Oriental Research
ASTI	*Annual of the Swedish Theological Institute*
ATAbh	Alttestamentliche Abhandlungen
ATANT	Abhandlungen zur Theologie des Alten und Neuen Testaments
ATD	Das Alte Testament deutsch
ATDan	Acta theologica danica
ATR	*Anglican Theological Review*
BA	*Biblical Archaeologist*
BARev	*Biblical Archaeology Review*
BASOR	*Bulletin of the American Schools of Oriental Research*
BBB	Bonner biblische Beiträge
BCSR	*Bulletin of the Council on the Study of Religion*
BDB	F. Brown, S. R. Driver, and C. A. Briggs, *A Hebrew and English Lexicon of the Old Testament*
BETL	Bibliotheca ephemeridum theologicarum lovaniensium
BEvT	Beiträge zur evangelischen Theologie
BHS	*Biblia hebraica stuttgartensia*
Bib	*Biblica*
BibB	Biblische Beiträge
BibLeb	*Bibel und Leben*
BibOr	Biblica et orientalia

BibS(N)	Biblische Studien (Neukirchen-Vluyn)
BJRL	Bulletin of the John Rylands University Library of Manchester
BKAT	Biblischer Kommentar: Altes Testament
BO	Bibliotheca orientalis
BR	Biblical Research
BSac	Bibliotheca Sacra
BT	The Bible Translator
BWANT	Beiträge zur Wissenschaft vom Alten und Neuen Testament
BZ	Biblische Zeitschrift
BZAW	Beihefte zur ZAW
CAT	Commentaire de l'Ancien Testament
CBC	Cambridge Bible Commentary
CBQ	Catholic Biblical Quarterly
ConBOT	Coniectanea biblica, Old Testament
CRAIBL	Comptes rendus de l'académie des inscriptions et belles-lettres
CRB	Cahiers de la RB
CTM	Concordia Theological Monthly
DBSup	Supplément au Dictionnaire de la Bible
EB	Echter Bibel
EdF	Erträge der Forschung
EKL	Evangelisches Kirchenlexikon
EncJud	Encyclopedia Judaica
EstBib	Estudios bíblicos
ETL	Ephemerides theologicae lovanienses
EvT	Evangelische Theologie
ExpTim	Expository Times
FRLANT	Forschungen zur Religion und Literatur des Alten und Neuen Testaments
HAT	Handbuch zum Alten Testament
HDR	Harvard Dissertations in Religion
HO	Handbuch der Orientalistik
HSM	Harvard Semitic Monographs
HTR	Harvard Theological Review
HUCA	Hebrew Union College Annual
HUCM	Monographs of the Hebrew Union College
IB	The Interpreter's Bible
ICC	International Critical Commentary
IDB	Interpreter's Dictionary of the Bible
IDBSup	Supplementary Volume to IDB
IEJ	Israel Exploration Journal
Int	Interpretation

IOSCS	International Organization for Septuagint and Cognate Studies
ITQ	*Irish Theological Quarterly*
JAAR	*Journal of the American Academy of Religion*
JANESCU	*Journal of the Ancient Near Eastern Society of Columbia University*
JAOS	*Journal of the American Oriental Society*
JBL	*Journal of Biblical Literature*
JBR	*Journal of Bible and Religion*
JCS	*Journal of Cuneiform Studies*
JDT	*Jahrbuch für deutsche Theologie*
JEA	*Journal of Egyptian Archaeology*
JNES	*Journal of Near Eastern Studies*
JPOS	*Journal of the Palestine Oriental Society*
JQR	*Jewish Quarterly Review*
JR	*Journal of Religion*
JSOT	*Journal for the Study of the Old Testament*
JSOTSup	*JSOT*, Supplement
JSS	*Journal of Semitic Studies*
JTC	*Journal for Theology and the Church*
JTS	*Journal of Theological Studies*
KAT	Kommentar zum Alten Testament
KD	*Kerygma und Dogma*
Kl. Schr.	*Kleine Schriften*
LUÅ	Lunds universitets årsskrift
MDOG	Mitteilungen der deutschen Orient-Gesellschaft
MGWJ	*Monatsschrift für Geschichte und Wissenschaft des Judentums*
MIO	*Mitteilungen des Instituts für Orientforschung*
MRS	Mission de Ras Shamra
NCB	New Century Bible
NICOT	New International Commentary on the Old Testament
OBO	Orbis biblicus et orientalis
Or	*Orientalia*
OrAnt	*Oriens antiquus*
OTL	Old Testament Library
OTS	*Oudtestamentische Studiën*
OTWSA	*Die Ou Testamentiese Werkgemeenskap in Suid-Afrika*
PEQ	*Palestine Exploration Quarterly*
PRU	*Le Palais Royal d'Ugarit*
PTMS	Pittsburgh Theological Monograph Series
RA	*Revue d'assyriologie et d'archéologie orientale*

RAI	Rencontre Assyriologique Internationale
RB	*Revue biblique*
RGG	*Die Religion in Geschichte und Gegenwart*, ed. K. Galling
RHA	*Revue hittite et asianique*
RHPR	*Revue d'histoire et de philosophie religieuses*
RLA	*Reallexikon der Assyriologie*
RoB	*Religion och Bibel*
RSO	*Rivisti degli studi orientali*
RTP	*Revue de théologie et de philosophie*
SANT	Studien zum Alten und Neuen Testament
SB	Sources bibliques
SBFLA	*Studii biblici franciscani liber annuus*
SBLDS	Society of Biblical Literature Dissertation Series
SBLMS	Society of Biblical Literature Monograph Series
SBLSBS	Society of Biblical Literature Sources for Biblical Study
SBS	Stuttgarter Bibelstudien
SBT	Studies in Biblical Theology
SEÅ	*Svensk exegetisk årsbok*
Sem	*Semitica*
SHVL	Skrifter utgivna av Kungl. Humanistiska Vetenskapssamfundet i Lund
SJLA	Studies in Judaism in Late Antiquity
SJT	*Scottish Journal of Theology*
SNTSMS	Society for New Testament Studies Monograph Series
SNVAO	Skrifter utgitt av Det Norske Videnskaps-Akademi i Oslo
SOTSMS	Society for Old Testament Studies Monograph Series
SPAW	Sitzungsberichte der preussischen Akademie der Wissenschaften
SQAW	Schriften und Quellen der alten Welt
SR	*Studies in Religion/Sciences religieuses*
SSN	Studia semitica neerlandica
ST	*Studia theologica*
SUNT	Studien zur Umwelt des Neuen Testaments
TBü	Theologische Bücherei
TD	*Theology Digest*
TLZ	*Theologische Literaturzeitung*
TRE	*Theologische Real-enzyklopädie*
TRu	*Theologische Rundschau*
TSK	*Theologische Studien und Kritiken*
TToday	*Theology Today*
TTZ	*Trierer theologische Zeitschrift*

TynBul	*Tyndale Bulletin*
TZ	*Theologische Zeitschrift*
UF	*Ugarit-Forschungen*
USQR	*Union Seminary Quarterly Review*
VD	*Verbum Domini*
VF	*Verkündigung und Forschung*
VT	*Vetus Testamentum*
VTSup	Vetus Testamentum, Supplements
WMANT	Wissenschaftliche Monographien zum Alten und Neuen Testament
WO	*Die Welt des Orients*
WTJ	*Westminster Theological Journal*
WZKM	*Wiener Zeitschrift für de Kunde des Morgenlandes*
ZA	*Zeitschrift für Assyriologie*
ZAW	*Zeitschrift für die alttestamenliche Wissenschaft*
ZDPV	*Zeitschrift des deutschen Palästina-Vereins*
ZTK	*Zeitschrift für Theologie und Kirche*

1

Israelite History

J. Maxwell Miller

I. SOURCES OF INFORMATION

The basic information available for writing a history of ancient Israel has not increased significantly since 1945. Primary data specifically relevant to this task are derived from three categories of sources: the biblical texts, other ancient Middle Eastern documents, and artifacts uncovered by archaeologists.

The Biblical Texts

The biblical account remains our primary source of information. Were we dependent upon other ancient documents and archaeological evidence available today, we would know very little more about ancient Israel than we know about the Ammonites, the Moabites, or the Edomites. Indeed, most of our information about these latter peoples is derived from the Bible also. Obviously the biblical texts have not expanded in size or content since 1945, and there have been no radically new developments in the methods by which scholars approach these texts. However, several critical studies have been published since the mid-1940s which have significant implications for using the biblical materials for reconstructing history. One thinks, for example, of M. Noth's *Überlieferungsgeschichtliche Studien I* and *Überlieferungsgeschichte des Pentateuch*, which appeared at the very beginning of the period under review and which quickly became standard works for analysis of the so-called historical books of the Hebrew Bible.

It should be observed—and Noth's studies illustrate this very well—that the various critical tools developed for analyzing ancient texts are by their very nature more useful for identifying characteristics and elements that tend to reduce confidence in the historical reliability of these texts than they are for identifying characteristics or elements that increase confidence. For example, source criticism of a biblical narrative relating some supposedly historical event may produce evidence that the narrative is composite or that it has been revised from time to time by various editors, each with a distinctive agenda far removed from critical historiography. Tradition criticism will focus on traditions that have been incorporated into the narrative and changes that occurred during the process of their oral transmission. Form criticism will focus on standardized patterns and expressions in the narrative which, by virtue of the fact that they are standardizations, are less useful for reconstructing the specifics of the particular event narrated. Yet none of these methodologies is very useful for determining whether the narrative in question is based on an actual historical event, nor can they aid well in recognizing historically reliable elements that have survived in the narrative as it stands today.

Obviously, historians cannot simply bypass critical analysis of the written sources on the grounds that the best tools available for this analysis tend to be more effective for pointing out problems than for verifying historicity. If the problems exist they must be taken seriously, and we need to be reminded from time to time that our critical tools have this negative bias.

Other Ancient Documents

Most of the ancient nonbiblical documents that have direct relevance for reconstructing the chronology and details of ancient Israel's history were already available before 1945. However, several exceptions deserve mention.

An inscribed stela from the reign of Adad-nirari III was discovered in 1967 during the excavations at Tell al-Rimah, Iraq (Page). Adad-nirari claims in the inscription to have conquered "the land of Amurru" and "the Hatti land" in a single year and to have collected tribute at that time from various kings, including "Joash (Ia'asu) of Samaria." The exact year of Adad-nirari's reign in which this tribute was paid remains uncertain.

Another new stela inscription, published by Louis Levine in 1972, parallels with minor variations a previously known section of Tiglath-pileser III's annals. Both this new inscription and the corresponding section of the annals include "Menachem (Me-ni-ḫi-im-me) of Samaria" among various local rulers who paid tribute to Tiglath-pileser before and/or during his ninth year (737 B.C.E.). Reports regarding the discovery of this second stela are vague. Apparently it was found in western Iran some time before 1967.

N. Na'aman's clarification of a fragmentary clay tablet that was already available before the turn of the century represents a more important development for biblical historians than either of the two inscriptions mentioned above. Earlier scholars had mistakenly attributed this fragment to Tiglath-pileser's reign and had reconstructed the text so that it seemed to refer to "Azariah (Az-ri-ya-a-u) of Judah." Na'aman demonstrated that the fragment derives from Sennacherib's reign and that the reference is to Hezekiah of Judah.

In 1956 D. J. Wiseman published from the British Museum archives a Babylonian chronicle that gives a year-by-year account of the period from 605 to 597 B.C.E. Among the events reported by the chronicle is the capture of Jerusalem by Nebuchadrezzar II in 597. This is our only non-biblical report of the fall of Jerusalem at the time of the exile, and it is especially important for biblical chronology since it provides an absolute date for the event.

Various ostraca, seal impressions, and papyrus fragments have been discovered in the Palestinian area since 1945. Among these are more than two hundred Hebrew and Aramaic ostraca recovered during the excavations at Tell Arad (Aharoni, 1968, 1975). Seventeen of the Arad ostraca (only nine are well enough preserved to be read with confidence) appear to be official letters dating from the last years of Judah's monarchical period. Several are addressed to one Eliashib, who apparently was commander of the military garrison of Arad at that time. In 1962 remnants of what must have been a large corpus of papyrus documents were discovered in a cave in the Wady Dâliyeh north of Jericho (Lapp, 1963; Cross, 1971). The corpus included letters and official documents of various sorts, apparently left in the cave by fugitives from Samaria at the time of Alexander the Great's conquest of Palestine.

Finally, mention should be made of the Mari (Tell Harîri) texts. These were discovered during the 1930s, and some of them were published at that time; however, they had only indirect relevance for Israelite history. The main publication of these texts (the ARM series) did not begin until 1946, and it is these texts that have figured significantly in recent discussions regarding the cultural context for and the historicity of the patriarchal narratives.

Artifacts

The years between the World Wars were very active and productive ones for Palestinian archaeology, and by the early 1940s general agreement had been reached regarding approximate dates and essential characteristics of the archaeological periods. Archaeological work in Palestine since 1945 has been largely a matter of sharpening up the picture and filling in details. Chapter 2 of this volume reviews the major developments in this regard, so it is necessary here to review only certain items that have played a specific role in treatments of Israelite history.

On the basis of his archaeological survey of the Transjordan conducted during the 1930s, N. Glueck (1940:114–57) concluded that the areas of ancient Edom and Moab were virtually devoid of sedentary occupation during the Middle and Late Bronze Ages—i.e., from ca. 2000 to the late 1200s B.C.E. This supposed gap in the occupation of this area became one of the key arguments for dating the exodus–conquest to the

thirteenth century, the point being that if the Israelites had passed
through southern Transjordan before that time there would have been
no Edomites or Moabites on the scene for them to encounter (see Num
20:14–21; Deut 2:29, etc.). This line of argument was rendered problematic during the 1950s and following, however, when several Edomite and
Moabite sites were excavated (Dhibân, excavated 1950–56; 'Arâ'ir, 1964–
66; Ḥesbân, 1968–76; Umm el-Biyarah, 1958–68; Tawilan, 1968–70; and
Buṣeirah, 1971–72). With the exception of 'Arâ'ir, none of these sites presented clear evidence of occupation before the twelfth or eleventh century
and in most cases much later. However, archaeological surveys currently
under way in central Moab and northern Edom are raising a problem from
the opposite direction. Contrary to Glueck's findings, these new surveys
indicate that there is a scattering of Late Bronze Age sites in both areas
(Weippert, 1979; Miller, 1979). The emerging picture is not yet clear; but
obviously the matter of Late Bronze/Early Iron settlement patterns in
southern Transjordan is more complex than Glueck's gap hypothesis presupposed, and the line of argument regarding the date of the exodus which
depended on that hypothesis will have to be discarded.

Archaeological evidence indicates widespread disturbances throughout the eastern Mediterranean world at the end of the Late Bronze Age.
Several cities in western Palestine were destroyed at that time, and
already in the 1930s W. F. Albright proposed that certain of these
destructions should be associated with the Israelite conquest (particularly
the destructions at Tell ed-Duweir, Tell Beit Mirsim, and Beitîn, which
he identified respectively as Lachish, Debir, and Bethel). This proposed
association found wide acceptance among biblical scholars and Palestinian archaeologists alike. It became customary during the next four
decades, in fact, to attribute the destruction of any city in Palestine at
the end of the Late Bronze Age to the invading Israelites, regardless of
whether the city in question is even mentioned in the biblical conquest
traditions.

Excavations at Tell el-Qedah from 1955 to 1958 seemed to confirm
this connection (Yadin, 1967). Tell el-Qedah almost certainly represents
the ruins of ancient Hazor, one of the three cities which the Bible specifically claims was destroyed by Joshua (see Josh 11:10–11; the other
two cities are Jericho and Ai), and here again there is evidence of a destruction at the end of the Late Bronze Age.

On the whole, however, archaeological findings since 1945 present
more problems than support for Albright's proposal. Specifically, it has
become increasingly apparent that the cities whose ruins present the best
examples of destructions at the end of the Late Bronze Age are not those
which the Bible associates with the conquest. Excavations in the ruins of
the cities which the Bible does associate with the conquest, on the other
hand, generally have produced little or no evidence even of Late Bronze

Age occupation, much less of destructions at the end of that period. Tell el-Qedah/Hazor turns out to be one of the exceptions rather than the rule (for a review of the evidence from the various sites and bibliographical data, see Miller [1977]). There are numerous issues involved—e.g., the complex matter of site identifications—and it perhaps would be an overstatement of the evidence to say that archaeology denies that a conquest of the sort described in the Bible occurred at the end of the Late Bronze Age. But it is certainly no longer possible, in the light of recent developments, to say that archaeology confirms such a conquest.

Regardless of how one understands the origins of Israel or the process by which the Israelites established their presence in western Palestine, it does seem clear that their emergence there as a self-conscious people had occurred already very early in the Iron Age. Are there any artifacts indicating their presence at that time? Albright called attention in 1940 to a particular ceramic form, the so-called collared-rim jar, which appears in the earliest Iron I phases of settlements throughout western Palestine, and proposed it as a "type fossil" characteristic specifically of the Israelite settlers. More recently, in 1970, Y. Shiloh made a similar argument for a certain type of four-room house: "In the light of the connection between the distribution of this type and the borders of the Israelite settlement, and in the light of its period of use and architectural characteristics, it would seem that the four-room house is an original Israelite concept" (180). Collared-rim jars have since turned up at a site deep within Ammonite territory, however, and houses typical of the ones to which Shiloh referred have been discovered well within the borders of ancient Moab (Ibrahim; Sauer). Obviously we are dealing in both cases with features characteristic of Early Iron Age Palestinian culture in general, not features that can be associated specifically with the Israelites.

King Solomon's building program provides the earliest instance, in this writer's opinion, where a connection can be made with some confidence between specific artifacts from Palestinian sites and specific details of Israel's history (see Miller [1975] for arguments against the supposed discovery of Saul's "palace-fort" at Tell el-Fûl). Yadin's discovery of a three-chambered gate and associated casemate wall at tenth-century Hazor, which led to his recognition of strikingly similar fortification systems at Megiddo (Tell el-Mutesellim) and Gezer (Tell Jezer), was the major breakthrough in this regard (1958, 1960). While his interpretation of the situation at Megiddo remains somewhat problematic (Aharoni, 1972; Yadin, 1973), it seems certain that these fortification systems are to be associated with Solomon's building program mentioned in 1 Kgs 9:15. It follows from Yadin's reinterpretation of the Megiddo stratigraphy, on the other hand, that the so-called Solomonic stables excavated there in the 1930s are not Solomonic after all but belong to a later period.

Indeed, they may not even be stables (Pritchard). Similarly, further investigation has shown that the supposed Solomonic smelting refinery excavated at Tell el-Kheleifeh (= Ezion-geber?) in 1938–40 is neither from the Solomonic period nor a smelting refinery (Rothenberg; Glueck, 1965).

As the record of artifacts pertaining to the period of Solomon comes into sharper focus, it is increasingly apparent that the size of his cities and the splendor of his buildings were rather modest by ancient Near Eastern standards. Even at Megiddo and Hazor the Solomonic remains are outclassed by those of a later building phase which can be dated to the ninth century B.C.E. and almost certainly is to be attributed to the Omride kings. At Megiddo, for example, it now seems that the famous water tunnel and the so-called Solomonic stables belong to the Omride period. Similar features are represented in the Omride phase of Hazor, which was more than double the size of the Solomonic city. Whether this pattern will continue as other sites are excavated remains to be seen. The available inscriptional evidence seems also to suggest that Omri and his son Ahab left a stronger impression on the other peoples of their day than did David, Solomon, or any of the other Israelite kings.

J. L. Starkey, who excavated Tell ed-Duweir during the 1930s, attributed the violent destruction of stratum III and the end of stratum II to Babylonian military activity in 597 and 586 B.C.E. respectively (1937a, 1937b). O. Tufnell reopened the issue in 1959, arguing that the stratum III destruction must have occurred somewhat earlier. Specifically, she attributed it to Sennacherib's invasion in 701. Albright's identification of Tell ed-Duweir as Lachish (1929; see esp. p. 3 n. 2) is generally accepted, and an Assyrian relief depicts Sennacherib's capture of Lachish. The issue is still debated, but the most recent evidence from other sites (e.g., Arad/Tell 'Arād and Beersheba/Tell es-Seba') as well as from excavations currently under way at Tell ed-Duweir seems to support Tufnell's position (Rainey, 1975). This calls for a reassessment of Nebuchadrezzar's dealings with Judah. There is less reason now to suppose that the Babylonian operation in 597 involved cities apart from Jerusalem.

The preceding review indicates that, while some advances have been made since 1945 in the ongoing attempt to correlate the archaeological record with the biblical account, this progress has been more than offset by the fact that so many of the proposed correlations that seemed rather certain during the 1940s are now turning out to be mistaken. This, plus a growing concern that Palestinian archaeology has been overly dominated by biblical interests, has led to a reactionary mood in some circles regarding the very concept of an interdisciplinary approach to archaeology and biblical studies (see, e.g., Dever, 1974, and his chapter in this volume). This reaction is not without some justification. "Biblical archaeologists" have had a tendency to begin with very shaky evidence and develop far-reaching conclusions that involve multiple layers of circular arguments. Yet there can be no question regarding the legitimacy (indeed the necessity!) of interdisciplinary biblical-archaeological studies. What we urgently need at this stage of research, then, is not a sharp separation of disciplines but a more realistic assessment of the nature of the evidence that various disciplines provide and more careful attention to the procedures by which different kinds of evidence are interrelated.

II. DEBATED ISSUES

While the basic information available for reconstructing the history of ancient Israel has not increased significantly since 1945, a lively debate has continued throughout the postwar years to the point that publications on Israelite history that were in the forefront during the mid-1940s are out of date today in many respects. Historical research is, after all, not simply a matter of collecting "facts" from the sources and combining these facts into a continuing story about people and events of times past. The sources must be evaluated and interpreted. The necessary exercise of judgment in the process of interpretation leaves room for disagreement. This is particularly true with regard to the history of biblical times, for which the sources are limited, selective, and often fragmentary.

Hardly a detail of Israelite history has escaped attention during the period under review. A comprehensive survey of the scholarly discussion with extensive bibliography is provided by Hayes and Miller (1977). For the purposes of this essay it will be useful to focus on five major questions in connection with which the points of agreement and disagreement among recent scholars become obvious. When does the history of Israel begin? How did the Israelites come to occupy the land of Canaan? What were the roots of the Israelite monarchy? To what extent are the chronological data and prophetical narratives incorporated into 1–2 Kings and 2 Chronicles reliable for historical reconstruction? Who came first, Ezra or Nehemiah?

The Point of Departure for Israelite History

M. Noth (1948) identified five traditions which, according to his analysis, originated independently among different groups of people, were combined gradually during the process of oral transmission, and eventually formed the basis of the Pentateuch. These five basic Pentateuchal traditions are, as Noth identified them: Guidance out of Egypt, Guidance into the Land of Canaan (das palästinische Kulturland), Promise to the Patriarchs, Guidance in the Wilderness, and Revelation at Sinai. Noth agreed that some or all of these traditions may hark back to historical people and events. He was, however, pessimistic about the possibility of actually reconstructing history on the basis of the traditions.

Moreover, he did not consider these traditions directly relevant to the history of Israel in any case since, in his opinion, they emerged from different groups of people and at a time when these groups had not yet been unified under the "all-Israel" concept. This unification occurred near the end of the Late Bronze Age, according to Noth, in connection with the establishment of an amphictyonic league (see below). Correspondingly, he began his treatment of Israel's history with the amphictyonic league (1950:9–15, 83–104).

W. F. Albright, on the other hand, called attention to certain names, customs, and sociopolitical circumstances in the patriarchal narratives which he believed pointed to the cultural milieu of the earliest phase of the Middle Bronze Age (MB I, ca. 2100–1900 B.C.E. according to his chronology; see Albright, 1935b, and references cited by Thompson: 4–5). Amorites begin to appear in the Mesopotamian documents about that time, and Palestine seems to have experienced a seminomadic interlude. Albright associated the two developments with each other, and thus emerged what came to be called the "Amorite hypothesis." Specifically, the entrance of the Hebrew patriarchs into Canaan was seen as part of a much larger Amorite movement that produced the seminomadic interlude. Influenced by this hypothesis, many scholars began to speak in terms of a "Patriarchal Age" which would have begun during MB I. Correspondingly, it seemed appropriate to begin Israel's history with the arrival of Amorite-Hebrew patriarchs in Palestine during the twentieth century B.C.E. (see, e.g., Albright, 1949:3–6; Bright, 1959:60–93).

While Albright's general approach to the patriarchal materials has been very influential during the postwar years, especially among English-speaking scholars, not all of those influenced by it have agreed with both the patriarchs/Amorites and the patriarchs/MB I connections. R. de Vaux, for example, who defended the Amorites/MB I connection, did so by associating the patriarchs with a second Amoritic influx in Palestine which occurred, according to his reckoning, during the nineteenth century B.C.E. (1976:66–68, 265–66). In other words, de Vaux associated the patriarchs with the second phase of the Middle Bronze Age (MB II A). Albright himself proposed a significant modification and expansion of the original hypothesis in a well-known paper, "Abraham the Hebrew," published in 1961. Specifically, he lowered the end date of MB I from ca. 1900 to ca. 1800 B.C.E., placed Abraham in the nineteenth century, and depicted him as a donkey caravaneer who frequented the trade routes from Palestine through the Negeb to Sinai. This proposal was rejected almost universally by scholars; indeed, by the 1960s the whole Albrightian approach to the patriarchal materials was encountering serious difficulties.

Several studies called attention to the fact that the names, customs, and the like reflected in the patriarchal narratives were not particularly characteristic of the Middle Bronze Age (Greenberg; Tucker; Van Seters, 1968).

B. Mazar, using arguments very similar to those of Albright, presented a case for associating the patriarchal traditions with the cultural milieu of the Early Iron Age: "In my view, it is much more within reason that the way of life and the ethnic and socio-political picture reflected in the patriarchal accounts generally correspond to the end of the period of the Judges and the beginning of the monarchy" (77). It remained for T. Thompson to work through Albright's treatment of the patriarchal materials systematically and to demonstrate that Albright's approach was methodologically unsound and that associating the patriarchs with any particular phase of the Bronze Age is altogether insufficient.

Noth's analysis of the Pentateuchal traditions has been challenged as well, on the grounds that he did not take archaeological data sufficiently into account (Bright, 1956) and that his criteria for identifying the basic Pentateuchal traditions are inadequate (B. W. Anderson; Polzin; see also studies such as Mittmann). The first of these charges is simply untrue (see Noth, 1960). The second calls into question the specific procedures and results of Noth's traditio-historical analysis, but not his assessment of the essential character of the patriarchal materials or his presumption that critical analysis of the texts themselves is the necessary starting point if they are to be used for historical reconstruction. It should be pointed out, moreover, that in spite of their methodological differences, Noth and Albright really were not so far apart when it actually came to using the patriarchal narratives for detailed historical reconstruction. Noth did not deny the historicity of the patriarchs; he insisted simply that, given the long and complicated tradition history of the patriarchal narratives, it is impossible to isolate at this late stage whatever authentic historical data these narratives may preserve. Albright had much to say about the "essential historicity" of these narratives, and he claimed to have identified the historical period in which the patriarchs lived. But he seems to have been as reluctant as Noth to make much of the biographical details about the patriarchs which the Pentateuchal narratives provide. In effect, the Albrightian approach was to locate the "Patriarchal Age" on the basis of certain general characteristics and clues recognized in the patriarchal narratives and then to fill in the details regarding this age, this supposed beginning point of Israel's history, on the basis of nonbiblical sources.

Although none of them has gained wide acceptance, three other positions regarding the patriarchal materials and/or the proper beginning point for a treatment of Israelite history deserve mention: (1) A few scholars, calling attention to social and legal parallels, the implications of the biblical genealogies, and other matters, have been inclined to associate the patriarchs with the Late Bronze Age (e.g., C. Gordon, 1940; 1958:28–31; O. Eissfeldt: 312–14). Generally, however, they have been as reluctant as Noth and Albright to make much of the biographical details about the patriarchs which the biblical narratives provide. (2) J. Van Seters (1975), on the basis of an extensive form and tradition analysis of the patriarchal narratives, concluded that they are, for the most part, a redactional creation of the exilic period. In other words, the patriarchal stories are pious fiction. (3) Some have expressed hopes that the Ebla archives (discovered in 1974 and following) will shed new light on the patriarchal question. D. N. Freedman in particular has gone so far as to claim that these archives provide new confirmation of the historicity of the patriarchs and to suggest that Abraham should be dated near the end of the Early Bronze Age (EB III, ca. 2800–2400 B.C.E.). Such claims are premature, to say the least.

For the moment, regardless of all that has been said about Mari, Nuzi, Ebla, etc., the Bible remains our only primary ancient source which actually mentions, or even alludes to, the Hebrew patriarchs. Ultimately, therefore, the question of the historicity of the patriarchs, to say nothing of their dates or biographical details, boils down to the question of the nature of the biblical account and its usefulness for historical reconstruction. There is always the possibility, of course, that nonbiblical sources will turn up in the future that will speak directly to the issue. But unless or until they do, any really convincing case for the historicity of the patriarchs or treatment of their life and times must be based on a comprehensive analysis of the biblical account itself.

Israelite Occupation of the Land of Canaan

A. Alt published a groundbreaking study in 1925, *Die Landnahme der Israeliten in Palästina*, in which he argued that the Israelite occupation of western Palestine began with gradual and generally peaceful movements of individual tribes and clans from the desert fringe into the central hill country. He was able to demonstrate on the basis of Egyptian sources, later confirmed by Palestinian archaeologists, that the central hill country was thinly populated during the Late Bronze Age. This meant that it would have been open to nomadic or seminomadic tribes who, according to his hypothesis, would have come each year with their small herds of cattle in search of summer pasturage. Each year these tribal groups would have penetrated farther into the interior of western Palestine, and over a period of time they would have learned agriculture and settled down to village life. In Alt's view, it was only at an advanced stage of their settlement in the land—namely, at the time of Saul and David—that the Israelite tribes came into serious conflict with, and actually conquered, the Canaanite city-states, most of which were situated in the lowlands.

Noth followed Alt's hypothesis, and it has been championed more recently by M. Weippert (1967). The hypothesis depends heavily on notions regarding desert nomads which recent studies have called into question (Kupper; Luke; Rowton). It also departs radically from the biblical account, particularly the book of Joshua, which claims a unified Israelite invasion of Canaan and decisive military conquest under Joshua.

Albright was convinced of the essential historicity of the biblical account and, as indicated above, associated the Israelite conquest with the numerous city destructions that occurred throughout Palestine in approximately the thirteenth century B.C.E. (i.e., at the end of the Late Bronze Age). The fact that this proposed correlation between the biblical account and archaeology has become increasingly problematic in the light of continued archaeological exploration was also indicated above. P. Lapp (1967) made the last systematic attempt to deal with the archaeological evidence in terms of a thirteenth-century Israelite conquest. Actually Lapp was exceedingly cautious on the matter, and J. Callaway published a study the following year in which he argued that in order to accommodate the biblical account with the archaeological evidence it would be necessary, first, to understand the "conquest" as a less unified and militarily successful effort than the Bible suggests and, second, to lower its date to at least the twelfth century B.C.E. Since then, two different scholars have attempted to demonstrate that the archaeological evidence would be less problematic if one dated the conquest considerably earlier—during the early fourteenth century (Waltke) or mid-fifteenth century (Bimson). It appears to the present writer that the archaeological evidence available at the moment neither supports, nor is easily accommodated with, any particular date for the Israelite conquest. In fact, the situation with regard to the conquest is not unlike that of the patriarchs. Were we dependent upon archaeological and other nonbiblical evidence alone, we would have no reason even to suppose that such a conquest ever occurred.

In 1962 G. E. Mendenhall advanced what might be called an "internal revolt" hypothesis regarding Israel's origins and occupation of Canaan. Specifically, he argued that Israel came into being as the result of a sociopolitical upheaval and retribalization that occurred in Palestine toward the end of the Late Bronze Age. Some of the people who constituted earliest Israel may have been recent arrivals from Egypt or semi-nomads from Transjordan seeking pasturage. For the most part, however, according to his view, Israel emerged from the heterogeneous population that had been in Canaan all along. This internal revolt hypothesis has been expounded recently in a massive volume by N. K. Gottwald, who explains that "early Israel was an eclectic formation of marginal and depressed Canaanite people, including 'feudalized' peasants (ḥupshu), 'apiru mercenaries and adventurers, transhumant pastoralists, tribally organized farmers and pastoral nomads (shosu), and probably also itinerant craftsmen and disaffected priests" (xxiii).

On the matter of whether Israel's ancestors invaded and conquered an indigenous Palestinian population or whether they emerged from this population, Mendenhall's hypothesis actually represents a shift of emphasis rather than an entirely new position. Even the biblical account, which clearly presupposes an invasion rather than a revolution, concedes in places that the Israelite conquerors allowed the indigenous population of Canaan to live on in their midst. Proponents of the internal revolt hypothesis presume, on the other hand, that some of the people who constituted earliest Israel may have been recent escapees from Egypt and pastoral nomads from the desert fringe. Indeed the main strength of Mendenhall's hypothesis is that it emphasizes the heterogeneous character of Israel's ancestry and recognizes that the tribalization of early Israel must have occurred largely in Palestine.

The crucial new elements, which are the least convincing aspects of the hypothesis, are the propositions that (1) Israel emerged from an apparently well-coordinated revolt that supposedly rocked the Canaanite city-states at the end of the Late Bronze Age, and (2) both this revolt and the subsequent tribalization of Israel represented a conscious effort on the part of oppressed peoples who were guided by a covenant theology and egalitarian principles. There is very little to be found in the biblical materials that can even be interpreted in terms of the hypothesized revolution from which the Israelite tribes supposedly emerged, much less evidence that actually calls for such a hypothesis (consider Gottwald's unconvincing efforts to establish a biblical basis for the hypothesis, pp. 214–19). The archaeological evidence for disturbances in Palestine at the end of the Late Bronze Age does not necessarily suggest a coordinated internal revolution any more than it necessarily suggests a pan-Israelite invasion from Transjordan. Literary analysis reveals that the covenant theology belongs primarily to later strata of the biblical materials, often the contexts in which the conquest motif is most prominent. It seems methodologically unsound, therefore, to place so much emphasis on one element—covenant—for understanding earliest Israel while essentially rejecting the other—conquest. Finally, as far as the egalitarian principles that supposedly guided the early Israelite revolutionaries are concerned, this is clearly a matter of projecting modern ideology back into ancient times. Actually, the internal revolt model might be more useful for dealing with developments at the time of Saul and David, but even these developments neither were determined by nor led to a social structure based on egalitarian principles.

The Roots of the Israelite Monarchy

In 1864 H. Ewald observed repeated occurrences of the number twelve in the biblical genealogies and noted a parallel in this regard with the "amphictyonic" leagues of ancient Greece and Italy. Noth explored the matter further in *Das System der zwölf Stämme Israels* (1930) and concluded that during the premonarchical period an Israelite tribal confederacy existed that was structurally similar to the European amphictyonies. He utilized the European amphictyonic model to elaborate on various aspects of this supposed Israelite tribal confederacy. Closely associated with the amphictyonic hypothesis, which soon gained wide acceptance, has been a heavy emphasis by many scholars during the postwar years on the role of charismatic leaders in premonarchical Israel. These leaders, such as Gideon and Deborah, were the ones who mustered Israel's troops in times of danger with no apparent political or military authority except their own bravery, the immediacy of the threat at hand, and the loyalty of the constituents of the amphictyonic league.

A. Alt argued, moreover, in two widely influential papers (1930, 1951), that this "charismatic ideal" was one of the roots of the Israelite monarchy and that it accounts for a noticeable difference between the royal ideologies of the separate Israelite kingdoms. Specifically, Alt depicted Saul as one of these charismatic leaders, a young farm boy who rose to the occasion at a time of Philistine oppression and led Israel to a series of spectacular victories. These initial victories were not sufficient, however, since the Philistines posed a permanent threat, and in response to this situation Saul's rule became permanent also. Regarding the royal ideologies of the separate Israelite and Judean kingdoms, Alt explained that the people of the North tended to hold on to the charismatic ideal from the days of the old tribal league and that the instability of rulership in the northern kingdom is to be understood largely in terms of an ongoing conflict between this ideal and the concept of dynastic succession. The situation was different in the southern kingdom, in his opinion, because Judah was dominated by the city-state of Jerusalem. Dynastic kingship was normal among the Canaanite city-states; this would have been true of Jerusalem when David conquered the city, and it was only natural that his descendants would continue to rule there after his death.

Both the amphictyonic model and the idea of the charismatic ideal have had far-reaching influence among biblical scholars during the period under review. Neither has gone unchallenged, however, and the concept of an early Israelite amphictyony has been under especially heavy attack during the past decade (Orlinsky; Fohrer; G. W. Anderson; Mayes). Opponents contend that, while there may be some parallels between the European leagues and the situation of the Israelite tribes prior to the establishment of the monarchy, these parallels are so general and/or elusive that it is altogether inappropriate to use a model derived from one to clarify and fill in details about the other. Moreover, it is not just a question of whether it is appropriate to speak of Israel's tribal league as an amphictyony. We need to rethink whether it is appropriate to speak in terms of a premonarchical Israelite "tribal league" at all. Obviously certain of the tribal groups settled in central Palestine on the eve of the establishment of the monarchy did feel a certain bond of kinship, and leaders such as Deborah, Saul, and David were able to capitalize on this. But scholars have overestimated the homogeneity and unity of these tribal groups (religiously as well as politically), and a good case has not been made (on the basis of a critical analysis of the narratives in Judges) that they were bound together by any sort of formal league.

The "charismatic ideal" does not stand or fall with the amphictyonic model, yet we will have to rethink this concept also over the next few years. It is not a question of whether charismatic leaders in the sense described above played a significant role in the early tribal wars, but whether it is an oversimplification to think of the role as a norm and whether too much has been made of the supposed charismatic ideal in later Israel's royal ideology. Perhaps more attention should be given to another sort of political leader in early Israel, one represented best by Abimelech and Jephthah. These appear to have been local military chieftains whose authority lay primarily in a band of professional or semiprofessional warriors whom they supported with the spoils from raids and gifts from the people whom they "protected." A case can be made for understanding the rise of Saul and David to power in terms of such roles (Miller, 1974). Buccellati, in his comprehensive study, *Cities and Nations of Ancient Syria* (1967), presented arguments against Alt's hypothesis that there was an inherent charismatic/dynastic conflict in the royal ideology of the northern kingdom. Buccellati's arguments are not overwhelming, but they do call for more caution than some of us have shown (Newman; Miller, 1967).

Chronological Data and Prophetical Narratives in Kings and Chronicles

1–2 Kings provide for the rulers of the separate Israelite and Judean kingdoms (1) a series of synchronistic reckonings that locate the beginning of each king's reign in relation to the reign of the contemporary ruler of the other kingdom and (2) a reckoning of the length of each king's reign. 2 Chronicles and the Mesopotamian documents offer some supplementary information, and the latter are particularly useful in that they provide occasional bench marks—e.g., they show that Ahab was on the throne in 851 B.C.E., Jehu in 841, Joash sometime between 805 and 796, that Samaria fell approximately 722, Jerusalem fell in 597, etc. Any comprehensive chronology of the separate kindoms, however, must depend primarily on the figures supplied in 1–2 Kings.

Unfortunately these figures present some problems that are not easily overcome. Different manuscripts provide different sets of figures. The figures provided in any given manuscript appear to be internally inconsistent. Calculations based on the biblical figures are difficult to correlate with the Mesopotamian "bench marks." We do not know what sort of calendar(s) or reckoning system(s) were used in the two kingdoms. Finally, the chronological data presented in 1–2 Kings belong to a more extensive chronological system, which begins in Genesis, ranges in coverage from creation to the exile, and shows evidence of having been constructed or adjusted to conform to an idealistic and schematic view of history. It is not surprising, therefore, that scholars disagree regarding the reliability of the biblical figures and that several competing chronologies for the period of the separate kingdoms have been advanced.

English-speaking scholars have tended during the postwar years to follow either the chronology published by E. R. Thiele in 1944 or the one published by W. F. Albright in 1945. The actual dates that Thiele and Albright proposed for the various kings are not so far apart. Yet there is a significant difference in the way they arrived at these dates, and this has not always been fully appreciated.

Thiele presupposed a high degree of accuracy for the figures supplied by the traditional Hebrew (Masoretic) manuscripts and explained the apparent inconsistencies (some within the Hebrew text itself and others vis-à-vis the Mesopotamian documents) by positing various coregencies, differences, and shifts in the calendars of the separate kingdoms, and changes in their methods of reckoning the beginnings and lengths of reigns. Correspondingly, his chronological system consists of very precise dates for the various kings and interlocking theories about when the various coregencies, calendar shifts, etc. supposedly occurred. The very precision and internal complexity of Thiele's chronology give it the appearance of being more methodologically sound than it really is and leave the misleading impression that he has demonstrated the accuracy of the biblical figures. This simply is not true. He has demonstrated only that the apparent inconsistencies in the Masoretic figures can be explained hypothetically in terms of unreported variables such as coregencies, calendar changes, variant reckoning procedures, and the like. Surely it can be seen that these variables allow enough latitude for one to deal in a similar fashion and reach equally precise conclusions with virtually any set of figures—for example, those provided by the Greek manuscripts.

Albright presumed the essential reliability of the biblical figures but recognized the possibility of scribal errors or secondary changes during the process of transmission and was willing to adjust the figures here and there in order to achieve harmony. Correspondingly, he offered only tentative dates and modified some of these during the course of his career: "I want to emphasize that my conclusions . . . are tentative, since we still lack a sufficiently large number of contemporary checks to warrant easy dogmatism. . . . I do not, however, believe that any of these dates (except possibly in the first half of the eighth century) are more than five years wrong" (1945:17). German scholars in recent years have tended to follow the chronology worked out by J. Begrich (revised later by A. Jepsen and R. Hanhart), whose approach was much more akin to that of Albright than to that of Thiele.

Studies in the Greek texts have revealed what appears to be a coherent system of synchronisms for the kings of the Omride period which differ from the synchronisms provided for these same kings by the Masoretic texts. Moreover, a strong case can be made for the priority of the Greek readings at this point (Miller, 1967b; Shenkel). W. R. Wifall, on the other hand, also on the basis of a comparative study of the Greek and Hebrew texts, has argued very persuasively that the chronological scheme originally presented in 1–2 Kings has undergone at least two major redactional revisions, the last of which involved an attempt to shift from a postdating reckoning system to an antedating reckoning system.

Regarding the prophetical narratives that have been incorporated into the books of Kings and Chronicles, the issue is twofold: (1) What sort of reliable historical information can be derived from these narratives? (2) Did the compilers of Kings and Chronicles place them in the proper historical contexts? The relevance of the first of these questions is obvious enough, and it is generally agreed that the prophetical narratives are useful for the historian's purposes primarily because they reflect the general religious, political, and sociological conditions of the periods from which they derive (allowing of course for changes that may have occurred in them during the process of transmission). The second question is less obvious but equally crucial. Since the prophetical narratives are generally vague on details apart from the miraculous deeds of the prophets, the periods from which they derive often cannot be established from the narratives themselves.

The period of the Omride kings has received considerable attention during recent years with precisely this second question at stake. There is much evidence to suggest that the Omrides, especially Omri himself and Ahab, were aggressive rulers over a stable and powerful nation. Only certain of the prophetical narratives that have been incorporated into the treatment of the Omride kings in 1–2 Kings suggest otherwise—i.e., the Elisha cycle (2 Kgs 2; 4:1–8:15; 13:14–21) and a narrative complex that describes three battles between a king of Israel (presumably Ahab) and Ben-hadad of Damascus (1 Kgs 20; 22:1–38). These particular narratives clearly reflect a period during which Israel was a pitifully weak nation whose kings were dominated by Yahwistic prophets on the one hand and the kings of Damascus on the other. Obviously a historian who takes these narratives into account will treat the Omride period differently from one who does not. But do these narratives in fact represent the Omride period? As early as the turn of the century, A. Kuenen and

R. Kittel observed that at least some of the Elisha narratives must belong in the later context of the Jehu dynasty. In 1942 A. Jepsen argued that the whole Elisha cycle belongs there, and the two battle accounts in 1 Kings 20 as well. This view has gained increasing support among scholars during the postwar years, and the center of discussion seems to have shifted from the question of whether some of the prophetical narratives associated with the Omride period are out of place to the questions of which ones are out of place and where they properly belong (C. F. Whitley; J. M. Miller, 1966; E. Lipiński).

The Dates of Ezra and Nehemiah

This last question may seem rather narrow in focus compared with the preceding four, but actually it is a focal point for a whole complex of historical issues pertaining to the postexilic period.

The arrangement of the books of Ezra and Nehemiah implies that Ezra preceded Nehemiah. This seems to be confirmed by Ezra 7:8 and Neh 1:1–3; 2:1, which place the beginnings of Ezra's and Nehemiah's careers in Jerusalem in the seventh and twentieth years respectively of the reign of Artaxerxes. A letter discovered among the Elephantine papyri seems to establish further that the Artaxerxes involved was Artaxerxes I (465–425 B.C.E.). Specifically, the letter is dated to the seventeenth year of Darius II (407 B.C.E.), addressed to a governor of Judah named Bagoas (possibly Nehemiah's successor), and refers to a high priest in Jerusalem named Johanan and to the sons of Sanballat, the governor of Samaria. Apparently this is Johanan the son of Eliashib, who in turn was a contemporary of Nehemiah (Neh 3:1; 12:10–11, 22, 13:28), and these are the sons of Sanballat, Nehemiah's well-known rival. The obvious conclusion, therefore, is that Ezra and Nehemiah came to Jerusalem in the seventh and twentieth years of Artaxerxes I, or in 458 and 445 B.C.E. respectively.

However, there is surprisingly little indication in the biblical materials of interaction between Ezra and Nehemiah, and scholars have gleaned various pieces of information that seem to make more sense when Ezra's career is dated later than that of Nehemiah. One of the main objections to the traditional arrangement, for example, is that Nehemiah is depicted as a contemporary of a high priest named Eliashib (Neh 3:1) while Ezra is depicted as a contemporary of one Jehohanan the son of Eliashib (Ezra 10:6). There is only one Eliashib in the priestly genealogy of Neh 12:10–11, and this Eliashib's grandson, Jonathan, is the only obvious candidate for Jehohanan, Ezra's contemporary. This Jonathan's name appears as Johanan in Neh 12:22–23; presumably he is the one to whom the Elephantine letter refers. If Nehemiah's contemporary was the ancestor of Ezra's contemporary, does it not follow that Nehemiah preceded Ezra?

Even before the turn of this century, van Hoonacker argued that, while Nehemiah's career is to be associated with Artaxerxes I, Ezra returned to Jerusalem in the seventh year of Artaxerxes II (398 B.C.E.). Championed by H. H. Rowley, this view gained wide acceptance among critical scholars especially during the 1940s and following. Another less influential suggestion was that Ezra returned during the thirty-seventh (rather than the seventh) year of Artaxerxes I, i.e., in 428 B.C.E. (Bright, 1960). This latter proposal leaves open the question of why, if their careers overlapped, there is so little indication of interaction between Ezra and Nehemiah. Moreover, there is no textual evidence for the necessary emendation.

Beginning in the late 1960s, scholarly interest began to shift away from chronology to the issues and parties that divided the postexilic community. Chronology has not been ignored altogether during the past decade, however, and one notices in this regard a trend back to the traditional arrangement—Ezra before Nehemiah, both during the reign of Artaxerxes I. Representing this trend are such diverse studies as U. Kellermann's *Nehemiah: Quellen, Überlieferung und Geschichte*, M. Smith's *Palestinian Parties and Politics that Shaped the Old Testament* (119–25), and F. M. Cross's 1974 presidential address to the Society of Biblical Literature.

Cross in particular has offered a rather interesting suggestion regarding the identities and chronological order of Ezra's and Nehemiah's respective priestly contemporaries, Johanan ben Eliashib and Eliashib. Observing instances of papponymy (the practice of naming a son after his grandfather) in the Wady Dâliyeh materials, he posits that the priestly family engaged in this practice and that a father-son combination has been dropped through haplography from the genealogy provided in Neh 12:10–11. In short, he reconstructs the genealogy as follows:

Jozadak	Neh 12:26
Jeshua	Neh 12:10–11, 26
Joiakim	Neh 12:10–11, 26
Eliashib Johanan	Dropped from the Neh 12:10–11 list through haplography; but these would have been the Eliashib and his son Johanan to whom Ezra 10:6 refers.
Eliashib	Nehemiah's contemporary. Neh 3:1; 12:10–11, 22–23
Joiada	Neh 12:10–11, 22
Johanan/Jonathan	Mentioned in Elephantine letter and Neh 12:10–11, 22–23
Jaddua	Neh 12:10–11

The possibility that haplography has occurred in Neh 12:10–11 is not unreasonable. However, the only argument of consequence in favor of Cross's reconstruction is that this list demands an explanation of some sort if one returns to the traditional Ezra-Nehemiah arrangement. If

Ezra preceded Nehemiah, then the Johanan ben Eliashib contemporary with Ezra must have been a different priest, earlier than the Johanan who descended from the Eliashib contemporary with Nehemiah. By the same measure, if there was an earlier Johanan ben Eliashib, then there must have been an earlier Eliashib also. The papponymy aspect of the argument and Cross's calculations regarding the average length of a priestly generation over against the time span to be accounted for are forced and have no direct relevance apart from assuring one that the hypothesis is at least plausible.

III. TRENDS IN THE DISCUSSION

The preceding has been only a very brief survey of the scholarly views pertaining to five selected questions about ancient Israelite history. These questions represent critical issues, however, and there is a noticeable pattern that is generally characteristic of studies in Israelite history since the mid-1940s.

"Altians" and "Albrightians"

During the first two decades of this period, from the mid-1940s through the mid-1960s, discussion tended to focus on the contrasting approaches and positions of what might be called the "Alt-Noth school" and the "Albright school." Certainly not all of the scholars contributing at that time to the study of Israelite history can be classified as "Altians" or "Albrightians" (e.g., H. S. Cazelles, O. Eissfeldt, K. Galling, H. L. Ginsberg, A. Jepsen, Y. Kaufmann, A. S. Kapelrud, B. Mazar, S. Mowinckel, E. Nielsen, H. M. Orlinsky, H. H. Rowley, H. Tadmor, and R. de Vaux). The approaches and positions advanced by Alt, Noth, and Albright clearly dominated the discussion, however, and a lively debate broke out between the two schools which reached its peak during the 1950s (see especially Bright, 1956; Wright, 1958, 1959; von Rad, 1960; Noth, 1960). Noth's *Geschichte Israels* (1950) illustrates the characteristic approaches and positions of the Alt-Noth school; Bright's *A History of Israel* (1959) does the same for the Albright school.

Actually the basic publications that set the respective directions of these two schools had appeared before the mid-1940s. Alt's basic studies were published in a series of lengthy essays between 1925 and 1940. His methodological approach and positions were developed significantly by Noth, whose own groundbreaking studies relating to biblical history appeared between 1930 and 1950. Albright's characteristic approach and views were hammered out in numerous short communications (most of them appearing in the *Bulletin of the American Schools of Oriental Research*) and several books published during the 1930s and 1940s. Although in later years Albright often revised his position with regard to details, the basics remained the same with one exception. This exception was his hypothesis advanced in 1961 that the Hebrew patriarchs were donkey caravaneers.

The crucial methodological difference was that the Alt-Noth school insisted on thoroughgoing critical analysis of the biblical texts as the proper starting point for reconstructing Israelite history, while the Albright school was inclined to disregard problems raised by critical analysis of these texts when it appeared that reasonable correlations could be made between the biblical claims and archaeological data. Obviously there is a case to be made for both sides. On the one hand, it is a basic tenet of historiography that a historian must analyze the sources with the best critical tools available before drawing historical conclusions from them. Moreover, given the very nature of archaeological evidence, any correlation between archaeology and the Bible involves a certain degree of speculation, and some of the correlations proposed by Albright and his students were clearly gratuitous. On the other hand, applying the critical procedures of biblical analysis—source criticism, tradition criticism, form criticism, etc.—also involves a high degree of subjectivity. Moreover, as indicated above, these procedures seem to be biased in that they are more effective for identifying characteristics and elements that reflect negatively on the historical reliability of an ancient document (a biblical narrative, for example) than they are for isolating historically reliable data that the same document may have preserved.

In addition to the methodological differences, there was also a tendency toward theological difference between the two schools. Namely, those who followed the Alt-Noth approach tended to make a sharp distinction between the actual events of ancient Israel's history and Israel's faith response to these events. They insisted (1) that the biblical narration of Israel's past is guided by the faith response, (2) that the real importance and authority of the Bible rests with its faith claims, and (3) that the validity of these claims does not depend upon whether they completely square with the actual course of events in terms of positivistic history (von Rad, 1943). Albright's followers, on the other hand, tended to be aligned with what has come to be called the "biblical theology movement." Those associated with this movement generally argued that the authority of the Bible resides in its overall faith claims and that the validity of these claims is not dependent upon the *detailed historical accuracy* of the biblical accounts. Since these faith claims focus precisely on God's mighty acts in history as recounted in the Bible, however, they held that this validity does require at least *essential* continuity between the biblical presentations of Israel's history and the actual course of events (e.g., Wright, 1952).

It should be emphasized, however, that the two schools did not represent opposite extremes but rather poles within an intermediate range of attitudes toward the Bible and its relationship to Israelite history. Indeed, it was the similarities between their approaches as well as the differences that made for such a lively debate. Considering the full range of biblical scholarship, apparent extremes would be the position of ultraconservative scholars on the one hand, for whom the Bible itself is an accurate and adequate treatment of Israelite history (Wood approaches this position), and the apparent position of some critical scholars on the other hand, who, as a result of their investigations, regard the biblical materials as useless for reconstructing history. Both the Altians and the Albrightians recognized that the biblical presentation of Israel's history is not entirely accurate as it stands; both were confident nevertheless that historically useful data could be derived from the biblical materials; and both insisted that the nonbiblical sources should be granted an integrity of their own rather than simply harmonized or explained away in deference to the biblical account. The fact that Alt and his students expended so much time and effort researching Israelite history is evidence that they were not nihilistic in this regard; the fact that Albright and his students so often revised the details of the biblical account of Israel's history in the light of the archaeological record is evidence that they were by no means fundamentalists.

Nevertheless, as one would expect from their methodological and theological presuppositions, Alt and his followers tended to be much less confident than the Albrightians regarding the reliability of the biblical materials for historical reconstruction, and the reconstructions they proposed tended to depart more radically from the biblical account. Albright and his students tended to follow the outline of the biblical account fairly closely, on the other hand, and to presuppose essential historicity, while making whatever adjustments seemed necessary to accommodate relevant nonbiblical (particularly archaeological) evidence.

Current Trends

The characteristic approaches and positions of the two schools held almost canonical status among their respective constituencies until the mid-1960s. They were challenged from time to time, of course, and not just by proponents of the opposite school. Already in 1962, for example, Orlinsky argued strongly against Noth's amphictyony hypothesis, which even the Albrightians found convincing.

Beginning in the late 1960s and especially during the 1970s, the challenges became much more vigorous and systematic. Moreover, the lines were no longer so clearly drawn between "Altians" and "Albrightians." The challenges to the cherished positions of the two schools came from within their respective circles as well as from without, and often these challenges were based on the same sorts of arguments as had been used earlier to bolster the positions now under attack. Thus, for example, Noth's traditio-historical analysis of the Pentateuch and his treatment of the Deuteronomic History have been called into question by more recent traditio-historical studies. Similarly, arguments based on names, customs, and the like—the sorts of arguments that Albright used to associate the patriarchs with MB I—have been used to associate them with MB II or the Early Iron Age. It is precisely the archaeological evidence that is turning out to be the most serious problem for Albright's dating and treatment of the conquest.

In short, scholarly research and discussion pertaining to Israelite history seem to have entered a new phase beginning in the late 1960s. This might be called a post-Alt/Albright phase, and it is not at all clear where the discussion will move next. At least three tendencies are noticeable:

(1) There are still some attempts to salvage the old approaches and positions. For example, while most scholars seem to have given up on the idea that the ancient nonbiblical documents will enable us to verify the historicity of the patriarchs and locate them chronologically, there are those who insist that where the Nuzi and Mari tablets failed the Ebla tablets will surely succeed. Freedman, for example, now proposes to date the patriarchs during the Early Bronze Age on the basis of the Ebla tablets. Methodologically, Bimson's treatment of the exodus-conquest is essentially the same as Albright's treatment. Namely, he tends to disregard problems raised by critical analysis of the biblical account but takes liberties with both the biblical account and the archaeological evidence in order to produce a "synthesis" between the two. The difference is that, whereas Albright attempted to synthesize in terms of a thirteenth-century exodus-conquest, Bimson opts for the mid-fifteenth century.

(2) Much attention is being given at the moment to the views advanced by G. E. Mendenhall, N. K. Gottwald, and a circle of scholars who take a sociological approach to biblical history. "Sociological approach," however, simply means that they wish to give more attention to sociological factors that might have influenced Israel's history, not that they are applying some new methodology developed by sociologists that would enable them to extract previously unavailable historical information from the sources. Much of what they propose, beginning with the "peasants' revolt" hypothesis, is bold speculation—as bold in its interpretation of the meager sociological information available for ancient Israel as in its interpretation of the biblical and archaeological evidence.

(3) The majority of biblical scholars seem inclined to defer historical questions at the moment, or at least to avoid some of the big issues, while pursuing more specialized interests (textual studies, literary analysis, archaeology, and the like). This is apparent, for example, among the second- and third-generation students of Albright active today in Palestinian archaeology. Although persons such as W. Dever, J. Seger, and

J. Sauer hold theological degrees and did their training when "Biblical Archaeology" was at the height of its popularity, their research interests seem to focus entirely on technical archaeological matters. Dever has been particularly outspoken in his concern for a sharper distinction between Palestinian archaeology and biblical studies as disciplines.

Two decades ago when the present writer began graduate studies, further research in the area of ancient Israelite history did not seem very promising. The Albrightian approach on the one hand and the Alt-Noth approach on the other seemed to cover the main options. Moreover, the implications of both options already had been explored in considerable detail. The situation is quite different today. Probably there is no other area of biblical studies so obviously in need at the moment of some fresh ideas based on solid research.

BIBLIOGRAPHY

Aharoni, Yohanan
　1968　　　　"'Arad: Its Inscriptions and Temple." *BA* 31: 2–32.
　1972　　　　"The Stratification of Israelite Megiddo." *JNES* 31: 302–11.
　1975　　　　*Arad Inscriptions*. Jerusalem: Bialik Institute/Israel Exploration Society (Hebrew).

Albright, William Foxwell
　1929　　　　"The American Excavations at Tell Beit Mirsim." *ZAW* 6: 1–17.
　1935a　　　"Archaeology and the Date of the Hebrew Conquest of Palestine." *BASOR* 58: 10–18.
　1935b　　　"Palestine in the Earliest Historical Period." *JPOS* 15: 193–234.
　1937　　　　"Further Light on the History of Israel from Lachish and Megiddo." *BASOR* 68: 22–26.
　1939　　　　"The Israelite Conquest of Canaan in the Light of Archaeology." *BASOR* 74: 11–23.
　1940　　　　Review of Lamon and Shipton, *Megiddo I*, and Shipton, *Notes on Megiddo Pottery*. *AJA* 44: 546–50.
　1945　　　　"The Chronology of the Divided Monarchy of Israel." *BASOR* 100: 16–22.
　1949　　　　*The Biblical Period*. Pittsburgh: The Biblical Colloquium (reprinted from *The Jews: Their History, Culture, and Religion*. Ed. L. Finkelstein).
　1961　　　　"Abraham the Hebrew: A New Archaeological Interpretation." *BASOR* 163: 36–54.

Alt, Albrecht
　1925　　　　*Die Landnahme der Israeliten in Palästina*. Leipzig: Reformationsprogramm der Universität. Reprinted

pp. 89–125 in *Kleine Schriften zur Geschichte des Volkes Israel.* Vol. 1. Munich: C. H. Beck, 1955. Translation: Pp. 173–221 in *Essays on Old Testament History and Religion.* Trans. R. A. Wilson. Garden City, NY: Doubleday, 1967.

1930   *Die Staatenbildung der Israeliten in Palästina.* Leipzig: Reformationsprogramm der Universität. Reprinted pp. 1–65 in *Kleine Schriften.* Vol. 2. Translation: "The Formation of the Israelite State in Palestine." Pp. 223–309 in *Essays on Old Testament History and Religion.*

1951   "Das Königtum in den Reichen Israel und Juda." *VT* 1: 2–22. Reprinted pp. 116–34 in *Kleine Schriften.* Vol. 2. Translation: "The Monarchy in the Kingdom of Israel and Judah." Pp. 311–35 in *Essays on Old Testament History and Religion.*

Anderson, Bernhard W.
1972   "Introduction." Pp. xiii–xxxii in M. Noth, *A History of Pentateuchal Traditions.* Trans. B. W. Anderson. Englewood Cliffs, NJ: Prentice-Hall.

Anderson, George W.
1970   "Israel: Amphictyony: 'AM; KAHAL; 'EDAH." Pp. 135–51 in *Translating and Understanding the Old Testament: Essays in Honor of H. G. May.* Ed. H. T. Frank and W. L. Reed. Nashville: Abingdon.

Begrich, Joachim
1929   *Die Chronologie der Könige von Israel und Judah.* Tübingen: J. C. B. Mohr.

Bimson, John J.
1978   *Redating the Exodus and Conquest.* JSOTSup 5. Sheffield: JSOT.

Bright, John
1956   *Early Israel in Recent History Writing.* SBT 19. London: SCM.

1959   *A History of Israel.* Philadelphia: Westminster.
1960   "The Date of Ezra's Mission to Jerusalem." Pp. 70–87 in *Yehezkel Kaufmann Jubilee Volume.* Ed. J. M. Haran. Jerusalem: Magnes.

Buccellati, Giorgio
1967   *Cities and Nations of Ancient Syria: An Essay on Political Institutions with Special Reference to the Israelite Kingdoms.* Studi Semitici 26. Rome: University of Rome.

Callaway, Joseph
1968   "New Evidence on the Conquest of 'Ai." *JBL* 87: 312–20.

Cross, Frank M.
1971   "Papyri of the Fourth Century B.C. from Dâliyeh." Pp. 45–69 in *New Directions in Biblical Archaeology*. Garden City, NY: Doubleday.
1974   "A Reconstruction of the Judean Restoration." Presidential address to the Society of Biblical Literature, published in *JBL* 94 (1975): 4–18.

Dever, William G.
1974   *Archaeology and Biblical Studies: Retrospects and Prospects*. William C. Winslow Lectures, 1972. Evanston, IL: Seabury–Western Theological Seminary.

Eissfeldt, Otto
1975   "Palestine in the Time of the Nineteenth Dynasty. (a) The Exodus and Wanderings." Pp. 307–30 in *Cambridge Ancient History* II/2. Ed. E. S. Edwards. Cambridge: Cambridge University Press.

Fohrer, Georg
1966   "Altes Testament—'Amphiktyonie' und 'Bund'?" *TLZ* 91: 801–16, 893–904.

Freedman, David Noel
1978   "The Real Story of the Ebla Tablets—Ebla and the Cities of the Plain." *BA* 41: 143–64.

Glueck, Nelson
1940   *The Other Side of the Jordan*. New Haven: ASOR.
1965   "Ezion-Geber." *BA* 28: 7–87.

Gordon, Cyrus H.
1940   "Biblical Customs and the Nuzi Tablets." *BA* 3: 1 12.
1958   "Abraham and the Merchants of Ura." *JNES* 17: 28–31.

Gottwald, Norman K.
1979   *The Tribes of Yahweh: A Sociology of the Religion of Liberated Israel, 1250–1050 B.C.E.* Maryknoll, NY: Orbis Books.

Greenberg, Moshe
1962   "Another Look at Rachel's Theft of the Teraphim." *JBL* 81: 239–48.

Hayes, John H., and J. Maxwell Miller, eds.
1977   *Israelite and Judaean History*. OTL. Philadelphia: Westminster.

Ibrahim, Moawiyah
1978   "The Collared-rim Jar of the Early Iron Age." Pp. 117–26 in *Archaeology and the Levant: Essays for Kathleen Kenyon*. Ed. R. Moorey and P. Parr. Warmaster: Aris & Phillips.

Jepsen, Alfred
1942   "Israel und Damaskus." *AfO* 14: 154–58.

Jepsen, Alfred, and Robert Hanhart
1964   *Untersuchungen zur israelitisch-jüdischen Chronologie.* BZAW 88. Berlin: Walter de Gruyter.

Kellermann, Ulrich
1967   *Nehemiah: Quellen, Überlieferung und Geschichte.* BZAW 102. Berlin: Walter de Gruyter.

Kupper, J. R.
1959   "Le role des nomades dans l'histoire de la Mesopotamie ancienne." *Journal of the Economic and Social History of the Orient* 2: 113–27.

Lapp, Paul
1963   "The Cave Clearances of the Wâdī ed-Dâliyeh." *Archaeological Newsletter of the American Schools of Oriental Research* #8. Cambridge, MA: ASOR.
1967   "The Conquest of Palestine in the Light of Archaeology." *CTM* 38: 283–300.

Levine, Louis D.
1972   "Two Neo-Assyrian Stelae from Iran." Pp. 11–24, 64–81 in *Art and Archaeology.* Occasional Paper 23. Toronto: Royal Ontario Museum.

Lipiński, Edouard
1969   "Le Ben-hadad II de la Bible et L'histoire." Pp. 157–73 in *Fifth World Congress of Jewish Studies.* Vol. I. Jerusalem: R. H. Hacohen.

Luke, John Tracy
1965   *Pastoralism and Politics in the Mari Period: A Re-Examination of the Character and Political Significance of the Major West Semitic Tribal Groups in the Middle Euphrates, c. 1828–1753 B.C.* (Ph.D. dissertation, University of Michigan; Ann Arbor: University Microfilms).

Mayes, Andrew D. H.
1974   *Israel in the Period of the Judges.* SBT 2/29. London: SCM.

Mazar, Benjamin
1969   "The Historical Background of the Book of Genesis." *JNES* 28: 73–83.

Mendenhall, George E.
1962   "The Hebrew Conquest of Palestine." *BA* 25: 66–87.

Miller, J. Maxwell
1966   "The Elisha Cycle and the Accounts of the Omride Wars." *JBL* 85: 441–54.
1967a   "The Fall of the House of Ahab." *VT* 17: 307–24.
1967b   "Another Look at the Chronology of the Early Divided Monarchy." *JBL* 86: 276–88.

1974 "Saul's Rise to Power: Some Observations Concerning I Sam. 9.1–10.16; 10.26–11.15 and 13.2–14.46." *CBQ* 36: 157–74.

1975 "Geba/Gibeah of Benjamin." *VT* 25: 145–66.

1977 "The Israelite Occupation of Canaan." Pp. 213–84 in *Israelite and Judaean History.* Ed. J. H. Hayes and J. M. Miller. Philadelphia: Westminster.

1979 "Archaeological Survey of Central Moab, 1978." *BASOR* 234: 43–52.

Mittmann, Siegfried
1975 *Deuteronomium 1, 1–6, 3 literarkritisch und traditions- geschichtlich untersucht.* BZAW 139. Berlin: Walter de Gruyter.

Na'aman, Nadav
1974 "Sennacherib's 'Letter to God' on his Campaign to Judah." *BASOR* 214. 25–39.

Newman, Murray
1962 *The People of the Covenant: A Study of Israel from Moses to the Monarchy.* New York: Abingdon.

Noth, Martin
1930 *Das System der zwölf Stämme Israels.* BWANT IV/1. Stuttgart: W. Kohlhammer.

1943 *Überlieferungsgeschichtliche Studien: Die sammelnden und bearbeitenden Geschichtswerke im Alten Testa- ment.* Schriften der Königsberger Gelehrten-Gesellschaft 18/2. Reissued separately; Tübingen: Max Niemeyer, 1957.

1948 *Überlieferungsgeschichte des Pentateuch.* Stuttgart: W. Kohlhammer. Trans. B. Anderson, *A History of Penta- teuchal Traditions.* Englewood Cliffs, NJ: Prentice-Hall, 1972.

1950 *Geschichte Israels.* Göttingen: Vandenhoeck & Ruprecht. 2d ed., 1954. Trans. P. R. Ackroyd. *The History of Israel.* Rev. ed. New York: Harper & Row, 1960.

1960 "Der Beitrag der Archäologie zur Geschichte Israels." Pp. 262–82 in *Congress Volume: Oxford, 1959.* VTSup 7. Leiden: E. J. Brill.

Orlinsky, Harry M.
1962 "The Tribal System of Israel and Related Groups in the Period of the Judges." Pp. 375–87 in *Studies and Essays in Honor of A. A. Neuman.* Ed. M. Ben-Horin, B. D. Weinryb, and S. Zeitlin. Philadelphia: Dropsie College.

Page, Stephanie
1968 "A Stela of Adad-nirari III and Nergal-ereš from Tell al Rimah." *Iraq* 30: 139–53.

Polzin, Robert
1976   "Martin Noth's *A History of Pentateuchal Traditions.*"
            BASOR 221: 113–20.

Pritchard, James B.
1970   "The Megiddo Stables: A Reassessment." Pp. 268–76 in
            *Near Eastern Archaeology in the Twentieth Century:
            Essays in Honor of Nelson Glueck.* Ed. J. A. Sanders.
            Garden City, NY: Doubleday.

Rad, Gerhard von
1943   "Grundprobleme einer biblischen Theologie des Alten
            Testaments." *TLZ* 68: 225–34.
1960   "History and the Patriarchs." *ExpTim* 72: 213–16.

Rainey, Anson
1975   "The Fate of Lachish during the Campaigns of Sen-
            nacherib and Nebuchadrezzar." Pp. 47–60 in *Investiga-
            tions at Lachish: The Sanctuary and the Residency
            (Lachish V).* Ed. Y. Aharoni. Publications of the Institute
            of Archaeology, 4. Tel Aviv: Gateway.

Rothenberg, Geno
1962   "Ancient Copper Industries in the Western Arabah."
            PEQ 94: 5–71.

Rowley, Harold Henry
1940   "The Chronological Order of Ezra and Nehemiah." Pp.
            117–49 in *Ignace Goldziher Memorial Volume,* I. Ed.
            S. Löwinger and J. Somogyi. Budapest: Globus. Re-
            printed pp. 135–68 in Rowley, *The Servant of the Lord.*
            London: Lutterworth, 1965.

Rowton, M. B.
1967   "The Physical Environment and the Problem of the
            Nomads." Pp. 109–21 in *La civilisation de Mari.* XVe
            Rencontre Assyriologique Internationale. Ed. J. R. Kup-
            per. Paris: Société de l'Edition "Les Belles Lettres."
1973   "Autonomy and Nomadism in Western Asia." *Or* 42:
            247–58.
1976   "Dimorphic Structure and the Problem of the 'Apiru-
            'Ibrim." *JNES* 35: 13–20.

Sauer, James A.
1979   "Iron I Pillard House in Moab." *BA* 42: 9.

Shenkel, James Donald
1968   *Chronology and Recensional Development in the Greek
            Text of Kings.* HSM 1. Cambridge, MA: Harvard
            University Press.

Shiloh, Yigael
1970   "The Four-Room House: Its Situation and Function in
            the Israelite City." *IEJ* 20: 180–90.

Smith, Morton
1971
Palestinian Parties and Politics that Shaped the Old Testament. New York: Columbia University Press.

Starkey, John L.
1937a
"Lachish as Illustrating Bible History." *PEQ* 69: 171–79.
1937b
"Excavations at Tell ed Duweir." *PEQ* 69: 228–41.

Thiele, Edwin R.
1944
"The Chronology of the Kings of Judah and Israel." *JNES* 3: 137–86. Expanded in *The Mysterious Numbers of the Hebrew Kings: A Reconstruction of the Chronology of the Kingdoms of Israel and Judah.* Grand Rapids: Eerdmans, 1965.

Thompson, Thomas L.
1974
The Historicity of the Patriarchal Narratives. BZAW 133. Berlin: Walter de Gruyter.

Tucker, Gene M.
1966
"The Legal Background of Genesis 23." *JBL* 85: 77–84.

Tufnell, Olga
1959
"Hazor, Samaria and Lachish." *PEQ* 91: 90–105.

Van Seters, John
1968
"The Problem of Childlessness in Near Eastern Law and the Patriarchs of Israel." *JBL* 87: 401–8.
1969
"Jacob's Marriages and Ancient Near Eastern Customs: A Reexamination." *HTR* 62: 377–95.
1975
Abraham in History and Tradition. New Haven: Yale University Press.

Vaux, Roland de
1946
"Les patriarches hébreux et les découvertes modernes." *RB* 53: 321–48; 55: 321–47; 56: 5–36.
1976
The Early History of Israel: To the Period of the Judges. London: Darton, Longman & Todd; Philadelphia: Westminster.

Waltke, Bruce K.
1972
"Palestinian Artifactual Evidence Supporting the Early Date of the Exodus." *BSac* 129: 33–47.

Weippert, Manfred
1967
Die Landnahme der israelitischen Stämme in der neueren wissenschaftlichen Diskussion. FRLANT 92. Göttingen: Vandenhoeck & Ruprecht. Trans. James D. Martin. *The Settlement of the Israelite Tribes in Palestine: A Critical Survey of Recent Scholarly Debate.* SBT 2/21. Naperville, IL: Allenson, 1971.
1979
"The Israelite 'Conquest' and Evidence from Transjordan." Pp. 15–34 in *Symposia.* Ed. F. M. Cross. Cambridge, MA: ASOR.

Whitley, Charles Francis
1952 "The Deuteronomic Presentation of the House of Omri."
VT 2: 137–52.

Wifall, Walter R.
1968 "The Chronology of the Divided Monarchy of Israel."
ZAW 80: 319–37.

Wiseman, Donald J.
1956 *Chronicles of the Chaldean Kings (625–556 BC) in the
British Museum.* London: British Museum.

Wood, Leon James
1970 *Survey of Israel's History.* Grand Rapids: Zondervan.

Wright, George Ernest
1952 *God Who Acts: Biblical Theology as Recital.* SBT 8.
London: SCM.
1958 "Archaeology and Old Testament Studies." *JBL* 77:
39–51.
1959 "Modern Issues in Biblical Studies—History and the
Patriarchs." *ExpTim* 71: 292–96.

Yadin, Yigael
1958 "Solomon's City Wall and Gate at Gezer." *IEJ* 8: 80–86.
1960 "New Light on Solomon's Megiddo." *BA* 23: 62–68.
1967 "Hazor." Pp. 244–63 in *Archaeology and Old Testament Study.* Ed. D. W. Thomas. London: Oxford University Press.
1973 "A Note of the Stratigraphy of Israelite Megiddo." *JNES*
32: 330.

2

Syro-Palestinian and Biblical Archaeology

William G. Dever

The state of Palestinian archaeology has been periodically surveyed by several authorities in the modern period. However, an examination of the standard treatments, including those written previously for the Society of Biblical Literature (see Albright, 1938, 1951, 1969; G. E. Wright, 1947, 1958, 1969b; Pritchard; Freedman, 1965; Lapp, 1969), will show that they have actually been general summaries of the recovery of the ancient Near Eastern context of the Bible. Most concentrated on the literary remains brought to light that might bear on problems of biblical history, literary criticism, or interpretation. Not until the 1970s did surveys discuss Syro-Palestinian or biblical *archaeology* as such or treat the problems of considering either as a *discipline* (Dever, 1974, 1976; Glock).

There is reason to believe that the earlier approach, although useful at the time, is no longer possible or desirable. (1) First, there has been a vast accumulation of new data from the post-1945 expansion of archaeological fieldwork in Palestine (i.e., southern Lebanon and Syria, Jordan, and Israel). The bulk and complexity of the excavated evidence—much of it not yet analyzed or published in detail—make it increasingly difficult even for specialists to single out the most significant discoveries, much less to synthesize the results of the field as a whole. (For a cursory summary of developments ca. 1950–75, however, see Dever, 1976, updating van Beek.)

(2) More important, in the last decade Syro-Palestinian archaeology has grown into a self-conscious discipline with its own aims and methods. Thus, it can no longer be subsumed under ancient Near Eastern studies (i.e., that aspect which deals with the recovery and interpretation of ancient texts) or considered simply a specialized branch of biblical studies that describes the material culture of ancient Israel (the original use of the term "archaeology" to denote "biblical antiquities"). Syro-Palestinian archaeology's stature as a branch of general archaeology now requires us to analyze it as a field of inquiry in itself and to render an account of its progress, its current research objectives and strategies, and its prospects. At the same time, it becomes possible to put biblical archaeology into critical perspective and to understand it as a unique chapter in American intellectual

history, both in relation to biblical studies and in relation to Syro-Palestinian archaeology.

The present essay therefore attempts to produce neither a comprehensive résumé of recent archaeological discoveries relating to the Bible nor a synthesis of the archaeological history of Palestine in the Bronze and Iron Ages.[1] It aims rather at a portrait of two disciplines during the crucial years of their development—one in the ascendancy, the other possibly in decline.

I. SYRO-PALESTINIAN ARCHAEOLOGY, 1945-80: RETROSPECTS AND PROSPECTS

Let us look first at the formative years of Syro-Palestinian archaeology, focusing especially on fieldwork, the development of theory and method, the growth of national schools, and the advent of professionalism.

1945-55: The Postwar Era

The end of World War II brought the prompt resumption of archaeological fieldwork in the Middle East. Early excavations in the former British Mandate territory of Palestine included those in what became the Hashemite Kingdom of Jordan: the work of the French under R. de Vaux at Tell el-Far'ah (north; biblical Tirzah; 1946-60); the excavation of the French, British, and Americans at Qumran and the Wâdî Murabba'at under de Vaux, L. Harding, and others (1949-56); the campaigns of the British under K. M. Kenyon at Jericho (1952-58); and American excavations under F. V. Winnett and successive directors at Dhibân (1950-56) and under J. B. Pritchard and others at Tulûl Abū el-'Alâyiq (NT Jericho; 1950-51). With the partition of Palestine, excavations were undertaken almost immediately in the new state of Israel, first by the Israelis themselves at Tell Qasileh under B. Maisler (Mazar, 1948-50); the somewhat later excavations under M. Dothan at 'Affûleh (1951) and at Kh. el-Bitar (1952-54) and under Mazar and N. Avigad at Beth-She'arim (1953-60) also belong to this formative phase.

Of greater long-term significance was the impetus toward national schools in both Jordan and Israel after 1948, although these would not flourish until the 1960s and 1970s. These were fostered initially by the growing local sponsorship of excavations, which became the pattern first

---

[1] As the title of this volume implies, this survey is intended largely for OT scholars, and therefore it is confined mostly to ancient Palestine (principally modern Israel, Jordan, and parts of Syria), and it focuses more on the Bronze and Iron Ages than on either prehistory or the Persian-Byzantine period. It also stresses excavation more than survey. Finally, being written from an American point of view, it may not always do full justice to other work. The writer is at work on another contribution to the Society of Biblical Literature Centennial Publications, a full-length history of the field.

in Israel and somewhat later in Jordan. Momentum toward independence was further built up by the establishment of new Departments of Antiquities in both countries, which not only gradually promulgated and enforced revised versions of the British Antiquities Laws but also began publication of their own organs. Replacing the *Quarterly of the Department of Antiquities in Palestine* (Vols. 1–15, 1931–51) were first the *Israel Exploration Journal*, published by the Israel Exploration Society beginning in 1950 (also the occasional series of memorial volumes in Hebrew, Eretz-Israel); and '*Atiqot: Journal of the Israel Department of Antiquities* (English Series 1955–, Hebrew Series 1966–). The *Annual of the Department of Antiquities in Jordan* was inaugurated by the British in 1951, but after their replacement by nationals in 1956 it continued to be published by the Jordanians (Vol. 4, 1960–). Trends already under way in the early 1950s also saw the eventual development of museums under the direction of the national antiquities departments: the Israel Museum was dedicated in 1965, and the old Palestine Archaeological Museum (established in 1938 as the Rockefeller Museum) was nationalized by the Jordanians in 1967 to supplement the opening at the Amman Archaeological Museum in 1960. Also, many smaller regional museums were founded in Israel and in Jordan from 1950 onward.

Finally, the Hebrew University in Jerusalem continued its Institute of Archaeology (see now its publication series *Qedem*, 1971–), followed later by other Institutes at Tel-Aviv (1968; see *Tel-Aviv*, 1974), at Beersheba (1973), and at Haifa (1974). And, to anticipate a bit, the University of Jordan in Amman included a Department of Archaeology and History from its founding in 1962 (graduate program 1973–); and a second archaeological program opened in 1979 at the new Yarmuk University. Already in the early 1950s, however, locally trained archaeologists were at work in both countries, though the full impact of a generation of younger archaeologists produced by the national schools would not be felt in Israel until the 1960s and in Jordan until the 1970s.

1950–60: A Revolution in Field Method and the Beginning of the National Schools

The next decade saw a golden age of excavation that surpassed even the heyday of the 1930s and brought with it advances in stratigraphic technique worthy of comparison with the first great breakthrough in archaeological method, Albright's development of refined ceramic typology in the 1930s.

The impetus came from the British, in the late Kathleen Kenyon's introduction of three-dimensional techniques of excavation and recording, brought to a fine art by R. E. M. Wheeler and others first at Romano-British sites and later in the Middle East in Wheeler's excavations at

Mohenjo Daro in the Indus Valley (see Wheeler; Kenyon, 1952). These newer methods were applied for the first time to the complex problems of multi-layered Palestinian mounds in Kenyon's excavations at Jericho in 1952–58 (and later in Jerusalem, 1961–67). Here she dug in smaller squares within a grid, usually on a five-by-five-meter module, leaving intervening catwalks or "baulks" that were then used to see the debris in section and to guide careful probing and stripping of the layers. Digging proceeded not by architectural strata as formerly, much less by artificial levées (as the French had employed at Byblos, Ugarit, and elsewhere), but rather by following the *natural* stratification of the mound, separating soil layers or "loci" by color, texture, and depositional character and history. The baulks were then drawn to scale, and the section-drawings became the basis of the interpretation and publication, all objects and architecture being related to the stratigraphy thereby illustrated.

This system introduced not only the third dimension in field archaeology but also the element of control that made it possible to separate and date debris layers and the objects they contained with greater accuracy as well as to recognize architectural sub-phasing more precisely. While the restricted exposure, slower pace, and mass of accumulated detail that characterized Kenyon's methods provoked controversy, the results have proven superior—especially in re-excavating sites dug previously, where there is little material left *in situ* and great care is essential. Indeed, the system worked so well that various adaptations of the so-called Wheeler-Kenyon (or better, "baulk/debris-layer") method came to be employed on nearly all British and American excavations in Jordan in the 1960s. Kenyon's own definitive statement on method appeared in this period (1952), and one may note work in the British tradition under P. J. Parr, Diana Kirkbride, Crystal-M. Bennett, G. R. H. Wright, and others at Petra (1955–68).

American contribution to the stratigraphic revolution also began in Jordan, principally in the excavation launched by G. E. Wright at Shechem in 1956, continued by him and others through 1973. Here Wright and his colleagues, including J. A. Callaway and L. E. Toombs, who had been trained at Jericho, deliberately set out to adapt Kenyon's methods, to complement them with the Albright-style ceramic typology in which Americans had traditionally excelled, and to train the first postwar generation of American field archaeologists—in this case, all from the background of the biblical archaeology school. Wright was followed by J. B. Pritchard at Gibeon, 1956–62 (but see the strictures of Lapp [1969:125] on Pritchard's methods). However, the full flowering of the American school did not come about until the maturation of the Shechem excavations in the mid-1960s—and in particular in the transfer of this tradition to Israel beginning with the Gezer excavation in 1964 and continuing with its derivatives in the 1970s. Other foreign schools working in Jordan in this period were affected to some degree by these improvements in method—de Vaux at Tell el-Far'ah (north) less so (1946–60; see Lapp, 1969:79), and the Dutch under H. J. Franken at Tell Deir 'Allā (1960–67) rather more so.[2]

Meanwhile, after the establishment of the state of Israel in 1948, the first task was to conserve the sites and to lay the groundwork for a national archaeological program. Although Mazar and others were already in the field before 1950, the Israeli school first came to international prominence with the large and superbly organized excavations of Y. Yadin and others at Hazor (1955–58), followed by Y. Aharoni at Ramat Raḥel (1954–62) and S. Yeivin at "Tel Gath" (= Tell esh-Sheikh Aḥmed el-'Areini, not biblical Gath; 1956–61). The distinctive features of the Israeli school during these early years were: (1) the concentrated effort to recover a national history, particularly of the Canaanite and Israelite eras; (2) excellent organization, resources, and technical facilities, such as only a local school can provide; (3) a preference for large-scale exposure of architecture at virgin sites, rather than more meticulously done soundings at re-excavated sites; and (4) an emphasis on building up a corpus of whole pottery found in situ, rather than detailed analysis of sherds. These objectives were admirable, but the inevitable isolation from developments in archaeology elsewhere in the 1950s meant that the Israeli school did not take full advantage of the stratigraphic revolution until the 1970s. As a consequence, some of the architectural phasing was imprecise, and interpretations have remained needlessly controversial. Furthermore, as with the British and American experiments in method, publication fell so far behind fieldwork that it was difficult to judge the merits of the various methods employed in the only way that counts—by evaluating the results obtained.

The Centre National Recherche Scientifique also worked in Israel under the direction of J. Perrot, chiefly at prehistoric sites such as 'Eynan ('Ain Mallaḥa; 1955–61), Tell Abu Maṭar (1952–54), Bir eṣ-Ṣafadi (1954–55), and Azor (1958–59).

Thus the developments of the relatively brief period of the 1950s did indeed constitute a revolution in field archaeology, the implications of which might not be fully understood until the 1970s but which would nevertheless ultimately transform the chaos of the earlier, architecturally

2 For virtually complete bibliography on recent theory and method in Syro-Palestinian archaeology, see the fundamental works of the British archaeologists Kenyon (1952) and Wheeler; the doctrinaire application of these and the polemical attack on American method in Franken and Franken-Battershill; American critique and adaptations in G. R. H. Wright, G. E. Wright (1969c, 1970), Lapp (1969, 1970), Dever (1971b, 1973, 1976, 1980b); and Israeli reaction in Aharoni (1973). One may note also the more detailed exposition of modern field technique in Dever and Lance (1978). On theory and method among American New World archaeologists, see n. 6 below.

oriented approach into the controlled and precise excavation of truly stratigraphic archaeology.

1960–70: A Discipline Comes of Age

Developments in Syro-Palestinian archaeology in the decade of the 1960s may best be described in terms of the advent of professionalism.

Excavations

There was a proliferation of excavations, many of them large, long-running projects. They were so numerous that only the major sites can be listed here.

American. American excavations in Jordan and Israel included those of G. E. Wright and his colleagues continuing at Shechem (1956–73); P. C. Hammond at Petra (1961–62); R. J. Bull in the Samaritan sanctuary on Mt. Gerazim (1964–68); P. W. Lapp at 'Arâq el-Emîr (1961–62), Ta'anach (1963–68), Tell er-Rumeith (1967), and Bâb edh-Dhrâ' (1965–67); J. A. Callaway at 'Ai (1964–69); G. E. Wright, W. G. Dever, H. D. Lance, and J. D. Seger at Gezer (in Israel, 1964–74); R. H. Smith at Pella (1967); J. B. Pritchard at Tell es-Sa'îdîyeh (1967); W. G. Dever at Kh. el-Kôm and Jebel el-Qa'aqîr (1967–71); and S. H. Horn, L. T. Geraty, and others at Ḥesbân (1968–78). These excavations not only marked the zenith of the American school's field operations; they also saw the further development of method and the emergence of a second generation of excavators trained since World War II. Moreover, they witnessed the impact of the influence of the American Schools of Oriental Research (with which virtually all the digs in Jordan were affiliated) in Israel. This was first felt in 1964–65, when the newly opened American school in West Jerusalem, the Hebrew Union College Biblical and Archaeological School (now the Nelson Glueck School of Biblical Archaeology), was staffed by Wright and his students and began the long-running Gezer operations. The school continued to be directed by Gezer-trained personnel for some time (W. G. Dever, 1966–71; J. D. Seger, 1971–74) and in the 1960s was the focus of the American school in Israel. After 1967 the old American School in East Jerusalem, now renamed the W. F. Albright Institute of Archaeological Research, was also in the Israeli sector and further consolidated American influence in Israel. In 1968 an ASOR affiliate in Amman was opened as the American Center for Oriental Research (ACOR) and continued to foster American archaeology in Jordan at Ḥesbân and many other sites (directed by J. A. Sauer, 1974–81, who was succeeded by D. W. McCreery, 1981–).

Israeli. The Israeli school came to full flower in the 1960s as well, with the very impressive excavations of Y. Yadin at Megiddo (1960–71);

Y. Aharoni, N. Avigad, P. Bar-Adon, Y. Yadin, and others in the caves in the Judean wilderness (1960–61); M. Stekelis at the Paleolithic site of 'Ubeidiya (1960–63); B. Mazar and Trude Dothan at 'En-gedi (1961–65); M. Dothan at Ashdod (1962–72); Aharoni and Ruth Amiran at Arad (1962–78); Yadin at Masada (1963–65); Aharoni at Lachish (1966–68); A. Biran at Dan (1966–79); Aharoni and others at Beersheba (1969–75); and especially B. Mazar, N. Avigad, M. Broshi, and numerous others at various sites in Old Jerusalem after 1967 (the Western Wall, the Jewish quarter, etc.). These excavations, which also saw the emergence of the younger generation of Israeli archaeologists, made several innovations and generally belied the monolithic character of the Israeli school of the 1950s—particularly after 1968, when the Tel-Aviv University inaugurated its Institute of Archaeology under Aharoni, rivaling that in Jerusalem and launching a vigorous, well-coordinated, and amply supported program of fieldwork concentrating on the Negev In addition, the end of the decade opened the West Bank, the Golan Heights, and the Sinai to Israeli exploration and salvage work and at the same time gave Israeli archaeologists an opportunity to examine (and to criticize) the older excavations of the British and Americans there. Insofar as this helped to overcome the isolation of the 1950s, it had a positive effect on the methodological debate, although the political ramifications stirred up other controversies.

French. The French now transferred many of their operations to Israel, where J. Perrot and others conducted excavations under the auspices of the Centre National Recherche Scientifique, mostly at prehistoric sites such as Munhata (1962–67), and Abu Ghosh and Beisamoun (1967–72).

British. The British worked exclusively in Jordan in this period: under Kenyon in Jerusalem (1961–67); under J. B. Hennessy at the Damascus Gate (1964–66), the Amman LB temple (1966), and at Telêilat al-Ghassûl (1967–); under Crystal-M. Bennett at the Iron Age sites of Buṣeirah (Bozrah), Umm el-Biyâra, and Ṭawilân (1964–); and under Diana Kirkbride at the Neolithic site of Beidha near Petra (1958–65). After 1967 the British School of Archaeology in Jerusalem (1919–) restricted its fieldwork in Israel to a survey of Islamic architecture in the Old City, which had the effect of concentrating British archaeological influence in Jordan thereafter.

German. The older Deutsches Evangelisches Institut für Altertumswissenschaft des Heiligen Landes (1902–) in Jerusalem, directed by Ute Lux, sponsored work on the Madeba mosaics (1964–75; see also Lux's excavations beneath the Erlöserkirche in Jerusalem, with E. W. Kruger, in 1970–71). Most German fieldwork of this period was limited to surveys, however, among which may be noted S. Mittmann's work in northern Transjordan (1963–66) and M. Weippert's work in the south beginning in the late 1960s. But younger German biblical scholars also showed interest in excavations in Israel and joined Israeli projects at Beersheba, Tel Masos, and elsewhere (V. Fritz, F. Maass, D. Conrad, and others). However, having been inactive in fieldwork in Palestine since the late 1930s, the Germans never regained their full momentum or made particularly significant contributions to recent developments in method (see below, however, on German participation in the debate on "Biblical Archaeology").

Dutch and Spanish. Finally, the Dutch under H. J. Franken and others conducted major excavations at Tell Deir 'Allā (1960–67), which not only contributed important finds but also played a prominent role in the controversy over method (see above). Spanish excavations were carried out by E. Olávarri at 'Arô'er on the Wâdī Môjib (1964–66).

Jordanian. The Jordanians themselves did not succeed in establishing an adequately supported and well-trained national school until the 1970s, but the early work of F. Zayidine at Samaria (1965–67) may be noted, along with the clearance of LB and Iron Age tombs at Irbid, Sahab, and Amman by R. Dajani and M. Ibrahim (1958–75), and work on the Citadel (1957–) and the Roman Forum at Amman (1964–67) by R. Dajani, F. Zayidine, A. Hadidi, and others.

New Trends

In addition to the sheer volume of excavated material—and perhaps more significant in the long run—were the specific new trends in both fieldwork and research in the 1960s that fostered the growth of Syro-Palestinian archaeology as an independent discipline. These trends can only be enumerated here, roughly in order of their appearance but not necessarily in order of importance.

Methodology. First, the pioneering improvements in excavation technique of the previous decade, sketched above, were more extensively tested, refined, and adapted to a variety of field problems, especially on American and Israeli excavations. Methodology grew more self-conscious, more sophisticated—and more controversial, particularly in Israel, where the Gezer excavations by mid-decade became the focus by attempting to introduce American innovations. The controversy had already come to a head in numerous discussions by the end of the decade, but it would not be fully reflected in the literature until the 1970s.[3]

---

[3] See, for instance, the first full-scale field reports based on the "Wheeler-Kenyon" (or "baulk-debris") methods in the Gezer preliminary volumes (Dever et al., 1970, 1975), and

Student volunteerism. While the first postwar generation of American excavators of Shechem had been devoted to field training, their successors at Gezer in the 1960s were even more dedicated to this task. In addition to recruiting and training a third generation of professionals on the staff, beginning in 1964 they structured the entire Gezer project around a field school for undergraduate and graduate students. This replaced hired native labor, familiar in both Israel and Jordan, with more than one hundred American student volunteers each season who did all the physical labor, helped work up the excavated material, and participated in an accredited academic program. The result was to emphasize the value of teamwork and also to demonstrate the superior benefits obtained with intelligent use of the more complex new methods. Student labor soon became an economic necessity as well, as costs mounted astronomically on excavations; by the 1970s it was the universal pattern on digs in Israel and in Jordan. No single development transformed the typical excavation between 1960 and 1970 more than student volunteerism.

Funding. In the 1960s the rise in costs, the growing demand for large staffs of specialists, and the massive influx of students from new orientations placed a typical American excavation project beyond the means or the inclination of theological seminaries to provide support, as they had done previously. By the mid-1960s, however, American excavations, having lost their exclusive identification with biblical studies, found it possible to qualify for large-scale financial support from the U.S. government, principally under the Public Law 480 program, which provided grants in soft currencies (counterpart funds), to be followed in the 1970s by the program of matching grants from the National Endowment for the Humanities. These grants were first made available to the Gezer excavations in 1966 and were later extended to nearly all American (and some joint) excavations in Israel and Jordan. They provided not only direct costs for fieldwork but also institutional overhead, for instance, to both the W. F. Albright and the Nelson Glueck schools in Jerusalem. At the same time, the necessity for raising matching funds in hard currency (and recruiting students) brought about the formation of large consortia of American universities and other institutions that will be noted presently, further reinforcing the secular shift. It is no exaggeration to say that these developments salvaged American archaeology in the Middle East as well as simultaneously transforming its earlier, almost exclusively biblical character beyond recognition.

An interdisciplinary approach. Closely related to the above was the first development of a truly interdisciplinary approach. The earliest

---

note the negative reaction of the Israeli archaeologist A. Kempinski (1972, 1976). Today the acceptance of British-American method in Israel is much more widespread.

employment of larger, more specialized staffs was seen in 1966 at Gezer, when a geologist became a member of the Core Staff. By the late 1960s, on some American and even a few Israeli excavations, traditional stratigraphers, architects, and ceramic typologists were working alongside geologists, geographers, paleo-ethno-botanists and zoologists, climatologists, hydrologists, physical and cultural anthropologists, ethnographers, historians of technology, computer programmers, and still other consultants in disciplines formerly thought quite remote from historical or biblical archaeology—but of course already familiar on prehistoric excavations.

At first the interest in allied disciplines was largely pragmatic and even naïve—a natural response to the general concern for improved method, the atmosphere of broader cooperative enterprises, and the greater availability of personnel and funding from new sources. But by the early 1970s, as Syro-Palestinian archaeologists became more familiar with American anthropology and the "New Archaeology" and also were now required to incorporate sophisticated research design into grant proposals for secular agencies, the basic approach to archaeology had changed. For the first time in its history, American archaeology in the Middle East began to develop and to articulate a *general theory* (see further below).

Thus, the era of the 1960s was one of rapid growth, of broadening horizons, and of stimulating controversy on crucial issues of theory and method. The trends sketched all too inadequately above were interrelated in a very complex fashion, of course, but their combined effect during this decade was simply to introduce a professionalism that soon would result in the establishment of Syro-Palestinian archaeology as an autonomous discipline—no longer a largely amateur affair or an adjunct of biblical studies, but a branch of general archaeology with its own integrity and its appropriate aims and methods. (For the impact on biblical archaeology, see below.) This third revolution will likely have even more far-reaching consequences than Albright's pioneering of ceramic chronology in the 1930s or Kenyon's introduction of stratigraphic methods in the 1950s, since it has altered the fundamental conception of the field, but it is still too early to predict what the precise result will be.

1970–80: The "New Archaeology"

It is hazardous to attempt to place a decade just coming to a close in historical perspective, but at least two significant trends that render the 1970s a new age may already be discerned.

The New Generation

The first trend is seen in the establishment of the new generation that emerged in the 1960s (actually the third since World War II). International

Palestinian archaeology was deprived of the pioneering generation—all of them closely associated with the foreign schools in Jerusalem during their formative years—by the deaths, within a cruelly brief period, of Martin Noth (1969), Paul Lapp (1970), Nelson Glueck (1971), W. F. Albright (1971), Roland de Vaux (1971), G. Ernest Wright (1974), and Kathleen Kenyon (1978). In the same period the Israelis suffered the loss of Michael Avi-Yonah (1974) and Yohanan Aharoni (1976). By the mid to late 1970s, Nahman Avigad, Benjamin Mazar, and Yigael Yadin (temporarily, to enter politics) had retired from the Hebrew University, Avraham Biran from the directorship of the Department of Antiquities, and Ruth Amiran from the Israel Museum. In Jordan, the first local archaeologist to direct the Department of Antiquities, Awni Dajani, died in 1968.

While this remarkable generation literally cannot be replaced, continuity in the field is ensured by a large and capable group of younger archaeologists, trained principally in the 1960s, which has come into the ascendancy. Without attempting a full listing, we may observe something of the scope and quality of their activity by characterizing the major excavations of the 1970s.

American projects. Among American projects in Israel, the Gezer excavations, which had played a pivotal role in the 1960s, continued under W. G. Dever (through 1971) and J. D. Seger (1972–74). The new multidisciplinary approach in method taken there was expanded and more firmly established in Israel when Gezer-trained staffs moved on to direct the new ASOR-sponsored projects at Tell el-Ḥesi (J. Worrell, L. E. Stager, G. L. Rose; 1970–); at the synagogue sites of Kh. Shema, Meiron, Gush Ḥalav, and Nabratein in Galilee (E. M. Meyers, Carol Meyers, J. F. Strange; 1970–); at Shechem (W. G. Dever; 1972–73); at Lahav (Tel Ḥalif; J. D. Seger, D. P. Cole; 1976–); at Be'er Resisim in the Central Negev (W. G. Dever; 1978–80; with R. Cohen); at Tell Yin'am (H. Liebwitz; 1976–); and at Tel Miqne (S. Gitin; 1981–; with T. Dothan). (Similar approaches were also being taken by more senior American excavators, in some cases influenced by Gezer, such as S. S. Weinberg with Sharon Herbert at Tel Anafa, 1968–81; G. van Beek at Tell Jemmeh, 1970–82; and R. J. Bull, L. E. Toombs, and others at Caesarea, 1971–.) This influence even extended further under Gezer-trained excavators who directed projects such as that at Tell Ḥesbân (1968–78) and Tell Jalul (1981–) in Jordan (L. T. Geraty); at Carthage in Tunisia (L. E. Stager; 1973–79); at Idalion in Cyprus (Stager, Anita Walker, Pamela Gaber; 1972–); at Tell Maskhuṭa in Egypt (J. S. Holladay, Jr.; 1978–); and even in the Belice Valley of Sicily (A. E. Leonard; 1974–79).

In Jordan, the same approach was seen in all American projects of the period, such as the major excavation at Ḥesbân (above) and at Bâb edh-Dhrâ' under W. E. Rast and R. T. Schaub (1975–81), as well as in

many smaller projects, such as B. de Vries's work at Umm al-Jimal
(1972–), and even in surveys like that of Moab by J. M. Miller (1979–),
of the Wâdi Ḥesa by B. Macdonald (1980), and others.

Meanwhile this generation of the Shechem-Gezer tradition assumed
the directorships of both American schools in Jerusalem, the Nelson
Glueck and the W. F. Albright institutes (P. W. Lapp, 1960–67; W. G.
Dever, 1968–75; J. D. Seger, 1971–73; E. M. Meyers, 1975–76; S. Gitin,
1980–) as well as that of the newly opened ASOR Center in Amman
(J. A. Sauer, 1975–81). They also took over positions of leadership in the
American Schools of Oriental Research, assumed editorships of some of
the major ASOR publications, especially the *Bulletin*, and established
themselves in academic positions at most of the North American universities that offered graduate programs in the field (Harvard, Chicago,
Pennsylvania, Duke, Toronto, Arizona, etc.). As these relative newcomers
on the scene begin to publish their fieldwork and research, a distinctive
point of view and methodology emerge. They confirm the ancestry of
these younger scholars in the American school but nevertheless show that
this generation has indeed come of age and represents a phenomenon
that may be designated the "new archaeology" (related to but not identical with the "New Archeology" [*sic*] in America; see below). Already
several monograph-length reports have appeared on Gezer, Shema, and
Ḥesbân, and shorter preliminary reports are available for other sites.

Israeli projects. Among Israeli projects, a few representing essentially the approach of the 1960s continued, as for example at Early
Bronze Age Arad under Amiran (1962–78); at Dan under Biran (1966–
79); at Beersheba under Aharoni (1968–74; 1975 directed by A. Rainey,
A. Kempinski, and Z. Herzog); and, of course, at many sites in Jerusalem, as well as in salvage and survey work everywhere but especially in
the occupied territories. The newer excavation projects being launched
in the 1970s, however, revealed the shape of things to come for the
Israeli school, especially in the excavations of the Tel-Aviv Institute of
Archaeology at Tel Masos under A. Kempinski (1972–75), at Tel Aphek
(Râs el-'Ain) under M. Kochavi and Pirhiya Beck (1972–), at Tel Michal
(1977–80) and Tell Jerisheh (1981–) under Z. Herzog, A. Rainey, and
others, and at Lachish under D. Ussishkin (1972–); of the Ben-Gurion
University of the Negev in Beersheba at Tel Shariya and at many sites in
the Sinai under E. Oren (1972–80); of the Haifa University at Acco
under M. Dothan (1973–); and of the Institute of Archaeology of the
Hebrew University of Jerusalem in the Negev and Sinai under O. Bar-
Yosef (1967–80), at Iron Age forts (including Kadesh-Barnea, 1976–81)
in the Negev under R. Cohen (1965–), at Tell Qasileh in Tel-Aviv under
A. Mazar (1971–74), at Deir el-Balaḥ in the Gaza Strip under Trude
Dothan (1972–), at Tel Mevorakh (1973–76) and Dor (1980–) under

E. Stern, at Yoqneam and Tel Qassis under A. Ben-Tor (1976–), at Tell Batash under A. Mazar (1977–), and in the City of David in Jerusalem under Y. Shiloh (1978–). It should be noted that the Israelis even dug at Athienu in Cyprus in 1971–72 under Trude Dothan and A. Ben-Tor—their first foreign excavation.

Part of the transition to younger leadership in this period was a changeover in the Department of Antiquities and Museums, which has been directed since 1974 by A. Eitan. The series of annual archaeological congresses begun by the Department in 1972, which provided a nation-wide forum for many younger Israeli excavators and often witnessed heated debates over methodology, definitely heightened the visibility of the newer Israeli school. We should not neglect to mention the many well-trained technicians and District Archaeological Officers employed by the Department or the numerous excellent regional museums maintained under its aegis. Also significant are the several amateur archaeological societies, such as the nationwide Friends of Antiquities, and dozens of kibbutz study groups. The Israel Exploration Society, whose publications enjoy wide circulation (notably the popular Hebrew periodical *Qadmoniot* and the leading technical quarterly, the *Israel Exploration Journal*), sponsors an annual meeting that draws thousands of participants from all over Israel. It is probably accurate to say that nowhere else in the world is there a comparable national enthusiasm for archaeology, which is virtually a secular religion.

This brief sketch, which has perforce passed over many important developments, has scarcely done justice to the extraordinary archaeological enterprise in Israel, but it may indicate something of its variety and vigor. However, as with the American school, archaeology has often made more sensational headlines than solid professional progress. For instance, publication lags far behind fieldwork—although this school has produced a number of standard reference works (below) as well as a growing number of preliminary and final reports. Nevertheless, the Israeli school now dominates the scene in Palestinian archaeology (or the "Archaeology of Eretz-Israel," as it is termed locally), both by sheer force of fieldwork and by the fact that it enjoys obvious advantages that threaten to place the foreign schools out of the competition.

British, French, and German projects. Apart from the American and the Israeli schools, there are few others to consider. The quiescence of the British, French, and German schools in the late 1960s has been noted. This was owing in part to their political policy, which virtually excluded them from Israel and the West Bank in the late 1960s and the 1970s (but not, of course, from Jordan and Syria). This policy was further complicated by the fact that, unlike the Americans and the Israelis, the other foreign schools had not succeeded in raising a generation of younger Syro-Palestinian archaeologists to succeed Kenyon, de Vaux, and Noth. Although the British had no one of the seniority of Kenyon, in the 1970s P. Parr, who had succeeded her as Lecturer in Palestinian Archaeology at the Institute of Archaeology of the University of London, dug at Tell Nebi Mend in Syria. Crystal-M. Bennett, who became director of the British School in Jerusalem, continued to work in Jordan, first at Buṣeirah and Ṭawilân (above) and later on the Amman Citadel (1975–); and J. B. Hennessy, who became Professor of Middle Eastern Archaeology in the University of Sidney, Australia, resumed excavations at Ghassûl (1976–) and Pella (1979–; with Americans under R. H. Smith). Younger British archaeologists had also worked on a smaller scale in Jordan (Kay Prag at Iktanu, 1966; and S. W. Helms at Jawa, 1973–75). In 1980 the British Institute at Amman for Archaeology and History opened, also under the direction of Bennett.

By contrast, the French worked almost exclusively in Israel, chiefly under J. Perrot and his younger colleagues at prehistoric sites such as Abu Ghosh and Beisamun (1967–72) and 'Eynan (1972–76) and also at Bronze and Iron Age sites. The older Dominican L'École Biblique et Archéologique Française in Jerusalem (1982–) resumed fieldwork at Tell Kisan near Acco in 1971 under de Vaux, directed thereafter by P. Prignaud (1972–74), then by J. Briend and J.-B. Humbert (1975–). (In 1980 the École Biblique also began part sponsorship of new excavations at Ribab and at the Byzantine site of Kh. es-Samra in Jordan.) In 1980 the Centre National Recherche Scientifique opened the Centre de Recherches Préhistoriques at the Mission Francaise Permanente (NRS) at Imwas, near Latroun, and commenced excavations at Tell Yarmuth under P. de Miroschedi (1980–). That the French also had long-range plans for Jordan, however, was indicated by the transfer of the Institut Francais d'archéologie du Proche Orient from Beirut to Amman in 1978.

The younger Germans joined several Israeli excavations (above) but also began excavations at 'Umm Qeis in northern Jordan, one of the cities of the Decapolis, under Ute Lux, E. W. Kruger, and others (1976–), with support from the Danish under S. Holm-Nielsen. And in 1976 the Germans opened a new sister school of the Jerusalem School in Amman.

Projects in Jordan. The development of indigenous archaeology in Jordan was delayed by political and economic vicissitudes, and it was some time before a small though impressive group of younger scholars who had been trained abroad could begin to take their place alongside the British and Americans who had been working there. Among them were Assam Barghouti, Adnan Hadidi (who became Director of the Department of Antiquities in 1977), Moawiyah Ibrahim, Nabil Khairy, Safwan Tell, Khair Yassine, and Fawzi Zayidine. They continued excavating the Amman Citadel and clearing many Bronze and Iron Age tombs near Amman as well as beginning larger-scale surveys and excavations elsewhere in Jordan. Principal projects were the excavations at Sahab under Ibrahim (1972–80), at Tell el-Mazar in the lower Jordan Valley under Yassine (1977–), and at Jerash under Barghouti (1977–). Also significant were cooperative excavation projects such as the resumption of work at Tell Deir 'Allā, co-directed by Ibrahim (1978–) in cooperation with the Dutch under H. J. Franken and G. Van Der Kooij, and the Jordan Valley Survey of Sauer, Ibrahim, and Yassine (1976).

Projects in Syria. In Syria there was little new fieldwork either by foreign or local archaeologists until the late 1960s and the early 1970s, owing to the political instability of the area and the general lack of well-trained nationals. The French resumed their fieldwork at Ugarit, while the Germans under A. Moortgat in 1960 began very important excavations which continue at Tell Chuera in the Habur. By far the most significant new project of the mid-1960s, as it now turns out, was the excavation of P. Matthiae and his Italian colleagues at Tell Mardikh, south of Aleppo, ancient Ebla (1964–), where the discovery of some twenty thousand fragments of twenty-fourth-century-B.C.E. cuneiform tablets in "proto-Canaanite" in 1975–77 is being hailed as the archaeological sensation of the century (for general orientation, see Matthiae, 1979, 1981; Biggs; and Gelb on the texts).

Also in the mid-1960s, the announcement of a new dam to be built by the Russians at Tabqa (modern Al Thaoura) on the Upper Euphrates launched a project to save the sites to be flooded by Lake Al Assad when the dam was completed in 1973. The first and second stages of the project in 1964–70 consisted mostly of survey done by the Syrians and a few foreign scholars (M. Van Loon and others). But between 1970 and 1974, with the assistance of UNESCO, a massive international salvage project was undertaken. The Americans at first participated only on a modest scale in cooperation with others under R. P. Harper and Harvard-Michigan auspices at Dibsi-Faraj and under Theresa H. Carter and Johns Hopkins auspices at Tell Frey (1972–73). But the several campaigns of the Milwaukee Public Museum under R. H. Dornemann at Tell Hadidi (1973–78) have produced extremely important stratified third- to second-millennium material. British work under T. A. Holland at Tell es-Sweihat (1973–75), sponsored by the Ashmolean Museum, concentrated on materials of the same horizon, while A. M. T. Moore and others fielded by Oxford produced an excellent Neolithic sequence at Tell Abu Hureira (1972–73). The French worked at Tell Aswad (1971) and at the pre-pottery Neolithic site of Mureybit (1971–74) under J. Cauvin, sponsored by the Centre National Recherche Scientifique, and at Meskeneh (Hittite "Emar"; 1972–74) under J. Cl. Margueron. German excavations at Habubu Kabira and Mumbaqat, sponsored by the Deutsche Orient-Gesellschaft and directed by E. Heinrich,

E. Strommenger, W. Orthmann, and H. Kühne, brought to light an enormous Early Dynastic fortified site at Habubu Kabira, as well as Middle Bronze Age material there and at Mumbaqat (1969–75). Other foreign excavations included those of the Dutch at Selenkehiye under M. Van Loon (1967–75) and H. J. Franken at Jebel Aruda (1972); of the Swiss under R. Stucky and others at Tell Hajj (1971); and of the Belgians under A. Finet at Tell Qannas (1967–74). The Syrians themselves participated in a number of these excavations and also directed their own project under A. Bouni (with the support of A. Bahnassi and the Directorate General of Antiquities and Museums) at Tell al-'Abd and 'Anab al-Safinah (1971–72) and at Tell Frey (1972–73). Although only scattered preliminary reports on these extremely important excavations on the Euphrates have appeared (see Freedman and Lundquist, 1979), it is already evident that, together with those at Ebla, these excavations will revolutionize our knowledge of Upper Syria in the third and second millennia B.C.E.

Apart from the Tabqa Dam projects, several newer American and British excavations were launched. First were those of the University of California at Los Angeles (license first issued to the Johns Hopkins University) under G. Buccellati and M. Kelley-Buccellati at Tell Asherah (ancient Terqa, on the Lower Euphrates near Mari; 1975–). Yale University worked at Tell Leilan in the Habur under H. Weiss (1978–). The British have been working on a small scale in southern Syria at Tell Nebi Mend (ancient Qadesh-on-the-Orontes) under P. J. Parr (1976–), with American participation; and soundings were carried out by J. Matthers at Tell Rifa'at, near Aleppo (1977).

The above review, although cursory, indicates that Syria—so incomparably rich but so sadly neglected in postwar archaeology—has suddenly come to the fore. However, much of the recent work has been salvage archaeology, and the conditions noted above that earlier hampered the development of a competent national school still remain to be dealt with. The best sources for archaeological news from Syria are *Syria: Revue d'Art Orientale et d'Archéologie* (1920–), and *Annales Archéologiques Arabes Syriennes* (1951–).

Projects in Lebanon. Lebanon has remained peripheral to this survey; it is not yet well known archaeologically, apart from the Classical period, and at the moment it would seem to have poor prospects. However, Americans have been able to do limited fieldwork there in the 1970s, of which one may note J. B. Pritchard's important excavation of the Phoenician coastal site of Sarafand (ancient Sarepta; 1967–75), and Patricia Bikai's soundings into Bronze and Iron Age levels at Tyre (1973–74).

The Germans had done significant survey work in the Beqa' under A. Kuschke (1954–) and have now undertaken excavations of major significance for method and for the history of the Beqa' under Kuschke,

R. Hachmann, and others at Kâmid el-Lôz (ancient Kumidi; 1963–).

Among the Lebanese themselves, while the redoubtable Emir Maurice Chehab continues as Director General of Antiquities, younger scholars like Roger Saideh have enjoyed increasing favor and support. The American University in Beirut offers some archaeological courses but has never sponsored excavations on any scale nor produced graduate students in the field. Thus Lebanon, despite its untapped riches, remains an archaeological backwater. However, archaeological discoveries are regularly reported in *Berytus* (1934–) and the *Bulletin du Musée de Beyrouth* (1937–).

The approach of the new generation. Based upon this survey of fieldwork in the 1970s in ancient Palestine and adjacent areas, let us try to summarize the significant differences in the approach of the younger generation, even though we may not yet have sufficient distance for critical perspective.

(1) First, the maturing of the national schools—manifest even earlier in Israel and now imminent in Jordan—meant that the last vestiges of the colonial era had disappeared. The new reality was reflected in the diminished role that the foreign institutes and schools played vis-à-vis the local authorities, to whom the initiative had now clearly passed; in the generally tighter antiquities laws and requirements for excavation permits (especially for prominent sites) being enforced by Departments of Antiquities, many of the provisions of which worked a special hardship on foreign excavators; and notably in the requirement that local archaeologists be incorporated into the staffs of some foreign excavations, sometimes even as co-directors.

(2) A further sign that the new generation was coming of age was more positive—the abatement of the earlier controversy over field method as a certain consensus was achieved. By the late 1970s, for instance, the use of stratigraphic techniques, section-drawings, extensive sampling and recording techniques, multidisciplinary staffs, and student trainees had become sufficiently accepted that there was little observable difference, for instance, between the better Israeli and American digs in the field. This agreement, however, was largely pragmatic; where *theory* was concerned, there was still wide divergence.

(3) The growth in scope, complexity, and staffing of archaeological projects generated pressure for cooperative efforts in recruitment and fund raising. For example, whereas Gezer had been sponsored principally by the Hebrew Union College, beginning in 1970 the typical larger American excavation had to create a consortium of schools and other institutions, which officially sponsored the project, supplied both students and staff, raised the matching funds now required by nearly all granting agencies, and often assumed a share of the finds and some responsibility for publication. Many of the Israeli excavations in the early 1970s also

solicited American funds, students, and occasional staff (Ashdod, Arad, the Western Wall, Dan, Lachish, Shariya, etc.). A model of even closer cooperation was the "joint excavation," such as those at Beersheba, Aphek, Acco, Tell Batashi, Tell Michal, Yoqneam, etc. (and note the earlier Japanese-Israeli partnership at Tell Zeror and the Italian-Israeli partnership at Ramat Raḥel). It was not until 1978, however, in the Central Negev Highlands Project, that one saw an excavation that featured co-sponsors and co-directors who were equal partners from fieldwork to publication—the Israel Department of Antiquities and the University of Arizona in affiliation with ASOR, under R. Cohen and W. G. Dever. (In 1981 the ASOR launched its first cooperative project with the Hebrew University, at Tel Miqne [Ekron], under the co-directorship of S. Gitin and T. Dothan—very likely the beginning of a significant trend.)

In Jordan, such joint excavations began later and obviously were characterized by a different balance and makeup, but one may observe a similar, growing pattern in both survey and excavation (the Jordan Valley Survey of Sauer and others and the resumption of work at Deir ʿAllā, above).

Finally, in 1978–79 "contract archaeology" made its debut in Israel and Jordan, when American construction firms doing projects in the Middle East began to be required by law to carry out cooperative "environmental impact" studies as they had been doing in federally funded projects in the United States: the Negev Salvage Project in Israel (1978–80); and, in Jordan, the Bâb edh-Dhrâʿ Township Survey (1977–78) and the Meqarin Dam Survey (Yarmuk-Zerqa area; 1978).

It would be naïve not to mention one danger in the increasing resort to local and to American government sources of support, although such is necessitated by the high cost and complexity of modern archaeology. The national schools in the Middle East run the risk of becoming nationalist, and American archaeology is increasingly becoming commercialized or heavily dependent on federal funds.

(4) Finally, while economic and political pressures have tended recently toward a retrenchment in fieldwork, the growing sophistication and ambition of current archaeological theory have exerted an expansive influence. Here is a paradox: Archaeology has become a luxury and at the same time an asset that no developing country can afford to neglect (certainly neither Israel nor Jordan). The result is that the *choice* of projects—particularly those locally sponsored—has become much more selective, more self-conscious, more public-minded (what is termed in American archaeology "cultural resource management"). In the future there will probably be fewer of the enormous, ten-year excavations at *tell* sites, such as characterized the 1960s and 1970s, and more smaller projects deliberately designed to answer specific questions—problem oriented excavations, digs at one-period sites, surface surveys, and regional studies.

The "New Archaeology"

The foregoing survey of the new generation of the 1970s leads us to the second current trend. By the end of the 1970s Syro-Palestinian archaeology was on the verge of becoming an independent discipline with its own theory, method, objectives, and support. The rationale for this had already been presented in several programmatic essays (Dever, 1971a, 1974, 1976). Whether welcomed as the inevitable evolution from amateurism to professionalism or lamented as the overspecialization of traditional biblical archaeology (below), this was a novel development, one that may be described as the triumph of the new archaeology. Influenced rather belatedly by the new archaeology in America, Syro-Palestinian archaeology by the mid-1970s was finally moving away from the classificatory-historical (descriptive) phase, with its particularistic and ideographic preoccupation and its inductive method, toward the explanatory phase, with its nomothetic orientation and its deductive reasoning.[4] It would be an oversimplification to say that traditional Near Eastern *historical* archaeology was giving way to the more characteristic *anthropological* archaeology of the Americanists, but the general contrast in orientation is pertinent.

Theory. Let us look first at the theory of the new archaeology. The fact that a theoretical groundwork was even beginning to be laid is itself significant. Palestinian archaeology from Petrie to the present has been so overwhelmingly pragmatic that almost nowhere in the literature will one find even a general definition of archaeology, much less a coherent body of archaeological theory. The major innovations of the new archaeology among the more avant-garde Syro-Palestinian specialists in the 1970s were all based on assumptions borrowed—often naïvely or even subconsciously—from American anthropology and archaeology. The most obvious were (1) the multidisciplinary orientation; (2) the consideration of environmental factors (ecology); (3) the value of ethnographic parallels; (4) the employment of general systems-theory (a holistic or systemic theory of culture), with its quantitative method; (5) the logic of explicitly scientific method, with its hypothesis testing; and (6) the behavioral-processualist goal (one school of cultural anthropology). These are precisely the fundamental tenets of the new archaeology of the 1960s in America (Willey and Sabloff: 183–97). Only the overriding evolutionary framework was missing, and that had been more or less assumed in Near Eastern archaeology from the beginning. The initial contribution

[4] The phase terms are adopted from Willey and Sabloff's very useful analysis of American archaeology ca. 1940 to 1960 and 1960 to the present (see especially pp. 172–211 and the extensive references there). This work, now in a revised edition (1980), is an excellent orientation to a literature largely unfamiliar to Palestinian and biblical archaeologists. The following section is an abridgment of the writer's longer discussion (Dever, 1980b); see also n. 6 below.

of the new archaeology—and perhaps its most lasting effect—was salutary: the attempt to produce the research designs in vogue in the 1970s forced Syro-Palestinian archaeologists, for the first time, to make *explicit* their presuppositions, their research goals, and their methodology. The field had advanced a long way toward becoming truly a discipline.

Method. In method, the innovations of the new archaeology follow quite logically from the incipient theory sketched above, although because of the typical pragmatic approach methodological advances actually preceded theory, in contrast to the new archaeology in America (see Willey and Sabloff: 191).

(1) The cultural evolutionary hypothesis, although rarely articulated, had been powerfully buttressed by the spectacular success of the previous generation's concentration on stratigraphy and ceramic typology, which had demonstrated deep in the mounds of the Middle East a long chronological and cultural sequence that lent itself admirably to analysis from an evolutionary perspective. More recently, however, ideological factors (art, philosophy, religion) as explanations of cultural change tend to be displaced by the newer emphasis on the environment and technology. This approach had the benefit of focusing attention on the potential of the new archaeology for explanation, in the sense of developing general covering laws capable of accounting for and not simply describing the process by which human society had evolved over time, as it so obviously had in the ancient Near East.

(2) The environmental approach, with its concern for "ecofacts" as well as artifacts and its determination to reconstruct past cultures as part of the ecosystem, naturally tended to concentrate fieldwork on regional surface surveys—especially of simpler, one-period sites—and on settlement-pattern studies (cf. the borrowing from cultural geography of spatial analysis—concepts such as site-catchment, rank-size hierarchies, etc.). In excavation, environmental archaeology would of course dictate a multidisciplinary staff of the sort we have described above.[5]

(3) The appreciation of the value of ethnography was relatively new. Near Eastern archaeology had previously been aware of the long continuity of peoples in the Middle East, but the lack of anthropological

[5] These newer field methods were in experimental use already in the late 1960s on American excavations such as Gezer, where E. S. Higgs, A. J. Legge, D. Webley, C. Vita-Finzi, and others did flotation and locational analysis beginning in 1968. They were expanded after 1971 at Ḥesi, Lahav, and other sites in Israel, as well as at Ḥesbân in Jordan. From 1978 on they were more fully implemented in the first American excavation project actually structured as "environmental archaeology," the Central Negev Highlands Project (see Cohen and Dever, 1978). However, little of the material is yet analyzed, and none of it has appeared in a fully integrated final excavation report. These techniques of retrieval and analysis were just beginning to appear on Israeli excavations in the late 1970s, and there is still great skepticism regarding their usefulness.

training meant that few archaeologists were equipped for ethnographic observation (except for the heavily romanticized accounts of native customs that sometimes accompanied the archaeologist's adventure story). Furthermore, the particularizing approach of most Near Eastern archaeology and the relative wealth of texts led to the general-comparative method, which focused largely on *Kulturgeschichte*, i.e., the reconstruction of past material cultures in a relatively antiquarian fashion. However, the new archaeology began to take its clues from anthropology and prehistory, for which analogies drawn from the study of modern preliterate societies had always been crucial. Thus ethnography as a tool of archaeology ("ethno-archaeology") was rediscovered. A single example of its use would be the study of modern seminomadic groups as models for understanding ethnic movements and socioeconomic change in the ancient Near East (see Dever 1977, 1980c and the references there).

(4) The adoption of general systems-theory has not been as pervasive or as deliberate as in current American archaeology, but a systemic view of culture has focused attention on various sub-systems that may leave archaeological traces. This has tended toward a more positive estimate of the range of the archaeological record (it consists of more than potsherds and architectural fragments) and the reliability of archaeological patterning as a reflection of patterned human behavior. The mass of factual data, however, that the newer techniques were capable of recovering presented the challenge of applying statistical and quantitative methods to the analysis of virtually unlimited variables and the possibility of building mathematical models similar to those used in the social sciences. Yet such multivariate statistical analysis will become feasible only as computers are fully applied to the manipulation of archaeological data, which is well under way in New World archaeology but not in Syro-Palestinian archaeology.

(5) The explicitly scientific method that is at the core of much American new archaeology (see Watson et al.) assumes that the testing of general covering laws (Hempel and others) and the explanation of cultural patterns in the scientific sense should be the major objectives of archaeology. This viewpoint has not been as widely adopted in Syro-Palestinian archaeology; most remain convinced that archaeology in the Near East is basically historical and not amenable to scientific (i.e., deductive) method. However, the *general* influence of the explicitly scientific school is seen in the deliberate development of research design, in the emphasis on problem solving, and in the testing of hypotheses in general, which increasingly characterized the more sophisticated American projects of Syro-Palestinian archaeology in the late 1970s. On a more pragmatic level, the use of consultants from the natural sciences has proved so helpful in such familiar areas as Radiocarbon 14 dating, geological analysis of sediments, study of skeletal materials (for instance)

that laboratory analysis is assumed by the new archaeology. Thermo-luminescent and neutron-activation analysis of pottery may be capable of dating and pinpointing the exact source of ceramics. Moreover, there are still newer experimental and very promising techniques of physical analysis—although the ultimate value of all this is limited by factors that will be considered presently. (On science in current archaeology, see Brothwell and Higgs.)

(6) The processualist/behavioralist approach, also fundamental to much of current American archaeology (see Schiffer, 1976, and the references there), is likewise too novel to have had much measurable effect on Syro-Palestinian archaeology. Yet its basic presupposition that the elucidation of the cultural process is the aim of archaeology has long been accepted by all but the most devout antiquarians, and the characteristic holistic concern typifies many of the most recent American excavations noted above.

(7) One final aspect of method is the workup, presentation, and publication of the results of the new archaeology. Here there are many practical advances in method. Field surveys are facilitated by such devices as the new Hewlett-Packard laser-beam transit. Photogrammetry, as well as balloon and boom photography, facilitates the drawing of site plans. Sherd-sawing and photo-mechanical drawing devices aid in the processing of pottery in the field. Computer printouts of field diaries and locus lists speed preparation for publication. In publication itself, the teamwork approach of multidisciplinary fieldwork has resulted in a new genre of preliminary reports (seen especially in the Ḥesbân volumes). Finally, the new orientation of the younger Syro-Palestinian archaeologists to a wider audience should be noted. They now routinely report not only to national meetings of Near Eastern and biblical scholars (SBL/AAR, AOS, etc.) but also to the meetings of the Archaeological Institute of America and even the Society of American Archaeologists. Gradually these archaeologists are publishing in professional archaeological journals such as the *Journal of Field Archaeology*, *American Antiquity*, and the *American Anthropologist*.

Summary

In summation of the foregoing review of the development of Syro-Palestinian archaeology from 1945 to the present, it may be said first that the discipline has grown almost exponentially in scope of fieldwork, has honed the tools of comparative ceramic typology and stratigraphy to a fine edge, and has brought to light a mass of new and in many cases startling evidence for the elucidation of a wide spatial-temporal range and succession of material cultures in the ancient Near East. Yet the development of a coherent body of explanatory theory and the synthesis and publication of the material have lagged far behind. In comparison with American archaeology, the formative period of the 1960s and 1970s appears to represent approximately the last of the descriptive-classificatory era and the transformation to a new integrative-explanatory phase. In that sense we are just where American archaeology was about 1950 (Willey and Sabloff: 94–197).[6] While it is only dimly perceived as yet, we stand on the threshold of a new age.

II. "BIBLICAL ARCHAEOLOGY," CA. 1945–80: A CRITIQUE

Against the above background it is now possible to assess the movement we shall call "biblical archaeology" and to place it in historical and intellectual perspective.

The Foundations and the Principal Architects, 1935–55

William Foxwell Albright

Although the expression "biblical antiquities" goes back to early classical writers, the term "biblical archaeology" did not arise until the late nineteenth century and did not come into current usage in Europe and America until the 1930s. However, the *technical* use of this term to denote a branch of Near Eastern archaeology relating to biblical studies, as well as a certain theological concept of the field, was an innovation of W. F. Albright and his protégé G. E. Wright.

Albright's first use of the term "biblical archaeology" appears to be in his popular Richard Lectures at the University of Virginia in 1932, published in 1935 as *The Archaeology of Palestine and the Bible* (1935, reprinted 1974), which was also his first written attack from an archaeological point of view on the European notions of biblical criticism prevailing in America, using his own recent excavations at Tell Beit Mirsim and other current fieldwork.

It is significant, however, that the term "biblical archaeology" is simply introduced as a surrogate for "Palestinian archaeology," used elsewhere throughout the volume, and that Albright's subject matter is actually the general progress of Near Eastern archaeology, particularly in epigraphic discoveries bearing on early biblical history. The same holds true for Albright's subsequent early works on the subject (1935, 1940a, 1940b), and even in the treatment where we should most expect to find a developed concept of biblical archaeology but do not, *Archaeology and the Religion of Israel* (1942). Indeed, the first *definition* of biblical archaeology that can be found in Albright's enormous published

---

6 For further orientation to the vast literature on the "new archaeology," see not only Willey and Sabloff but also S. R. and L. R. Binford; Watson et al.; L. R. Binford; Redman; Schiffer (1976, 1978–79); Dever (1980b).

body of work is again in a popular lecture in 1966, where he states (1969:13): "I shall use the term 'biblical archaeology' here to refer to all Bible Lands—from India to Spain, and from southern Russia to South Arabia—and to the whole history of those lands from about 10,000 B.C., or even earlier, to the present time" (see also 1969:1).

In all these and other treatments, it seems clear in retrospect that Albright was remarkably consistent in the enterprise he sometimes called biblical archaeology. (1) His point of departure was the inadequacy of early twentieth-century Protestant liberal theology's evolutionary approach to the history of Israel's religion, which he regarded as a unique phenomenon in the ancient Near East. (2) His *method* was to provide a corrective to literary criticism by bringing to bear on biblical literature the external evidence increasingly provided by the recent archaeological revolution, which he believed was poorly understood by European scholars. (3) The consistent focus of his attack was certain *historical issues* which he isolated as crucial in American biblical studies and which he expected would be amenable to a solution by archaeological means—the historicity of the patriarchs, Moses and monotheism, (somewhat later) the background of the Israelite conquest/settlement of Canaan, and the period of the Assyrian-Babylonian destructions and the exile.

Two conclusions seem inescapable: (1) Albright did not consider himself either a professional archaeologist or a biblical scholar, but rather an Orientalist; (2) he never intended to found a *separate* school, much less an academic discipline, of biblical archaeology. His major contribution to archaeology lay in fact in the field of Syro-Palestinian archaeology (his own term, 1938), where his pioneering fieldwork noted above, his scholarly synthesis in *The Archaeology of Palestine* (1949) and in innumerable articles, and his influence through his students established him as the leading authority.

George Ernest Wright

We turn now to G. E. Wright, the other principal architect of biblical archaeology, even though the full thrust of his own distinctive contribution was not felt until the next phase.[7] In the 1930s and 1940s Wright attained preeminence first as a Syro-Palestinian archaeologist, Albright's most brilliant protégé, and later as an Old Testament scholar (see 1944, 1946, 1950, 1951). His provocative monograph *God Who Acts: Biblical Theology as Recital* (1952), in particular, served to establish him as a pivotal figure in the biblical theology movement of the period (see later, 1958, 1963, 1966, 1969a). The ambivalence in Wright's dual career was

---

[7] The following section is abridged from the writer's fuller treatment (Dever, 1980a).

overcome not only by his frequent insistence that philosophically archaeology and biblical studies belonged together (1947:76; 1957:17; 1969b: 160) but also by his skillful balancing of the two concerns in his actual fieldwork and archaeological research.

The Heyday of Biblical Archaeology: 1955–70

We shall continue our assessment principally on the basis of Wright's own contribution to the development of biblical archaeology since Albright's role was now minimal.

The 1950s

That Wright shared his mentor Albright's general view of archaeology and ancient Near Eastern studies was already clear from his founding of *The Biblical Archaeologist* (1938–) as well as from a few early works (see 1950). By the mid-1950s, however, Wright began to combine his theological and archaeological interests in a more deliberate and self-conscious fashion. An earlier programmatic essay of 1947—largely overlooked now but significantly entitled "The Present State of Biblical Archaeology"—had already presented Wright's first (and almost his only) theoretical definition of what he meant by biblical archaeology (1947:74):

> To me, at least, biblical archaeology is a special "armchair" variety of general archaeology, which studies the discoveries of the excavators and gleans from them every fact that throws a direct, indirect, or even diffused light upon the Bible. It must be intelligently concerned with stratigraphy and typology, upon which the method of modern archaeology rests, but its chief concern is not with strata or pots or methodology. Its central and absorbing interest is the understanding and exposition of the Scriptures.

He produced a full-scale text in his *Biblical Archaeology* (1957; on p. 17 he gives virtually the same definition as the above).

Biblical Archaeology was a popular handbook. Apart from the brief introductory portion it was a straightforward summary of the discoveries of Near Eastern archaeology that might be pertinent to biblical studies. But it provoked a stormy exchange of views with biblical scholars in Germany. In addition to several shorter critical reviews, there were the substantive responses of K. Elliger and especially of M. Noth (1957, 1960b). Wright replied on the general theme of archaeology's contribution to Old Testament history (1958) and on the historicity of the patriarchs in particular (1960), to which G. von Rad responded in the next issue of the same journal (1960/61) and again later (1963).

The heat (if not the light) generated by this brief controversy in the late 1950s would be inexplicable as a response to Wright the archaeologist. It was not that, but rather was a long-delayed reaction from Continental biblical scholars to Albright's—and now Wright's—attempt since the late 1930s to characterize the Alt-Noth-von Rad school, to document its nihilism (Albright's term already in 1939) where the positive contributions of archaeology to the premonarchical history of Israel are concerned, and finally to reject the theological presuppositions—as well as the form-critical and tradition-historical methods—of the reworking of the Hexateuch on which the Americans felt that the entire German reconstruction of Israel's early history rested (see especially Noth, 1960b:262–63; but note also the exchange between Wright, 1960, and von Rad, 1960/61; and see the summary of views in Soggin, 1960). Further polarizing the discussion, both the German and American schools very shortly and largely independently produced monumental histories of Israel in English: Noth in 1958 (from the German edition of 1950) and J. Bright in 1959 (revised 1972; see also Bright, 1956, for a sharp, if somewhat polemical, juxtaposition of the views of the two schools). And in 1957, the same year as Wright's *Biblical Archaeology*, there appeared the German edition of von Rad's first volume of his massive and influential *Old Testament Theology* (1957; and see also his *Genesis* commentary of 1949–53 [English translation 1961]). Thus, it is clear that the issues being addressed in this classic contretemps over biblical archaeology were not archaeological in the strict sense at all, but were theological and, secondarily, historical. The *specific* issue was, in fact, the possibility of reconstructing a historical setting for the patriarchal era (see the most recent review, with full references, in Dever, 1977).

A few other ripples in these troubled waters may be noted. Another of Albright's protégés, Nelson Glueck, became embroiled in the controversy in the late 1950s, when he began to characterize his MB I sites in the Negev from his survey of 1952–onward as representing the "Age of Abraham." The Germans specifically challenged this equation in the discussion over the patriarchs (Noth, 1960b:265). At the same time, Glueck was bitterly attacked by his *Landsmann* J. J. Finkelstein and subsequently defended with equal vigor by Wright in a minor classic entitled "Is Glueck's Aim to Prove that the Bible is True?" (1959). Wright said no, but suspicions lingered about Glueck as well as about the entire American approach.

Repercussions of the general controversy even made the popular press. The work of the German journalist Werner Keller, *Und die Bibel hat doch Recht: Forscher beweisen die historische Wahrheit* (1955), does not, of course, represent biblical archaeology as a serious enterprise. It is significant, however, partly because it was a runaway best-seller and also because several scholars took it as a popular manifestation of biblical archaeology and the dangers to which that could lead (see W. Stählin, "Auch darin hat die Bibel Recht," 1964; and cf. de Vaux, 1970:68, etc.).

The 1960s

It remains to consider the 1960s briefly, even though both movements—biblical theology and biblical archaeology—had apparently run their course. The question addressed here is whether there was any causal relationship between them that might have hastened the downfall of both. That both movements evolved simultaneously in the 1940s and the 1950s and that someone like Wright could be a prime mover in both suggest that there *was* such a relationship. Particularly troubling was Wright's coupling of theology and archaeology in the 1950s in a way that raised fundamental questions of historiography. Suspicions were perhaps justified when Wright the archaeologist could declare: "To participate in Biblical faith means that we must indeed take history seriously as the primary data of the faith. . . . In Biblical faith everything depends upon whether the central events actually occurred" (1952:127, 126). Later, critics would charge of his *Shechem: The Biography of a Biblical City* (1965)—Wright's only attempt at a full-scale synthesis of archaeology, history, and biblical criticism—that it distorted both the biblical and the archaeological record and that his theological presuppositions were chiefly to blame.

In his obituary of biblical theology Childs has observed: "The Biblical Theology Movement underwent a period of slow dissolution beginning in the late fifties. The breakdown resulted from pressure from inside and outside that brought it to a virtual end as a major force in American theology in the early sixties" (87). Of concern here is Childs's very sharp criticism of Wright's use of the category of "revelation in history." L. Gilkey accused Wright of equivocation in his adoption of the Old Testament language describing "God's miraculous action in history" without (evidently) accepting its literal meaning. K. Stendahl's prescient article in the *Interpreter's Dictionary of the Bible*—which, it later turned out, had "struck a blow at the very heart of the movement" (Childs, 1970:79)—pointed out concerning Wright's (and von Rad's) theology that its emphasis on the community of faith's living and growing historical memory of "God's saving acts" brought us to a parting of the ways between Jews and Christians. Stendahl furthermore concluded: "But once we have accepted history as the fabric of biblical theology, we are thrown back to the same choice of faith which faced the first century. History does not answer such questions: it only poses them" (424). In the course of several perceptive critiques of biblical theology (1974, and especially 1976a, b), J. Barr has suggested that the influence of Wright's *God Who Acts* was due primarily to its "fundamental rhetorical character," but that analyzed closely it becomes clear that "it left concealed the whole strongly historicistic and naturalistic attitude with which a man like Wright as a historian and archaeologist looked upon actual historical events" (1976a:3).

Wright's reply to these criticisms (1963, 1966, 1968) left no doubt about his abiding interests in theology, as witnessed also by his last book, *The Old Testament and Theology* (1969a). But in fact by the early 1960s he had already moved on to other concerns, specifically archaeology. In 1956, Wright launched the Drew-McCormick-ASOR excavations at Shechem, which were to have such a profound influence in shaping the next generation of Syro-Palestinian archaeologists (above). Then in 1958 Wright left McCormick Theological Seminary for Harvard, where for the first time he had doctoral students—including some of the younger Shechem staff and nearly all of the later Gezer staff mentioned above—involved with him in an active program of fieldwork at Shechem, Gezer, and other sites. In 1966 he became president of ASOR, a post he held until his death in 1974. Wright gave his last and most productive years to his first love, archaeology.

Meanwhile, the inquest into the death of biblical theology continued (Hasel), as did the critique of the American school's use of archaeology in the reconstruction of early Israelite history (see M. Weippert; and especially T. L. Thompson's 1974 polemic, which can only be understood as a belated attack on the Albright-Wright school, with the historicity of the patriarchs once again at the fore). Nevertheless, by the 1960s the biblical theology movement of the 1950s was dead;[8] and with its passing, we suggest, American-style biblical archaeology had also suffered a mortal blow, even though the extent would not be apparent until the early 1970s.

Before turning to the 1970s, a final retrospect seems in order. It is clear now that the general *theological* presuppositions of Wright's biblical archaeology grew out of the "revelation in history" theme so characteristic of the biblical theology movement of the 1950s. Not only were the formulations of this theme weak theologically, but as applied to *history and archaeology* they led to a number of debatable premises. The first was that faith is dependent upon, or at least enhanced by, a demonstration of the historicity of biblical events. The second premise followed naturally from the first: archaeology deals with *realia* and thus is uniquely capable of producing not only an independent witness to history but an adequate explanation of it. Here the misgivings were many. The assumption that archaeology is somehow more objective because it deals with things rather than with ideas, that here the role of interpretation is less crucial than in the analysis of texts, and particularly the implication that archaeological data where available take precedence over literary evidence—methodologically all this now seems ingenuous.

---

[8] The writer is aware, of course, that "biblical theology" dates back to the nineteenth century. On signs of its revival again in the 1970s, see Hasel.

Despite these obvious theoretical weaknesses of biblical archaeology, however, Wright made the enterprise appear to work. He overcame the apparent contradictions simply by insisting that archaeology and biblical studies *belonged* together (above). In addition, there were certain qualities of Wright that enabled him to combine all aspects of biblical and ancient Near Eastern studies in a delightful if sometimes bafflingly eclectic fashion, notably his pragmatism and his sense of vocation. It need not be emphasized that Wright's rationale for conceiving archaeology as part of biblical studies was a uniquely personal blend of his own temperament and the temper of his times. His position, often misunderstood even by his contemporaries, certainly cannot be taken as determinative for Syro-Palestinian archaeology today.

The Decline, 1970s and Beyond

If it is argued that biblical archaeology was moribund by the 1970s, we need to ask what went wrong.

First, it is noteworthy that by the late 1960s other leading biblical archaeologists were shying away from Wright's early positivist position, especially J. B. Pritchard, R. de Vaux (1965, 1970), B. Mazar, and even Wright's protégé, P. Lapp (1969). Wright (1969b) and Albright (1969) themselves, when they returned to the debate at the end of the decade, were already somewhat on the defensive. For Wright's more mature views, we have only two popular articles (1971, 1974), but the change in his thinking toward the end of his life is clear and remarkable, even to the extent of embracing much of the new archaeology sketched above.

Second, the natural momentum generated by the school that Wright himself launched in the 1960s, together with his students at Shechem, Gezer, and elsewhere, pushed biblical archaeology in the 1970s irresistibly toward the professionalism and secularization we have noted, and thus toward status as a field of research more and more independent of biblical studies. It could be implied from what we have said that, inasmuch as biblical archaeology was an intellectual construct of Albright and Wright, it died with them. But in a more profound sense it did not die at all; it evolved naturally, perhaps inevitably, into the discipline of Syro-Palestinian archaeology whose progress we have charted above. In the end, no one was more responsible for that beneficent development than Wright himself.

From the foregoing analysis, principally of the work of Albright and Wright, it is possible now to suggest certain deficiencies of the biblical archaeology movement of the 1950s and the early 1960s. (1) First, biblical archaeology was *parochial*; it was almost exclusively the province of American, postliberal Protestant Old Testament scholars—as a glance at any excavation staff of the period will show. It largely ignored the long

secular tradition in this country, as well as Continental scholarship and
the rising national movements in the Middle East.

(2) A second deficiency was that biblical archaeology never really
had a *methodology* in the proper sense of that term. It had an approach,
a point of view, a practical rationale—but as a putative *discipline* it had
no method of its own, either theological or archaeological. It took for its
issues the problems of certain schools of biblical interpretation at the
time, and it borrowed (in some cases even perfected) some of the technical apparatus, along with much of the data, of field archaeology. But it
did not develop either a coherent body of theory or a research design
appropriate to its avowed aims, and in fact it showed no interest in
doing so. The reasons are difficult to analyze, but this shortcoming, perhaps more than any other, may have been responsible for its disintegra-
tion. Furthermore, the lack of methodology meant that the fundamental
historical-theological issues were never resolved, neither the general
questions of faith and history, nor the specific questions of the historicity
of the patriarchs, the Israelite conquest, and the like. (For the latest
surveys that document the inconclusive nature of the quest, see Dever,
1977; Miller's chapter in Hayes and Miller: 213–84; and, although too
polemical always to be balanced or reliable, Thompson.)

(3) The most serious deficiency of biblical archaeology, however, was
the basic reactionary character that we have noted above. The passing of
the theological schools that Albright and Wright sought to combat
through the archaeological revolution left biblical archaeology without
an adequate rationale. In particular, association with the biblical theology movement of the 1950s was detrimental, for the collapse of this
movement made the classic formulation of biblical archaeology (especially that of Wright) obsolete within a very short time.

The fact that the present treatment has been able to survey Syro-
Palestinian and biblical archaeology separately for the first time means
that a new stage has been reached in which not only is a certain style of
archaeology past, but the mid-1970s *debate* over it (see Dever, 1974,
1976; Glock) is also passé. The new archaeology, with all its attendant
problems, is here to stay, and it is a full-time professional discipline with
adequate personnel and support, both in America and in the Middle
East. Although it may be largely a matter of semantics, we propose to
call this discipline "Syro-Palestinian archaeology," thus accurately delim-
iting its geographical, chronological, and cultural spheres, as in other
branches of archaeology.

This leaves us with the question: Then what *was* biblical archaeology? And what can it *still* be, if anything? On the basis of the analysis
above, certain conclusions can now be summarized. Biblical archaeology
was a uniquely American phenomenon, a reactionary movement growing out of the theological climate of the 1930s and reaching its climax by

the end of the 1960s. The movement made use of the results of archaeology in the lands of the Bible, but it really represents a chapter in the history of American biblical studies. Meanwhile, parallel to it, Syro-Palestinian archaeology had also been developing during this period as a "secular" branch of Near Eastern archaeology, and by the late 1970s it had emerged to dominate the field as an *academic* discipline. Biblical archaeology—or, stated accurately, the archaeology of Syria-Palestine in the biblical period—may indeed survive, although not in the classic 1950s sense. But it is not a surrogate for Syro-Palestinian archaeology, or even a discipline at all in the academic sense; it is a sub-branch of biblical studies, an *interdisciplinary* pursuit that seeks to utilize the pertinent results of archaeological research to elucidate the historical and cultural setting of the Bible. In short, biblical archaeology is what it *always* was, except for its brief bid in the Albright-Wright era to dominate the field of Syro-Palestinian archaeology. The crucial issue for biblical archaeology, properly conceived as a dialogue, has always been (and is even more so now) its understanding and use of archaeology on the one hand, its understanding of the issues in biblical studies that are fitting subjects for archaeological illumination on the other—and the proper relationship *between* the two.

III. NEW VISTAS AND NEW RELATIONSHIPS:
1980 AND BEYOND

In looking forward to a more constructive dialogue between Syro-Palestinian archaeology and biblical studies, it is necessary first to look at what archaeology will need to achieve before it can be a full partner in the discussion.

Prospects for Syro-Palestinian Archaeology

The challenge is for Syro-Palestinian archaeology to remain viable and especially to attain the status of a full-fledged discipline in the next generation. There are several essentials, particularly applicable to the American school, which has contributed so much to biblical studies.

Cooperative Ventures

An effective archaeological presence in the Middle East, in the face of increasing local competition, rising costs, and diminishing resources, must be maintained by developing new patterns of cooperation with the emerging secular national schools in both Israel and the Arab countries—even though that may radically transform archaeology as we have conceived it.

Fieldwork

A vigorous program of fieldwork, undertaken with the most advanced methods and adequately supported, must be maintained, even if on a somewhat smaller scale. Otherwise our participation will be reduced to armchair archaeology, increasingly dependent on data produced and interpreted by others for their own interests.

Research Design

Since we cannot and do not need to do everything ourselves, however, we must develop research strategies that will maximize our contribution to Syro-Palestinian archaeology, building on our traditional strengths to complement the work of others. Our focus should be on innovative methods, highly selective field projects, and superior critical and integrative scholarship.

Publication

Nothing is more urgent in the near future than the reinterpretation, synthesis, and publication of the vast data recovered through the remarkable progress of archaeological fieldwork in the last generation, much of it inaccessible to the nonspecialist historian or biblical exegete.

Professional Personnel

All these desiderata will be achieved in vain unless we can recruit, train, and place the next generation of specialists in the field. Syro-Palestinian archaeology has always been marginal, but now that it must look to secular sources for acceptance and support, all the paraphernalia of a respectable academic discipline must be created: a coherent, self-conscious body of theory; appropriate methods and objectives; professional standards; institutional and financial backing; research and teaching positions; graduate programs, including field and laboratory schools; learned societies and journals; scholarly monographs, general textbooks, and teaching aids; and access to the mainstream of intellectual and cultural life, as well as enlightened public support. A pioneering generation of new archaeologists, building on past progress, has already achieved some of this, but much more is required.[9]

In order to contribute to biblical studies Syro-Palestinian archaeology must not only develop as a discipline but must also design and carry out

---

[9] Principal progress is due to the American Schools of Oriental Research, an offshoot of the SBL that has fostered most American work in the field since 1900 and continues to expand.

specific research projects in Bronze and Iron Age studies that may produce new data relevant to select problems in biblical research. Furthermore, archaeological specialists should take much more responsibility for ensuring that the results of survey and excavation are made accessible to biblical scholars through publications geared to the nonspecialist.

At this point, since a comprehensive summary of recent discoveries has been beyond our state-of-the-art review, it may be helpful to provide a brief guide for biblical scholars to some of the archaeological tools we already possess, even though these simply underline the need for better resources.

For topography we have several good recent atlases (Baly and Tushingham; May; and especially Aharoni and Avi-Yonah), as well as a first-class handbook on historical geography (Aharoni, 1967). Many of the sites and subjects listed in our survey above are not only published in preliminary reports in the scholarly journals but now can also be found conveniently in authoritative yet nontechnical works such as *Archaeology and Old Testament Studies* (Thomas); *Peoples of Old Testament Times* (Wiseman); and under pertinent headings in *The Interpreter's Dictionary of the Bible, Supplementary Volume* (Crim). Special mention must be made of the new four-volume *Encyclopedia of Archaeological Excavations in the Holy Land* (Avi-Yonah and Stern); this contains bibliography and authoritative, well-illustrated résumés of hundreds of sites in Israel and Jordan—often written by the directors or staff members themselves—and is now the most convenient single source of archaeological information for amateurs and professionals alike. The only reliable textbook available is the revised edition of *Archaeology in the Holy Land* (Kenyon, 1979).[10] Good, up-to-date surveys of particular periods are still lacking (but see provisionally Dever, 1977, on the Bronze Age; 1980b on the Early Iron Age; and the references there). Among more specialized topics, the pottery of Palestine is now well treated in a recent, lavishly illustrated handbook by a leading authority (Amiran). *The Biblical Archaeologist* provides reliable semipopular accounts of current discoveries; on a more scholarly level, we have the *Israel Exploration Journal*, the *Bulletin of the American Schools of Oriental Research*, and the *Revue biblique*, all of which carry shorter news items as well as full-length critical discussions. Finally, mention must also be made of a comprehensive bibliography for Palestinian sites up to 1970 (Vogel). The field of Old Testament studies in its relation to archaeology has been recently surveyed by Lance, but no comparable up-to-date study exists for the New Testament.

---

[10] The classic work of Albright (1949) is now out of print. It will be replaced by a comprehensive new text under ASOR auspices, edited by the writer with an international team of archaeologists.

What Syro-Palestinian Archaeology and Biblical Studies
Can Contribute to Each Other

Biblical Studies

It has been argued above that the concerns of biblical studies can no longer dominate the burgeoning field of Syro-Palestinian archaeology or even provide its basic agenda. But if the central task of historical archaeology (in contrast to anthropological archaeology) is to correlate the literary and nonliterary remains, and if specialized knowledge of each is now required, then obviously the archaeologist working in ancient Syria-Palestine must turn to the biblical exegete and the historian for technical assistance. This does not obviate the necessity, however, for the archaeologist to be equipped with at least a working knowledge of Northwest Semitic languages and literatures as well as of biblical criticism.

Syro-Palestinian Archaeology

The potential contribution of Syro-Palestinian archaeology to biblical studies is evidently much greater than the other way around. First, however, let us emphasize what archaeology *cannot* do. In its present stage of development, much less in the past, Syro-Palestinian archaeology cannot be expected to make definitive contributions to several basic problems, which unfortunately include many of those with which biblical scholars have been preoccupied: (1) chronology, which beyond certain broad limits, like those determined by ceramic or Radiocarbon 14 dating, depends more upon texts for the biblical period; (2) the whole question of ethnicity in the archaeological record (for instance, how are Philistines or Israelites to be recognized and compared in ceramics or architecture?); (3) political history, which seeks to relate such phenomena as destruction levels directly to events described in the literary sources; and (4) the confirmation of the meaning of texts, either in their historical or religious dimensions.

What Near Eastern archaeology in general, and Syro-Palestinian archaeology in particular, *can* contribute consists, for instance, of the following, examples of which could be multiplied many times over. (1) Archaeology recovers a broad spectrum of ancient Near Eastern peoples and places that not only provides a general setting for biblical events but also offers limitless possibilities for cross-cultural comparisons. One has only to think what Ugarit and Qumran have done to revitalize biblical studies—and now Ebla brings to light the whole prehistory of Canaanite culture. A generation ago, the Philistines were barely known outside the Bible, but now we can characterize their material culture almost more confidently than that of their early Israelite contemporaries. (2) Archaeology provides a specific spatial-temporal-cultural context for events, much of which the biblical narratives do not supply. Thus we are more and more able to reconstruct in detail the complex cultural milieu out of which the early Israelite state rose in Canaan and the impact of the Assyrian-Babylonian campaigns that precipitated its downfall; or the social, economic, and religious Sitz im Leben in which the Hebrew prophets proclaimed their message; or the cultural cross-currents of life in cosmopolitan Jerusalem and in the Galilean diaspora in Jesus' time; or the sophisticated world of Late Antiquity in which church and synagogue flourished. (3) Archaeology continues to provide rich remains of the material culture to supplement and complement the literary remains—town-planning and administration, defenses, weapons and utensils, royal and domestic architecture, sanctuaries, bizarre cult objects, tombs, pottery, luxury goods and imports, artistically executed ivories and seals, and a phenomenally expanding corpus of ostraca and other epigraphic materials. All this not only illuminates daily life in biblical times in a manner impossible to reconstruct from the biblical texts, but it also sheds light on the broader cultural context of political and socioeconomic conditions, religion and philosophy, arts and letters, technology, trade, and international relations. (4) Archaeology increasingly provides an alternate perspective from which to view narratives and events in the biblical texts—not necessarily contradictory, but in some senses corrective. In astonishing discoveries like the eighth-century syncretistic sanctuary at Kuntillet Ajrud in Sinai (Meshel), archaeology brings to light folk religion, a glimpse of the counterculture barely suspected heretofore. The Bible usually gives us the official version—what was viewed as normative behavior; archaeology occasionally may be able to reconstruct what *really* happened. (5) Finally, archaeology may provide corroborative detail for particular biblical texts, either corrupted in transmission or simply obscure until an unexpected discovery yields the clue to their interpretation. Of course, extra-biblical texts are most welcome, as for instance the Ugaritic liturgical texts that have recently elucidated early Hebrew poetry; but stratigraphic evidence and artifacts may be just as eloquent.

In short, archaeology—in the broad sense of the deliberate or chance recovery of ancient remains, including epigraphic evidence—is obviously our *only* possible source of new factual data capable of elucidating the Bible, without which we are reduced to the endless manipulation of the received texts or the application of ingenious but frequently inconclusive hypotheses. In that sense Albright's confidence in the external evidence provided by archaeology was not misplaced, merely premature. It may be that the future of biblical studies will rest largely with the increasing sophistication of archaeology—especially in its use of social and anthropological theory and its growing explanatory potential—in combination with improved historical and text-critical studies.

Yet the uncompleted agenda is long. In the future, Syro-Palestinian archaeology, in particular, must concentrate on broadening our knowledge of the world of the Bible, especially in the recovery of Bronze and Iron Age Syria and Transjordan. Insufficiently known periods, like that of the Israelite settlement in Canaan, and the postexilic horizon, must be explored with renewed vigor and new techniques. Expanded regional surveys, ecological analyses, demographic studies, and examination of human skeletal remains could yield invaluable information about the population of Palestine in the biblical period.

The illumination of the cult of ancient Israel is potentially one of the most promising aspects of the new archaeology, especially with its systemic view of culture, yet research here is still in its infancy. Nearly intact Canaanite temples are now known in Palestine from a dozen sites such as Hazor, Beth-shan, Megiddo, Shechem, Tell Kitan, Mevorakh, Lachish, and elsewere, but there is no penetrating study of the material remains as evidence for cult practice. Well-preserved Philistine temples have been uncovered in Palestine, especially the twelfth- to the eleventh-century series at Tell Qasile, with an extraordinary wealth of data, but again the preliminary publications hardly go beyond architectural descriptions. For the Iron Age, numerous local shrines come to light, along with material from domestic areas and tombs, such as altars, braziers, incense stands, *kernoi*, "Astarte" figurines, and other obviously cultic items, yet the implications of these are curiously left unexamined.

New Testament archaeology scarcely exists as a field of inquiry, much less an academic discipline. But on our analogy of the progress and potential of Syro-Palestinian archaeology above, a separate branch of archaeology should now be cultivated, perhaps as the archaeology of Late Antiquity or of Early Judaism and Christianity, related to the study of classical archaeology.[11]

Conclusion

To the question "What was unique about ancient Israel?" the archaeologist, on the basis of the picture of the indigenous material culture he pieces together, may answer "nothing." Yet in the larger context of human culture, every society reveals both universal and particular dimensions, aspects of its own unique pattern of adaptation. Ancient Israel is no exception. As Albright long ago observed, placing the Bible in its original setting makes it more intelligible and therefore more credible. The Bible may thus seem more human and less divine, but that need not preclude faith. And finally the interpretation of both texts and

---

[11] The most promising fieldwork and synthesis are being done by the ASOR-Duke project at sites in Upper Galilee, under the direction of E. M. Meyers, Carol Meyers, and J. F. Strange (1970–). See now Meyers and Strange (1981).

artifacts *is* a matter of faith—that is, of intuition and empathy as well as of knowledge.

In the end, the primary datum is the witness of the biblical text itself. As the late Père de Vaux—whose masterly balance of faith and criticism in the use of archaeology has never been surpassed—observed (1970:78):

> One will always have to reconstruct biblical history by starting with the texts, and the texts must be interpreted by the methods of literary criticism, tradition criticism and historical criticism. Archaeology does not confirm the text, which is what it is; it can only confirm the interpretation which we give it.

BIBLIOGRAPHY

Aharoni, Yohanan
1967   *Land of the Bible: A Historical Geography*. Trans. A. F. Rainey. Philadelphia: Westminster.
1973   "Remarks on the Israeli Method of Excavation." Pp. 48–53 (Hebrew) in *I. Dunayevsky Memorial Volume*. Eretz-Israel 11. Jerusalem: Israel Exploration Society, 1973. (English summary, p. 23.)

Aharoni, Yohanan, and Michael Avi-Yonah
1968   *The Macmillan Bible Atlas*. New York: Macmillan.

Albright, William Foxwell
1935   *The Archaeology of Palestine and the Bible*. Reprint, 1974. Cambridge, MA: ASOR.
1938   "The Present State of Syro-Palestinian Archaeology." Pp. 1–46 in *The Harverford Symposium on Archaeology and the Bible*. Ed. E. Grant. New Haven: ASOR.
1940a   *From the Stone Age to Christianity: Monotheism and the Historical Process*. Baltimore: Johns Hopkins University Press.
1940b   "The Ancient Near East and the Religion of Israel." *JBL* 59: 85–112.
1942   *Archaeology and the Religion of Israel*. Baltimore: Johns Hopkins University Press.
1949   *The Archaeology of Palestine*. Harmondsworth: Penguin Books.
1951   "The Old Testament and the Archaeology of Palestine." Pp. 1–26 in *The Old Testament and Modern Study*. Ed. H. H. Rowley. Oxford: Oxford University Press.
1969   "The Impact of Archaeology on Biblical Research—1966." Pp. 1–14 in *New Directions in Biblical Archaeology*. Ed. D. N. Freedman and J. C. Greenfield. Garden City, NY: Doubleday.

1970　　　　　　　　"The Phenomenon of Israeli Archaeology." Pp. 57–63 in *Near Eastern Archaeology in the Twentieth Century: Essays in Honor of Nelson Glueck.* Ed. J. A. Sanders. Garden City, NY: Doubleday.

Amiran, Ruth
1969　　　　　　　　*Ancient Pottery of the Holy Land.* New Brunswick, NJ: Rutgers University Press.

Avi-Yonah, Michael, and Ephraim Stern, eds.
1975–78　　　　　　*Encyclopedia of Archaeological Excavations in the Holy Land.* Vols. I–IV. Jerusalem: Masada Press.

Baly, Denis, and A. D. Tushingham
1971　　　　　　　　*Atlas of the Biblical World.* New York: World.

Barr, James
1974　　　　　　　　"Trends and Prospects in Biblical Theology." *JTS* 25: 265–82.
1976a　　　　　　　"Story and History in Biblical Theology." *JR* 56: 1–17.
1976b　　　　　　　"Biblical Theology." Pp. 104–11 in *IDBSup.*

Beek, Gus van
1962　　　　　　　　"Archaeology." Pp. 195–207 in *IDB*, Vol. 1.

Biggs, Robert D.
1980　　　　　　　　"The Ebla Tablets: An Interim Perspective." *BA* 43: 76–87.

Binford, Lewis Roberts
1972　　　　　　　　*An Archaeological Perspective.* New York: Seminar Press.

Binford, Sally R., and Lewis Roberts Binford, eds.
1968　　　　　　　　*New Perspectives in Archaeology.* Chicago: Aldine.

Bright, John
1956　　　　　　　　*Early Israel in Recent History Writing: A Study in Method.* SBT 19. Chicago: Allenson.
1959　　　　　　　　*A History of Israel.* Philadelphia: Westminster. Rev. ed., 1972.

Brothwell, Don, and Eric S. Higgs
1969　　　　　　　　*Science in Archaeology: A Survey of Progress in Archaeology.* Rev. ed. London: Thames and Hudson.

Childs, Brevard S.
1970　　　　　　　　*Biblical Theology in Crisis.* Philadelphia: Westminster.

Cohen, Rudolph, and William G. Dever
1978　　　　　　　　"The Pilot Season of the 'Central Negev Highlands Project.'" *BASOR* 232: 29–45.

Dever, William G.
1971a　　　　　　　"'Biblical Archaeology'—or 'The Archaeology of Syria-Palestine?'" *Christian News from Israel* 22: 21–23.

1971b   "Archaeological Methods and Results: A Review of Two
                 Recent Publications." *Or* 40: 459–71.
1973   "Two Approaches to Archaeological Method—the Archi-
                 tectural and the Stratigraphic." Pp. 1–8 in *I. Dun-
                 ayersky Memorial Volume*. Eretz-Israel 11. Jerusalem:
                 Israel Exploration Society.
1974   *Archaeology and Biblical Studies: Retrospects and Pros-
                 pects*. Evanston, IL: Seabury-Western.
1976   "Archaeology." Pp. 44–52 in *IDBSup*.
1977   "The Patriarchal Traditions. Palestine in the Second Mil-
                 lennium BCE: The Archaeological Picture." Pp. 70–120
                 in *Israelite and Judaean History*. Ed. J. H. Hayes and
                 J. M. Miller. Philadelphia: Westminster.
1980a   "Biblical Theology and Biblical Archaeology: An Appre-
                 ciation of G. Ernest Wright." *HTR* 73: 1–15.
1980b   "The Impact of the 'New Archaeology' on Syro-
                 Palestinian Archaeology." *BASOR* 242: 15–29.
1980c   "New Vistas on the 'EB IV—MB I' Horizon in Syria-
                 Palestine." *BASOR* 237: 31–59.
1982   "Monumental Architecture in Ancient Israel in the
                 Period of the United Monarchy." Pp. 269–306 in *Studies
                 in the Period of David and Solomon and Other Essays*.
                 Papers read at the International Symposium for Biblical
                 Studies, Tokyo, 5–7 December 1979. Winona Lake, IN:
                 Eisenbrauns; Tokyo: Yamakawa-Shuppansha.

Dever, William G., and H. Darrell Lance, eds.
1978   *A Manual for Field Archaeologists*. New York: Hebrew
                 Union College.

Dever, William G., H. Darrell Lance, and G. Ernest Wright
1970   *Gezer I. Preliminary Report of the 1964–66 Seasons*.
                 Jerusalem: Hebrew Union College Biblical and Archaeo-
                 logical School.

Dever, William G., et al.
1975   *Gezer II. Report of the 1967–70 Seasons in Fields I–II*.
                 Jerusalem: Nelson Glueck School of Biblical Archaeol-
                 ogy.

Elliger, Karl
1959   Review of G. E. Wright, *Biblische Archäologie*. *TLZ* 84:
                 94–98.

Finkelstein, Jacob J.
1959   "The Bible, Archaeology, and History: Have the Excava-
                 tions Corroborated Scripture?" *Commentary* 27: 341–49.

Franken, Hendricus J., and C. A. Franken-Battershill
1963   *A Primer of Old Testament Archaeology*. Leiden: E. J.
                 Brill.

Freedman, David Noel
1965   "The Biblical Languages." Pp. 294–312 in *The Bible in
                       Modern Scholarship*. Ed. J. Philip Hyatt. Nashville:
                       Abingdon.

Freedman, David Noel, and Jonas C. Greenfield, eds.
1969   *New Directions in Biblical Archaeology*. Garden City,
                       NY: Doubleday.

Freedman, David Noel, and John M. Lundquist
1979   *Archaeological Reports from the Tabqa Dam Proj-
                       ect—Euphrates Valley, Syria*. Cambridge, MA: ASOR.

Gelb, Ignace J.
1977   "Thoughts about Ibla: A Preliminary Evaluation, March
                       1977." *Syro-Mesopotamian Studies* 1: 3–28.

Gilkey, Langdon
1961   "Cosmology, Ontology, and the Travail of Biblical Lan-
                       guage." *JR* 41: 194–205.

Glock, Albert E.
Forthcoming   "Biblical Archaeology—An Emerging Discipline?" in
                       The Archaeology of Jordan and Other Studies. Ed.
                       L. T. Geraty.

Glueck, Nelson
1955   "The Age of Abraham in the Negev." *BA* 18: 2–9.

Hasel, Gerhard
1972   *Old Testament Theology: Basic Issues in the Current
                       Debate*. Grand Rapids: Baker Book House (revised edi-
                       tion, 1975).

Hayes, John H., and J. Maxwell Miller, eds.
1977   *Israelite and Judaean History*. Philadelphia: Westmin-
                       ster.

Keller, Werner
1955   *Und die Bibel hat doch Recht: Forscher beweisen die
                       historische Wahrheit*. Düsseldorf: Econ-Verlag.

Kempinski, Aharon
1972   Review of W. G. Dever et al., *Gezer I*. *Israel Explora-
                       tion Journal* 22: 183–86.
1976   Review of W. G. Dever et al., *Gezer II*. *Israel Explora-
                       tion Journal* 26: 210–14.

Kenyon, Kathleen M.
1952   *Beginning in Archaeology*. New York: Frederik A.
                       Praeger.
1979   *Archaeology in the Holy Land*. 4th ed. London: Ernest
                       Benn.

Lance, H. Darrell
1981   *The Old Testament and the Archaeologist*. Philadelphia: Fortress.

Lapp, Paul W.
1969   *Biblical Archaeology and History*. Cleveland: World.
1970   "The Tell Deir Alla Challenge to Palestinian Archaeology." *VT* 20: 243–56.

Matthiae, Paolo
1979   *Ebla in the Period of the Amorite Dynasties and the Dynasties of Akkad: Recent Archaeological Discoveries at Tell Mardikh (1975)*. Malibu, CA: Undena Publications.
1981   *Ebla, An Empire Recovered*. Garden City, NY: Doubleday.

May, Herbert G., ed.
1974   *Oxford Bible Atlas*. Oxford: Oxford University Press. 2d ed., 1974.

Mazar, Benjamin
1969   "The Historical Background of the Book of Genesis." *JNES* 24: 73–83.

Meshel, Ze'ev
1979   "Did Yahweh Have a Consort?" *BARev* 2: 24–34.

Meyers, Eric M., and James F. Strange
1981   *Archaeology, The Rabbis, and Early Christianity*. Nashville: Abingdon.

Noth, Martin
1957   "Hat die Bibel doch Recht?" Pp. 7–22 in *Festschrift für Günther Dehn zum 75. Geburtstag*. Neukirchen-Vluyn: Neukirchener Verlag.
1960a   *The History of Israel*. Trans. from second German edition, 1958. New York: A. & C. Black.
1960b   "Der Beitrag der Archäologie zur Geschichte Israels." Pp. 262–82 in *Congress Volume: Oxford, 1959*. VTSup 7; Leiden: Brill. = Pp. 34–52 in *Aufsätze zur biblischen Landes- und Altertumskunde*, Vol. 1. Ed. H. W. Wolff. Neukirchen-Vluyn: Neukirchener Verlag.

Pritchard, James B.
1965   "Culture and History." Pp. 313–24 in *The Bible in Modern Scholarship*. Ed. J. P. Hyatt. Nashville: Abingdon.

Rad, Gerhard von
1957   *Theologie des Alten Testaments*, Vol. 1. Munich: Chr. Kaiser. English trans., 1962.
1960/61   "History of the Patriarchs." *ExpTim* 72: 213–16.
1961   *Genesis*. London: SCM. German original, 1949–53.

Redman, Charles L., ed.
1973   *Research and Theory in Current Archaeology.* New York: John Wiley and Sons.

Sauer, James A.
Forthcoming   *The Archaeology of Jordan.*

Schiffer, Michael B.
1976   *Behavioral Archaeology.* New York: Academic Press.

Schiffer, Michael B., ed.
1978–79   *Advances in Archaeological Method and Theory.* 2 vols. New York: Academic Press.

Soggin, J. Alberto
1960   "Ancient Biblical Traditions and Modern Archaeological Discoveries." *BA* 23: 95–100.

Stählin, W.
1964   *Auch darin hat die Bibel Recht.* Stuttgart: Evang. Verl.-werk.

Stendahl, Krister
1962   "Biblical Theology, Contemporary." Pp. 418–32 in *IDB*, Vol. 1.

Thomas, D. Winton, ed.
1967   *Archaeology and Old Testament Study.* Oxford: Clarendon.

Thompson, Thomas L.
1974   *The Historicity of the Patriarchal Narratives. The Quest for the Historical Abraham.* New York: Walter de Gruyter.

Vaux, Roland de
1965   "Method in the Study of Early Hebrew History." Pp. 15–29 in *The Bible in Modern Scholarship.* Ed. J. P. Hyatt. Nashville: Abingdon.
1970   "On Right and Wrong Uses of Archaeology." Pp. 64–80 in *Near Eastern Archaeology in the Twentieth Century: Essays in Honor of Nelson Glueck.* Ed. J. A. Sanders. Garden City, NY: Doubleday.

Vogel, Eleanor K.
1974   *Bibliography of Holy Land Sites.* Cambridge, MA: ASOR.

Watson, Patty J., Steven A. LeBlanc, and Charles L. Redman
1971   *Explanation in Archaeology: An Explicitly Scientific Approach.* New York: Columbia University Press.

Weippert, Manfred
1971   *The Settlement of the Israelite Tribes in Palestine: A Critical Survey of Recent Scholarly Debate.* London: SCM. German original, 1967.

Wheeler, Robert E. M.
1954   *Archaeology from the Earth*. Oxford: Clarendon.

Willey, Gordon R., and Jeremy A. Sabloff
1974   *A History of American Archaeology*. San Francisco: W. H. Freeman. Rev. ed., 1980.

Wiseman, Donald J.
1973   *Peoples of Old Testament Times*. Oxford: Clarendon.

Wright, G. Ernest
1944   *The Challenge of Israel's Faith*. Chicago: University of Chicago Press.
1946   "Neo-Orthodoxy and the Bible." *JBR* 14: 87–93.
1947   "The Present State of Biblical Archaeology." Pp. 74–97 in *The Study of the Bible Today and Tomorrow*. Ed. H. R. Willoughby. Chicago: University of Chicago Press.
1950   *The Old Testament Against its Environment*. London: SCM.
1951   "The Study of the Old Testament." Pp. 17–44 in *Protestant Thought in the Twentieth Century*. Ed. A. S. Nash. New York: Macmillan.
1952   *God Who Acts: Biblical Theology as Recital*. SBT 8. London: SCM.
1957   *Biblical Archaeology*. Philadelphia: Westminster.
1958   "Archaeology and Old Testament Studies." *JBL* 77: 39–51.
1959   "Is Glueck's Aim to Prove that the Bible is True?" *BA* 22: 101–8.
1960   "Modern Issues in Biblical Studies: History and the Patriarchs." *ExpTim* 71: 3–7.
1963   "History and Reality: The Importance of Israel's 'Historical' Symbols for the Christian Faith." Pp. 176–79 in *The Old Testament and Christian Faith*. Ed. Bernhard W. Anderson. New York: Harper & Row.
1965   *Shechem: The Biography of a Biblical City*. New York: McGraw-Hill.
1966   "Reflections Concerning Old Testament Theology." Pp. 376–88 in *Studia Biblica et Semitica Th. C. Vriezen*. Wageningen: H. Veenman.
1968   Review of J. Barr, *Old and New in Interpretation*. *Int* 22: 83–89.
1969a   *The Old Testament and Theology*. New York: Harper & Row.
1969b   "Biblical Archaeology Today." Pp. 149–65 in *New Directions in Biblical Archaeology*. Ed. D. N. Freedman and J. C. Greenfield. Garden City, NY: Doubleday.

1969c   "Archaeological Method in Palestine—An American Interpretation." Pp. 125–29 in *W. F. Albright Volume*. Ed. A. Malamat. Eretz-Israel 9. Jerusalem: Israel Exploration Society.

1970   "The Phenomenon of American Archaeology in the Near East." Pp. 3–40 in *Near Eastern Archaeology in the Twentieth Century: Essays in Honor of Nelson Glueck*. Ed. J. A. Sanders. Garden City, NY: Doubleday.

1971   "What Archaeology Can and Cannot Do." *BA* 34: 70–76.

1974   "The 'New' Archaeology." *BA* 38: 104–15.

Wright, G. R. H.

1966   "A Method of Excavation Common in Palestine." *ZDPV* 82: 113–24.

3

The Ancient Near Eastern Environment

J. J. M. Roberts

In 1951, W. F. Albright contributed two chapters to H. H. Rowley's *The Old Testament and Modern Study*, the second of which was entitled, "The Old Testament and the Archaeology of the Ancient East." Albright used the term "archaeology" to include the reading and interpretation of orthographic remains, and it was this textual evidence that was central in his survey of scholarly advances in the understanding of the ancient Near East that shed light on biblical studies. Thus his article provides a convenient starting point for the present survey of the field, which will emphasize the main corpora of Near Eastern texts and the main currents of their interpretation that have influenced Old Testament studies in the three decades since Albright's essay. Many of the new insights that the ancient Near Eastern environment has offered to biblical studies stem from further work in areas that Albright had already seen as important, and some of these insights confirm his earlier and often brilliant intuitions. In other cases, new discoveries that seemed to promise much have turned out to be largely sterile, at least regarding biblical studies, while some areas that had appeared to be mined out have begun to yield new treasures to more recent investigators. Moreover, there have been new textual discoveries, some of such an age and wealth as would have astounded even Albright.

I. COLLECTIONS OF TEXTS

Byblos, Alalakh, Nuzi

Albright called the finds at Byblos disappointing (1951:29), and nothing during this intervening period has changed that judgment. The Phoenician inscriptions discovered there have contributed to our understanding of the Phoenician language and orthography, but the religious or historical content of these texts is quite inconsequential (see below). The earlier Byblian syllabic remains undeciphered despite the persistent efforts of Mendenhall and others.

The excavations at Alalakh appeared more promising. Albright had the statue of Idri-mi (Smith), which shed light on life in Northern Syria and Palestine around 1450 B.C.E., but the subsequent publication of the

Alalakh tablets (Wiseman, 1953, 1954, 1959a, 1959b) provided relatively little of direct bearing on biblical studies. Their main contribution was to provide a better understanding of the historical and sociological developments in Syria against which some of the later biblical statements could be seen in a clearer light (Wiseman, 1967; Mendelsohn, 1955, 1959; and Dietrich, 1966, 1969). The distribution of these texts between the seventeenth and fifteenth centuries, for example, revealed an increasing Hurrian element in the population as well as changes in the structure of the society such as the rise of the *maryannu* chariot-warrior class. Apart from Idri-mi's autobiography, the treaty texts (Wiseman, 1953:25–32), and one text in which a camel was mistakenly alleged to appear (Wiseman, 1959a:29; Lambert, 1960a), the Alalakh tablets have not figured largely in specifically biblical discussions.

The Nuzi texts are a different matter. The publication of these texts has continued apace until now about four thousand of the approximately five thousand tablets recovered from Yoghlan Tepe (ancient Nuzi) and Kirkuk (ancient Arrapkha) have appeared (Eichler, 1976:635; for a comprehensive bibliography see Dietrich, 1972b). Additional Nuzi-type texts have also been discovered at Tell-al-Fahhar and Tell er-Rimah (Eichler, 1976:635). E. A. Speiser thought that these texts provided the legal background for understanding many of the customs reflected in the patriarchal narratives. He, along with Cyrus Gordon (1954), A. E. Draffkorn-Kilmer (1957), and others (Eichler, 1976:636), espoused this view in a number of detailed articles (Speiser, 1955, 1963) and popularized it in his influential commentary on Genesis (1964). The conclusions of Speiser and company were generally accepted among the students of Albright, and this view was disseminated further in the writings of G. E. Wright and in both editions of John Bright's *A History of Israel* (1959:71, 1972:68). It was also adopted by de Vaux in his early study on the Hebrew patriarchs (1946, 1948, 1949). Only recently have scholars begun reevaluating the worth of these Nuzi parallels for understanding the Bible (de Vaux, 1971:224–43).

Critics have contested the importance of the Nuzi parallels from the Mesopotamian side on two grounds: they have argued either (1) that the interpretation assigned to Nuzi texts is itself untenable, in which case the parallel can no longer be drawn, or (2) that the given Nuzi custom is not unique but simply a reflection of general Mesopotamian legal practice, in which case the parallel, although it still exists, loses much of its value for historical reconstruction (Eichler, 1976:635; Thompson: 294). As examples of the first type of argument, one may cite the role of the Nuzi house gods and the sistership contracts. It now appears that the household gods did not function as tokens of inheritance rights; hence the explanation of Rachel's theft of the teraphim based on that understanding of Nuzi law falls to the ground (Greenberg, 1962). New evidence has also weakened the view that a husband at Nuzi could enhance his wife's standing in Hurrian society by adopting her as his sister prior to marrying her (Skaist: 17; Eichler, 1977), thus casting doubt on Speiser's explanation of the origin of the stories in which a patriarch claims his wife as his sister. As examples of the second type of argument, one may point to the discussion of the customs of inheritance and concubinage. Scholars have questioned whether the right of the firstborn or the practice of a childless wife providing her husband with a slave to bear children for her are limited to Nuzi (Eichler, 1976). Alleged parallels have been sought elsewhere, in the Old Babylonian and Old Assyrian periods, or even in much later periods (Van Seters, 1968, 1969, 1975:70, 91). Moreover, the value of such parallels has also been questioned from the biblical side, particularly in the new exegetical program espoused by Childs. Do these parallels aid in the exegetical task, or is their value limited to historical reconstruction? Do they really enlighten the reader to what the present biblical text is trying to say, or are they important only for the historical and necessarily hypothetical reconstruction of earlier forms of the tradition? If the latter, can one show how this earlier form of the tradition was transformed into the present text? If there is an unbridgeable gap between the reconstructed "historical" kernel or earlier form of the tradition and the text to be exegeted, one may well question whether such reconstruction is anything more than a futile exercise of the creative imagination. It is too early to say whether this reaction to the earlier excessive stress on the Nuzi parallels is itself excessive, but future biblical scholarship will have to be more critical in the treatment of all alleged parallels.

Ugarit

Albright's estimate of the importance of Ugaritic for the future development of biblical studies has proved correct. Since he wrote, Ugaritology has developed into a quasi-independent specialization, and new texts as well as many new tools have contributed to the better elucidation of these difficult texts. The most important texts earlier known, as well as some previously unedited alphabetic texts, were published in a fine edition by A. Herdner (1963). Other new alphabetic texts were published under the editorship of C. Schaeffer in *PRU* II, V, and VI, in *Ugaritica* V, and in works by Virolleaud, Fisher (1971), Herdner (1972), Caquot and Masson (1977), and Bordreuil. The most important editions of syllabic texts appeared in *PRU* III, IV, VI, and in *Ugaritica* V. Whitaker produced a very useful concordance of the alphabetic Ugaritic literature; M. Dietrich and others contributed a basic bibliography (1973) as well as a concordance to the differing and often confusing systems for numbering the texts (1972a). A specialized new annual, *Ugarit-Forschungen*, edited by Bergerhof and others, was introduced in 1969, and it now runs to ten volumes. Craigie began editing "Newsletter for Ugaritic Studies" in 1972, and it has proved very helpful in keeping up with what is going on in the field. Cyrus Gordon's periodically updated *Ugaritic Textbook* still provides the best grammatical introduction to Ugaritic as well as the best glossary. The glossary, however, should be supplemented with Aistleitner's dictionary, and G. R. Driver's *Canaanite Myths and Legends* also contains a glossary as well as a helpful discussion and translation of the more important mythological and epic texts known at the time. This last work has just recently been revised and reedited by J. C. L. Gibson. H. L. Ginsberg's translation of the Ugaritic myths, epics, and legends in *ANET* remains one of the most useful, but the more recent translation by Caquot, Sznycer, and Herdner as well as Coogan's popular treatment should also be mentioned.

The study of Ugaritic language and literature has had an impact on several areas of biblical studies. The light that the Ugaritic texts have thrown on Canaanite religion and culture has provided a helpful foil against which to discuss Israelite religion, and numerous studies have been devoted to Ugaritic religion (Pope, 1955; Kapelrud, 1969; Oldenburg; Gese, 1970; de Moor, 1970, 1971, 1972; Cassuto; van Zijl) and to a comparison of Ugaritic and Israelite beliefs (Kaiser; Habel; Gray, 1965; Kapelrud, 1963; Schmidt; Clifford; Miller, 1973b; Albright, 1968; Cross, 1973). Sometimes an excessive emphasis has been placed on the undeniable contrast between Israelite and Canaanite beliefs, but in the better treatments of the subject attention has been given to the elements of continuity between Israel and her pagan environment as well as to those features of discontinuity (Miller, 1973a).

The Ugaritic language has also contributed to a better understanding of Hebrew lexicography, syntax, and prosody. A glance through the third edition of Köhler-Baumgartner's *Hebräisches und aramäisches Lexikon zum Alten Testament* is enough to form some conception of the influence of Ugaritic studies on recent Hebrew lexicography. To cite one example (although it is taken from that part of the alphabet not yet reached by Köhler-Baumgartner's third edition), the forms תשׁתע and ונשׁתעה, found in Isa 41:10, 23, were erroneously listed under the root שׁעה in BDB (1043) despite the fact that both forms occurred in parallel with the root ירא. When the Ugaritic cognate *tt'* also appeared in parallel with *yr'*, it was finally realized that שׁתע was, in fact, a separate verb, synonymous with ירא, meaning "to fear." Many other lexicographical suggestions derived from Ugaritic may be found in the writings of M. Dahood and his students (see Martinez), although by no means all are persuasive. James Barr (39–61) has strongly criticized Dahood's lack of sound method in his lexicographical suggestions, and the criticism was certainly telling at points. Barr demonstrated, for instance, that Dahood's attractive interpretation of מגן as "suzerain"—in this case based on

Phoenician material rather than Ugaritic—was unfortunately devoid of any textual foundation, being based merely on a misunderstood passage in a French article (Barr: 45–48).

In the area of syntax Ugaritic's enclitic -*m* (C. H. Gordon, 1965: 103–4), emphatic *l*- and *k*- (1965:76), *l*- meaning "from" (1965:92), and its use of both imperfect and perfect forms for past tense in poetry (1965:114), to mention only a few items, have led to the discovery of these same features in Hebrew and in many cases have thereby explained long-standing cruxes in the biblical texts (Hummel; Noetscher; Gordis; Fitzmyer; Held, 1962; Moran, 1961). Unfortunately, enthusiasm for the Ugaritic explanation has led Dahood and his students to introduce these and other far less certain features of Ugaritic or later Phoenician syntax and morphology into a discussion of the biblical text even at those points where the traditional text presents no difficulties. An atomistic approach to both the Ugaritic texts and the biblical text compounds the problem. One can never be sure that a proposed rendering of a Ugaritic passage cited by Dahood as support for a new rendering of a biblical text really makes any sense in the original Ugaritic context unless one goes to the trouble of working through the extended context of the Ugaritic passage for oneself. For this reason Dahood's very suggestive and stimulating commentary on Psalms (1966–70) is also extremely frustrating. It is almost as though the writer abdicated responsibility to be self-critical of new insights and foisted off the whole burden of that onerous task on the unfortunate reader.

Much of the recent discussion of the relative date of early Israelite poetry hinges on the comparative data provided by Ugaritic. Albright had already laid the theoretical basis for this attempt at typological-sequence dating of Hebrew poetry at the beginning of our period (1944, 1950), but his work has been followed up in that of his students Cross and Freedman (1948, 1950; Cross 1955, 1968; Freedman 1971, 1972, 1976) and has received independent confirmation in the recent work of D. A. Robertson. The underlying assumption is that poetry, like any other human activity, will show a typological development over a period of time. By comparing undated Hebrew poetry with Ugaritic poetry of the middle of the second millennium and with dated Hebrew poetry of the eighth century and later, one can establish a relative chronology of the undated material based on its closer resemblances to one end or the other of the scale. Robertson worked exclusively with linguistic features in his analysis, while Albright, Cross, and Freedman also noted prosodic patterns—types of parallelism, meter, etc.—and historical allusions. Freedman's latest work in this area (1976) adds the criterion of divine epithets. Despite the different criteria, all agree in dating Exod 15:1–18 to the premonarchical period. There is less agreement on some of the other texts, but Judges 5, the Balaam oracles in Numbers 23–24, Genesis 49, Deuteronomy 32 (significant variation) and 33,

Psalm 18 (= 1 Samuel 22), 29, and 68 are generally considered relatively ancient. D. W. Goodwin's unfortunate attack on the method of Albright and his students was demolished in a devastating response by Cross and Freedman (1972). Goodwin simply restated older views without refuting the arguments against them and without considering the new inscriptional evidence that had accumulated in the interval since the last article he considered had appeared. While many European critics still do not accept the datings proposed by Cross and Freedman, discounting Goodwin's feeble attempt, no reasoned critique of the approach has appeared. Norin, who does take the method seriously in his recent study of Exodus 15, ends up by accepting a very early date for the original form of that poem.

Dating is only one area in which the stylistic analysis of Ugaritic poetry has contributed to a better understanding of Hebrew material. The discovery in Ugaritic of so-called parallel pairs or A and B words, i.e., the regular recurrence in the same sequence of parallel words in parallel stichs (Held, 1957), led to the study of the same phenomenon in Hebrew poetry (Boling; Melamed) and eventually to the major research tool edited by Fisher (1972–75). Some of the recent stylistic study of Hebrew poetry, in fact, with its attention to chiastic arrangement, inclusio, and other features, received its stimulus from earlier work on Ugaritic.

Although some critics have made unsound use of the Ugaritic material or overplayed its importance to the virtual exclusion of other comparative material and others have warned of the dangers of pan-Ugaritism (Donner, 1967; van der Lugt), it is unlikely that biblical studies can or should return to a pre-Ugaritic approach. The advances have been many and substantial. If one may hazard a personal opinion, however, despite the new texts and the mass of secondary literature the work of translating Ugaritic has not progressed substantially beyond the point represented by Ginsberg's *ANET* translation. Much remains obscure, and the proliferation of secondary studies has convincingly removed relatively few of these lexical obscurities. One wonders how much farther one can press without substantial new additions to our corpus of Ugaritic texts. Such is certainly possible. In the meantime biblical studies could profit from a far more self-critical application of those insights that Ugaritic studies have already provided.

Mari

Albright was also on target in his estimate of the importance of the Mari texts for biblical studies. The texts continue to appear with no immediate end in sight. So far thirteen volumes of autographed copies have appeared in the series *ARM*, and the companion translation series *ARMT* now numbers eighteen volumes, although two of these do not contain texts. In addition numerous other texts have been published in various journals, and these are now listed in *ARMT* 17/1. Well over a thousand letters and two thousand economic, juridical, and administrative texts have been published. Most of the texts date to a relatively short span (1800–1760 B.C.E.) during the Old Babylonian period, which makes Old Babylonian Mari one of the best-documented societies in antiquity. This material is important for OT studies not only for general historical background but also because Israel's ancestors probably originated among just such tribal groups as are described in the Mari texts. Biblical tradition places Abraham's family in Harran prior to his migration to Canaan, and part of his family, with which the patriarchs maintained contact, remained in the region. This same Harran region figures prominently in the Mari texts as an area in which nomadic groups moved. Moreover, there are linguistic, sociological, and religious connections between Israel and the Amorites of the Mari texts that have been taken to suggest a genetic link. Even if this link cannot be established, the well-documented character of the tribal society at Mari provides important comparative material for understanding the early tribal society in premonarchic Israel.

The question of the linguistic classification of the Semitic but non-Akkadian language attested at Mari in many of the proper names as well as in certain lexicographical items has been hotly debated (Moran, 1961:56–57). Theo Bauer had classified similar names from previously known Old Babylonian sources as East Canaanite, and M. Noth invoked the term proto-Aramaic. But H. B. Huffmon's fundamental study of the Mari names (1965), I. J. Gelb's analysis of Amorite grammar (1958), and G. Buccellati's work on the Amorites of the Ur III period have demonstrated the value of retaining the traditional designation Amorite. This language was, as Moran so aptly puts it, "an ancient and venerable uncle of both Canaanite and Aramaic, who was, it should be stressed, a colorful personality with an individuality bordering on eccentricity" (1961: 57). These linguistic studies are important for OT scholarship, even if one cannot make this Northwest Semitic language the immediate ancestor of either Canaanite or Aramaic. Many of the names in the early patriarchal tradition seem to come from the same linguistic strata as the Amorite names, and that has encouraged scholars to connect the migrations of the patriarchs to the Amorite movements of the beginning of the second millennium (de Vaux, 1971:193–94). Such a view also finds support in Malamat's comparative study of early Israelite and Mari tribal society based largely on the series of West Semitic terms used at Mari to denote tribal units, forms of settlements, and positions of authority (1967). In the religious realm, one may point to the appearance of prophetic phenomena at Mari closely paralleling the later phenomena in Israel. The majority of these prophetic texts have been superbly translated and discussed from the Assyriological side by Moran (1969b, with references to the earlier literature), and their relationship to the Hebrew

Bible has been investigated in detail by J.-G. Heintz, F. Ellermeier (with reference to the many earlier studies), and most recently by E. Noort. In the meantime an additional dream text has appeared (Dossin), although it does not change the overall picture presented by the texts. One should also note the resemblances between the ban in Mari and in early Israel (Malamat, 1966).

Despite the many points of contact between later Israel and the Amorite society reflected in the Mari texts, however, there remains a significant chronological gap. The oldest biblical narratives are hardly earlier than the tenth century, some eight hundred years after the Mari period, and it is likely that the biblical narrators of the patriarchal stories have telescoped into three generations a process of centuries. The "Patriarchal Age" as a concrete and well-defined period of time, therefore, is problematic, and that in turn renders the quest for a genetic relationship problematic, although not impossible (Malamat, 1967:131).

In any case the discovery of the Mari texts has provided scholars with a far better analogy for understanding the tribal society of the patriarchs and of later premonarchic Israel than the earlier model provided by the bedouin of the classical Arabic sources. J.-R. Kupper's fundamental study showed that the seminomads of the Mari region were primarily sheep and goat herders and therefore were tied to the margins of the cultivated lands. Moreover, as later studies particularly emphasized (Luke; Rowton, 1967, 1973a, 1973b, 1974, 1976; Liverani, 1970, 1973; Dever; Matthews), the nomads of the Mari region were in a constant symbiotic relationship with the settled agricultural towns and villages, and there was movement back and forth between the two sides of this dimorphic society. The impact of these studies on the Hebrew Bible has up to now focused largely on the period of the conquest and settlement. These studies served to lessen the contrast between the seminomadic Israelite shepherds infiltrating into Canaan and the Canaanite farmers already settled in the land (Gottwald, 1974, 1975). This is particularly true of Luke's study, since he denied that the Mari material reflected the influx of any significant new element of population.

Taken with the anarchic portrayal of Canaanite society pictured in the Amarna letters, this new conception provided support for the thesis of Luke's teacher, Mendenhall, that the Israelite conquest of Palestine was by revolution rather than by settlement (1962; see also de Geus). There was neither invasion nor piecemeal infiltration, but a peasant revolt against the oppressive structures of Canaanite feudal society. Gottwald has corrected and further elaborated Mendenhall's views in his massive new book (1979), but while very suggestive the work fails to live up to its advance billing. The sociological jargon and Marxist ideology double the size of the book without making it any more convincing, and the sometimes arbitrary treatment of the biblical material—e.g., his discussion of the meaning of יֹשֵׁב

(1979:519–34)—objectionable in itself, becomes even more objectionable in a work as polemical as this.

Other scholars who have maintained a more traditional picture of Amorite movement into Mesopotamia have seen the long-term infiltration of Amorites into the Fertile Crescent as support for an analogous, largely peaceful infiltration of Israel into Canaan (Weippert). One may question, however, whether either of these treatments has dealt adequately with the Mesopotamian evidence. There may have been Amorite elements in Mesopotamia for a very long time, but prosopography gives evidence for a heavy new influx in the Ur III and Isin-Larsa period, and some of the evidence suggests invasion rather than simple infiltration. One cannot simply ignore references to the "Amorite wall which keeps the nomads far away" or to the "Amorites who break in like a southstorm" or to "Amorites, people from the steppe, have pressed into the settled land" (Edzard, 1957:33–34). One should also be a bit more cautious about totally dismissing the evidence from the literary texts; even if they do reflect urban prejudices against the outsider, those prejudices, however warped, are rooted in experience. Moreover, one should note the number of military titles in the Old Babylonian period that are composed with MARTU as one element (Edzard, 1957:37; Sasson [12 n. 4] discusses only three of these titles: GAL.MAR.TU, UGULA.MAR.TU, and DUB.SAR.MAR.TU). One should also note the reference to the "council of the Amorites" in one of the letters inadequately edited by K. A. Al-A'dami (19: IM 49341, Pl. 1), which suggests an Amorite tribal organization that extended beyond the individual city-state, at least in the period before the Amorites were totally assimilated into the Mesopotamian city-state system. That in turn calls to mind possible analogies to the Israelite tribal assemblies and their conflict with particular Canaanite city-states.

However much or little the new sociological model of Luke, Gottwald, and Rowton has to be revised back toward more traditional models, one can only agree with Dever, against Van Seters (1975:17) and Thompson (85–88), that "the Mari material provides the best available data . . . for promising research on patriarchal backgrounds" (116–17). As a final point one should note the similarity between the Amorite genealogical traditions and the early genealogical traditions of the Bible (Kraus, 1965b; Finkelstein, 1966; Malamat, 1968). Wilson's recent study of these has shed new light on the function of the genealogical material (1977), and if, as seems likely, the Tudija of the Assyrian genealogical tradition has now turned up as a historical personage in the Ebla texts (Pettinato, 1976e:48), it means that these genealogical traditions in the Bible must be treated with new respect as historiographical sources whether that was their original function or not.

Ebla

The mention of Ebla invokes the most sensational discovery of epigraphic remains in the Near East since Albright's essay. Tell Mardikh, ancient Ebla, is situated in Syria about thirty-five miles (sixty kilometers) southwest of Aleppo and sixty miles (one hundred kilometers) northeast of Ugarit. There in 1974, after ten seasons of relatively modest finds, the Italian excavators, under the direction of P. Matthiae, discovered an archive of some forty-two cuneiform tablets and fragments dating to the last half of the third millennium B.C.E. The following year they uncovered some sixteen thousand additional tablets and fragments of the same period. The story of this remarkable discovery has been widely reported in the popular press, in semipopular journals (Matthiae, 1976b; Pettinato, 1976e; La Fay), and in a notably well-informed, well-documented semipopular book (Bermant and Weitzman), so it need not be repeated here. The implications of this discovery for biblical scholarship, however, do merit discussion.

There is no question that this discovery will force fundamental revisions in scholarly reconstructions of the early history of the ancient Near East. Syria no longer remains a silent bridge between the two great literate, riverine cultures of Egypt and Mesopotamia. It is clear from the Ebla discoveries that Syria had an advanced and vigorous culture of its own. Ebla itself was a powerful kingdom, treated on an equal footing with the most powerful states of the time (Gelb, 1977:15), and the many references to other Syrian and Palestinian cities reported in the texts (Pettinato, 1976e:46) probably indicate an economic network with other flourishing urban centers. Thus these texts will enable the future historian to correct and fill in the rather sketchy picture of early Syro-Palestinian history provided up to now by archaeology and the relatively few relevant texts from Egypt and Mesopotamia.

Since the general history of the ancient Near East provides the setting in which biblical scholars do their work, these advances in our understanding offered by the Ebla texts will certainly affect the direction of biblical studies. Much that has been written recently on the direct connections between Ebla and the Bible, however, seems curiously premature. While various scholars have seen photographs of some of the tablets, only a few have been adequately published (Pettinato, 1976c and 1977); for the rest one is dependent on Pettinato's reports, based on his preliminary readings. Preliminary readings normally require significant corrections after more extensive study, however, so they offer a very insecure foundation for elaborate hypothetical reconstructions. D. N. Freedman's recent (1978) defense of the historical accuracy of Genesis 14 on the basis of an unpublished Ebla tablet is a case in point. This tablet, TM.75.G.1860, which was reported to list the cities of the plain in the same order as Genesis 14 (i.e., Sodom, Gomorrah, Admah, Zeboiim, and Bela), provides the key for his whole reconstruction, including his attempt to redate Abraham to the mid-third millennium B.C.E. Yet, prior to the publication of his article, in time to include it in a box insert, Freedman received a letter from M. Dahood informing him that Pettinato had changed his reading of the third and fourth city names and that, in any case, the third and fourth city names were not in the same tablet (143). In short, Freedman's premature reconstruction was left hanging in the air.

Equally premature is Dahood's attempt (1978) to explain anomalous Ugaritic forms from the newly discovered Eblaite language. Pettinato has established that the Ebla scribes used the Sumerian writing system in an Old Akkadian syllabary to write their own Eblaite language and that this language was a Semitic language (1975). It remains debatable, however, whether this language should be classified as proto-Canaanite. Gelb has argued on the data presented by Pettinato that Eblaite's closest affinities are with Old Akkadian and Amorite (1977:28). His view has also been criticized; indeed Ullendorf (154) argues that from Gelb's own assessment there is insufficient ground for choosing either Akkadian or Ugaritic as having the closer affinities with Eblaite; the question should be considered unanswerable until more texts are published and available for grammatical analysis. Up to now the analyses of Eblaite have been based primarily on information derived from proper names, but proper names are notoriously difficult to interpret even when their reading is not in doubt. When too few texts have been published to provide any control on which syllabic values one should assign to multiple-value signs, such analysis becomes even more problematic. This is why many cuneiformists remain unconvinced by Pettinato's claim that the divine name Ya(w), a shortened form of Yahweh, has appeared in the Ebla tablets (1976e:49). Even if the reading -yà were correct, one need not explain the element as a divine name, but one should note that the sign in the Old Akkadian syllabary has the more common values ni, lí, and ì (Gelb, 1961:81–82). While it is doubtful in most cases whether Pettinato's reading -yà will survive closer scrutiny, his case would be much stronger if this element ever appeared as an independent name, not just as an element of a composite personal name.

Unfortunately, the premature rhapsodies over the connections between Ebla and the Bible have not only contaminated popular literature on the Bible with possible misinformation that may persist indefinitely; they have also created political problems that can only hinder the scholarly evaluation of the new evidence from Ebla. The Syrians, who are perhaps too sensitive to the possible political implications of these ancient texts (all of which seem very remote, if not absurd, to the average Western scholar), were very disturbed by Freedman and Pettinato's emphasis on the importance of these texts for biblical studies (Shanks: 48–50). This, together with the quarrel between Pettinato and Matthiae over the dating of the texts, has led to Pettinato's fall from favor. The publication of the texts has been taken out of his hands and assigned to an international committee composed of G. Buccellati, D. O. Edzard, P. Fronzaroli, P. Garelli, H. Klengel, J.-R. Kupper, G. Pettinato, F. Rashid, and E. Sollberger under the presidency of Matthiae (Matthiae, 1978: 334). Although Pettinato was assigned several volumes of texts, continuing difficulties have led him to resign from the committee, and Shanks, in reporting this development, hints at an intentional suppression of certain crucial Ebla texts by the Syrians (43–50). Such a fear seems a trifle premature. There has almost always been a big gap between new discoveries and adequate publications; many of the most important Dead Sea scrolls still have not appeared. One ought to give the committee a chance to do their work without further poisoning the air by conspiracy theories. On the other hand, scholars have a legitimate interest in the prompt publication of important new discoveries. One can only hope that the committee, with the support of the Syrian authorities, will provide a new model of scholarly responsibility by the rapid publication of these important new texts. In the meantime scholars would do well to learn from the debates over past discoveries. Sensational interpretations have seldom stood the test of time. The cautious interpretation is more useful because it is most often more nearly correct.[1]

Amarna

Work has continued on the Amarna tablets. These cuneiform texts discovered in Egypt in 1887 consist primarily of diplomatic correspondence between the Egyptian courts of Amenophis III and Amenophis IV (Akhenaten) and their allies or vassals in Western Asia. Since many of them come from vassal kings in Palestine and are often written in a barbaric Akkadian that betrays the native West Semitic language of the

---

[1] Since this manuscript was completed, the discussion on Ebla has continued. Robert Biggs published a thoughtful review of the present state of the discussion. There occurred an interchange of views between Alfonso Archi, Pettinato's replacement as epigrapher for the excavation, and Pettinato (1980); this debate was represented, partly in summary and partly in detail, along with photographs of several texts in BA 43 (1980) 200–216. Even more significant is Pettinato's decision to proceed with the publication of the texts despite the creation of the international committee. So far two volumes have appeared in the series, Materiali epigrafici di Ebla, published by the University of Naples Press. The first is a catalogue of the texts, Catalogo dei testi cuneiformi di Tell Mardikh-Ebla (1979), and the second is a transliteration and translation of fifty economic texts with extensive commentary, Testi amministrativi della biblioteca L. 2769 (1980). Additional volumes are in preparation. Although one could wish that the volumes would include photographs, it is very encouraging that the texts are beginning to appear.

writer, these texts are important for the history, culture, and languages of Palestine in the period prior to the Israelite conquest. Following up on suggestions of Albright, Moran has contributed a number of important studies (1950b, 1960, 1961, 1969a, 1973, 1975a, 1975b), of which one should especially note his still unpublished dissertation on the Byblos dialect (1950a). He has also promised a new translation of all the Amarna texts, but this has not yet appeared. Rainey published a supplement (1970) to Knudtzon's still basic edition, and one should also note the historical studies of Campbell (1964, 1965), Kitchen, Klengel (1964, 1965–70), and Helck (1971). Space forbids listing all the other studies that have appeared, scattered through the journals, but one should mention the discovery of some new Amarna-type tablets at ancient Kumidi (Edzard, 1973; Wilhelm).

The Amarna material has figured largely in such historical questions as the nature of the Israelite occupation or conquest of Palestine and the disputed relationship between the widely attested 'apiru and the Hebrews. Both questions continue to occupy biblical scholars. Bottéro (1954) and Greenberg (1955) both argued for a sociological understanding of the term 'apiru, but de Vaux in his last treatment of the topic still argued for an ethnic interpretation of the designation (1971:106–12). Nonetheless, the ethnic interpretation is clearly a minority point of view. Gottwald (1979) hardly even acknowledges its existence in his extensive discussion of 'apiru and 'ibrî.

II. AREAS OF RESEARCH

For the later periods there has not been any comparable publication of new collections of texts. This is one reason why comparative work on the Hebrew Bible has tended to concentrate on the extra-biblical material from the second millennium rather than on the first millennium, even though the Hebrew Bible itself is basically a literary product of the first millennium. Another reason for this paradoxical state of affairs is the scholarly fascination with origins, and Israel's origins were indubitably in the second millennium. Important work has been done in the later periods, however, and it will be mentioned in the following survey of the major areas of Near Eastern research bearing on the Hebrew Bible.

Historiography

Although they do not compare in sheer quantity to the mass of new texts from the second and third millenniums B.C.E., there have appeared some new texts from the later periods that affect the study of ancient Israel. One thinks especially of the discovery of the continuation of the Neo-Babylonian chronicle (Wiseman, 1961), which has enabled biblical scholars to reconstruct the late history of Judah with far more accuracy

(Bright, 1972:323 nn. 40–41; Malamat, 1974). One should also note the inscription of Adad-nirari III (Page), which mentions the tribute of Joash of Samaria, thus adding a complicating factor to the already troublesome chronology of the divided kingdom (Donner, 1970; Tadmor, 1973). The major advances in the understanding of the historiographical material, however, have come from new studies of earlier known material. One thinks of the historical studies of Tadmor (1961, 1970, 1975) and Brinkman (1964, 1968), Borger's edition of the Esarhaddon inscriptions (1956), Borger's (1961) and Schramm's introductions to the Assyrian royal inscriptions, Grayson's new translations of the Assyrian inscriptions (1972, 1976), his new edition of the Assyrian and Babylonian chronicles (1975a), and his smaller study of related historiographical literature (1975b).

Grayson's work on the broader historiographical literature has a bearing on two related questions. He rejected the view, recently resurrected by Lambert (1972), that the Babylonian chronicles simply arose out of Mesopotamian divination (1966). Grayson's more pronounced appreciation of the Mesopotamian historiographic achievement together with his new edition of the chronicles, following the important discussion of Albrektson, raises the possibility of a more adequate comparison of Israelite and Mesopotamian historiography. A significant attempt has been made along this line by Cancik, although he primarily concentrates on the comparison of Hittite and Israelite material. One should also mention Gese's earlier study (1958a), but the task more likely requires a new approach with a much broader base (Roberts, 1976).

The other question raised by Grayson's work is closely connected; it is the question of the genre and function of a particular historiographical work. Here Egyptian, Hittite, and Mesopotamian parallels may all be helpful in gaining a better understanding of the Israelite historiographical literature. A. Hermann, followed by S. Herrmann (1953/54; 1973: 212), argued for the Israelite adaptation of the Egyptian *Königsnovelle* in explaining 2 Samuel 7 and 1 Kings 8. Although the analysis as they present it can be criticized both from the standpoint of the Egyptological definition of the genre (Spalinger, 1973) and from the standpoint of its applicability to the alleged biblical parallels (Kutsch, 1961), a more careful analysis on both sides of the comparative equation, such as in the recent work of M. Görg, may yet yield positive results. On the Hittite side one may point to Wolf's treatment of Hattusilis's apology as a possible parallel to the history of David's rise to power. Tsevat justly criticized Wolf's failure to apply sound form-critical method in his study, but that weakness should not be allowed to obscure Wolf's valid insights. Hoffner has returned to the question with positive results in his "Propaganda and Political Justification in Hittite Historiography" (1975b), and P. Machinist has similarly stressed the political aspect of an important piece of Mesopotamian historiographical literature in his treatment of the epic of Tukulti-Ninurta. Finally, one may note the comparative use of Mesopotamian texts of various genres dealing with the return of captured images in the recent discussion of the ark narrative in 1 Samuel (Miller and Roberts, with the earlier literature cited there) and T. W. Mann's similarly extensive use of comparative material in his study of the typology of exaltation.

At this point one may also refer to the interpretative work done on the Phoenician, Aramaic, Moabite, Ammonite, Edomite, and Hebrew inscriptions. Their interpretation has affected the reconstruction of Israel's history and religion, and it has improved the linguistic understanding of the Hebrew and Aramaic languages in which the OT text is written. (See the chapter by Dever in this volume.)

Religion

Hymns and Prayers

The study of Israelite hymns and prayers went through a period in the 1920s and the 1930s when a great deal of attention was paid to Egyptian and Mesopotamian parallels. In the 1940s attention was shifted to the newly discovered Ugaritic parallels (Patton; Coppens). Although only a few Ugaritic texts have been published that could by any stretch of the imagination be called hymns or prayers, it is this concern for Ugaritic parallels that still dominates the important Psalms commentary of Dahood.

In the meantime, however, a revival of interest in the more strictly comparative material of the broader Near Eastern region has taken place. Falkenstein and von Soden's translation of Sumerian and Akkadian hymns and prayers provided a handy tool for comparing a wide range of hymns and prayers, while Ebeling's edition of the Akkadian *šu-illa* prayers gave biblical scholars access to a large corpus of one general class—whether one can speak of one genre is questionable (Lambert, 1974–77)—of prayers comparable to the individual lament of the biblical psalms. The publication of the Sultantepe tablets (Gurney and Finkelstein; Gurney and Hulin) supplemented this collection with a number of nicely preserved duplicates as well as some new texts and generated new interest in Akkadian hymns and prayers. Lambert published three long literary prayers of the Babylonians in 1960, and similar individual articles continue to appear in the Assyriological literature to the present. One may note particularly Lambert's article on the DINGIR.ŠÀ.DIB.BA prayers (1974) and von Soden's recent treatment of two royal Assyrian prayers to Ištar (1974–77).

In 1962 E. R. Dalglish wrote a valuable comparative study on Psalm 51 in which he tried to apply form-critical principles to the Mesopotamian as well as the biblical material. Following this, Hallo pointed to the importance of the Sumerian material as providing a point of comparison for the interpretation of the biblical text (1968). He was primarily concerned with the individual prayer, but he discussed other genres as well, and one should especially note the congregational lament. Several of these have been recently published (Kramer, 1969a:611–19; Kutscher), but they have yet to be fully utilized in the exegetical treatment of this genre of psalms to which the book of Lamentations also belongs. One should also note the renewed work on the Egyptian comparative material by Barucq and the possibility for comparison with the Hittite material, which has never been fully exploited (Gurney, 1948; Güterbock; Houwink ten Cate).

Gerstenberger's recent work on Psalms (1971) is a major advance in the right direction. In the meantime, however, a whole spate of new tools that should ease the task of the biblical scholar attempting to understand the psalms in the light of the general Near Eastern background has appeared. Werner Mayer's excellent new study of the *šu-illa* prayers, heavily influenced as it is by biblical form criticism, particularly that of Gerstenberger, should make it easier for the biblical scholar to make methodologically legitimate comparisons. The additional texts available to Mayer, some of which are now published in copies by Loretz and Mayer, make Mayer's study the most complete and accurate treatment of the *šu-illa* prayers and a necessary supplement and corrective to both Ebeling's edition and the earlier form-critical study of Kunstmann. Nonetheless, Mayer's volume is not the final word; there are still unpublished texts, and the form-critical work has not yet been carried through with the thoroughness it deserves (Lambert, 1974–77). Returning to the positive, one should note the new French translation of Babylonian hymns and prayers by M.-J. Seux. Taken together with the older works, it and Mayer's volume provide the biblical scholar with a rich corpus for comparative purposes. Moreover, Jan Assmann's new translation of Egyptian hymns and prayers opens up new possibilities for serious comparative work on the Egyptian side as well. The number of texts represented and the clear types into which they fall should make form-critical analysis relatively easy and thereby provide some of the methodological control necessary for worthwhile comparative work.

Myth, Ritual, Magic

The period since Albright wrote has seen the recovery of significant portions of the Babylonian creation epic (Lambert and Parker; Grayson, 1969), publication of the Atrahasis (Lambert and Millard) and Erra epics (Cagni, 1969, 1970), and smaller additions to other Babylonian epics and myths (Grayson, 1969; Hecker). One should also note the appearance of a number of Sumerian (Kramer, 1969b; Alster, 1972; Ferrara; Cooper,

1978; Farber-Flügge) and Hittite (Hoffner, 1975a) myths and epics.

The Atrahasis epic, in particular, has had an important influence on biblical studies since this epic connects the creation of humanity and the flood in a historical sequence just as the Genesis account does. Comparative studies between the two texts have concentrated on the reason for the flood in the two narratives. One school of thought sees a similarity in that the flood in both stories is caused by human evil. This is not so clear in the Babylonian account, but such an interpretation is assigned to the text based on a moral understanding of the "noise" made by humanity. Such an interpretation tries to connect the motif of "noise" to the "outcry" of the Sodom and Gomorrah story and, in fact, often sees this later story as a simple variant of the basically similar flood story (Pettinato, 1971b). The other, far more persuasive, school of thought sees rather a contrast between the biblical and Mesopotamian reasons for the flood. The biblical account blames the flood on moral evil (Frymer-Kensky), but the Atrahasis epic sees the problem in what one might call natural evil, in the problem of overpopulation (Draffkorn-Kilmer, 1972; Moran, 1971). Needless to say, the nature of the deity involved in the two accounts varies considerably. For the view of creation and the position of the gods in Atrahasis, note especially the articles of Moran (1970) and Jacobsen (1977) where earlier literature is discussed.

The creation epic has also figured prominently in biblical discussions, particularly in the ongoing debate over the alleged enthronement festival in Israel. There is no room to enter into that debate, which is well treated in the fine comparative study by Lipinski, except to note the new material relevant to the discussion that has emerged from the extra-biblical material. The myth and ritual school's view of a pattern of divine kingship common to the whole Near East was severely criticized by Frankfort, who pointed to striking differences between the Egyptian and Mesopotamian views of the king. Even the divinity of the Egyptian king, however, has been questioned. Goedicke stressed the divinity of the office of the king rather than his person, and Posener has been even more critical of the alleged divinity of the Pharaoh. Such criticism has reduced the contrast between Egyptian and Mesopotamian conceptions of kingship, but at the same time it has also reduced the "divine" element in both conceptions, a central tenet of the myth and ritual school. Moving to the Mesopotamian side, reconstructions of the Babylonian new year festival have tended to ignore regional and temporal differences in the quest for a common pattern, and the resulting reconstructions are therefore subject to question. To mention only one point, most reconstructions include the death and resurrection of Marduk, but the one text that was thought to tell of Marduk's resurrection has been shown by von Soden to be something quite different (1952–55, 1957). The text actually uses mythological material to justify Sennacherib's sack of Babylon. A similar use of mythological material to interpret or justify historical events for political reasons can be seen in the much earlier Sumerian composition *The Exaltation of Inanna* (Hallo and van Dijk; cf. Roberts, 1973:341), and Jacobsen has argued that it is a significant feature in most of the combat myths of later Mesopotamian history (1975:72–77). Even the great creation epic was written, according to Jacobsen, to celebrate a historical event: Babylon's victory over the Sealand (1975:76). Such a development obviously has significant implications for biblical studies where one can find a similar political use of myth (Roberts, 1973).

The numerous ritual texts from the ancient Near East also have a potential value for biblical scholarship that has not yet been fully exploited. *Maqlu* (Meier) and *Shurpu* (Reiner) have been mined for their rich contribution to curse formulas (Hillers, 1964), and Jacob Milgrom, in particular, has drawn upon Hittite material in explaining Israelite ritual (1970, 1976a, 1976b), but much remains unused. In addition to the Mari prophecies and the Neo-Assyrian prophetic texts, for instance, the enormous amount of new material on Babylonian divinatory practice (RAI 14, 1966; Bottéro, 1974 and bibliography) would appear to be ready-made for the new interest in the "social location" of the Israelite prophets. It has not been totally overlooked (Long, 1973), but this discussion has seemed to prefer more remote, relatively modern analogies (Long, 1977). These analogies have their place, but there is much that one can still learn from the more ancient parallels (Roberts, 1977a; Barré). A fine summary and a good use of this material can be found in Robert Wilson's new monograph (1980). One should also note the potential value of such ritual series as the "opening of the mouth" ceremony (Borger, 1975:85) for gaining a better understanding of ancient Near Eastern idolatry and hence of the prophetic polemic against idolatry.

Law

The major collections of Near Eastern law were already known at the time Albright wrote, but our understanding of them has increased in the intervening period. New translations or editions of some of the collections have appeared (Yaron; Cardascia; Finet), but even more important, detailed interpretative work such as that of Finkelstein (1973) has opened our eyes to the significance of these corpora as collections, or perhaps even revisions, of traditional case law, and has made clear the basic continuity of the biblical collections with these antecedents. F. R. Kraus's (1958, 1965a) and Finkelstein's (1965) treatments of the Babylonian *mišarum* edicts, moreover, have provided possible legal parallels for such Israelite institutions as the Sabbath Year and the Jubilee Year, which were once regarded as purely utopian constructs.

Albrecht Alt's classic study of the origins of Israelite law remains a formative influence although it has required significant modification. On form-critical grounds he made a sharp distinction between casuistic or case law, common to the ancient Near Eastern legal tradition and adapted from it by Israel, and the so-called apodictic or categorical law, typified by the Ten Commandments, which he regarded as uniquely Israelite and derived from religious instruction in the cult. Several criticisms have been leveled against his category of apodictic law (Nielsen: 56–93). The category as he defines it is not a unit, since some radically different formulations have been subsumed under one category. Moreover, the apodictic command is neither peculiarly Israelite nor necessarily cultic—examples have been found in Near Eastern laws, ritual instructions, and Hittite treaties. These observations could be accommodated by slight modifications of Alt's theory, but E. Gerstenberger (1965) raised a more fundamental objection when he denied that the apodictic command originated in a cultic setting and argued instead that it arose in the ethos of early Israelite tribal society as instruction given by clan heads and elders to the youth (*Sippenweisheit*). His treatment was suggestive and has been favorably received by many scholars, but there are serious grammatical difficulties with Gerstenberger's attempt to remove the distinction between the Hebrew negatives לא and אל (Bright, 1973). If that distinction cannot be erased, most of Gerstenberger's examples of apodictic law in the wisdom collections vanish, and Bright's alternate explanation of an original Israelite setting in the covenant stipulations, later transmitted in various channels—cultic recitation, priestly instruction, prophetic word, legal debates among the village elders, and family instruction—appears a more adequate model for understanding the origins and development of this kind of legal material.

Covenant

No area of the Near Eastern background of the Hebrew Bible has been more discussed in recent years than the international treaty. Since Mendenhall initiated the biblical discussion with his little booklet in 1955, the comparative treaty material has multiplied dramatically. McCarthy was able to take account of most of the new material in his standard treatment of the question (1963), but new material since then, such as the Hittite version of the Aziru treaty (Freydank), forced McCarthy to revise some of his earlier conclusions in his more recent work (1972). McCarthy's very thorough work tended to dampen discussion of these parallels despite the fact that many of the scholars who had worked on this material earlier were far from agreeing with McCarthy's assessment of the material (Huffmon, 1966; Huffmon and Parker; Hillers, 1969; Mendenhall, 1973). This, in turn, has resulted in a perceptible shift in

much OT discussion of covenant back to a narrowly biblical base, which
can be seen in Kutsch's widely quoted definition of ברית as "obligation"
(1967) and in Perlitt's return to Wellhausen's view of covenant as a late
theological novelty in Israel. This is a false step, an attempt to gain a
bogus security in the constricted womb of pure OT studies. Whatever the
excesses of the comparative work done on biblical covenant and Near
Eastern treaty, it should have made clear that the reality involved could
not be apprehended by a simple syntactical study of a single Hebrew
word (see McCarthy, 1974:103). If genuine progress is to be made in this
area, it will come from a continued firsthand acquaintance with the
extra-biblical material conjoined with careful analysis of the biblical texts.
Examples of this type of approach may be seen in M. Weinfeld's
interesting comparison of the Davidic covenant to the royal grant and in
P. Riemann's thoughtful reappraisal of the Mosaic covenant.

Wisdom

The wisdom literature is another area in which our understanding of
the Near Eastern background has advanced significantly in the last three
decades. Edmund Gordon's *Sumerian Proverbs*, recently supplemented
by Alster (1978), and W. G. Lambert's *Babylonian Wisdom Literature*
(1960b) were significant milestones in a better understanding of the Mesopotamian material, but one must also note Kramer's treatment of the
Sumerian "Man and his God" (1955, 1969c) and Nougayrol's publication
of "Une version ancienne du 'Juste souffrant'" (1952). These together
with the new texts discovered at Ugarit (Nougayrol, 1968:265–300)—
providing, among other things, evidence of a possible cultural link
between Canaan and the Babylonian tradition—testified to a long intellectual tradition in which the problem of individual suffering was
treated, and they thus have an important bearing on the interpretation
of Job (Roberts, 1977b; see more recently Müller). Sjöberg's studies on
the Sumerian schools (1972, 1973, 1975a, 1975b) helped to clarify the
part these may have played in the continuity of that tradition. A number
of summarizing studies appeared (Kuhl, 1953, 1954; Gray, 1970), including the oft-cited work by Gese (1958b). At the same time significant
work was also being done on the Egyptian wisdom material. Williams
(1961) and Couroyer (1963, 1968) refuted Drioton's (1957, 1959) attempt
to trace the Wisdom of Amenemope back to a Semitic original.
Gardiner's work on the onomastica was used by von Rad to explain Job
38. Other currents in Egyptian wisdom literature were mediated to biblical scholars in the works of McKane, Schmid, and Gemser.

Some of the attempts to explain biblical material from the background of international wisdom, however, seem a bit excessive. One may
question whether Israelite wisdom had any conception equivalent to the

Egyptian *maat*, and certainly the influence of the Egyptian encyclopae-
dic lists on biblical literature has been highly overrated. Hillers has
shown that the background for Psalm 148, far from being sought in the
Egyptian lists, may be found in a hymnic tradition reaching back to pre-
Israelite Mesopotamia and Egypt, in which other gods, as deified elements of creation, join in praising the deity being worshiped (1978).

Love Poetry

One should also look at the recent attempts to find a background for
understanding the Song of Songs. Gerleman has stressed the Egyptian
parallels, and the recent work of White has added some relevant material (Williams, 1977:499). Schmökel (1952, 1956) and Cooper (1971)
have pointed to cuneiform parallels, and if one takes at all seriously the
possibility that these songs originated in a fertility cult, one cannot overlook the rather peculiar "love" lyrics published by Lambert (1975). All of
this material, together with a mass of nontextual comparative evidence,
has been assembled in the massive new commentary by Pope (1977), but
it is still too early to say how much this will clarify the text of this most
peculiar of biblical books.

Collections of Pictures and Texts in Translation

Finally, one should note the major collections of ancient Near Eastern texts and pictures relating to the Bible. The two standard collections
have been those of Gressmann (1926, 1927) and Pritchard (1969). A bit
less expensive is Beyerlin's collection of texts made for the ATD series,
which has now been translated into English for the OT Library series.
D. Winton Thomas edited a collection of texts prepared by the Society
for Old Testament Study, and Kurt Galling's collection of historical texts
should also be mentioned. Although the iconographic evidence has never
been entirely ignored in OT scholarship, it has never received quite the
same serious treatment that has been accorded the ancient Near Eastern
texts. This exclusively textual orientation has been a serious flaw in the
approach of many biblical scholars. Spalinger's study (1978) of a Canaanite human sacrifice depicted on an Egyptian relief points up the
value of the pictorial evidence for understanding the OT backgrounds.
Even more impressive, however, has been Othmar Keel's series of exciting exegetical studies (1974, 1977a, 1977b) which have systematically
incorporated the pictorial evidence, including that of the seals, into the
exegetical process. This is perhaps the most promising direction taken in
recent biblical scholarship's use of the comparative material. One can
only hope that scholars will begin to give serious attention to non-
epigraphic evidence in a more self-critical fashion.

III. SUMMARY

It is difficult in a summary statement to do justice to the complexity of the ebb and flow of the study of OT backgrounds over the last thirty years. The tendency has been to overstress the importance of the background material in the first flush of discovery, and then, when the flaws in the early interpretations have become obvious, to swing to the other extreme of largely ignoring the comparative material. Very often in this latter phase of the discussion many of the biblical scholars involved no longer controlled the primary sources for the extra-biblical evidence. This lack of first-hand acquaintance with the nonbiblical material is a growing problem in the field. It is partly a reflex of the growing complexity of the broader field of ancient Near Eastern studies: no one can master the whole field any longer. Partly it reflects a conscious theological decision about the appropriate task of the OT scholar (Childs), and partly it may reflect a loss of nerve, a decision to settle for a more controllable albeit more restricted vision.

In any case, the perceptible shift away from the larger picture bodes ill for the exegetical task. The concern for biblical backgrounds has had its abuses and exaggerations. There is a need for a far more rigorous attempt to understand both the OT material and the nonbiblical material in their own settings, and before making comparative judgments one should also be clear that the material being compared or contrasted is really comparable (Saggs: 1–29). But, despite the abuses and the need for a more self-critical methodology, the attention to extra-biblical sources has brought new understanding to the biblical text. If it has never proven a particular interpretation, it has certainly ruled out some and suggested others. However, if this light from the East is to continue shining and grow brighter, biblical scholars must continue to be conversant with fields outside their own discipline. To some extent one can and must depend on experts in these related fields, but unless one has some first-hand acquaintance with the texts and physical remains with which these related fields deal, one will hardly be able to choose which expert's judgment to follow. There is no substitute for knowledge of the primary sources.

BIBLIOGRAPHY

Aistleitner, Joseph
1963   *Wörterbuch der Ugaritischen Sprache.* Berichte über die Verhandlungen der Sächsischen Akademie der Wissenschaften zu Leipzig. Phil.-hist. Klasse 106/3. Berlin: Akademie Verlag.

Al-A'dami, Khalid Ahmad
1967   "Old Babylonian Letters from ed-Der." *Sumer* 23: 151–66.

Albrektson, Bertil
1967   *History and the Gods: An Essay on the Idea of Historical Events as Divine Manifestations in the Ancient Near East and in Israel.* Lund: CWK Gleerup.

Albright, William F.
1944   "The Oracles of Balaam." *JBL* 63: 207–33.
1950   "The Psalm of Habakkuk." Pp. 1–18 in *Studies in Old Testament Prophecy.* Edinburgh: T. & T. Clark.
1951   "The Old Testament and the Archaeology of the Ancient East." Pp. 27–47 in *The Old Testament and Modern Study.* Ed. H. H. Rowley. Oxford: Clarendon.
1968   *Yahweh and the Gods of Canaan.* Garden City, NY: Doubleday.

Alster, Bendt
1972   *Dumuzi's Dream: Aspects of Oral Poetry in a Sumerian Myth.* Mesopotamia, 1. Copenhagen: Akademisk Forlag.
1978   "Sumerian Proverb Collection Seven." *RA* 72: 97–112.

Alt, Albrecht
1934   *Die Ursprünge des israelitischen Rechts.* Berichte über die Verhandlungen der Sächsischen Akademie der Wissenschaften zu Leipzig. Phil.-hist. Klasse 86/1. Leipzig: S. Hirzel. Reprinted pp. 278 332 in *Kleine Schriften zur Geschichte des Volkes Israel,* 1. Munich: C. H. Beck, 1968.

Archi, Alfonso
1979   "The Epigraphic Evidence from Ebla and the Old Testament." *Bib* 60: 556–66.

Archives royales de Mari 1–
1946   Textes cunéiformes, Musée du Louvre, XXII–. Paris: Paul Geuthner.

Archives royales de Mari, transcrite et traduite, I–XIX
1950–77   Ed. André Parrot and Georges Dossin. Paris: Imprimerie Nationale.

Assman, Jan
1975   *Ägyptische Hymnen und Gebete.* Zurich and Munich: Artemis-Verlag.

Barr, James
1974   "Philology and Exegesis: Some General Remarks, with Illustrations from Job 3." Pp. 39–61 in *Questions disputées d'Ancien Testament.* Ed. C. Brekelmans. Leuven: University Press.

Barré, M. L.
1978   "New Light on the Interpretation of Hosea vi 2." *VT* 28: 129–41.

Barucq, André
1962   *L'expression de la louange divine et de la prière dans la Bible et en Égypte.* Bibliothèque d'étude, 33. Cairo: Institut français d'archéologie orientale.

Bauer, Theodor
1926   *Die Ostkanaanäer.* Leipzig: Asia Major.

Bergerhof, K., M. Dietrich, O. Loretz, and J. C. de Moor
1969   *Ugarit-Forschungen.* Neukirchen-Vluyn: Neukirchener Verlag.

Bermant, Chaim, and Michael Weitzman
1979   *Ebla: An Archaeological Enigma.* London: Weidenfeld and Nicolson.

Beyerlin, Walter, ed.
1978   *Near Eastern Texts Relating to the Old Testament.* Philadelphia: Westminster.

Biggs, Robert
1980   "The Ebla Tablets: An Interim Perspective." *BA* 43: 76–86.

Boling, Robert G.
1960   "'Synonymous' Parallelism in the Psalms." *JSS* 5: 221–55.

Bordreuil, Pierre
1975   "Nouveaux textes économiques en cunéiformes alphabétiques de Ras Shamra-Ougarit (34e campagne 1973)." *Sem* 25: 19–29.

Borger, Riekele
1956   *Die Inschriften Asarhaddons, Königs von Assyrien.* AfO Beih. 9. Graz: E. Weidner.
1961   *Einleitung in die assyrischen Königsinschriften*, I. Leiden: E. J. Brill.
1967–75   *Handbuch der Keilschriftliteratur*, I–III. Berlin and New York: Walter de Gruyter.

Bottéro, Jean
1954   *Le problème des Habiru à la 4ᵉ Rencontre assyrio-logique internationale.* Cahiers de la Société asiatique, 12. Paris: Imprimerie Nationale.
1974   "Symptômes, signes, écritures en Mésopotamie ancienne." Pp. 70–197 in *Divination et Rationalité.* Paris: Éditions du Seuil.

Bright, John
1959   *A History of Israel.* Philadelphia: Westminster. 2d ed., 1972.
1973   "The Apodictic Prohibition: Some Observations." *JBL* 92: 185–204.

Brinkman, A. J.
1964   "Merodach-Baladan II." Pp. 6–53 in *Studies Presented to A. L. Oppenheim.* Chicago: Oriental Institute.
1968   *A Political History of Post-Kassite Babylonia 1158–722 B.C.* AnOr 43. Rome: Pontifical Biblical Institute.

Buccellati, Giorgio
1966   *The Amorites of the Ur III Period.* Naples: Instituto Orientale di Napoli.

Cagni, Luigi
1969   *L'epopea di Erra.* Studi Semitici 34. Rome: Instituto di Studi del Vicino Oriente.
1970   *Das Erra-Epos Keilschrifttext.* Rome: Pontifical Biblical Institute.

Campbell, Edward F., Jr.
1964   *The Chronology of the Amarna Letters.* Baltimore: Johns Hopkins University Press.
1965   "Shechem in the Amarna Archive." Pp. 191–207 in *Shechem: The Biography of a Biblical City.* Ed. G. E. Wright. New York and Toronto: McGraw-Hill.

Cancik, Hubert
1976   *Grundzüge der hethitischen und alttestamentlichen Geschichtsschreibung.* Wiesbaden: Otto Harrassowitz.

Caquot, André, Maurice Sznycer, and Andrée Herdner
1974   *Textes Ougaritiques: I. Mythes et Légendes.* Paris: Éditions du Cerf.

Caquot, André, and Emilia Masson
1977   "Tablettes Ougaritiques du Louvre." *Sem* 27: 5–19.

Cardascia, Guillaume
1969   *Les lois assyriennes.* Littératures anciennes du proche-orient. Paris: Éditions du Cerf.

Cassuto, Umberto
1971   *The Goddess Anath.* Jerusalem: Magnes. Hebrew original in 1951.

Childs, Brevard S.
1979   *Introduction to the Old Testament as Scripture.* Philadelphia: Fortress.

Clifford, Richard J.
1972   *The Cosmic Mountain in Canaan and the Old Testament.* Cambridge, MA: Harvard University Press.

Cohen, Mark E.
1974   *Balag-Compositions: Sumerian Lamentation Liturgies of the Second and First Millennium* B.C. Sources from the Ancient Near East, 1/2. Malibu, CA: Undena.

Coogan, Michael David
1978   *Stories from Ancient Canaan.* Philadelphia: Westminster.

Cooper, Jerrold S.
1971   "New Cuneiform Parallels to the Song of Songs." *JBL* 90: 157–62.
1978   *The Return of Ninurta to Nippur.* AnOr 52. Rome: Pontifical Biblical Institute.

Coppens, Joseph
1946   "Les parallèles du Psautier avec les textes de Ras Shamra-Ougarit." *Bulletin d'histoire et d'exegesis de AT* 18: 113–42.

Couroyer, B.
1963   "L'origine égyptienne de la Sagesse d'Amenemopé." *RB* 70: 208–24.
1968   "Amenemopé XXIV, 13–18." *RB* 75: 549–61.

Craigie, P. E., ed.
1972–   *Newsletter for Ugaritic Studies.* Calgary, Alberta, Canada: Religious Studies Program, University of Calgary.

Cross, Frank M.
1954   "The Evolution of the Proto-Canaanite Alphabet." *BASOR* 132: 15–24.
1955   "The Song of Miriam." *JNES* 14: 237–50.
1961   "The Development of the Jewish Scripts." Pp. 133–202 in *The Bible and the Ancient Near East: Essays in Honor of William Foxwell Albright.* Ed. G. E. Wright. Garden City, NY: Doubleday.
1967   "The Origin and Early Evolution of the Alphabet." Pp. 8–24 in *E. L. Sukenik Memorial Volume (1899–1953).* Eretz-Israel 8. Jerusalem: Israel Exploration Society.
1968   "Song of the Sea and Canaanite Myth." *JTC* 5: 1–25.
1973   *Canaanite Myth and Hebrew Epic.* Cambridge, MA: Harvard University Press.
1974   "Leaves from an Epigraphist's Notebook." *CBQ* 36: 486–94.

Cross, Frank M., and David N. Freedman
1948   "The Blessing of Moses." *JBL* 67: 191–210.
1950   *Studies in Ancient Yahwistic Poetry.* Baltimore: Authors. Published as SBLDS 21. Missoula, MT: Scholars Press.
1952   *Early Hebrew Orthography: A Study of the Epigraphic Evidence.* New Haven: American Oriental Society.
1972   "Some Observations on Early Hebrew." *Bib* 53: 413–20.

Dahood, Mitchell
1966–70   *Psalms.* 3 vols. AB 16, 17, 17a. Garden City, NY: Doubleday.
1978   "Ebla, Ugarit and the Old Testament." Pp. 81–112 in *Congress Volume: Göttingen, 1977.* VTSup 29. Leiden: E. J. Brill.

Dalglish, Edward R.
1962   *Psalm Fifty-One in the Light of Ancient Near Eastern Patternism.* Leiden: E. J. Brill.

Dever, William G.
1977   "Palestine in the Second Millennium BCE: The Archaeological Picture." Pp. 70–120 in *Israelite and Judaean History.* Ed. J. H. Hayes and J. M. Miller. Philadelphia: Westminster.

Dietrich, Manfred, and O. Loretz
1966, 1969   "Die soziale Struktur von Alalah und Ugarit." *WO* 3: 188–205; 5: 57–93.
1972a   *Konkordanz der ugaritischen Textzählungen.* AOAT 19. Kevelaer: Verlag Butzon und Bercker.
1972b   *Nuzi-Bibliographie.* AOAT Sonderreihe 11. Kevelaer: Verlag Butzon und Bercker.
1973   *Ugarit-Bibliographie 1928–66.* AOAT 20. Kevelaer: Verlag Butzon und Bercker.

Donner, Herbert
1967   "Ugaritismen in der Psalmenforschung." *ZAW* 79: 322–50.
1970   "Adadnirari III und die Vasallen des Westens." Pp. 49–59 in *Archäologie und Altes Testament* (Festschrift Kurt Galling). Ed. A. Kuschke and E. Kutsch. Tübingen: J. C. B. Mohr.

Dossin, G.
1975   "Tablettes de Mari." *RA* 69: 23–30.

Draffkorn-Kilmer, Anne E.
1957   "*Ilāni/Elohim.*" *JBL* 76: 216–24.
1972   "The Mesopotamian Concept of Overpopulation and Its Solution as Represented in the Mythology." *Or* 41: 160–77.

Drioton, Etienne
1957				"Sur la Sagesse d'Aménémopé." Pp. 254–80 in *Mélanges
				bibliques redigés en l'honneur de André Robert*. Ed.
				H. Cazelles. Paris: Bloud & Gay.
1959				"Le livre des Proverbes et la Sagesse d'Aménémopé." Pp.
				229–41 in *Sacra Pagina: Miscellanea biblica congressus
				internationalis Catholici de re biblica*, vol. 1. Ed.
				J. Coppens. BETL 12. Gembloux: Duculot; Paris:
				Gabalda.

Driver, G. R.
1956				*Canaanite Myth and Legends*. Old Testament Studies,
				3. Edinburgh: T. & T. Clark.

Ebeling, Erich
1953				*Die akkadische Gebetsserie 'Handerhebung' von neuem
				gesammelt und herausgegeben*. Berlin: Akademie Ver-
				lag.

Edzard, Dietz Otto
1957				*Die 'zweite Zwischenzeit' Babyloniens*. Wiesbaden: Otto
				Harrassowitz.
1973				"Die Tontafeln von Kāmid el-Lōz." Pp. 50–62 in *Kamid
				el-Loz-Kumidi*. Ed. D. O. Edzard et al. Saarbrücker
				Beiträge zur Altextumskunde, 7. Bonn: Rudolf Habelt.

Eichler, Harry L.
1973				*Indenture at Nuzi: The Personal Tidennūtu Contract
				and its Mesopotamian Analogues*. New Haven and
				London: Yale University Press.
1976				"Nuzi." Pp. 635–36 in *IDBSup*.
1977				"Another Look at Nuzi Sisterhood Contracts." Pp. 45–59
				in *Essays on the Ancient Near East in Memory of
				Jacob Joel Finkelstein*. Ed. Maria de Jong Ellis. Mem-
				oirs of the Connecticut Academy of Arts and Sciences,
				19. Hamden, CT: Archon Books.

Ellermeier, Friedrich
1968				*Prophetie in Mari und Israel*. Herzberg am Harz:
				E. Jungfer.

Falkenstein, Adam, and Wolfram von Soden
1953				*Sumerische und akkadische Hymnen und Gebete*.
				Zurich and Stuttgart: Artemis-Verlag.

Farber-Flügge, Gertrud
1973				*Der Mythos "Inanna und Enki" unter besonderer
				Berücksichtigung der Liste der m e*. Studia Pohl 10.
				Rome: Pontifical Biblical Institute.

Ferrara, A. J.
1973				*Nanna-Suen's Journey to Nippur*. Studia Pohl: Series
				Maior, 2. Rome: Pontifical Biblical Institute.

Finet, André
1978   *Le code de Hammurapi* Littératures anciennes du
                      proche-orient. Paris: Éditions du Cerf.

Finkelstein, J. J.
1965   "Some New *Misharum* Material and its Implications."
                      Pp. 233–46 in *Studies in Honor of Benno Landsberger
                      on his Seventy-Fifth Birthday, April 21, 1965.* AS 16.
                      Chicago: University of Chicago Press.
1966   "The Genealogy of the Hammurapi Dynasty." *JCS* 20:
                      95–118.
1973   "The Goring Ox: Some Historical Perspectives on Deo-
                      dards, Forfeitures, Wrongful Death and the Western
                      Notion of Sovereignty." *Temple Law Quarterly* 46:
                      169–290.

Fisher, Loren R., ed.
1971   *The Claremont Ras Shamra Tablets.* AnOr 48. Rome:
                      Pontifical Biblical Institute.
1972, 1975   *Ras Shamra Parallels: The Texts from Ugarit and the
                      Hebrew Bible.* 2 vols. Rome: Pontifical Biblical Institute.

Fitzmyer, Joseph A.
1956   "*le* as a Proposition and a Particle in Micah 5,1(5,2)."
                      CBQ 18: 10–13.

Frankfort, Henri
1948   *Kingship and the Gods.* Chicago: University of Chicago
                      Press.

Freedman, David N.
1071   Prologomenon to G. B. Gray's *The Forms of Hebrew
                      Poetry.* New York: Ktav.
1972   "Psalm XXIX in the Hebrew Poetic Tradition." *VT* 22:
                      144–45.
1976   "Divine Names and Titles in Early Hebrew Poetry." Pp.
                      55–102 in *Magnalia Dei: The Mighty Acts of God:
                      Essays on the Bible and Archaeology in Memory of
                      G. Ernest Wright.* Ed. F. M. Cross, W. E. Lemke, P. D.
                      Miller. Garden City, NY: Doubleday.
1977   "A Letter to the Readers." *BA* 40: 2–4.
1978   "The Real Story of the Ebla Tablets: Ebla and the Cities
                      of the Plain." *BA* 41: 143–64.

Freedman, Nadezhda
1977   "The Nuzi Ebla." *BA* 40: 32–33.

Freydank, Helmut
1960   "Eine hethitische Fassung des Vertrags zwischen dem
                      Hethiterkönig Šuppiluliuma und Aziru von Amurru."
                      MIO 7: 35–81.

Frymer-Kensky, T.
1977   "The Atrahasis Epic and Its Significance for our Under-
           standing of Genesis 1–9." *BA* 40: 147–55.

Galling, Kurt
1950   *Textbuch zur Geschichte Israels.* Tübingen: J. C. B.
           Mohr. 2d ed., 1968.

Gardiner, Alan H.
1947   *Ancient Egyptian Onomastica* 1–3. London: Oxford
           University Press.

Gelb, Ignace J.
1958   *La lingua degli Amoriti.* Rendiconti delle sedute Del'
           accademia Nazionale dei Lincei. Class di Science morali,
           storiche e filologiche, XIII: 143–64. Atti della Accademia
           Nazionale dei Lincei.
1961   *Old Akkadian Writing and Grammar.* 2d ed. Chicago:
           University of Chicago Press.
1977   "Thoughts About Ibla: A Preliminary Evaluation, March,
           1977." *Syro-Mesopotamian Studies* 1: 113–30.

Gemser, B.
1960   "The Instructions of Onchsheshonqy and Biblical Wis-
           dom Literature." Pp. 102–28 in *Congress Volume:
           Oxford, 1959.* VTSup 7. Leiden: E. J. Brill.

Gerleman, Gillis
1965   *Ruth: Das Hohelied.* BKAT 18. Neukirchen-Vluyn:
           Neukirchener Verlag.

Gerstenberger, Erhard
1965   *Wesen und Herkunft des "apodiktischen Rechts."*
           WMANT 20. Neukirchen-Vluyn: Neukirchener Verlag.
1971   *Der bittende Mensch: Bittritual und Klagelied des Ein-
           zelnen im Alten Testament.* Habil.-Schrift, Heidelberg.
           Now published: WMANT 51. Neukirchen-Vluyn: Neu-
           kirchener Verlag.

Gese, Hartmut
1958a   "Geschichtliches Denken im Alten Orient und im Alten
           Testament." *ZTK* 55: 127–45.
1958b   *Lehre und Wirklichkeit in der alten Weisheit.* Tübin-
           gen: J. C. B. Mohr.
1970   "Die Religionen Altsyriens." *Die Religionen der
           Menschheit* X, 2: 1–232.

Geus, C. H. J. de
1976   *The Tribes of Israel.* Assen and Amsterdam: Van
           Gorcum.

Gibson, J. C. L.
1978   *Canaanite Myths and Legends.* Edinburgh: T. & T.
           Clark.

Ginsberg, H. L.
1955   "Ugaritic Myths, Epics and Legends." Pp. 120–55 in
              ANET. 2d ed. Ed. J. Pritchard. Princeton: Princeton
              University Press.

Goedicke, Hans
1960   *Die Stellung der Königs im alten Reich*. Ägyptologische
              Abhandlungen, 2. Wiesbaden: Otto Harrassowitz.

Goodwin, Donald Watson
1969   *Text-Restoration Methods in Contemporary U.S.A. Bib-
              lical Scholarship*. Pubblicazioni del Seminario di Semitis-
              tica, Ricerche 5. Naples: Instituto Orientale di Napoli.

Gordis, Robert
1943   "The Asseverative Kaph in Ugaritic and Hebrew." *JAOS*
              63: 176–78.

Gordon, Cyrus H.
1940   "Biblical Customs and the Nuzi Tablets." *BA* 3: 1–12.
1954   "The Patriarchal Narratives." *JNES* 13: 56–59.
1965   *Ugaritic Textbook*. AnOr 38. Rome: Pontifical Biblical
              Institute.

Gordon, Edmund I.
1959   *Sumerian Proverbs: Glimpses of Everyday Life in An-
              cient Mesopotamia*. Philadelphia: University Museum.

Görg, Manfred
1975   *Gott König Reden in Israel und Ägypten*. BWANT
              105. Stuttgart: W. Kohlhammer.

Gottwald, Norman K.
1974   "Were the Early Israelites Pastoral Nomads?" Pp.
              223–55 in *Rhetorical Criticism: Essays in Honor of
              James Muilenburg*. Ed. J. J. Jackson and M. Kessler.
              PTMS 1. Pittsburgh: Pickwick.
1975   "Domain Assumptions and Societal Models in the Study
              of Pre-Monarchic Israel." Pp. 89–100 in *Congress Vol-
              ume: Edinburgh, 1974*. VTSup 28. Leiden: E. J. Brill.
1979   *The Tribes of Yahweh: A Sociology of the Religion of
              Liberated Israel 1250–1050 B.C.E.* Maryknoll, NY: Orbis
              Books.

Gray, John
1957   *The Legacy of Canaan*. VTSup 5. Leiden: E. J. Brill.
              2d ed., 1965.
1970   "The Book of Job in the Context of Near Eastern Litera-
              ture." *ZAW* 82: 251–69.

Grayson, Albert K.
1966   "Divination and the Babylonian Chronicles." Pp. 69–76
                in *La divination en Mesopotamie ancienne*, XIVe. Ren-
                contre Assyriologique Internationale. Paris: Presses Uni-
                versitaires de France.
1969   "Akkadian Myths and Epics." Pp. 501–18 in *ANET*. Ed.
                J. Pritchard. Princeton: Princeton University Press.
1972, 1976   *Assyrian Royal Inscriptions*, 1–2. Records of the Ancient
                Near East. Wiesbaden: Otto Harrassowitz.
1975a   *Assyrian and Babylonian Chronicles*. Texts from Cunei-
                form Sources, 5. Locust Valley, NY: J. J. Augustin.
1975b   *Babylonian Historical-Literary Texts*. Toronto and
                Buffalo: University of Toronto Press.

Green, Margaret Whitney
1975   "Eridu in Sumerian Literature." Ph.D. dissertation,
                Department of Near Eastern Languages and Civiliza-
                tions, University of Chicago.

Greenberg, Moshe
1955   *The Hab/piru*. New Haven: American Oriental Society.
1962   "Another Look at Rachel's Theft of the Teraphim." *JBL*
                81: 239–48.

Gressmann, Hugo
1926   *Altorientalische Texte zum Alten Testament*. 2d ed.
                Berlin and Leipzig: Walter de Gruyter.
1927   *Altorientalische Bilder zum Alten Testament*. Berlin
                and Leipzig: Walter de Gruyter.

Gröndahl, Franke
1967   *Die Personennamen der Texte aus Ugarit*. Studia Pohl
                1. Rome: Pontifical Biblical Institute.

Gurney, Oliver R.
1948   "Hittite Prayers of Mursili II." *Annals of Archaeology
                and Anthropology* 27: 1–163.

Gurney, Oliver R., and J. J. Finkelstein
1957   *The Sultantepe Tablets*, I. London: British Institute of
                Archaeology at Ankara.

Gurney, Oliver R., and P. Hulin
1964   *The Sultantepe Tablets*, II. London: British Institute of
                Archaeology at Ankara.

Güterbock, H. G.
1958   "The Composition of Hittite Prayers to the Sun." *JAOS*
                78: 237–45.

Habel, Norman
1964   *Yahweh Versus Baal*. New York: Bookman Associates.

Hallo, William W.
1968   "Individual Prayer in Sumerian: The Continuity of a

Tradition." Pp. 71–89 in *Essays in Memory of E. A. Speiser*. Ed. W. W. Hallo. *JAOS* 88/1 and AOS 53.

1976   "The Royal Correspondence of Larsa: A Sumerian Prototype for the Prayer of Hezekiah?" Pp. 209–24 in *Kramer Anniversary Volume*. AOAT 25. Neukirchen-Vluyn: Neukirchener Verlag.

Hallo, William W., and J. J. A. van Dijk
1968   *The Exaltation of Inanna*. New Haven and London: Yale University.

Hecker, Karl
1974   *Untersuchungen zur akkadischen Epik*. AOAT Sonderreihe. Neukirchen-Vluyn: Neukirchener Verlag.

Heintz, Jean-Georges
1969   "Oracles prophétiques et 'guerre sainte' selon les archives royales de Mari et l'Ancien Testament." Pp. 112–38 in *Congress Volume: Rome, 1968*. VTSup 17. Leiden: E. J. Brill.

Helck, Wolfgang
1971   *Die Beziehungen Ägyptens zu Vorderasien im 3. und 2. Jahrtausend v. Chr.* 2d ed. Ägyptologische Abhandlungen, 5. Wiesbaden: Otto Harrassowitz.

Held, Moshe
1957   "Studies in Ugaritic Lexicography and Poetic Style." Ph.D. dissertation, Johns Hopkins University.
1962   "The YQTL QTL (QTL YQTL) Sequence of Identical Verbs in Biblical Hebrew and in Ugaritic." Pp. 281–90 in *Studies and Essays in Honor of Abraham A. Neuman*. Ed. M. Ben-Horin, B. D. Weinryb, and S. Zeitlin. Leiden: E. J. Brill.

Herdner, Andrée
1963   *Corpus des tablettes en cunéiformes alphabétiques découvertes à Ras Shamra-Ugarit de 1929 à 1939*. MRS 10. Paris: Imprimerie Nationale.
1972   "Une prière à Baal des Ugaritiens en danger." *CRAIBL* 693–97, 698–703.

Hermann, Alfred
1938   "Die ägyptische Königsnovelle." Leipziger Ägyptologische Studien, 10. Glückstadt: Augustin.

Herrmann, Siegfried
1953/54   "Die Königsnovelle in Ägypten und in Israel." *Wissenschaftliche Zeitschrift der Karl-Marx-Universität*. 3: 33–44, 87–91.
1973   *Geschichte Israels in alttestamentlicher Zeit*. Munich: Chr. Kaiser.

Hillers, Delbert R.
1964   *Treaty-Curses and the Old Testament Prophets*. BibOr 16. Rome: Pontifical Biblical Institute.
1969   *Covenant: The History of a Biblical Idea*. Baltimore: Johns Hopkins University Press.
1978   "A Study of Psalm 148." *CBQ* 40: 322–34.

Hoffner, H. A., Jr.
1975a   "Hittite Mythological Texts: A Survey." Pp. 136–45 in *Unity and Diversity*. Ed. H. Goedicke and J. J. M. Roberts. Baltimore and London: Johns Hopkins University Press.
1975b   "Propaganda and Political Justification in Hittite Historiography." Pp. 49–62 in *Unity and Diversity*.

Hoftijzer, J., and G. van der Kooij
1976   *Aramaic Texts from Deir 'Alla*. Leiden: E. J. Brill.

Houwink ten Cate, Ph. H. J.
1969   "Hittite Royal Prayer." *Numen* 16: 81–98.

Huffmon, Herbert B.
1965   *Amorite Personal Names in the Mari Texts*. Baltimore: Johns Hopkins University Press.
1966   "The Treaty Background of Hebrew Yādaʿ." *BASOR* 181: 31–37.

Huffmon, Herbert B., and Simon B. Parker
1966   "A Further Note on the Treaty Background of Hebrew Yādaʿ." *BASOR* 184: 36–38.

Hummel, H. D.
1957   "Enclitic *mem* in Early Northwest Semitic, especially Hebrew." *JBL* 76: 85–107.

Jacobsen, Thorkild
1975   "Religious Drama in Ancient Mesopotamia." Pp. 65–97 in *Unity and Diversity*. Ed. H. Goedicke and J. J. M. Roberts. Baltimore and London: Johns Hopkins University Press.
1977   "Inuma ilu awilum." Pp. 113–17 in *Essays on the Ancient Near East in Memory of Jacob Joel Finkelstein*. Memoirs of the Connecticut Academy of Arts and Sciences, 19. Hamden, CT: Archon Books.

Kaiser, Otto
1962   *Die mythische Bedeutung des Meeres in Agypten, Ugarit, und Israel*. 2d ed. BZAW 78. Berlin: A. Töpelmann.

Kapelrud, Arvid S.
1963   *The Ras Shamra Discoveries and the Old Testament*. Norman: University of Oklahoma Press.
1969   *The Violent Goddess*. Oslo: Universitetsforlaget.

Keel, Othmar
 1969   *Feinde und Gottesleugner*. Stuttgart: Katholisches Bibel-
        werk.
 1974   *Wirkmächtige Siegeszeichen im Alten Testament*. OBO
        5. Göttingen: Vandenhoeck & Ruprecht.
 1977a   *Vögel als Boten*. OBO 14. Göttingen: Vandenhoeck &
        Ruprecht.
 1977b   *Jahwe-Visionen und Siegelkunst*. SBS 84/85. Stuttgart:
        Katholisches Bibelwerk.
 1978   *The Symbolism of the Biblical World*. New York: Sea-
        bury. German original in 1972.

Kitchen, Kenneth A.
 1962   *Suppiluliuma and the Amarna Pharaohs*. Liverpool:
        Liverpool University.

Klengel, Evelyn, and Horst Klengel
 1970   *Die Hettiter: Geschichte und Umwelt*. Vienna and Mu-
        nich: Verlag Anton Schroll.

Klengel, Horst
 1964   "Aziru von Amurru und seine Rolle in der Geschichte
        der Amarnazeit." *MIO* 10: 57–83.
 1965, 1969, 1970 *Geschichte Syriens im 2. Jahrtausend v.u.Z*, 1–3. Berlin:
        Akademie Verlag.
 1972   *Zwischen Zelt und Palast—die Begegnung von No-
        maden und Sesshaften im alten Vorderasien*. Leipzig:
        Koehler & Ameorng.

Knudtzon, Jorgen Alexander
 1915   *Die El-Amarna-Tafeln*, 1–2. Vorderasiatische Biblio-
        thek, 2. Leipzig. J. C. Hinrichs. Photostatic reprint.
        Aaden: Otto Zeller, 1964.

Koehler, Ludwig, and Walter Baumgartner
 1967–   *Hebräisches und aramäisches Lexikon zum Alten Tes-
        tament*. Leiden: E. J. Brill.

Kramer, Samuel Noah
 1955   "'Man and his God': A Sumerian Variation on the 'Job'
        Motif." Pp. 170–82 in *Wisdom in Israel and in the
        Ancient Near East*. Ed. M. Noth and D. W. Thomas.
        VTSup 3. Leiden: E. J. Brill.
 1969a   "Lamentation over the Destruction of Sumer and Ur."
        Pp. 611–19 in *ANET*. Ed. J. B. Pritchard. Princeton:
        Princeton University Press.
 1969b   "The Curse of Agade: The Ekur Avenged." Pp. 646–51
        in *ANET*. Ed. J. B. Pritchard. Princeton: Princeton Uni-
        versity Press.
 1969c   "'Man and his God': A Sumerian Variation of the 'Job'
        Motif." Pp. 589–91 in *ANET*. Ed. J. B. Pritchard.
        Princeton: Princeton University Press.

Kraus, Fritz R.
1958   *Ein Edikt des Königs Ammi-saduqa von Babylon.*
        Studia et documenta ad iuru orientis antiqui pertinentia,
        5. Leiden: E. J. Brill.
1965a   "Ein Edikt des Königs Samsu-iluna von Babylon." Pp.
        225–31 in *Studies in Honor of Benno Landsberger on
        his Seventy-Fifth Birthday, April 21, 1965.* AS 16. Chi-
        cago: University of Chicago Press.
1965b   *Könige, die in Zelten wohnten.* Mededelingen der
        Koninklijke Nederlandse Akademie van Wetenschappen
        (Afd. Letterkunde, N. R. 28/2). Amsterdam: Noord-
        Hollandsche Uitgevers Maatschappij.

Kuhl, C.
1953   "Neuere Literarkritik des Buches Hiob." *TRu* 21: 163–
        205, 257–317.
1954   "Von Hiobbuche und seinen Problemen." *TRu* 22:
        261–316.

Kümmel, Hans Martin
1967   *Ersatzrituale für den hethitischen König.* Studien zu
        den Bogazköy-Texten. Wiesbaden: Otto Harrassowitz.

Kunstmann, Walter G.
1932   *Die babylonische Gebetsbeschwörung.* Leipzig: J. C.
        Hinrichs.

Kupper, Jean-Robert
1957   *Les nomades en Mésopotamie au temps des rois de
        Mari.* Bibliothèque de la Faculté de Philosophie et
        Lettres de l'Université de Liège, Fascicule 142. Paris:
        Société d' Édition "Les Belles Lettres."

Kutsch, E.
1961   "Die Dynastie von Gottes Gnaden." *ZTK* 58: 137–53.
1967   "Gesetz und Gnade. Probleme des alttestamentlichen
        Bundesgriffs." *ZAW* 79: 18–35.

Kutscher, R.
1975   *Oh Angry Sea (a-ab-ba/hu-luh-ha): The History of a
        Sumerian Congregational Lament.* New Haven and
        London: Yale University Press.

LaFay, Howard
1978   "Ebla, Splendor of an Unknown Empire." *National Geo-
        graphic* 154: 730–59.

Lambert, W. G.
1959/60 "Three Literary Prayers of the Babylonians." *AfO* 19:
        47–66.
1960a   "The Domesticated Camel in the Second Millennium—
        Evidence from Alalakh and Ugarit." *BASOR* 160:42–43.
1960b   *Babylonian Wisdom Literature.* Oxford: Clarendon.

1972   "Destiny and Divine Intervention in Babylon and
               Israel." *OTS* 17: 65–72.
1974   "DINGIR.ŠÀ.DIB.BA Incantations." *JNES* 33: 267–322.
1974–77   Review of Werner Mayer, *Untersuchungen zur Form-
               ensprache der babylonische "Gebetsbeschwörungen."*
               AfO 25: 197–99.
1975   "The Problem of the Love Lyrics." Pp. 98–135 in *Unity
               and Diversity*. Ed. H. Goedicke and J. J. M. Roberts.
               Baltimore and London: Johns Hopkins University Press.

Lambert, W. G., and Alan R. Millard
    1969   *Atra-hasis: The Babylonian Story of the Flood*. Oxford:
               Clarendon.

Lambert, W. G., and Simon B. Parker
    1966   *Enuma Eliš: The Babylonian Epic of Creation, the
               Cuneiform Text*. Oxford: Clarendon.

Lehmann, Johannes
    1975   *Die Hethiter. Volk der tausend Götter*. Munich and
               Vienna: C. Bertelsmann Verlag.

Lipinski, Edouard
    1965   *La royauté de Yahwe dans la poésie et le culte de
               l'ancien Israël*. Brussels: Paleis der Academiën.

Liverani, M.
    1970   "Per una considerazione storica del problema amorreo."
               OrAnt 9: 5–27.

    1973   "The Amorites." Pp. 100–133 in *Peoples of Old Testa-
               ment Times*. Ed. D. J. Wiseman. Oxford: Clarendon.

Long, Burke O.
    1973   "The Effect of Divination upon Israelite Literature."
               JBL 92: 489–97.

    1977   "Prophetic Authority as Social Reality." Pp. 3–20 in
               *Canon and Authority: Essays in Old Testament Reli-
               gion and Theology*. Ed. G. W. Coats and B. O. Long.
               Philadelphia: Fortress.

Loretz, Oswald, and W. R. Mayer
    1978   *Šu-ila-Gebete*. Supplement zu L. W. King, *Babylonian
               Magic and Sorcery*. AOAT 34. Neukirchen-Vluyn: Neu-
               kirchener Verlag.

Lugt, P. van der
    1974   "The Spectre of Pan-Ugaritism." *BO* 31: 3–26.

Luke, John T.
    1965   "Pastoralism and Politics in the Mari Period: A Re-
               Examination of the Character and Political Significance
               of the Major West Semitic Tribal Groups on the Middle
               Euphrates, c. 1828–1753 B.C." Ph.D. dissertation, Univer-
               sity of Michigan.

McCarthy, Dennis J.
1963   *Treaty and Covenant: A Study in Form in the Ancient Oriental Documents and the Old Testament.* AnBib 21. Rome: Pontifical Biblical Institute.
1972   *Old Testament Covenant: A Survey of Current Opinions.* Atlanta: John Knox.
1974   "Covenant-relationships." Pp. 91–103 in *Questions disputées d'Ancien Testament, Méthode et Théologie.* Ed. C. Brekelmans. BETL 33. Leuven: University Press.

Machinist, P.
1976   "Literature as Politics: The Tukulti-Ninurta Epic and the Bible." *CBQ* 38: 455–82.

McKane, William
1970   *Proverbs: A New Approach.* OTL. Philadelphia: Westminster.

Malamat, Abraham
1966   "The Ban in Mari and in the Bible." Pp. 40–49 in *Biblical Essays.* University of Stellenbosch.
1967   "Aspects of Tribal Societies in Mari and Israel." Pp. 129–38 in *XVe Rencontre Assyriologique Internationale: La civilisation de Mari.* Ed. J. R. Kupper. Paris: Société d'Édition "Les Belles Lettres."
1968   "King Lists of the Old Babylonian Period and Biblical Genealogies." *JAOS* 88: 163–73.
1974   "The Twilight of Judah: In the Egyptian-Babylonian Maelstrom." Pp. 123–45 in *Congress Volume: Edinburgh, 1974.* VTSup 28. Leiden: E. J. Brill.

Mann, Thomas W.
1977   *Divine Presence and Guidance in Israelite Traditions: The Typology of Exaltation.* Baltimore and London: Johns Hopkins University Press.

Martinez, Ernest R.
1967   *Hebrew-Ugaritic Index to the Writings of Mitchell J. Dahood.* Rome: Pontifical Biblical Institute.

Marzal, Angel
1976   *Gleanings from the Wisdom of Mari.* Studia Pohl 11. Rome: Pontifical Biblical Institute.

Matthews, Victor Harold
1978   *Pastoral Nomadism in the Mari Kingdom (ca. 1830–1760 B.C.).* ASOR Dissertation Series, 3. Cambridge, MA: ASOR.

Matthiae, Paolo
1975   "Ebla nel periodo delle dinastie amoree e della dinastia di Akkadi-Scoperte archaeologiche recenti a tell Mardikh." *Or* 44: 337–60.

1976a   "Aspetti amministrativi e topografici di Ebla nel III mil-
               lennio Av. Cr.: B. Considerazioni archeologiche." *RSO*
               50: 16–30.
1976b   "Ebla in the Late Early Syrian Period: The Royal Palace
               and the State Archives." *BA* 39: 94–113.
1978   "Tell Mardikh-Ebla." *Or* 47: 334–35.

Mayer, Werner
1976   *Untersuchungen zur Formensprache der babylonischen
               "Gebetsbeschwörungen."* Studia Pohl, Series Maior 5.
               Rome: Pontifical Biblical Institute.

Meier, Gerhard
1937   *Die assyrische Beschwörungssammlung Maqlû. AfO*
               Beih. 2. Berlin: Selbstverlag des Herausgebers.

Melamed, E. Z.
1961   "Break-up of Stereotype Phrases as an Artistic Device in
               Biblical Poetry." Pp. 115–53 in *Studies in the Bible.*
               Ed. C. Rabin. Scripta Hierosolymitana, 8. Jerusalem:
               Magnes.

Mendelsohn, I.
1955   "On Slavery in Alalakh." *IEJ* 5: 65–72.
1959   "On Marriage at Alalakh." Pp. 351–57 in *Essays on Jew-
               ish Life and Thought.* New York: Columbia University
               Press.

Mendenhall, George E.
1955   *Law and Covenant in Israel and the Ancient Near
               East.* Pittsburgh: Biblical Colloquium.
1962   "The Hebrew Conquest of Palestine." *BA* 25: 66–87.
1973   *The Tenth Generation: The Origins of the Biblical Tra-
               dition.* Baltimore and London: Johns Hopkins University
               Press.

Milgrom, Jacob
1970   *Studies in Levitical Terminology,* 1. Berkeley: Univer-
               sity of California Press.
1976a   *Cult and Conscience: The Asham and the Priestly Doc-
               trine of Repentance.* SJLA 18. Leiden: E. J. Brill.
1976b   "The Concept of MA'AL in the Bible and the Ancient
               Near East." *JAOS* 96: 236–47.

Miller, Patrick D., Jr.
1973a   "God and the Gods." *Affirmation* 1/5: 37–62.
1973b   *The Divine Warrior in Early Israel.* Cambridge, MA:
               Harvard University Press.

Miller, Patrick D., Jr., and J. J. M. Roberts
1977   *The Hand of the Lord.* Baltimore and London: Johns
               Hopkins University Press.

Moor, Johannes C. de
1970   "The Semitic Pantheon of Ugarit." *UF* 2: 187–228.
1971   *The Seasonal Pattern in the Ugaritic Myth of Ba'lu.*
                AOAT 16. Kevelaer: Verlag Butzon & Bercker.
1972   *New Year with Canaanites and Israelites.* Kampen:
                J. H. Kok.

Moran, William L.
1950a   "A Syntactical Study of the Dialect of Byblos as Re-
                flected in the Amarna Tablets." Ph.D. dissertation, Johns
                Hopkins University.
1950b   "The Use of Canaanite Infinitive Absolute as a Finite
                Verb in the Amarna Letters from Byblos." *JCS* 4:
                169–72.
1960   "Early Canaanite *yaqtula.*" *Or* 29: 1–19.
1961   "The Hebrew Language in its Northwest Semitic Back-
                ground." Pp. 54–72 in *The Bible and the Ancient Near
                East.* Ed. G. E. Wright. Garden City, NY: Doubleday.
1969a   "The Death of Abdi-Asirta." Pp. 94–99 in *W. F.
                Albright Volume.* Ed. A. Malamat. Eretz-Israel 9, Jeru-
                salem: Israel Exploration Society.
1969b   "New Evidence from Mari on the History of Prophecy."
                Bib 50: 15–56.
1970   "The Creation of Man in Atrahasis I 192–248." *BASOR*
                200: 48–56.
1971   "Atrahasis: The Babylonian Story of the Flood." *Bib* 52:
                51–61.
1973   "The Dual Personal Pronouns in Western Peripheral
                Akkadian." *BASOR* 211: 50–53.
1975a   "The Syrian Scribe of the Jerusalem Amarna Letters."
                Pp. 146–66 in *Unity and Diversity.* Ed. H. Goedicke
                and J. J. M. Roberts. Baltimore and London: Johns Hop-
                kins University Press.
1975b   "Amarna Glosses." *RA* 69: 147–58.

Müller, Hans-Peter
1978   *Das Hiobproblem.* Darmstadt: Wissenschaftliche Buch-
                gesellschaft.

Nielsen, Eduard
1965   *The Ten Commandments in New Perspective: A
                Traditio-Historical Approach.* SBT 2/7. London: SCM.

Noetscher, F.
1953   "Zum emphatischen Lamed." *VT* 3: 372–80.

Noort, Edward
1977   *Untersuchungen zum Gottesbescheid in Mari: Die
                "Mariprophetie" in der alttestamentlichen Forschung.*
                AOAT 202. Neukirchen-Vluyn: Neukirchener Verlag.

Norin, Stig I. L.
1977   *Er spaltete das Meer: Die Auszugsüberlieferung in Psalmen und Kult des alten Israel.* ConBOT 9. Lund: CWK Gleerup.

Noth, Martin
1961   *Die Ursprünge des alten Israel im Lichte neuer Quellen.* Arbeitsgemeinschaft für Forschung des Landes Nordrhein-Westfalen Geisteswissenschaften 94. Cologne and Opladen: Westdeutscher Verlag.

Nougayrol, J.
1952   "Une version ancienne du 'juste souffrant.'" *RB* 59: 239–50.
1968   "Choix de textes littéraires." Pp. 265–319 in *Ugaritica* V. MRS 16. Paris: Imprimerie Nationale.

Oldenburg, U.
1060   *The Conflict between El and Baʿal in Canaanite Religion.* Leiden: E. J. Brill.

Page, S.
1968   "A Stela of Adad-nirari III and Nergal-ereš from Tell al Rimah." *Iraq* 30: 139–53.

Patton, John H.
1944   *Canaanite Parallels in the Book of Psalms.* Baltimore: Johns Hopkins University Press.

Perlitt, Lothar
1969   *Bundestheologie im Alten Testament.* WMANT 36. Neukirchen-Vluyn: Neukirchener Verlag.

Petschow, H.
1965   "Zur Systematik und Gesetztechnik im Codex Hammurabi." *ZA* 57: 146–72.

Pettinato, Giovanni
1971a   *Das altorientalische Menschenbild und die sumerischen und akkadischen Schöpfungsmythen.* Abhandlungen der Heidelberger Akademie der Wissenschaften, Philosophisch-historische Klasse. Heidelberg: Carl Winter—Universitätsverlag.
1971b   "Die Bestrafung des Menschengeschlechts durch die Sintflut." *Or* 37: 165–200.
1975   "Testi cuneiformi del 3. millennio in paleo-cananeo rinvenuti nella campagna 1974 a Tell Mardikh-Ebla." *Or* 44: 361–74.
1976a   "Aspetti amministrativi e topografici di Ebla nel III millennio Av. Cr.: A. Documentazione epigraffici." *RSO* 50: 1–14.
1976b   "Carchimiš-KĀR-kamiš: Le prime attestagioni den III Millennio." *OrAnt* 15: 11–15.

1976c   "Ed lu e ad Ebla: La recostruzione delle prime 63 righe sulla base di TM. 75.G.1488." *OrAnt* 15: 169–78.
1976d   "Ibla (Ebla) A. Philologisch." *RLA* 5: 9–13.
1976e   "The Royal Archives of Tell Mardikh-Ebla." *BA* 39: 44–52.
1977   "Al Calendario di Ebla al Tempo del Re Ibbi-Sipis sulla base di Tm.75.G.427." *AfO* 25: 1–36.
1980   "Ebla e la Bibbia." *OrAnt* 19: 49–72.

Pope, Marvin H.
1955   *El in the Ugaritic Texts*. VTSup 2. Leiden: E. J. Brill.
1977   *Song of Songs*. AB 7C. Garden City, NY: Doubleday.

Posener, Georges
1960   *De la divinité du Pharaon*. Cahiers de la Société Asiatique, 15. Paris: Imprimerie Nationale.

Pritchard, James B.
1969   *Ancient Near Eastern Texts*. 3d ed. Princeton: Princeton University Press.

Rad, Gerhard von
1955   "Hiob xxxviii und die altägyptische Weisheit." Pp. 293–301 in *Wisdom in Israel and in the Ancient Near East*. Ed. M. Noth and D. W. Thomas. VTSup 3. Leiden: E. J. Brill.

Rainey, Anson F.
1970   *El Amarna Tablets 359–379*. AOAT 8. Neukirchen-Vluyn: Neukirchener Verlag.
1976   "Tell el Amarna." P. 869 in *IDBSup*.

Reiner, Erica
1958   *Šurpu: A Collection of Sumerian and Akkadian Incantations*. AfO Beiheft, 11. Graz. Reprinted, Osnabrück: Biblio-Verlag, 1970.

Rencontre Assyriologique Internationale 14
1966   *La divination en Mésopotamie ancienne et dans les régions voisines*. Paris: Presses Universitaires de France.

Riemann, P. A.
1976   "Covenant, Mosaic." Pp. 192–97 in *IDBSup*.

Roberts, J. J. M.
1973   "The Davidic Origin of the Zion Tradition," *JBL* 92: 329–44.
1976   "Myth *Versus* History: Relaying the Comparative Foundations." *CBQ* 38: 1–13.
1977a   "Of Signs, Prophets, and Time Limits: A Note on Ps 74:9." *CBQ* 39: 474–81.
1977b   "Job and the Israelite Religious Tradition." *ZAW* 89: 107–14.

Robertson, David A.
1972   Linguistic Evidence in Dating Early Hebrew Poetry.
                 SBLDS 8. Missoula, MT. Scholars Press.

Römer, Willem H. Ph.
1971   Frauenbriefe über Religion, Politik und Privatleben in
                 Mari. AOAT 12. Neukirchen-Vluyn: Neukirchener Ver-
                 lag.

Rowton, M. B.
1967   "The Physical Environment and the Problem of the
                 Nomads." Pp. 109–21 in XVe Rencontre Assyriologique
                 Internationale: La civilisation de Mari. Ed. J. R.
                 Kupper. Paris: Société d'Édition "Les Belles Lettres."
1973a   "Autonomy and Nomadism in Western Asia." Or 42:
                 247–58.
1973b   "Urban Autonomy in a Nomadic Environment." JNES
                 32: 201–15.
1974   "Enclosed Nomadism." Journal of Economic and Social
                 History of the Orient 17: 1–30.
1976   "Dimorphic Structure and the Problem of the 'Apirû-
                 'Ibrîm." JNES 35: 13–20.

Saggs, H. W. F.
1978   The Encounter with the Divine in Mesopotamia and
                 Israel. London: Athlone.

Sasson, Jack
1969   The Military Establishments at Mari. Studia Pohl 3.
                 Rome: Pontifical Biblical Institute.

Schaeffer, Claude F. A., ed.
1955–   Ugaritica V. MRS 16. Paris: Imprimerie Nationale.
1968   Le palais royal d'Ugarit 1–VI. MRS. Paris: Imprimerie
                 Nationale.

Schmid, Hans H.
1966   Wesen und Geschichte der Weisheit: Eine Untersuch-
                 ung zur altorientalischen und israelitischen Weisheits-
                 literatur. BZAW 101. Berlin: A. Töpelmann.

Schmidt, Werner H.
1966   Königtum Gottes in Ugarit und Israel. 2d ed. BZAW
                 80. Berlin: A. Töpelmann.

Schmökel, Hartmut
1952   "Zur kultischen Deutung des Hoheliedes." ZAW 64:
                 148–55.
1956   Heilige Hochzeit und Hoheslied. Abhandlungen für die
                 Kunde des Morgenlandes, 23/1. Wiesbaden: Deutsche
                 Morgenländische Gesellschaft.

Schramm, Wolfgang
    1973   *Einleitung in die assyrischen Königsinschriften*, 2. Lei-
                   den: E. J. Brill.

Seux, Marie-Joseph
    1976   *Hymnes et prières aux dieux de Babylonie et d'Assyrie*.
                   Paris: Éditions du Cerf.

Shanks, Hershel
    1979   "Syria Tries to Influence Ebla Scholarship." *BARev* 5/2:
                   37–50.

Sjöberg, A. W.
    1972   "In Praise of the Scribal Art." *JCS* 24: 126–31.
    1973   "Der Vater und sein missratener Sohn." *JCS* 25: 105–69.
    1975a   "Der Examenstext A." *ZA* 64: 137–76.
    1975b   "The Old Babylonian Eduba." Pp. 159–70 in *Sumero-
                   logical Studies in Honor of Thorkild Jacobsen on his
                   Seventieth Birthday, June 7, 1974*. AS 20. Chicago and
                   London: University of Chicago Press.

Skaist, A.
    1969   "The Authority of the Brother at Arrapha and Nuzi."
                   JAOS 89: 10–17.

Smith, Sidney
    1949   *The Statue of Idri-mi*. London: British Institute of
                   Archaeology in Ankara.

Soden, Wolfram von
    1952–55   "Gibt es ein Zeugnis, dass die Babylonier an Marduks
                   Wiederauferstehung glaubten?" *ZA* 16–17: 130–66.
    1957   "Ein neues Bruchstück des assyrischen Kömmentars zum
                   Marduk-Ordal." *ZA* 52: 224–34.
    1965   "Das Fragen nach der Gerechtigkeit Gottes im Alten
                   Orient." *MIO* 96: 41–59.
    1971   "Der grosse Hymnus an Nabu." *ZA* 61: 44–71.
    1974–77   "Zwei Königsgebete an Ištar aus Assyrien." *AfO* 25:
                   37–49.

Spalinger, A. J.
    1973   "Aspects of the Military Documents of the Ancient
                   Egyptians." Ph.D. dissertation, Yale University.
    1978   "A Canaanite Ritual Found in Egyptian Reliefs." *The
                   Society for the Study of Egyptian Antiquities Journal*
                   8/2: 47–60.

Speiser, E. A.
    1940   "Of Shoes and Shekels." *BASOR* 77: 15–18.
    1955   "I Know not the Day of my Death." *JBL* 74: 252–56.
    1963   "The Wife-Sister Motif in the Patriarchal Narratives."
                   Pp. 15–28 in *The Lown Institute Studies and Texts*:

Volume 1, *Biblical and Other Studies*. Ed. A. Altmann. Cambridge, MA: Harvard University Press.

1964   *Genesis*. AB 1. Garden City, NY. Doubleday.

Szlechter, Emile
1951   *Les lois d'Ešnunna*. Paris: Centre Nationale de la Recherche Scientifique.

Tadmor, Hayim
1958   "The Campaigns of Sargon II of Assur: A Chronological Historical Study." *JCS* 12: 22–40, 77–100.
1961   "Azriyau of Yaudi." Pp. 232–71 in *Studies in the Bible*. Ed. C. Rabin. Scripta hierosolymitana, 8. Jerusalem: Magnes.
1970   "*Ḥ'rwt lšwrwt hptyḥh šl hḥwzh h'rmw myspyrh*." Pp. 397–401 in *Samuel Yeivin Jubilee Volume*. Jerusalem: Israel Society for Biblical Research (Hebrew).
1973   "The Historical Inscriptions of Adad-nirari III." *Iraq* 35: 141–50.
1975   "Assyria and the West: The Ninth Century and its Aftermath." Pp. 36–48 in *Unity and Diversity*. Ed. H. Goedicke and J. J. M. Roberts. Baltimore and London: Johns Hopkins University Press.

Thomas, D. Winton
1958   *Documents from Old Testament Times*. London: Thomas Nelson & Sons.

Thompson, Thomas L.
1974   *The Historicity of the Patriarchal Narratives: The Quest for the Historical Abraham*. BZAW 133. Berlin: Walter de Gruyter.

Tocci, Franco Michelini
1960   *La siria nell'eta di Mari*. Studi Semitici 3. Rome: Centro di Studi Semitici, University of Rome.

Tsevat, Matitiahu
1968   Review of H. M. Wolf's *The Apology of Hattusilis*. . . . *JBL* 87: 458–61.

Ullendorff, Edward
1978   Review of I. J. Gelb, "Thoughts about Ibla . . ." (1977). *JSS* 23: 151–54.

Van Seters, John
1968   "The Problem of Childlessness in Near Eastern Law and the Patriarchs of Israel." *JBL* 87: 401–8.
1969   "Jacob's Marriages and the Ancient Near East." *HTR* 62: 377–95.
1975   *Abraham in History and Tradition*. New Haven and London: Yale University Press.

Vaux, Roland de
1946, 1948, 1949   "Les patriarches hébreux et les découvertes modernes."
                   RB 53: 321–48; 55: 321–47; 56: 5–36.
1971   *Histoire ancienne d'Israel.* Paris: Gabalda. English
                   trans., 1978.

Virolleaud, Charles
1960   "Un nouvel épisode du mythe ugaritique de Baal."
                   CRAIBL: 180–86.

Weinfeld, M.
1976   "Covenant, Davidic." Pp. 188–92 in *IDBSup*.

Weippert, Manfred
1967   *Die Landnahme der israelitischen Stämme in der
                   neueren wissenschaftlichen Diskussion.* FRLANT 92.
                   Göttingen: Vandenhoeck & Ruprecht. English trans.,
                   1971.

Whitaker, Richard E.
1972   A *Concordance of the Ugaritic Literature.* Cambridge,
                   MA: Harvard University Press.

White, John B.
1978   A *Study of the Language of Love in the Song of Songs
                   and Ancient Egyptian Poetry.* SBLDS 38. Missoula, MT:
                   Scholars Press.

Wilhelm, G.
1973   "Ein Brief der Amarna Zeit aus Kāmid el-Lōz (KL
                   72:600)." *ZA* 63: 69–75.

Williams, Ronald J.
1961   "The Alleged Semitic Original of the *Wisdom of Amen-
                   emope*." *JEA* 47: 100–106.
1977   "II. Ägypten und Israel." Pp. 492–505 in *TRE* 1/4. Ber-
                   lin and New York: Walter de Gruyter.

Wilson, Robert R.
1977   *Genealogy and History in the Biblical World.* New
                   Haven and London: Yale University Press.
1980   *Prophecy and Society in Ancient Israel.* Philadelphia:
                   Fortress.

Wiseman, Donald J.
1953   *The Alalakh Tablets.* London: British Institute of
                   Archaeology in Ankara.
1954   "Supplementary Copies of Alalakh Tablets." *JCS* 8:
                   1–30.
1959a   "Ration Lists from Alalakh VII." *JCS* 13: 19–33.
1959b   "Ration Lists from Alalakh IV." *JCS* 13: 50–62.
1961   *Chronicles of Chaldaean Kings (626–556 B.C.) in the
                   British Museum.* London: Trustees of the British
                   Museum.

1967   "Alalakh." Pp. 119–35 in *Archaeology and Old Testament Study*. Ed. D. Winton Thomas. Oxford: Clarendon.

1976   "Alalakh Texts." Pp. 16–17 in *IDBSup*.

Wolf, Herbert Marlin
1967   *The Apology of Hattusilis Compared with Other Political Self-Justifications of the Ancient Near East*. Ann Arbor: University Microfilms.

Yaron, Reuven
1969   *The Laws of Eshnunna*. Jerusalem: Magnes.

Zijl, Peter J. van
1972   *Baal*. AOAT 10. Kevelaer: Verlag Butzon und Bercker.

4

Criticism of Literary Features, Form, Tradition, and Redaction

Rolf Knierim

I. INTRODUCTION: ON HISTORICAL EXEGESIS

This review focuses on the development of the historical-critical method in the exegesis of the Hebrew Bible during the period following the Second World War. Although reference to actual exegetical results in the various areas of OT study will occasionally be unavoidable, the review will not concentrate on them since they will be discussed elsewhere in this volume. Textual criticism and translation, areas normally considered parts of the historical-critical method, will also be treated separately.

It is the task of exegesis to interpret the Hebrew Bible as ancient literature, i.e., as written texts that came into existence in a distinct historical milieu and certainly do not exist without it. The methodology required for this task is to be distinguished from methods in, e.g., archaeological, topographical, or historical research,[1] despite the fact that these fields contribute a wealth of background information on the historical nature of the texts and a critical correlative to their historical assessment. Yet the time has come, especially in the light of the upsurge of additional methods of interpretation in recent years, to affirm that the method of historical interpretation must also be distinguished from hermeneutical methods which concentrate on the principles of relevance, validity, or accessibility of the ancient texts for us. This distinction must be upheld regardless of whether those methods are based on theological or philosophical preconceptions such as those offered by existentialism, universal history, process philosophy, aestheticism, psychology, Marxist philosophy, or any sort of meta-historical understanding of language. The distinction says nothing about or against the value of these hermeneutical systems, nor does it imply anything about the proper interrelationship of exegesis and hermeneutic in a system of interpretation encompassing both, a system on which there is as yet no general agreement. It merely emphasizes the need for a methodology that accounts in principle for the historical nature of the OT texts.

---

[1] For a good example of this point, see C. C. Smith (71–106).

Unless one can show that this nature is irrelevant, an appropriate methodology must begin with it, and it must also be accounted for in the area of hermeneutic itself.[2]

The so-called historical-critical method has been both attacked and defended. This essay will point out some of the arguments that are no longer intrinsic to the method or are not adequately formulated and should therefore be abandoned or modified.

Biblical criticism, and with it historical exegesis, has been regarded as indispensable since the breakthrough of scientific studies in the field during the eighteenth century (Kraus, 1956:455). This does not mean, however, that the philosophical assumptions of the eighteenth century provide the reason for our historical study of the Bible. The dependence of the Old (and New) Testament on human and historical conditions is real and universal (Kraus, 1956:455, quoting Noth). In other words, historical exegesis is necessary because of the "historicality" of the Old Testament and not because of our dependence on the eighteenth century. Therefore, a statement such as Baumgärtel's (1185), that the autonomy of human thinking remains normative for biblical criticism, calls for qualification precisely because "autonomy" does not necessarily mean for us what it meant two hundred years ago. Suffice it to say that historical exegesis presupposes that autonomy of human judgment by which the interpreter is aware of the circle in historical interpretation and becomes subject to the heteronomy of the materials to be interpreted just as much as he/she is subject to our current assumptions. Yet one may add that the discovery of the circle itself, linking both the interpreter and the interpreted, does not dissolve the task of historical exegesis.

It should also be understood that historical exegesis is no longer based on or identified by the source theory of the Eichhorn-Graf-Wellhausen school and its philosophical assumptions and historical reconstructions, or by the method of classical literary criticism as a whole (Kuhl, 1957:1231). While much is still owed to that school, historical exegesis must be identified by the historicality of the text itself and not

---

[2] This position is affirmed by Kaiser and Kümmel (10), Koch (1969:102ff., 106ff.; and 3d German edition, 1974:336), Barth and Steck (xii, 2, 106), Fohrer et al. (12), Baumgärtel (1184–86); in principle also by Cazelles (101: "Not all biblical texts are historical . . . , but all have a historical 'coefficient,' even if it is only the date of composition [or adaptation]. Failure to grasp this could well falsify their interpretation"), Fichtner (1221: "Die E.[xegese] at-licher Texte hat nach der wissenschaftlichen Methode der Auslegung *antiker* Texte zu geschehen" [emphasis added]), Keck and Tucker (296, although their formulation could be interpreted differently: "The same methods of exegesis are applicable to the Bible as to any other document"; cf., however, 297, section b., second paragraph and especially the third paragraph), Hesse (1915), Kraus (1956:455: ". . . unerlässliche Aufgabe wissenschaftlicher Erforschung der Heiligen Schrift," following Noth's programmatic statement that the human and historical qualification of the OT word is real and limitless), and also by Krentz (61–63) and Habel.

by a certain view of that historicality. The historicality of the text is fundamental. Our understanding of the nature of the text is changing, but not our understanding of its basic *historicality*. It is therefore essential that we distinguish between the recognition of the historicality of the texts, which is the essence of historical exegesis, and the more or less successful attempts to locate the texts historically (Fichtner: 1222; Horst: 1124), to define authorship (Grobel: 412), etc. A statement such as Grobel's (412) that, "as with all literature, the answer to such questions is necessarily largely subjective," can at best be taken with reference to the unavoidable difficulties confronting each interpreter, in which case it becomes a truism. However, it must not be understood as discrediting historical exegesis on the grounds of "subjectivism."

Furthermore, it has been said that OT exegesis must, on the one hand, elucidate the historical facts as much as possible because God acts in history and that it must, on the other hand, also investigate how this history is presented in the Hebrew Bible (Fichtner: 1222). This statement amalgamates two separate methods: its latter part belongs indeed to historical exegesis, but its former part belongs to the task of history writing and not to exegesis. Inasmuch as exegesis is affected by this task, it must elucidate the historical circumstances of the texts, which again cannot be done without the support of historical research. The volume edited by Hayes and Miller is a telling example of this point. The statement that God acts in history may be itself a result of historical exegesis, but it is not the reason for or the basis of it. A similarly false reason is given by Kraus (1956:456), who defends historical criticism with reference to the historical intentions of the OT literature and says, "denn das AT ist im wesentlichen ein Geschichtsbuch und nimmt also allerorts auf die Historie Bezug." While it is true that much (but not all) of the OT is preoccupied with history, it is not true that this preoccupation is the reason for historical exegesis. Again, the reason for historical exegesis is the historicality of the texts themselves and not their preoccupation with history.

A word must be added about the role of theology in exegesis. There was a time, also in the Society of Biblical Literature, when the inclusion of the theology of a text into its exegesis was considered unscientific speculation. Only "philological" and "historical" data were admissible, as if the theology—or the content and intention of a text and the people responsible for its existence—is not at least as much a part of its historicality as its philological phenomena and its historical context! In the meantime it has been acknowledged that the Bible is a "book of faith" (Grobel: 413; De Vries: 416), and it must be insisted that this "faith," wherever and however it is present in the texts, receive its proper place in historical exegesis. Otherwise, OT exegesis will fail to be what historical exegesis must be—a comprehensive effort to recover all data and all levels of meaning present in the text.

The atomization of methods and results in historical exegesis has become a major concern for everybody. Some have called it a scandal. Krentz, reporting on this situation, has said, "The *miserere*, the wretched state, of the discipline shows that exegesis has reached a crisis situation" (85). The situation is indeed critical, but it is senseless to push the panic button. The facts are irreversible, and in all probability the same development would occur were we to undo history and start over. More important, we belong to a privileged generation that has experienced and contributed to an enormous explosion of knowledge. Despite the dilemma caused by this explosion, constructive things have been, and are, happening both in published and unpublished ways, and the Bible, including both Testaments, is seriously studied, taught, and read by people in our day as seldom before. It could be that in the future people will be able to create a synthesis out of the indispensable raw materials that our atomistic generation has handed them. In the meantime, we should interpret our situation and draw appropriate consequences.

One of these consequences is that historical exegesis cannot be abandoned or replaced. Neither the atomization of its insights nor the contradictory results nor the degree of difficulty imposed by the nature of the texts nor the pluralism and imperfection of the methods themselves can exempt interpreters from the need to explain the historicality of the texts. As long as this reality confronts us, our options are either to improve the methods we have or to develop others that are better suited to explain the same phenomena. Significant efforts have been undertaken in recent years to improve existing methods, whereas better substitutes are nowhere in sight. Also, methodological shortcuts attempting either to supply us with an uncomplicated historical picture or to offer a quick, direct hermeneutical access to the texts are basically unrealistic.

One such substitute could be a simplistic application of canon criticism. Canon criticism, understood properly, is necessary as a part of historical exegesis; as such it may be an alternative expression for what has generally been called "tradition history." However, should it propose concentrating on the finally "canonized" text *at the expense of* the historical growth of the total tradition, it would be condemned to failure.

The new literary criticism as "the disciplinary study of pure literature" (Robertson, 1977:3) is another case in point. Robertson (1976:547) says, "These scholars . . . are united in considering the Bible primarily and fundamentally as a literary document (as opposed, e.g., to considering it as a historical or theological document). . . . Their enterprise, viewed in the context of Western culture as a whole, is part of a turning away from a preoccupation with history and a turning toward language." It should be pointed out that—apart from the questions of the promise of this approach, its methodological appropriateness for the OT literature, its integrity, and also its own current atomization—the formulations through which Robertson sets this method apart from historical exegesis seem essentially guided by the goals set by this field of study and not by the current understanding of historical exegesis. For historical exegesis, studying the OT as "historical" and "theological" is not "opposed" to studying it as a "literary document," and the concern with history is secondary and subordinate to the primary interest in the language of the texts. After all, historical exegesis has had a long-standing interest in and need for an Israelite *Literaturgeschichte* inherited from Gunkel (Horst: 1124ff.; Koch, 1969:102ff.). The difference, therefore, is between the inclusion and the exclusion of the historicality of the OT literature in our methods; the difference is not a historical and a theological assessment of the OT literature "as opposed" to a purely literary assessment in the context of Western culture.

Another possible shortcut could be to replace the concern for "the conscious reflection of the author or the reader" by the concern for the "unconscious" in the texts as emphasized by psychology and structuralism (discussed by Cazelles: 99–100). This objection does not affect the possibility of the all-pervading presence of the unconscious. If the unconscious is understood as a metahistorical reality, it can complement historical exegesis. However, if concern for this reality is intended to replace the search for the historically determined realities, one would first have to prove that human historicality—and that of God's presence on this level, as the texts describe it—is nonexistent and hence irrelevant for interpretation. Since "the text as it stands" is "the point of departure" (so Cazelles: 99), one would have to know that this text is merely the point of departure in the search for something else but not the focus of interpretation in its historical context and contingency.

Finally, Richter's postulate that the expression *"historisch-kritische Wissenschaft"* itself is no longer applicable (1971:17–18) must be mentioned. Richter is correct in saying that this expression grew out of the opposition to a type of systematic interpretation, that the cause for this opposition is no longer given, and that the "philological method" itself depends on systematic concepts. Thus, he wants to replace the traditional expression by the more encompassing term *(kritische) Literaturwissenschaft*. Ultimately, the search for the best expression, while not unimportant, is of secondary concern. What matters is that in such a *Literaturwissenschaft* the one factor that cannot be ignored in the work on the OT literature is its historicality, which is different from the historicality of, e.g., our own literatures. Hence, while the exegesis of the OT literature must be in tune with the method of *Literaturwissenschaft*, it must account for that specific kind of historicality. This is necessary because the term *Literaturwissenschaft* does not by definition express the differentiation between historically and societally different types of literature. It could be understood in the sense in which Robertson understands literary criticism, in which case Richter's term would be inappropriate for the exegesis of our historically determined texts. This must be stated apart from the question of what results a comparison of Richter's and Robertson's methods would yield. For these reasons, and not because of the origin of the term, we still prefer the expression "historical (-critical) exegesis." Moreover, Richter's own methodology, his exegetical publications, and those of his students are demonstrations of historical exegesis.

Another insight drawn from the critical situation is that the methods of historical exegesis, which were developed in the epistemological contexts of their time and emerged one by one in historical succession, need to be reconceptualized and integrated with one another. The order of presentation in our methodological textbooks and articles, as well as the different methodological systematizations, points out the problem. This problem has received increasing attention in recent years, and it will be addressed more specifically in the final section of this review. We begin with a discussion of each method and will conclude with a review of the problem of an integrated exegetical methodology.

II. THE INDIVIDUAL METHODS

Literary Features

The Heritage: Traditional Literary Criticism

The study of literary features originated in traditional literary criticism of the Hebrew Bible. Around the turn of this century, literary criticism had developed into the literary-critical school. Its representatives, above all Wellhausen, had placed the literary-critical analysis of the scriptures in the center of their work (Eissfeldt, 1960:388–89). During the following decades this priority was supplanted by the plurality of methodological approaches generated by the rise of the religio-historical school, form criticism, and tradition history. At first this resulted in a diversification of the roles literary criticism continued to play in OT exegesis. While many scholars started early and of course in varying ways—and with varying success—to combine literary criticism with other methods, particularly with form criticism and tradition history, other scholars continued to isolate literary criticism from these new methods, never integrating them all together in their publications. Probably the most striking and certainly the last example of this stance was G. Hölscher, whose *Geschichte der israelitischen und jüdischen Religion* (1922) was totally religio-historical in nature and had very little to do with literary criticism while his *Geschichtsschreibung in Israel* (1952) is exclusively based on the method of the literary-critical school. A comparison of the first edition of Eissfeldt's *Einleitung in das Alte Testament* (1934) with the second edition (1956) shows literary criticism emerging from its isolation. While the first edition was strictly confined to the summary of literary-critical work, which along with a history of Israelite literature was one of the two main objectives of the literary-critical school, the second edition includes the results of form criticism—the discussion of the preliterary genres and their settings. Both progress and deficiency are clearly visible in this edition, progress in the adaptation of the results of a different method and deficiency in the juxtaposition of methods without their integration. This, then, was the place where literary criticism stood as a discipline in the mid-1950s—moving toward a broadening of its base but not yet free of an isolationist stance. Even though the alternatives had long been under way, literary critics were not yet capable of realizing that their discipline might have to become part of an overarching exegetical method. An extreme reflex of this stance is a remark by G. Hölscher after G. von Rad had become Hölscher's successor at Heidelberg in 1949 (also the year in which the first part of von Rad's commentary on Genesis appeared). Hölscher commented: "Das ist das Ende der Wissenschaft."[3] The impulses for change had to come from elsewhere.

In the early 1950s, von Rad tried to persuade Eissfeldt to write a compendium for students on the literary-critical method; Eissfeldt answered that it could all be found in his introduction.[4] It was only in subsequent years that summaries of the method began to appear in reference works such as *EKL*, *RGG*[3], *IDB*, and others, and more recently in *IDBSup* and in methodologically oriented monographs; see, among others, Barth and Steck (27–36), Baumgärtel (1186), Boecker (110–11), Cazelles (100), Fichtner (1221), Fohrer et al. (44–57), Freedman (723), Fretheim (838), Grobel (412), Habel (1–17), Horst (1124), Kaiser and Kümmel (15–18), Keck (547), Keck and Tucker (296–303), Koch (1969: 68–78), Kraus (1956: 455–56), Kuhl (1957:1227–32), Rendtorff (1977), Richter (1971:50–69), O. H. Steck (1975:27–36).

All these publications affirm literary criticism as a legitimate exegetical method. Yet none considers it the sole method to be used in isolation. While most of them reflect the understanding of *traditional* literary criticism, some see it in a *refined* way (Barth and Steck), some in an *alternative* way (Lohfink; Muilenburg; Schulte). Some redefine it in a *new* way (Richter; Fohrer et al.), and others *subordinate it to a different* method altogether (Horst and Koch to form criticism, and Rendtorff to tradition history). The consensus on the need for literary criticism as such is based on the literary-historical character of the texts. Any attempt to deny this factor and to replace literary criticism with other

---

[3] The remark was made to the late Dr. Erich Thier, lecturer in social ethics at the Theology Faculty, Heidelberg University, and was related to me orally by Thier in 1961 while we were neighbors in Heidelberg.

[4] Related to me by von Rad around 1959.

methods such as oral tradition history (Engnell) or form criticism (Reventlow) remains unpromising. On the other hand, the diverse positions presently expressed on the method itself indicate that its methodology has now become a central problem which in all probability is bound to stay with us for some time. In the following, we will attempt to outline the major methodological problems.

The Methodological Problem in Literary Criticism

Traditional literary criticism was guided by interest in the integrity or compositeness of texts; in the identification of such texts or layers of them as parts of larger literary works or layers (such as primary and secondary sources), as fragments, or as redactional additions (such as introductions or conclusions, expansions, appendixes, brackets, glosses, etc.); in the reconstruction of the literary history of a text in the context of the larger work (with major emphasis on the "original" or "authentic" layers); in the correlation of the literary history with the history of Israel; and in the assessment of the theology or religion especially of the sources. At present there is agreement on one goal of the literary-critical task: to establish the literary integrity or compositeness of a text unit. (The terms "integrity" or "compositeness" refer only to whether a text unit stems from the same hand, not to whether the text is "original" [ursprünglich, "Urtext"], authentic [echt], or uniform [stylistically homogeneous or heterogeneous].) In the case of composite texts, the task is to separate the layers from one another and to establish their relative chronology. On every other question, however, there is a partial, if not a significant, diversity of opinion.

The relationship of small literary units to larger literary corpora (so-called sources), a problem only recently addressed in literary criticism, has become a point of major methodological diversity. The problem was programmed into the history of literary criticism, especially in the interaction between actual literary-critical work and its methodological design. As long as literary observations could be explained either by the source or fragment hypothesis, literary criticism did not have to be identified as source criticism. However, as soon as the (new) documentary hypothesis about the Hexateuch had won out over the fragment hypothesis, literary criticism was defined as source criticism per se, even though numerous scholars continued to refute it as the sole solution to the problem.[5] Wellhausen himself is probably responsible more than anyone else for this development. His *Die Composition des Hexateuchs* is involved with the assumption and discussion of the *Quellen* (from the first sentence to the last). This development probably explains why many

---

[5] See Eissfeldt (1956:132–43).

have defined literary criticism as, or have related it simply to, source criticism (Baumgärtel· 1186; Horst: 1124; Kuhl, 1957:1231; Fichtner: 1221; Keck and Tucker: 300; Fretheim: 838; Tucker in Robertson, 1977:viii; Koch, 1969:70), while others have understood it as also dealing with (short) texts themselves (Kraus, 1956:455; Grobel: 412; Kaiser: 16; Keck: 547 ["Analyzes texts . . . , possible use of sources . . . ,"]; Habel: 6, although heavily involved with the discussion of sources; and Barth and Steck: 27 ["Einzeltexte . . . und grössere Textkomplexe . . . ,"]). Most recently, however, coming from text linguistics on the one hand, Richter (1971:50–72), Fohrer et al. (44–57), and Hardmeier (28–51), and on the other hand Rendtorff (1977), coming from tradition history, have insisted that literary criticism be dissociated from source criticism altogether and strictly confined to the smallest text units. The correlation of such units is considered to be a task of redaction criticism.[6]

To a certain extent, the differences in these positions are fundamental. Since they cannot be further analyzed in this paper, only four remarks will be made. (1) It is interesting to observe two reversed developments in literary criticism and in form criticism respectively. Form criticism, originally concerned with small units, has expanded its range to include larger literary works. By contrast, literary criticism, originally concerned with larger works, has turned its attention to small units. (2) It should be clear that, methodologically speaking, the identification of literary criticism with source criticism is wrong. The determination of sources is a possible result of literary-critical work but not its methodological principle. (3) A tension is emerging between two principles in the methodology of literary criticism—the concern for the integrity or the compositeness of a unit and the programmatic confinement to small units. These principles are neither congruous nor interchangeable. Large works as well as small units can have literary integrity. In either case the integrity of a text depends on whether or not it is the product of the same literary hand. It remains to be seen, therefore, whether larger works, where they exist, can be excluded from the proper literary-critical task. For as long as literary criticism is preoccupied with the integrity of texts, its accounting for both small units and large works through discernment of their constituent elements seems to be a genuine proposition. (4) The exclusion of larger works from literary-critical work is problematic also because it subordinates their determination to redaction criticism, suggesting that the distinctions held between authors, collectors, and strata on the one hand and editors or redactors of smaller or larger works on the other be abandoned. For example, the Deuteronomistic history, whether one sees it with Noth or with Cross (1973b),

---

[6] For demonstrations of this understanding see, among others, Richter (1963, 1970), Zenger, and Hardmeier.

could only be understood as the work of a redactor; similar problems exist in the prophetic literature. In this respect, Weimar's approach, starting with the analysis of (small) units in order to arrive at a more refined picture of the larger works and then proceeding to the analysis of the redactional combination of these works, is not without reason.[7]

Methodological problems are involved also in the relationship between the literary history or the *Literaturgeschichte* of the OT and the history of Israel. Initially, literary criticism combined the chronology of its assumed sources with the history of Israel. This combination proved to rest on, among other things, a simplistic understanding of the nature of the OT literature. Neither the layers of tradition in it nor its total range or generic character could be accounted for (see Koch, 1969: 70–72). This deficit was theoretically discharged by Gunkel's proposal of a history of Israelite literature, initially outlined by Gunkel and Gressmann and carried out once by Hempel in 1934. This legacy has been upheld by Koch with his "Scheme for a Literary History of the Bible," designed in the framework of the "History of Biblical Interpretation and the History of Language" (1969:106–8; 1974:333–42; see also Rendtorff, 1977). But an updated implementation of the program is still to come. The reasons for the delay must be sought less in form criticism than in literary criticism itself. Both the attention directed to the OT as literature, with a host of revisions of and alternatives to the method, and the mushrooming new results indicate that literary criticism will have to play a conspicuous role in the foreseeable future before a new OT *Literaturgeschichte* can be written.

The problem of chronology is a major case in point. Among those who assume the existence of Pentateuchal sources, the opinions conflict sharply. While Kilian, Weimar, and Schulte have recently confirmed the existence of the old sources, Van Seters, Schmid, and Rendtorff have ascribed the sources (Van Seters, Schmid) or the unifying layers (Rendtorff) to the Deuteronomic time and thereafter. The situation is compounded further if one looks at the Sinai pericope. Perlitt, denying the Elohistic origin of Exod 19:3–8, ascribes it to the time shortly before 587 B.C.E. (179). Zenger, meanwhile, also assuming the existence of the older sources and denying the Elohistic origin of Exod 19:3bβ–9b, ascribes this passage to the second Deuteronomistic redaction following the first post-exilic redaction (164–65). Mittmann's discussion, both agreeing and disagreeing with these two scholars on related passages, complicates the problem even more. To be sure, all the scholars mentioned here operate on a methodological level much more refined and even more rigid than traditional literary criticism has used, especially in terms of attention to

---

[7] This judgment is independent of Weimar's actual results, especially his contention that E is "vollständig überliefert" (165), which he has not substantiated.

the text. And yet, while one may assume that the same methodological criteria are at work for all of them, their results vary on both general and specific points. One may explain these differences as the unavoidable limit set by the texts beyond which there is room only for "subjective" conjecture. It seems, however, that the diversity still points back to the problem of method itself, i.e., to the problem of what weight the specific criteria such as tensions, breaks, brackets, doublets, style, and content have in any given case and on what small or broad basis decisions can be justified. Here the method itself is in need of further development. Of particular interest at this point is Barth and Steck's statement that doublets, parallels, variations in vocabulary, differences in rhetoric and style, distinct thematic and phraseological features, and gaps or unevennesses in texts can no longer be considered the sole criteria for literary-critical analysis. They are relative and can become valid only when evaluated together with the observations on form, content, and the traditions in a text. This evaluation of the literary-critical criteria is certainly different from that of Richter and Fohrer et al., who believe that these criteria alone should be the basis for the determination of the literary layers of a text. These different positions are in need of further critical comparison in conjunction with the testing of the methodological models through actual exegetical work, most preferably on the same texts. The new beginnings have been promising, but the future will have to show which model, in its overall design as well as in its specifics, best serves the goal acknowledged by all—to establish the relative chronology within texts.

Another case in point is a new awareness of the relativity of words such as author, collector, originality, or authenticity in literary criticism. Schmid, for example, wants to avoid the concept of "author" and to do more justice to the literary phenomena by assuming a Yahwistic "stratum," a *Schicht* (17–18).[8] Rendtorff too speaks of *Bearbeitungsschichten* (1977:158–73). Related to this stance is Kilian's renewed inclusion of the activity of "collectors" and "revisers" (*Sammler und Bearbeiter*) into the concept of "author" (304). A particularly interesting example is the difference in the interpretations of Gen 1:1–2:4a by Steck and Schmidt. Schmidt has argued that this creation story is the result of the reinterpretation of an older text, a *Tatbericht*. In other words, he had identified two "sources" in the present text. By contrast, Steck has argued that the text has a genuine integrity dictated by the intention of its author. The fact that this author also uses older concepts by no means points to different sources (1975: esp. 243–48). The difference between these positions affects the criteria for establishing the integrity or compositeness of

---

[8] This proposal is not new, of course. Already Gunkel preferred to speak of *Schichten* rather than "sources."

a text as much as for identifying an author. Finally, suffice it to say that
words such as originality or authenticity are commonly understood in
the sense of an oldest discernible layer, but no longer in the sense of
Urtext or *Echtheit* versus less relevant secondary accretions.

Last but not least, H. Schulte proposes to solve the problem of the
Yahwist through investigation of *Epochenstil* and the isolation of the
specific theme "justice" and the genre *Führungsgeschichte* in the literary
corpora of an epoch. Hence, the work of the Yahwist probably extends
to 1 Kgs 2:46 (218), and its author can be identified as the grandson of
Abiathar (218). To be sure, operation with *Epochenstil* is another
attempt to stay away from the concept of *Autorenstil* and converges
with the concept of strata, which attempts to account for the stylistic
complexity in a work, or the work of an author. However, while others
who assume strata have opted for circles of authors, Schulte identifies the
author personally, including the time of his work—between 910 and 900
B.C.E. plus or minus thirty years (216). Indeed, it is difficult to see how
the detection of the same theme and genre in various passages of several
works of an epoch is enough to determine a specific author and the procedure of his literary activities. This must be said, quite apart from the
question of whether J belonged to the tenth century—or indeed even
existed—and apart from the fact that Schulte's approach to literary criticism stands at the opposite end of the method suggested by structural
linguistics.

Alternative Approaches

Before the resurgence of traditional literary criticism in the 1960s
(e.g. Fohrer, 1964; Elliger, 1966) and the emergence of structural linguistics as a force in literary criticism, two major proposals were introduced
that called attention to the Hebrew Bible as literature. One came from
James Muilenburg, the other from Norbert Lohfink. Their approaches
both rest on the methods of the classical science of literature.[9] Their
different emphases seem to reflect more their individual reactions against
specific aspects of the exegetical situation than basically different
understandings of the science of literature. Generally speaking, their
contributions were particularly important because they arose from the
exegesis of texts (Deutero-Isaiah and Deuteronomy, respectively) that lay
outside the narrative corpora, the domain of traditional literary criticism.
Implied in this diversity of OT texts and methods is the overall question of
whether the same method and the same process are commensurate with

---

[9] The denunciation of this method as "aesthetic" is beside the point. The aestheticism of
this method has itself been understood since Greco-Roman antiquity to be subject to
norms intrinsic to higher literature. A different question is whether its norms and categorie-
ries can be assumed to be partly or universally at work in the Israelite literature.

each of these literary types. This question has received insufficient attention in the literary-critical discussion.

Because form criticism had become increasingly preoccupied with the typical forces at work behind the texts, Lohfink called for a new recognition of the texts as texts. Influenced by Wellek and Warren and by Alonso-Schökel, he proposed a "New Style Criticism" as the literary-critical task (10, 13). Its model was the analysis of the language in the context of the whole text and not on the lexical and syntactical level only (15).

Lohfink's method and his results have been criticized, and his actual results appear to have been surpassed (see Perlitt and Mittmann). It remains to be seen whether the method as such is to be discarded or if some of it will survive, and how. His particular kind of methodological correlation of literary criticism and form criticism certainly promised more than it could deliver. His attempt to identify an a priori accepted genre ("Covenant Formulary") in the stylistic structure of the text was just as indefensible as the literary-critical analysis of texts on the a priori assumption of sources.

Meanwhile, literary criticism had already received another impulse through Muilenburg's "rhetorical criticism." Muilenburg too was dissatisfied with form criticism's one-sided concentration on the originally short units and their generic typicality. In addition to that work, he called attention to the creative role of individual authors in smaller units as well as larger compositions. He proposed to analyze their style by identifying the rhetorical devices used in them. In turn, such analysis would allow him to recognize the individual oral style behind the written style and to establish the interdependence of written and oral literature (1953; 1956; 1969).[10]

The viability of his criteria for identifying the style of compositions themselves, for demarcating rhetorical criticism from form criticism (compare the dependence of Lohfink's stylistic criteria on form criticism), and for correlating written and oral style may be questionable, but his call for the recognition of both the typicality and the individuality, the short units and the larger compositions, the oral and the written, and for the correlation of all in an integrated method remains a substantial legacy for exegesis. Thus, it is not coincidental that Muilenburg has generated a significant tradition of studies by his own students and others (see, e.g., Jackson and Kessler; Anderson: ix–xviii; Melugin: 1–10, 175–78).

Finally, it must be noted that impulses from the science of literature or from stylistic criticism have also come from others. For example, M. Weiss proposes a method of "Total-Interpretation" of a biblical text as a holistic literary phenomenon. There are also new insights coming

---

[10] For a discussion of oral literature, see the essay by Robert C. Culley in this volume.

from the study of the ancient Near Eastern literature, particularly for poetry, but also for prose literature (Cross and Freedman, 1975; Robertson, 1972). In general, the new periodical *Semeia* now provides a specific outlet for new literary-critical studies, indeed for "experimental" work.

It is evident that the new concentration on the Hebrew Bible as literature has generated an enormous resurgence of literary criticism in our generation. At the same time, the variety and diversity of models indicate that a consensus on the description of the literary-critical task is not yet in sight. Nevertheless, the situation in which we find ourselves is in no way comparable to the situation of literary criticism a generation ago.

Form

The Development of the Discussion

The exegetical interest in form had its beginnings in literary criticism, for which the determination of the structure or composition of larger literary works (the sources) was a major ingredient of methodology (Baumgärtel: 1186; Kraus, 1956:455; Grobel: 412; Keck: 547 ["Analyzes texts in order to determine their structure and composition"]; Hölscher, 1952:46–60, 196–209).[11] However, it was in the form-critical method that the determination of form as typical form gained a central place. Form criticism had started with the isolation of the small original units, the determination of their presumed oral origin (the so-called setting in life), and the generic classification of these units and of their function. This scope was broadened by von Rad, who investigated larger literary works form-critically (see Rendtorff, 1956:1304). Von Rad's impulse was carried in a specific direction by H. W. Wolff's works on the kerygmatic nature of J, E, D, and of "kerygmatic units" in the prophetic literature. The state of that development was the basis for the first German edition of Koch's *Was ist Formgeschichte?* (1964).

During the late 1960s and the early 1970s, the methodological discussion began to erupt as it had not done since the days of Gunkel. Major factors contributing to this development have been the impulses from ancient Near Eastern studies, especially on treaty and covenant, from the new stylistic and rhetorical criticism, from the study of oral literature, from structuralism, especially structural linguistics, and from careful scrutiny of the form-critical assumptions by some form critics themselves. Affected were the understanding of form or structure, genre, setting, function and/or intention, their interdependence, the relationship of genre and

---

[11] See Wellhausen's *Die Composition des Hexateuchs* (emphasis added). It would be interesting to study specifically Wellhausen's explicit and implicit arguments for "composition." Of course, literary criticism's understanding of "structure" or "composition" has to be distinguished from that in other fields.

text, and of literature and orality. This state of the discussion is for the most part summarily, although often controversially, reflected in the latest German and English editions of Koch's work, in the exegetical methodologies of Richter, Steck, Fohrer et al., and in Tucker's article, which also lists most of the pertinent bibliography. Instead of recounting this development,[12] the following will attempt to highlight the points most central to the recent debate and to the future of form criticism.

The Focus of the Current Debate

What was in the past variously suggested by literary criticism, and not unambiguously by form criticism, has now received central attention—the structure of the text itself (Richter, 1971:72–120; Fohrer et al.: 57–89; Koch, 1974:304–30, 1976:21–28; Campbell: 55–178; Hardmeier: 28–153). With some variations, a text is understood as an organic linguistic entity, as the elementary and self-contained unit of linguistic (oral or written) expression in a communication event. In principle, it supersedes the entities of the word and sentence levels. It is a "macrosyntactical unit" (Koch, 1976:11). Influenced by structural linguistics, one has accepted the assumption that a text involves both an element of expression and an element of signification and that, hence, as a whole it is a semantic phenomenon. The structure in which this phenomenon exists becomes the focus of analysis. This was also seen by Richter (1971:92–120) and Fohrer et al. (57–80), although "signification" and "content" are apparently not clearly distinguished by Richter. This compromises his assertion of the interdependence of expression and signification in the text structure and probably accounts for his belief that "content" (signification?) plays no role in the investigation of the history of forms (1971:120). Of course, Barth and Steck (104–8) and Koch have questioned whether the discussion of content can be dissociated from the analysis of the structure of a text, particularly with regard to the influence of content on the historicality of a text. Whatever the answer to that question may be, the analysis of structure in the correlation of external (expression) and internal (signification) structure is certainly within the domain of historical exegesis since it deals with the Hebrew text and its intrinsic components. On the critique of this issue, see Hardmeier (44–51).

Different from the task of the structural analysis of a text as such is the question where or when in the exegetical process such analysis should be done. As is well known, Richter—followed by Fohrer et al.— has assigned it to a place within a seemingly logical, at any rate rigidly determined, sequential order. Their proposal has met with widespread opposition, but it nevertheless continues to be practiced in exegetical

12 See my discussion (1973).

work. Three alternatives are conceivable. (1) The structural analysis of a text may be subsumed under literary criticism. This would not be new and would mean that the determination of the literary integrity of a text would be combined with—and supported by—the determination of its structure. In my own opinion, the integrity of a text cannot be ascertained at all without also, even primarily, the determination of its structural integrity. (2) The structural analysis may be subsumed under form criticism. This would mean that form criticism would finally incorporate the structural analysis of texts as texts into its methodology and, more important, that such analysis would become the starting point as well as the controlling basis for the subsequent identification of genre exemplars in the texts and the genres underneath them. (3) It may be done in isolation. This would highlight the distinctiveness of this methodological step and add a new method to those already known.

One may be tempted to evaluate these alternatives pragmatically rather than programmatically, but more is involved. It seems that neither the new emphasis on structural analysis of texts nor the demarcation of the distinctiveness of this step necessitates the introduction of a new exegetical method; methodological differentiation does not mean methodological separation. It also seems as though the methodological isolation of analyzing text structure deprives us of executing in actual exegesis what our assumptions about the nature of "text" suggest—its semantic and hierarchic unity, i.e., the interdependence not only of its elements of expression and signification but also of the individual (style, syntax, grammar) and the typical in its surface structure, and of the surface structure and depth structure as well.

More difficult is the question whether to subsume the analysis of text structure under literary criticism or form criticism. As the analysis of a text's integrity, the step belongs to literary criticism. As the analysis of a genre exemplar, it belongs to form criticism. Moreover, as the analysis of both the individuality (rhetorical nature) and the typicality interdependent in a unit, it stands at the intersection of both methods. This result leads, ultimately, to the question of the methodological relationship between literary criticism and form criticism. Literary criticism is not concerned with the typical—except in the concept of an Israelite *Literaturgeschichte*. The interest of form criticism in the individual phenomenon has been ambiguous, but it has this potential. If the structural analysis of texts and of their individuality is considered an essential ingredient in determining their literary integrity, and if form criticism incorporates such structural analysis into its methodology, then the best place for it, possibly including the literary-critical task, seems to be as the initial step of the form-critical method. This possibility is part of Koch's long-standing position, which he and his team have now exemplified in the three volumes *Amos, untersucht mit den Methoden einer strukturalen Formgeschichte*, including an extensive introduction on the method and design of the work. (For a discussion of the nomenclature of the various form-critical steps and for its critique, see now Hardmeier [283–93].)

Text and Genre

Scholars have become increasingly articulate and united in emphasizing that the detection of generic structures in a controlled way can occur only through comparison of the semantic structures of text entities. Even Koch and Richter agree on this point (Koch, 1973:811, 1976:22). The discussion about the so-called Covenant Formulary exemplifies the importance of this insight (Perlitt; McCarthy). Another case in point is provided by the different assessments of the rituals in Leviticus 1–7 by Rendtorff (1963) and Elliger. Indeed, approaching this problem through the text structures shows that the generic pattern of those rituals as claimed by Rendtorff cannot by verified.

The problem of understanding the defining genre has been discussed intensively. There is agreement that typical conventions of communication underneath the texts govern the typical structure of the texts, even though they are not identical with the structures of individual texts, and that the generic text structures can be detected only through the synchronic and diachronic comparison of text structures.

Within this agreement, however, there are different emphases. Barth and Steck emphasize the correlation of form and content of a genre in the framework of its history, and they propose to use the word *Form-geschichte* for the exegetical process and the word *Gattungsgeschichte* for the history of a specific genre in a definitive setting (59–69). Richter—his caricature of traditional form criticism aside (1971:127–28; Koch, 1973:811)—sees genre on the basis of form alone, exclusive of content, as the structural pattern of a group of similar forms (1971:131). Similarly Fohrer et al. speak of a *Strukturschema* (90) and differentiate between, among other things, the setting of genres and their history (93–97). Koch, on the other hand, understands genre as a texteme, as a structural or linguistic pattern (*Sprachmuster, Strukturmuster*; 1976:11) or as a "syntax of macrostructures" (1973:812) which is dependent on setting (custom and institutions, 1976:24; 1969) and which provides the generative rules for the text performance so that individual texts can be regarded by definition as exemplars of genres (1976:11).

The latest and at the same time most comprehensive critical and constructive treatment of the subject was submitted by Hardmeier. It discusses all the relevant literature (except for Koch, 1976) and will have to be given central attention in future methodological discussion. Constitutive for Hardmeier's point of departure—as for Koch—is an advanced understanding of linguistic theory according to which texts are parts of linguistic acts of communication (52–105). The texts are products of the linguistic competence of societies and the generative factors in these societies. Inherent in these factors are semantically oriented "plans," abstract depth structures, or generic structures. These generic structures govern the structures of individual texts normatively. They are only detectable in the surface texts, although these surface texts also have components of text, individuality detectable particularly in their stylistic variability. Thus, the task is to distinguish the signals for the genre exemplar from those of individuality in the texts (258–301) and to develop the criteria for discovering the semantic components of genre exemplars.

There is no room here for a further report of Hardmeier's own development of this last point, but it is obvious that a methodology must distinguish between the conceptual model within which exegesis is done and the heuristic problem of verifying genre exemplars in texts and genres underneath them. The quest for verification is decisive: in our search for exemplars in the texts, we have only the texts and cannot presuppose what must be found out (i.e., the problem of circular conclusions). Naturally, this problem has been seen by Koch, Barth and Steck, Richter, Fohrer et al., Hardmeier, and others, and proposals have been made. However, one wonders what it means when Richter identifies a genre as an *Erzählung* (1971:142), a very general term, and speaks of a *prophetische Erzählung* (143) on the basis that such a narration has two parts: a speech prompting an action and an execution report. This pattern is certainly not typical only for prophetic narrations (see also Koch, 1973:810).

Occasionally, one refers to generic *termini* in the Hebrew literature itself (Fohrer et al.: 92–93; Hardmeier: 263, 284). Most recently, Kraus has proposed to reestablish our designations of the genres of the psalms based on the generic superscriptions of the psalms themselves (1978: 14–29) and has made a first effort in this direction.

The task referred to here is thorny. A discussion of Klaus Koch's generic identification of 2 Kgs 1:6 (1974:309–14) demonstrates this difficulty. Koch is chosen, not because he might be wrong or because others have already solved the problem, but because he has submitted a detailed example of his approach. Koch detects in 2 Kgs 1:6 a genre (exemplar) *Profezeiung* (P) with the following genre indicators: *Botenformel* v.6aa$_5$ (BF), *Lage-Hinweis* v.6aβ (LH), *Unheils-Wort* v.6ba (UW), and *Abschliessende Charakteristik* v.6bβ (AC). The rules generating the transformation from the genre (P) to the text are charted in a *Baumgraph* on p. 314. The following sets of questions arise.[13]

First is a question concerning the generic structure. The whole prophecy (P) is subdivided into two parts, a *Rubrik* (BF) and a *Korpus*

---

[13] In the following, Koch's abbreviations noted above are used.

consisting of three parts itself: LH, UW, and AC. What is the relationship of the three parts of the *Korpus*? Koch juxtaposes them on the same level. Syntactically, this is difficult to verify, for AC (6bβ) is subordinate to UW (6bα) and not a second reference to LH (6aβ) in juxtaposition to UW. It seems that we have two sentences, not three, and that the indicators לכן and כי, since they indicate generic components, must also be considered in view of their syntactical function and not in isolation from it. The syntactical order, however, can also be seen as a signal of two genre indicators which would affect the structure of the genre exemplar. What, then, are the criteria that verify the genre indicators?

Second, there are questions concerning the chosen generic terminology. (a) The messenger formula (BF) "thus Yahweh has spoken" is said to be a sort of legitimation (309), which is a definition according to function. And while agreeing with this, because this definition may be important for the determination of a genre "prophecy" one must ask whether such a legitimizing BF did not also belong to the legitimation of nonprophetic messengers, apart from the fact that the BF is not unequivocally prophetic as such.

(b) What constitutes the determination of v.6aβ as LH? Koch, in his German translation, renders the passage in two separate sentences: "Kein Dasein eines Gottes in Israel? Du—sendend, zu ersuchen . . . !" Leaving aside the question whether this translation is the only possible one, what constitutes its definition as LH? Is it the statement in question form in the first sentence (presupposing: there is a God in Israel), or that in the second sentence, or both sentences together? Certainly, LH is not impossible, but what makes it unequivocal? Could it not be understood as an accusation in two parts, in which the first part rationalizes or substantiates the accusation proper by pointing to the alternative—just as the LH (or accusation?) has this function with regard to the following UW? Also, one may expect that the word LH can be expressed in a variety of verbal forms, one of which is the second person address, but this does not mean that every second person address form is to be generically classified as an LH. How do we determine the genre indicator in the second person address form in the second part of our passage? The same question can be asked with regard to the relationship of the question in the first part of the passage. And finally, LH is not by definition a genre indicator for "prophecy," nor does it denote as such the semantic correlation to the following UW, i.e., the direct reason for the UW. This correlation was the reason Westermann rejected the words *Scheltwort* and *Drohwort*, which denoted unrelated entities, and replaced them with *Begründung* and *Ankündigung* (1960:46–49).

(c) Koch's choice of the term *Unheilsweissagung* (UW) is at least partly the result of his opposition to the judicial interpretation of these prophetic words as *Gericht*. Although the controversy about this issue is not unrelated to the generic definition of our passage, its a priori solution is not required for the evaluation of the problems concerning us here. We can, therefore, let UW stand. The term AC, however, is problematic. The word *"Abschliessend"* is at least ambiguous because it can mean the conclusion of the preceding part (UW) or of the whole. Syntactically, it belongs to the preceding. Structurally, Koch sets it on the same level as LH and UW and, hence, signalizes the conclusion of the whole as a self-contained entity. In what sense can this designation be understood as a genre indicator, and if it is so understood, why for "prophecy"? The same question affects the word *Charakteristik* in AC. This term is not confined to a certain tense. The word "you shall surely die," however, is future oriented, like the UW. Which establishes the genre indicator for "prophecy" in this sentence—*Charakteristik* or its future orientation? If it is the former, what is the basis for calling this sentence a *Charakteristik*? If it is the latter, is the word *Charakteristik* then a clear designation for what is characteristic in the sentence, i.e., for an indication of its generic nature? Finally, why is AC as such a genre indicator of "prophecy"?

Obviously, neither the LH nor the AC, taken independently, indicates unequivocally a genre "prophecy." And certainly this should not be expected, for it is their interdependence that determines which genre they indicate. In this case, however, the only indisputable genre indicator in the *Korpus* is the UW, which would then also determine the generic nature of the LH and AC. But this result raises new questions: Does every "prophecy" announcing evil, or every UW for that matter, have this threefold structure? And, if UW constitutes the whole structure, why call it "prophecy" and not "UW"? This definition would be supported just as much by the BF as that of prophecy. In this case, the BF would qualify the UW as a "prophetic UW," which appears in Koch's scheme as one of the two *subdivisions* of "prophecy." An implication of this is that the *supergenre* "prophecy" would then be constituted by the BF indicating the "prophetic," regardless of the nature of *this* corpus. Moreover, in its structural pattern the indicator UW would have to be replaced by a different indicator such as *Weissagung* (W), because UW indicates only prophecy of evil. Applied to the specific text laid out in Koch's *Baumgraph*, this means that this text reflects the pattern of the subgenre UW regardless of whether or not it belongs to a supergenre P and should, therefore, be superscribed with "(prophetic) UW" and not with P.

Finally, the *Baumgraph* identifying the two major parts as *Rubrik* (BF) and *Korpus* does not present the generic identity of this corpus. *Korpus* says nothing about "prophecy." Presumably what is meant is "prophecy proper."

A third set of questions arises in regard to the context. Verses 5 and 6 are part of a larger context and its language; our unit should be understood in its horizon. At least three observations are pertinent. The messenger scenario is quite explicit in the total chapter, in the introduction to our unit as well as in the parallel of vv 3–4. Furthermore, the officers sent to Elijah call him "man of God," not "prophet" (vv 9, 10, 11, 12, 13). Finally, the king's own reaction (vv 7–8) does not focus on the prophecy or whatever else it might be called. What was the generic horizon that guided or influenced the narrator? Does this context show unequivocal evidence of a genre "prophecy" in the speeches of the מלאך יהוה and the messengers?

In conclusion, in order to establish the structure and to determine the genre indicators of our unit within the immediate text unit and not without it, it seems important to encounter at least the immediate text unit in which it stands. The text unit is given in vv 5–8 and its structure seems to signal that vv 5–6 are a genre exemplar of dialogue and part of it, a substantiated, directly addressed, announcement of death (evil) in the framework of a messenger speech.[14]

At any rate, the question at this point is methodological, i.e., *how* can we *verify* a genre exemplar and identify a genre when confronting a text, and not which of the propositions is finally correct. Once again we are indebted to Koch for his intensive effort to correlate form criticism as a whole with semantic linguistics, a first attempt of this kind which

---

[14] The structure itself is as follows:

Report of the return of the messengers (5–8)	
I. Statement about the return	5a
II. Dialogue	5b–8
A. First round	5–6
1. (King's) question (introduction + question)	5b
2. Answer (of messengers)	6
a. Narrative introduction	$6aa_1$
b. Answer	$6aa_2$–b
1) Statement about event	$6aa_2$
2) Statement about speech	$6aa_3$–b
a) Narrative introduction	$6aa_3$
b) Speech	$6aa_4$–b
(1) Messenger commission	$6aa_5$
(2) Messenger speech	$6aa_6$–b
(a) Messenger formula	$6aa_6$
(b) Message	$6a\beta$–b
a. Accusation	$6a\beta$
aa. Rhetorical question	$6a\beta_1$
bb. Statement of fact	$6a\beta_2$
β. Announcement of death (evil)	6b
aa. Announcement proper	$6ba$
bb. Reason	$6b\beta$
B. Second round	7–8a
C. Conclusion	8b

This format of the structure already contains the depth structure and could be directly transposed into the format of a *Baumgraph*, just as Koch's *Baumgraph* can be directly transposed into this format.

signaled a new era in the field. The further clarification of this issue is certainly one of the most important tasks immediately ahead, and progress on other important questions such as the relationship between oral and written language (see the essay by Robert C. Culley in this volume) and especially the determination of setting depends on it.

Additional Developments

In addition to the issues discussed thus far, developments in or relative to form criticism are emerging that deserve our attention.

We currently experience a distinct interest in the sociology of ancient Israel. The most recent works by Gerstenberger, Morton Smith, Gottwald, and Wilson are cases in point. While Gerstenberger has demonstrated in the Complaints of the Individual the remaining validity of a controlled reconstruction of a setting in the ancient Near East and the OT through the classical approach of form criticism itself, Smith, Gottwald, and Wilson, each in his own way and on different subjects, have endeavored to describe societal realities in Israel through a sociologically controlled interpretation of the wider evidence.

For form criticism, the societal settings behind the texts are assumed to be the decisive generative forces for the emergence of generic texts. This assumption, however, has always meant that a comprehensive sociological picture of Israel's history is indispensable for form-critical work. The only problem is that we have never had such a comprehensive picture, let alone the problem of the sometimes dubious reconstruction of settings via dubiously identified text patterns. In view of this desideratum, the above mentioned works, besides some others, indicate not so much a new direction in form criticism itself—or in the sociology of religion for that matter—but certainly the execution of a long-standing program that is also decisive for the completion of the form-critical program. A new direction would evolve, however, if the sociological study of Israel's history and the study of the genres of the OT literature, each in its own right, would be programmatically correlated. Of such a programmatic correlation we have at best embryonic indications but neither a program nor an execution.

The attention to text structures has also opened the way, actually for the first time, for the correlation of the form critical method with the methods of rhetorical criticism and the criticism of literature. If one compares the text structures identifiable through the criteria of rhetoric, of literature, and of genre (form-critically speaking) with one another, the discrepancies in one and the same text are obvious. The acrostic or any prosodic structure of a psalm, e.g., is very different from, and in principle independent of, the generic structure of the psalm. Evidently, each of these structures is intrinsic to the textual phenomenon, and it makes no sense for us to carry out a methodological warfare among these different approaches. Instead, a methodology is necessary that enables us to correlate these approaches in such a way that the interrelationship of the rhetorical, literary, and generic structures in the same texts can be determined, i.e., the place and function of each of them in the hierarchy of semantic-linguistic units. Such a methodology has not yet been developed sufficiently. But actual studies in this direction are under way. Such studies should help us to advance our methodology just as much as they yield fresh exegetical insights. At any rate, this convergence of methods raises additional questions also for form criticism.

The relationship between orality and literality in many of our texts has long been of preeminent interest in form criticism. In fact, the assumption of the oral background of the OT literature stood at the cradle of the form-critical movement. What has always been a problem, however, is the lack of sufficient criteria by which to ascertain with certainty the degree and kind of oral language in our written texts. In spite of intensive work in this area during the last half-generation, definitive results and methodological concepts have remained elusive. Nevertheless, we are moving forward. In the area of Hebrew prosody, Michael H. Floyd has recently submitted the latest, and so far the most comprehensive, theory by which oral language can be discerned in Hebrew poetry. And in the area of royal judicial (prose) narratives, Charles Mabee has, through form-critical interpretation, established criteria that allow us to see the degree to which those written narratives reflect—or do not reflect—the language of actual oral judiciary processes. In both cases the results indicate that, while oral language does or may stand behind the written texts generally, the written texts are phenomena sui generis. They reflect a significant distance from the realm of oral language and cannot be considered as intending primary reproductions of oral texts. This development indicates that form-critical work as such must take seriously the problems of structure, genre, setting, and function/intention of written texts as literature in their own right in order to be better equipped or inquiring into the relationship between the written text and the oral background. The time is passing rapidly in which one could prematurely jump to conclusions about oral tradition before doing what must be done first: the form-critical assessment of the written text itself. The methodological consequences from this new direction as well as the substantive results promise to be far-reaching.

In conclusion, one more problem must be pointed out that needs to be taken up within form criticism. It concerns the methodological differentiation between form history and form sociology, between the diachronic and the synchronic aspects in form-critical work. It makes a difference whether we speak about, e.g., an oral or a written tradition that stands—diachronically—*behind* a Genesis story and has led to it throughout a process lasting centuries, or whether we speak about a setting that lies—synchronically—*underneath* a complaint psalm. The forces at work that generate each of these two text types seem to be quite different and, hence, in need of a differentiating methodological description. However, the systematic methodological clarification of this item and its application to the entirety of the OT literature is very much in the beginning stages.

Tradition

We are fortunate to have available a comprehensive account of the history of traditio-historical research by D. Knight (1973).[15] The results of this study are presupposed here, and we can attempt to systematize the current situation.

Current Methodological Positions

There seem to be some points of essential agreement. (1) We differentiate between the transmitted subject matters and the process of transmission; they are now called respectively traditions and transmission. (2) There is agreement that for the processes in both tradition and transmission we have to account for the possibilities of continuity as well as discontinuity. (3) There is agreement that oral and written influences are interdependent in the transmission of traditions. Oral transmission and written transmission are not by definition mutually exclusive, nor are they to be assigned to separate historical epochs. The determination of which of the two carried the process at a given time, or of the type of their interdependence, depends on the actual observations of specific materials. (4) There is agreement among those who have addressed the methodological issue that transmission history and tradition history deal with the transmission of the tradition of text units, whereas genre history is considered a separate question to be discussed together with genre (see Koch, 1969:38–39; Richter, 1971:142–64; Barth and Steck: 37–47, 70–78; Fohrer et al.: 99–136).

However, there are differences and disagreements. Whereas Barth and Steck (37) and Fohrer et al. (117) confine transmission history to the oral stage, Koch (1969:38–54) and Richter (1971:152) speak of both the oral and the (possibly) written stage.[16] On the question of whether form, content, or both are the subjects of inquiry, there are also variations.

---

[15] See also the essays from several contributors in the volume edited by Knight (1977) on a variety of aspects of the field.

[16] See, e.g., Noth, who used *Überlieferungsgeschichte* for the oral stages in his *Überlieferungsgeschichte des Pentateuch* and for the written stages in his *Überlieferungsgeschichtliche Studien*.

Barth and Steck, in the section on *Überlieferungsgeschichte* (37–45), seem to allow for both form and content while in their separate section on *Traditionsgeschichte* (70–78) they seem to allow for content only (conceptions, ideas, motifs). For Koch (38–54) and Richter (156), however, the emphasis on the forms is predominant while content is subordinate, whereas Fohrer et al. speak of "fixed semantic syndromes" of texts (108). Furthermore, Koch and Barth and Steck concentrate on the prehistory of—the conceptions of—text units in their entirety, especially Barth and Steck in *Traditionsgeschichte* (70), in contrast to the history of parts or elements of texts. Richter (1971:152–58) and Fohrer et al. (108), on the other hand, concentrate on generic elements in the units in form and content. The concentration on units in their entirety takes place for Richter (1971:72–125) in a separate exegetical step: the investigation of the history of a group of forms (or a form-group) and of the forms of a group. For Fohrer et al., the same concern is associated with genre criticism (81–99).

There is, finally, a remarkable terminological confusion that affects all the points just mentioned. Thus, the term *Traditionsgeschichte* is used by Kaiser (19–24) for that which grew out of *Formgeschichte*, i.e., the history of forms and genres. Koch did not use it in 1964/1969. For Barth and Steck, it means only the history of conceptions and ideas to be researched analytically and synthetically. For Richter and Fohrer et al., it refers predominantly to the forms to be researched synthetically. The latter authors use *Traditions-Kritik* for the analytical process, *Überlieferungs-Kritik* for the analysis, and *Überlieferungsgeschichte* for the synthesis. Koch and Barth and Steck use *Überlieferungsgeschichte* for the designation of the historical process and not as a methodological term, but they too have their differences. For Koch, it describes the whole object of study, whereas it is confined for Barth and Steck to the process of transmission.

To be sure, all these terminological distinctions were generated by legitimate concerns, and we must not lay subjective blame on the scholars responsible for them. Nevertheless, the situation is a nuisance, and students as well as experts could spend their hours on more important things than on the analysis of the same words for different things or on different words for the same things in the various methodological and exegetical publications. While it is impossible to achieve rapid terminological uniformity because of the substantive differences, one could expect terminological consistency within a system. The book by Fohrer et al. is a case in point: they use the words *Kritik* and *Geschichte* as terms for methodological procedures, which is already problematical because *Geschichte* is not used only in this sense. The problem is aggravated by the fact that under *Kritik* they separate *Überlieferungs-Kritik* from *Kompositions-Kritik* and *Redaktions-Kritik* (118–19), whereas their *Überlieferungs-Geschichte*, the synthetic reconstruction, encompasses both the transmission of oral or written units and their composition and redaction (122). Hence, one should use sets of terminology that keep the designation of steps of research clearly separate from that of subjects researched. The traditional terms "analysis" and "synthesis" still make sense as names of the method. If they were adopted for all the exegetical steps, one could reserve the word "history" for both tradition and transmission and agree on the already used expression "History of the Transmission of Traditions" for the interdependence of tradition and transmission and for the entire field as well.

The substantive differences mentioned above are reflected not only in the methodologies but also in actual research. This item will be discussed in other sections of this volume, but two examples may be mentioned here.

In studies on the transmission of traditions, there are significant differences of both process and results between M. Sæbø and P. D. Hanson in their studies on Zechariah 9–14. While both combine the two aspects of tradition and transmission, Sæbø arrives at his results through exegesis of the history of the forms of his texts, while Hanson arrives at his results through exegesis of the traditional motif that determines the pattern of his texts (280–380).[17] Another example is the difference between Cross's approach to and results in his study of the Gilgal cult (1973a:90–142) and E. Otto's study, which is analogous to Koch's approach demonstrated in 1969 (38–57).

Finally, the problem of the relationship of the history of the transmission of traditions to history itself must be mentioned. It should be self-evident that the two areas involve separate methodologies just as they deal with distinguishable realities. It is also evident that in some corpora of tradition the insight into the history of the transmission of the traditions reveals how exceedingly difficult it is to ascertain anything specific about the historicity of the events themselves. The studies by Van Seters, Thompson, and Dever and Clark on the patriarchs are recent documentations of that difficulty. The methodological problem is whether to emphasize the distinctiveness of transmission history apart from the history of which it speaks,[18] or whether we have to accept Fohrer's "tradition comes from history" (1964:7, my translation). How can one affirm such a statement as a universal methodological principle in the context under debate? On the other hand, when disconnecting transmission history from history, are we not in danger of reestablishing a metahistory despite our reassurances of the hermeneutical circle in our understanding of transmission history? At least, do we not separate transmission history from a non-history before the tradition (see Kuhl, 1959b:1530; Coats: 913–14)?

---

[17] See also Steck (1967) who basically deals with the transmission of *Vorstellungen*.
[18] See Koch's restrained position (1969:54–56).

Tradition and the Exegetical Task

The terminological and substantive differences mentioned above indicate that the methodology of the field is still influenced by the cumulative effect of its historical evolution (see Paulsen). This is true of the system of steps within the method and also of the relationship of the method itself to the other exegetical methods. When Gunkel (like Eichhorn) proposed in *Schöpfung und Chaos* to consider the entire transmission of the tradition in a text, i.e., to consider texts as traditions, he spoke—as a historian of religion—of the history of their subject matter, of their *Stoff und Vorstellung*. In his *Die Sagen der Genesis*, the emphasis was on the genres and their history. And in his *Einleitung zu den Psalmen* (never translated into English!) there was more of an emphasis on the generic forms than anywhere else. Furthermore, for Gunkel, who introduced the word *Überlieferungsgeschichte* before *Form-Geschichte*, there was no substantial difference between the two because both meant the attention to the prehistory of texts.[19] Some of the current differences still reflect the shifts in Gunkel's own work, from which different methodological emphases have emerged. While Gunkel did not understand these shifts as changes in method, neither did he balance them in an explicit, integrated methodology.[20]

Furthermore, Gunkel did not intend to introduce a new method in addition to the literary criticism prevailing at his time. He meant to replace literary criticism with a superior holistic method better suited to explain the reality of the texts. This method is now one among others in our methodology. Most important perhaps is the fact that he was not so much interested in developing a method for the sake of methodology as in developing it as an exegete who needed an approach to the texts that was commensurate with their reality. This reality was *the phenomenon of the history of transmission of tradition in the texts*. In this regard, we still have nothing better to say. From this vantage point, however, it seems that, while we are greatly indebted to the scholars who have refined and correlated the methodology, we still have to press toward the formulation of a methodology in which the integrity of the text history is

[19] Kaiser's statement that "tradition criticism arises quite independently out of form criticism or genre criticism" (22–23) reflects this view although historically, i.e., in the progress of Gunkel's research, genre history grew out of tradition transmission history. The English translation quoted here uses the terms tradition *criticism* and form *criticism*, thus obscuring precisely the very reason for Kaiser's statement, which is the assumption of history (*Geschichte*) as the basis for the coherence of *Formgeschichte* and *Traditionsgeschichte* (cf. Kaiser and Kümmel, 1963 [German original]:22).

[20] Those differences affect especially the relationship of the ideas and forms of genre history and transmission/tradition history, the current methodological separation of genre history from text history, and the relationship of transmission history to the history of religions and culture.

demonstrated in the exposition of the unavoidable complexity of the exegetical steps. In view of this goal, in which the methodological system is to be oriented to the reality of the texts, it is most important that the system be freed from the unintentional but actual influences of the historical growth of the method.

Redaction

The work and understanding of redaction criticism were an outgrowth of the nineteenth-century literary-critical school, especially its Pentateuchal criticism. Its understanding is best reflected by Eissfeldt: "Pentateuchal criticism has become accustomed to use a unified terminology in so far as it denotes as redactors those who brought the material together, in distinction to the compilers or authors of the individual 'documents,' 'books' or 'sources'" (1965:239) or: "There is a distinction, for the most part clearly recognizable, between the author, organically shaping the material, and the redactor working mechanically" (1965:240). A redactor is understood in opposition to an author (see Koch, 1969:57).

This understanding has changed significantly through the influence of form criticism, and the most recent methodologies by Koch (1969: 57–59), Richter (1971:165–73), and Barth and Steck (48–53) reflect this change (see also Wharton). For all of them, redaction history concerns the entire history of the *written* texts (i.e., larger texts) from their first to their last literary layer, including the last gloss. Redaction is defined by the opposition "oral–written" (Koch; Barth and Steck) or "small and composed literary units" (Richter). Fohrer et al. are an exception (136–47). They distinguish between "composition" for layers before the final literary edition and "redaction" for their final composition. Here, "redaction" is defined by the opposition "earlier–later compositions" within the written tradition. Thus, we are currently confronted with three different methodological definitions of redaction.

The differences between the traditional understanding and the understanding expressed by Koch, Richter, and Barth and Steck are also reflected in exegetical publications in which redaction-critical/historical studies have been mushrooming during the last half-generation. A random sample shows that Thiel (e.g., 33–42), Rietzschel (e.g., 127–79), Wanke (e.g., 144–49), Mittmann (e.g., 168–69), Fuss (390–406), and Kilian (e.g., 284–313) operate essentially on the traditional assumptions of redaction criticism. They regard redactions as secondary compilations of primary sources, basic layers or blocks of literary traditions written by authors. Richter's position on the *Retterbuch* in Judges (1963) as expressed in his *Traditions-geschichtliche Untersuchungen* is not clear. He does not emphasize redaction criticism, but he distinguishes between oral and written traditions on the one hand and between a *Verfasser*

(1963:329–43, with elaborate emphasis!) and successive *Erweiterungen* within the written traditions on the other. If Richter understood the whole literary history as redaction history in 1963 (as suggested in 1971), then his "author" is also a redactor, and a subsequent distinction between an author-redactor and expansion-redactors becomes necessary. If he did not understand the whole literary history as redaction history, then he operated on the traditional distinction between author and redactors, a position different from the one taken in 1971.

On the other hand, Seitz (e.g., 303–5), Weimar (e.g., 91, 161–68), Zenger (e.g., 161–63), and Barth (e.g., 79–92, 208, 277) operate on the assumptions advanced by Koch, Richter, and Barth and Steck. They use the term "redactors" for the composers of original literary works or of blocks of original traditions (Barth, Seitz) as well as for the combiners of "sources," such as the "Jehovist" (JE), even though they describe the activities of those combiners in the sense of the work of authors (Zenger, Weimar). On the ambivalence on this issue in traditional redaction criticism, see Eissfeldt (1965:239).

These differences are by and large more than terminological. They result in part from a different understanding of the nature of the OT literature and in part from the different designs of the exegetical system. However, their existence indicates the need for a more critical clarification than has been offered so far of all the factors involving redaction criticism and its relationship to related exegetical steps. There is no room here for this task, nor for an analysis of the specific differences between the individual designs presented or practiced so far and their causes, but a few suggestions are in order.

First, the understanding of redaction and redactor should, speaking methodologically, be the same for all the literatures with which we are concerned and not be oriented to certain parts of the Hebrew Bible and the specific kinds of their literary transmission alone. It is precisely because of the different kinds of literary transmission of the various corpora of the OT literature (and within these corpora) that we need a consistent understanding of redactional activities that allows us to determine what is redactional in all of them and what is other than redactional.

Second, it can be observed in virtually all the publications past and present that verbs such as collect, compose, compile, combine, connect, assemble, and their respective nouns are used for the description of the activities of authors as well as of secondary redactors. It seems that this is not primarily the result of the fluctuating usage of words. Rather it indicates that—to say it in the traditional framework—both authors and redactors can use *techniques* of collecting, composing, compiling, combining, and connecting. In other words, these activities as such constitute neither a difference between authors and redactors nor the activities of redactors alone, if one understands under redaction the total process of

the literary transmission of corpora. If this were so, one would have to
add activities such as framing, expanding, adding, amending, inserting,
interpolating, glossing, etc., and one would also have to reintroduce the
figure "author" as one among several subcategories of those carrying on
redactional activity. In sum, all the emphasis would have to rest on the
distinctions within redactional activities, and the term redaction would
become a superterm for almost all the literary activities concerning at
least larger corpora—in essence synonymous with the creation and the
transmission of literary corpora.

Third, the antipathy of the traditional form-critical movement
against the concept of author is known. There was good reason. To be
sure, the understanding of redactors as opposed to authors must not be,
and is no longer, depreciated as "mechanistic" or irrelevant, even as one
may still—or again—prefer to admit to different degrees of literary
creativity in our literature. However, the fact that we should not uncriti-
cally carry the notion of modern authorship into our concept of ancient
Israelite texts does not mean that there are no authors to be found there.
In some cases, it is indeed difficult to distinguish between what was
newly created by an author and a corpus edited by a redactor. This
difficulty comes partly from our insufficient insights and partly from the
material itself, in which both factors interpenetrate. Such interpenetra-
tions should be appreciated wherever they occur. Fohrer et al. could be
on the right track in using "composers" for this phenomenon, but it is not
typical for the totality of the OT literature. In many cases, one can
clearly distinguish between the work characteristic of an ancient author
and that of redactors. So long as we must not abandon the concept of
author in principle, we will have to account for it methodologically. If
we subsume it under "redactional activity," assuming that all redactors
were authors or all authors were redactors, we lose the unavoidable distinction between characteristically different types of literary activities,
and we also confuse the meanings of both words, which have exactly
referred to those different types of literary activity in our modern languages. This distinction is even more important because both terms,
author and redactor, refer to literary activities, which is why literary
activity as such (e.g., vis-à-vis orality) cannot be identified with redaction
history alone, even as it was not identified with authors alone in the
literary-critical school.

Finally, one should also avoid understanding redaction history as a
term for a specific exegetical step rather than as a description of the
phenomenon of the history of redaction itself. Barth and Steck (48)
understand it as the process of *synthesis*, which is preceded by literary
criticism as analysis (27–34). The assignment of literary criticism and
redaction history to two separate exegetical processes, analysis and synthesis, evokes the question of the balance of their system, in which

analysis and synthesis appear as correlative processes in the one method of *Überlieferungsgeschichte*.

III. THE UNITY OF HISTORICAL EXEGESIS

The work of OT scholarship during the last generation has been characterized by intensive methodological efforts, a process that has by no means come to an end. These efforts have focused not only on the individual methods but also on the method for the methods. Exegesis of texts is more than the application of individual methods, or even their cumulative application. At stake is the methodological unity in the plurality of the methods, a unity that should be commensurate with the unity and wholeness of the texts. This problem is generally recognized (see Grobel: 412–13; Fichtner: 1221–23; Cazelles: 100; Keck and Tucker: 296–300; Fretheim: 839; Kaiser: 24; Koch, 1976:100–110; Barth and Steck: 81–84; Richter, 1971:179–87; Fohrer et al.: 27–30, 148–71; Rendtorff, 1977:82, 143; among others). It is also recognized that the historical succession in which the methods emerged means neither that one method has replaced the others nor that the order in which we may apply them has to follow the sequence of their historical emergence (see Kuhl, 1957:1227). The historically developed methods must become parts of an exegetical system that has an integrity of its own.

However, there are differences among those who use and describe these methods systematically, quite apart from those who do exegesis in different ways. The partially controversial discussion surrounding the latest methodological designs already points to the need for further clarification of major problems intrinsic to the system's approach.

We can refer only in passing to the increasing number of publications in which selected methods are combined either explicitly or actually in exegetical work. The variability of such combinations seems to be as broad as the number of methods allows.[21] In many instances, these combinations are dictated by specific interests of the authors. In some, however, they seem to or do imply an author's understanding that he/she is doing *comprehensive* exegesis defined in principle by the dominant role of one method or a combination of methods.[22] The variety in these approaches also points to major differences in the systemic assumptions.

---

[21] For example, literary criticism is combined with form criticism, history, history of religion, rhetorical criticism, redaction criticism, linguistics, tradition history. In addition, form criticism is combined with tradition history, and tradition history with redaction criticism. See on this issue Horst (1124), Fichtner (1222), Kuhl (1959b:1530), and the titles in the bibliography of this essay.

[22] See, e.g., Richter (1963), tradition history; Koch (1976), structural form criticism; Mittmann, literary criticism and tradition history; Weimar, redaction history; Rendtorff (1977), tradition history.

This fact can be observed in the systemic differences in commentaries and commentary series.

In the published methodologies themselves, two issues are of particular importance: the sequence in which the exegetical steps should be employed and the supremacy of one method over all the others. Until the late 1960s, the sequence of the steps in exegesis does not seem to have been a methodological problem. It had been inherited from the exegetical tradition and consisted of the order of the methods' historical emergence, augmented where necessary by methods known from the classical philological tradition. Kaiser's arrangement of the steps (1963, trans. 1967)—text criticism, meter, literary criticism, form criticism, tradition history, concluding exegesis—is a clear example for both the cumulative character of the system and its self-evident logic.

The situation changed when Richter (1971) made a methodological issue out of the custom by demanding an unalterable sequence of steps consistent with an understanding of a science of OT literature: (1) exegesis of smaller units in the order literary criticism, form(s), genre, tradition (whereby the exegesis of forms, genre, and tradition has to branch out synchronically and diachronically); (2) exegesis of the large corpora—compositions and redactions; (3) content. Fohrer et al. have adopted Richter's system with some refinements. These refinements consist of the addition of text criticism; an extra step for linguistic analysis after literary criticism; the division of tradition criticism into criticism of motif, tradition, and transmission; an explicit separation of composition criticism and redaction criticism; the application of all these steps to small units (except in part for redaction criticism); and the detailed and comprehensive exegesis of content, followed by the theological critique. However, they also leave no doubt that the sequence of steps is necessary because of the *Sache* (27).

Barth and Steck outline a different basic sequence. First they undertake *analytical* steps moving backwards from text criticism to the Hebrew text. They then determine the text's oldest layer form-critically and from there move to the oral prestages through tradition history. They reverse the process to *synthesis*, by which tradition history is complemented by transmission history. Redaction history follows, and the comprehensive *Einzelexegese* concludes the process.

The similarities and differences in these models cannot be further analyzed at this point. Nonetheless, they are sufficient to indicate that the sequence of steps as such has become a methodological problem and that the clarification of this issue is now an urgent task for both substantive and didactic reasons.

Also at issue is the question of whether any particular method should govern all of exegesis. Koch's view on the matter is known. He has upgraded it (1976) by the concept of an all-encompassing *strukturale*

Formgeschichte. Richter, Barth and Steck, and Fohrer have no such concept. For them, the all-encompassing step, if any, is the final comprehensive exegesis or the final synthesis that pulls together the results of all the previous steps. Rendtorff, on the other hand, proposes—on the basis of a forceful critique of the entire traditional model of exegesis—to reconstruct the exegetical method under the guidance of transmission history. It seems that Weimar is moving toward redaction history as the encompassing model.

To be sure, in all of these cases the proposed dominant method is understood as pervading all the other methods without replacing them and not as one segment of the methodology alone. And in each case the reasons for a model are substantial and in no way mechanical. Yet just because this is the case, the different models suggest substantive and heuristic differences of larger proportions and once more indicate the transitional stage of the present methodological situation.

It is not the task of this review to outline the program of an exegetical methodology, but a few points should be mentioned which affect such a program. The very first task seems to be that we distinguish between our description of the specific exegetical steps and the traditional labels for our methods. Exegetical steps are means of access to the texts; these steps are developed in accordance with questions suggested by the texts. Some of these means of access are no longer necessarily to be associated with the traditional label of a specific method. The cluster of terms such as style, form, forms, form-group, groups of forms, structure, composition, rhetorical or generic pattern, etc., and their diverse associations with literary criticism, form criticism, rhetorical criticism, redaction criticism, or their separate application, are a case in point. Another case of (mis)labeling is work being done under form *Geschichte* that is in fact either form sociology or tradition history (regardless of whether it is done analytically and/or synthetically). Form criticism has never seriously distinguished between the two steps. The fact that both aspects should not be separated does not mean that they must not be distinguished methodologically. In sum, the current situation no longer supports the assumption of a self-evident congruity of our descriptions of methodical steps and our traditional labels.

A second task should be to conceptualize the correlation of these steps in a system that responds to an integrated approach evoked by the texts and at the same time reflects the critical interdependence of method and actual exegetical work. With regard to the plurality of text traditions in the Hebrew Bible, it may still be asked whether we have to speak about systems in which the steps are applied selectively and in variable correlations. In other words, the question is whether or not we should allow for variability in the system of steps itself. The question of the sequence of steps is certainly important, but it can be addressed only in conjunction with their systemic conceptualization, and not before or without it. In this regard, none of the proposals submitted so far in the methodologies has remained uncontested. In fact, each raises serious questions at certain points, regardless of the contention of unalterable sequence.

The almost universal positioning of redaction criticism demonstrates this point. Richter said (1971) that no one has as yet demanded that it stand at the beginning; such a demand seemed to be absurd. Yet since then it has been advocated at least theoretically by Koch (1976: I, 31–32, 78ff.). Indeed, the rationale for this advocacy seems to be much stronger than is generally recognized. In fact, all the OT literature is without exception before us on the level of the final redaction. This final redaction implies not only mechanical work such as framing, glossing, etc. of preserved texts but also selecting, regrouping, recomposing, etc. of texts, and even reformulating of traditional texts themselves. Theoretically, we cannot legitimately assume that we have any text before us in its pre-redactional form and content unless we can show evidence for that fact. It is much more problematic first to establish original texts from the present texts and then to identify the later layers than to identify the latest layers first and then to inquire into their prehistory. Even the famous delimitation of small units accorded to literary criticism ignores the fact that the texts of those units—their beginnings and ends, their position in the context, and their form and content—are at least also, even primarily, redactional phenomena. We cannot assume their present form to be older unless we have shown that they are not redactional. Such an assumption would require an *e silentio* redaction-critical judgment at the beginning, which is not exactly methodologically controlled exegesis. This factor alone raises questions about the methodological legitimacy of an exclusive focus on the small units at the beginning of the process with the redaction-critical step at its end. Certainly, it does not suggest a total reversal of the process, but it does raise the possibility, if not the necessity, of focusing from the outset on the interdependence of larger redactional works and their smaller units. If that were so, the conceptualization of the sequence of steps in the system would for this reason alone have to look quite different from anything that we have seen so far.

It is frequently asserted that the redactional layers are *also* deserving of interpretation, and not only the separate "sources." This assertion, legitimate as it is, is not a serious methodological issue. The methodological issue is the question of the *place* where redaction criticism comes into exegesis. Our exegetical tradition suggests that redaction criticism continues to be an appendix to literary criticism and that its proper role in the methodological system has not yet received the attention it deserves. This deficit affects our concept of the system in its entirety.

The question of the supremacy of one method over the others is too complex to be pursued in detail here. The differences of the proposals made are more than terminological in nature and affect the conceptualization of a holistic, integrated methodology. In this regard, it is important that we distinguish between a holistic conceptualization of the entire OT literature and a holistic conceptualization of the exegesis of texts. Nevertheless, the texts too are subject to such claims from form criticism, tradition history, science of literature, and perhaps redaction criticism. In this regard it is important that any claim distinguish between the usage of a label for a particular step as distinct from others and the usage of the same label for the process involving all the steps. If one considers that the unity of the system must be commensurate with the unity of the texts and recognizes that all of the aspects implied in the steps must play their role in setting forth that unity which must in one way or the other happen in a final all-encompassing step, one could conclude that the more neutral term "historical exegesis" is sufficient for the time being.

Finally, historical exegesis should always be aware of the anthropological factor in the texts. This does not mean the human mind underneath the texts, nor does it mean that the focus of exegesis should move away from the texts to the humans behind them. The anthropological factor is the presence of the speakers and writers in their texts. These texts did not come into existence mechanically, even where redactors may have operated only mechanically. They owe their existence to human beings, i.e., to their concerns, attentions, efforts, decisions, learnedness, and intentions. These humans speak in the texts and are part of their historicality. To ignore this factor could mean another idealistic or mechanistic misunderstanding of the phenomenon "text": idealistic where the texts are treated as expendable shells of ideas or of meaning to be abstracted from the shells even where one stresses their semantic nature; and mechanistic where they are treated only as texts at our disposal despite our claims to the validity of the hermeneutical circle, while the humans who produced them are barred from their own texts by our methodologically sophisticated historical exegesis. These human beings were part of their historical texts. In fact, they are the real sources of the texts. The inclusion of this factor into the historicality of the texts is as important as the historical exegesis of the texts themselves. Taken seriously, it could add a set of questions to our methodology which so far has virtually totally eluded us. And surely, inasmuch as these human texts were concerned with theological matters, their theological concerns must also be an intrinsic part of historical exegesis, or it does not do its job. This means that the "theological critique" has to be part of all the exegetical steps and should not be relegated to a separate step at the very end of the exegetical process, as Fohrer et al. suggest (156–71). At the very least, the inclusion of the anthropological factor into historical exegesis can help us to encounter the spirit breathing in the texts and to avoid being killed by seeing only their letter.[23]

BIBLIOGRAPHY

Alonso-Schökel, Luis
  1960a   "Genera Litteraria." *VD* 38: 3–15.
  1960b   "Die stilistische Analyse bei den Propheten." Pp. 154–64
                      in *Congress Volume: Oxford, 1959.* VTSup 7. Leiden:
                      E. J. Brill.

Anderson, Bernhard
  1974   "The New Frontier of Rhetorical Criticism: A Tribute to
                      James Muilenburg." Pp. ix–xviii in *Rhetorical Criticism:
                      Essays in Honor of James Muilenburg.* Ed. J. J. Jackson
                      and M. Kessler. PTMS 1. Pittsburgh: Pickwick.

Barth, Hermann
  1977   *Die Jesaja-Worte in der Josiazeit.* WMANT 48.
                      Neukirchen-Vluyn: Neukirchener Verlag.

Barth, Hermann, and Odil Hannes Steck
  1973   *Exegese des Alten Testaments.* 4th ed. Neukirchen-
                      Vluyn: Neukirchener Verlag.

Baumgärtel, Friedrich
  1957   "Bibelkritik, I. AT." Cols. 1184–88 in *RGG*, Vol. 1. 3d
                      ed. Tübingen: J. C. B. Mohr (Paul Siebeck).

Boecker, Hans Jochen
  1959   "Pentateuch." Cols. 109–14 in *EKL*, Vol. 3. Göttingen:
                      Vandenhoeck & Ruprecht.

Campbell, Antony F.
  1975   *The Ark Narrative (1 Sam 4–6; 2 Sam 6): A Form-
                      critical and Traditio-historical Study.* SBLDS 16. Mis-
                      soula, MT: Scholars Press.

Cazelles, Henri
  1976   "Biblical Criticism, OT." Pp. 98–102 in *IDBSup.*

Coats, George W.
  1976   "Tradition Criticism, OT." Pp. 912–14 in *IDBSup.*

Coote, Robert B.
  1976   "Tradition, Oral, OT." Pp. 914–16 in *IDBSup.*

[23] The manuscript of this essay was completed in September 1979. Once more I am greatly indebted to Mrs. Eleanor Johnston, my research associate in 1979 at the Institute for Antiquity and Christianity, for shepherding this article from my manuscript to the volume editors, and also to the editors themselves for their efforts. I dedicate this essay to Klaus Koch, eminent scholar, colleague, and friend, who in more than one way has set new horizons for OT studies and certainly for the methodological discussion itself.

1976   "Tradition, Oral, OT." Pp. 914–16 in *IDBSup*.

Cross, Frank Moore, Jr.
1973a   "The Cultus of the Israelite League." Pp. 77–144 in
                        Canaanite Myth and Hebrew Epic. Cambridge, MA:
                        Harvard University Press.
1973b   "The Themes of the Book of Kings and the Structure of
                        the Deuteronomistic History." Pp. 274–89 in *Canaanite
                        Myth and Hebrew Epic*. Cambridge, MA: Harvard Uni-
                        versity Press.

Cross, Frank Moore, Jr., and David Noel Freedman
1975   *Studies in Ancient Yahwistic Poetry*. SBLDS 21. Mis-
                        soula, MT: Scholars Press.

Dever, William G., and W. Malcolm Clark
1977   "The Patriarchal Traditions." Pp. 70–148 in *Israelite
                        and Judaean History*. Ed. John H. Hayes and J. Max
                        well Miller. Philadelphia: Westminster.

De Vries, Simon J.
1962   "Biblical Criticism, History of." Pp. 413–18 in *IDB*, Vol.
                        1. Nashville: Abingdon.

Eissfeldt, Otto
1956   *Einleitung in das Alte Testament*. 2d ed. (1st ed. 1934).
                        Tübingen: J. C. B. Mohr (Paul Siebeck).
1960   "Literarkritische Schule." Cols. 388–90 in *RGG*, Vol. 4.
                        3d ed. Tübingen: J. C. B. Mohr (Paul Siebeck).
1965   *The Old Testament, An Introduction*. Trans. Peter R.
                        Ackroyd from 3d German ed. (1964). New York and
                        Evanston: Harper & Row.

Elliger, Karl
1966   *Leviticus*. HAT 4. Tübingen: J. C. B. Mohr (Paul
                        Siebeck).

Engnell, Ivan
1969   *A Rigid Scrutiny: Critical Essays on the Old Testament*.
                        Trans. John T. Willis. Nashville: Vanderbilt University.

Fichtner, Johannes
1956   "Exegese I. Des AT." Cols. 1220–25 in *EKL*, Vol. 1. Göt-
                        tingen: Vandenhoeck & Ruprecht.

Floyd, Michael H.
1980   "Oral Tradition as a Problematic Factor in the Historical
                        Interpretation of Poems in the Law and the Prophets."
                        Ph.D. dissertation, Claremont Graduate School.

Fohrer, Georg
1964   *Überlieferung und Geschichte des Exodus*. BZAW 91.
                        Berlin: A. Töpelmann.

Fohrer, Georg, et al.
1973   *Exegese des Alten Testaments*. Heidelberg: Quelle und

Meyer.

Freedman, David Noel
1962   "Pentateuch." Pp. 711–27 in *IDB*, Vol. 3.

Fretheim, Terence E.
1976   "Source Criticism, OT." Pp. 838–39 in *IDBSup*.

Fuss, Werner
1972   *Die deuteronomistische Pentateuchredaktion in Exodus 3–17*. BZAW 126. Berlin and New York: Walter de Gruyter.

Gerstenberger, Erhard
1980   *Der bittende Mensch*. WMANT 51. Neukirchen-Vluyn: Neukirchener Verlag.

Gottwald, Norman K.
1979   *The Tribes of Yahweh*. Maryknoll, NY: Orbis Books.

Grobel, Kendrick
1962   "Biblical Criticism." Pp. 407–13 in *IDB*, Vol. 1.

Habel, Norman
1971   *Literary Criticism of the Old Testament*. Philadelphia: Fortress.

Hanson, Paul D.
1975   *The Dawn of Apocalyptic*. Philadelphia: Fortress.

Hardmeier, Christof
1978   *Texttheorie und biblische Exegese*. BEvT 79. Munich: Chr. Kaiser.

Hayes, John, and J. Maxwell Miller, eds.
1977   *Israelite and Judaean History*. Philadelphia: Westminster.

Hempel, Johannes
1934   *Die althebräische Literatur*. Handbuch der Literaturwissenschaft. Wildpart-Potzdam: Akademische Verlagsgesellschaft Athenaion.

Hesse, Franz
1961   "Schriftauslegung I. Im AT." Cols. 1513–15 in *RGG*, Vol. 5. 3d ed. Tübingen: J. C. B. Mohr (Paul Siebeck).

Hölscher, Gustav
1922   *Geschichte der israelitischen und jüdischen Religion*. Giessen: A. Töpelmann.
1952   *Geschichtsschreibung in Israel*. Lund: CWK Gleerup.

Horst, Friedrich
1958   "Literaturgeschichte, I. Des AT." Cols. 1124–26 in *EKL*, Vol. 2. Göttingen: Vandenhoeck & Ruprecht.

Jackson, Jared J., and Martin Kessler, eds.
1974   *Rhetorical Criticism: Essays in Honor of James*

Kaiser, Otto, and Werner Georg Kümmel
1967   *Exegetical Method.* Trans. E. V. N. Goetchius. New
              York: Seabury. German original: *Einführung in die exe-
              getischen Methoden.* Munich: Chr. Kaiser, 1963.

Keck, Leander E.
1976   "Literary criticism." P. 547 in *IDBSup.*

Keck, Leander E., and Gene M. Tucker
1976   "Exegesis." Pp. 296–303 in *IDBSup.*

Kilian, Rudolf
1966   *Die vorpriesterlichen Abrahamsüberlieferungen.* BBB
              24. Bonn: Peter Hanstein.

Knierim, Rolf
1973   "Old Testament Form Criticism Reconsidered." *Int* 27:
              435–68.

Knight, Douglas A.
1973   *Rediscovering the Traditions of Israel.* SBLDS 9. Mis-
              soula, MT: Society of Biblical Literature.

Knight, Douglas A., ed.
1977   *Tradition and Theology in the Old Testament.* Phila-
              delphia: Fortress.

Koch, Klaus
1964   *Was ist Formgeschichte?* Neukirchen-Vluyn: Neukirch-
              ener Verlag.
1969   *The Growth of the Biblical Tradition: The Form-
              Critical Method.* Trans. S. M. Cupitt from 2d German
              ed. New York: Charles Scribner's Sons.
1973   "Reichen die formgeschichtlichen Methoden für die
              Gegenwartsaufgaben der Bibelwissenschaft zu?" *TLZ* 98:
              801–14.
1974   *Was ist Formgeschichte?* 3d ed. Neukirchen-Vluyn:
              Neukirchener Verlag.
1976   *Amos.* AOAT 20. Neukirchen-Vluyn: Neukirchener Ver-
              lag.

Köhler, Ludwig
1923   *Deuterojesaja (Jesaja 40–55) stilkritisch untersucht.*
              BZAW 37. Giessen: A. Töpelmann.

Kraus, Hans-Joachim
1956   "Bibelkritik, I. AT." Cols. 454–57 in *EKL*, Vol. 1. Göt-
              tingen: Vandenhoeck & Ruprecht.
1978   *Psalmen.* 5th ed. BKAT 15/1–2. Neukirchen-Vluyn:
              Neukirchener Verlag.

Krentz, Edgar
1975   *The Historical Critical Method.* Philadelphia: Fortress.

Kuhl, Curt
1957 "Bibelwissenschaft, geschichtlich: I. Bibelwissenschaft des AT." Cols. 1227–36 in *RGG*, Vol. 1. 3d ed. Tübingen: J. C. B. Mohr (Paul Siebeck).
1959a "Traditionswesen in Israel." Cols. 1476–79 in *EKL*, Vol. 3. Göttingen: Vandenhoeck & Ruprecht.
1959b "Überlieferungsgeschichtliche Forschung." Cols. 1525–30 in *EKL*, Vol. 3. Göttingen: Vandenhoeck & Ruprecht.

Lohfink, Norbert
1963 *Das Hauptgebot*. AnBib 20. Rome: Pontifical Biblical Institute.

Mabee, Charles
1977 "The Problem of Setting in Hebrew Royal Judicial Narratives." Ph.D. dissertation, Claremont Graduate School. See also *VT* 30: 192–207; *ZAW* 92: 89–107.

McCarthy, Dennis J.
1978 *Treaty and Covenant*. AnBib 21A. Rome: Pontifical Biblical Institute.

Melugin, Roy F.
1976 *The Formation of Isaiah 40–55*. BZAW 141. Berlin and New York: Walter de Gruyter.

Mittmann, Siegfried
1975 *Deuteronomium 1:1–6:3 literarkritisch und traditionsgeschichtlich untersucht*. BZAW 139. Berlin and New York: Walter de Gruyter.

Muilenburg, James
1953 "A Study in Hebrew Rhetoric: Repetition and Style." Pp. 97–111 in *Congress Volume: Copenhagen, 1953*. VTSup 1. Leiden: E. J. Brill.
1956 "The Book of Isaiah: Chapters 40–66, Introduction and Exegesis." Pp. 381–419, 422–773 in *IB*, Vol. 5. New York and Nashville: Abingdon.
1969 "Form Criticism and Beyond." *JBL* 88: 1–18.

Noth, Martin
1957 *Überlieferungsgeschichtliche Studien*. 2d ed. (1st ed., 1943). Darmstadt: Wissenschaftliche Buchgesellschaft.

Otto, Eckart
1975 *Das Mazzotfest in Gilgal*. BWANT 107. Stuttgart: W. Kohlhammer.

Paulsen, Henning
1978 "Traditionsgeschichtliche Methode und religionsgeschichtliche Schule." *ZTK* 75: 20–55.

Perlitt, Lothar
1969   *Bundestheologie im Alten Testament.* WMANT 36.
                Neukirchen-Vluyn: Neukirchener Verlag.

Rast, Walter E.
1972   *Tradition History and the Old Testament.* Philadel-
                phia: Fortress.

Rendtorff, Rolf
1956   "Formen und Gattungen, I. AT." Cols. 1303–10 in *EKL*,
                Vol. 1. Göttingen: Vandenhoeck & Ruprecht.
1963   *Die Gesetze in der Priesterschrift.* 2d ed. FRLANT 62.
                Göttingen: Vandenhoeck & Ruprecht.
1971   "Beobachtungen zur altisraelitischen Geschichtsschrei-
                bung anhand der Geschichte vom Aufstieg Davids." Pp.
                428–39 in *Probleme biblischer Theologie: Gerhard von
                Rad zum 70. Geburtstag.* Ed. H. W. Wolff. Munich:
                Chr. Kaiser.
1977   *Das überlieferungsgeschichtliche Problem des Penta-
                teuch.* BZAW 147. Berlin and New York: Walter
                de Gruyter.

Reventlow, Henning Graf
1961   *Das Heiligkeitsgesetz formgeschichtlich untersucht.*
                WMANT 6. Neukirchen-Vluyn: Neukirchener Verlag.

Richter, Wolfgang
1963   *Traditionsgeschichtliche Untersuchungen zum Richter-
                buch.* BBB 18. Bonn: Peter Hanstein.
1970   *Die sogenannten vorprophetischen Berufungsberichte.*
                FRLANT 101. Göttingen: Vandenhoeck & Ruprecht.
1971   *Exegese als Literaturwissenschaft.* Göttingen: Vanden-
                hoeck & Ruprecht.

Rietzschel, Claus
1966   *Das Problem der Urrolle.* Gütersloh: Mohn.

Robertson, David A.
1972   *Linguistic Evidence in Dating Early Hebrew Poetry.*
                SBLDS 3. Missoula, MT: Society of Biblical Literature.
1976   "Literature, The Bible as." Pp. 547–51 in *IDBSup.*
1977   *The Old Testament and the Literary Critic.* Philadel-
                phia: Fortress.

Sæbø, Magne
1969   *Sacharja 9–14: Untersuchungen von Text und Form.*
                WMANT 34. Neukirchen-Vluyn: Neukirchener Verlag.

Schmid, Hans Heinrich
1976   *Der sogenannte Jahwist.* Zurich: Theologischer Verlag.

Schmidt, Werner H.
1964   *Die Schöpfungsgeschichte der Priesterschrift.* WMANT
                17. Neukirchen-Vluyn: Neukirchener Verlag.

Schulte, Hannelis
1972   *Die Entstehung der Geschichtsschreibung im Alten Israel.* BZAW 128. Berlin and New York: Walter de Gruyter.

Seitz, Gottfried
1971   *Redaktionsgeschichtliche Studien zum Deuteronomium.* BWANT 93. Stuttgart: W. Kohlhammer.

Smith, Clyde Curry
1977   "Jehu and the Black Obelisk of Shalmaneser III." Pp. 71–106 in *Scripture in History and Theology: Essays in Honor of J. Coert Rylaarsdam.* Ed. A. L. Merrill and T. W. Overholt. PTMS 17. Pittsburgh: Pickwick.

Smith, Morton
1971   *Palestinian Parties and Politics that Shaped the Old Testament.* New York and London: Columbia University Press.

Steck, Karl Gerhard
1959   "Tradition." Pp. 1471–76 in *EKL*, Vol. 3. Göttingen: Vandenhoeck & Ruprecht.

Steck, Odil Hannes
1967   *Israel und das gewaltsame Geschick der Propheten.* WMANT 23. Neukirchen-Vluyn: Neukirchener Verlag.
1975   *Der Schöpfungsbericht der Priesterschrift.* FRLANT 115. Göttingen: Vandenhoeck & Ruprecht.

Thiel, Winfried
1973   *Die deuteronomistische Redaktion von Jeremia 1–25.* WMANT 41. Neukirchen-Vluyn: Neukirchener Verlag.

Thompson, Thomas L.
1974   *The Historicity of the Patriarchal Narratives.* BZAW 133. Berlin and New York: Walter de Gruyter.

Tucker, Gene M.
1976   "Form Criticism, OT." Pp. 342–45 in *IDBSup.*

Van Seters, John
1975   *Abraham in History and Tradition.* New Haven: Yale University Press.

Wanke, Gunther
1971   *Untersuchungen zur sogenannten Baruchschrift.* BZAW 122. Berlin: Walter de Gruyter.

Weimar, Peter
1977   *Untersuchungen zur Redaktionsgeschichte des Pentateuch.* BZAW 146. Berlin and New York: Walter de Gruyter.

Weiss, Meir
1972   "Die Methode der 'Total-Interpretation'" Pp. 88–112 in
              Congress Volume: Uppsala, 1971. VTSup 22. Leiden:
              E. J. Brill.

Wellek, Rene, and Austin Warren
1975   *Theory of Literature*. 3d ed. New York and London:
              Harcourt Brace Jovanovich.

Wellhausen, Julius
1963   *Die Composition des Hexateuchs und der historischen
              Bücher des Alten Testaments*. 4th ed. (2d ed., 1889).
              Berlin: Walter de Gruyter.

Westermann, Claus
1967   *Basic Forms of Prophetic Speech*. Trans. H. C. White
              from *Grundformen prophetischer Rede*, 1960. Philadel-
              phia: Westminster.

Wharton, James A.
1976   "Redaction Criticism, OT." Pp. 729–32 in *IDBSup*.

Wilson, Robert R.
1980   *Prophecy and Society in Ancient Israel*. Philadelphia:
              Fortress.

Wolff, Hans Walter
1964   *Gesammelte Studien zum Alten Testament*. TBü 22.
              Munich: Chr. Kaiser.

Zenger, Erich
1971   *Die Sinaitheophanie: Untersuchungen zu Jahwist und
              Elohist*. Forschung zur Bibel 3. Würzburg: Echter-
              Verlag.

5

Exploring New Directions

Robert C. Culley

THE OLD AND THE NEW

No discipline is static. New directions are always emerging, and this is true of biblical studies. Frequently the impulse to try something new comes from other disciplines and even from scholars outside biblical studies who for one reason or another turn to the Bible as the object of their analysis. The word "new" is used descriptively. What is new is not necessarily better than what is old.

It is not new for biblical studies to turn to other disciplines. The Hebrew Bible is an ancient religious text with its setting in the ancient Near East. Both the text and the setting have been major focuses in OT studies for some time. Almost any approach or method that can be applied to texts, history, culture, religion, and faith is potentially useful in biblical studies. Thus, archaeology, history, philology, various kinds of textual analysis, as well as anthropological and sociological theories of religion and society, have been employed by biblical scholars and have found their place in OT studies.

More recently stimulus for new work in biblical studies has come from approaches like structuralism and phenomenology or disciplines like folklore, sociology, and anthropology. Substantial work is now appearing in which biblical scholars make extensive use of methods derived from these areas or apply the results of fieldwork in folklore, sociology, and anthropology. The application of even more recent approaches like cybernetics, information theory, and systems analysis can only be noted (Wagner; Buss, 1979; Andersen, 1976).

Structuralism, phenomenology, folklore, sociology, and anthropology have served as broad headings in organizing material for this chapter. However, it is clear that these headings can provide only a general indication of the kinds of topics to be discussed. The list is heterogeneous. Structuralism and phenomenology can refer to broad philosophical stances or ways of dealing with reality. Or, these terms can refer to methods used at a lower level and found in several disciplines (e.g., structural analysis). On the other hand, folklore, sociology, and anthropology designate disciplines each of which embraces a whole range of perspectives and methods.

In order to provide a clear structure for this chapter some further modifications of this list of headings will be necessary. A distinction will be made between those scholars who direct their attention principally to the text of the Hebrew Bible and those who concentrate more on the social and cultural setting from which the text arose. Those scholars who focus on the text do so because they are interested in the nature of language. Most but not all structuralist analysis of biblical texts betrays this interest. But so do other analytic methods like discourse analysis and narrative analysis, and so these will be set alongside structural analysis. Phenomenology too, at least as it will be treated here, concerns itself with the question of language, as we will see in Paul Ricoeur's work on symbol, forms of discourse, and text. On the other hand, the folkloristic, anthropological, and sociological approaches in biblical research tend to focus on the context or setting of the text, on the society, religion, and culture of ancient Israel, although the text is still important as the major source of information for reconstructing these aspects of the world of that people.

There are at least two good reasons for paying attention to new directions. First, while it is true that some of these experiments will remain marginal and others will disappear, there will be those that will persist and develop into significant movements in biblical studies of the future. Second, examining new directions may lead to a reconsideration of older more established approaches. When this is done, the question of method in biblical studies is posed. Even though a preoccupation with method may lead to fundamental philosophical questions seemingly far from the rich biblical tradition that has attracted scholars in the first place, it is not an idle exercise to reflect on what we are doing when we study the Bible. If some sense of humility is thereby evoked, the results must be considered salutary.

In choosing books and articles for comment and discussion here, we have given priority to those works which have made explicit and substantial use of perspectives, methods, theories, or fieldwork from the disciplines mentioned above. Even with that restriction we have also usually had to limit our attention to only the more recent developments.

I. FOCUS ON TEXT: THE NATURE OF LANGUAGE

While the approaches that focus on text are in many respects quite different, they do share an interest in the biblical text as a structure of language, and they desire to explore the implications of this (for some discussion, see Zaborski).

To study the Bible as language may include viewing it as literature. This perspective can only be noted here. In his book *Exegese als Literaturwissenschaft*, Wolfgang Richter argued that biblical study was first and foremost the study of literature. For him this meant working with methods of textual analysis already well established in biblical studies but also modifying them significantly so that they would deal only with literary questions (for further discussion, see the chapter by Rolf Knierim in the present volume). Luis Alonso-Schökel, his colleagues, and his students have long been concerned with literary style in the Hebrew Bible. On this side of the Atlantic, students of James Muilenburg have actively pursued literary questions of structure, style, and form under the heading of rhetorical criticism (see, for example, Jackson and Kessler). Finally, one can point to a rather different literary approach to the Bible in the writings of David Robertson (see the discussion by Knierim).

The subject of the text as language will be reviewed under four headings: discourse analysis; narrative analysis; structural analysis; and symbol, forms of discourse, and text as these are discussed in the work of Paul Ricoeur. The impetus for this kind of study has come from a rather wide range of fields, disciplines, and scholars outside biblical studies: linguistics (for a discussion of different models of text analysis, see Gülich and Raible; Dressler); folklore (Propp; Jason, 1977a, 1977b; Jason and Segal); the social anthropologist Claude Lévi-Strauss (his classic article on the analysis of myth); French literary structuralists (Greimas, 1966, 1970, 1977); and Paul Ricoeur, who came to the problem of language through his philosophical investigation, which, according to his own description, is both existential and phenomenological.

Discourse Analysis

Discourse analysis, at least as the term will be used here, applies the study of grammar to larger elements of discourse than simply phrases, clauses, and sentences (for a general description, see Newman). Discourse analysis is still very new to biblical studies. While some initial discussion of this approach with regard to OT prose texts may be found scattered through the work of Francis Andersen on the Hebrew sentence, the only extended analysis of a Hebrew prose text to appear so far is a treatment of the flood story by Robert Longacre, a linguist. Both Andersen and Longacre use a tagmemic approach which, because it is hierarchical, is flexible enough to take account of structures larger than the phrase and clause. In fact, tagmemic analysis can be expanded to consider structures of content as well. Richter's work also touches on this larger perception of grammar.

Longacre. Discourse analysis as described by Longacre is an attempt to cope with elements of texts larger than the phrase and the clause usually treated by grammar. Many new factors need to be accounted for and described: genre classification, overall discourse structure (beginnings, endings, episodes, high points), cast of participants, author viewpoint, and strands of cohesion (see Longacre and Levinson for the theory). Longacre distinguishes between a formal or surface structure (the formal features of grammar extended to cover larger units like paragraph and discourse) and a notional (semantic) or deep structure, which consists of "more elusive categories such as an inciting incident, rising tension, climax, dénouement . . . final suspense, and wrap-up" (260). First, Longacre identifies paragraphs by means of any grammatical markers present, such as introductory and concluding circumstantial clauses. Next, the thematic participant for each paragraph is identified, under the assumption that a paragraph usually highlights only one such participant. Paragraphs are also classified according to their internal structure (e.g., execution paragraph, sequence paragraph). Then the function of each paragraph is determined with regard to its position on the main story line (preview, aperture, paragraph in the rising tension, peak or climax, paragraph in the loosening tension, or wrap-up).

Longacre's work looks sufficiently important that more analysis of this type should be done on biblical texts so that a serious evaluation can be made. One should note how this approach not only covers a whole range of features on the formal level but also probes into the structure of content dealing with features like plot. The flood story is not an ideal text with which to initiate the study of rules for discourse in biblical Hebrew prose, for this story has long been considered by most scholars to be a composite work. A more restricted kind of discourse analysis, applied this time to a poetic text, may be seen in an article by William A. Smalley where he investigates chiasm in Amos as a form of patterned recursion, a special case of the recursion essential to all discourse whereby continuity and cohesion are produced.

Richter. Certain parallels to this kind of discourse analysis may be found in the work of Wolfgang Richter as well as that of some of his colleagues and students (notably Gross; Schweizer; and the monographs now appearing in the *Münchener Universitätsschriften: Fachbereich Kath. Theologie*, edited by Richter). While Richter does not use the term "discourse analysis," the element in his model that is called "structural form" consists of a similar analysis of those formal grammatical features of texts which indicate continuity through clauses linked together or which show breaks in the text. For example, the charts in the books by Gross and Schweizer show the features considered to be important for recognizing where clauses are bound together to form subsections of texts and where breaks occur to mark divisions between subsections. Three things seem to be especially significant for establishing breaks in the text: pronominal subjects referring back to nouns, pronominal suffixes referring back to nouns, and direct speeches. It is argued that these features will not cross over a major break in the text;

consequently, they are useful for establishing subsections. So far this approach has been confined to the formal side of the text rather than to content (but see Gross, 1979).

Narrative Analysis

While Longacre did make some attempt to describe narrative action and participants, his discussion of these aspects of narrative did not go very far. In the approach that will be called here "narrative analysis," most of the attention is focused on two features important to narrative: narrative action, or plot, and the major roles that participants can assume in narrative action.

A very influential figure in narrative (and structuralist) analysis is the Russian folklorist, Vladimir Propp, who some decades ago produced a classic study of a group of one hundred Russian fairy tales. Although the tales presented a wide variety of characters who performed many different actions, Propp noticed that this bewildering variety could be reduced to a basic set of seven roles and thirty-one narrative actions or functions. Using his one hundred tales and reducing them to the functions of the *dramatis personae*, Propp argued that all these tales could be reduced to one basic type, that is, they shared a common structure. While Propp's analysis was very specifically related to the group of tales he studied, many other scholars realized that his work contained important insights into narrative in general. Some have tried to apply his model of thirty-one functions directly to stories from narrative traditions other than Russian. Others have preferred to select elements from Propp's model that seem capable of generalization and to modify them so that they can be applied more widely. As far as the Hebrew Bible is concerned, a direct application of Propp can be found in a brief section of Jack Sasson's book on Ruth. It is understandable that the results are mixed, since Propp's model was developed for Russian fairy tales and not biblical narratives (on the use of Propp, see de Pury, 1975, 2:479–81, 497; 1979).

Culley. My own work (1974, 1975, 1976a, 1976b, 1978a, 1978b) is more closely related to the approach of Propp than to any of the other approaches to narrative discussed in this chapter. I have not tried to apply his list of thirty-one functions to biblical narratives. Since most OT narratives are relatively short, the simple application of Propp's analysis did not seem to me to be appropriate. It struck me as useful, however, to do what Propp did when he developed his method, that is, to gather together similar narratives in order to see what they had in common.

My own work has gone through two stages. At the start, I collected and compared some of the shortest stories to be found in biblical Hebrew. In my view the shortest stories would consist of the bare essentials of narrative, thereby making it possible to identify those features with regard to the action and the characters which would appear to be basic and indispensable. These stories were grouped according to similarity in narrative action: rescue from a difficult situation (miracle stories), escape from a difficult situation (deception stories), and punishment of a wrong (punishment stories). More recently my attention has shifted to longer and more complex narratives in order to see how basic patterns like the ones found in very short stories are combined to form longer narratives. Larger narratives seem to be constructed by combining sequences of action in various ways. By "sequences" or "action sequences" I mean the movement in narrative usually referred to as that from conflict to resolution or from tension to dénouement, although these terms are usually applied to the main action in a story. Traditional stories like those found in the Hebrew Bible seem to have more than one such movement portraying a transition from a situation of unbalance or incompleteness to a situation of balance or completeness. A wrong is committed and then punished. A dangerous or difficult situation develops, and a rescue or escape is accomplished. Such action sequences were labeled in terms of the action they describe, for example, wrong/wrong punished, difficulty/difficulty removed, and danger/danger averted.

There is much more to narrative than narrative action. Nevertheless, narrative action is especially important because it provides a framework within which the other elements of narrative, such as participants, are integrated. Before examining other elements in narrative, it would seem to be important to establish reliable and relevant ways of describing narrative action.

Jason. Mention should be made of an analysis of 1 Samuel 17 by a folklorist, Heda Jason (1979). Her approach, which she calls ethnopoetic, was developed over a number of years in several publications (see esp. 1977a, 1977b). Characteristic of Jason's method is her desire to examine folklore texts first of all as literature, that is, as works of art. Only after this has been done, she argues, can texts be interpreted as items of culture, or as communications, or as materials to be viewed in a sociological or psychological framework (1977b:VII). In the case of 1 Samuel 17, Jason uses her analysis to try to answer two questions: Does the text come from oral literature? To which genre does it belong? The examination of the text involves both narrative syntax, having to do with plot structure and character roles, and narrative semantics, dealing with matters of content and features like space and time. In testing for genre, Jason applies Propp's model for the heroic fairy tale and also that of another scholar, A. Skaftymov, developed for a certain kind of Russian epic. As a result of this analysis, Jason concludes that 1 Samuel 17 is a short prose record of a romantic epic possibly composed in verse. It is an oral work, or at least an imitation of such. These conclusions are perhaps less important than the fact that Jason has demonstrated how one may apply a model developed for folklore to biblical narrative.

Structural Analysis

Structuralism is so broad a phenomenon that most writers try to avoid summing it up in a definition. It can refer to a philosophical perspective, but more often it designates a method of analysis applied to languages and literary texts as well as a wide range of other phenomena. The definition of Jean Piaget stresses three characteristics of structuralism: the study of wholes, the study of these wholes as systems of transformations, and the study of these systems as self-regulating or closed. (But see the challenging and provocative statement in Kovacs, 1978.) In this section attention will be limited to structural analysis of literary texts—in this case biblical texts. The discussion will be arranged according to two major figures who have had great influence on the development of structural analysis of texts: Claude Lévi-Strauss, especially his article on the analysis of myth; and A. J. Greimas, who has for some years been developing a broad theory of text analysis (1966, 1970, 1977). While both have stimulated work on biblical texts, Greimas has perhaps had more impact on biblical scholars (see Beauchamp; Detweiler; Crossan, 1978; Bryce, 1977; McKnight).

Those Influenced by Lévi-Strauss

Leach. One of the earliest attempts at a structural analysis of texts in the Hebrew Bible was an application of the myth analysis of Lévi-Strauss. A British anthropologist, Edmund Leach, treated the early chapters of Genesis (1965, 1969a) and the last part of 2 Samuel (1969b). Following Lévi-Strauss, Leach assumes that myths are organized around insoluble paradoxes basic to existence (life/death, male/female). By multiplying variations, myth seeks to soften and thereby mediate these paradoxes. This method of analysis works with a set of versions or variants of a myth in order to establish the oppositions and mediations operating in the set. Plot is ignored. The real meaning of myth lies beneath the surface at the level where oppositions are mediated. This meaning is held to be the product of the unconscious mind at work within a group or society.

Three brief illustrations of Leach's analysis may be mentioned. In Genesis 1, Leach proposes a number of oppositions and mediations (e.g., sea/dry land, mediated by vegetation). Death is opposed to life; the first three days of creation where things are static are opposed to the last three days of creation where things are moving. No mediation is mentioned. In Genesis 2–3, the oppositions, some mediated and some not, are ones like Adam (living) coming from dust (static, dead). In the throne succession narrative of 2 Samuel, a major contradiction is mediated: land as a gift from God to Israel (basis for rule against intermarriage) and the land as conquered from foreigners (which led to intermarriage). Thus, oppositions of endogamy/exogamy and legitimacy/illegitimacy are basic oppositions the story seeks to blur.

Intriguing as these proposals are, they pose problems. For example, if the structure of oppositions and mediations is by definition hidden in the text, then it is both easy and difficult to argue for their presence. At the same time, there are many obvious and important aspects of these biblical texts, such as narrative action or plot, which are left out of Leach's analysis. Then, of course, there is the problem of presuppositions. Does myth really work this way? At the least, however, Leach has directed attention to a level of the text that may require more attention than it has received so far (for critique, see esp. Pitt-Rivers: 128–31, 135–41, 168; Culley, 1972b; Rogerson, 1974:109–12; Detweiler: 128–30).

Casalis. An instructive contrast to Leach may be found in an article by Mathieu Casalis in which he applies the work of Lévi-Strauss to Genesis 2–3 and 6–9. Casalis relates his work to the death of God debate in which, as he puts it, the death of the Absolute Signified has resulted in the liberation of the signifier. The divine center has collapsed. The semiology of myths not only rests on the conviction that the "subject" is an illusion but helps to destroy this illusion (compare Crossan, 1975). In contrast to Leach, Casalis relates the Genesis stories by proposing that they all have a pattern featuring the opposition wet/dry. Too much wet means no life (flood, pre-creation of P) while too much dry means no life (pre-creation of J). But a balance of the two means life (e.g., water and earth yield humanity).

Polzin. While the structural analysis of Robert Polzin has drawn on a number of sources and differs in many ways from that of other structuralists, he has been influenced more by Lévi-Strauss than by Greimas or Propp. For Polzin, structuralism is a "hermeneutical enterprise" that is "neither a science nor a distinctive methodology" (1977:1). In calling structural analysis a hermeneutic he appears to be fusing two phases in the process of interpretation that other structuralists are inclined to keep separate: explanation (the descriptive or exegetical phase) and understanding (the phase of appropriation). Other structuralists usually argue that they are seeking a method which is scientific in the sense that they are striving for a rigorous statement and an exacting analytical model (Charpentier: 53; Patte in the introduction to Calloud, 1976). Furthermore, Polzin argues that structuralism is three things: (1) objective, being self-conscious about the object; (2) deductive, producing a hypothetical deductive model; and (3) subjective, being self-conscious about the subject who is doing the analyzing. This inclusion of the subject in the process is not characteristic of structuralists, who are often chided for ignoring or even destroying the subject (see Casalis, above).

Polzin's analysis of texts, Job (1977:54–125) and Genesis 12, 20, and 26 (1975), shows that he is both flexible and eclectic. In the study of Job he draws on elements from Lévi-Strauss (his formula for myth), Greimas, Roland Barthes, T. Todorov, and group theory in mathematics. The Genesis article, on the other hand, refrains from overt references to other approaches, saying only that the approach is synchronic (analysis of the text as it stands), and concentrates on certain transformations (for a response, see Miscall). Three topics (wealth, progeny, and adultery) are traced in these three stories. It is argued that only in the last story are these three found in a satisfactory relationship.

Polzin's approach is in large part intuitive, and this is consonant with the role he gives the subject in interpretation. He feels free to pick and choose elements and features from many different methods since he uses these more to stimulate thinking about the text rather than to build a method. In fact, he seems now to be moving toward a broader formalist approach (1979).

Those Influenced by Greimas

The general theory being developed by Greimas is complex, to say the least, and no attempt will be made here to describe it. It will be sufficient to see how biblical scholars understand and use Greimas.

CADIR. A few analyses of OT texts have been produced by scholars associated with the Centre pour l'Analyse du Discours Religieux (CADIR) and have appeared in their journal, *Sémiotique et Bible* (1976, 1977a, 1977b). A full statement of their appropriation of the Greimasian model may be found in *Analyse Sémiotique des Textes*, which includes an analysis of Genesis 11. The description that follows is based on this book and an article by Jean Calloud (1979). Generally speaking, a structural or semiotic method aims at a formal description of the fundamental structures of a text associated with meaning. The question is not primarily what the text means but rather what makes meaning possible. How is the text able to say what it says? An essential tool is a language of description (metalanguage) different from ordinary language and capable of describing accurately the play of relationships among signifying elements in a text. Meaning is the effect produced by this play. It is also assumed that meaning is only possible through difference, and so it is the opposites and oppositions in the system of the text that produce the architecture of meaning.

With regard to narrative, a model has been developed in which analysis proceeds on two levels. The first is called the surface level. This is not the text as it stands but a first level of abstraction. This surface level is divided into two components, narrative and discursive. The narrative component views narrative as a series of states and transformations. States relate a subject to an object. The subject either possesses the object (S∨O) or does not (S∧O). Transformations, or performances, show changes from one state to another: subjects lose and gain objects. This usually happens through the intervention of another subject who takes or gives the object. The formula for this is A(S) —→[(S∨O) —→(S∧O)], that is, an action is taken by one subject which causes another subject to lose an object. For example, a villain steals the king's daughter, to put it in terms of Propp's fairy tales. Such a story would go on to relate the king's selection of and preparation of a hero who would pursue and confront the villain. The hero would win the battle and bring the daughter home to the acclamation of all. A series of states and transformations that moves from an initial state of loss to a final state of restoration (or possibly the reverse) is called a narrative program. A narrative program has four basic operations or performances: manipulation (getting the hero to act), competence (preparing the hero for the task), performance (confrontation between the hero and the villain resulting in the domination of the one over the other), and sanction (recognition of the hero or villain for who they are). Since it is held in this theory that a story is polemic in nature, a narrative program concerning a hero is always opposed by an anti-program concerning a villain.

The second component in the surface level is the discursive component. This is concerned with the units of content which clothe, so to speak, narrative programs. Units of content are called figures. A story like the Tower of Babel has several figures, such as tower, city, making bricks. These form part of a trajectory running through the story, and all have to do with construction. Other trajectories consisting of figures from the story have to do with language and displacement. These trajectories can be related to the roles of actors.

The second major level of the narrative model is the deep level. Here one is concerned with the logic of the relationships. Semiological isotopies are identified. For example, in the Tower of Babel story, a language isotopy contains the opposition /one language/ vs. /many languages/. A sociopolitical isotopy brings the oppositions /settled/ vs. /scattered/ or /unity of people/ vs. /plurality of people/. The major analytic device used here is the semiotic square, on which the basic oppositions and relationships can be displayed.

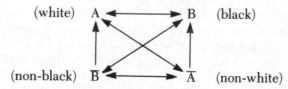

This is a relational model in which two contraries, A and B, are related to two other contraries, non-A and non-B, which are also contradictions of the first two terms. That is to say, white is contrary to black as by implication non-black is to non-white. White is contradictory to non-white as black is to non-black. The oppositions sought are those established by the text. Once all the oppositions established by the text are identified, one may search for a general opposition that includes and sums up all the others. For Genesis 11, it is suggested that /distinct/ vs. /indistinct/ does this. Indistinct describes the lack of distinction in having one language and one place whereas distinct describes the distinction produced by several languages and several places. It is also argued that the plot of narrative, translated into a movement of logic, can be traced on this square (e.g., A to $\overline{A}$ to B).

Patte. Since Daniel Patte and Judson Parker have done an analysis of Genesis 2–3, a brief mention should be made of Patte's approach, which has otherwise been applied to NT texts. Patte has also been influenced by Greimas, but he differs from CADIR in significant ways. Patte claims that his goal is to uncover the system of deep values presupposed by a given text (that is, the coherent vision of life and world) and to establish the specific symbolic system of a text (Parker and Patte; Patte and Patte). His analysis proceeds at two levels, a narrative level and a level of symbolic organization. For Patte, a narrative program is simply a subject causing the transfer of an object to a receiver, $S(O \longrightarrow R)$, and each verb manifests a program. The semiotic square is used for the symbolic, or semantic, analysis.

The methods developed by CADIR and Patte are relatively complex and are continually being modified in significant ways. A substantial critique will only be possible when many more biblical narrative texts have been examined by scholars using these methods. Even at this stage, however, it must be admitted that a study of these approaches leads one to ask many of the important questions about the nature of narrative. Some real insights are gained into the phenomenon of literature and the kinds of constraints and rules that govern its production. Nevertheless, one may raise some questions. First, how adequate is the language of description? Is this metalanguage appropriate for the task? For example, it is not clear that narrative actions are best described in terms of the exchange of objects. Similarly, the four-phase narrative program of CADIR does not, in my experience, fit biblical material as well as it should. Second, the controlled, scientific nature claimed by these methods seems to be weakest at the point where the analyst fills in the formulas and semiotic squares with material from the text being studied. This activity relies heavily on the intuition and judgment of the investigator.

Jobling. The work of David Jobling will be mentioned here even though he draws on both Propp and Lévi-Strauss as well as Greimas. Jobling's analysis has two aspects: a narrative stage following the original lead of Propp and a semantic analysis based on Lévi-Strauss, both being filtered through Greimas. He starts with the notion of a "well-formed" story, which is Propp's scheme reduced to its barest essentials, a movement from villainy or lack to defeat of the villain or liquidation of the lack. For Jobling, the semantic material is best arranged according to codes (cultural structures like geography and cosmology) and isotopies (more general abstracts like the supernatural).

Jobling has produced four analyses of biblical stories: Jonathan, Numbers 11–12, Ahab and Elijah, and Genesis 2–3 (1978a, 1978b). His approach may be seen from his study of Numbers 11–12, in which he explores the relationship of four stories: the punishment with fire, the quails, the elders, and the challenge by Miriam and Aaron. Viewed in this order (syntagmatically), these stories relate the breakdown and the establishment of the proper role of Moses. Viewed superimposed one on another (paradigmatically), the logic of the narratives appears as an opposition between unity and diversity. The semantic analysis of these chapters is mapped out in three codes: geographical (Egypt—desert—Canaan), topographical (tent—camp—outside the camp), and vertical (above the earth—earth—below the earth), all of which are sufficiently homologous to permit arrangement in a semantic configuration. There are two isotopies: unity and diversity, and communication of knowledge. The Genesis article argues that the basic movement of the garden story is one from lack (no man to till the soil) to the liquidation of lack (man, outside the garden, tills the soil). This illustrates a tendency of structuralists (see also Parker and Patte) to view lack/liquidation of lack as the basic movement, even where the text does not very obviously suggest it (Culley, 1978b).

Only brief mention can be made of the further variety of work being done. Greimas's narrative model has been applied by Glendon Bryce (1978) to a wisdom text and by Rémi Lack to a poetic wisdom text, Psalm 1. Roland Barthes has analyzed Genesis 32 using a mixture of procedures, and this has been discussed by Hugh White (1975; also Roth). White's analysis of Genesis 2–3 (1978) seeks to add a further dimension to Greimas by drawing on E. Benveniste, J. L. Austin, and J. R. Searle, that is, the aspect of the production of texts. Following a comment by Jean Calloud, White argues that one should not focus on the text as statement (what is said) as Greimas does to the exclusion of the text as production (speaking). White wants "to illuminate the system of constraints which stem from the act of speech and serve to shape the surface of the narrative . . ." (122). Walter Gross has used the study of 1 Kings 13 to try to develop a method for role analysis.

Symbol, Forms of Discourse, and Text

This final section will be devoted to those writings of Paul Ricoeur in which he discusses OT texts. He has turned to biblical material at several stages of his own work in philosophy, which has more and more become focused on the problem of language. His comments on biblical texts have also begun to have an impact on biblical scholars. Ricoeur's views will be discussed under three headings: symbol, forms of discourse, and text.

In *The Symbolism of Evil* Ricoeur addressed the problem of how symbolic language can be related to the work of philosophy (see Rogerson, 1974:128–44; Detweiler: 57–62). While symbolic language is not reflective thought, Ricoeur argues that symbols give rise to thought. They are primary language and emerge directly and spontaneously out of experience. In a secondary stage, symbols are arranged into a narrative form, the myth, which is still not reflective thought. In order to discover the intention of symbols Ricoeur examines their double structure: that of a literal or obvious meaning and that to which the symbol points by analogy. The first part of the book investigates the experience of fault by means of OT symbols related to evil, gathered under three headings: defilement, sin, and guilt. The notions of the stain, the deviation, and the burden are examined not only in themselves but also in their dynamic relationship to each other. This interplay is important because it transforms, deepens, and modifies the meaning of each so that the notions of interiority and subjectivity (guilt) remain in a blend with notions of exteriority and objectivity (pure—impure).

The second part of the book turns to myth. Ricoeur places the Adamic myth of the fall (Genesis 2–3) in a typology with the creation-through-struggle myth from Mesopotamia and the Greek myths of the tragic type and the exiled-soul type. This is done to see where evil is located in each tradition. In the Adamic myth, evil arises unexpectedly in a good creation. The interior and exterior dimensions of evil are displayed by having evil diffused through three characters. The man is responsible for his act, yet the serpent shows that evil did not originate with humanity. The woman introduces the idea of temptation and the notion that the slide into evil is imperceptible.

At a later stage in his thinking, Ricoeur has turned his attention to the forms of discourse in the Bible (1977). He speaks at one point of biblical polyphony (1979: 219). For him it is not only important to notice that there are different forms in the Hebrew Bible—narrative, prophetic, legal, sapiential, and cultic—and to try to describe the nature of each literary mode. Ricoeur goes beyond this and, as he did with symbols and myths, endeavors to assess how these forms affect each other and what kinds of creative tensions are produced once they are placed together in the same canonical space. For example, with regard to narrative and prophecy, the one consolidates with stories the founding of a people while the other dislocates this with the threat of destruction. In a sense, this interest in forms of discourse may reflect the influence of the *einfache Formen* of André Jolles on biblical scholars, especially von Rad whom Ricoeur mentions in this regard (1975–76:23; see also Rogerson, 1978:73–82).

The notion of text not only as written discourse but also as a literary work has become a central preoccupation for Ricoeur (1975–76; 1979: 216–17). According to Ricoeur, writing gives a work a certain autonomy not only from the author but also from the audience. Nevertheless, the text still remains discourse, something said to someone about something. He argues that texts refer to reality but in an indirect and special way (compare Crossan, 1975). He speaks of a second-order reference. The text throws out before the reader a world, a recreation of reality by means of the imagination. Thus, following his increasing concern with the nature of language, Ricoeur's hermeneutical theory has moved from hermeneutics as the interpretation of the double structure of symbols to hermeneutics as the explication of the world that is unfolded in front of each text (1975–76:25–26, 1979:217).

Perhaps the importance of Ricoeur for biblical scholars is that he invites them to explore dimensions of the Bible such as symbol, metaphor, forms of discourse, and text in ways that have not received a great deal of attention in biblical scholarship so far.

II. FOCUS ON CONTEXT: SOCIETY AND CULTURE

While the approaches to be discussed under this heading are varied, they are similar to the extent that they display an interest in some aspect of the social or cultural setting of the texts that comprise the Hebrew scriptures. The texts function here primarily as a means of gaining access to something that lies behind them, a social or cultural phenomenon that could not be reconstructed apart from evidence provided by the text. This is not to say that all the scholars who use this approach are interested in the text only as a means of reconstruction. For many, the purpose of reconstructing the social and cultural background is to understand the text better, all of which implies, nevertheless, a certain view of how texts are to be interpreted. The disciplines to be discussed here are folklore, anthropology, and sociology.

Folklore

For some time now, OT research has made use of folklore theory and literature collected by folklorists (Hahn, 44–82; Rogerson, 1978: 66–73). This has often meant collecting stories, accounts, and descriptions that appear to be parallel to the biblical stories and customs.

Recently, T. H. Gaster has attempted to assemble everything that he could find in terms of folklore and mythology that might be comparable to the Hebrew Bible, although the starting point for this study was a much earlier work, *Folklore in the Old Testament*, by Sir James Fraser. Discussion of literary categories like myth, legend, and proverb by OT scholars has often included some reference to work done by folklorists. Similarly, oral tradition, an important theme in folklore studies, has been the subject of discussion for some time among biblical scholars, especially the Scandinavians (for a survey, see Knight, 1973:215–399). Nevertheless, a careful and consistent use of methods used in folklore and of the results of folklore analysis has not been common. Recent work of this sort on the Hebrew Bible may be discussed under two headings, oral tradition and motif analysis.

Oral Tradition

Since sophisticated field studies of oral tradition by folklorists, anthropologists, and students of comparative literature are relatively recent, application of such studies to written texts like the Hebrew Bible, which may have an oral background, has been limited (for general comments, see Coote, 1976a; Culley, 1976a; Long, 1976a). Albert B. Lord's *Singer of Tales* is still a basic study for the application of oral fieldwork to texts like Homer and Beowulf, although there are some others (Culley, 1976a:1–11; more recently Finnegan).

Following Milman Parry, Lord has argued that some kinds of orally composed poetry can be identified by the presence to a very high degree of traditional language in the form of stock phrases (formulas and formulaic phrases) and stock scenes and descriptions (themes). These are apparently used by poets to compose traditional poems rapidly during performance. With regard to formulaic language, both Stanley Gevirtz and William Whallon applied some aspects of the work of Parry and Lord to biblical texts as early as 1963. My own work on the psalms (1967) presented a collection of repeated phrases which fitted Lord's definition of formula and formulaic phrase. The amount of material was sufficiently large to suggest that it was a body of traditional language, possibly having its origin in oral formulaic composition. Fixed pairs (traditional pairing of synonyms in parallel lines) had also been considered formulaic by Gevirtz and Whallon. In his book, Whallon lists both word pairs and repeated phrases as formulaic (1969). P. B. Yoder has argued that all formulaic language in Hebrew poetry can be reduced to fixed pairs (see also Watters, who rejects the oral origin of these).

Oral composition in Job has been studied by William J. Urbrock (1975, 1976), who concludes that there are strong indications that oral antecedents lie behind the book. The evidence adduced is of two kinds.

First, there is formulaic language in the form of traditional word pairs (the basic building blocks for composing parallel cola) and in the form of colon-length formulas and formulaic systems (175 examples, of which 137 are taken to be good evidence). Urbrock is on the whole more generous in determining formulas than I would be, since he does not ask for as high a degree of formal and semantic identity or similarity.

Urbrock breaks some new ground by seeking to identify themes in Job. For Lord a theme was a recurrent block of narrative like a stock scene or a description without an exact word-for-word repetition. Urbrock presents fifteen examples of repeated groups of ideas that appear more than once in Job or other biblical writings. These are associated with individual complaints, the didactic traditions, and the hymnic traditions. Within themes, Urbrock identifies components he calls "motifs." As with formulas, Urbrock is rather generous in his inclusion of similar material, and his definitions of theme and motif are very general. In some cases there is similarity in wording; in others there is only similarity in contents or subject matter. Nevertheless, the amount and kind of material collected by Urbrock are significant and will bear further study concerning whether or not they constitute signs of oral composition.

Analysis for signs of oral composition has significant restrictions, especially with biblical material. We are working with very limited amounts of material compared with that in field studies, or even in other ancient texts. This means that the results are suggestive rather than definitive. Another problem is that fieldwork in oral tradition has not progressed as rapidly as might be hoped, and there is much more that we need to know about traditional language in oral cultures.

Inger Ljung has made an attempt to use the notion of formulaic language in the psalms in order to test the hypothesis that there is a group of *Ebed YHWH* psalms that are rituals or reflections of rituals depicting the suffering of the sacral king in the annual festival. Assuming that the use of formulaic language is probably linked to genre, Ljung seeks to show by a very detailed analysis of the formulaic language collected in my book and of the psalms in which this language appears that no group of psalms emerges that could be called an *Ebed YHWH* genre. While it is worth exploring how the notion of formulaic language in the psalms can be used in critical studies, my own inclination is to be hesitant in view of the fragmentary nature of the collection of phrases that may be formulaic.

Biblical prose has also been examined for oral characteristics. Here one looks for repeated narrative elements like the themes in poetic tradition, that is, stock scenes and descriptions useful in building narratives during poetic performance. David Gunn has collected some stereotypical passages with significant linguistic similarities. Using the work of Parry, Lord, and others, he concludes that this is clearly a traditional style, possibly oral in origin (1974). More stereotyped material is presented in another article (1976) where he argues for a traditional language, although perhaps not oral traditional language (for critique, see Van Seters). My own work (1976b) outlined some field studies of oral prose and then applied the results to some of the doublets in the Hebrew narrative traditions. No clear case could be made that the doublets were the result of oral tradition, although this remains possible for some.

These discussions of oral tradition focus on the historical setting of the text in the sense that an attempt is being made, with the use of comparative material, to reconstruct the way composition took place. At the very least, the nature of oral composition in all its complexity is more clearly understood by biblical scholars (for the problem of oral tradition and historicity, see Culley, 1972a; Wilson, 1977a). This new perception might lead to some new ideas about textual criticism (Coote, 1976b). Or, insights gained from the study of oral poets and their poetry may lead to a deeper understanding of language, literature, and text (e.g., the kinds of questions raised by Wittig). This line of thought leads back to the types of issues raised in the first section of this chapter where the focus was on text. On the other hand, a study of traditional poets and artists leads back into the setting where one may see the close relationship between traditional poet and audience (community).

Motifs

Discussion of motifs, if the word is used in a very broad sense, has not been absent from biblical studies, although serious attempts to exploit folklore research are less frequent. One may point to Gaster's book, where he gives a brief index of biblical motifs that fit the headings in Stith Thompson's standard *Motif-Index of Folk-Literature*.

In comparing Israelite and ancient Near Eastern tales, Dorothy Irvin, in her *Mytharion*, brings together both the study of motifs and oral tradition in a project she believes is a continuation of the work of Gunkel. With regard to motifs, Irvin turns to the work of Stith Thompson, although she favors a more limited definition of motif: "a plot element which moves the story forward a step." On the basis of Parry's description of how epithets function in oral composition, Irvin proposes an element that she calls a "traditional episode." Motifs and traditional episodes are then examined in Genesis 16, 18–19, 21, and 28 along with stories from Sumerian, Akkadian, Hittite, Ugaritic, and Egyptian traditions. While Irvin has made use of Thompson's index, she does not find it especially useful. In her view there is need for a similar system for ancient Near Eastern material. While Irvin's work moves in the right direction, further clarification is necessary regarding motif. Are we dealing with form or content? Are motifs universals apt to be present in all folk literature or traditional episodes used by a particular culture in the composition of tales? It would be more fruitful to relate motifs to Lord's theme rather than Parry's formula. Motifs might also be considered in relation to structural and narrative analysis.

A much more limited study by S. Niditch and R. Doran, a formal approach to Daniel 2, Genesis 41, and Aḥiqar, seeks to define form on the basis of motifs and patterning shared by specific works. They work with a tale type from Thompson. The question of how motifs should be defined may be raised here as well.

Anthropology and Sociology

While anthropology and sociology are separate disciplines, there is a certain amount of overlap especially when both are applied to the study of a culture in the past. Impact from these disciplines on biblical studies has not been lacking in the past (Hahn; for anthropology: Rogerson, 1978; Wilson, 1979a; for sociology: Gottwald and Frick). The work of W. Robertson Smith has been significant far beyond biblical studies (Muilenburg). W. F. Albright frequently showed interest in questions posed by these disciplines, for example, his reflections on the development of human thinking in the light of the theory of Lucien Lévy-Bruhl (Albright, 1964:51–53, 66–67). The life and institutions of Israel have received extensive comment (for example, de Vaux). Recent studies making substantial use of anthropology and/or sociology fall into three categories; anthropologists who have turned to the Bible, biblical scholars who have drawn on anthropological research, and biblical scholars who have sought to exploit sociological theory.

Anthropologists and the Bible

In his book *Culture and Communication*, Edmund Leach uses rituals described in the OT to support his thesis that culture communicates and to illustrate the use of structural analysis in social anthropology. For example, when he discusses the ritual of sacrifice, he takes as a specific example the use of sacrifice in the consecration of Aaron (for discussion, see Collins). In order to do this, Leach assumes that Exodus 28–29 and Leviticus 1–10, 16 are reasonably accurate descriptions of the ritual. Two models of religious ritual are employed: one of metaphysical space with divine and human spheres overlapping in a liminal zone, and one of metaphysical time with a transitional movement from normal to abnormal time and back again. Using these two models, Leach seeks to understand sacrifice, with its metaphor of death, as communication between the divine and the human. In the consecration of Aaron, sacrifice is used to mark stages of transition to a new status and to separate impurities from him. The scapegoat is the reverse. The impurities are loaded on the goat which is driven off with them.

Another anthropologist, Mary Douglas, has treated biblical material both in *Purity and Danger* and in some subsequent articles (1973, 1975: 153–72, 249–75). In *Purity and Danger*, she raises the problem of the rationale for the distinction between clean and unclean animals in Leviticus. Douglas suggests that the notion of holiness (unity, perfection, and integrity) can be related to the threefold scheme of the world presented in Genesis (earth, water, and firmament). The clean animals of Leviticus are those which fit clearly into these categories. The unclean are those which mix characteristics of more than one sphere. Douglas argues that the rituals of purity and impurity sought to create unity in experience, a definite attempt to impose order on a disorderly existence. In the light of some criticism of this proposal, Douglas has subsequently sought to clarify the issue by exploring analogies to this purity structure in other areas of the culture of Israel. For example, the meal places restrictions on which animals may be eaten, demands the removal of blood from the meat, and requires the separation of milk and meat (1975:249–75). Other analogies are suggested. There is the distinction between Israel and other nations. A further analogy is that between the temple and the human body. Another is that between the temple and its courts of increasing degrees of purity and the classification of animals according to holiness. Douglas argues that in all these rules and patternings the same message of the value of purity and the rejection of impurity comes through. The period when all this operated in Israelite society is taken to be that of the Priestly tradition (1975:308).

If pursued with great care, the approaches of Leach and Douglas may lead to some intriguing analysis of Israelite society. Leach is doing structural analysis, while Douglas is doing something very close to it. The object of the analysis is ritual practice of various kinds rather than texts although the only sources for ritual practices are texts.

In contrast to these approaches is the study of the story of Dinah, Genesis 34, by the anthropologist Julian Pitt-Rivers (126–71). In his view, traditional discourse embraces a whole range of material running from myth (morally indifferent, related to imagination) on the one hand to codes of divine injunction (morally charged, related to action) on the other. Genesis lies at a transition point between these two poles so that most of the Genesis stories are injunctions related to reality. Furthermore, and again in contrast to Leach, the stories of Genesis form a progressive sequence such that problems that arise in the early parts of the sequence are worked through to a resolution toward the end. For example, Pitt-Rivers argues that the wife-sister stories reflect one view of the treatment of women: they may be given as an act of sexual hospitality to establish an alliance, a custom known to anthropologists. He calls this a conciliatory marriage strategy, which would be appropriate for nonsettled peoples needing the protection of settled peoples. The story of Dinah reflects a progression in that access now becomes restricted by means of an aggressive strategy that denies women to outsiders but allows their women to be taken. Here, Pitt-Rivers argues, a notion of sexual honor is introduced that is appropriate to the military dominance of a people which has become settled. In Numbers 25, before the end of the Pentateuch, a defensive strategy (keeping women and taking no outsiders) is determined to be the wisest course in the long term. Pitt-Rivers's approach provides a very useful contrast to that of Leach and Douglas and raises many substantial issues.

Biblical Scholars and Anthropology

A major contribution to the subject of anthropology and the Hebrew Bible has been made by Robert R. Wilson in two books, one on genealogies and the other on prophecy (1977a, 1980; see also 1975, 1979b). These studies are important not only for the contribution they make to our understanding of genealogies and prophecy but also for the careful attention paid to the problem of method in comparative study.

Wilson argues that the use of anthropological data for biblical studies should be governed by six guidelines (1980:15–16). (1) Comparative material must be "collected systematically by a trained scholar." (2) The comparative material must be "properly interpreted in its own context before any attempt is made to apply it to the biblical text." (3) A wide range of societies that contain the phenomenon should be used. (4) One should concentrate on data and avoid the interpretative framework in which the sociologists or anthropologists have placed the data. (5) The comparative material must really be comparable to the biblical data. (6) The biblical text must be the controlling factor.

In his book on genealogies, Wilson begins with an examination of oral genealogies in living societies in order to establish some formal characteristics (segmentation, depth, fluidity, internal structure) and functions (domestic, political-jural, religious). After a review of ancient Near Eastern examples, biblical material is investigated (Genesis 4, 5, 36: genealogies of the twelve tribes), and similarities to and differences from the anthropological and ancient Near Eastern examples are noted. Wilson concludes that genealogies are not normally produced for historical records but rather for domestic, political-jural, and religious purposes. Oral and written genealogies are similar to each other although written ones tend to become frozen while oral ones are open to continual change. Nevertheless, there are ways in which the genealogy may yield important information for the historian.

The book on prophecy follows a similar pattern. From an examination of field studies Wilson proposes that prophets, shamans, mediums, and diviners may all be defined as intermediaries since they are individuals who mediate between the divine and human worlds. Such figures always have a group of supporters and usually assume stereotyped characteristics of speech and behavior. Central intermediaries are connected to the established religion and seek to maintain stability in society. Peripheral intermediaries are on the fringe of society and may seek either to speed up or slow down social change.

In biblical prophetic traditions, Wilson isolates an Ephraimitic tradition as represented in the Deuteronomistic history, in the Elohist tradition, and in the prophets Hosea and Jeremiah. This he distinguishes from a Judean tradition, which is much smaller in scale. Applying the description of an intermediary deduced from anthropological studies, Wilson argues that a relatively coherent picture results. The model for the Ephraimitic tradition was the Mosaic prophet, whose role was to act as the only legitimate channel of communication between God and people or people and God. While Ephraimitic prophecy began with social maintenance functions, with the monarchy the prophets became peripheral, supported by marginal groups who sought social change.

Wilson's work on prophecy is not an isolated phenomenon (for a survey of discussion on prophecy and society, see Wilson, 1977b). As early as 1963, the sociologist Peter Berger had argued that the prophets, as charismatics, may nevertheless have worked within traditional institutions, the cult in particular. A number of others have tried to draw on anthropological and sociological research: H. Huffmon on the origins of prophecy, Robert Carroll on the theory of cognitive dissonance and the prophets (1973–74, but see now 1979), Thomas Overholt on the Ghost Dance and the prophetic process, Simon Parker on the question of possession trance, and Burke Long on prophetic authority (1977, and reference there to his other articles).

The concept of Sitz im Leben is also being examined seriously in the light of anthropological and sociological research. On the basis of a review of some field studies by anthropologists, Burke Long suggests that biblical scholars must give up the idea that every genre was related to a primary, definitive setting (1976b; compare Knierim: 463–66). For Martin Buss, a restatement of the concept of setting will necessarily involve the use of anthropological and sociological models (1978). One may also note Douglas Knight's proposal to expand and reorganize the notion of Sitz im Leben into a study of matrices all of which may be potentially related to a given text (societal, institutional, mental, cultural, ideological, literary), thus making room for both anthropology and sociology within the approaches that can be used (1974).

Biblical Scholars and Sociology

While there have been attempts to use sociological models in analyzing the period of the judges (Malamat) and the postexilic period

(Hanson), Norman Gottwald's book on the premonarchic period of ancient Israel must be considered a major contribution to a sociological approach in biblical studies. At the same time, one would need to mention the work of George Mendenhall, whose writings have done so much to stimulate recent interest in sociological analysis. While Mendenhall clearly works with notions of how societies function, he does not relate his work very explicitly to a particular sociological model nor to sociological discussion (1962, 1973, 1978; for Gottwald's critique see 1979:599–602). Mendenhall's theory of the conquest as a peasant revolt has become a central element in Gottwald's approach.

Gottwald's aim in *The Tribes of Yahweh* is to reconstruct the origin and early development of Israel. While sociological method becomes a major instrument in this task, he does not see it as a replacement for but rather a complement to traditional approaches. Accepting the revolt model for the conquest, Gottwald seeks to broaden and deepen this hypothesis by an analysis of the social structures in existence during the early period. Current sociological and anthropological discussion is used to define the nature of the association of tribes which was early Israel. This includes a full discussion of nomadism, which in Gottwald's view did not play a major role in the early period. On a scale of social development that runs from band society, to tribal society, to chiefdoms, and finally to state, Gottwald places Israel at the tribal stage. However, this stage is seen as a retribalization, a movement back out of and in opposition to the stage of the city-state. This movement developed into a tribal association with the coming together of several groups marginal to Canaanite society, one being the Moses group, which contributed the experiences of Egypt and the cult of Yahweh. Viewed in this way, the peasant revolt is a rejection of the city-state and its social and political values. Israel chose, according to Gottwald, a "sociopolitical egalitarianism" as opposed to an "imperial-feudal hierarchic state."

Two levels may be distinguished in Gottwald's analysis. At the first level, he employs what he calls a structural-functional model in order to describe ancient Israel as a total social system. A social system is "the whole complex of communal interaction involving functions, roles, institutions, customs, norms, and symbols" (18). Religion functions as a component of this system coherently related to all other components. However, a structural-cultural model has, according to Gottwald, certain limitations in that it simply identifies relationships but cannot cope with origins and change. It cannot indicate priorities by telling which elements are more important than others. Therefore, Gottwald introduces a second level of analysis that he calls a historical cultural-material model, derived from Karl Marx. This model gives social relations priority over religious formations. As Gottwald remarks, "The historical cultural-material hypothesis is that Yahwism is derivable from the social system as a whole and meaningful only in the frame of reference and realm of discourse provided by social relations of which it was a particular form of symbolic expression" (647). Nevertheless, he does give religion a more positive, even creative, role than one would expect from a historical materialist perspective.

Gottwald has presented his method in some detail and with great enthusiasm and force. He expects and will get vigorous reactions. Even with the aid of sociological methods, which are helpful, the reconstruction of the earliest period of Israel will remain controversial, simply because of the relative lack of evidence for that period. His choice of methods has been clear and deliberate with a sensitivity to the fact that methodological decisions may operate on different levels. He uses a structural-functional model at a descriptive level. However, while this model might be compatible with a number of perspectives at a higher level, he selects a historical cultural-material model, which establishes his axioms and presuppositions. This recalls somewhat Ricoeur's argument that interpretation has two phases, one where description occurs and one where appropriation occurs. Now that a number of approaches and models are being introduced into biblical studies from anthropology and sociology by Wilson, Gottwald, and others, one is beginning to feel the need for competent persons to map out the methodological choices and options that are available from these disciplines in order to gain some perspective on individual contributions like that of Gottwald (Kovacs is working in this direction).

Finally, two studies may be mentioned which examine the role of the city in ancient Israel. The first is a full-length study by Frank Frick, *The City in Ancient Israel*. Urban studies, a bundle of disciplines in which sociology plays a major role, is used to tackle the problem of the city in preexilic Israel. Frick emphasizes both the functionally causal analysis of sociology and social anthropology and the historical-contextual analysis of the culture historian and the archaeologist. James Flanagan is interested in the shift of David's capital from Hebron to Jerusalem. He tries to clarify the importance of this shift by drawing on a distinction made by some sociologists between cities that are orthogenetic centers (carrying on an older tradition—Hebron) and others that are heterogenetic centers (introducing new modes in conflict with the old—Jerusalem).

III. FINAL COMMENTS

Because most of the approaches mentioned are quite recent developments, it is not yet possible to work out substantial critiques of these new directions. Comments have been made at several points along the way to indicate my own evaluations and impressions. In the same vein some general observations can be added.

In one form or another language will likely become an important topic in future biblical studies. In which particular form or forms the subject of language will be pursued in biblical texts is not clear at the moment. We have noticed that texts have been engaged at several levels: literary and grammatical, structural and hermeneutical. There is no reason why biblical scholars should not examine the language dimension of the biblical text with all its complex structures, including the literary structures produced by the imagination, with the same intensity and thoroughness that scholars have devoted to the study of the links texts have with their settings, their historical dimensions. In my view, one of the interesting questions for further discussions pertains to the ways in which literary texts can be said to refer to something outside themselves (Ricoeur; Crossan).

It seems equally clear that sociological and anthropological perspectives are attracting a significant response among biblical scholars, and this will likely increase and become more important as time goes on. Since these approaches, along with folklore, are used on the whole by biblical scholars to reconstruct various aspects of ancient Israel, these methods are easily linked to historical studies. As indicated earlier, there is now a need to plot out the various aims and strategies available from these disciplines in order to gain some sense of the implications of choosing various options. With the new sense developing of the relative autonomy of texts as literary structures, it may be necessary to readdress from our new perspective the old problem of how biblical texts reflect their setting. More subtlety may be required in using these texts as sources for aspects of their setting, like society, culture, and religion.

While the distinction between text-oriented approaches and context-oriented approaches has been useful, it is striking to notice that the methods used on both sides, language analysis and social science analysis, are very similar. They are cross-cultural, oriented toward phenomena that are widely, if not universally, found through space and time (language, narrative, society, prophecy, the city). While interest in the general phenomenon does not exclude interest in specific examples of the general, biblical scholars are in fact mainly interested in ancient Israel. One needs to consider how the general and the specific can or should be related when biblical scholars bring together the study of language and the biblical text or ancient Israel and sociological-anthropological approaches (note the care of Wilson).

Biblical studies is an amalgam of many different approaches, old and new, which involve many tensions crisscrossing each other: the general vs. the specific, the historical vs. the literary, and focus on text vs. focus on context (see Buccellati's comments on method in Near Eastern studies). What kind of model will relate different approaches and methods, aims and interests, levels and dimensions? Crossan suggests a concept of field (1977). Buss explores the suitability of a communications model (1979). Kovacs discusses how structuralism and the social sciences may be related in such a way that a number of fundamental issues are brought together and a foundation laid for hermeneutics. It remains to be seen how discussion will develop on this topic. The challenge is certainly there.

BIBLIOGRAPHY

Albright, William Foxwell
1964   History, Archaeology and Christian Humanism. New York: McGraw-Hill.

Alonso-Schökel, Luis
1972   The Inspired Word. New York: Herder and Herder.

Andersen, Francis I.
1974   The Sentence in Biblical Hebrew. Janua Linguarum, Series Practica 231. The Hague: Mouton.
1976   "Style and Authorship." The Tyndale Paper 21.

Barthes, Roland
1974   "The Struggle with the Angel: Textual Analysis of Genesis 32:23-33." Pp. 21-33 in Structural Analysis and Biblical Exegesis. Ed. R. Barthes, F. Bovon et al. Trans. Alfred M. Johnson, Jr. PTMS 3. Pittsburgh: Pickwick.

Beauchamp, Paul
1972   "L'analyse structurale et l'exégèse biblique." Pp. 113-28 in Congress Volume: Uppsala, 1971 VTSup 22. Leiden: E. J. Brill.

Berger, Peter L.
1963   "Charisma and Religious Innovation: The Social Location of Israelite Prophecy." American Sociological Review 28: 940-50.

Bryce, Glendon E.
1977   "Structuralism and History: The Structure of the Narrative in Myth, Folktale, and the Synoptic Gospels." Pp. 301-42 in Scripture in History and Theology: Essays in Honor of J. Coert Rylaarsdam. Ed. Arthur L. Merrill and Thomas W. Overholt. PTMS 17. Pittsburgh: Pickwick.
1978   "The Structural Analysis of Didactic Texts." Pp. 107-21 in Biblical and Near Eastern Studies: Essays in Honor of William Sanford La Sor. Ed. Gary A. Tuttle. Grand Rapids: Eerdmans.

Buccellati, Giorgio
1973   "Methodological Concerns and the Program of Ancient Near Eastern Studies." *Or* 42: 9–20.

Buss, Martin J.
1978   "The Idea of Sitz im Leben—History and Critique." *ZAW* 90: 157–70.
1979   "Understanding Communication." Pp. 3–44 in *Encounter with the Text*. Semeia Supplements. Ed. Martin J. Buss. Philadelphia: Fortress; Missoula, MT: Scholars Press.

CADIR
1976   "Abraham et Abimelek: Genèse 20." *Sémiotique et Bible* 4: 23–38.
1977a   "Abraham et Abimelek: Genèse 20 (suite)." *Sémiotique et Bible* 5: 7–28.
1977b   "Approche du Livre de Jonas: Propositions et Questions." *Sémiotique et Bible* 7: 30–40 = "An Approach to the Book of Jonah: Suggestions and Questions." *Semeia* 15: 85–96.

Calloud, Jean
1976   *Structural Analysis of Narrative*. Semeia Supplements. Trans. Daniel Patte. Philadelphia: Fortress; Missoula, MT: Scholars Press.
1979   "A Few Comments on Structural Semiotics: A Brief Review of a Method and Some Explanation of Procedures." *Semeia* 15: 51–83.

Carroll, Robert P.
1973–74   "Prophecy, Dissonance and Jeremiah xxvi." *Transactions of the Glasgow University Oriental Society* 25: 12–23.
1979   *When Prophecy Failed: Cognitive Dissonance in the Prophetic Traditions of the Old Testament*. New York: Seabury.

Casalis, Mathieu
1976   "The Dry and the Wet: A Semiological Analysis of Creation and Flood Myths." *Semiotica* 17: 35–67.

Charpentier, Etienne, ed.
1976   *Une initiation à l'analyse structurale*. Cahiers Evangile 16. Paris: Éditions du Cerf.

Collins, John J.
1977   "The Meaning of Sacrifice: A Contrast of Methods." *BR* 22: 19–34.

Coote, Robert B.
1976a   "Tradition, Oral, OT." Pp. 914–16 in *IDBSup*.
1976b   "The Application of the Oral Theory to Biblical Hebrew Literature." *Semeia* 5: 51–64.

Crossan, John Dominic
1975   *The Dark Interval: Towards a Theology of Story*. Niles,
              Il.: Argus Communications.
1977   "Perspectives and Methods in Contemporary Biblical
              Criticism." *BR* 22: 39–49.
1978   "Waking the Bible: Biblical Hermeneutic and Literary
              Imagination." *Int* 32: 269–85.

Culley, Robert C.
1967   *Oral Formulaic Language in the Biblical Psalms*. Tor-
              onto: University of Toronto Press.
1972a   "Oral Tradition and Historicity." Pp. 102–16 in *Studies
              on the Ancient Palestinian World*. Ed. J. W. Wevers
              and D. B. Redford. Toronto: University of Toronto.
1972b   "Some Comments on Structural Analysis and Biblical
              Studies." Pp. 129–42 in *Congress Volume: Uppsala,
              1971*. VTSup 88. Leiden: E. J. Brill
1974   "Structural Analysis: Is it Done with Mirrors?" *Int* 28:
              165–81.
1975   "Themes and Variations in Three Groups of OT Narra-
              tives." *Semeia* 3: 3–13.
1976a   "Oral Tradition and the OT: Some Recent Discussion."
              Semeia 5: 1–33.
1976b   *Studies in the Structure of Hebrew Narrative*. Semeia
              Supplements. Philadelphia: Fortress; Missoula, MT:
              Scholars Press.
1978a   "Analyse alttestamentlicher Erzählungen: Erträge der
              jüngsten Methodendiskussion." *Biblische Notizen* 6:
              26–30.
1978b   "Action Sequences in Gen 2–3." Pp. 51–59 in *SBL Semi-
              nar Papers*, Vol. 1. Ed. Paul J. Achtemeier. Missoula,
              MT: Scholars Press.

Detweiler, Robert
1978   *Story, Sign, and Self: Phenomenology and Structural-
              ism as Literary Critical Methods*. Semeia Supplements.
              Philadelphia: Fortress; Missoula, MT: Scholars Press.

Douglas, Mary
1970   *Purity and Danger: An Analysis of Pollution and
              Taboo*. Harmondsworth: Penquin Books
1973   "Critique and Commentary." Pp. 137–42 in Jacob Neus-
              ner, *The Idea of Purity in Ancient Judaism*. Leiden:
              E. J. Brill.
1975   *Implicit Meanings*. Boston: Routledge and Kegan Paul.

Dressler, Wolfgang U., ed.
1978   *Current Trends in Textlinguistics*. Berlin: Walter
              de Gruyter.

Finnegan, Ruth
1977   *Oral Poetry*. Cambridge: Cambridge University Press.

Flanagan, James W.
1978   "The Relocation of the Davidic Capital." *JAAR* 46: 224–44.

Fraser, James G.
1918   *Folklore in the Old Testament*. London: Macmillan.

Frick, Frank S.
1977   *The City in Ancient Israel*. SBLDS 36. Missoula, MT: Scholars Press.

Gaster, Theodor H.
1969   *Myth, Legend, and Custom in the Old Testament*. New York: Harper & Row.

Gevirtz, Stanley
1963   *Patterns in the Early Poetry of Israel*. Studies in Ancient Oriental Civilization, 32. Chicago: University of Chicago Press.

Gottwald, Norman K.
1979   *The Tribes of Yahweh: A Sociology of the Religion of Liberated Israel, 1250–1050 B.C.E.* Maryknoll, NY: Orbis Books.

Gottwald, Norman K., and Frank S. Frick
1976   "The Social World of Ancient Israel." Pp. 110–19 in *The Bible and Liberation*. Ed. Norman K. Gottwald and Antoinette C. Wire. Berkeley: Radical Religion.

Greimas, A. J.
1966   *Semantique structurale*. Paris: Larousse.
1970   *Du sens: Essais sémiotiques*. Paris: Seuil.
1977   "Elements of a Narrative Grammar." *Diacritics* 7: 23–40 = "Elements d'une grammaire narrative." Pp. 157–83 in *Du sens: Essais sémiotiques*.

Gross, Walter
1974   *Bileam*. SANT 38. Munich: Kösel.
1979   "Lying Prophet and Disobedient Man of God in 1 Kings 13: Role Analysis as an Instrument of Theological Interpretation of an OT Narrative Text." *Semeia* 15: 97–135.

Groupe d'Entrevernes
1979   *Analyse sémiotique des textes*. Lyon: Presses Universitaires de Lyon.

Gülich, Elizabeth, and Wolfgang Raible
1977   *Linguistic Textmodelle*. Uni-Taschenbücher 130. Munich: Wilhelm Fink.

Gunn, David
 1974   "Narrative Patterns and Oral Tradition in Judges and Samuel." *VT* 24: 286–317.
 1976   "Traditional Composition in the 'Succession Narrative.'" *VT* 26: 214–29.

Hahn, Herbert F.
 1966   *The Old Testament in Modern Research*. Philadelphia: Fortress.

Hanson, Paul D.
 1975   *The Dawn of Apocalyptic*. Philadelphia: Fortress.

Huffmon, Herbert B.
 1976   "Origins of Prophecy." Pp. 171–86 in *Magnalia Dei, The Mighty Acts of God: Essays on the Bible and Archaeology in Memory of G. Ernest Wright*. Ed. Frank Moore Cross, Werner E. Lemke, and Patrick D. Miller, Jr. Garden City, NY: Doubleday.

Irvin, Dorothy
 1978   *Mytharion: The Comparison of Tales from the Old Testament and the Ancient Near East*. AOAT 32. Neukirchen-Vluyn: Neukirchener Verlag.

Jackson, Jared J., and Martin Kessler, eds.
 1974   *Rhetorical Criticism: Essays in Honor of James Muilenburg*. PTMS 1. Pittsburgh: Pickwick.

Jason, Heda
 1977a   "A Model for Narrative Structure in Oral Literature." Pp. 99–139 in *Patterns in Oral Literature*. Ed. Heda Jason and Dimitri Segal. The Hague: Mouton.
 1977b   *Ethnopoetry: Form, Content, Function*. Forum Theologiae Linguisticae, 11. Bonn: Linguistica Biblica.
 1979   "The Story of David and Goliath: A Folk Epic?" *Bib* 60: 36–70.

Jason, Heda, and Dimitri Segal, eds.
 1977   *Patterns in Oral Literature*. The Hague: Mouton.

Jobling, David
 1978a   "A Structural Analysis of Genesis 2:4b–3:24." Pp. 61–69 in *SBL Seminar Papers*, Vol. 1. Ed. Paul J. Achtemeier. Missoula, MT: Scholars Press.
 1978b   *The Sense of Biblical Narrative: Three Structural Analyses in the Old Testament*. JSOTSup 7. Sheffield: JSOT.

Knierim, Rolf
 1973   "Old Testament Form Criticism Reconsidered." *Int* 27: 435–68.

Knight, Douglas A.

1973 *Rediscovering the Traditions of Israel: The Develop-ment of the Traditio-Historical Research of the Old Testament, with Special Consideration of Scandinavian Contributions.* SBLDS 9. Missoula, MT: Scholars Press. Rev. ed., 1975.

1974 "The Understanding of 'Sitz im Leben' in Form Criti-cism." Pp. 105–25 in *SBL Seminar Papers*, Vol. 1. Ed. George MacRae. Missoula, MT: Scholars Press.

Kovacs, Brian Watson

1978 "Philosophical Foundations for Structuralism." *Semeia* 10: 85–105.

1979 "Philosophical Issues in Sociological Structuralism: A Bridge from the Social Sciences to Hermeneutics." *USQR* 34: 149–57.

Lack, Rémi

1976 "Le Psaume 1—Une Analyse structurale." *Bib* 57: 154–67.

Leach, Edmund

1965 "Lévi-Strauss in the Garden of Eden: An Examination of Some Recent Developments in the Analysis of Myth." Pp. 574–81 in *Reader in Comparative Religion.* 2d ed. Ed. William A. Lessa and Evon Z. Vogt. New York: Harper & Row.

1969a "Genesis as Myth." Pp. 7–23 in *Genesis as Myth and Other Essays.* London: Jonathan Cape = *Discovery* 23 (1962): 30–35 = Pp. 1–13 in *Myth and Cosmos.* Ed. John Middleton. New York: Natural History Press.

1969b "The Legitimacy of Solomon." Pp. 25–83 in *Genesis as Myth and Other Essays.* London: Jonathan Cape.

1976 *Culture and Communication: The Logic by Which Symbols are Connected.* Themes in the Social Sciences. London: Cambridge University Press.

Lévi-Strauss, Claude

1967 "The Structural Study of Myth." Pp. 202–27 in *Struc-tural Anthropology.* Trans. C. Jacobson and B. G. Schoepf. Garden City, NY: Doubleday, Anchor.

Ljung, Inger

1978 *Tradition and Interpretation: A Study of the Use and Application of Formulaic Language in the So-Called Ebed YHWH-Psalms.* ConBOT 12. Lund: CWK Gleerup.

Long, Burke O.

1975 "The Social Setting for Prophetic Miracle Stories." *Semeia* 3: 46–63.

1976a "Recent Field Studies in Oral Literature and their Bear-ing on OT Criticism." *VT* 26: 187–98.

1976b   "Recent Field Studies in Oral Literature and the Ques-
               tion of *Sitz im Leben.*" *Semeia* 5: 35–49.
1977   "Prophetic Authority as Social Reality." Pp. 3–20 in
               Canon and Authority. Ed. George W. Coats and
               Burke O. Long. Philadelphia: Fortress.

Longaoro, Robert E.
1976   "The Discourse Structure of the Flood Narrative." Pp.
               235–61 in *SBL Seminar Papers.* Ed. George MacRae.
               Missoula, MT: Scholars Press = "The Discourse of the
               Flood Narrative." *JAAR* 47 Supplement (March 1979).

Longacre, Robert E., and Stephen Levinson
1978   "Field Analysis of Discourse." Pp. 103–22 in *Current
               Trends in Textlinguistics.* Ed. Wolfgang Dressler. Ber-
               lin: Walter de Gruyter.

Lord, Albert B.
1960   *Singer of Tales.* Harvard Studies in Comparative Litera-
               ture, 24. Cambridge, MA: Harvard University Press.

McKnight, Edgar V.
1978   *Meaning in Texts: The Historical Shaping of a Narra-
               tive Hermeneutics.* Philadelphia: Fortress.

Malamat, Abraham
1976   "Charismatic Leadership in the Book of Judges." Pp.
               152–68 in *Magnalia Dei: The Mighty Acts of God.* Ed.
               F. M. Cross, Werner E. Lemke, and Patrick D. Miller,
               Jr. Garden City, NY: Doubleday.

Mendenhall, George E.
1962   "The Hebrew Conquest of Palestine." *BA* 15: 66–87.
1973   *The Tenth Generation: The Origins of the Biblical Tra-
               dition.* Baltimore: Johns Hopkins University Press.
1978   "Between Theology and Archaeology." *JSOT* 7: 28–34.

Miscall, Peter D.
1979   "Literary Unity in Old Testament Narrative." *Semeia*
               15: 27–44.

Muilenburg, James
1969   "Prolegomenon." Pp. 1–27 in W. Robertson Smith, *Lec-
               tures on the Religion of the Semites.* New York: Ktav.

Newman, B. M.
1976   "Discourse Structure." Pp. 237–41 in *IDBSup.*

Niditch, Susan, and Robert Doran
1977   "The Success Story of the Wise Courtier: A Formal
               Approach." *JBL* 96: 179–93.

Overholt, Thomas W.
1974   "The Ghost Dance of 1980 and the Nature of the Pro-
               phetic Process." *Ethnohistory* 21: 37–63.

Parker, Judson F., and Daniel Patte
1978   "Structural Exegesis of Genesis 2 and 3." Pp. 141–59 in *SBL Seminar Papers*, Vol. 1., Ed. Paul J. Achtemeier. Missoula, MT: Scholars Press.

Parker, Simon B.
1978   "Possession Trance and Prophecy in Pre-Exilic Israel." *VT* 28: 271–85.

Parry, Milman
1930   "Studies in the Epic Technique of Oral Verse-Making I: Homer and Homeric Style." *Harvard Studies in Classical Philology* 41: 73–147.

Patte, Daniel
1976   *What is Structural Exegesis?* Guides to Biblical Scholarship: New Testament Series. Philadelphia: Fortress.

Patte, Daniel, and Aline Patte
1978   *Structural Exegesis—From Theory to Practice.* Philadelphia: Fortress.

Piaget, Jean
1970   *Structuralism.* Trans. and ed. Chaninah Maschler. New York: Harper & Row.

Pitt-Rivers, Julian
1977   *The Fate of Shechem or the Politics of Sex: Essays in the Anthropology of the Mediterranean.* Cambridge: University Press.

Polzin, Robert M.
1975   "'The Ancestress of Israel in Danger' in Danger." *Semeia* 3: 81–98.
1977   *Biblical Structuralism: Method and Subjectivity in the Study of Ancient Texts.* Semeia Supplements. Philadelphia: Fortress; Missoula, MT: Scholars Press.
1979   "A Few Comments on Structural Semiotics." *Semeia* 15: 45–50.

Propp, Vladimir
1968   *Morphology of the Folktale.* 2d ed. Austin, TX: University of Texas.

Pury, Albert de
1975   *Promesse divine et légende cultuelle dans le cycle de Jacob.* 2 vols. Etudes bibliques. Paris: J. Gabalda.
1979   "Jakob an Jabbok, Gen 32, 23–33 im Licht einer alt-irischen Erzählung." *TZ* 35: 18–34.

Reagan, Charles, and David Stewart
1978   *The Philosophy of Paul Ricoeur: An Anthology of His Work.* Boston: Beacon.

Richter, Wolfgang
1971   *Exegese als Literaturwissenschaft*. Göttingen: Vandenhoeck & Ruprecht.

Ricoeur, Paul
1969   *The Symbolism of Evil*. Trans. Emerson Buchanan. Boston: Beacon.
1975–76   "Philosophical Hermeneutics and Theological Hermeneutics." *SR* 5: 14–33.
1977   "Toward a Hermeneutic of the Idea of Revelation." *HTR* 70: 1–37.
1979   "Naming God." *USQR* 34: 215–27.

Robertson, David
1977   *The Old Testament and the Literary Critic*. Guides to Biblical Scholarship: Old Testament Series. Philadelphia: Fortress.

Rogerson, J. W.
1974   *Myth in Old Testament Interpretation*. BZAW 134. Berlin: Walter de Gruyter.
1978   *Anthropology and the Old Testament*. Oxford: Blackwell.

Roth, Wolfgang
1977   "Structural Interpretations of 'Jacob at the Jabbok' (Genesis 32:22–32)." *BR* 22: 51–62.

Sasson, Jack M.
1979   *Ruth: A New Translation with a Philological Commentary and a Formalist-Folklorist Interpretation*. Johns Hopkins Near Eastern Studies. Baltimore: Johns Hopkins University.

Schweizer, Harald
1974   *Elischa in den Kriegen: Literaturwissenschaftliche Untersuchung von 2 Kön 3; 6,8–23; 6,24–7,20*. SANT 37. Munich: Kösel-Verlag.

Smalley, William A.
1979   "Recursion Patterns and the Sectioning of Amos." *BT* 30: 118–27.

Thompson, Stith
1946   *The Folktale*. New York: Dryden.

Urbrock, William J.
1975   "Evidences of Oral-Formulaic Composition in the Poetry of Job." Dissertation, Harvard University.
1976   "Oral Antecedents to Job: A Survey of Formulas and Formulaic Systems." *Semeia* 5: 111–37.

Van Seters, John
1976   "Oral Patterns or Literary Conventions in Biblical Narrative." *Semeia* 5: 139–54.

Vaux, Roland de
1962   *Ancient Israel: Its Life and Institutions.* Trans. John
                     McHugh. London: Darton, Longman, and Todd.

Wagner, Norman E.
1976–77   "General System Theory, Cybernetics and Old Testament
                     Tradition." *SR* 6: 597–605.

Watters, William R.
1976   *Formula Criticism and the Poetry of the Old Testament.*
                     BZAW 138. Berlin: Walter de Gruyter.

Whallon, William
1963   "Formulaic Poetry in the Old Testament." *Comparative
                     Literature* 15: 1–14.
1969   *Formula, Character, and Context.* Publications of the
                     Center of Hellenic Studies. Cambridge, MA: Harvard
                     University Press.

White, Hugh C.
1975   "French Structuralism and OT Narrative Analysis: Roland
                     Barthes." *Semeia* 3: 99–127.
1978   "Direct and Third Person Discourse in the Narrative of
                     the 'Fall.'" Pp. 121–40 in *SBL Seminar Papers*, Vol. 1. Ed.
                     Paul J. Achtemeier. Missoula, MT: Scholars Press.

Wilson, Robert R.
1975   "The Old Testament Genealogies in Recent Research."
                     JBL 94: 169–89.
1977a   *Genealogy and History in the Biblical World.* Yale Near
                     Eastern Researches, 7. New Haven: Yale University Press.
1977b   "Prophecy and Society in Ancient Israel: The Present State
                     of the Inquiry." Pp. 341–58 in *SBL Seminar Papers*. Ed.
                     Paul J. Achtemeier. Missoula, MT: Scholars Press.
1979a   "Anthropology and the Study of the Old Testament."
                     USQR 34: 175–81.
1979b   "Prophecy and Ecstasy: A Reexamination." *JBL* 98:
                     321–37.
1980   *Prophecy and Society in Ancient Israel.* Philadelphia:
                     Fortress.

Wittig, Susan
1976   "Theories of Formulaic Narrative." *Semeia* 5: 65–83.

Yoder, P. B.
1970   "Fixed Word Pairs and the Composition of Hebrew
                     Poetry." Ph.D. dissertation, University of Pennsylvania.
1971   "A-B Pairs and Oral Composition in Hebrew Poetry." *VT*
                     21: 470–89.

Zaborski, Andrzej
1974   "Structural Methods and Old Testament Studies." *Folia
                     Orientalia* 15: 263–68.

6

Israelite Religion

Patrick D. Miller

I. THE DECLINE AND RISE
OF THE HISTORY OF RELIGIONS

The sharpest impression one receives in looking back over the past thirty-five years of the study of Israel's religion is the very different status held by history-of-religion studies at the beginning of that period compared with the present. The fifteen years after World War II were a time when various factors contributed to and reflected a lack of interest, if not a negative attitude, toward the history of religion. The last fifteen years have seen a significant recrudescence of history-of-religion studies. While there are exceptions to both these generalizations, it is clear that there was in the early sixties a swinging of the pendulum from a heavy emphasis on (biblical) theology to renewed interest in (history of) religion. What was true for religion and history of religions in general was also true of the study of Israel's religion. Some analysis of that swing is a major part of any survey of this period. The following paragraphs will seek to characterize that movement in broad outline (see Barr; and P. D. Miller, 1978).

The first part of this century saw the rise to prominence of history-of-religion studies arising out of the increasing data coming from Near Eastern excavations and centering in the "pan-Babylonian school" as it influenced Old Testament studies but more especially in the work of Hermann Gunkel and Hugo Gressmann as well as Sigmund Mowinckel. These scholars looked not only at the texts but also at the religious phenomena behind the texts. They asked questions about beginnings, development, and relationships. Their concerns, their tools, and their data were therefore *phenomenological*, *historical*, and *comparative*. The characteristics and components of Israel's religion were examined in various ways as the historians of religion sought to extrapolate from the biblical texts—sometimes on the basis of explicit statement, at other times by inference—what took place and what conceptions or "ideology" underlay the religious practices. They also inquired into the original form of the practices and ideas and how and why they developed and changed. They were especially interested in the influences from outside Israel that helped to create these religious elements or affected and shaped them in some way. Such methodological questions, while refined, elaborated, and illustrated in various ways, were central to the study of religion from the beginning and have remained so down to the present. *Theological* concerns were much less to the fore. They were not entirely absent, particularly in Gunkel (Klatt: 74ff.; P. D. Miller, 1973:41–42), but the history of religions tended to undercut theological work as it relativized the sacred literature out of which theological systems were constructed, challenging claims to uniqueness, absoluteness, revelation, and finality.

It was in part against just such a tendency that Karl Barth launched his massive theological attack and carried much of continental theology with him from the 1930s on. The negative attitude toward religion that appears so strongly in Volume I of Barth's *Church Dogmatics* contributed to a deemphasis on the worth of phenomenological and historical analysis of religious movements at the same time that many were finding that the investigations of the *religionsgeschichtliche Schule* and those associated with it had not opened up the scriptures for a clearer, more relevant hearing by modern men and women.

In America the impact of Barth's theological revolution was probably less on systematic theology than it was on biblical study with the mushrooming interest in biblical theology (Childs, 1970), a development attested by the growth of biblical theology courses in the theological schools and the consequent decline of courses in the history of the religion of Israel, a tendency that is still present in seminary curricula. The postwar period saw a significant renewal of theological and hermeneutical interest in the Bible generally, but especially in the OT. Both for its paradigmatic character at this time and for its widespread influence, one may cite the work of G. Ernest Wright, particularly in his two monographs, *The Old Testament Against Its Environment* and *God Who Acts*. The former work reveals its focus in the title. It is an attempt to argue for the revelatory uniqueness of Israel's faith by laying her religion alongside that of her Near Eastern neighbors to demonstrate both its singular character and its superiority as a religious expression. He acknowledges regularly his indebtedness to W. F Albright, Thorkild Jacobsen, and Henri Frankfort, all three of whom had produced major works in the study of Israelite and Mesopotamian religions affirming the distinctiveness of the former against the latter.[1] Wright's work is a study

---

[1] Albright's classic work (1940) continued to have major impact on OT studies until the 1960s. His massive history of the religion of Israel remains unpublished though it exists in manuscript form. He did update the earlier work, particularly in light of the growth of knowledge of Ugaritic and Phoenician materials, in his last major book (1968). The subtitle of this work, as well as the regular use of the term "pagan" to characterize Canaanite religion, demonstrates the continuity with Albright's earlier stance and with that of his more theologically oriented and intentionally apologetic student Wright. Albright here as

of Israel's religion. It deals with the phenomena appropriate to that study: notions of the divine world, how the relationship between deity and human creature is structured (covenant), kingship, magic and divination, and the cult. Wright was selective to a definite degree and made theological judgments based on his comparison of Israelite and Near Eastern religions, an approach that turned out to be more useful to theologians than to historians of religion. Some of his analyses of the differences, however, may hold up better than is presently recognized.

His book *God Who Acts* continued the earlier work and provided an even clearer theological statement. Indeed, it was the unofficial prolegomenon to the OT theology that he never wrote. Here Wright emphasized history as the realm of God's activity. One sees history as the primary locus or context of divine revelation rather than human religion. This conclusion leads to an emphasis on a *theological* reading of the biblical materials rather than a *history-of-religions* reading. Indeed, it was because the latter approach seemed to lead to a positivistic, disinterested analysis of the Bible that Wright moved in a different direction.

Wright was not alone in the postwar years. Many other OT scholars shared his views. Virtually all of them were deeply concerned to overcome the distance between the world/time/religion of the Bible and that of the contemporary age. Indeed, that concern comes legitimately to the fore in any interpretive reading of the scriptures. Wright shared it with one of his chief protagonists, Rudolf Bultmann; but while Bultmann sought to overcome the distance between these worlds by demythologizing the religious thought of the ancient world into a mode of thought more compatible with the modern temper, Wright and other OT colleagues concerned with the place of the OT in the community of faith sought, in the words of Krister

---

always clearly affirmed and sought to demonstrate the religious and cultural influence of Canaan on Israel, but he still spoke of "irruptions of paganism into Israel" or claimed that Israelite authors were able to utilize this contribution "without permitting it seriously to distort their monotheistic approach" (180).

The most influential works of Frankfort were his essays on myth and reality co-authored with his wife (1946), later republished and widely read in a paperback version (1949), and *Kingship and the Gods*. While the former work continues to be read and used (a new edition in paper has just appeared under the original title), the essays by the Frankforts that were crucial for Wright contain judgments about the logic and thought of ancient men and women, their sense of the relationship between myth and reality, that are more speculative and less certainly to be inferred from Near Eastern texts than the manner of their presentation would suggest.

Jacobsen's principal contribution was his essay on Mesopotamian thought. His influence on Wright is something of an anomaly, for in all his works on Mesopotamian religion, he has manifested a deeply empathetic understanding and appreciation of its various dimensions and developments that would seem to be less conducive to Wright's vigorous apologetic in behalf of Yahwism against other contemporary religious expression. Jacobsen has, however, always held to the view that Israel's religion opened up possibilities that may have been incipient in Mesopotamian religion but did not develop out of it (e.g., 1949:233; 1976:164).

Stendahl, to turn the "experience of the distance and strangeness of biblical thought" into a "creative asset rather than . . . a destructive and burdensome liability" (420).

The situation vis à vis the study of Israel's religion was not significantly different on the Continent, although the unified biblical theology approach of this side of the Atlantic was not duplicated there. Barth's impact was felt, however, and the interest in OT theology and hermeneutics in the twenty years after the war was, if anything, even stronger. As Wright is probably the best representative of what was happening in this country, so Gerhard von Rad stood at the forefront of the trends on the Continent. He produced the most comprehensive and important OT theology since that of Walther Eichrodt in the 1930s, and he was at the center of the group of scholars working on the *Biblischer Kommentar* who sought to wrestle explicitly with the hermeneutical issues involved in interpreting the OT. Indicative of the meaning of this for the history of the religion of Israel is von Rad's handling of that subject in his *Old Testament Theology*. He prefaced the work with a hundred-page chapter entitled "A History of Yahwism and of the Sacral Institutions of Israel." But how that should be integrated into the theology of the OT is not clear. It seems to be left up in the air, disconnected from all that follows. Von Rad's methodological presuppositions, his prolegomena, are given *after* this history of Israel's religion is laid out. Indeed, he finally regards the idea of "the religion of Israel" as problematical, a methodological assumption fully consistent with his approach and valid if one has in mind a static, noncomplex reality.

Von Rad was certainly not atypical. The period up to the mid to late 1960s has been called the golden age of OT theology (Dentan). And the debate about how the OT is to be understood in relation to the NT and in relation to the present communities of faith involved many public participants (Mays). A perceptible shift began, however, in the 1960s, a revival of interest in the history of Israel's religion. It must not be assumed that the field lay fully dormant in the years after the war. Otto Eissfeldt continued to devote himself vigorously to the examination of many questions having to do with Israel's religion and its Near Eastern environment, including the significance of the Ugaritic and Phoenician texts for Israel's religion, the origins of Yahweh and his relationship to the gods of Canaan, cultic places and actions, and the relation of myth and ritual (1962–72). Scandinavian scholarship, best represented by Ivan Engnell and Sigmund Mowinckel but including a number of other major figures such as Widengren, Kapelrud, and Hvidberg, focused attention especially on the religious character of Israel's king, stirring up conversation among themselves and other scholars, particularly advocates of the so-called myth and ritual school in Great Britain (Hooke, 1933, 1935, 1958). The issues involved revolved around whether the appropriate modifying adjective for Israel's kingship is "sacral" or "divine." Tied up in that question are many other complex and debated matters: the degree of influence of other Near Eastern cultures, especially that of Ugarit, on Israel's notion of kingship, the nature of kingship in Ugarit and Mesopotamia, the relationship of myth to ritual, the place of the psalms in the cultic activity of Israel, and the role of the king in the Israelite festival(s). The reaction of German OT scholars to these developments in Scandinavia and Great Britain tended to be negative (see below).

Jewish scholarship was not influenced significantly by these theological and hermeneutical developments of the postwar era.[2] Most of Yehezkel Kaufmann's multivolume *History of Israelite Religion* appeared in the decade after the war (1937–56; 1960). It is a very individual work that nevertheless manifests some interesting comparisons with what was taking place in American biblical theology. Both affirmed a focus on the historical over against the natural and the mythological. Kaufmann and Wright saw the Wellhausenist approach to Israel's literature and religion as radically wrong and set that approach as a principal target of attack. Both of these scholars maintained the monotheistic character of Israel's religion and its sharp divergence in essentials and in details from the polytheistic pagan religions of the ancient Near East. Kaufmann went even further, however, arguing that the gulf between Israelite religion and paganism was so great that the former could not even understand the latter. While there may have been some unconscious influences, Israelite religion saw pagan religion simply as fetishism. The idolatries posed no serious threat to the primacy and uniqueness of the God of Israel. Even popular religion did not have a serious rootage in paganism (see below).

While many would find Kaufmann's position extreme in its sharp separation of Israelite religion from the influence of her neighbors, his great work has had continuing influence on biblical scholarship, Jewish and non-Jewish. It is somewhat ironic that at the same time that Kaufmann was producing his *History* other Jewish scholars, particularly H. L. Ginsberg and Umberto Cassuto, were doing first-rate interpretive work on the Ugaritic literature that would help lay the foundations for the continuing effort to examine the relationship between Canaanite religion and Israelite religion. Indeed, the contribution of Jewish scholars to the interpretation of the Ugaritic texts and their significance for the history of Israel's religion has continued without break since the war, and the names of Matitiahu Tsevat, Cyrus Gordon, Moshe Held, Nahum Sarna, Baruch Levine, and

---

2 Martin Buber's work was influential in this period. It was not, however, his straightforward OT writing that had a large impact. Rather, it was his more theological and philosophical study, *I and Thou*, a work that was particularly congruent with Protestant theological conversation at the time.

Jonas Greenfield are identified in a major way with the study of the Ugaritic literature and its implications for Israelite religion.

These continuing investigations into Israel's religion in its Near Eastern context contributed to a revival of interest in the history and character of that religion. Several other developments were a part of the renewal that began in the late 1950s and the early 1960s. Questions began to be raised about the notions of revelation that divorced it from the realities of the religious life out of which it had come (Koch, Rendtorff, Barr). Focus on the theology of the OT and hermeneutical issues tended to draw attention more to methodological concerns than to substantive and material ones and sometimes blurred the dynamic of Israelite faith in favor of a more static presentation. Further, much of the consensus that had been present under the rubric of biblical theology began to erode because biblical scholars had begun to approach the material afresh with phenomenological, historical, and comparative questions (Childs, 1970).

This renewed interest in Israel's religion is reflected in many ways and in many persons. Only some of the most obvious landmarks of that shift can be noted here:

(1) The intensified interest in the ancient Near East and the exploding knowledge of Israel's environment on the basis of epigraphic and other discoveries in Palestine proper and in Egypt, Syria, and Mesopotamia have opened up new possibilities for our understanding of Israel's religion. One has only to think of the number of sanctuaries uncovered in Palestine, inscriptions having to do with prayer, judicial matters, and cultic activities, extensive references to and detailed myths about the gods of Canaan, and the existence now of some thirty to thirty-five occurrences of the name Yahweh with various epithets in inscriptional contexts, to recognize that much new material is available and still being digested for its implications for Israel's religion.[3]

---

[3] Three examples of the ways in which these data may seem both to confirm and to challenge the picture of Israelite religion given in the Bible are offered by way of illustration. (1) In all of the places but one (at Kuntillet Ajrud the data are ambiguous) where there are multiple uses of the divine name, YHWH is the only deity mentioned in Hebrew preexilic inscriptions. One can add to that the Moabite evidence, which clearly identifies Yahweh as the god of the northern kingdom of Israel. At Arad there existed a cultic center of some sort that must be judged Yahwistic in light of the exclusive use of the name Yahweh in the letters. This is consistent with the biblical data about the primacy of Yahweh and his place as the sole deity of Israel. (2) Among theophoric personal names in all Hebrew inscriptions only 6 to 7 percent are explicitly non-Yahwistic, and most of these are "Baal" names on the Samaria Ostraca, exactly where one might expect Baal names in the light of the biblical evidence. (3) In two Judaean sites, however, Khirbet el Qom and Kuntillet Ajrud, we now have multiple references to yhwh w'šrth, "Yahweh and his asherah," a phrase whose meaning is much debated and—on the basis of the biblical evidence—hardly what one would expect in a Yahwistic context.

(2) Several essays appeared about the same time in Germany pressing for a renewal of attention to the history of religion and offering methodological suggestions in that regard. Prominent among these were articles by Klaus Koch and Rolf Rendtorff (1963) which sought to lay out the implications of the Alt-Noth approach to the origins of Israel for understanding the beginnings of her religion. They pointed out that prior to Israel's settlement, various strands and aspects of the ancient Near Eastern world—clan religion and Canaanite religion, Hittite treaties, and Baal imagery—came together in a complex way. The particularity of Israel's religion is in the result of this coming together, not in any single element, which can always be paralleled. This means that there is no single revelatory moment; there is no single religious mediator, and Israel's religious origins and particularity must be seen in and through the religious world and not only over against it.[4]

Claus Westermann called for close attention to the *religionsgeschichtliche* background of Israel's religion because that is a part of understanding the OT for itself, the literal sense of the text. To exclude these dimensions from exegesis is not to deal with the OT as we have it but only a postulated OT. One must, however, not deal with parallels in particulars—a single phenomenon, concept, epithet, etc. That can have no significance, or it can indeed be misleading. Rather, one must seek to work with phenomenological unities, basic structures in Israelite faith, when comparisons are being made (1964, 1974). Westermann, then, sought to illustrate this point by several examples, such as the primeval history, the relation of law and commandment, and the Psalter.[5]

Some of the assumptions about Israel's history that were built into Koch's and Rendtorff's approach no longer belong to a general consensus (e.g., the amphictyonic structure of Israel, the early relation of Israelite covenant to Hittite treaty), but the basic direction they charted is sound. They appropriately called for a *religious* and *phenomenological* analysis of Israel's faith that would not sharply separate the religious and the theological. Any theological interpretation of Israel's existence will have to grow out of an awareness of Israel's continuity with her religious world not simply in terms of religion being *like* that of Egypt, Mesopotamia, and Canaan but in the recognition of a complex interaction with that world at many points, sometimes out of it, sometimes against it, often in a kind of creative tension that appropriates much from the milieu while

---

[4] Friedrich Baumgärtel made a vigorous double response to this approach, especially the work of Koch. He affirmed the revelatory character of Israelite faith and the radically different character of Israel's God as evidenced, for example, in the absence of a female consort, the transcendent rather than immanent character of Yahweh vis à vis the natural elements, and the personal, historical sphere of Yahweh's activity rather than the natural.

[5] Even more important in this regard is Westermann's careful use of parallel material from the ancient Near East in his great commentary, *Genesis 1–11* (1976).

giving it a new shape that may produce a rather sharp disjunction. Westermann is certainly correct in arguing that one must examine basic structures of Israel's religion in relation to that of other religions of the Near East. Such parallels or analogies will more likely illumine that religion than will minor and very particular parallels. There may be times, however, when less significant matters are in fact clarified by the data from other cultures. One thinks, for example, of the *marzēaḥ*, which is alluded to only twice in the OT (Amos 6:7 and Jer 16:5) but may be understood in some detail as a socioreligious institution on the basis of Aramaic and Ugaritic evidence (Miller, 1971), or the *asherah* of the OT, which has to be interpreted on the basis of OT contexts but only as they are placed in the context of Ugaritic, Phoenician, Arabic, and Akkadian sources.[6]

(3) The 1960s also witnessed the appearance of several major surveys of the history of Israel's religion, by Vriezen, Ringgren, Fohrer, and Schmidt (1968). The last focused only on the notion of deity in Israel, but within that more narrow focus Schmidt examined Israel's belief about God historically and comparatively, producing a historical survey that is judicious and constructive. It is in some respects as close to OT theology as it is to the history of Israel's religion. Ringgren's work is a general survey with considerable attention and indebtedness to Scandinavian scholarship. His primary focus is on the period of the monarchy. Ringgren, Vriezen, and Fohrer all provide competent textbooks for the study of the history of Israel's religion. They draw upon the numerous recent individual studies of particular aspects of that religion, sometimes engaging in rather vigorous debate with some of the dominant points of view of Noth and von Rad (e.g., Vriezen). All of these are useful and balanced works. No single one has established itself as preeminent or representing a consensus of the field.

(4) The most substantive new construct for the history of Israel's religion is that put forth by Frank M. Cross in several articles, but especially in his book *Canaanite Myth and Hebrew Epic*, which is not a full history of Israel's religion but in its various chapters moves from origins to postexilic times laying out basic directions and theses for understanding that history. The study represents much independent research and a heavy focus on linguistic, literary, and religious evidence from the Near East. At the same time he engages in conversation with some of the dominant approaches to that religion, including Wellhausen (with whom

---

[6] That is even more clearly the case now with the presence of the expression *yhwh w'šrth* in epigraphic sources from preexilic Judaean sites. It is an unusual expression that must inform and be informed by OT references in its interpretation, as well as by Ugaritic evidence where an analogous expression is found when El refers to *laṭrty*, for "my Aṭirat" (*PRU*, II, 39).

he is not infrequently in agreement while differing radically with his basic approach), the myth and ritual school of Scandinavia and Great Britain, and the history-of-redemption approach, which he associates with Noth, von Rad, and their successors in Germany.

For Cross, the "idealistic and romantic presuppositions" that undergirded the work of W. Vatke and Wellhausen and were inherited by Gunkel and other literary and form critics are still overly influential when the archaeological discoveries of this century and even before have significantly discredited them. Assumptions, for example, that qualities such as length, complexity, and rationality belong to later stages of development and, therefore, can only reflect the religion and literature of a late period, or the reverse, i.e., that brevity, simplicity, and primitiveness clearly belong to earliest stages, are no longer warranted on the basis of the evidence. This does not mean that Cross sees no order or development in Israel's religion. On the contrary, typologies and order are essential ingredients of his whole approach whether he is dealing with linguistic, literary, historical, archaeological, or religious matters or with a complex of these.[7] But that development and order must be worked out or perceived in relation to the milieu or context of Israel's life and the continuities between Israel's religion and the culture out of which it came. Further, to understand that religion, one must come to some realization of how Israel dealt with myth and history. Here Cross rejects either a notion that Israel's religion represented a historicizing of originally mythic elements or the reverse, a mythologizing of historical experience. The following paragraph is indicative of his approach and a major clue to his understanding of the history of Israel's religion:

> Characteristic of the religion of Israel is a perennial and unrelaxed tension between the mythic and the historical. Concern with this aspect of Israel's religious expression gives some unity to the essays to follow. Israel's religion emerged from a mythopoeic past under the impact of certain historical experiences which stimulated the creation of an epic cycle and its associated covenant rites of the early time. This epic, rather than the Canaanite cosmogonic myth, was featured in the ritual drama of the old Israelite cultus. At the same time the epic events and their interpretation were shaped strongly by inherited mythic patterns and language, so that they gained a vertical dimension in addition to their horizontal, historical stance. In this tension between mythic and historical elements the meaning of Israel's history became transparent. (1973:viii)

[7] Note his critical response to Yehezkel Kaufmann's work: "The empirical historian must describe novel configurations in Israel's religion as having their origin in an orderly set of relationships which follow the usual typological sequences of historical change" (1973:viii).

Cross regards the term "epic" as the best designation of the "constitutive genre of Israel's religious expression" (1973:viii).[8] That genre includes the JE sources of the early monarchy, the Deuteronomistic history, and the Chronicler's work (in which he includes Ezra and Nehemiah). Other sources are used by Cross, but the epic tradition is the key: "Israel's choice of the epic form to express religious reality, and the elevation of this form in their cultic drama, illustrates both the linkage of the religion of Israel to its Canaanite past and the appearance of novelty in Israel's peculiar religious concern with the 'historical'" (1973:ix). The volume *Canaanite Myth and Hebrew Epic* is in one sense, as its subtitle suggests, only a collection of essays. At the same time it is a programmatic treatment of the history of the religion of Israel that takes up significant aspects of that history from beginning to end and, building upon the work of the past, takes a generally fresh approach to familiar issues. The treatment of the origins of the God of Israel is an example. It is easily the most significant and comprehensive study of the origins of Israel's religion prior to the league since Alt's study, *Der Gott der Väter*, in 1929. It is indebted to Alt's analysis of patriarchal clan religion while offering a major revision of Alt's understanding of El worship. Here Cross draws upon Ugaritic literature, inscriptional evidence, and sources that range across the Mediterranean world from Old Akkadian to Punic. This wide-ranging mastery and use of Near Eastern data alongside the biblical evidence is fundamental to his reconstruction. More than his mentor Albright, Cross gives primary attention to the biblical texts themselves, but they are placed in conversation with the extra-biblical data, not for the sake of demonstrating parallels—an endeavor in which Cross seems singularly uninterested—but in order to understand the religion of Israel more accurately. His interpretation of the origins of Yahwism out of the worship of tutelary clan deities identified with the high god El of Amorite and Canaanite religion, his emphasis on the seminal character of the imagery of Yahweh as Divine Warrior, and his general treatment of the early cultus[9] and particularly the impact of images and patterns from the mythology of Baal have exerted widespread influence, not only among his students where the influence is obvious in the dissertations

---

[8] Characteristic of the epic genre is the interpretation of historical events that combines mythic and historical features in various ways and proportions. This designation is preferable to "historical" because "epic" refers to the interaction of a people and their god(s) in the temporal realm whereas "historical" assumes only human agency. "Myth," on the other hand, refers to primordial events and seeks static structures of meaning.

[9] Cross's argument for David's establishment of a co-priesthood of both Mushite (Abiathar) and Aaronic (Zadok) lineage is another good example of his building upon work of the past that has been widely followed (i.e., Wellhausen's analysis of the history of the priesthood and his claim that Moses is the dominant figure of the early traditions) while breaking significantly with past consensus (i.e., in arguing against Wellhausen's assumption that Zadok did not belong to the Aaronite line) (1973:195–215).

and other works that have come out under his direction but also among biblical scholars generally.

II. METHODOLOGICAL ISSUES

Uniqueness versus Commonality

The methodological problem of uniqueness vs. commonality or continuity vs. discontinuity lies both in discovering with some certainty where uniqueness may be found or what constitutes genuine continuity or commonality and in the meaning of that commonality.

The worship of a deity whom one addresses in prayer and to whom one ascribes power is certainly an element—indeed a very fundamental one—that Israel's religion shared with her neighbors, but it can hardly be identified as a significant point of continuity in describing that religion. Were one to find Yahweh listed as a prominent deity in the pantheon of Moab, Byblos, Ugarit, or Mari, that would be a common religious datum of marked importance. What one encounters throughout Israel's religion is an ongoing process of appropriation and transformation of aspects of the divine world and cultic ordering as they were manifest in her environment (Fohrer: 101-6). The extent to which one may speak of a conscious borrowing as over against a less conscious use of the religious ideology and paraphernalia available to Israel at various stages of her history is debatable. The notion of religious "borrowing" is no more or less appropriate for Israel than for Moab or Edom or, for that matter, Aramaean religion in its various forms. More accurate would be the notion of inheritance, i.e., Israel, taking form as a community of faith, inherited religious elements from the world in which it came into being. As uncertain as the idea of conscious borrowing is the view that Israel consciously rejected elements of Canaanite or other Near Eastern religions (Fohrer: 104-5). To be sure, there are significant moments in the history of Israel's religion when it quite explicitly rejected certain options that were available, and indeed some rejections were present always and at the heart of that religion. But that is not the same as simply regarding elements absent from Israel's religion as being consciously rejected. At least one should make such claims on more extensive and sophisticated bases than argument from silence. The focus of analysis should be on what is chosen and present in the paradigm of Israel's religion, not on what is absent, unless rejection can be identified in the paradigm as a conscious element.

While various proposals have been put forward to identify central elements of discontinuity or uniqueness in Israel's religion,[10] the most

[10] Fohrer claims that Yahweh, unlike other gods, does not act within the cycle of nature so as to be indistinguishable from it but deals rather with the fate of human beings and nations

likely candidates are the initial demands of the Decalogue, the claim of exclusive worship by Yahweh, and the aniconic requirement (Schmidt, 1968, 1969). These demands belong together form-critically in the Decalogue and in the history of Israel's religion. They run throughout the history of that religion and often function as the decisive elements over against the intrusion of other religious paradigms.[11] Even more fundamental, the absence of Yahweh from other Near Eastern pantheons, the exclusion of any other deities from Israel's "pantheon," and the emphasis upon the name of the deity all combine to point to Yahweh as the centrally distinctive aspect of Israel's religion. That is, the uniqueness of that religion is in the deity worshiped. Yet even as one affirms this major point of discontinuity, one is immediately thrust into the realm of commonality, for in most respects Yahweh appears in the texts as a typical Late Bronze/Iron Age god. He has a name and character, anthropomorphic form, associations with a people or nation, a dwelling place in the heavens, an entourage, associations with nature, and typical roles, e.g., father, creator, judge, warrior, and king. Consequently, one cannot describe Israel's religion accurately by focusing on elements of discontinuity. The commonality looms large and must play a role in any description and assessment.

Any formal efforts at such description and assessment must wrestle with the balance and interaction of these two dimensions.

In many methodological issues in the study of the OT, there are underlying theological questions or issues either hiding beneath the surface or explicitly asserted. That is certainly the case here. The issue may be stated succinctly: To what extent is the uniqueness of Israel's faith, however understood, the category or element that ensures, enhances, or is necessary for its revelatory and truth claims? G. E. Wright asserted the utter uniqueness of Israel's faith and saw there the principal indicator of its revelatory character. The failure of his analysis to carry the day in the long run only sharpens the issue. If the structure of Israel's faith must be seen in closer relationship to the religious world in which it took shape, how is one to integrate that reality into any theological understanding of

---

directly and that Yahweh is set apart as a God of ethical demands (79). The former element is less clearly identified as unique in the nature of Yahweh in the light of the work of B. Albrektson, who has demonstrated that the "idea of historical events as divine revelation must be counted among the similarities" (114).

Another proposal is that of Vriezen, following Baumgartner, who lists the absence of the element of sex in deity, the repudiation of magical rites to induce fecundity, and the absence of the idea of the dying and rising god as three important points of difference between Israelite and Canaanite Phoenician religion (73).

[11] One notes, for example, other legal formulations that grow out of the first commandment or are analogous to it in the Hexateuch, the historical books, the Psalms, and the prophets; the jealousy of Yahweh; the role of the Shema in Deuteronomy; and the attitude of Deutero-Isaiah to the gods and the idols.

the OT or judgments about its religious and revelatory priority over other religious expressions of that time?[12]

Antiquity versus Late Retrojections

To what extent is the material before us an authentic presentation of the religious views and practices of the period about which it speaks, and to what extent does it reflect the later period from which it comes to us? Here clearly we confront the challenge of Wellhausen. The problem is a complex one and not easily handled. The conclusions one reaches are usually the result of assumptions as much as data. The difficulty of dating material is obvious. The presumption is usually that the tradition as we receive it is in fairly late form, though Albright, Cross, Freedman, their students, and others have produced some criteria that enhance the possibility of determining what is earlier, at least regarding poetry (Cross and Freedman; Freedman; Robertson). At the opposite end of the spectrum is the work of John Van Seters, a student of F. V. Winnett, who places virtually the whole of the OT literature in the exilic and postexilic eras. His work also sharpens the issue at the point of deciding whether or not literature whose written form shows clear signs of late formulation can tell us of earlier concepts and practices. For Van Seters a work illumines primarily its own age. For Cross, as an opposite example, much information about the whole course of Israel's religion is imbedded in the OT narratives when they are analyzed in relation to comparative data and when typologies are developed carefully.

The concern for origins is obviously an aspect of this issue. That is in part because a grasp of the beginning point should allow one to perceive and understand the ongoing history with greater clarity as well as simply claiming a larger perception of the history of Israel's religion than one will find if all the material is late and reflects only its own time. But here too there is probably a significant theological issue involved: Does greater antiquity give to practices and ideas a higher theological priority or enhance their truth claims? For example, does one give to the Decalogue a higher theological and ethical weight if it belongs to the actual foundations of Israel's religion rather than being a sort of late pastiche of customs and laws that developed in Israel? The reconstruction of the history of Israel's religion does not depend upon the answer to that question, but it can be affected by the assumptions of those who carry out that reconstruction.[13]

---

12 For some preliminary proposals about dealing with this issue, see P. D. Miller, 1973.

13 There is at present a counteremphasis in OT studies that focuses the primary interpretive and theological attention on the latest form of the text, but this approach evidences little interest in the history of Israel's religion whether early or late (e.g., Childs, 1979).

Organizing the History of Israel's Religion

Any attempt to recreate or describe Israel's religion will organize that history in some way. But will that organization seek to clarify and set forth an essential structure or portray Israel's religion in terms of various stages, or will it set forth with little overt schematization a complex phenomenon that resists organization if one is to portray it faithfully? Although Frank Cross's work in some ways represents the first category, focusing on the tension between the mythic and the historical as a fundamental characteristic of Israel's religion, his elaboration of that religion is complex and resists the effort to set forth the history of Israel's religion in neat or ordered stages (1973). Werner Schmidt also has seen an inner coherence to Israel's religion in the persistence of the power of the first commandment. In a very basic way one may describe the history of Israelite religion in terms of what it has done with or about that commandment. Yet another important effort to uncover and describe the inner structure of Israelite religion is found in the work of George Mendenhall, who in a number of studies—and on the basis of a broad range of data—has argued that the basic structure of Israelite religion is the covenant, which shaped its character and differentiated it from other religions. The elements of that structure are present at the beginning and were never lost.

The effort to understand Israel's religion in terms of various stages is seen in Fohrer's *History*; he describes several influences (Mosaic Yahwism, kingship, prophecy, Deuteronomic theology, and incipient eschatology) that shaped Israel's religion in an essentially sequential way. Fohrer is of course aware that the changes and stages evolve and that influences persist into new periods. Ringgren, on the other hand, ostensibly develops a picture of Israel's religion on a historical basis, but the religion of the monarchy takes up two-thirds of his discussion and the religion of the patriarchs, Moses, the judges, the exilic period, and the postexilic period takes up the remaining third of the presentation. There is no overarching structure perceived in the religion beyond what one might lay out in a phenomenological analysis of any religion.

Again, one may suggest an underlying theological issue here while not claiming that it controls the formulations. That issue has to do with whether or not there are stages (Mosaic, prophetic, etc.) in Israel's religious history or aspects (prophetic, priestly, Deuteronomic, legal, etc.) that, either implicitly or explicitly, are regarded as normative. We are probably more careful than Wellhausen about letting our value judgments and theological predispositions shape our results, but they still may be matters of concern or influences. Or we may simply argue that the data force upon us a view about what should be regarded as normative. An important example of this is to be found in the works of George

Mendenhall and Norman Gottwald. While the work of these two scholars has been done independently, there are lines of continuity between them, and they have engaged in an ongoing dialogue. For both scholars, sociological and anthropological tools are important, and in both cases the premonarchical period is normative. That is where Gottwald sees the formation of the egalitarian society, which went against the grain of ancient Near Eastern cultures but became normative for Israel, even if often suppressed.[14] Mendenhall and Gottwald both see the monarchy as a negative development, the breakdown of the egalitarian society under the kingship of Yahweh and "a reversion to the old Bronze Age paganism" (Mendenhall, 1975:158).

The Nature of the Religion

A final methodological issue is the problem of deciding which religion is to be studied. Is the proper subject of investigation the Yahwism described in the biblical sources as normative, or is it the popular religion which may have been very different from or even opposed to Yahwism? But here already one encounters a critical issue of debate— the nature and character of popular religion or piety in Israel and the basis for defining it. The recrudescence of interest in the history of Israel's religion has brought with it a renewed attention to this question but hardly a consensus about either the nature of popular piety or the sources for its reconstruction. For some the popular religion consisted of those practices and beliefs against which the representatives of official or normative Yahwism—e.g., prophets, Deuteronomists—inveighed with great vigor. C. J. Labuschagne represents this perspective with the following definition: "Popular theology is the result of a process of corruption and perversion of true Yahwism, imperceptibly moving with the prevailing spirit of the times, like a putrefaction transmuting one living cell after the other" (123).

For Yehezkel Kaufmann, understanding popular religion is crucial for understanding the nature of Yahwism. He sees a distinction between public, royally promoted cults and the private practices of individuals. But that distinction operated within acceptable and unacceptable Yahwistic practices. The crucial thing is that the popular religion was Yahwistic and not a Canaanized, paganized syncretism. Kaufmann perceives the popular religion negatively as idolatrous. But it was a "vestigial idolatry," the worship of Yahweh in pagan ways, not the worship of other gods. It happened within a religion of the folk that was nonmythological and monotheistic.

---

[14] One clearly infers from Gottwald's writings and his views on political and social concerns that the *egalitarian paradigm* of Israel has continuing relevance.

More recent studies of this issue have been less inclined to define popular religion or piety negatively as a syncretizing and paganizing of Yahwism. Rather it is to be understood as an inner-Israelite aspect of Yahwism distinct from the official cult. The most extensive work in this area has been done by R. Albertz (1978), at least in part under the theological influences of his teacher, Claus Westermann. Others, however, have sought to demonstrate a more positive place or role for popular religion, among them James Crenshaw, Martin Rose, H. Vorländer, and E. Gerstenberger. The characteristics of this popular religion are perceived somewhat differently by these various scholars, but there are common threads running through some of the analyses. Popular religion or piety functions more within the realm of the family than within the large social or religious community. It focuses on the individual and the personal more than on the whole community.[15] The personal relation with the deity who protects and guides is central.[16]

Differences exist in the understanding of what popular religion was in Israel, created to a large degree by different judgments about the appropriate sources from which to learn about that religion. Does one draw from the description of the practices of the people that are described as contrary to Yahwism in such sources as the Deuteronomistic history, and if so how does one separate these non-Yahwistic practices from the public, official cult in which the king is often at the center of things? One of the primary sources in the estimation of some scholars is the rather extensive amount of quotation of the views of the people in the oracles of the prophets. Crenshaw (1970) has fairly accurately described the main themes in these citations of the views of the people. Whether one has here a popular religion or the changing views of the audiences of the prophets is not entirely clear. Albertz (1978) has focused attention on the individual laments, which are also the basis of Gerstenberger's investigations, and on the data of patriarchal religion. In addition he sees in the personal names of Israelites (as well as of Babylonians) clues to aspects of personal religion. Here is a fruitful avenue of investigation, though one must ask whether it is really possible to mark off a core of personal piety distinguishable from the official cult when many of the verbs and nouns can be and are used in Yahwistic expressions that would be associated with the Yahwism of the sanctuary and the community. Along with the

[15] Crenshaw sets up a somewhat different description of what he calls the *vox populi*, each characteristic having both negative and positive dimensions: (1) confidence in God's faithfulness, (2) satisfaction with traditional religion, (3) defiance in the face of prophets who hold a different view, (4) despair when hope seems dead, (5) doubt about the justice of God, and (6) historical pragmatism (1971:24).

[16] This may be compared with the description of personal religion given by Thorkild Jacobsen (1976:147–64). Albertz has sought to show that the distinction between official cult and popular religion was much the same in Israel and Mesopotamia (1978).

names from the OT one needs to examine the large onomasticon from the ever-increasing corpus of Hebrew inscriptions as well as the inscriptions themselves and anepigraphic data from the excavation of biblical sites. These data are quite revealing. Very little of the epigraphic material can be related to the temple cultus though there are references to it. Rather, we have to do with letters, administrative matters, disputes, contracts, grave inscriptions, and prayers of people in hiding far from the official shrines. But in all of this it is clear that Yahweh and Yahweh alone is the deity with whom the writers and those about whom they write have to do. The theophoric names are almost entirely composed of *yhwh* forms or *'ēl*. Only in the several *b'l* names on the Samaria ostraca does one find exceptions. One is not surprised to find exceptions there, but these are only a very small part of the epigraphic onomasticon, and even they exist alongside a significant number of Yahwistic names. The name "Yahweh" itself is now widely attested in Judaean inscriptions (over thirty examples) and there are no references to other deities.[17] Here the evidence, insofar as it testifies to popular religious ideas, is completely consistent with the normative Yahwism of the OT and the official cultus. But an important variation occurs in the texts from Kuntillet Ajrud and Khirbet el Qom, where reference is made to "Yahweh and his asherah" (*yhwh w'šrth*). These references, appearing in contexts that seem to deal with the piety of Yahwists, apparently accept a religious component of some sort (cult object, sanctuary, or consort) that is universally condemned in the literature of the OT but seems to have existed alongside Yahwism. In a similar way artifactual evidence confirms the OT picture of the worship of Yahweh while also modifying it. This can be seen in the absence of male figurines or idols from Israelite and Judaean sites while female figurines exist in abundance. The former is consistent with the OT picture; the female figurines, however interpreted, are not.

The issue of public and personal official and popular religion will continue to be a center of attention in OT research. It is likely that we will have to reckon with a more complex differentiation than the two levels indicate to this point, as has already been suggested by Westenholz for Mesopotamia[18] and Albertz for Israel (1978:297). But any account of Israelite religion will have to reckon with this complexity and the limited character of the official picture of Yahwism provided by the OT. The theological issue that creeps in is a familiar one. It has to do with the

[17] That assumes the references to El and Baal in the texts from Kuntillet Ajrud are from a Phoenician source.

[18] Westenholz sees four levels with the early Akkadian religion but without sharp boundaries between them: (1) the popular religion; (2) the religion of practitioners not attached to the temples (i.e., presumably certain kinds of incantation priests); (3) the religion of practitioners attached to the temples (i.e., the official cult); (4) the official religion of the ruling family in each city state, notably that of the Akkadian kings and their family.

potential disparity between the official cultus and theology as portrayed in the OT and the actual historical reality. For some interpreters a historical judgment that the official religion described to us as a partial, or a minority, report has the potential of raising questions about the authenticity and authority of either the official or normative worship of Yahweh or the various other levels or alternatives. The theological problem of relativism that arises when Israel's religion is seen in commonality with the world of ancient Near Eastern religions now moves internally into our picture of Israelite religion. What is the true religion of Israel, and what is the theological significance of the answer or the inability to answer that question?

III. SOME FURTHER ASPECTS OF ISRAEL'S RELIGION

There are a number of other particular issues in the study of Israel's religion not alluded to above that have received major attention since World War II. The careful and perceptive survey by W. Zimmerli has focused on several of these at a depth that precludes the necessity of going over all the same subjects in these pages.

Among the issues that have been prominent in this period, the role of the king in the religion of Israel has been among the most discussed and debated. The case for the divine character of Israel's king was most strongly argued by the advocates of the myth and ritual school in Great Britain (Hooke, 1933, 1935, 1958) and by some Scandinavian scholars, particularly Ivan Engnell (1943) but including also his teacher Geo Widengren and his student Gösta Ahlström. At the heart of these investigations was the claim to see in the ancient Near East a cultic pattern that centered upon the king who was of divine origin and in some fashion was to be identified with the deity. He was not only the cultic leader but was also in some sense the god-king, who went through various rites, including dying and reviving, to insure the renewal of life and nature, and to demonstrate or recreate the victory of the deity over hostile forces of every sort. The details of this analysis varied from scholar to scholar, but the heart of the matter for all was the view that the king not only had a sacral role but was also in some way divine.

The post–World War II period has been characterized primarily by reaction to this position and a general retreat to a more moderate view. The reaction came in part from students of the ancient Near East, particularly Frankfort (1948, 1951) with regard to the role of the king in Mesopotamia, and from various scholars who investigated kingship in the Ugaritic texts. The former argued vigorously against the existence of any common cultic pattern around the king, much less the particular one being claimed by the proponents of divine kingship. They also argued in detail and effectively that while the Egyptian pharaoh may have had some clear standing and identification as divine, that was not at all true of Mesopotamian kings. De Langhe, Rainey (1965), Gray (1969), and others have challenged the divine kingship-cultic pattern approach to the Ugaritic texts. It is clear that the king had a significant role in the religious activities of Ugarit (though there are only hints of that) and that at least some of the kings were seen as having an intimate relationship with the deity. But the continuing study of the Ugaritic texts confirms a *sacral*, not a divine, character to the kings of Ugarit.

From the OT side the reaction was equally vigorous if not more so. De Fraine, Bernhardt, and Noth (1965) challenged and indeed denied the existence of the god-king ideology in Israel or the existence of a cultic pattern associated with it centering in *hieros gamos* and the king's ritual suffering, dying, and reviving. The cultic character of the psalms is heavily exaggerated when it leads to a widespread reading of a single ritual pattern, a pattern that can be assumed only if one accepts its existence outside the Israelite milieu, which has become less and less tenable. Royal characteristics applied to premonarchical leaders of Israel, which are indeed present, cannot tell us anything of a god-king ideology. Most important, the history of the monarchy in Israel with the frequent prophetic critique and rejection of it stands firmly against the notion that central to Israel's religion were a belief in the divine character of the king and a ritual celebration around the king's sacred marriage and/or mock death and resurrection.

The work of Engnell and others of his disposition has had the salutary effect of bringing to the fore the sacral character of the role of the king in Israel and his importance for the faith and religion of Israel. Efforts to play down this aspect of religion are a distortion of the religion of Israel as it existed from the beginning of the monarchy on. Indeed it is likely that the king's presence or role in the psalms—and thus to some extent in the cultic activities out of which they come—was probably more extensive than often assumed (Mowinckel, 1962:42–80; Eaton).[19] The effort of Georg Fohrer to deny altogether the sacral character of the king does not correspond to the picture given in Israel or elsewhere. The general—but not universal—consensus at the moment in the study of Israel's kingship appears to consist of a recognition that the king had a unique relationship to Yahweh expressed primarily in filial and covenantal terms, participated in a major way in the festival(s), prayer, and sacrifice, functioned as the agent of the deity, and represented the

[19] Mowinckel's analysis of the relationship of the king to the deity and his role in the cult is a modified and more balanced form of the position advocated by Engnell, Widengren, and the exponents of the myth and ritual school. Mowinckel speaks of the king as having "something of the 'divine' in him" (1962:57), but he is careful to explicate this dimension ("superhuman and supernatural power, wisdom and insight") and deny any identification of the king with Yahweh. The king is for Mowinckel truly a *ben 'ēl*.

people to Yahweh. The most extensive elaboration of such a view is found in A. R. Johnson's *Sacral Kingship in Ancient Israel*, but variations of this moderate position are found in other scholars. Ringgren and Mettinger demonstrate a tendency among Scandinavian scholars toward a more moderate view that emphasizes the divine sonship of the king and his sacral functions as distinct from divine kingship. Both Mettinger and Cross (1973) emphasize the importance of the promises to David and the Davidic covenant for understanding the relationship of king and deity. Both also demonstrate—in different ways and with some different conclusions—that there was not just one ideology of kingship in every time and place. Significant differences existed between Israel and Judah, and there were changes in that ideology over time.

Two closely related issues that have received serious attention partly as a result of the study of kingship and partly as a result of the impact of the Ugaritic texts are the place of the kingship of Yahweh in Israel's religious development and the nature of Israel's primary religious festival. Both issues, as well as the various efforts to describe the cultic sacral role of the king, represent efforts to find *the unifying center* of Israelite religion—a center which, depending upon the view espoused, incorporates other dimensions of that religion to a greater or lesser degree. With regard to the matter of Israel's major festival, three hypotheses have dominated the scholarly discussion. H.-J. Kraus proposed that the Feast of Tabernacles was the primary festival during the monarchy. It centered in a celebration of Yahweh's choice of David as king and of Zion as his abode (1951; 1966:179–88). Such texts as 2 Samuel 6 and 7, 1 Kings 8, and Psalm 132 provide the basic clues to this Royal Zion Festival. For Artur Weiser, the center of the cultus was the Covenant Festival, celebrated at the new year in the autumn. It had as its aim to renew the encounter between God and his people as well as the covenant bond established at Sinai. The center of the festival, therefore, was the theophany of Yahweh, dramatically represented in some fashion, but the occasion was liturgically complex and included such matters as the proclamation of the divine name, recital of the Heilsgeschichte, renewal of the covenant, and renunciation of foreign gods. Many texts in the Psalter and elsewhere have served as a foundation for Weiser's hypothesis. Indeed, the very plurality of texts he invokes has been as much a problem for credibility as the rather meager evidence Kraus assembles to support the notion of a Royal Zion Festival.

Both of these proposals have drawn some adherents among students and others, but neither has stood the test of time in a significant way. Nor has either hypothesis provoked the extent of reaction pro and con aroused by the third and earliest reconstruction of Israel's major festival—the Enthronement Festival of Yahweh as proposed by Sigmund Mowinckel. While his basic analysis was set forth over half a century ago, he restated it in forthright fashion shortly after World War II in a form that was eventually translated into English (1962). It has continued to be the subject of much discussion and controversy.

There is no need at this stage of our history to rehearse the details of the Enthronement Festival as Mowinckel reconstructed it. Suffice it to say that he sees this as the primary cultic event in Israel, occurring at the new year Feast of Tabernacles. It is a multifaceted cultic occasion that centers in the declaration "Yahweh has become king" (*yhwh mālak*), but it includes in various ways celebration of his creative activity, victory over all other gods, Yahweh's judgment of gods and nations, the election of Israel, and the covenant made at Sinai. The core of psalms reflecting this festival are the enthronement psalms (47, 93, 96, 97, 98, 99), but Mowinckel draws many other psalms into the picture in connection with various facets of the festival. This last move is crucial. For Mowinckel, the problem with a form-critical approach is that it remains too much on the purely formal level and does not move—as it should—to a truly *cult-functional* interpretation, according to which one discerns important inner correspondences between psalms which outwardly appear to belong to different groups but which are in fact governed by similar ideas and conceptions and thus should be seen together as belonging to a particular cultic, i.e., festival, occasion.

Without rehearsing the various responses to Mowinckel or the discussions among Weiser, Kraus, and Mowinckel—a review that is unnecessary in the light of the recent excellent discussion of the debate by John Gray (1979:7–38), who is sympathetic to Mowinckel's position—several observations can be made: (1) The few allusions to the fall festival suggest that it had the prominence ascribed to it above as the central cultic occasion during the monarchy. One may assume that a number of psalms and other hymns were related to it, not necessarily as many as or the same ones as Mowinckel—or Weiser—has suggested. (2) There is a clear stress upon Yahweh's rule or kingship as a central and climactic element not only in enthronement psalms proper but elsewhere in psalms and poetry. It belongs to earlier rather than later elements of Israel's religious thought as evidenced by its prominence in early Israelite poetry (Exod 15:18; Num 23:21; Deut 33:5; Pss 68.25, 24.9). (3) The expression *yhwh mālak* probably means "Yahweh has become king (and thus reigns)." The analyses of Lipiński (1963) and Gray (1979:20–25) are important here. As they, Mowinckel, and others have recognized, such a translation neither denies the eternal character of Yahweh's reign nor implies anything about a dying and rising god. The expression is more a proclamation of Yahweh's enthronement and rule than an actual royal investiture. (4) There is in several poems (e.g. Exodus 15, Deuteronomy 33, Psalm 68) a pattern that includes Yahweh's coming to deliver and create a people and his victory, which leads to the celebration of kingship and the establishment of his sanctuary. In this pattern Near Eastern mythic elements and Israel's historical experience come together. It is reflected or hinted at in various places in the OT and probably was a major influence on the central festival. (5) Kraus's emphasis on Yahweh's election of David and Jerusalem is appropriate, but it is viewed *too* narrowly and in isolation from or over against other notes that are sounded in harmony with these themes. The choice of Jerusalem would inevitably and early have had larger connotations than simply establishing this city as the place of the temple. It also is the place where Yahweh dwells, is enthroned, and rules. The ark goes up in victory as well as to establish or choose a sanctuary. Kraus tends to ignore the mythic and cosmic overtones in the choosing of Zion, but they are there from the earliest times in the so-called ark narrative (P. D. Miller and Roberts), Psalms 47, 68, and 132. (6) Along these lines Cross has suggested a possibly fruitful direction in underscoring the joining of the motif of exodus and conquest with the motif of creation and kingship in the royal cult. Yahweh enters in victory, having delivered his people, but this is also the ascent of the king to the throne. The institution of kingship and the temple bring the latter, which has many mythological overtones, more to the fore, and these are united with the interest in the choice of David and Zion (1973:91–111).

The one issue that has dominated the discussion of Israel's religion in a way comparable to the question of divine and human kingship is the role of covenant. Eichrodt had claimed the dominating character of covenant in the 1930s in his great *Theology of the Old Testament*, and G. Ernest Wright and others had affirmed its theological significance. But it was a small monograph by George Mendenhall entitled *Law and Covenant in Israel and the Ancient Near East* that sparked the contemporary debate and a renewal of interest in the subject. The significance of Mendenhall's work was that he suggested analogies from the Near East, i.e., Hittite treaties as published and analyzed by E. F. Weidner, J. Friedrich, and V. Korošec, which served to provide a more solid form-critical base for understanding the structure of covenant and gave it a viable setting in the second millennium. His work was paralleled independently on the Continent by Klaus Baltzer. Their works together provided a viable basis for developing the earlier intimations of Alt, von Rad, and Weiser that regular occasions of covenant renewal played a significant part in Israel's religion.

A spate of studies followed these foundational works, some in critical conflict, some elaborating and developing even further the implications of Mendenhall's and Baltzer's discoveries. The criticism centered upon several issues that are still important matters of debate: How did Israel know the treaty forms of the Hittites? Can one date the origins of Israel's covenant by comparison with Hittite treaties? Should first-millennium Aramaic and Akkadian treaties be included, and are there significant differences? Is it legitimate to compare a literary form that is self-contained outside the Bible with a reconstructed form that has to be drawn together from different strata of materials? How many and which elements need to be present in a biblical context to enable one to conclude that in fact the treaty form has been taken over? Can one uncover a liturgical form, i.e., covenant renewal ceremony, from a literary form, i.e., treaty or covenant document?

While these questions were being raised and discussed, various biblical elements were being tied into the treaty form: the love of God commanded in Deuteronomy (Moran), *ṭôb/ṭôbâ* (= friendship) terminology (Moran; Hillers, 1964b; Fox), the knowledge of God and Yahweh's knowledge of Israel (Huffmon, 1966; Huffmon and Parker), the prophetic lawsuit (Huffmon, 1959; Wright, 1962; Harvey), the OT curses (Fensham; Hillers, 1964b), and Priestly covenant formulations (Hillers, 1969:158–68). The verdict is still out on many of these questions and issues, though some important matters seem to be settled, e.g., the unlikelihood that exodus/settlement and Sinai traditions belonged to separate festival occasions in the light of the intimate relationship of the historical prologue and the stipulations in the treaty form (Huffmon, 1965). The impact of the treaty forms on Israel's religious thought can no longer be denied, though we may never know how direct that influence was. Deuteronomy is clearly a covenant document having many affinities with treaty forms (Huffmon, 1965). But the antecedents of this treaty-covenant relationship in Deuteronomy are much debated. L. Perlitt has argued vigorously that the notion of covenant did not exist in Israel prior to the Deuteronomic era. A more balanced and plausible view has been set forth by D. McCarthy who sees pre Deuteronomistic signs of the covenant formulary in Exod 19:3–8, Joshua 24, and 1 Samuel 12, "the oldest evidence for the covenant formulary" (McCarthy, 1978:284). McCarthy holds covenant to be an ancient concept that was originally cultic at Sinai with sacrifice, blood rites, and a covenant meal. Over a long period of time covenant developed toward expression in a structure analogous to the treaty form in Deuteronomy, which was word-centered rather than ritual-centered as at the beginning.

Allusion to Lothar Perlitt's study of covenant theology serves to identify a significant trend in the last two decades, i.e., a return to positions espoused long ago by Julius Wellhausen. The correlation is sometimes intentional, sometimes not. In some cases there are partial affinities. In a number of instances, e.g., the challenge to notions of an early central sanctuary or the claim for a late origin of the covenant, scholars have returned to positions closer to the views of Wellhausen (P. D. Miller, 1982).

A very important modification of the general understanding of religious developments during the time of Assyrian domination has come from two studies prepared independently but reaching somewhat similar conclusions. Against the standard notion that the idolatry and syncretism represented by the presence of Assyrian deities within the Jerusalem temple were the result of imposition of the cult of Aššur and the worship of Assyrian deities generally, John McKay and Morton Cogan have demonstrated, on somewhat different grounds, that nations under Assyrian rule were not forced to adopt Assyrian gods once they were conquered by Assyria. Vassal states had no cultic obligations (so Cogan). Judah's adoption of pagan cults, probably accentuated during the era of Assyrian domination, was a much more complex and autonomous action, probably involving Assyrian mediation. One significant result of this revision is the realization that the reforms of Hezekiah and Josiah were not primarily acts of political rebellion, throwing off the yoke of Assyrian rule by removing the Assyrian gods from the cultus. Such actions would not have signaled in a large way the beginning of rebellion. These reforms were rather a more genuinely religious reaction against a lengthy and steadily increasing tendency toward idolatry and syncretism on the part of Judah, a tendency shaped by Mesopotamian, Aramean, and Canaanite influences.

Efforts to comprehend the complexities of sacrifice and sanctuary in Israel's religion have continued in this period. With regard to the former, the primary advances have been on two fronts: the impact of comparative data and the formal analysis of ritual texts. The accumulation of texts and terminology—especially Ugaritic—from the Near Eastern world has provided a broader basis for comparison of practices and has allowed us to see how much Israel shared a technical sacrificial terminology with her neighbors at very early stages. The extra-biblical data, however, are themselves often very cursory and elusive concerning the details of ritual practices and the distinctions in character among the types of offerings. The most painstaking efforts to interpret the various sacrifices, their order, and their administration have been carried on by Baruch Levine and Jacob Milgrom with important contributions by Anson Rainey (1970) as well as others. Levine has made an important breakthrough in methodology by identifying two primary categories or forms of ritual texts: *prescriptive* texts, which contain instructions for the priests to guide them in carrying out the ritual, e.g., Leviticus 1–7; and *descriptive* texts, which are documents reporting how or when a certain rite was carried out, e.g., Leviticus 8–9, Numbers 7, and 1 Kgs 8:64 (1963, 1965). These categories apply not only to Israelite ritual texts but also to Near Eastern ritual texts generally. Both Levine and Rainey have sought also to uncover the relationship between order and procedure in the administration of sacrifice.

The meaning and character of sacrifice generally and of the individual sacrifices have been the subject of major attention by Levine (1971,

1974) and Milgrom. Building on the earlier work of George Gray and taking account of comparative data, Levine has argued the case for understanding Israelite sacrifice primarily as gift (Levine, 1971). Levine proposes as an "organizing principle, the proposition that the God of Israel desired the sacrifices of his people as a form of tribute to him as their sovereign, in return for which he would grant them the blessings of life" (xxxii; similarly Milgrom, 1976a). For Levine this notion is epito-mized in the šĕlāmîm sacrifice, which while undergoing changes in its history always reflected "the notion of sacrifice as an efficacious gift of greeting" (1974:52). Levine and Milgrom part company in their under-standing of the expiatory offerings. For example, the 'āšām sacrifice was not, in Levine's analysis, an altar sacrifice consumed by fire but "a cultic offering presented to the deity in the form of silver or other objects of value in expiation for certain offenses" (1974:99), while the ḥaṭṭā't "rep-resents the coalescence of two rites: the one a rite of riddance and the other a gift of expiation" (1974:108). That is, the ḥaṭṭā't of the priests reflected a priestly duty to rid the sanctuary of contamination created by priestly offenses; the ḥaṭṭā't of the people, however, was a gift to the priesthood for their services on behalf of the people (1974:108). Mil-grom, on the other hand, sees the function of the 'āšām as dealing with the infringements on or profanation of the realm of the sacred, i.e., holy things, while the ḥaṭṭā't seems to overcome the more serious contamina-tion of the holy, an occurrence that is always sinful and dangerous (1976a:127).

During the same period Rolf Rendtorff devoted a major monograph to the same subject (1967). His aim is to identify some of the critical points for the question of the inner Israelite history of the sacrificial cult. He seeks with some care to identify the different spheres of tradition dealing with the subject and on that basis to uncover something of that history. Rendtorff concludes that the picture of the 'ôlâ sacrifice main-tains an astonishing continuity, while the other types of sacrifice evi-dence continual evolution and change. In the course of his analysis Rendtorff not only sketches a history of these types of sacrifice and the sacrificial cultus, but he concludes that the traditions of the Priestly texts cannot be dismissed out of hand as "late." The cultic theology of the Priestly texts has clear connections to the words of the prophets and even earlier texts.

The sanctuary or shrine as a phenomenon in Israel's religion is a matter of some complexity as well as obscurity. Four areas stand out in the study of this subject over the last forty years:

(1) In the period after World War II Martin Noth's amphictyonic hypothesis as a way of understanding the organization of early Israel dominated the scene and with it the assumption that in the early period as well as later on the primary cultic occasions of the tribes of Israel took

place at a central sanctuary. The major debate was over the location of the central shrine. Albright and those associated with him argued for Shiloh as the primary location, though it may at some time have been at other spots such as Gilgal or Shechem (Albright, 1940:282; Bright: 162), while Noth and others who followed his lead have suggested that the central sanctuary was originally at Shechem and then moved to Bethel and/or Gilgal before finally ending up at Shiloh (Noth, 1965:91–97). During the last decade or more, however, the consensus has disappeared as a result of significant criticism of Noth's hypothesis. A number of voices have challenged the existence of any such unified organization as an amphictyony in early Israel (e.g., Mayes; de Geus). That challenge has for the most part included a denial that the tribes shared any central shrine prior to the time of Saul and David. The multiplicity of major shrines attested in the historical books has led many, but not all, to the view that these shrines served different clans and purposes rather than all the tribes at different times.[20]

(2) The relationship of tent, tabernacle, and ark remains a knotty problem. The claim that tent and ark were historically separate shrines associated with different tribal units and/or different purposes has continued to attract exponents (e.g., Haran, 1960; Maier; Görg; Schmitt; Fritz) even though some, particularly those who have argued for more unity in the early tribal structure of Israel, have maintained the early association of tent and ark that is presented in the biblical material (e.g., Bright; Beyerlin: 112–20). The reassessment of the Priestly traditions leading to an awareness that these include more ancient elements and traditions than was once thought has resulted in a new evaluation of the tabernacle traditions. Menahem Haran has suggested that the Priestly tabernacle is a partial reflection of the Shiloh sanctuary. Frank Cross, followed later by Richard Clifford, pointed out important similarities between the abode of El in the second-millennium Ugaritic texts and the tabernacle description in P (Cross, 1961; Clifford). Rather than being a retrojection from the exile or later based upon the temple, the tabernacle description in Cross's analysis probably rests in part on traditions of the tent-shrine erected by David (cf. Haran, 1962; Davies). In their description of the tabernacles and their discriminating use of forms of *yšb* for God's heavenly dwelling but *škn* for his earthly "tenting," the Priestly

[20] The work of Roland de Vaux provides a good example of the changing perspective during this period. In his *Ancient Israel*, published between 1958 and 1961, he maintained the then pervasive thesis that Israel had many sanctuaries but one was the central sanctuary for the tribal confederation. But in his unfinished history of Israel, originally published 1971–73 and translated in 1978 as *The Early History of Israel*, de Vaux mounted a major attack on the amphictyonic hypothesis that included a detailed argument against the view that the Israelite tribes had a central sanctuary during the period of the judges.

theologians blended together traditions from the past with sophisticated theological construction.

(3) Recent decades have seen the discovery of a number of sanctuaries in Palestine. Bronze Age temples have been discovered at Hazor, Amman, Lachish, Tell Kittan, and Tell Mevorakh. Some of these sites, as is typical of other excavated cities, reveal a series of cult places, one above the other over a broad span of time, indicating the tenacity of local tradition in preserving and maintaining the location of holy places.

Even more significant is the discovery in several places of sanctuaries or temples in Israelite excavation levels. The most famous of these is the temple at Arad, which existed during the first half of the monarchy. Other cult places or shrines have been identified in Israelite levels at Lachish, Beer-sheba, and possibly Kuntillet Ajrud. In the latter case it is doubtful that we are dealing with a temple, and the non-Yahwistic as well as Yahwistic elements in the inscriptions give an unclear picture of the character of the site. In addition, the discovery of an eighth-century seal referring to a "priest of Dor" suggests that there was a sanctuary there also (Avigad).

The significance of these shrines is debated. It is likely that they are Israelite or Judean sanctuaries, and indeed probably Yahwistic in most cases. J. M. Miller has proposed a close relationship between the Jerusalem temple and the Arad temple, "an extension of the Zion cult" headed by Korahites, who are referred to on an ostracon found there. In a study of the Arad and Jerusalem temples, V. Fritz has argued against this conclusion, maintaining the independence of the sanctuary and priesthood at Arad. Fritz claims further that there were two traditions of temple structure in Israel. One was the "long room" type modeled on the so-called Syrian temple type and thus of non-Israelite origin. This is represented in the Jerusalem temple. The Arad temple is an example of the "broad room" type, an ancient Israelite temple type that is modeled on the Israelite house structure. The same type is found in the Hellenistic Lachish temple known as the "solar shrine."

The excavator of Arad, Y. Aharoni, put forth a theory to explain the existence of these sanctuaries outside Jerusalem as well as others alluded to in the Bible. He suggested that they represent a series of sanctuaries built as a necessary part of the royal administrative and military centers set up along the borders. While Fritz has claimed that these sanctuaries cannot all be related to the concern for maintenance of borders, the hypothesis may provide at least partial explanation for some of these Israelite cultic centers.

(4) Finally, there has been considerable attention given to one particular type of cult place, the bāmâ or high place. The discussion in recent times has been sparked by Albright's identification of the high places with funerary shrines associated with the cult of the ancestors

(1957). He regarded the *bāmôt* as burial cairns or stone mounds or a stele set up in honor of someone. The *bêt bāmôt* would be a house of stelae like the stelae temple found at Hazor or the open-air sanctuary with large standing stones found at Gezer. The funerary associations of the *bāmâ* are disputed by some (e.g., Vaught, 1974; Barrick) and Albright's interpretation remains a highly uncertain hypothesis. His view, however, does suggest why the *bāmôt* became increasingly identified as paganizing elements, an attitude accentuated by the associations of *maṣṣēbâ* and *'ašērâ* with the high place. At a minimum it is likely that the high place was a raised elevation, platform, or mound often alongside or near a sanctuary and set up primarily for the purpose of sacrifices. A number of high places have been identified in excavations, but the absence of written remains and the uncertainty of the picture given by the biblical records caution against an overly easy identification of opèn areas, mounds, or platforms with *bāmôt*.

That many issues in the history of Israel's religion would remain untouched or lightly skimmed in these pages was an assumption from the beginning. Yet even this summary presentation shows how fertile scholarship of the last thirty-five years has been in this area and indicates at least something of the rich possibilities on the horizon. New artifacts and inscriptions, continued assimilation of the finds from such places as Ebla, Ugarit, and Mari, as well as the refinements and reconstructions arising from the study of the biblical data, will further sharpen and focus our view of Israel's religion.

BIBLIOGRAPHY

Aharoni, Yohanan
  1969   "Arad: Its Inscriptions and Temple." *BA* 31: 2–32.
Ahlström, Gösta
  1959   *Psalm 89: Eine Liturgie aus dem Ritual des leidenden Königs.* Lund: Gleerup.

Albertz, Rainer
  1974   *Weltschöpfung und Menschenschöpfung. Untersucht bei Deuterojesaja, Hiob und den Psalmen.* Calwer Theologische Monographien, 3. Stuttgart: Calwer.
  1978   *Persönliche Frömmigkeit und offizielle Religion. Religionsinterner Pluralismus in Israel und Babylon.* Calwer Theologische Monographien, 9. Stuttgart: Calwer.

Albrektson, Bertil
  1967   *History and the Gods: An Essay on the Idea of Historical Events as Divine Manifestations in the Ancient Near East and in Israel.* ConBOT 1. Lund: Gleerup.

Albright, William F.
1940   From the Stone Age to Christianity: Monotheism and
           the Historical Process. Baltimore: Johns Hopkins Univer-
           sity Press.
1957   "The High Place in Ancient Palestine." Pp. 242–58 in Vo-
           lume du Congres, Strasbourg, 1956. VTSup 4. Leiden:
           E. J. Brill.
1968   Yahweh and the Gods of Canaan. Garden City, NY:
           Doubleday.

Avigad, Nahman
1975   "The Priest of Dor." IEJ 25: 101–6.

Baltzer, Klaus
1971   The Covenant Formulary in Old Testament, Jewish, and
           Early Christian Writings. Trans. D. E. Green. Philadel-
           phia: Fortress.

Barr, James
1966   Old and New in Interpretation. Philadelphia: West-
           minster.

Barrick, W. Boyd
1975   "The Funerary Character of 'High Places.'" VT 25:
           565–95.

Baumgärtel, Friedrich
1963   "Der Tod des Religionsstifter." KD 9: 223–33.
1967   "Das Offenbarungszeugnis des Alten Testaments in Lichte
           der religionsgeschichtlichvergleichenen Forschung." ZTK
           64: 393–422.

Bernhardt, Karl-Heinz
1961   Das Problem der altorientalischen Königsideologie im
           Alten Testament: Unter besonderer Berücksichtigung
           der Geschichte der Psalmen exegesis dargestellt und
           kritisch gewürdigt. VTSup 8. Leiden: E. J. Brill.

Beyerlin, Walter
1965   Origins and History of the Oldest Sinaitic Traditions.
           Trans. S. Rudman. Oxford: Basil Blackwell.

Bright, John
1972   A History of Israel. 2d ed. Philadelphia: Westminster.

Cassuto, Umberto
1951/1971 Ha-'Elā 'Anath. Jerusalem: Bialik Institute. English trans.
           I. Abrahams, The Goddess Anath. Jerusalem: Magnes.
1974   Biblical and Oriental Studies. Vol. 1: Bible. Jerusalem:
           Magnes.
1975   Biblical and Oriental Studies. Vol. 2: Bible and Ancient
           Oriental Texts. Jerusalem: Magnes.

Childs, Brevard S.
1970   Biblical Theology in Crisis. Philadelphia: Westminster.

1979   *Introduction to the Old Testament as Scripture.* Phila-
                       delphia: Westminster.

Clifford, Richard J.
1971   "The Tent of El and the Israelite Tent of Meeting." *CBQ*
                       33: 221–27.

Cogan, Morton
1974   *Imperialism and Religion: Assyria, Judah and Israel in
                       the Eighth and Seventh Centuries B.C.E.* SBLMS 19.
                       Missoula, MT: Scholars Press.

Crenshaw, James
1970   "Popular Questioning of the Justice of God in Ancient
                       Israel." *ZAW* 82: 380–85.
1971   *Prophetic Conflict.* BZAW 124. Berlin: Walter de
                       Gruyter.

Cross, Frank M.
1961   "The Priestly Tabernacle." Pp. 208–28 in *The Biblical
                       Archaeologist Reader.* Ed. G. Ernest Wright and D. N.
                       Freedman. Garden City, NY: Doubleday.
1973   *Canaanite Myth and Hebrew Epic.* Cambridge, MA:
                       Harvard University Press.

Cross, Frank M., and David Noel Freedman
1975   *Studies in Ancient Yahwistic Poetry.* SBLDS 21. Mis-
                       soula, MT: Scholars Press.

Davies, G. Henton
1962   "Tabernacle." Pp. 498–506 in *IDB*, Vol. 4.

Dentan, Robert C.
1963   *A Preface to Old Testament Theology.* New Haven: Yale
                       University Press.

Eaton, John R.
1976   *Kingship and the Psalms.* SBT 2d series 32. London:
                       SCM.

Eissfeldt, Otto
1962–72   *Kleine Schriften.* 6 vols. Tübingen: J. C. B. Mohr.

Engnell, Ivan
1943   *Studies in Divine Kingship in the Ancient Near East.*
                       Uppsala: Almqvist and Wiksell.
1963   *A Rigid Scrutiny: Critical Essays on the Old Testament.*
                       Trans. and ed. J. T. Willis. Nashville: Vanderbilt Univer-
                       sity Press.

Fensham, F. Charles
1962   "Maledictions and Benedictions in Ancient Near Eastern
                       Vassal-Treaties and the Old Testament." *ZAW* 74: 1–9.
1963   "Common Trends in Curses of the Near Eastern Treaties
                       and *Kudurru*-Inscriptions Compared with Maledictions of
                       Amos and Isaiah." *ZAW* 75: 155–75.

Fohrer, Georg
1972 *History of Israelite Religion.* Trans. D. E. Green. New York: Abingdon.

Fox, Michael
1973 "*Ṭôb* as Covenant Terminology." *BASOR* 209: 41–42.

Fraine, J. de
1954 *L'aspect religieux de la royauté Israélite: L'institution monarchique dans l'Ancien Testament et dans les textes Mesopotamiens.* AnBib 2. Rome: Pontifical Biblical Institute.

Frankfort, Henri
1948 *Kingship and the Gods.* Chicago: University of Chicago.
1951 *The Problem of Similarity in Ancient Near Eastern Religions.* Oxford: Oxford University Press.

Frankfort, H., and H. A. Frankfort
1946/1949 "Myth and Reality" and "The Emancipation of Thought from Myth." Pp. 8–27 and 363–88 in *The Intellectual Adventure of Ancient Man.* Chicago: University of Chicago Press; and pp. 11–36 and 237–63 in *Before Philosophy.* Harmondsworth: Penguin.

Freedman, David N.
1980 *Pottery, Poetry, and Prophecy: Studies in Early Hebrew Poetry.* Winona Lake, IN: Eisenbrauns.

Fritz, Volkmar
1977 *Tempel und Zelt: Studien zum Tempelbau in Israel und zu dem Zeltheiligtum der Priesterschrift.* WMANT 47. Neukirchen-Vluyn: Neukirchener Verlag.

Gerstenberger, Erhard
1971/1980 *Der bittende Mensch: Bittritual und Klagelied des Einzelnen im Alten Testament.* Habilitationsschrift, Heidelberg. Published as *Der bittende Mensch.* WMANT 51. Neukirchen-Vluyn: Neukirchener Verlag.

Geus, C. H. J. de
1976 *The Tribes of Israel. An Investigation into some of the Presuppositions of Martin Noth's Amphictyony Hypothesis.* Studia Semitica Neerlandica 18. Assen: Van Gorcum.

Ginsberg, H. L.
1936 *The Ugarit Texts* (Hebrew). Jerusalem: Bialik Institute.
1955 "Ugaritic Myths, Epics, and Legends." Pp. 129–55 in *Ancient Near Eastern Texts Relating to the Old Testament.* 2d ed. Ed. J. B. Pritchard. Princeton: Princeton University Press.

Görg, Manfred
1967 *Das Zelt der Begegnung: Untersuchung der sakralen Zelttraditionen Altisraels.* BBB 27. Bonn: Peter Hanstein.

Gottwald, Norman
1979   *The Tribes of Yahweh: A Sociology of the Religion of Liberated Israel 1250–1050 B.C.E.* Maryknoll, NY: Orbis Books.

Gray, John
1969   "Sacral Kingship in Ugarit." Pp. 289–302 in *Ugaritica* VI. Paris: Geuthner.
1979   *The Biblical Doctrine of the Reign of God.* Edinburgh: T. & T. Clark.

Haran, Menahem
1960   "The Nature of the 'Ohel Mo'edh in Pentateuchal Sources." *JSS* 5: 50–65.
1962   "Shiloh and Jerusalem: The Origin of the Priestly Tabernacle in the Pentateuch." *JBL* 81: 14–24.

Harvey, Julien
1962   "Le '*rîb*-Pattern,' réquisitoire prophétique sur la rupture de l'alliance." *Bib* 43: 172–96.
1967   *Le Plaidoyer prophétique contre Israël après la rupture de l'alliance.* Montreal: Les Editions Bellarmin.

Hillers, Delbert R.
1964a   "A Note on Some Treaty Terminology in the Old Testament." *BASOR* 176: 46–47.
1964b   *Treaty-Curses and the Old Testament Prophets.* BibOr 16. Rome: Pontifical Biblical Institute.
1969   *Covenant. The History of an Idea.* Baltimore: Johns Hopkins University Press.

Hooke, S. H.
1933   *Myth and Ritual.* London: Oxford University Press.
1935   *The Labyrinth.* London: Oxford University Press.
1958   *Myth, Ritual, and Kingship.* London: Oxford University Press.

Huffmon, Herbert B.
1959   "The Covenant Lawsuit and the Prophets." *JBL* 78: 286–95.
1965   "The Exodus, Sinai, and the Credo." *CBQ* 27: 101–13.
1966   "The Treaty Background of Hebrew *Yada'*." *BASOR* 181: 31–37.

Huffmon, Herbert B., and Simon B. Parker
1966   "A Further Note on the Treaty Background of Hebrew *Yada'*." *BASOR* 184: 36–38.

Hvidberg, Flemming F.
1962   *Weeping and Laughter in the Old Testament.* Leiden: E. J. Brill.

Jacobsen, Thorkild
1946/1949 "Mesopotamia." Pp. 125–219 in *The Intellectual Adventure of Ancient Man.* Chicago: University of Chicago Press; and pp. 137–234 in *Before Philosophy.* Harmondsworth: Penguin.
1970 *Toward the Image of Tammuz.* Cambridge, MA: Harvard University Press.
1976 *The Treasures of Darkness. A History of Mesopotamian Religion.* New Haven: Yale University Press.

Johnson, Aubrey R.
1967 *Sacral Kingship in Ancient Israel.* 2d ed. Cardiff: University of Wales.

Kapelrud, Arvid
1963 *The Ras Shamra Discoveries and the Old Testament.* Trans. G. W. Anderson. Norman: University of Oklahoma Press.
1979 *God and His Friends in the Old Testament.* Oslo: Universitets-forlaget.

Kaufmann, Yehezkel
1937–56 *Tôl^edôt Ha'emunâh Hayyiśrā'ēlît.* 8 vols. Tel Aviv: Bialik Institute.
1960 *The Religion of Israel.* Trans. M. Greenberg. Chicago: University of Chicago Press.

Klatt, Werner
1969 *Hermann Gunkel.* FRLANT 100. Göttingen: Vandenhoeck & Ruprecht.

Koch, Klaus
1962 "Der Tod des Religionsstifters." *KD* 8: 100–123.

Kraus, Hans-Joachim
1951 *Die Königsherrschaft Gottes im Alten Testament.* Tübingen: J. C. B. Mohr.
1966 *Worship in Israel.* Trans. G. Buswell. Richmond: John Knox.

Labuschagne, C. J.
1964–65 "Amos' Conception of God and the Popular Theology of His Time." Pp. 122–33 in *Studies on the Books of Hosea and Amos. Papers read at 7th and 8th meetings of Die OT Werkgemeenskap in Suid Afrika.*

Langhe, R. de
1958 "Myth, Ritual, and Kingship in the Ras Shamra Tablets." Pp. 122–48 in *Myth, Ritual, and Kingship.* Ed. S. H. Hooke. London: Oxford University Press.

Levine, Baruch A.
1963 "Ugaritic Descriptive Rituals." *JCS* 17: 105–12.

1965   "The Descriptive Tabernacle Texts of the Pentateuch."
                JAOS 85: 307–18.
1971   "Prolegomenon." Pp. VII–XLIV in G. B. Gray, *Sacrifice
                in the Old Testament: Its Theory and Practice.* Library
                of Biblical Studies. New York: Ktav.
1974   *In the Presence of the Lord: A Study of Cult and Some
                Cultic Terms in Ancient Israel.* SJLA 5. Leiden: E. J.
                Brill.

Lipiński, Edouard
1963   "*Yāhweh mâlāk.*" *Bib* 44: 405–60.
1965   *La royauté de Yahwé dans la poésie et la culte de l'ancien
                Israel.* Brussels: Koninklijkie Academie.

McCarthy, Dennis J.
1978   *Treaty and Covenant.* AnBib 21A. Rome: Pontifical Bibli-
                cal Institute.

McKay, John
1973   *Religion in Judah Under the Assyrians.* SBT 2d series 26.
                London: SCM.

Maier, Johann
1965   *Das altisraelitische Ladeheiligtum.* BZAW 93. Berlin:
                Walter de Gruyter.

Mayes, A. D. H.
1974   *Israel in the Period of the Judges.* SBT 2d series 29. Lon-
                don: SCM.

Mays, James L.
1976   "Historical and Canonical: Recent Discussion about the
                Old Testament and the Christian Faith." Pp. 510–28 in
                Magnalia Dei: The Mighty Acts of God. Ed. F. M. Cross,
                W. Lemke, and P. D. Miller, Jr. Garden City, NY: Double-
                day.

Mendenhall, George E.
1955   *Law and Covenant in Israel and the Ancient Near East.*
                Pittsburgh: The Presbyterian Board of Colportage of
                Western Pennsylvania. (Reprint of *BA* 17: 26–46, 49–76.)
1961   "Biblical History in Transition." Pp. 32–53 in *The Bible
                and the Ancient Near East.* Ed. G. E. Wright. Garden
                City, NY: Doubleday.
1973   *The Tenth Generation: The Origins of the Biblical Tra-
                dition.* Baltimore: Johns Hopkins University Press.
1975   "The Monarchy." *Int* 29: 155–70.

Mettinger, Trygve
1976   *King and Messiah: The Civil and Sacral Legitimation of
                the Israelite Kings.* ConBOT 8. Lund: Gleerup.

Milgrom, Jacob
1971   "Sin-Offering or Purification Offering?" *VT* 21: 237–39.

1976a   "Sacrifices and Offerings, OT." Pp. 763–71 in *IDBSup*.

1976b   *Cult and Conscience: The Asham and the Priestly Doctrine of Repentance*. SJLA 18. Leiden: E. J. Brill.

Miller, J. Maxwell
1970   "The Korahites in Southern Judah." *CBQ* 32: 58–68.

Miller, Patrick D.
1971   "The *Mrzḥ* Text." Pp. 37–48 in *The Claremont Ras Shamra Tablets*. Ed. L. H. Fisher. Rome: Pontifical Biblical Institute.

1973   "God and the Gods: History of Religion as an Approach and Context for Bible and Theology." *Affirmation* I/5: 37–62.

1983   "Wellhausen as Historian of Religion." Pp. 61–73 in *Julius Wellhausen and His Prolegomena to the History of Israel. Semeia* 25. Chico, CA: Scholars Press.

Miller, Patrick D., and J. J. M. Roberts
1977   *The Hand of the Lord: A Reassessment of the "Ark Narrative" of 1 Samuel*. Baltimore: Johns Hopkins University Press.

Moran, William L.
1963   "The Ancient Near Eastern Background of the Love of God in Deuteronomy." *CBQ* 25: 173–76.

Mowinckel, Sigmund
1953   *Religion und Kultus*. Göttingen: Vandenhoeck & Ruprecht.

1956   *He That Cometh: The Messiah Concept in the Old Testament and Later Judaism*. Trans. G. W. Anderson. New York: Abingdon.

1962   *The Psalms in Israel's Worship*. Trans. D. R. Ap-Thomas. Oxford: Blackwell.

Noth, Martin
1960   *The History of Israel*. 2d ed. Trans. P. R. Ackroyd. New York: Harper & Row.

1965   "God, King, People in the Old Testament: A Methodological Debate with a Contemporary School of Thought." Pp. 20–48 in *The Bultmann School of Biblical Interpretation: New Directions? JTC*. Ed. R. W. Funk. New York: Harper.

Perlitt, Lothar
1969   *Bundestheologie im Alten Testament*. WMANT 36. Neukirchen-Vluyn: Neukirchener Verlag.

Rad, Gerhard von
1962   *Old Testament Theology*. Vol. I. Trans. D. M. G. Stalker. New York: Harper and Bros.

Rainey, Anson F.
1965   "The Kingdom of Ugarit." *BA* 28: 102–25.
1970   "The Order of Sacrifices in Old Testament Ritual Texts." *Bib* 51: 485–98.

Rendtorff, Rolf
1963   "Die Entstehung der israelitischen Religion als religions-geschichtliches und theologisches Problem." *TLZ* 88: 735–46.
1967   *Studien zur Geschichte des opfers im Alten Israel.* WMANT 24. Neukirchen-Vluyn: Neukirchener Verlag.

Ringgren, Helmer
1966   *Israelite Religion.* Trans. D. E. Green. Philadelphia: Fortress.

Robertson, David A.
1972   *Linguistic Evidence in Dating Early Hebrew Poetry.* SBLDS 2. Missoula, MT: Scholars Press.

Rose, Martin
1975   *Die Ausschliesslichkeitanspruch Jahwes: Deuterono-mische Schultheologie und die Volksfrömmigkeit in der späten Königskeit.* BWANT 106. Stuttgart: W. Kohlhammer.

Schmidt, Werner H.
1968   *Alttestamentlicher Glaube und Seine Umwelt: Zur Geschichte des alttestamentlichen Gottesverständnis.* Neukirchen-Vluyn: Neukirchener Verlag.
1969   *Das erste Gebot.* Theologische Existenz heute 165. Munich: Chr. Kaiser.

Schmitt, Rainer
1972   *Zelt und Lade als Thema alttestamentlicher Wissen-schaft.* Gütersloh: Mohn.

Stendahl, Krister
1962   "Biblical Theology, Contemporary." Pp. 418–32 in *IDB*, Vol. 1.

Van Seters, John
1975   *Abraham in History and Tradition.* New Haven: Yale University Press.

Vaught, Patrick
1974   *The Meaning of 'bāmâ' in the Old Testament. A Study of Etymological, Textual and Archaeological Evidence.* SOTSMS 3. London: Cambridge University Press.

Vaux, Roland de
1961   *Ancient Israel: Its Life and Institutions.* Trans. John McHugh. New York: McGraw-Hill.
1978   *The Early History of Israel.* Trans. D. Smith. Philadel-phia: Westminster.

Vorländer, H.
1975   *Mein Gott. Die Vorstellungen vom persönlichen Gott im Alten Orient und im Alten Testament.* AOAT 23. Neukirchen-Vluyn: Neukirchener Verlag.

Vriezen, Th. C.
1967   *The Religion of Ancient Israel.* Trans. H. Hoskins. Philadelphia: Westminster.

Weiser, Artur
1950   "Zur Frage nach dem Beziehungen der Psalmen zum Kult. Die Darstellung der Theophanie in den Psalmen und im Festkult." Pp. 513–31 in *Festschrift Alfred Bertholet.* Ed. W. Baumgartner. Tübingen: J. C. B. Mohr.
1962   *The Psalms.* 5th ed. Trans. H. Hartwell. Philadelphia: Westminister.

Westenholz, A.
1976   "The Earliest Akkadian Pantheon." *Or* 45: 215–16.

Westermann, C.
1964   "Das Verhältnis des Jahweglaubens zu den ausserisraelitischen Religionen." Pp. 189–218 in *Forschung am Alten Testament.* TBü 24. Munich: Chr. Kaiser.
1974   "Sinn und Grenze religionsgeschichtliche Parallelen." Pp. 84–95 in *Forschung am Alten Testament.* II. TBü 55. Munich: Chr. Kaiser.
1976   *Genesis: Kapitel 1–11.* BKAT 1/1. Neukirchen-Vluyn: Neukirchener Verlag.

Widengren, Geo
1955   *Sakrales Königtum im Alten Testament und im Judentum.* Stuttgart: W. Kohlhammer.

Wright, G. Ernest
1950   *The Old Testament Against Its Environment.* SBT 2. London: SCM.
1952   *God Who Acts. Biblical Theology as Recital.* SBT 8. London: SCM.
1962   "The Lawsuit of God: A Form-Critical Study of Deuteronomy 32." Pp. 26–67 in *Israel's Prophetic Heritage.* Ed. B. W. Anderson and W. Harrelson. New York: Harper and Bros.

Zimmerli, Walther
1979   "The History of Israelite Religion." Pp. 351–84 in *Tradition and Interpretation: Essays by Members of the Society for Old Testament Study.* Ed. G. W. Anderson. Oxford: Oxford University Press.

7

Theology of the Hebrew Bible

George W. Coats

A review of contributions to a theology of the Hebrew Bible since 1945 might contain nothing more than a bibliography with annotations, and even in that configuration some items of importance would doubtless drop out. Thus, this review begins with a disclaimer. It is not a review of the chronology of the discipline with all the works in each facet of the period tucked into their appropriate places. It is a sketch of the facets that seem most significant for an understanding of the discipline. The arbitrary quality is, moreover, not limited to a choice of books and articles. It comes to expression more sharply in the structure of the sketch. This study builds on key works that have either exerted direct influence on subsequent contributions to the discussion or in some other manner have qualified as characteristic for a group of publications concerned with the discipline. It is necessary to observe also that much of the history of publication in the discipline derives from the context of Christian theology and thus emerges under a more particularistic rubric, Old Testament Theology. It is thus an accident of the discipline's history that configurations appear predominantly Christian. These key works, then, show something of the achievements of OT scholars contributing to a theology of the Hebrew Bible.

The focal issue for each group in the review is methodology. What, in the final analysis, will count as a theology of the Hebrew Bible? The question is, of course, a matter of content. What substance will a given method explore? Before the period under review, an OT theology might have developed a selection of assertions from the Hebrew Bible according to the categories of a Christian systematic theology. Since 1933 such a procedure has fallen under severe criticism, and new proposals for understanding the content of an OT theology have emerged. Moreover, OT theology has not developed its content as an amorphous set of observations. A fundamental question of methodology and content concerns the cohesion of the subject. In what manner can an OT theology develop a sense of unity not only for its own presentation, but also for the substance it presents? To what extent is the OT a unified subject? But the question is broader, for the OT stands in a number of contexts that enlarge the potentials for understanding its unity. In what manner can the theologian describe the relationship between the OT and the NT, or between the Hebrew Bible and the Mishnah or the Talmud? The concepts and traditions basic for the Hebrew Bible move into the NT or the Rabbinic tradition. The assumption of the sketch is thus that no OT theology can be judged adequate unless it attempts to show the position of the OT in its contexts (see Jacob: 12–13).

I. THE HISTORY OF THE DISCIPLINE

A most helpful method for contributing to the discipline of OT theology is to review its history in order to determine what has been done and what yet needs to be done. In a perceptive chronology of the period, Brevard S. Childs described a consensus among biblical scholars as a biblical theology movement (1970:13–87). The elements of consensus were (1) a concern for the theological nature of the biblical text in contrast to the arid historical and linguistic exegesis of the previous period; (2) a conviction that the Bible must stand as a unity, at least as a unity in diversity, rather than fall into two distinct or even unrelated camps; (3) a strong emphasis on the revelation of God in history; (4) an assertion that the Bible contains a distinctive approach to matters of faith; and (5) a passionate appeal to the distinctive character of the OT in contrast to its environment.

The movement developed a marked crisis, however. And the crisis signaled the demise of the consensus at the center of the discipline (Childs, 1970:61–87). The first issue concerned the relationship between history as it can be reconstructed by the historian equipped with the latest scientific tools for historical research and history as it is reported in the Bible. This issue was primarily a matter of method. An obvious distinction between reconstructed history and its biblical counterpart emerged in the discussions of the discipline. In what manner could the gap between them be bridged? A similar problem appeared in the use of biblical and theological language. To use biblical language to speak of divine event and then to use the same language to refer to the same events in a naturalistic sense revealed a problematic equivocation in method (Gilkey). Again, some doubt about the unity of biblical tradition signaled a move away from the concerns of the movement. Sharp criticism was leveled against those who would draw an easy distinction between the OT and its environment (Albrektson) or those who would maintain a simplistic conception of distinctive mentality in the OT (Barr, 1961). Finally, the consensus concerning a theological dimension broke down with the dissolution of a theological program at large.

It is important to note, however, that Childs did not review the history of the movement just to demonstrate the crisis that choked it. He moved beyond his description of the era to a proposal for a new program in OT theology. Described under the rubrics of "canon criticism," his program embraced not only hermeneutical reflections on the context for exploring particular Hebrew scripture but also the contributions of that reflection to moral theology.

An additional review of the history of the discipline will illustrate the pattern of this section. Gerhard Hasel (1972) isolated four problems in recent publications: (1) methodology; (2) the question of history, history of traditions, and salvation history; (3) the center of the OT and OT theology; and (4) the relationship between the Testaments. Then, on the basis of his review, he too proposed new directions for OT theology, each focused on matters of methodology: (1) A biblical theology must involve both historical and theological methodologies. (2) The starting point for a biblical theological method must be both historical and theological. (3) The subject of the discipline will be the theologies that appear in the OT, "a summary interpretation and explanation of the Old Testament writings or blocks of writings" (1972:90). (4) The presentation of the theologies in the OT will follow the date of origin as nearly as it can be fixed for the particular books in the OT, not the canonical order. (5) The work will display not only the theology of the various books of the OT but also the major themes that run across several books in the OT. (6) Finally, the theologian will seek to determine whether there is a theology of the OT that transcends the diversity of theologies and longitudinal themes so obviously characteristic for the OT (see also Dentan, Kraus).

II. OLD TESTAMENT THEOLOGY
AS A DESCRIPTIVE DISCIPLINE

Closely related to the contributions to an OT theology by describing the history of the discipline is a group of contributions to the field developed as descriptions of OT content. OT theology need not be restricted to a Christian pursuit or a Jewish pursuit. It would appear that if there is a theology of the OT to perceive, anyone might penetrate it regardless of the particular faith commitment embraced. The clarion call for a theology that would be open to discussion by members of any faith group appears in Krister Stendahl's article on biblical theology. Stendahl pointed out that the discipline has, either explicitly or implicitly, drawn a distinction between what the biblical witness meant to its own period and what it means to the current audience. He did not denigrate the task of theologians to present the witness of the various biblical texts to the present day, but that task cannot be achieved without a careful, descriptive preparation. "This makes it the more imperative to have the 'original' spelled out with the highest degree of perception in its own terms. This is the nucleus of all biblical theology . . ." (422). The movement from the descriptive pursuit to the question of meaning for the current audience is the field of hermeneutics. The principles that control the move should receive careful examination before the effort to relate the text to the present begins. Otherwise, the field becomes simply a jumble of ad hoc pious interpretations. But the final stage, the work of hermeneutics, is nonetheless a central, if not the central, stage that emerges from the nucleus of descriptive biblical theology. To this end Stendahl concluded, "The question as to the meaning of the Bible in the present—as distinguished from the meaning in the past as stated by descriptive biblical theology—receives its theological answer from the canonical status of scripture" (429). The key element in biblical hermeneutics is thus an explanation of "canon." Stendahl did not leave the field of biblical theology simply in the realm of objective, descriptive pursuits, open to the agnostic as well as the Christian and Jew. On the contrary, he placed the focus of a biblical theology in the context of faith. "To be sure, the church 'chose' its canon. But it did so under the impact of the acts of God . . ." (429). It is significant that the power of that canon, the end product of the hermeneutic, comes to expression for Stendahl in the pulpit (431). The future of OT theology would thus be bound up with the future of preaching. Nevertheless, one cannot fail to hear that the starting point for a biblical theology is the task of describing what the content of the text was for its own period.

A part of the same cloth that comprised Stendahl's influential appeal for descriptive theology was the monograph by G. Ernest Wright, *God Who Acts*. The content of an OT theology for Wright could not stand apart from the content of a NT theology. The subject for the monograph was thus a biblical theology, and its content was a recital of the principal events that comprise God's revelation. But that recital appears not as an effort to spell out what the OT means for the contemporary pulpit but as a description of the events as they occurred and became significant for their first witnesses. There was an important sense, then, of the objective in Wright's enterprise (1952:23 and passim). The biblical theologian works primarily as a historian, with the tools of the historian the major elements of methodology (13).

Yet, at just this point a crucial problem in Wright's presentation appears, for history entails not simply the events of the past that might be reconstructed in a more or less objective pursuit but also the *traditions* that relate those events to the audience of the day (1952:38 and passim). Wright was certainly on the mark to insist, for example, that "to refuse to take history seriously as the revelation of the will, purpose, and nature of God is the simplest escape from the Biblical God and one which leaves us with an idol of our own imagining" (58). But the issue of methodology is dominant. One cannot proceed simply with the methods of the historian, as if the task were to describe more adequately the original event which the first witnesses described inadequately. One must raise the question of tradition, and that question introduces a literary methodology. Wright observed, "Biblical theology must begin, therefore, with the primary question as to why the Bible possesses the historical nature it does" (58). But what precisely is the character of that historical nature, comprised as it is by tradition? Wright continued: biblical theology "must point in the first instance to this confessional recital of traditional and historical events . . ." (58). But does that double character not suggest that the method must probe not only events as they were in their original, objective nature but also in the tradition as it emerged around the event? Indeed, one may ask whether the one or the other is primary, or even whether the one is possible without the other. The method must, then, embrace procedure for evaluating not only the objectivity of the historical events but also the potential for recognizing and incorporating to some degree the subjectivity of the traditions about the events. The method would thus be as much a literary as a historical one (see also 1969).

This last point did not come to full expression in Wright's monograph. His focus remained on history. Thus, he observed that biblical theology is not concerned primarily with abstractions but with telling the story created by the history (1969: passim). For him, telling the story is a historical task, not a literary one. It is a recital of history, not a presentation of a literary art form. "It is, therefore, the objectivity of God's historical acts which are the focus of attention, not the subjectivity of inner, emotional, diffuse, and mystical experience" (1952:55). Yet, the double character of the task was not ignored. History gives the OT theologian knowledge of what God and people have done, but closely associated with the event is the word that interprets the event. "By means of human agents God provides each event with an accompanying Word of interpretation, so that the latter is an integral part of the former . . ." (1952:84). Moreover, the OT event with its word is incomplete without its context in the NT event with its word. The events and their words hang together in a significant theological continuum. Wright used the term "typological" to describe this point: "Typology when rightly understood and used takes historical data seriously; persons, acts and events possess a typological meaning when they are understood to have been fixed or directed by God so that they point toward the future" (1952:61).

III. OLD TESTAMENT THEOLOGY
AS A KERYGMATIC DISCIPLINE

The double character of content in an OT theology leads to consideration of contributions that address the questions of tradition and history even more directly. These contributions remain at least in part quite descriptive in their method. Their task was to identify the essential elements of OT theology and to describe them in theological terms. That descriptive task began to enlarge its compass, however, particularly when the traditio-historical context that binds OT and NT together emerged as a serious element in the discussion. The question is not simply whether traditions that have a history in the OT continue their history into the NT. The question becomes one of authority seated in the OT for the life of faith, either for the church or the synagogue. Thus, method for an OT theology· develops a combination of descriptive procedures with normative assumptions.

A Cross-Section Method

Discussion of contributions to OT theology controlled by a "cross-section" method begins with the monumental *Theology of the Old Testament* by Walther Eichrodt (1933). The assumption is that his work represented not only a high-water mark in the discipline but also a formative influence on subsequent efforts to write an OT theology. The review of this section encompasses, therefore, not only the work of Eichrodt, whose *Theology* appeared in English during the period defined for this paper but also a series of works within the period, each raising the kind of questions that were at the base of Eichrodt's method.

Eichrodt's theology was epoch-making because he broke decisively with the pattern of exposition current at the time, which sought structural unity from the categories of systematic theology. In its place Eichrodt displayed a cross-section of the OT defined by a category native to the OT witness. That central category was, of course, the covenant between God and Israel (1961, I:36–45). Out of that category, he found evidence that would, in his opinion, resolve "the problem of how to understand the realm of Old Testament belief in its structural unity and how, by examining on the one hand its religious environment and on the other its essential coherence with the New Testament, to illuminate its profoundest meaning" (1961, I:31). The covenant suggested an organization of the structural unity in the OT around the themes of the special nature of the Israelite faith in God: God and the people, God and the world, and God and man (1961, I:33; McKenzie: 84).

A series of contributions to an OT theology follows Eichrodt's quest for a center of OT faith. For example, Rudolph Smend's quest for the center of the OT reflects the same kind of method as Eichrodt's. Indeed, his results are strikingly similar to those produced by Eichrodt. The center of the OT lies in the covenantal formulary: "Yahweh the God of Israel, Israel the people of Yahweh" (see also Kaiser: 12–13). Smend recognized, however, that the middle of the OT is not so much a conceptual pattern as it is a constructive key for understanding a tension with theological import: God stands in relationship to Israel. Those developments which constitute the substance of an OT theology occur within the context of that tension (1970:46–59).

In the same vein Gerhard Hasel argued that the center for an OT theology should be the concept of God (1974:63; see also McKenzie: 26). Hasel's formulation, however, runs the risk of overgeneralization. To say that the center of the witness in the OT is God fails to capture the particularity of the tradition, and the door would be open to include anything that might develop a random reference to God. Indeed, it may well be that the methodological procedure itself carries the tendency to overgeneralize, a problem latent also in Eichrodt's work. With one concept to serve as the middle of an OT theology, how can the particular configurations of its various stages come adequately to light? Does the OT not require a procedure that will capture the tension produced by various "centers"?

The more recent works by Walther Zimmerli and Samuel Terrien demonstrate this methodological development quite well. Zimmerli developed his OT theology on the basis of his insight that the center of the OT is the name of God (1975:97–118, 1978:17–27). The one who is known by the tetragrammaton is the one who effects the fullest shape of Israel's theology, who molds the moral fabric of Israel's life. But in fact Zimmerli changed the nature of the question. In his efforts to probe an OT theology, the name of Yahweh was not a "conceptual" center, as if it were the primary idea that binds all the OT together. Rather, the name of God functioned for Zimmerli as a living foil, pulling the people who witness the name to a more adequate experience of divine grace. Concepts or themes may multiply. Indeed, traditions may change their configurations as they appear in new contexts. But the principal point for a structure in an OT theology, thus, the middle of the OT, is the dynamic created by the living Lord of the tradition. He observed: "The center of the Old Testament which we are seeking to exhibit is in no case something conceived by us, but in every case that which seizes us and calls us forward" (1975:109). It is not a concept; it is a dynamic. It therefore calls for a procedure that will give full weight to its dynamism. Moreover, this dynamic allows Zimmerli to conclude that the OT is a book that is open to the future. The dynamic that preserves continued life into the future is the dynamic that offers relationship with the NT. Even though Zimmerli does not consider that relationship as a substantive part of his OT theology, the framework for probing the question is there.

Terrien adopted "the elusive presence" of God in his relationships with Israel as the constructive center of his OT theology (xxiii; see also Clements: 40–46; Jacob: 52–54). From this center he wrote a theology that covers the entire canon of the OT, placing it at the same time into its NT context. One may object that once again the principle suffers from an overgeneralization. At what point in the OT would one not expect to find some formative role for a notion of God's presence, or at least its counterpart, a notion of God's absence? Nevertheless, Terrien's description of presence and absence fills a pressing need for a systematic exploration of a key motif. Of particular importance is his discussion of the negative pole. The presence makes God known not only as savior but also as judge and executioner. But how can one speak of God's absence from creation? Would not such a tradition mean a return to chaos? Terrien expounds the central theme, however, as a dynamic pole held in tension with presence and casts both as the "elusive" presence, the presence of a God who refuses to be bound in any particular box. The God who is absent reminds the creation of his past presence. The absence points beyond itself to the God who seeks out his people, the God who wills his presence. Apparent absence is the sign of presence elusive to perception (see also Clements: 40–46).

Thus, Terrien emphasized his position regarding "die Mitte des Alten Testaments." Presence is not a "concept" that stands at any point in the history of the tradition as a static datum. Rather, Terrien, like Zimmerli, saw the center of the OT as a dynamic process. "The study of the motif of 'the presence of God' may prove more fruitful than other motifs in providing a unifying and yet dynamic principle which will account not only for the homogeneity of the Old Testament literature in its totality . . . but also for the historical and thematic continuity which unites Hebraism and large aspects of Judaism with nascent Christianity" (556). So, for Terrien, as for Zimmerli, the methodological question cannot be cast simply as a quest for the central concept. Concept becomes tradition. And the tradition shows the homogeneity of OT and NT, not by founding a uniform structure or isolating a static concept but by revealing substance that takes on new shape when it enters new contexts.

A Traditio-Historical Method

It would be a mistake if the review of the period left the impression that a consensus for finding "die Mitte des Alten Testaments" controlled contributions to a kerygmatic theology of the OT. Gerhard von Rad, for example, objected vigorously to the notion that the OT reveals a center that might function as the organizational key for an OT theology. The OT does not contain a single center, but many centers, not a single theology derived from a key concept, but many theologies. An OT theology must give voice to these competing items, allowing each to speak its own word, comparing each with its predecessors in order to show how the tradition grew in the process of its move from one generation to another. Moreover, each new generation adds a dimension to the tradition that becomes fundamental for the tradition's content. The new tradition cannot be interpreted without the context that gives it life. But the new context also adds a dimension to the old that influences the way intention in the whole can be described.

One can see this process especially in the Deuteronomistic historian. But the process does not support a conclusion, as Hasel suggested, that von Rad defends a secret "Mitte" for the OT in contradiction to his own methodological claims (1972:61). The Deuteronomistic history is not a concept that grounds the structure of the OT witness but the result of an applied method for evaluating history. That method now appears as von Rad's basic tool for developing an OT theology.

It should be clear, in the light of Hasel's remark, that the juxtaposition of a cross-section method and a traditio-historical method in this review does not imply that the task of a biblical theology is simply discovering the right conceptual center. It is not correct to suggest that the primary issue between Eichrodt and von Rad is whether the central concept for organizing the discipline is the covenant between God and Israel or the tradition history of the Pentateuch, as for example D. G. Spriggs maintains (10). The primary issue is rather a methodological one. Can an OT theology emerge satisfactorily from a single central concept? Or does the diversity of OT traditions demand a procedure that will embrace a series of divergent concepts?

Von Rad identified his method as a traditio-historical one (1965, II:321). It is a method at home in the OT itself, as is clear in the Deuteronomistic history, or Deutero-Isaiah's use of the exodus tradition for addressing a generation of people in exile. Moreover, he asserts, "everything that follows [in his own presentation of OT theology] is really intended simply to carry this familiar procedure a stage further by trying to understand that the way in which the Old Testament is absorbed in the New is the logical end of a process initiated by the Old Testament itself . . ." (1965, II:321, cf. 326–27). Or in a related direction, "one particular way by which the Old Testament was understood . . . is the well-known typological interpretation . . . whose purpose was to establish a correspondence between an event in the Old Testament and another in the New" (1965, II:329). This call for typological interpretation should not be taken as an open door for multiple esoteric readings that might generate a range of equally esoteric doctrines. On the contrary, his typological interpretation, remarkably similar to that suggested by Wright, unfolds under the strictest of controls, the product of his tradition history. It works on the assumption of unity in revelation between the OT and the NT. "The same God who revealed himself in Christ has also left his footprints in the history of the Old Testament covenant people . . . we have to do with *one* divine discourse here to the fathers through the prophets, there to us through Christ" (1963:36).

Von Rad developed his insight into the history of OT traditions as the structural framework for an OT theology. The first part of his work treats the principal themes of tradition in the Hexateuch as theological elaborations of basic cultic, confessional articles of Israelite faith. In addition, he sets these themes of tradition into relationship with a new complex of traditions about the anointed king. The traditions, at times complementary, at times contradictory, carry the content of theology constitutive for the Hebrew Bible: (1) the primeval history, (2) the history of the patriarchs, (3) the deliverance from Egypt, (4) the divine revelation at Sinai, (5) the wandering in the wilderness, and (6) the granting of the land of Canaan. In addition he develops a section on the conception of Moses and his office as a significant theological bond that relates to points (3) through (6). These themes reveal what Israel said about her own theology. The final part of the first volume explores Israel's response to God's acts celebrated in the themes of Hexateuchal theology. The dominant poles in this section are the Psalms and the wisdom tradition. It is not clear that wisdom fits the scheme as a response invoked by the celebration of God's acts in the Hexateuch. Indeed, von Rad focused the issues for an OT theology in treating the wisdom tradition: "But what is to happen when wisdom proceeds to understand itself as the representative of the most central concepts of Jahwism, and, bypassing the saving history, goes on to legitimise itself straight from Creation?" (1962:453). Perhaps it is precisely the position of a theology about creation and its corollary, a theological anthropology, that can facilitate a more adequate definition of the contributions of wisdom tradition to an OT theology (Brueggemann, 1972).

The second part of the *Theology* treats general introductory questions about theology in the prophets and then sets out an exploration of the individual prophets according to their appropriation of the Hexateuchal—and other—themes. It is precisely here that the typological scheme emerges most clearly. If for Hosea the traditions about wilderness and covenant are crucial, for the Second Isaiah the same tradition facilitates depiction of a new wilderness journey. Perhaps the key to the entire program appears finally with exploration of relationships between the OT and the NT.

The discipline did not embrace von Rad's method and theological content without objection. A significant series of critical questions came from Walther Eichrodt, Franz Hesse, and Roland de Vaux, among others. The opening point of criticism suggested that von Rad separated too radically between real history as reconstructed by the disciplines of historical research and the tradition's history, which offers the plane for his theological commentary. The second point is that to examine the history of OT traditions produces not a theology but a history of religion. Thus, two pressing questions summarize the responses to von Rad's theology: (1) What constitutes an OT theology? In what manner does it require a complementary pole, a NT theology, in order to complete its task? (2) Where in the field of discussion does the question of truth appear? Particularly, how is one to relate the theology of traditions to the truth claims of reconstructed history? It is, of course, relevant to ask whether any particular event with significant theological content, such as the exodus, really happened. But does the question of truth admit an answer simply in terms of evidence for reconstructing the event? Or does the answer lie in Israel's manner of witnessing to that event? In that case, the task of theology is not to reproduce the historical events described in the lines of the text. The methods for an OT theology would be primarily literary, the task an effort to define significance in a particular literary creation. The historical disciplines are most relevant, then, in helping to determine what a witness meant, in defining the intention of the text. The truth claims of the text would reside not so much in the accuracy of historical projection but rather in the perception and depth of the assertion.

Hermeneutical Implications

The period under review has witnessed a new focus on issues of OT hermeneutics, at least in part out of the stimulation of von Rad's theology and the responses to it. A number of approaches to the topic are represented by a collection edited by Claus Westermann (1963), with the lead essay appropriately von Rad's exploration of typology as a method into hermeneutical problems. Rudolf Bultmann's essay depicting the OT as a history of failure stimulated some continuing discussion on the value of the OT for Christians (50–75), a point witnessed by both a response in the collection by Claus Westermann (123–33) and a provocative response outside the collection by Rolf Rendtorff (1960:27–40). Perhaps the most significant essay in the collection is the contribution from Walther Zimmerli (1963:89–122). Zimmerli proposed that the hermeneutical issues related to the OT appear most clearly in a span of tension created by narratives that describe God's promise to his people and the corresponding narratives about the fulfillment of those promises or the potentials for fulfillment at some point in the future. The weight of the observation rests, of course, on the important role of promise in the Genesis narrative. God promises a progeny and a land. Then the Pentateuchal narrative, indeed much of the OT, develops in a way that demonstrates fulfillment. Some critical comment concerning the adequacy of proposals for the role of the promise, as for example in the review by J. Hoftijzer, suggests that other theological structures may be required in order to perceive the character of the biblical tradition. It is not difficult to conclude, however, that the effort to penetrate the hermeneutical issues with the structure of promise-fulfillment has carried significant weight in the period (Childs, 1979:150–52).

Hans Walter Wolff pushed this point a step further in his program for hermeneutics of the OT. The OT contains documents that present the history of Israel as the history of the people of Yahweh. An OT theology must allow the text to witness to the dynamic established by the God of the people. That dynamic is as present in the contemporary exercise of theology, particularly in the proclamation of the witness from the pulpit, as it was for the ancient people of Yahweh. The method of hermeneutics subordinates the hearer to the given text. That subordination may emphasize the people's life "under a *divine law*, which is continually proclaimed anew" (1963:169). It will typically emphasize that the divine law appears in a context "in which it is firmly surrounded by God's saving deeds for Israel and his covenant with Israel, and is given as God's help for life" (1963:170). Indeed, it will suggest that the NT constitutes the primary viable context of the OT, the historical goal, the only workable analogy that makes the divine law significant in its succeeding generations. Wolff's method is thus closely related to von Rad's typology.

> If the essential presupposition of typology is correct, that the Old Testament does not bear witness to a strange god, but to the Father of Jesus, then it must be allowed to speak completely with the kerygma that is its own. But then typology does not lead only to historical understanding, but also at the same time to an exposition of the Old Testament that is *proclamation*, in as far as the God of Israel is the God of the Church, is God today, in as far, therefore, as the character of the Old Testament as address is also relevant to us. (1963:186)

It cannot surprise anyone that von Rad's colleague in Heidelberg, Claus Westermann, shows significant influence in his theology from the basic orientation von Rad proposed. For Westermann, theology for the OT begins as storytelling. "'The Old Testament tells the story' (von Rad); but the story which the Old Testament tells can be equated neither with the concept of history . . . nor with a religious or salvation history. . . . We have to go back behind these alternatives to a broader concept of history, in which both have not yet been separated . . ." (1979:25). A theology of the OT facilitates telling that story. Moreover, a major part of the story belongs to the law. Westermann makes a functional distinction between law, tied to a human institution and associated with punishment, and the commandments, direct proceedings between God and people. Laws vary from situation to situation, but the commandments constitute a direct and immediate word of God. It is "necessary and indispensable for the relationship of God to man" (1979:76). In this form, it represents a crucial basis for the moral content of OT theology (see the comments below).

To organize this section of the review under the rubric of a kerygmatic discipline suggests some significant position for the work of Hans Walter Wolff. His review of the kerygma of the Yahwist emphasized the contribution of God's chosen as the instrument of blessing for the peoples of the world who stand under a curse (1975c). The Elohist focuses on the "fear of God" as a theological watchword that would meet the crisis posed by the pressure to accommodate faith to the surrounding culture

(1975a). In the Deuteronomistic history, the kerygma calls for Israel's repentance and return to Yahweh. Moreover, the content of the kerygma develops specific moral qualities. It contains an appeal for obedience to the Mosaic law (1975b). Walter Brueggemann added a fourth article to the series, emphasizing the kerygmatic intention in P as a proclamation of the phrase, "be fruitful and multiply, fill the land, subdue it and have dominion," to a people who had lost the land and perhaps the courage to return to it (1975a). In a summary statement for the series, Brueggemann suggested that the goal of kerygmatic exegesis "is to locate in any given text the confessing stance of the faithful community—a stance which will be both protest and affirmation. That confessional stance is found in a particular kerygmatic formulation which announces the end of an old order, now rejected, and gives the 'news' of a new order reflecting Yahweh's purpose and power" (1975b:31–32). That kerygmatic intention constitutes also the center of interest for the work of von Rad: "Out of von Rad's study of the credo [a basic study leading to his OT theology] has come the fresh interest among Old Testament studies in the kerygmatic question. Because von Rad has shown that texts are refashioned by the credo and do not have their original meaning, the question of the faith confessed by Israel is the primary one to put to each text" (1975b:29).

IV. OLD TESTAMENT THEOLOGY
IN THE CONTEXT OF THE CANON

In some manner a product of the mode for OT theology set by von Rad, the call for the work of that theology to be done in the context of the Christian canon is one of the most stimulating advancements in the period under discussion. Brevard Childs advanced the colors of canon criticism as a necessary operation in an OT theology. The question for canon criticism is different from the one that grounds the work of von Rad. It is not simply an inquiry into the tradition history that shapes an old complex into a new one. It is an inquiry into the influence the community of faith exerts on the final shape of any particular text. But the procedure is fundamentally the same. The canon constitutes a new level in the process that brings a tradition from its origin to its present shape. To explore that level, whether in terms that probe a quotation of the tradition in the NT or in some other manner that opens a new setting adopted by the tradition, is a necessary stage in writing the tradition's history.

Childs's contribution to an OT theology appears most clearly in his commentary on Exodus (1974). An example illustrates the point: In his commentary on the Passover, Exod 12:1–13:13, he sets out a significant display of form-critical and traditio-historical work. In the final form of

the text, word and event stand together as a result of the narrator's effort
to link command with narrative. "The biblical writer does not conceive
of the event as primary or 'objective' from which an influential, subjective deduction of its meaning is drawn. . . . The event is never uninter-
preted" (1974:204). Rather, the event comprises both action and word.
Moreover, the tradition reveals a dialectic between redemption as hope
and redemption as memory. In this dialectic the character of Passover
emerges most graphically. This tradition already appears with a distinct
orientation toward new stages. Furthermore, the NT offers that development. "The effect of understanding the Old Testament passover traditions in the light of the New Testament is to affirm the hope of Israel in
so far as it foreshadowed God's true redemption" (1974:213). Without
the NT context, "the passover rite can lead to distortion" (1974:213). It
can remain simply a political liberation. In the NT context, the passover
"becomes a symbol of the cost to God of Israel's redemption" (1974:213).
The context for interpreting the OT is thus effectively described. But for
Childs the interpretation is genuinely a dialectic. "The New Testament
not only fulfills the Old, but equally important the Old Testament
interprets the New" (1974:213). The interpretation allows the Christian
community to see not only what redemption in the exodus from Egypt
means but also what redemption in Jesus Christ means. He emphasized
three points: (1) The political overtones of Israel's deliverance are a part
of the whole biblical message. (2) Passover warns that redemption theology must not overlook the collective nature of God's intervention.
(3) The eschatological dimension of redemption must not be lost through
an overconcentration on the death of Christ. The point to be illustrated
here, however, is not the particularity of comment on the Passover. It is
the methodological perspective. The NT does not validate the OT any
more than the OT validates the NT. Rather, the relationship between
the Testaments is dialectical. Together, as poles in the canon, OT and
NT comprise the context for pursuing biblical theology.

Childs clarifies his method still further in his *Introduction* (1979).
Here it is clear that the key stage for an OT theology resides in the final
form of the text, the shape established as canon by the community of
faith. Moreover, it is this stage, not some hypothetical stage preceding it,
that witnesses to the character of the community of faith. The Passover,
not the Festival of Unleavened Bread or any other prior stage, functions
in the canonical process with the NT. The center of canon criticism for
Childs, then, is essentially synchronic.

James A. Sanders (1976) connects the canon with Israel's attempt to
discover and preserve self-identity, and as a consequence he opens the
issues of "canonical criticism" more directly to the dimensions of depth
suggested by the history of the tradition. The canon is the product of generations which regularly reinterpreted the sacred traditions to meet the

changing needs of their lives. It is characterized by a necessary stability that insures that it can be repeated from generation to generation; but it also reveals a marked adaptability. Moreover, the adaptability facilitates its growth from stage to stage and its plurality, preserving in any given stage the signs of diversity in its history of authoritative meaning.

Ronald E. Clements also approaches the task of a biblical theology from the context of canon:

> It has therefore been a welcome feature of recent approaches to the problem of biblical theology to have rediscovered the notion of canon as a central feature of the Old Testament. . . . At a very basic level we can see that it is because the Old Testament forms a canon . . . that we can expect to find in it a 'theology', and not just a report of ancient religious ideas. (15)

Clements then develops his treatment of OT theology around the diverse understandings of God reflected in the canon with its complement of perspectives about the people of God. Perhaps of most importance is his observation of a key to a canonical theology: "It is precisely the concept of a canon that raises questions about the authority of the Old Testament and its ability to present us with a theology which can be meaningful in the twentieth century" (19). The question of authority is already resident in the OT itself in the manner of presentation for key figures such as Moses, David, and Solomon (170–74). Authority resides in the validation of tradition established by reference to these figures. However, authority derives not simply from a claim for origin in Moses or David but in a confirmation of continuity between Moses or David and each succeeding generation (174).

James Barr addresses the topic of authority in scripture first by observing that authority resides in a relationship between community and text. One can embrace a notion of authority without absolutizing the text (1976a). Dewey Beegle makes the assertion for a conservative audience: Infallibility belongs to God. According to Beegle, scripture witnesses to that infallibility, but it remains the product of human beings. God's activity in the production of scripture and thus divine authority at the basis of scripture "did not extend to inerrant transmission, either oral or written, and neither did it guarantee an absolute inerrancy of the original documents. What the Spirit's activity did guarantee was selectivity of events and accuracy of reporting and interpretation sufficient to achieve God's purpose . . ." (307). The reality of its authority is thus derived and not immediate. Moreover, authority typically accrues to some particular part of the canon, a theme or a book, rather than to the whole. It is not unusual to employ terms like "a canon within the canon" as the functional source of authority. But there are dangers with such terms, dangers that apply also to Eichrodt's procedure in establishing a central theme as the theological center of OT theology. The danger is not simply that one part of the canon is relegated to an inferior position but rather that the elements chosen to be central gain too great a status. The problem is that the elevated element becomes absolutized and beyond criticism (Barr, 1973:161). In the history of the discipline, the danger also appears in the tendency for the locus of authority to shift from one theme to another. What was once of central importance may move to a peripheral rank. The issue of authority in the text thus collapses into a marked element of subjectivity. This facet has been expressed, furthermore, in the importance placed on relevance. Barr observes, "Scripture, as a work of the past and so understood, feeds and illuminates the understanding of modern men and women. . . . Within the church and the situation of faith it builds and enriches the faith in which people are able to see their own situation more clearly and to judge their actions more rightly" (1976a:797).

V. A MORAL THEOLOGY OF THE OLD TESTAMENT

This pattern relates to the important role of ethics in biblical theology. There is no way that twentieth-century theologians can say that their contemporaries should follow the ethical principles of the Bible just because they are in the Bible. "The Bible is not in fact a problem-solver" (Barr, 1973:142). Why, then, make reference to the Bible at all, whether for moral guidance or theological construction? Barr develops a notion of the Bible as a part of the tradition that constitutes the effective model for Christian life, "the classical model for understanding." The authority of the Bible becomes, therefore, not an absolute standard by which behavior can be judged but a sufficient standard that facilitates contemporary behavior. "The 'authority'—or whatever we call it—of the Old Testament will never be permanently established. Questionings of it and debates about its value are likely to continue and are part of the living process of its appropriation anew within the churches in each generation" (1971:40).

A programmatic essay by Bruce C. Birch and Larry L. Rasmussen (1976), suggesting a methodology for bridging the disciplines of biblical study and Christian ethics, shows marked influence of the theology of Gerhard von Rad and Brevard S. Childs, among others. The authors' first concern is a demonstration of basic methodology for doing ethics for the sake of biblical students and a demonstration of a corresponding methodology for doing biblical study for the sake of students in ethics. The motivation for developing the program lies in a gap in theological literature. Although many theologians recognize a natural correspondence between the two fields, not many publications for students working in both fields can be found. Yet, their motivation is not simply to chart a

pattern for an interdisciplinary course. The authors perceive a fundamental connection between the two fields that proves suggestive not only
from the perspective of a theological curriculum but also for the necessary work of Christian theology itself.

In accord with the suggestion in the introduction of this review,
Birch and Rasmussen assume the unity of biblical tradition, set their
program in the context of the theological perspectives of the Christian
church, and recognize the importance of methodological issues. A primary contribution to the discussion of OT theology is their recognition
that concepts about biblical authority commonly underlie warrants for
making ethical decisions and building moral character. "Authority
derives from acknowledgment of a source's right to influence us, not
from absolute power that operates apart from the affirmation of the
community. . . . The claim to be scripture establishes an authority for
the Bible that must be taken into account, but its authority is not absolute" (1976:144). The authors expound the nature of this limited authority in terms of (1) the functional role scripture has played in the history
of the Christian church, thus suggesting that if one's interest is in *Christian* ethics one's identification as a Christian requires primary reference
to scripture, and (2) the common ground between the present context for
Christian ethics and the past context for the witness of scripture, namely,
the active presence of God. So despite a limiting element in the character of biblical authority, the Bible constitutes a necessary element in the
enterprise of Christian ethics.

The next step in advancing the concerns of these authors is a necessary part of the enterprise of biblical, or more particularly OT, theology.
Childs has suggested that such may be the case by showing how a new
program for OT theology can lead to moral conclusions. "This issue at
stake, theologically speaking, is the understanding of the nature of man's
decision for God. Seen from one perspective, the issue is unequivocal in
its character, the clear call to discipleship. In another sense, it is a living
and deciding among the variety of relationships in which we live . . .
seeking to live an obedient life" (1970:180). That call for discipleship
emerges from biblical tradition. The second essay by Birch and Rasmussen (1978) points in a similar direction. Biblical resources provide a
perspective for analyzing moral problems. For example, a theology
derived from OT creation tradition depicts the human creature as the
subject of moral responsibility. "A broader Biblical understanding of
humanity, nature, and God could help us toward a redefinition of the
scope of human interest and responsibility" (1978:124). That responsibility places the human creature squarely before a moral relationship with
nature and the environment as well as with the human community.

Yet, the participants in the discussion of OT theology might well
consider whether they have the luxury of choosing a dialogue with

Christian ethics, as if such a dialogue were one among several possibilities. The question can be explored as an extension of the debate about the relationship between OT theology and history. The persisting questions about the nature of history and the corresponding methodology for writing an OT theology that will not simply abstract principles from history suggest that another dimension of history requires attention. It is now widely recognized that history is not simply a collection of *bruta facta*, from which theological meaning can be abstracted. The only data available for writing history are interpreted ones. But the interpretation of historical data in the OT does not proceed in a haphazard way (Rendtorff, 1961). Rather, the data reveal, among other facets, a marked moral dimension. Thus, the event at the Sea is not simply a complex of causes and effects but the combination that gives Israel knowledge of God as "Yahweh who brought you out of Egypt." But that assertion is not simply an abstraction from the event. The event reminds Israel that she was a slave in Egypt, and that God brought her out. But it also reminds her that because God brought her out of her slavery, she should also defend and redeem slaves. At that moment, history becomes moral; it communicates present obligation. Furthermore, that obligation becomes the center of Israel's theology. For Israel there could be no separation between the good news that God redeems his people and the consequent law that the people ought to redeem their neighbors. It follows that a crucial segment of an OT theology, relatively little discussed in the era of the biblical theology movement, is the law (see McKenzie: 257–66). Indeed, this point could be deduced from the OT itself, since by far the most extensive body of tradition organized around a single theme concerns the law. Moreover, a second segment arising within the same area of interest would be the wisdom tradition and its contribution to ethics (McKenzie: 203–33). One of the most stimulating publications within this frame of OT theology was *In Man We Trust* by Walter Brueggemann. The achievement of this book was not simply its assertion that wisdom morality demanded its just hearing alongside the work done on the historical traditions. It was the recognition that wisdom embraced a theological anthropology that did not wallow in a sense of guilt and worthlessness but rather affirmed the potential of the human creature for moral maturity (1972:78–114). The question that remains is whether such an anthropology is limited to OT wisdom. Or does it exert its presence in other traditions?

VI. CONCLUSIONS

A summary of the review suggests not only the major issues of the past decades in OT theology but also some hint about directions for the discussion in the coming decades. The following four points do not imply that the entire period can be reduced to these issues alone but rather that the period highlighted these points in a kind of natural continuum.

(1) The problems and perspectives posed by the history of Israel have formed a basic element in the discussion. Israel achieved her distinctive theology at least in part from her conviction not only that God acted in her history on her behalf but also that God communicated knowledge to Israel about himself in the process. That knowledge becomes the content of Israel's theology. It is important to relate the history of Israel that communicates such knowledge to genuine historical event (see Hesse, 1960:26). The element of interpretation remains a crucial part of genuine history. There is no way that event can become history without the word that makes clear its meaning. This facet of the discussion has dominated the period and will doubtless continue as a part of the debate. However, it is necessary to see that the discipline has moved beyond this point to new issues, related to the problems of theology and history but nonetheless developing new positions of the controlling question.

(2) The unity of the OT in itself, as well as the unity of the Christian canon, has been a part of the discussion of OT theology throughout the period. The recent discussion of "canon criticism" has given this topic new impetus. It places the issues on a new plane, with a new set of questions. The issues are not simply whether concepts and traditions carry over from the OT to the NT. They are not even whether typology can give new insights into the relationship. They are to explore (1) how the emergence of these traditions as scripture influences the shape they assume for the community, and (2) how their emergence as scripture influences the shape of the community. This development in the discussion will certainly provoke new contributions to the field of OT theology.

(3) The position of the OT as canon raises the issues of the authority that the OT might have for the communities in which it lives (Clements: 19).

(4) As a consequence of discussion about the issues of authority in scripture, OT theology has developed some interest in moral problems. Both of these final two points call for renewed attention in the coming decades.

How, then, might these goals be accomplished? Method must make itself the servant of the text, so that the witness of the text to its own kerygma may effectively be heard. No one method can rule the field, but rather any method that can accomplish that task deserves its day. To find a single theme that captures the unity of the canon does not appear a viable pursuit. Rather, a variety of themes might illumine the character of the kerygma in the witness. This goal might call for new, comprehensive surveys of OT theology. But the need at this moment is not to test the merit of an entire system. It is to develop a discussion characterized by probing into a wide range of concepts and traditions. It may be anticipated, then, that the significant advances in OT theology for the next decade will come in the form of short probes, fundamental exegesis, perhaps programmatic suggestions, but nonetheless particular in scope.

BIBLIOGRAPHY

Albrektson, Bertil
1967   *History and the Gods.* Lund: Gleerup.

Barr, James
1961   *The Semantics of Biblical Language.* London: Oxford University Press.
1969   "The Authority of the Bible." *Ecumenical Review* 21: 135–66.
1971   "The Old Testament and the New Crisis of Biblical Authority." *Int* 25: 24–40.
1973   *The Bible in the Modern World.* New York: Harper & Row.
1976a   "Authority of Scripture." Pp. 794–97 in *IDBSup.*
1976b   "Biblical Theology." Pp. 104–11 in *IDBSup.*

Barton, John
1978   "Understanding Old Testament Ethics." *JSOT* 9: 44–64.

Beegle, Dewey M.
1973   *Scripture, Tradition, and Infallibility.* Grand Rapids: Eerdmans.

Birch, Bruce C., and Larry L. Rasmussen
1976   *Bible and Ethics in the Christian Life.* Minneapolis: Augsburg.
1978   *The Predicament of the Prosperous.* Philadelphia: Westminster.

Bright, John
1967   *The Authority of the Old Testament.* Nashville: Abingdon.

Brueggemann, Walter
1970   "The Triumphalist Tendency in Exegetical History." *JAAR* 38: 367–80.
1972   *In Man We Trust: The Neglected Side of Biblical Faith.* Richmond: John Knox.
1975a   "The Kerygma of the Priestly Writers." Pp. 101–13 in *The Vitality of Old Testament Traditions.* Atlanta: John Knox.
1975b   "Wolff's Kerygmatic Methodology." Pp. 29–39 in *The Vitality of Old Testament Traditions.* Atlanta: John Knox.

Bultmann, Rudolf
1963 "The Significance of the Old Testament for the Christian Faith." In *The Old Testament and Christian Faith*. Ed. Bernhard W. Anderson. New York: Harper & Row.

Childs, Brevard S.
1970 *Biblical Theology in Crisis*. Philadelphia: Westminster.
1974 *The Book of Exodus: A Critical, Theological Commentary*. Philadelphia: Westminster.
1979 *Introduction to the Old Testament as Scripture*. Philadelphia: Fortress.

Clements, Ronald E.
1978 *Old Testament Theology: A Fresh Approach*. London: Marshall, Morgan, and Scott.

Dentan, Robert
1963 *Preface to Old Testament Theology*. New York: Seabury.

Eichrodt, Walther
1933 *Theologie des Alten Testaments*. Berlin: Evangelische Verlagsanstalt.
1961 *Theology of the Old Testament*, I. Trans. J. A. Baker. Philadelphia: Westminster.

Fohrer, Georg
1972 *Theologische Grundstrukturen des Alten Testaments*. Berlin: Walter de Gruyter.

Gilkey, Langdon
1961 "Cosmology, Ontology, and the Travail of Biblical Language." *JR* 41: 194–205.

Hasel, Gerhard
1972 *Old Testament Theology: Basic Issues in the Current Debate*. Grand Rapids: Eerdmans.
1974 "The Problem of the Center in the Old Testament Debate." ZAW 86: 65–82.

Hesse, Franz
1960 "Kerygma oder geschichtliche Wirklichkeit? Kritische Fragen zu Gerhard von Rads 'Theologie des Alten Testaments, I. Teil.'" *ZTK* 57: 17–26.
1971 *Abschied von der Heilsgeschichte*. Theologische Studien, 108. Zurich: EVZ.

Hoftijzer, J.
1956 *Die Verheissungen an die drei Erzväter*. Leiden: F. J. Brill.

Imschoot, Paul van
1954 *Theology of the Old Testament*. New York: Desclee.

Jacob, Edmond
1958   *Theology of the Old Testament.* Trans. A. W. Heathcote and P. J. Allcock. London: Hodder and Stoughton. (Original French edition 1955.)

Kaiser, Walter C.
1978   *Toward an Old Testament Theology.* Grand Rapids: Zondervan.

Knierim, Rolf
1971   "Offenbarung im Alten Testament." Pp. 206–35 in *Probleme biblischer Theologie.* Ed. Hans Walter Wolff. Munich: Chr. Kaiser.

Kraus, H.-J.
1970   *Die Biblische Theologie: Ihre Geschichte und Problematik.* Neukirchen-Vluyn: Neukirchener Verlag.

McKenzie, John L.
1974   *A Theology of the Old Testament.* New York: Doubleday.

Muilenburg, J.
1961   *The Way of Israel: Biblical Faith and Ethics.* New York: Harper & Row.

Rad, Gerhard von
1962   *Old Testament Theology,* I. Trans. D. M. G. Stalker. New York: Harper & Row.
1963   "Typological Interpretation of the Old Testament." Pp. 17–39 in *Essays on Old Testament Hermeneutics.* Ed. Claus Westermann. Richmond: John Knox.
1965   *Old Testament Theology,* II. Trans. D. M. G. Stalker. New York: Harper & Row.

Rendtorff, Rolf
1960   "Hermeneutik des Alten Testaments als Frage nach der Geschichte." *ZTK* 57: 27–40.
1961   "Die Offenbarungsvorstellungen im Alten Israel." Pp. 21–41 in *Offenbarung als Geschichte.* Ed. W. Pannenberg. Göttingen: Vandenhoeck & Ruprecht.

Sanders, James A.
1972   *Torah and Canon.* Philadelphia: Fortress.
1976   "Adaptable for Life: The Nature and Function of Canon." Pp. 531–60 in *Magnalia Dei: Essays on the Bible and Archaeology in Memory of G. Ernest Wright.* Ed. Frank Moore Cross, Jr., Werner E. Lemke, and Patrick D. Miller, Jr. Garden City: Doubleday.

Smend, Rudolph
1970   *Die Mitte des Alten Testaments.* Theologische Studien, 101. Zurich: EVZ.

1977   "Tradition and History: A Complex Relation." Pp. 49–68 in *Tradition and Theology in the Old Testament*. Ed. Douglas A. Knight. Philadelphia: Fortress.

Spriggs, D. G.
1974   *Two Old Testament Theologies: A Comparative Evaluation of the Contributions of Eichrodt and von Rad to our Understanding of the Nature of Old Testament Theology*. SBT 2/30. London: SCM.

Stendahl, Krister
1962   "Contemporary Biblical Theology." Pp. 418–32 in *IDB*, Vol. 1.

Terrien, Samuel
1978   *The Elusive Presence: Toward a New Biblical Theology*. New York: Harper & Row.

Vaux, Roland de
1965   "Method in the Study of Early Hebrew History." Pp. 15–29 in *The Bible in Modern Scholarship*. Ed. J. Philip Hyatt. Nashville: Abingdon.
1971   "Is It Possible to Write a 'Theology of the Old Testament'?" Pp. 49–62 in *The Bible and the Ancient Near East*. Ed. G. E. Wright. Garden City: Doubleday.

Vriezen, Th. C.
1958   *An Outline of Old Testament Theology*. Oxford: Blackwell.

Westermann, Claus
1963   "The Interpretation of the Old Testament." Pp. 40–49 in *Essays on Old Testament Hermeneutics*. Ed. Claus Westermann. Richmond: John Knox.
1978   *Theologie des Alten Testaments in Grundzugen*. Göttingen: Vandenhoeck & Ruprecht.
1979   *What Does the Old Testament Say About God?* Atlanta: John Knox.

Wolff, Hans Walter
1963   "The Hermeneutics of the Old Testament." Pp. 160–99 in *Essays on Old Testament Hermeneutics*. Ed. Claus Westermann. Richmond: John Knox.
1975a   "The Elohistic Fragments in the Pentateuch." Pp. 69–82 in *The Vitality of Old Testament Traditions*. Atlanta: John Knox. = *Int* 26 (1972) 158–73.
1975b   "The Kerygma of the Deuteronomic Historical Work." Pp. 83–100 in *The Vitality of Old Testament Traditions*. Atlanta: John Knox.
1975c   "The Kerygma of the Yahwist." Pp. 41–66 in *The Vitality of Old Testament Traditions*. Atlanta: John Knox. = *Int* 20 (1966) 131–58.

Wright, G. Ernest
  1952   *God Who Acts: Biblical Theology as Recital*. SBT 8.
               London: SCM.
  1963   "History and Reality: The Importance of Israel's 'His-
               torical' Symbols for the Christian Faith." Pp. 176–99 in
               The Old Testament and Christian Faith. Ed. Bernhard
               W. Anderson. New York: Harper & Row.
  1969   *The Old Testament and Theology*. New York: Harper
               & Row.

Zimmerli, Walther
  1963   "Promise and Fulfillment." Pp. 89–122 in *Essays on Old
               Testament Hermeneutics*. Ed. Claus Westermann.
               Richmond: John Knox.
  1971   "Alttestamentliche Traditionsgeschichte und Theologie."
               Pp. 632–47 in *Probleme biblischer Theologie*. Ed. Hans
               Walter Wolff. Munich: Chr. Kaiser.
  1975   "Zum Problem der 'Mitte des Alten Testaments.'" *EvT*
               35: 97–118.
  1978   *Old Testament Theology in Outline*. Atlanta: John
               Knox.

8

The Pentateuch

Douglas A. Knight

It would be difficult to overestimate the role that the Pentateuch has played in the course of biblical scholarship. In all likelihood, these first five books have been subjected to scrutiny more than any other single block of the Bible, with the sole possible exception of the Gospels. It is significant that the Pentateuch has generally served as the staging ground for many if not most of the critical questions and methods that later spread to other areas of the biblical literature. Consider the following examples. Eight centuries ago Ibn Ezra wrote a commentary on the Pentateuch in which he delicately asked whether Moses could in fact have written all parts of the books normally attributed to him; subsequently, of course, such questioning of traditional authorship has extended to all parts of the Pentateuch as well as to, for example, Davidic composition of the psalms, Solomonic responsibility for wisdom literature, the origin of the prophetic writings, the authorship of the Gospels, the writer of various Pauline letters, to say nothing of the source of many of Jesus' sayings. Second, even before source criticism the idea that oral and written traditions might have been transmitted from generation to generation was proposed in the sixteenth and seventeenth centuries in the Hexateuchal studies of such scholars as John Calvin, Martin Chemnitz, Andreas Masius, Blaise Pascal, Baruch Spinoza, and Richard Simon; again, this notion has become common fare throughout the range of biblical studies, with the special twentieth-century perception that such traditions would not have been handed down passively but would have actually developed in the course of their transmission. Third, source criticism, as is well known, was first proposed for Genesis in the eighteenth century, initially by Henning Bernhard Witter in 1711 and then by Jean Astruc in 1753; now it is commonplace for scholars to inquire about the unitary or composite character of biblical passages and the authorship, date, and provenance of any sources we may discover. Fourth, the method of Religionsgeschichte seems, as can best be determined, to have emerged from a circle of friends that included Albert Eichhorn, Wilhelm Wrede, Hermann Gunkel, Wilhelm Bousset, Hugo Gressmann, and Ernst Troeltsch, but Gunkel's landmark study of 1895, *Schöpfung und Chaos*, was one of the very first full attempts to study a

portion of biblical literature from this perspective. Fifth, form criticism
of biblical literature originated with Gunkel's commentary on Genesis in
1901; it is now inconceivable to conduct critical exegesis without attention
to form, genre, Sitz im Leben, and intention. In all of these cases—and
many more could be added to them—the Pentateuch was the literary
material that first invited closer study and presented in the process other
problems demanding attention. The majority of biblical criticism holds
itself in debt to these five books of the Torah.

However, the vital importance of the Pentateuch extends beyond its
role in the development of critical methods, for it has long been used as
the primary key to understanding Israel's history, society, religion, and
morality. These are all addressed matter-of-factly in these ancient writings. The creation of the world, the origin of the people, the institution
of religion, the ordering of family and social life—all are recounted in
narratives, genealogies, laws, and speeches. But they were not presented
simply out of antiquarian interest, as if merely to record what occurred
in earliest times. Rather, this literature seems to be designed to lay out
the program for Israel's life in later periods: settlement, monarchy, exile,
and reconstruction. This is evident quite explicitly in the Mosaic sermons
in Deuteronomy, but it cannot be mistaken elsewhere as well—from the
relationship with neighboring peoples implied in eponymous ancestral
stories, to the details for the temple building, to the cultic and moral
ordinances for a settled agricultural and urban life. Of course, historical
criticism has argued persuasively that most of these details stem not from
the pre-settlement period as they purport to do, but instead are projected
from later centuries back into the ancestral and Mosaic times. Thus the
Pentateuch, which ends with the death of Moses (generally thought to
have occurred in the thirteenth century B.C.E.), serves actually as a major
source for our reconstruction of the cultural and religious life of the
people from that point all the way down to the fifth century. This itself
could scarcely be accomplished were it not for the division of the literature into documentary sources that could then be dated to successive
periods. Such use of the Pentateuch in historiography is nowhere more
evident than in the work of Julius Wellhausen (especially 1878).

Given these two factors—that the Pentateuch has so often served as
the subject matter for innovative criticism throughout the history of
biblical scholarship and that this literature is of crucial importance for
our study of Israel's cultural history—it is all the more disconcerting to
observe that uncertainties and disputes at very fundamental points are
prevalent in current Pentateuchal studies. Not long ago it seemed that
real clarity had been achieved, but the state of affairs has now turned.
These general problems of method and interpretation deserve attention
at this point before we focus on more specific parts of Pentateuchal
research.

I. A SYNTHESIS AND ITS DISSOLUTION

It would be fair to say that Gerhard von Rad and Martin Noth have offered the most significant comprehensive work on the Pentateuch in modern biblical scholarship. Wellhausen's decisive contributions, in comparison, were limited primarily to source criticism (1876–77), in which he amassed the findings of his predecessors and ordered them cogently into the Grafian sequence of JEDP, a structure that in general has held now for a century—no small achievement. However, Wellhausen's work on the Pentateuch included little more than drawing—very extensively, to be sure—on its postulated documents for his reconstruction of the history of Israel and its religion. He produced no commentaries, theologies, or further critical studies of the whole. Gunkel did write a nonpareil commentary on one of its books, Genesis, but his seminal form-critical work on this literature was left to be applied by others to the rest of the Pentateuch. He also presented no in-depth analysis of the whole. In contrast, both von Rad and Noth devoted themselves massively and repeatedly to the Pentateuch. For von Rad, the comprehensive proposal came in 1938 in his *Form-Critical Problem of the Hexateuch*. He added to this numerous other studies including commentaries on Genesis (1953) and Deuteronomy (1964) and a major section in his *Old Testament Theology* (1st ed. in 1957). Similarly, Noth offered his general study in the form of an even more detailed, intensive analysis, *A History of Pentateuchal Traditions*, first published in 1948 and several times reprinted and translated. Beyond this seminal study Noth wrote commentaries on Exodus (1959), Numbers (1966), and Leviticus (1962), but these were not as closely related to his 1948 monograph as was his 1950 *History of Israel*, in which he demonstrated how this history should be understood in the light of his reconstructed development of the Pentateuchal traditions.

Between the two of them, von Rad and Noth managed to put together a critical synthesis that has informed nearly two generations of students and scholars. For all of the critical responses that they have received from the very beginning—and there have always been dissenting voices—their combined view of the origins of the Pentateuch long survived as the ruling hypothesis about how the Pentateuch came to be. What is especially important in this regard is the hermeneutical assumption: that the meaning(s) or intentions which a given text had at its origin and during its subsequent development are relevant for our understanding of the text in its present form. Thus most subsequent commentaries on the books of the Torah have been overwhelmingly concerned with focusing exegetically on this period of formation rather than on the longer postbiblical period in which the church and the synagogue interpreted these texts, often quite differently. So the critical framework that von Rad and Noth provided has had an impact not only in the area of literary history but also in exegetical interpretation and in historiography.

Before saying more about this hypothesis and its subsequent demise, one might well ask whether it is even proper to consider the separate work of von Rad and of Noth as indeed parts of a common synthesis. To be sure, the two did not explicitly collaborate on any specific project, an important exception being the development of the influential series, Biblischer Kommentar. Furthermore, von Rad's primary interest in theological questions was noticeably at variance with Noth's preoccupation with historical matters. However, the two critics themselves viewed their work as complementary to each other. On the second page of his 1948 volume Noth referred favorably to von Rad's earlier study of the "confessions/creeds" which gave a very early order to the series of themes that were essential for the faith of the Israelite tribes, confessions that were recited repeatedly in the early cult (also 1948:48). What Noth then attempted to do beyond this was to determine the nature and origin of these individual themes and to show how they were gradually filled out with innumerable other independent traditions. Von Rad, for his part, emphasized in later editions of his *Form-Critical Problem of the Hexateuch* that he wished it to be read in conjunction with Noth's volume. The various differences between the two seem to pale in comparison with the central preoccupation of both: to move the discussion beyond the then prevalent "stalemate" and "boredom" in Pentateuchal work (as von Rad [1938:1] described it at the time) and, in Noth's words, "to understand, in a manner that is historically responsible and proper, the essential content and important concerns of the Pentateuch—which, from its manifold beginnings, variously rooted in cultic situations, to the final stages in the process of its emergence, claims recognition as a great document of faith" (1948:3f.; Eng. tr. 3). Above all, in this the concern—again as Noth three times emphasized it (1948:4, 161, v)—is more to raise the proper questions than to offer definitive solutions.

The main features in this von Rad/Noth synthesis can be described as follows, without attempting to note all of the differences between the two. For both von Rad and Noth the Pentateuch as we have it is decidedly an "Endstadium," the final stage in a long process of development. Their primary task was not to engage in a literary-critical analysis of its smaller elements, but instead to try to recover this history of growth. They pictured this consistently as a living process, often oral; the operative category for it is "Vergegenwärtigung," understood in both senses of reinterpretation and actualization—a legitimatizing process in which one generation receives the traditions from the past and then has the opportunity to reaffirm them, adjusting them as they find appropriate, before passing them to the next generation. These traditions thus have to do with matters of vital importance to the Israelites' faith, society, and self-understanding. As a rule, the Pentateuch is based on innumerable traditions that were at first largely independent of one another. Only in the course of time did they become fused together, a process that von Rad and Noth sought to unlock. Noth concentrated much more on the precompositional stage; von Rad, on the compositional period. Noth identified five central themes that served as crystallization points for much that is in the Pentateuch: Promise to the Patriarchs, Guidance out of Egypt, Guidance in the Wilderness, Revelation at Sinai, and Guidance into the Arable Land. Each of these may well rest on some kernel of historical fact involving one or another group, but in no instance did all of Israel experience any one of these. Von Rad dealt also with these five themes, although he linked the exodus and conquest into one complex (hence also his insistence on a Hexateuch) and stressed especially the independence of the Sinai tradition from the others.

Perhaps the main difference between the two scholars, however, lies in how they viewed the merger of these themes. Noth set it in the period prior to the Yahwist, whereas von Rad attributed this decisive change to the compositional work of the Yahwist himself. For Noth, during the settlement period the Israelite tribes became aligned in the form of an amphictyony, with a central cult and several institutional functions in common (1930). It was in this cultic context that the themes merged together and that much of the remaining traditions were introduced into the whole. Von Rad postulated that the faith of Israel in this premonarchic period would have been expressed in a creedal form (the best example is in Deut 26.5b–9) and that such confessional statements would have provided the outline for the later composition. But he attributed to the Yahwist this innovation of creating a linear narrative based on the exodus–wilderness–conquest complex, through the "Einbau" (inclusion) of the Sinai tradition, the "Ausbau" (extension) of the ancestral traditions, and the "Vorbau" (addition at the beginning) of the primeval history. However, neither one considered this merger of the themes to be accidental or arbitrary, even though they tended to give different reasons for it: Noth, the development of the amphictyonic community; von Rad, the theological intentionality of the Yahwist. They agreed on seeing this early period as the formative stage of the faith as well as of the traditions, and wherever possible they tried to attribute these processes to specific groups, cultic celebrations, and geographical locations. They also shared a heuristic dichotomy between tradition and history, that is, between Israel's picture of her history and the historical-critical reconstruction of what actually happened. This discrepancy was not a problem for either of them: von Rad tied the kerygmatic, heilsgeschichtlich theology to Israel's traditional interpretation of her past, and Noth used these traditions themselves as indicators not of presettlement history but

of the beliefs and ideas of the settled tribes. And finally, these two scholars were fully persuaded that this early formative period was so important that it must necessarily be penetrated if the structure and contents
of the present Pentateuch, both as a whole and in its details, are to be
understood properly. Small wonder, then, that von Rad in his commentary on Genesis gave explicit exegetical preference to the Yahwistic and
Elohistic levels of the text—even though he clearly admitted that "the
question of whether the preacher and teacher are also tied to this hermeneutical point of departure is another question entirely" (1953:31; Eng.
tr. 1961:40). While both von Rad and Noth maintained a critical interest
in the later Pentateuchal stages as well, for them the early period carried
special significance.

A historical hypothesis can be considered valid only if it manages to
explain all the evidence better than any other hypothesis can. Seen in
this light, it is no wonder that the von Rad/Noth synthesis had the
degree of success it has enjoyed since the 1940s. No other rival hypothesis concerning the growth of the Pentateuch has been so comprehen-
sively and cogently developed nor so widely accepted during this period.
However, so many specific features of this proposal have gradually fallen
victim to attack that the cohesion of the whole has steadily eroded. Some
of the most serious criticisms should be mentioned before we move on to
the primary dilemma facing Pentateuchal studies today.

(1) One of the key items of the synthesis is von Rad's suggestion that
there were creedal statements in the pre-Yahwistic period that set the
central themes in order and thereby served as the outline according to
which the Pentateuch was arranged. The antiquity of these creeds has
now been effectively repudiated by Brevard Childs (1967), Wolfgang
Richter (1967), J. Philip Hyatt, Leonhard Rost, and others. The confessions cited by von Rad contain too many Deuteronomistic elements to be
dated any earlier than probably the seventh century. They are, therefore, in the nature more of theological summaries or systematic recapitu-
lations at the end of the developmental process than of ancient faith
statements that from an early point onward affected this process itself.

(2) Related to this, the antiquity of covenantal theology itself has
been persuasively discounted by Lothar Perlitt. Both von Rad and Noth
had, like Albrecht Alt before them, envisioned a covenant-renewal festival at Shechem when the Sinai theme would have been reactualized, and
they regarded this as probably the oldest extensive tradition preserved in
the Hebrew Bible. But Perlitt has undercut this thoroughly now by tracing the theological concept of covenant no earlier than the seventh century. Of course, this also affects the hypotheses advanced by George
Mendenhall and others.

(3) Because the "creeds" were unanimous in omitting the Sinai revelation from their concatenation of the heilsgeschichtlich events, von Rad

and Noth both concluded that this theme was wholly independent of the others. This has been roundly challenged by A. S. van der Woude, Walter Beyerlin, and others on the grounds of literary and theological affinities or by positing a covenant/treaty model, the latter of course a questionable point.

(4) The formative period of the Pentateuchal traditions reputedly occurred during the stage of oral transmission, with several folkloristic characteristics indicating this. John Van Seters (1975), however, has disputed that one can comfortably determine such orality from the written literature.

(5) Like Gunkel and Alt before them, von Rad and especially Noth considered many of the cultic, geographical, and popular narratives to be etiologically based. John Bright, Brevard Childs (1963), and Burke O. Long have cautioned, however, against prematurely discounting the authenticity of such traditions, for the etiological elements could in many cases be secondary redactional additions.

(6) Although most literary critics before him had normally maintained that the sources J and E were independent of each other, Noth made the interesting suggestion that preceding these two was a G source, a "Grundlage," comprising already in the amphictyonic period the elements common to both J and E (1948:40–44; Eng. tr. 38–41). This proposal has not been convincing to such scholars as Hannelis Schulte in her study of the Joseph story or Van Seters in his work on the Abraham narrative; they attribute such common materials rather to author-editors who succeeded one another and made use of their predecessor's work, in other words through a series of literary dependency and redaction.

(7) By elevating the five themes to a position of supremacy in the early formation of the Pentateuch, von Rad and Noth unwittingly reduced all else to secondary or even less importance. Stated differently, the scheme was allowed sometimes to control the data, rather than vice versa. Thus for Noth especially, the traditions that serve merely to fill out the themes or in some way to connect them together include much of the Isaac and Jacob stories, the Joseph narrative, genealogies, itineraries, the plagues account, much of the wilderness tradition, the story of the Midianites in Exodus 18, the golden calf apostasy and covenant renewal in Exodus 32 and 34, and several other traditions as well. However, the element that has produced the most contrary response from scholars is the role assigned to the figure of Moses. According to Noth, the main reliable historical information we have about Moses is the tradition of his marriage to a foreign woman and the tradition about his grave. Just as Moses plays a negligible role outside the Pentateuch in the Hebrew Bible, so also he is not indispensable to any of the five themes— but belongs instead to the narrative elaboration as a linking element among several of the themes (1948:172–91; Eng. tr. 156–75). Noth's

thesis regarding Moses has met with a storm of protest—not all of which, however, is argued as carefully or researched as thoroughly as is Noth's initial proposal.

(8) For both Noth and von Rad, the primary Sitz im Leben for the pre-Yahwistic developments was the amphictyony in its cultic, political, and military functions. As suggestive as this amphictyonic model seemed to be after Noth first elaborated it in 1930, it has not proved itself resilient to such attacks as those of Harry Orlinsky and Georg Fohrer (1966). Noth had maintained that it was through the amphictyony that the traditions attained their all-Israel orientation, so this matter needs to be reconsidered now also. Add to this the massive sociological proposal by Norman Gottwald and others: that Israel came into existence not through migration into the land but through a peasant uprising against the exploitative Canaanite overlords. What remains for the critic is a welter of hypotheses but no firm consensus regarding institutional, social, or cultic structures that could have aided the growth of the Pentateuchal traditions. For that matter, there seems now to be as little agreement on the emergence of Israel and the origin of Yahwism as there ever has been, although additional material data now coming to light should assist on this question (see the discussion in the chapter by J. M. Miller in this volume).

(9) Von Rad's division between scientific history and the theological interpretation of history has come under fire from several sides. Franz Hesse called it "double-tracking" and insisted that the actual course of Israel's history, not simply Israel's interpretation of it, must be the vital arena of God's activity. In line with this, others have attempted—often through an illegitimate use of archaeological finds—to confirm the historical veracity of Pentateuchal events, customs, and other evidences. Thomas Thompson and John Van Seters, in separate monographs, have firmly refuted any such efforts at isolating elements in the ancestral narratives that might point unequivocally to the second millennium B.C.E. Although this would seem to make tradition and history even more distinct from each other than von Rad and Noth maintained, one must admit that the issue is far from settled in many scholars' eyes.

(10) The idea of Heilsgeschichte, on the other hand, seems to have gone the way of the Biblical Theology movement (Childs, 1970: Barr: 65ff.). It is too selective in highlighting only major historical junctures as occasions where God acts, as if the regular cultic interaction between God and humans is of much less importance. Second, it becomes too readily a theology of deliverance rather than a theology of justice with moral claims on humanity. Third, it is too facilely turned into a type of kerygmatic theology, in which one attempts to reduce the complexity of the literature and history to a primary kerygma. For example, Hans Walter Wolff (see the articles reprinted in Brueggemann and Wolff)

finds the kerygmatic message of the Yahwist in the charge to Israel to be
a blessing to the world; for the Elohist, the kerygma is the call to "fear
God"; and for the Deuteronomist it is the call to repentance and return.
There is little willingness among scholars anymore to bypass the varied
nature of the literature in order to arrive at such simple reductions.

(11) At the level of the literary sources there has also occurred a
serious departure from the Wellhausen/von Rad/Noth schema. Most
notably, the Yahwistic source has come under heavy fire. John Van
Seters has been insistent on dating this source closer to the exile, and
Hans Heinrich Schmid wanted to consider it in terms of a much longer
redactional period than the traditional dating in the tenth century would
allow. Rolf Rendtorff (1977), in a very thorough criticism, even accused
von Rad of departing from the normal source-critical model in arguing
so strongly that the Yahwist was a theologian, rather than a literary document. The E material was also seen by Van Seters and others as more
of a redactional level than a separate source. There continues to be considerably divided opinion on whether and how much the Deuteronomists
laid their hands on the Pentateuch. And finally, several critics remain
unconvinced by Noth's provocative proposal (1948:7–19) that P was a
separate source document that became the framework into which J and
E were incorporated to make the final Pentateuch. Frank Cross, among
others, maintained that it is much more likely that P was not a separate
source but rather represented the final redaction of the JE material.
Further complicating the discussion is the argument by several Jerusalem scholars that P is in fact a document of the preexilic period.

(12) To conclude this list we can simply point to the general lack of
unanimity on where the Pentateuch ends. That is, in terms of literary
history does the book of Deuteronomy belong more with Genesis–
Numbers or with Joshua–Kings, the so-called Deuteronomistic History?
This question is tied as well to the problem of where the conquest tradition belongs. On these points von Rad and Noth themselves disagreed.
While von Rad spoke of a Hexateuch that ended with the conquest narrative, Noth preferred the notion of a Pentateuch—although with the
bulk of Deuteronomy excluded he virtually operated with a Tetrateuch
(as did Engnell more explicitly). A similar divergence on such a major
point as this continues to the present.

Reference has been made here only to rather general points of contention. It hardly needs to be said that many of von Rad's and Noth's interpretations of specific literary units have also faced substantial and telling
criticism. The important point for us is that Pentateuchal studies is hardly
in a favorable position at the present point. The synthesis that explained
so much about the formative history and meaning of the literature has
met with such formidable opposition at individual points that only with
multiple reservations can one defend it any longer. Heuristically, it still

continues to prompt productive debate—not the least with regard to the determination of the right questions to ask of the text. However, there is no other grand plan, at the present, which promises to take the place of this influential proposal.

II. HISTORY OF THE PENTATEUCHAL LITERATURE

Pentateuchal research has largely followed Gunkel's lead (1906) in reconstructing a history of the literature ("Literaturgeschichte") from the earliest origins on down to the last stages. There has been, in comparison, remarkably little synchronic study of pericopes; examples of the exceptions are R. Polzin and D. Patte. Somewhat more attention has been focused on stylistics, for example, with regard to Hebrew narrative art (see the volume edited in 1975 by R. Culley, as well as other studies). Yet most scholars, like von Rad and Noth, have sought instead to clarify the ways in which the literature came into existence. What specifically comes under scrutiny in any study may be as short as a portion of a verse or as long as an entire book. Similarly, attention can shift variously from oral tradition to genre to documentary source to redaction. There would be few scholars who would not understand their individual analyses to be contributions to the larger program of reconstructing the development of the literature along its full course of growth. There can be both theological and historical motivations for this enterprise, as we noted above to be the case also for von Rad and Noth.

Preliterary Tradition

In the section above we have described in some detail the work of von Rad and Noth and various points of critical reaction to it. It was in regard to the preliterary stage of the development of traditions that these two scholars made some of their most important contributions, not the least in their basic insistence that this period holds vital information for the proper understanding of the text. Most researchers of the Pentateuch have tended to agree with this, even if opinions vary on many specific points. A detailed study of traditio-historical work since its inception is available in Knight, 1975; therefore, our comments here can be limited to a few general aspects of it in Pentateuchal studies.

Especially notable is the increased attention given to oral tradition. Literary materials could not only be remembered but also could actually be created at the oral stage. A tradition could thereby emerge as an expression of anything that was important to the ongoing life of the community. Scholarship has often envisioned an oral stage for almost every one of the various Pentateuchal literary forms: narrative, laws, songs, and even lists; there has also been a similar inquiry for most other literary sections of the Hebrew Bible, particularly the prophetic and psalmic literature. Although such research dates back to Gunkel and his predecessors, Scandinavians such as H. S. Nyberg, I. Engnell, and S. Mowinckel have been especially strong proponents of it in the past forty years—and with a distinctive direction. In several studies they have argued that very much of the Hebrew Bible originated as "oral literature," in part in cultic contexts and in part in other institutional or everyday situations. In contrast to Mowinckel, Nyberg and Engnell maintained that the oral process had a type of "Schmelzofen" effect, causing the tradition leading up to a given text to become so fused within itself that any layers of meaning stemming from various periods could not be distinguished from one another. For Engnell, the methodological implication of this was that scholars must virtually abandon source criticism in favor of tradition history, which is not oriented toward a "book-view" or an *interpretatio europeica moderna* of this ancient Hebrew literature. With respect to the Pentateuch, he adjusted the standard sigla to phrases (e.g., the "P-work" or the "D-group") or set them in double quotation marks ("J," "E," "P"). There was not actually a Pentateuch but a Tetrateuch (without "D"), and "P" was not a documentary source but the last transmitter and editor of it. Following a debate with Mowinckel over critical method, Engnell seemed to modify his position somewhat about the extent of oral tradition in the Hebrew Bible, but he continued to argue stridently against attempts to stratify the tradition into primary and secondary elements. The influence of Nyberg and Engnell on such matters has steadily decreased over the years among other Scandinavian scholars, while researchers elsewhere have tended to consider it an idiosyncratic turn in scholarship. (For a full discussion of this traditio-historical work, see Knight, 1975:217–399; specifically also Engnell; Nyberg, 1947, 1972.)

However, the emphasis on oral means of transmission and oral devices in the literature has not been lost. Most scholars now recognize that a strict dichotomy between oral and written tradition is probably inappropriate, that both could have continued alongside each other and contributed to each other, that the oral probably preceded the written during the growth of the tradition but that oral interpretation could have continued long after a written text became fixed (note, e.g., the oral law in early Judaism) and that long compositions or cycles of traditions, if not actually created in written form, must have been committed early to writing rather than been retained solely as oral literature. Very often it is difficult or impossible to determine whether a given composition existed first in oral or written form; Noth (1948:41; Eng. tr. 39) acknowledged this for the Pentateuchal "Grundlage," his postulated source for the common elements in J and E. As indicated above concerning the dissolution of the von Rad/Noth synthesis, J. Van Seters (especially 131–48) has even questioned whether oral tradition can be identified on the basis of

our present written texts except at a few isolated points where folkloristic
criteria point clearly to preliterary genres. Most scholars tend to attribute
a greater role to the oral prehistory of the biblical text than this (see,
e.g., the various articles in Culley, 1976), with some recognition also of
its theological implications (R. Lapointe).

As will be seen in the sections below on source and redaction criticism, F. Winnett, J. Van Seters, H. H. Schmid, R. Rendtorff, and others
have sought to shift the emphasis from tradition history to a history of
successive literary developments, which would then be studied by redaction criticism. Rendtorff's work (1977) is especially important at this
point. Briefly stated, the traditio-historical problem of the Pentateuch in
his view does not concern itself with the smaller, independent traditions
that arose and circulated at the very earliest period in Israel's history
(Gunkel's project), nor does it have to do with the compilation of the
bulk of the epic tradition by the Yahwist (von Rad's contribution).
Rather, he observed that what has been neglected is the stage in between
when the independent, often disparate traditions became gathered
together into "larger units," prior to the time when these various units
were in turn structured together to make our present Pentateuch. He
surveyed the numerous such units identifiable in the Pentateuch, but he
spent the bulk of his analysis in an attempt to reconstruct this traditio-
historical stage for the ancestral traditions. Here, for example, he dealt
with such units as the Abraham cycle, the Isaac traditions, the Jacob
traditions, and the Joseph story. In attempting to determine how and
why the various traditions came together to form each of these originally
separate units, Rendtorff focused especially on literary and thematic
elements (such as the types of promise to the ancestors) rather than on
geographic, social/political, or cultic circumstances (such as Noth elevated as criteria). This study of literary and thematic elements holding
the units together constitutes in fact one of the primary contributions of
this book, although Rendtorff failed to relate them adequately to the
other factors just mentioned and thereby did not create a plausible setting for these traditio-historical developments. After thus executing his
brief analysis of the formation of these larger units, Rendtorff turned to
a criticism of recent Pentateuchal research and then to the implications
of his study. His basic thesis in this regard was that there were no continuous "sources" in the sense of comprehensive drafts of Pentateuchal
materials, such as scholars for a century have seen in J and P. He based
this thesis in part on the lack of consensus among scholars about the
precise extent and characteristics of J and P, in part on the lack of solid
evidence for these source documents in the Pentateuch or even in the
preexilic prophetic literature, in part on the lack of continuity among
the larger units, and furthermore in part on the simple fact that with the
multitude of these larger units in the Pentateuch the sources J and P are

no longer really necessary. At most they might represent editorial reworkings of the materials. Rendtorff concluded in fact that only at the level of the Deuteronomistic redaction did any editor have the comprehensive Pentateuch on which to work. Having thus called into serious question the standard results of source criticism, the book concluded with some further observations about how important the origin of the several larger units is for the overall understanding of the Pentateuch and its development.

Rendtorff's critique is suggestive, especially for the attention which he drew to the "larger units" in the Pentateuch, but substantially more analyses of texts and units are needed if his thesis is to be established. In the face of his work and that of the others who prefer to think of the Pentateuchal growth as mainly a literary process of successive redactions, one still cannot lose the sense that more can be said about the developmental process than just this. Very much of the Pentateuchal research in recent decades has focused on the larger cycles of similar materials or on the five themes of Noth, with results that are admittedly hypothetical but nonetheless often plausible (for a brief overview of such studies see, among others, R. Smend, 1978:96–100). To the extent that these forays into the uncharted terrains of preliterary (as well as literary) traditions provide us with reasonable insights, they will continue to be pursued.

Literary Development

Of all the stages in the history of the Pentateuchal literature, the documentary sources have enjoyed the longest and most thorough scrutiny. Indeed, source criticism, which attempts to identify the literary sources that may have served as the basis for the final text, was the first of the historical-critical exegetical methods to develop after the seventeenth-century onset of modern biblical criticism. The eighteenth and nineteenth centuries saw this work produce a succession of different proposals: the older documentary hypothesis, the fragment hypothesis, the supplementary hypothesis, and finally the new documentary hypothesis. It is the latter that has continued to have an impact up to the present, above all because of Julius Wellhausen's cogent presentation of the literary evidence (1876–77) and the relation of these sources to the history of Israel, especially to the history of its religion (1878; for an appraisal of Wellhausen's significance, see the volume edited by D. Knight, 1982). Following the suggestion of Eduard Reuss and Karl Heinrich Graf, Wellhausen envisioned four primary sources set in the following order: J (ca. 850 B.C.E.), E (ca. 700), D (ca. 623), and P (500–450). In the following decades and still to the present this delineation has for most scholars continued to represent the base point of Pentateuchal criticism. Modifications were offered up through the 1930s in primarily two

different areas: proposing alternate dates for the sources or subdividing
the various sources into multiple strands. However, these were generally
intended by the source critics to be little more than adjustments to the
established scheme. (For detailed discussions of source criticism during
that period, see especially Houtman; Kraus.) It is significant, however,
that most of the early source critics assumed that to identify the literary
sources was sufficient for explaining the origins of the Pentateuch.

Yet by the 1940s there was a different mood afoot. With attention
being turned increasingly to other stages in the history of the Pentateuchal literature—especially to the genres and the traditions—scholars
began to sense, as Gunkel had earlier proposed, that much, if not most,
of the creative activity had already occurred well before the sources
were written. Most critics tended to consider the problem of source
delineation to be basically resolved, and they presupposed this Well-
hausenian structure for the work which they preferred to conduct.
Already in his landmark study of 1938 Gerhard von Rad noted that
source criticism had come to a halt—and in the eyes of some had even
gone too far. Both in this area and in the study of the smaller units he
observed a "Stillstand" and a "Forschungsmüdigkeit" which had regretta-
bly taken hold, especially among younger scholars (1938:1). A mere
decade later, however, Martin Noth referred to "the continuing lively
debate over the literary-critical analysis of the Pentateuch" (1948:5; Eng.
tr. 6). These divergent evaluations are due to several elements. Noth
engaged in more explicit source criticism than did von Rad and offered
several novel proposals. Noth tended to relate such source investigation
to the history of the literature, whereas for von Rad the theological
aspects were more important, especially as these related to the final
compositions. Noth could also, of course, look back on a decade of
increased attack on source criticism from several sides, especially from
Scandinavian scholars (see Knight, 1975). Finally, von Rad's own contributions to the relationship between the theologizing Yahwist and the
final state of the Pentateuch/Hexateuch reopened questions about the
significance of the sources. Actually, the years following 1938 would
confirm von Rad's comment only for the specific matter of source division, that is, the assigning of texts to one continuous source document or
another. Even Noth (1948:4–44) and most commentators since that time
have tended to follow the division elaborated by Wellhausen. Nonetheless, the debate has hardly been stagnant if one considers the fundamental questions that have been and still are raised, issues that have to do
with the whole literary development of the Pentateuch from initial written sources on down to final redactions.

The Yahwistic Literature (J)

The liveliness of this discussion can be seen immediately with the source that has traditionally been set as the first: J. Although there is some divergence among scholars on questions of composition, the greatest variance of views—and thereby the most unsettled questions of vital significance for the understanding of J—is to be found on matters of origin and intention.

The literary composition of J, which embraces the largest single narrative block in the Pentateuch, has long been suspect of "Mehrschichtigkeit." Earlier generations of scholars have at times fragmented J into multiple strata. This source-critical tendency has been largely abandoned, except at one specific point. O. Eissfeldt divided J into two sources—the older termed the Lay source (L) and dated ca. 950–850 B.C.E. and the younger simply called J and assigned anywhere between 900 and 721. He first gave graphic portrayal of these sources in his *Hexateuch–Synopse* (1922, repr. 1962) and continued to argue this division in his influential *Introduction*. Notably, these sources were traced beyond the Pentateuch into the books of Joshua and Judges. Just as significant, Eissfeldt maintained that the two sources stemmed from opposing circles: L from groups committed to the nomadic ideal and to the unity of Israel despite its division into two kingdoms after 922; and, in direct contrast, J from circles enthusiastically interested in agricultural life and in the national political power and cult. Georg Fohrer's modification of this division (1969:173–79) consisted especially in renaming L with N (= Nomadic source) and setting it not before but after J as a conservative reaction against J's satisfaction with the arable land ("Kulturlandbegeisterung"). Previously, C. A. Simpson (1948), one of the other main proponents of a divided J source during the period since 1945, assigned his J1 source to the southern tribes and considered that the J2 source had then, in the period around 900 B.C.E., used and revised J1 in the light of additional traditions from the Joseph tribes. Later, around 700 B.C.E., E reworked all the material in a thoroughgoing manner in the light of other northern interests. Simpson furthermore posited a complex subsequent redactional history of these sources. Eissfeldt, Simpson, and Fohrer have not found wide support for their proposals, which to many appear to be rather artificial and improbable divisions of J. By far the dominant inclination has been to account traditio-historically or redaction-critically for any materials in J that seem to deviate from its usual character.

On this point of its character, one can find descriptions of J—with greater or lesser detail but with little substantial deviation from each other—in any number of introductory volumes on the Hebrew Bible. R. Smend (1967:27–87), Peter F. Ellis (225–95), and others have reproduced the text in translation, joining all parts together into a flowing narrative. Henri Cazelles (771–91) provided an overview with source-critical notes about the materials that are assigned to J; commentators, of course, usually do the same for their respective books. A list of Hebrew words and forms that are distinctive to J can be found in Simpson (403–9), and Ellis (113–46) described some of the primary literary techniques used by the Yahwist; Aage Bentzen (2: 45–51) discussed both sets of criteria with reference to the problem of distinguishing between J and E. With few exceptions (especially U. Cassuto and I. Engnell), scholars have tended not to contest these matters to any degree approaching their disputes over how the data are to be interpreted.

The problem of date looms largest—and consequently the questions of audience, place, and intention are necessarily attached to it as well. Few scholars would deny that some or even most of the J material may extend back in time to the premonarchic period of settlement. Noth argued forcefully that "the actual formation of Pentateuchal tradition is to be placed essentially in the period of prestate tribal life" (1948:248; Eng. tr. 229), and for him this included not only the source "G" but also many other narratives that were subsequently used in J, E, and P to fill out the traditional materials in each. Furthermore, it is often maintained by scholars that these pre-J and pre-E traditions were not necessarily still in the form of disparate small units when they were incorporated into J or E, for there could well have existed cycles or collections—for example, stories about the ancestors, early laws, descriptions of the wanderings of the people—in oral or written form before the extensive written sources later emerged. Thus the question of the origin of the various *contents* of a given source tends to be held separate from the question of when the *whole* was constituted as a documentary source.

The most common date assigned to the origin of J is the period of the early monarchy. Von Rad associated it with a "Solomonic humanism" (1962:68–69; Eng. tr. 55), a period of enlightenment under Solomon marked by political security, a nationalistic spirit, building programs, new interest in culture and the arts, and an appreciation of human existence. "What else is the Jahwist's wonderful work but one great attempt to make Israel's past relevant to the spirit of a new age by reviewing and, above all, spiritualizing it?" (1962:69; Eng. tr. 55). Even though von Rad's notion of a "Solomonic Enlightenment" may be somewhat excessive (see, e.g., the critique by J. Crenshaw [16–20]), the vast majority of interpreters have followed him in dating J somewhere between the mid tenth and the late ninth century (see, e.g., the seven observations supporting a Solomonic date in H. P. Müller [52]). This Yahwistic history is thereby associated with the succession narrative and other literary productions of this monarchy, all seen as examples of Israel's initial efforts in historiography (von Rad, 1944; Hölscher; Schulte). Not only did J first emerge as a written source in this period; but also it is seen to represent "Hoftheologie," and its author is considered a "court theologian"

(Richter, 1966; Brueggemann, 1968)—although how officially sanctioned is unclear. W. von Soden proposed Nathan or his disciple as the author of J or substantial parts of it, with a certain prophetic-type critique of Solomon to be found in Genesis 3 and 11 (cf. also M.-L. Henry). Adherents to this early dating of J vary in assigning it to the reign of David, Solomon, or Rehoboam, but they quite uniformly agree to its southern provenance. J was thus a collection of old narratives that were gathered together at that point in order to celebrate the new monarchy by recounting God's beneficent dealings in Israel's earlier past history. H. W. Wolff (1964) identified Gen 12:1–3 as the key indicator of J's theological kerygma: YHWH's promise of blessing to Abraham, which was becoming fulfilled in J's period when the early monarchy was established and secured (see also L. Schmidt).

A very different conception of J has emerged in recent years, a view that challenges directly the position held by those scholars who trace their critical heritage back to Noth, von Rad, and Wellhausen. In 1964 Frederick V. Winnett delivered his Presidential Address to the Society of Biblical Literature, which was published in 1065 under the provocative, if not iconoclastic, title "Re-examining the Foundations." The "foundations" he examined were those represented in the foregoing description of the J source. In a word, Winnett disputed the idea of two parallel strands, J and E, running through the book of Genesis, and in its place he proposed a succession of "official revisions," extensive supplementations by later hands. The emphasis on "official" is important because it is improbable that various scribes along the way would have been permitted to "tamper" with the narrative, introducing glosses and interpolations without the sanction of the basically conservative religious body for whom this narrative was so important (1965:12). Winnett posited an early J document, probably cultic in origin, which was composed of Abraham and Jacob stories linked together sequentially. The first official revision was E's work of supplementing—not altering—this J source still in the preexilic period. However, the book of Genesis owes its present form to the major revision done by the author whom Winnett called "Late J" and dated in the postexilic period. This Late J composed the primeval history on the basis of diverse sources ("mainly oral but possibly some written" [1965:18]), incorporated the Abraham-Jacob narrative as revised by E, and drew on the E story of Joseph, recasting it to give Judah a more prominent role. The impetus for this work by the Late J, whose outlook was notably universalistic and monotheistic, was the fall of Jerusalem in 587 B.C.E. There was a later official revision of Late J's Genesis by P about 400 B.C.E. The major achievement by P, however, was the creation of the Pentateuch: prefixing Genesis to the Mosaic tradition in the books of Exodus and Numbers (the latter two books were also significantly revised by P) and detaching the book of

Deuteronomy from the Deuteronomistic History in order to append it to the Mosaic tradition. This means, then, that the book of Genesis is later than Exodus and Numbers, and thus that the promises of land in Genesis do not presuppose a JE narrative extending as far as the story of the conquest and settlement of Canaan. In an earlier study (1949) Winnett had also disputed the theory of parallel J and E strands in Exodus and Numbers, so his study challenged the regnant documentary hypothesis not merely for Genesis but for the entire Pentateuch as well.

Winnett's proposal has not won the day among Pentateuchal scholars, but it has had a strong impact on several researchers, particularly some of his own students. These, together with other scholars who have independently reached similar conclusions, have pressed the critical questions to the point where they must be faced directly. To some extent P. Volz and W. Rudolph anticipated part of the argument already in 1933 when they maintained that only J could be considered an authentic "source" and that E was not an independent narrative strand but rather a later redactor and supplementer. S. Sandmel, only four years before Winnett's article, defined the developmental growth of the Pentateuch as a process of midrashic augmentation, that is, one in which subsequent redactors would have been loath to alter their received text in any way other than to add new materials to it—thus a "process of neutralizing by addition" (120). N. Wagner questioned whether one could legitimately assume that what we identify as J or E in Genesis is the same J or E found in Exodus, or even whether there is a common origin for all J (or E) materials in the various parts of the book of Genesis itself.

Three other lengthy studies, from independent contexts yet all within three years of each other, have heightened the issue. J. Van Seters, in a 1975 publication dedicated to his teacher, Winnett, limited his attention to the Abrahamic tradition in Genesis. Methodologically, as we have mentioned above, Van Seters disputed the claims of tradition historians who have attempted to retrace the development of these materials in the realm of oral tradition. Like T. L. Thompson, furthermore, Van Seters found nothing that could reliably be dated in the second millennium B.C.E.; the question of Abraham's historicity is thereby left wholly unanswerable. His literary analysis produced a picture very similar to Winnett's. There was a pre-Yahwistic first stage comprised of only the stories of Abraham in Egypt (Gen 12:10–20), Hagar's flight (16:1–12), and Isaac's birth (18:1a, 10–14; 21:2, 6–7). This was followed by a pre-Yahwistic supplement ("E"), the story of Abraham and Abimelech (20:1–17; 21:25–26, 28–31a). The Yahwist, working in the exilic period and addressing the despair of the exilic community, drew on these sources, added new materials of his own, and thus composed the whole Abrahamic cycle. Later, the Priestly writer added some genealogical and chronological details as well as the episodes found in Genesis 17 and 23. Finally, Genesis 14 was inserted, bringing the literary development to a close. Van Seters thus followed—although without managing to prove them to the satisfaction of most subsequent researchers—Winnett's basic tenets: a series of successive supplements of the previous written tradition; doubt about the existence of E as a separate Pentateuchal source; an exilic or postexilic date for the Yahwist, who was primarily responsible for the composition; and P as a later supplementary revision.

The next monographic study came from the pen of Hans Heinrich Schmid (1976), who acknowledged early in his discussion the contributions of Winnett and Van Seters to the current upheaval in Pentateuchal research. Schmid's analysis focused on J materials in several blocks of literature beyond Genesis: the call of Moses, the Egyptian plagues, the Reed Sea crossing, the wilderness wanderings, the Sinai pericope, as well as the promises to the ancestors. His conclusion coincided with that of Winnett and Van Seters in that he did not find it tenable to date the Yahwist's comprehensive theological redaction and interpretation in the Solomonic period. However, more so than did the other two, Schmid based his argument on evidence about preexilic prophecy and the Deuteronomic-Deuteronomistic tradition. For him, the Yahwist presupposed the preexilic prophets at numerous points, a clear indication of a late date. Significantly, Schmid advocated that the "so-called Yahwist" should not be seen as an individual collector, author, or theologian; rather, the "Yahwist" was a "Redaktions- und Interpretationsprozess" (1967:167) which took place during approximately the same time frame as that of the Deuteronomic-Deuteronomistic group and shared some viewpoints with it. This would conform well to the thesis of L. Perlitt that a full "covenantal theology" was a product of this Deuteronomic-Deuteronomistic movement, for such a theology is also reflected in some of the J pieces of the Pentateuch.

Work by a third scholar has further extended the dilemma. R. Rendtorff's 1977 monograph was discussed above concerning general matters of tradition history. His thesis about the Yahwist was advanced in 1975 and reissued in English translation in 1977 together with brief responses by Van Seters, Schmid, and R. N. Whybray. Rendtorff accused von Rad of turning a literary problem into a theological issue insofar as he considered the Yahwist as a theologian rather than a literary source. This fundamentally changed the type of question being asked of the text, for the emphasis was drawn away from the literary characteristics of the sources. It also led to an interest in determining the role that this Yahwist had in theologically shaping the Pentateuch. Rendtorff, in contrast, understood the Yahwist neither as a personality nor as a comprehensive theological editing of the materials. Even more clearly in 1977 (e.g., 112) he maintained that the Yahwistic work could hardly be understood in the sense of the usual documentary hypothesis, that is, as an extensive narrative running through the Pentateuch. At most J, like P, might represent editorial reworkings of the materials. Only at the level of the Deuteronomistic redaction did an editor have the whole Pentateuch to work on.

The state of research on J is currently in a rather perplexing condition. The majority of scholars quite clearly adhere more to the views of Wellhausen and von Rad, with the earlier date and ideological intention quite in keeping with the early monarchy. However, the critiques by those described above have shaken confidence in the usual hypothesis. Even if the Yahwist does not emerge as an exilic or postexilic source, it will henceforth be much more difficult to disregard the suggestion that there was redactional activity in the Yahwistic vein over the course of several centuries down to and probably including the exilic period.

There has been significantly less fundamental critique of the other three documents—E, D, and P—during the past three decades in comparison with what the J source has had to endure. Some of the substantial questions about these three have already been described above, especially the issue of whether they were comprehensive sources or, rather, supplementary revisions over the long redactional history of the Pentateuch. We will consequently restrict our comments to only a few other distinctive points about each.

The Elohistic Literature (E)

The Elohistic source received a substantial challenge in the 1930s by P. Volz and W. Rudolph, first by both together in a volume on Genesis and then later by Rudolph in a study of Exodus through Joshua. They argued that E could not have existed as an independent narrative with substantial scope, as the traditional form of the documentary hypothesis claimed. Instead, E represented a redactional stage in which additions were made to the Yahwistic source document. Volz (Volz and Rudolph: 135–42) even went on to posit that P was also not an independent narrative source but a redactional level, although Rudolph (1938:253–55) differed with him on this point. The problem regarding E, of course, is its fragmentary character, a point that virtually every writer on the subject makes at the very outset. On the whole, there is less significant disagreement among scholars on the identification and interpretation of E texts, however, than there is on the question of origin.

Noth (1948:36–44, 247ff.; Eng. tr. 33–41, 228ff.) upheld the documentary hypothesis despite the argument of Volz and Rudolph. For him, E constituted a whole narrative parallel to J on which a redactor drew in order to augment J, which served as the literary basis. E must have been much more extensive, but it was primarily the special materials that

were taken from it to be added to J. Originally J and E existed independently, although they were both based on the older source G, which
contained mainly those traditions that they both had in common. Noth
even considered E, taken as a whole, to have been closer to G than was J.
Other studies, for example, A. W. Jenks and K. Jaroš as well as most
commentaries, have followed this view of E as a narrative source with its
own distinctive provenance (usually the north), theological intention
(e.g., for Wolff [1969] it is "the fear of God" and the opposition to syncretism), and literary style.

The dissenting position follows closely that of Volz and Rudolph and
has been mentioned above in the discussion of J. According to Winnett,
Van Seters, and others, E is not a separate source but a redactional
supplementation of the old Yahwistic narrative, the latter being indeed
sparse at many points. H.-C. Schmitt even carried this argument further
in his recent study of the Joseph narrative. Without considering E to be
a documentary source, Schmitt proposed that E was a redactor, yet even
more than this insofar as E brought together the narrative blocks that
had been distinct until then—the ancestral tradition, the Joseph story,
and at least the Moses story in Exodus 1–3—thereby producing a new
and continuous historical composition. This thesis is suggestive, but like
others it serves primarily to emphasize the open questions that still exist
about the E materials.

The Deuteronomic Literature (D)

The D source may seem to pose fewer problems because of its supposed confinement to the book of Deuteronomy, thus not being present
throughout the whole Pentateuch to the same extent as the other primary sources. This, however, would be to mask the real difficulties that
have continued to confront researchers: Is there an older core to the
present book of Deuteronomy, and what can be known about its origin?
How does this core relate to its literary context? Furthermore, is there a
close connection between it and redactional strata outside the book of
Deuteronomy?

It has long been held that Deuteronomy 12–26 constituted an "Urdeu-
teronomium," a core of laws to which the remaining chapters subsequently
were added. The roots of this legal corpus normally have been found in the
northern kingdom prior to its fall in 722 B.C.E. R. P. Merendino attempted
to identify the parts of this old Deuteronomic law through a careful
analysis of both form and content, and he concluded that there were
several smaller, originally independent series of laws (cultic laws, apodictic
laws, abomination laws, marriage laws, humanitarian laws) that were
brought together to form this core. G. Seitz focused in his study mainly on
the Deuteronomic redaction of these earlier materials, finding especially

an emphasis on humanitarian aspects, apostasy, and cultic unity at this
level. Although it has often enough been thought that many of the laws
themselves date back to very early times and have some affinity to the Book
of the Covenant in Exodus 21–23, P. C. Craigie has revived the traditional
dating of the whole book to an even earlier period. Arguing on the basis of
the covenantal form and significance of the book, he found "it not unreasonable to assume that the book comes from the time of Moses or shortly
thereafter" (28). Few would concur with Craigie on this point about the
book, although it is clear that there were pre-Deuteronomic laws in the collection. More form-critical and comparative legal study is necessary before
we can hope to understand better the relation of such early laws to the first
Deuteronomic corpus. As Seitz, Merendino, A. D. H. Mayes, and others
have sensed, the proper approach to this is to attempt to determine what
the Deuteronomic redactor added to the received legal sources.

Since W. M. L. de Wette in the early nineteenth century it has been
common to identify Deuteronomy, or only the Deuteronomic core
(chaps. 12–26), with the "book of the law" that was discovered in the
Jerusalem temple during Josiah's reign, as recounted in 2 Kings 22–23.
As much support as this thesis has found in recent decades, substantial
questions have also been raised. Mayes (85–103) presented these in his
full review of the issue and concluded that the story in 2 Kings 22–23
was introduced later by the Deuteronomist and that there was thus no
immediate relation between Josiah and the Deuteronomic corpus of
laws. S. Mittmann, in his study of Deut 1:1–6:3, furthermore concluded
that the law preached in Deuteronomy did not exist apart from the historical introduction in these opening chapters. This is quite in contrast to
the opinion introduced by M. Noth (1943) that Deuteronomy 1–3(4) was
written by the exilic Deuteronomist not so much as a part of the book of
Deuteronomy but as an introduction to the whole Deuteronomistic History. However these matters are viewed, one can hardly escape the conclusion that the book of Deuteronomy experienced a rather long and
complex series of redactions, perhaps even in the sense of a supplementary hypothesis, until its present form was reached.

The authorship of Deuteronomy, without its latest redactions, has
proved difficult to resolve. Von Rad (1947) advocated that the "country
Levites," who were in allegiance with the reform-minded "people of the
land," were responsible for it, while Mayes attributed it to Levites with
priestly prerogatives who were attached to the Jerusalem temple. E. W.
Nicholson argued that prophets of the north stood behind it, whereas
M. Weinfeld proposed scribes of the Jerusalem court because of the connections that he identified between Deuteronomy and wisdom. Several
scholars have maintained that the form of the book of Deuteronomy had
some connection with a covenantal form—whether because of a

covenant-making or covenant-renewing festival (von Rad, 1938:30–37; Eng. tr. 33–40) or through a covenant formulary based on the form of international treaties (K. Baltzer and others). As with other matters, such questions will likely need different answers depending on the redactional level under consideration.

The Priestly Literature (P)

Issues similar to those facing J, E, and D have confronted the P source in recent decades—with not totally dissimilar results. First, the dating of P has been set in widely divergent periods. J. G. Vink assigned it to the Persian period; most others have dated it in the exilic or post-exilic age. Quite differently, Y. Kaufmann (174–211) considered it pre-exilic, in fact pre-Deuteronomic, before the idea of cultic centralization began to rise under Hezekiah. This early dating has also received some support from A. Hurvitz on the basis of a linguistic comparison of P with Ezekiel, Ezra-Nehemiah, Chronicles, and the Mishnah; he concluded that P idioms and terminology do not presuppose the exilic or postexilic period as do the others. Yet to whichever period P as a whole is dated, the problem of its sources remains pertinent. There has been a consensus that JE existed before P and that P could not have been unacquainted with such a significant historical narrative. Beyond that, one has looked for such other sources as a "Toledoth-Book" (Noth, 1948:9ff.; Eng. tr. 10ff.; modifying the earlier view of von Rad, 1934), certain narrative blocks, and various legal collections (e.g., Leviticus 1–7; 11–15; and 17–26, the "Holiness Code"; see Rendtorff, 1954; Koch; Reventlow; and Kilian). In virtually all such cases P would have edited the received materials before inserting them into the P history, some stylistic aspects of which process are depicted well by S. E. McEvenue.

The essential critical problem, although not original to this recent period of research, parallels that of the other documents: What, precisely is P—a source or a redaction? Noth (1948:7–19, 228ff.; Eng. tr. 8–19, 228ff.) was unequivocal in identifying P as an intact narrative independent of other sources, and he then posited that this P served as the literary basis into which JE was woven. P was normative for the final Pentateuch, beginning at Genesis 1 and ending at Deuteronomy 34. Thus for Noth it was not simply an editorial process of combining JE and P together but rather of fitting JE into P. Quite a different view has been proposed by F. M. Cross (293–325). Noting the absence of numerous important Pentateuchal traditions, the presence of various framing devices, the occurrence of archaizing language, and other evidences, Cross argued that P could only be considered a redactional stage and not an independent narrative document. The basis was JE, which the Priestly tradent edited and supplemented with Priestly lore during the latter

period of the exile, the purpose being to revive the Sinaitic covenant and
to aid the restoration of Israel. Rendtorff (1977:112–42) maintained just
as strongly that P was not a continuous narrative but rather a redactional
level, comprised especially of chronological and some theological texts
that were made to link the previous traditions together. Winnett and
Van Seters have taken similar positions, as we have seen above. Also
regarding P we find, therefore, a situation in which careful studies and
bold argumentation have combined to unsettle old positions in favor of a
more redaction-critical view of the development of the Pentateuch.

The Pentateuch as a Whole

Much more scholarly attention has been devoted—as might well be
expected given the predominant critical methods—to the meaning and
history of parts of the Pentateuch than to the nature of the Pentateuch as
a whole. Nonetheless, the latter has been a matter of concern with
respect especially to three questions: extent, literary basis, and intention.

We have already indicated that von Rad and Noth themselves disagreed on where the Pentateuch as a literary unity actually ends. The
problem involves both the book of Deuteronomy and the conquest tradition. In his 1943 publication Noth tied Deuteronomy as well as the conquest narrative in Joshua to the Deuteronomistic History, which runs
through the books of Kings; and thereby he was left with essentially a
Tetrateuch plus some P materials at the end of Deuteronomy. Von Rad,
for his part, considered the conquest narrative to be the natural conclusion to the creedal affirmation that begins with the promises to the
ancestors, including the promise of the land. Scholars have had difficulty
in moving the discussion beyond this difference of opinion, even if the
word "Pentateuch" is much more frequently used than either "Tetrateuch" or "Hexateuch." Mowinckel (1964b; 1964a) found in the book of
Joshua some traces of both J and P concerning a conquest of the land,
but above all a Deuteronomistic redaction which made such fragments
into a full history of the conquest by "all-Israel." For him, then, there
was never a Tetrateuch nor a Hexateuch in the sense of an independent
historical work—but only a Pentateuch with the D laws incorporated
and the J and P conquest materials included in the Deuteronomistic
History (1964b:77). However, the more difficult problem has been associated with the book of Deuteronomy. Ever since Noth's 1943 study scholars have been inclined to see in Deuteronomy the ideological basis for
the following Deuteronomistic History, and in some cases (e.g., W. Fuss)
also to identify a Deuteronomistic redactional layer in the earlier books
of the Pentateuch. In all of this, however, it is extremely difficult to
move beyond the ancient tradition of a canonical corpus of five books,

that is, with Deuteronomy connected with what precedes it more than with what follows it.

On what literary basis was the Pentateuch formed? For Noth (1948:7–19; Eng. tr. 8–19), P was an extensive narrative work and served as the literary framework into which JE was incorporated; however, this was not simply a matter of adding JE to P but rather a process in which P drew on JE to enrich its own narrative. The opposing position of Winnett, Van Seters, Cross, Schmid, and Rendtorff has been detailed above: that P was not a distinct source but rather a redactional layer, a reworking of JE. This point is far from resolution at present, and it will scarcely be adjudicated until more work has been done on the nature of redactional activity itself, the various postulated redactional layers have been compared, and the distinctively P materials (both narrative and laws) have been further examined for internal and stylistic coherence.

Not unrelated to these issues is the question of the Pentateuch's intention or purpose. Noth (1948:267–71; Eng. tr. 248–51) assigned it no greater significance traditio-historically than merely the literary adding together of all of the source materials, even if later synagogue and church have seen in this whole a theological unity that it originally did not have. For Noth, there was such similarity among the separate documentary sources in their narration of the course of Israel's history that their amalgamation did not affect this theological affirmation. Quite a different approach to this question of the meaning of the final compilation of the Pentateuch has more recently emerged, however. J. A. Sanders, J. Blenkinsopp, and B. S. Childs (1979) have all called attention to the role that the formation of the Pentateuch as authoritative or "canonical" literature played for the community. This process, especially in the postexilic period, involved a corporate search for meaning as well as a need to regularize the people's relation to their God. All three of these scholars as well as S. Tengström, R. Rendtorff (1977), and D. J. A. Clines assigned a key role to the theme of promise, especially as articulated to the ancestors. Here and also in the establishment of the law, the Pentateuch constituted a compelling message that helped to shape and preserve the people as much as the people had molded and retained the literature. This reciprocal relationship between community and text, together with the many other suggestive proposals reviewed above, will continue to command further inquiry in future Pentateuchal research.[1]

[1] I wish to express sincere appreciation for the Fulbright Grant and the Vanderbilt University Fellowship which supported my work on this essay during a sabbatical leave in Jerusalem in 1981–82.

BIBLIOGRAPHY

Baltzer, Klaus
1964   *Das Bundesformular*. WMANT 4. 2d ed. Neukirchen-Vluyn: Neukirchener Verlag. English trans., 1971.

Barr, James
1966   *Old and New in Interpretation: A Study of the Two Testaments*. London: SCM.

Bentzen, Aage
1952   *Introduction to the Old Testament*. 2 vols. 2d ed. Copenhagen: G. E. C. Gad.

Beyerlin, Walter
1961   *Herkunft und Geschichte der ältesten Sinaitraditionen*. Tübingen: J. C. B. Mohr (Paul Siebeck). English trans., 1965.

Blenkinsopp, Joseph
1977   *Prophecy and Canon: A Contribution to the Study of Jewish Origins*. Notre Dame, IN: University of Notre Dame Press.

Bright, John
1956   *Early Israel in Recent History Writing: A Study in Method*. SBT 19. London: SCM.

Brueggemann, Walter
1968   "David and His Theologian." *CBQ* 30: 156–81.

Brueggemann, Walter, and Hans Walter Wolff
1975   *The Vitality of Old Testament Traditions*. Atlanta: John Knox.

Cassuto, U.
1961   *The Documentary Hypothesis and the Composition of the Pentateuch*. Jerusalem: Magnes. Hebrew original, 1941.

Cazelles, Henri
1966   "Pentateuque: IV, Le nouveau 'status quaestionis.'" *DBSup* 7. 736–858.

Childs, Brevard S.
1963   "A Study of the Formula 'Until this Day.'" *JBL* 82: 279–92.
1967   "Deuteronomic Formulae of the Exodus Traditions." Pp. 30–39 in *Hebräische Wortforschung: Festschrift zum 80. Geburtstag von Walter Baumgartner*. VTSup 16. Leiden: E. J. Brill.
1970   *Biblical Theology in Crisis*. Philadelphia: Westminster.
1979   *Introduction to the Old Testament as Scripture*. Philadelphia: Fortress.

Clements, Ronald E.
1970   "Pentateuchal Problems." Pp. 96–124 in *Tradition and Interpretation: Essays by Members of the Society for Old Testament Study*. Ed. George W. Anderson. Oxford: Clarendon.

Clines, David J. A.
1978   *The Theme of the Pentateuch*. JSOTSup 10. Sheffield: Department of Biblical Studies, University of Sheffield.

Craigie, Peter C.
1976   *The Book of Deuteronomy*. NICOT. Grand Rapids: Eerdmans.

Crenshaw, James L.
1976   "Prolegomenon." Pp. 1–60 in *Studies in Ancient Israelite Wisdom*. New York: Ktav.

Cross, Frank M.
1973   *Canaanite Myth and Hebrew Epic: Essays in the History of the Religion of Israel*. Cambridge, MA: Harvard University Press.

Culley, Robert C., ed.
1975   *Classical Hebrew Narrative*. Semeia 3. Missoula, MT: Scholars Press.
1976   *Oral Tradition and Old Testament Studies*. Semeia 5. Missoula, MT: Scholars Press.

Eissfeldt, Otto
1922   *Hexateuch-Synopse: Die Erzählung der fünf Bücher Mose und des Buches Josua mit dem Anfange des Richterbuches*. Leipzig: J. C. Hinrichs. Reprinted, Darmstadt: Wissenschaftliche Buchgesellschaft, 1962.
1964   *Einleitung in das Alte Testament: Entstehungsgeschichte des Alten Testaments*. 3d ed. Tübingen: J. C. B. Mohr (Paul Siebeck). 1st ed., 1934. English trans., 1965.

Ellis, Peter F.
1968   *The Yahwist: The Bible's First Theologian*. Collegeville, MN: Liturgical Press.

Engnell, Ivan
1945   *Gamla Testamentet: En traditionshistorisk inledning*, I. Stockholm: Svenska Kyrkans Diakonistyrelses Bokförlag.

Fohrer, Georg
1966   "Altes Testament—'Amphictyonie' und 'Bund'?" *TLZ* 91: cols. 801–16, 893–904. Rev. and reprinted pp. 84–119 in *Studien zur alttestamentlichen Theologie und Geschichte (1949–1966)*. BZAW 115. Berlin: Walter de Gruyter, 1969.

1969   *Einleitung in das Alte Testament.* 11th ed. Heidelberg: Quelle & Meyer. English trans., 1968.

Fuss, Werner
1972   *Die deuteronomistische Pentateuchredaktion in Exodus 3–17.* BZAW 126. Berlin: Walter de Gruyter.

Gottwald, Norman K.
1979   *The Tribes of Yahweh: A Sociology of the Religion of Liberated Israel 1250–1050 B.C.E.* Maryknoll, NY: Orbis Books.

Gunkel, Hermann
1895   *Schöpfung und Chaos in Urzeit und Endzeit: Eine religionsgeschichtliche Untersuchung über Gen 1 und Ap Joh 12,* mit Beiträgen von Heinrich Zimmern. Göttingen: Vandenhoeck & Ruprecht.
1901   *Genesis, übersetzt und erklärt.* Göttingen: Vandenhoeck & Ruprecht. 7th ed., 1966.
1906   "Die israelitische Literatur." *Die Kultur der Gegenwart* 1/7: 51–102. 2d ed., 1925. Reprinted separately, Darmstadt: Wissenschaftliche Buchgesellschaft, 1963.

Henry, Marie-Louise
1960   *Jahwist und Priesterschrift: Zwei Glaubenszeugnisse des Alten Testaments.* Arbeiten zur Theologie, 3. Stuttgart: Calwer.

Hesse, Franz
1958   "Die Erforschung der Geschichte Israels als theologische Aufgabe." *KD* 4: 1–19.

Hölscher, Gustav
1952   *Geschichtsschreibung in Israel: Untersuchungen zum Jahvisten und Elohisten.* Skriften utgivna av Kungl. Humanistika Vetenskapssamfundet i Lund, 50. Lund: Gleerup.

Houtman, C.
1980   *Inleiding in de Pentateuch: Een beschrijving van de geschiedenis van het onderzoek naar het ontstaan en de compositie van de eerste vijf boeken van het Oude Testament met een terugblik en een evaluatie.* Kampen: J. H. Kok.

Hurvitz, Avi
1974   "The Evidence of Language in Dating the Priestly Code: A Linguistic Study in Technical Idioms and Terminology." *RB* 81: 25–46.

Hyatt, J. Philip
1970   "Were There an Ancient Historical Credo in Israel and an Independent Sinai Tradition?" Pp. 152–70 in *Translating and Understanding the Old Testament: Essays*

in Honor of Herbert Gordon May. Ed. H. T. Frank and W. L. Reed. Nashville and New York: Abingdon.

Jaroš, Karl
1974   *Die Stellung des Elohisten zur kanaanäischen Religion.* OBO 4. Göttingen: Vandenhoeck & Ruprecht.

Jenks, Alan W.
1977   *The Elohist and North Israelite Traditions.* SBLMS 22. Missoula, MT: Scholars Press.

Kaufmann, Yehezkel
1960   *The Religion of Israel: From its Beginnings to the Babylonian Exile.* Trans. and abridged by Moshe Greenberg. New York: Schocken Books. Hebrew original, 1938–56.

Kilian, Rudolf
1963   *Literarkritische und formgeschichtliche Untersuchung des Heiligkeitsgesetzes.* BBB 19. Bonn: Peter Hanstein.

Knight, Douglas A.
1975   *Rediscovering the Traditions of Israel.* Rev. ed. SBLDS 9. Missoula, MT: Scholars Press.

Knight, Douglas A., ed.
1982   *Julius Wellhausen and His* Prolegomena to the History of Israel. *Semeia* 25. Chico, CA: Scholars Press.

Koch, Klaus
1959   *Die Priesterschrift von Exodus 25 bis Leviticus 16: Eine überlieferungsgeschichtliche und literarkritische Untersuchung.* FRLANT 71. Göttingen: Vandenhoeck & Ruprecht.

Kraus, Hans-Joachim
1969   *Geschichte der historisch-kritischen Erforschung des Alten Testaments.* 2d ed. Neukirchen-Vluyn: Neukirchener Verlag.

Lapointe, Roger
1977   "Tradition and Language: The Import of Oral Expression." Pp. 125–42 in *Tradition and Theology in the Old Testament,* ed. D. A. Knight. Philadelphia: Fortress; London: S.P.C.K.

Long, Burke O.
1968   *The Problem of Etiological Narrative in the Old Testament.* BZAW 108. Berlin: A. Töpelmann.

McEvenue, Sean E.
1971   *The Narrative Style of the Priestly Writer.* AnBib 50. Rome: Biblical Institute Press.

Mayes, A. D. H.
1979   *Deuteronomy.* NCB. London: Oliphants.

Mendenhall, George E.
1955   *Law and Covenant in Israel and the Ancient Near East.* Pittsburg: Biblical Colloquium.

Merendino, Rosario Pius
1969   *Das deuteronomische Gesetz: Eine literarkritische, gattungs- und überlieferungsgeschichtliche Untersuchung zu Dt 12–26.* BBB 31. Bonn: Peter Hanstein.

Mittmann, Siegfried
1975   *Deuteronomium 1,1–6,3: Literarkritisch und traditionsgeschichtliche Untersucht.* BZAW 139. Berlin and New York: Walter de Gruyter.

Mowinckel, Sigmund
1964a   *Erwägungen zur Pentateuchquellenfrage.* Oslo: Universitetsforlaget.
1964b   *Tetrateuch—Pentateuch—Hexateuch: Die Berichte über die Landnahme in den drei altisraelitischen Geschichtswerken.* BZAW 90. Berlin: A. Töpelmann.

Müller, Hans-Peter
1969   *Ursprünge und Strukturen alttestamentlicher Eschatologie.* BZAW 109. Berlin: A. Töpelmann.

Nicholson, E. W.
1967   *Deuteronomy and Tradition.* Philadelphia: Fortress.

Noth, Martin
1930   *Das System der zwölf Stämme Israels.* BWANT 4/1. Stuttgart: W. Kohlhammer. Reprinted, Darmstadt: Wissenschaftliche Buchgesellschaft, 1966.
1943   *Überlieferungsgeschichtliche Studien: Die sammelnden und bearbeitenden Geschichtswerke im Alten Testament.* Halle: Max Niemeyer. 3d ed., Tübingen: Max Niemeyer, 1967.
1948   *Überlieferungsgeschichte des Pentateuch.* Stuttgart: W. Kohlhammer. 3d ed., 1966. English trans., *A History of Pentateuchal Traditions.* Trans. with an introduction by B. W. Anderson. Englewood Cliffs, NJ: Prentice-Hall, 1972. Reprinted, Chico, CA: Scholars Press, 1981.
1950   *Geschichte Israels.* Göttingen: Vandenhoeck & Ruprecht. English trans., 1958.
1959   *Das zweite Buch Mose, Exodus, übersetzt und erklärt.* ATD 5. Göttingen: Vandenhoeck & Ruprecht. 4th ed., 1968. English trans., 1962.
1962   *Das dritte Buch Mose, Leviticus, übersetzt und erklärt.* ATD 6. Göttingen: Vandenhoeck & Ruprecht. 2d. ed., 1966. English trans. 1965.
1966   *Das vierte Buch Mose, Numeri, übersetzt und erklärt.* ATD 7. Göttingen: Vandenhoeck & Ruprecht. English trans., 1968.

Nyberg, Henrik Samuel

1947   "Korah's uppror (Num. 16f.): Ett bidrag till frågan om traditionshistorisk metod." SEÅ 12: 230–52.

1972   "Die schwedischen Beiträge zur alttestamentlichen Forschung in deisem Jahrhundert." Pp. 1–10 in *Congress Volume: Uppsala, 1971.* VTSup 22. Leiden: E. J. Brill.

Orlinsky, Harry M.

1962   "The Tribal System of Israel and Related Groups in the Period of the Judges." *OrAnt* 1: 11–20.

Patte, Daniel, ed.

1980   *Genesis 2 and 3: Kaleidoscopic Structural Readings.* *Semeia* 18. Chico, CA: Scholars Press.

Perlitt, Lothar

1969   *Bundestheologie im Alten Testament.* WMANT 36. Neukirchen-Vluyn: Neukirchener Verlag.

Polzin, Robert M.

1977   *Biblical Structuralism: Method and Subjectivity in the Study of Ancient Texts.* Semeia Supplements. Philadelphia: Fortress; Missoula, MT: Scholars Press.

Rad, Gerhard von

1934   *Die Priesterschrift im Hexateuch.* BWANT 65. Stuttgart: W. Kohlhammer.

1938   *Das formgeschichtliche Problem des Hexateuch.* BWANT 78. Stuttgart: W. Kohlhammer. Reprinted, pp. 9–86 in *Gesammelte Studien zum Alten Testament.* 3d ed. Munich: Chr. Kaiser, 1965. English trans., "The Form Critical Problem of the Hexateuch," pp. 1–78 in *The Problem of the Hexateuch and Other Essays.* Edinburgh and London: Oliver & Boyd, 1966.

1944   "Der Anfang der Geschichtsschreibung im alten Israel." *Archiv für Kulturgeschichte* 32: 1–42. Reprinted, pp. 148–88 in *Gesammelte Studien zum Alten Testament.* Munich: Chr. Kaiser. English trans., pp. 166–204 in *The Problem of the Hexateuch and Other Essays.* Edinburgh and London: Oliver & Boyd, 1966.

1947   *Deuteronomium-Studien.* FRLANT 58. Göttingen: Vandenhoeck & Ruprecht. English trans., 1953.

1953   *Das erste Buch Mose, Genesis, übersetzt und erklärt.* ATD 2–4. Göttingen: Vandenhoeck & Ruprecht. 9th ed., 1972. English trans., 1961; rev. ed., 1972.

1962   *Theologie des Alten Testaments. I: Die Theologie der geschichtlichen Überlieferungen Israels.* 4th ed. Munich: Chr. Kaiser. 1st ed., 1957. English trans., *Old Testament Theology. I: The Theology of Israel's Historical Traditions.* Trans. D. M. G. Stalker. Edinburgh and London: Oliver & Boyd, 1962.

1964   *Das fünfte Buch Mose, Deuteronomium, übersetzt und erklärt.* ATD 8. Göttingen: Vandenhoeck & Ruprecht. 2d ed., 1968. English trans., 1966.

Rendtorff, Rolf
1954   *Die Gesetze in der Priesterschrift.* FRLANT 62. Göttingen: Vandenhoeck & Ruprecht. 2d ed., 1963.
1975   "Der 'Jahwist' als Theologe? Zum Dilemma der Pentateuchkritik." Pp. 158–66 in *Congress Volume: Edinburgh, 1974.* VTSup 28. Leiden: E. J. Brill. English trans., "The 'Yahwist' as Theologian? The Dilemma of Pentateuchal Criticism." *JSOT* 3 (1977) 2–10.
1977   *Das überlieferungsgeschichtliche Problem des Pentateuch.* BZAW 147. Berlin: Walter de Gruyter.

Reventlow, H. Graf
1961   *Das Heiligkeitsgesetz formgeschichtlich untersucht.* WMANT 6. Neukirchen: Neukirchener Verlag.

Richter, Wolfgang
1966   "Urgeschichte und Hoftheologie." *BZ* 10: 96–105.
1967   "Beobachtungen zur theologischen Systembildung in der alttestamentlichen Literatur anhand des 'kleinen geschichtlichen Credo.'" Pp. 175–212 in vol. I of *Wahrheit und Verkündigung: Festschrift M. Schmaus.* Ed. L. Scheffczyk. Munich/Paderborn/Vienna: Ferdinand Schoningh.

Rost, Leonhard
1965   *Das kleine Credo und andere Studien zum Alten Testament.* Heidelberg: Quelle & Meyer.

Rudolph, Wilhelm
1938   *Der "Elohist" von Exodus bis Josua.* BZAW 68. Berlin: A. Töpelmann.

Sanders, James A.
1972   *Torah and Canon.* Philadelphia: Fortress.

Sandmel, Samuel
1961   "The Haggada within Scripture." *JBL* 80: 105–22.

Schmid, Hans Heinrich
1976   *Der sogenannte Jahwist: Beobachtungen und Fragen zur Pentateuchforschung.* Zurich: Theologischer Verlag.

Schmidt, Ludwig
1977   "Überlegungen zum Jahwisten." *EvT* 37: 230–47.

Schmitt, Hans-Christoph
1980   *Die nichtpriesterliche Josephsgeschichte: Ein Beitrag zur neuesten Pentateuchkritik.* BZAW 154. Berlin and New York: Walter de Gruyter.

Schulte, Hannelis
1972   Die Entstehung der Geschichtsschreibung im Alten
               Israel. BZAW 128. Berlin and New York: Walter de
               Gruyter.

Seitz, Gottfried
1971   Redaktionsgeschichtliche Studien zum Deuterono-
               mium. BWANT 13. Stuttgart: W. Kohlhammer.

Simpson, Cuthbert Aikman
1948   The Early Traditions of Israel: A Critical Analysis of
               the Pre-deuteronomistic Narrative of the Hexateuch.
               Oxford: Basil Blackwell.

Smend, Rudolf
1967   Biblische Zeugnisse: Literatur des alten Israel. Frank-
               furt am Main: Fischer Bücherei.
1978   Die Entstehung des Alten Testaments. Stuttgart: W.
               Kohlhammer.

Soden, Wolfram von
1974   "Verschlüsselte Kritik an Salomo in der Urgeschichte des
               Jahwisten?" WO 7,2: 228–40.

Tengström, Sven
1976   Die Hexateucherzählung: Eine literaturgeschichtliche
               Studie. ConBOT 7. Lund: Gleerup.

Thompson, Thomas L.
1974   The Historicity of the Patriarchal Narratives. BZAW
               133. Berlin: Walter de Gruyter.

Van Seters, John
1975   Abraham in History and Tradition. New Haven: Yale
               University Press.

Vink, J. G.
1969   "The Date and Origin of the Priestly Code in the Old
               Testament." OTS 11: 1–144.

Volz, Paul, and Wilhelm Rudolph
1933   Der Elohist als Erzähler: Ein Irrweg der Pentateuch-
               kritik? BZAW 63. Giessen: A. Töpelmann.

Wagner, Norman E.
1967   "Pentateuchal Criticism: No Clear Future." CJT 13:
               225–32.

Weinfeld, Moshe
1972   Deuteronomy and the Deuteronomic School. Oxford:
               Oxford University Press.

Wellhausen, Julius
1876–77   "Die Composition des Hexateuchs." JDT 21: 392–450,
               531–602; 22: 407–79. Reprinted, pp. 1–208 in Die Com-
               position des Hexateuchs und der historischen Bücher

des Alten Testaments. 3d ed. Berlin: Georg Reimer, 1899.

1878   *Geschichte Israels. In zwei Bänden. Erster Band.* Berlin: G. Reimer. 2d ed., *Prolegomena zur Geschichte Israels.* Berlin: G. Reimer, 1883. English trans., *Prolegomena to the History of Israel.* With Preface by W. Robertson Smith. Edinburgh: Adam & Charles Black, 1885. Reprinted, New York: Meridian Books, 1957.

Winnett, Frederick V.

1949   *The Mosaic Tradition.* Toronto: University of Toronto Press.

1965   "Re-examining the Foundations." *JBL* 84: 1–19.

Wolff, Hans Walter

1964   "Das Kerygma des Jahwisten." *EvT* 24: 73–98. Reprinted, pp. 345–73 in *Gesammelte Studien zum Alten Testament.* Munich: Chr. Kaiser, 1964. English trans., pp. 41–66 in Brueggemann and Wolff.

1969   "Zur Thematik der elohistischen Fragmente im Pentateuch." *EvT* 29: 59–72. Reprinted, pp. 402–17 in *Gesammelte Studien zum Alten Testament.* 2d ed. Munich: Chr. Kaiser, 1975. English trans., pp. 67–82 in Brueggemann and Wolff.

Woude, Adam Simon van der

1960   *Uittocht en Sinai.* Nijkerk: C. F. Callenbach.

9

The Historical Literature

Peter R. Ackroyd

A separate chapter in this volume is devoted to the history of Israel; the present one therefore excludes any discussion of problems of historical reconstruction or of the nature of OT historiography. In this respect, while there is inevitably much overlap, this survey differs from that offered by J. Roy Porter where the title "Old Testament Historiography" sets out a different aim. (For an earlier survey see Snaith.) The concern here is to examine the books themselves and the ways in which the handling and interpretation of them have been forwarded in the last thirty years or so. The discussion is restricted to two groups of biblical books, the first being those from Joshua to 2 Kings, often described as the Deuteronomistic history. (The use of the two terms, Deuteronomic and Deuteronomistic, though common, is apt to be confusing since it is not always clear that they are used in a sufficiently precise manner. For a recent comment, see Clements, 1980:104.) The second is the group comprising Chronicles, Ezra, and Nehemiah, in which the continuity of the two parts that form Chronicles and the continuity of Ezra and Nehemiah are guaranteed by the main textual tradition. In both cases major problems in recent discussion have concerned the precise interrelationship between the books in each of these groups, and these questions will be taken up subsequently. But a further area of study has been the relationship between the two groups themselves in view of the substantial measure of overlap between the books of Chronicles on the one hand and the material of Samuel/Kings on the other. These questions of relationship invite attention first to an underlying issue, that of the text, since any discussion of the use of one work by another, such as is normally assumed for the position as between Chronicles and Samuel/Kings, must depend on the resolving of questions regarding the precise text that the later work may be assumed to have used.

I. TEXTUAL QUESTIONS

The Qumran discoveries at the beginning of the period under survey provided a new impetus in the investigation of the history of the MT and its relationship to the alternative forms both in Hebrew and in the versions available to us. While publication of the relevant textual material from Qumran has been slow and piecemeal (for references, see Sanders; Fitzmyer)—a full-scale analysis of one of the Samuel texts is only now in prospect (Ulrich)—its importance for the recognition of alternative text forms is evident. The study of the versions, and in particular the LXX, reveals the markedly deviant texts that exist (see Jellicoe), and these deviations are underlined by some of the Qumran material. The MT does not stand alone; side by side with it are alternative forms that must be considered in their own right. Discussion of the books, limited, as is often the case, to the single form attested by the Hebrew in its Masoretic shape, inevitably offers only a partial view of the problems of their development.

What appears from the textual evidence is clear also in the comparison that can be made between alternative presentations as these are most clearly seen in the books of Samuel and Kings on the one hand and the books of Chronicles on the other (Gerleman; Allen). For a full consideration of the latter, the detailed examination of the parallels between, for example, genealogical lists and those to be found predominantly in the Pentateuch is not only an important element in textual study and tradition history but also a point at which clues may be detected to the particular slant of the Chronicler's own approach (see below). Such synoptic study, however, is not to be limited to these broader comparisons or even to the consideration of detailed parallel passages, sometimes so close as to be virtually identical (e.g., 2 Chr 4:10–22; 1 Kgs 7:39b–50), at others widely divergent (e.g., 2 Chronicles 28; 2 Kings 16; see Ackroyd, 1968a: 65–68; Williamson, 1977). It must also include the alternative texts for particular sections of material: thus the major part of 2 Kings 18–20 appears in Isaiah 36–39, but the divergencies make it appropriate to designate these as alternative forms (see Ackroyd, 1974; Childs, 1967), and their function within different compilations needs to be considered (see Ackroyd, 1978, 1981a). A further parallel may be detected, although less precisely demonstrated, between 2 Kings 24–25, its very close but slightly deviant form in Jeremiah 52, and the longer and more elaborate form to be found in Jeremiah 37–44 (see Pohlmann, 1978, for a closer analysis) and the strongly divergent 2 Chronicles 36 (Ackroyd, 1968b).

The discussion of these variant forms raises questions of a wider purport which impinge upon the problems to be discussed in relation to the books of Chronicles. The evaluation of the sources used by the latter requires a more nuanced appraisal than the oversimple view that the Chronicler used Samuel and Kings. For while this is in a general sense true, the precise nature of the text so used, what precisely it contained, and how far detailed consideration of differences in detail makes possible an adequate assessment of the particular line of thought represented by Chronicles, raise much more delicate issues. The very strict method advocated by Lemke, perhaps too narrowly conceived (Ackroyd, 1967), would stress the use of the nonparallel passages for the assessment of the Chronicler, and the uncertainty about the underlying text must put many question marks against the meticulous analysis of exegetical method expounded by Willi. While his listing of different exegetical procedures and levels serves to underline the richness of the Chronicler's activity—although the divisions between the different procedures are not always as neatly to be made as he supposes—the discussion of textual differences does not take sufficient account of the uncertainties. If it is exaggeration to say that every copy of an ancient work is a new edition, it is nevertheless important to recognize the degree to which ongoing transmission imparts gradual or substantial modification both as a result of scribal inadvertence and as a result of exposition of an older text in the light of new circumstances. The comparison of parallel texts provides one way into such an area of investigation.

The question here impinges on others closely related to the origin and extent and nature of the works in question. The problems of the relationship between Chronicles and Samuel/Kings suggest that the former used an expanded version of the latter, perhaps the "midrash" of the Kings referred to in 2 Chronicles (Eissfeldt, 1965:533–34; Rudolph, 1954: 402–3, 1955:xi and n. 2). Discussion of hypothetical earlier forms of the Chronicler's work and hence the dating of what may be regarded as the "basic work" to which later additions were made rest upon certain assumptions about literary history. A further problem arises in regard to the relationship between the Hebrew text and the Greek 1 Esdras (Pohlmann, 1970; Williamson, 1977). A similar debate is observable in regard to the formation of the books regarded as the Deuteronomistic history (Joshua to Kings) from Noth (1943) onward. As will be indicated below, issues dominating much of the discussion include the possibility of a final edition in the exilic age, preceded by earlier forms, and the more complex question of various levels of Deuteronomistic editing, representing stages in the final evolution of the work. In part at least, such discussions inevitably handle only hypothetical reconstructions of earlier forms and point to the continuous and ongoing formation of these books. The particular structures we now possess represent moments of "freezing" of texts at particular points and by no means provide a full picture. Some of the discussion of date and structure needs to be more thoroughly correlated with such clues as we have to the ongoing process and to the very wide variety of texts which either exist or can plausibly be postulated. Textual history and literary history are here as elsewhere parts of the same discipline (Talmon, 1970).

II. JOSHUA TO KINGS: THE DEUTERONOMISTIC WORK

The development of Pentateuchal criticism had an important offshoot in the attempts made to trace the continuation of the older "sources" in the books that follow in the canon. The supposition that a Hexateuch, Heptateuch, Octateuch, or Enneateuch could be demonstrated derives in part from the endeavor to trace these sources and in part from a belief that a work is likely to cover a period up to or nearly up to its date of composition, a belief which is, however, not supported by a consideration of the "Priestly work." The main part of these developments precedes the period that we are here surveying (see Eissfeldt, 1965:241–48, for a short critical discussion; Radjawane: 178–80), but they have their importance in that they represent one of the approaches to the books we are here considering, an approach that continues to operate in recent discussion.

A substantially new direction was imparted to the discussion by the work of Noth (1943: Part I), arguing for a single "Deuteronomistic work," a view presented independently by Engnell (1945; see also 1970) and developed in a number of studies (Jepsen; Boecker) and widely accepted. The persistence of the source approach is to be seen in Hölscher (1941–42, but again 1952), and in Eissfeldt (1947, 1948, 1965), who offers sharp criticism of Noth's methods and of his treatment of the material. Criticism continues in von Rad (1953, 1965b), particularly because of his conception of a Hexateuch, and in Weiser, Fohrer (1970), and Kaiser. Recent assessments of the discussion (e.g., Janssen; Wolff; Soggin, 1967, 1976 [1980]; Lohfink, 1967; Radjawane), while recognizing the literary problems and the diversity within the books, which make the idea of a single unified work not entirely satisfactory, nevertheless acknowledge the weight of evidence that points in the direction of an underlying assumption such as that of Noth (see also Clements, 1974). The presentation of both the function and the nature of the work itself and the process of its final styling would now differ considerably from his (Porter: 132–52; see also Miller in Hayes and Miller: 217–21). The unified work, however precisely described, may then be held to stand alongside the "Priestly work," comprising essentially but not necessarily only Genesis to Numbers, and the "Chronistic work" (see below).

Further definition within this area of discussion may be set out as follows, although the subsections overlap: (a) consideration of the individual books and their structure and of the nature and extent of their underlying sources; (b) possible stages in the formation of the work; and (c) the final shaping and its context. Together with these go discussions also of particular aspects of the material, recently with considerable attention to the nature and function of narratives within the larger structure.

The Individual Books and Underlying Sources

Commentaries tend to be based on the accepted canonical divisions of the text, but while there are clear practical reasons for such a procedure it must be recognized that the divisions are themselves artificial. Joshua and Judges overlap in the treatment of Joshua's death and in certain detailed material, although essentially their style and presentation are radically different. The Samuel birth narratives read as a continuation of the judges stories, with Judges 17–21 as a separate collection of "appendixes" to what precedes—or in some measure as an "introduction" to what follows. Similarly, the final stages of the David story run over into Kings, with a break created by the "appendixes" of 2 Samuel 20–24 (on the function of these chapters, see Cazelles, 1955).

A fuller review of commentaries published during the period may be found in Ackroyd (1976a) and in Childs (1979). For earlier surveys, see Snaith, Jenni, and also Kaiser (134–68) on trends and problems. The following comments are inevitably selective.

The commentary by Soggin (1970) on Joshua stands markedly in the Noth tradition; another on Judges will follow. Gray (1907), also in that tradition and also handling both Joshua and Judges, is at points more critical and offers a closer evaluation of elements of historical material preserved in the text in its final form. Much recent discussion here has turned on problems of the nature and origin of particular sections of the material, with sharply divergent views both regarding Joshua 1–12—the relation of the material to Gilgal affirmed by Noth and Soggin is followed up particularly by Langlamet (1969, 1971) and others (see Porter: 149 n. 110)—and also regarding the lists of Joshua 18–19 (21), with a large number of specialist studies (see Miller in Hayes and Miller: 230–36). A study by A. Auld is particularly concerned with the latter chapters and their relation to Numbers and to the problem of the "Tetrateuch-Pentateuch-Hexateuch" debate.

Literary analysis has been very rigidly applied to Judges by C. A. Simpson, with a refinement that is far from convincing, and in detailed discussion by H. Schulte, who traces the "J" work through the books of Judges and Samuel into the period of the early divided kingdoms. R. G. Boling's commentary on Judges attempts an oversimple explanation of the structure of the book with too little analysis of the stages of its development (see the discussion in *JSOT* 1: 30–52) and rather more confidence in chronology than would be admitted either by de Vaux ("impossible to establish a chronology" [a note in his manuscript cited in the preface, 1978:xx]) or by the discussions in Hayes and Miller (241–43). The analysis of the pre-Deuteronomic stages in the formation of the book has exposed its complexity (Beyerlin; Richter, 1963, 1964; van Rossum); the studies point further to the problems of distinguishing the various stages in the formation of the

Deuteronomistic Work as a whole.

The detailed commentary by H. J. Stoebe on 1 Samuel concentrates heavily on individual points of text and interpretation but also offers an assessment of history and of the patterns of presentation. Too much historical assumption is made by P. Kyle McCarter, whose commentary stands strongly in the Albright tradition. However, it has the important advantage of making use of the Qumran textual material.

The older idea of a court history of David has been largely replaced by L. Rost's hypothesis of a succession narrative in 2 Samuel (6) 9–20, 1 Kings 1–2; this assumes that a degree of unity of origin and function can be traced in these chapters. But difficulty appears here in view of the variety of opinions about what constitutes the function and how far there is unity. There have been numerous discussions attempting some clarification of the nature and function of the assumed unified narrative (Blenkinsopp, 1965; von Rad, 1965a; Delekat; Brueggemann; Whybray; Flanagan; Würthwein, 1974; Veijola, 1975; Van Seters, 1981:156–67). The possibility of an anti-Davidic propaganda element, subsequently modified, has been brought out by Delekat and Würthwein (critique by Mettinger: 29) and most recently by Van Seters, who sees the section as a postexilic addition to the narratives to counter later "messianic" trends. Differences of dating range from such a very late date to that most often maintained—an early, almost eye-witness account. If different levels (see Würthwein) are detectable, then there is no single answer to the question of dating; equally, if the limits of the supposed separate narrative are not as closely fixed as is often assumed (Gunn, 1978, and in some degree also Van Seters, 1981: especially 157–58) then it is clear that we must question the propriety of ascribing a single function to what is not sufficiently demonstrated to be a totally separable work. The assumption of such a single function, of complete unity of attitude, appears difficult to maintain (Ackroyd, 1981b).

A number of other recent studies have, in fact, examined sections of the books of Samuel in such a way as to raise doubts about the existence of actual independent preexisting works. Various studies of the so-called Ark narrative (Schicklberger; Campbell; for a summary and critical discussion, see Miller and Roberts, although their own arguments for an early date and for a particular function do not carry conviction) attempt some degree of isolation of particular chapters as having some independent status. A recent study by Gunn (1980) is devoted to the Saul narratives and their particular nature as narrative, although this is not with a view to discovering an independent source. Studies of the origins of the monarchy and the different levels of material (Birch; Clements, 1974; Boecker) and of the rise to power of David (Rendtorff; Grønbæk; Conrad; Mettinger; Lemche; see Kaiser: 158–59) extend over narrower or wider areas of the material but in some measure overlap other proposed divisions. R. A. Carlson, in a study based on traditio-historical assumptions, divides the major part of 2 Samuel into a positive section (David under the blessing) and a negative (David under the curse); but suggestive as this approach is in its appraisal of the wider structures of the material, it may be questioned whether there is really so precise a division.

The variety of the material in these books (see Weiser) suggests rather that the explanation of their present form may be much more complex and less unified. The attempt to detect a single function for particular parts or for the whole remains unsuccessful, and in any case the function of any one section must now be seen in the context of the whole group of books.

The books of Kings have been well served by commentators in the past generation. The major critical and textual study of J. A. Montgomery and H. S. Gehman is complemented by the greater concern with history and chronology in Gray (1970). Noth (1968) developed his understanding of the Deuteronomistic material in the first part of his unfinished commentary, a task to be taken up in due course by Rudolf Smend. The corresponding first half of a commentary by Würthwein (1977) attempts a detailed literary analysis, with some cautious reservations, to indicate pre-Deuteronomic, Deuteronomic, and post-Deuteronomic stages. Within the books of Kings, special studies have been made of many individual chapters and sections, particularly of the Elijah and Elisha narratives (Fohrer, 1957; Steck; Schmitt), and of particular genres (e.g., Lohfink, 1978).

Stages in the Formation of the Books as a Whole

The single stage view of Noth has been seen to be too simplified. The same must almost certainly be said of the two-stage theory associated particularly with Cross (1973; see also Freedman, 1976). The assumption of this view that only relatively minor touching up was undertaken in the exilic period and that the work was virtually complete in its first major recension under Josiah does not appear to be warranted. On the one hand, it becomes increasingly clear that there is more in these books that reflects the exilic age and possibly also even later situations than such a view would allow (for examples, see Diepold; Clements, 1980:66–67, and his forthcoming study of 2 Kings 20; Ackroyd, 1974, and later studies). On the other hand, the work of Smend and Dietrich (see also Würthwein, 1974; and Mittmann, whose study of Deut 1:1–6:3 and its redactional levels suggests consequences for the books that follow; for other references, see Kaiser: 174) points to a large number of stages in the formation of the work, and hence at least some extension of the period over which the process was operating (see also Veijola, 1975, 1977). How far these stages can be identified with precision remains more open.

The Final Form and Its Context

Wider questions must also be asked about the function of the whole work and hence about its context. The place of origin, whether Palestine or Babylonia, remains undetermined (see Janssen: 16–18; Japhet, 1973; Ackroyd, 1968a:65–68; Nicholson). The negative appraisal of Noth has been seen to be less than adequate to explain the whole purpose of the work, and various definitions of purpose have been proposed (Wolff; McCarthy; Lohfink, 1967; Soggin, 1967; Weinfeld; Weippert; Wyatt). There is a balance to be held here between the attempt to subsume everything within a single pattern—which hardly does justice to the varieties of the material or to the richness of the editorial processes involved in the four very different sections of the work, roughly delineated by the division into four books—and the recognition of differing levels which, having reference to different situations and perhaps to quite different locales, may be held to point to something more like an ongoing exegetical tradition. The homiletic quality of much of the work may suggest that there is some degree of chance in its eventual shaping and that momentary needs may have dictated the presence of what are in effect only minor sidelines of interpretation.

Questions concerning the unity and diversity within the Deuteronomistic work remain open. A concern with the canonical shape of the books as they stand (Childs, 1979) invites a greater interest in what they are in their final form and how they function. Almost in parallel with this are recent studies that concentrate on the narratives, studies that for the most part look at elements within the whole range of these books (so, e.g., Carlson; Gunn, 1978, 1980, as well as preliminary studies; Long; Conroy; Jobling; Talmon, 1978; Murray; and also some sections of *Semeia* 3 [1975]). The recognition that the present shape of the material provides something more than the sum of its component parts, and the renewed application of literary theories—different from those of earlier generations—to the biblical writings offer illumination of the impact that a particular sequence makes without necessarily assuming an independent source. Such studies do not obviate the need for analysis, but they recognize that the work of the postulated compilers is more than an editorial process; it involves a measure of creative writing in which the handling, ordering, and shaping of already existing and presumably familiar material have been undertaken. Polzin attempts such an overall view of the whole Deuteronomistic work, the first volume (1980) covering the books from Deuteronomy to Judges. There is clearly scope for approaches of this kind with sensitivity to the literary quality of the material, although questions may be raised about the validity of particular literary and structuralist theories which in some instances underlie recent work. But the understanding of a literary work and of the relationship among author, text, and reader is a matter of importance here as elsewhere. The views of Goulder (1974, 1978; and see below on the Chronistic work), stressing the homiletical aspects in association with a particular lectionary theory, may not in themselves provide a fully satisfying answer; but the questions he raises about the viability of some of the literary theories about these biblical books and his stress on the importance of finding a function for individual passages such as could be used within the religious life of the community are questions that invite full attention to the possible ways of discovering real contexts not simply for composition but also for use. The very complexity of the present texts and their various forms imply repeated use and indeed an exegetical process that must be postulated even if the possibility of its exact description may be recognized as doubtful.

III. CHRONICLES, EZRA, AND NEHEMIAH

Recent surveys of the problems of these books may be found in Porter (152–62), Childs (1979:624–55), Ackroyd (1976a for the books of Chronicles; see also Richards), and Talmon (1976) and Klein for Ezra and Nehemiah. The main areas of discussion to be considered may be arranged conveniently under three headings: the unity of the group, the sources and their use, and the purpose or purposes of the books. Inevitably the three are interrelated.

Unity?

(1) The debate about the single authorship or unity of compilation of the books of Chronicles on the one hand and Ezra-Nehemiah on the other is of long standing. Early Jewish tradition (see Talmon, 1976: 317–18) affirms unity, and it has often been maintained that the overlap between the two works (2 Chr 36:22–23, Ezra 1:1–3a) and the continuity of text in 1 Esdras, as well as general similarities of style, confirm this. The description of the whole as a "Chronistic work" (see Noth, 1943: Part II, followed in much of the more recent discussion) underlines this; but it may be recognized, also regarding the problems of unity and diversity in the Deuteronomistic work, that such a title may be held to point only to a general *Tendenz* or to some rather looser concept of relationship than simple identity of author or compiler. The marked separateness of the Nehemiah memoir or memorial (e.g., Mowinckel; Kellermann; also In der Smitten, 1972) raises one very clearly separate question, that of possible insertions into the work.

The discussion of the question of unity has been particularly sharpened recently. A consideration of the commentaries of the past generation shows diverse ways of treating the books. Rudolph (1949, 1955) assumes the unity or essential unity of the whole work, although he treated Ezra-Nehemiah first and Chronicles second. Unity is assumed by Myers (1965), Galling (but with a particular view of levels within the work), and Michaeli; the list could be multiplied. In some series the two have been treated separately: Elmslie rejects unity in handling Chronicles alone, while Bowman in the same volume affirms it in handling Ezra-Nehemiah; Brockington accepts unity, although the forthcoming Chronicles volume by Williamson will reject it (see below). Conservative discussions do not follow any precise line: Harrison eventually appears to argue for separation; Young appears to be undecided, although he apparently considers it possible that Ezra was the author of Chronicles and that Nehemiah definitely wrote his own book, including the Ezra sections within it.

A marked move toward separating the two works has appeared in recent discussion, particularly clearly articulated by Japhet (1968, 1971, 1977) and taken somewhat further by Williamson (1977; for a useful critical review see Cazelles, 1979; cf. Mosis: 214 n. 23; Polzin, 1976). The arguments here are of two kinds: the linguistic usage in the two works is held to be distinct, and the ideology is different. The linguistic arguments are impressive, and their detail deserves close attention; but in some measure at least they are rendered problematic by the nature of the sources used. Particularly in the books of Ezra and Nehemiah, the distinctive character of the Nehemiah material makes arguments based on that material less than reliable. Earlier sources are used in Ezra 1–6, and how far they have been subsequently modified remains uncertain. The remaining material may also in part be based on sources, but it is in any case open to question whether conclusions can be drawn in such limited material in a statistically viable manner. The ideological differences are equally hard to appraise (see below). The separation of the works has certainly become much more widely accepted, as may be seen in the very diverse studies of Willi, Welten, Braun (1979), and the recent summarizing statement by Porter (154).

(2) In some measure the question of unity involves that of the degree to which the books as we now have them are seen as having been supplemented by major sections at some point in their formation. Here the primary example is that of the Nehemiah material. Clearly, the Nehemiah memoir or memorial has independent standing, at one stage having existed separately as an apology for Nehemiah or as a kind of votive offering asking divine blessing for him (Mowinckel; Kellermann); nevertheless, at some point it has been included in the larger work (In der Smitten, 1972). The distinction between such "addition" and a view proposing more than one edition of the work as a whole is marginal; nor is there a clearly marked distinction between this and the discussion of sources. Arguments for the later addition of the whole or substantial parts of 1 Chronicles 1–9—already in Welch (185ff.) and taken further by Noth (1943:117–22), Rudolph (1955) and Cross (1975)—have been

given full critical examination by Williamson (1977), whose well-argued conclusion is that such separation is unsatisfactory (see also Johnson). A similar position exists in regard to 1 Chronicles 23–27 (see Williamson, 1979b, for a critical discussion). Smaller insertions have been postulated for the psalm material in 1 Chronicles 16 (Butler; Loader) and in Ezra 9 and Nehemiah 9, but the probable use in these passages of already existing psalm material—this being quite clear, although variously interpreted, for 1 Chronicles 16—itself explains something of the apparent lack of consonance between the ideas of these passages and their context. Prayers, such as that in Nehemiah 1, have also been seen as additions, but again the same essential point applies.

(3) The move from this to the hypothesis of more than one edition of the books is a small one. A thoroughgoing two-edition theory is presented by Galling, specifically criticized by Welten (189–91); a more general three-edition theory is advocated by Cross (1975). The former provides a precise textual analysis of the whole work, while the latter provides only an overall picture that would need detailed examination (see also Freedman, 1961; Newsome). In some degree this too overlaps into the area of source analysis, since the relationship between Chronicles and Samuel/Kings, which is clearly no simple one (see Eissfeldt, 1965:531–35 for a summary), raises the question whether we should think in terms of an ongoing and continually modified presentation of the narratives. Thus insofar as 1 and 2 Chronicles handle essentially only the southern kingdom—with some few significant exceptions, notably for the reigns of Jehoshaphat (2 Chronicles 18) and Ahaz (2 Chronicles 28)—this could suggest the existence of a "shortened" form of the books of Kings omitting all or most of the northern material. That such a presentation should be taken on further to cover the immediate postexilic period, covering the first six chapters of what is now the book of Ezra, is a possibility worth considering, but there is no evidence that the work ever ended at that point. Its continuance at a further editorial stage to cover the essential moment of Ezra and eventually to be supplemented with Nehemiah also makes good sense. But then we may ask whether we are in reality dealing with a series of editions or whether we should postulate the existence over a considerable period of time, as also seems probable in the case of the Deuteronomistic writings, of a "school of thought," more or less precisely conceived, related in its style also to a "Priestly" school, responsible for the ongoing development of the Pentateuchal (Tetrateuchal) material. Is it then from such an ongoing school that various forms of the work emerged, of which essentially the only one that survives is the biblical books? Alongside this, as another part of the same process, is the problematically related 1 Esdras (Pohlmann, 1970, and critique by Williamson, 1977; Myers, 1974). In any case the continuation of this line is to be seen in later presentations, in Josephus's

Antiquities, in Pseudo-Philo's *Biblical Antiquities*, which offers a retelling from Adam to Saul (thus corresponding to 1 Chronicles 1–10), and, probably much later, in the Samaritan Chronicles.

The Sources and Their Use

The basic discussion for our period is again to be found in Noth (1943:131–50; see also Brunet), who considers primarily the apparently direct relationships between sections of the work as it now stands and other parts of the biblical text. Thus, details of the links between 1 Chronicles 1–9 and the Pentateuchal text are considered; 1 Chronicles 10–2 Chronicles 36 has as its main source the books of Samuel and Kings in their traditional form, assuming that other material found here is not from independent sources but is owing to the Chronicler's own method and, particularly for the prophetic references, is linked to his imitation of the Deuteronomistic work. Only for the details of military fortifications and war narratives does Noth envisage independent material. It is these last particular elements that are fully investigated by Welten. With the recognition that this material, as well as lists of names and the like, has been much used, often positively, in recent assessments of archaeological work (especially Myers, 1965, and bibliographical references in Welten: 9–10, and in North), Welten assesses it much more radically, examining its function and style and seeing it as more relevant to the particular purpose of the Chronicler, especially since these elements may on occasion be associated with accounts of reform or with moralizing comments. His belief is that only very small fragments of early material may here be traced. The discussion is of particular value in offering a critique of attempts to use distinctive material from the books of Chronicles for historical reconstruction of the preexilic period. Even if Welten is too negative, his work draws attention to the fact that the discussion of sources and their identification cannot be separated from the question of what the Chronicler actually does with the material he presents. In relation to the major compilation of Samuel-Kings, the complexity of this matter is very evident. The supposition that Chronicles depends on an earlier form of that material (Rehm) clearly does not do justice to the evidence (Noth, 1943:138–39), but the actual form in which the Chronicler knew what we know as Samuel-Kings remains problematic. If (see above) we speak of the "midrash of the Kings," as a general title to cover the wide variety of indications given of an extended form of those books, the reconstruction of this remains purely hypothetical. More value may derive, as in other instances (Childs, 1979), from considering the work as we have it and endeavoring to assess its particular viewpoint.

Similar considerations apply to the books of Ezra and Nehemiah (see Myers, 1965:XLVIII–LII). The lack of reference to sources, apart from the Aramaic documents of Ezra 4–6 and 7, makes their discovery less clear. Whether Nehemiah is a source (Noth, 1943) or an addition (see above) is also uncertain, although the latter appears more probable. Stress on the differences within the material of both Ezra 1–6 and Ezra 7–10 together with Nehemiah 8–9 argues for the existence of more than one form underlying these (Ackroyd, 1970), but the reconstruction of alternative narratives is not a viable possibility. The relationship between the narratives incorporated in Ezra 1–6 and the two prophetic collections Haggai and Zechariah 1–8 also remains an unresolved question. There are indications of alternative presentations of the traditions concerning the reestablishment of the Judaean community and the rebuilding of the temple, to which the two prophetic collections contribute some variant information, suggesting that those chapters of the book of Ezra offer a now partly harmonized depiction of the period. Whether part of the Chronicler's work or not, this section needs to be assessed within the overall function of the writings grouped together as Chronicles, Ezra, and Nehemiah.

Full-scale investigations of the Nehemiah (Kellermann) and Ezra (In der Smitten, 1973) traditions, both biblical and nonbiblical, provide in themselves certain pointers back into the earlier stages, insofar as the later forms of the material provide some clues to the degree to which the two figures have been handled together, with some amount of cross-influence, and a resulting problematic history of the period (Ackroyd, 1970:24–27).

Theology and Purpose

If few would now follow C. C. Torrey in his depiction of the Chronicler as one with a highly gifted literary imagination—greater stress being laid on the sources and their handling—it is nevertheless in part to Torrey that the more positive evaluation of the Chronicler may be attributed. He had the great merit of taking this group of books seriously not as history but as a particular style of presentation of the traditions of Israel from the beginnings to the period of Nehemiah and Ezra. Inevitably here again differences of assessment will depend in part at least on the literary analysis. The denial of community of outlook to Chronicles on the one hand and Ezra-Nehemiah on the other (Japhet, 1977; Williamson, 1977; Braun, 1979) is drawn out by detailed investigation of the handling of particular themes: that of Williamson on the theme of "Israel" clearly delineated for the books of Chronicles needs a counterbalancing analysis of the ways in which the Ezra-Nehemiah material differs (see also Braun, 1976). Cazelles (1979) expresses doubts, which the present writer shares, about how fundamental the supposed differences really are. But such distinctions do not seem to take sufficient account of the differences of level in the sources being reproduced or handled. More generalizing accounts (e.g., Freedman, 1961; Ackroyd, 1967; Mosis; Newsome) inevitably suffer by being insufficiently analytical of the text while recognizing the degree to which there is a relatedness between the various books. Both Willi and Welten hold the separate books together, while attributing them to different points of literary origin. Braun (1979; see also his earlier contributions) traces an ongoing relationship. Comparisons with the Priestly work (Porter) tend to be more generalized than precise.

Attempts to correlate the work or works with a specific period of postexilic life—in part assessed on the evidently very unclear indications of date (see above on the theory of different editions)—tend in some degree to be linked to assumptions about the postexilic period and its theology (Blenkinsopp, 1980). The development of various views of a central "establishment" line of thought, in which the Chronicler, however precisely conceived, is seen as a prime example, sets the work over against an ongoing prophetic, visionary, or proto-apocalyptic style (Plöger: 106–12; Hanson: 209–79). Rudolph's influential assessment of the sense in the Chronicler that the community has achieved an embodiment of the promises of the past (1954, 1955) and the exclusion therefore of any eschatological element here have come recently under criticism with attempts to define how far a wider and ongoing outlook is to be detected. The idealization of the past—particularly of David and Solomon but also of Hezekiah (Braun, 1973, 1976; Williamson, 1977)—the hesitation about the present (Mosis; Ackroyd, 1976b), and the affirmation of a particular kind of eschatological thinking (Stinespring; Caquot; Williamson, 1979a) raise questions as yet insufficiently resolved for it to be felt that any clearly defined pattern of thought has yet been detected. Along with this must be stressed the degree to which the discerning of purpose in a work or works that we know only from itself and from comparison with other known accounts of the same traditions must inevitably be in some degree subjective. While we may assume deliberate selectiveness of treatment, the problems of purpose are related to those of text and to the extent to which accidental factors may have influenced the survival of a particular form rather than another. Indeed, it may be more appropriate to see less than complete unity and a more varied homiletic tendency. If Goulder (1974, 1978) attempts to prove too much with his lectionary theories, the emphasis he lays on "sermonizing"— which if further developed would allow for a considerable degree of diversity within a partly unified pattern—could here too do more justice to the material than the endeavor to discover literary unity or precise levels of editorial activity. This too allows for further investigation of exposition in relation to known or postulated needs in the postexilic period.

IV. CONCLUSION

If any summarizing conclusion can be drawn in relation to these two major collections of writings, it must be that many of the older and more simplified presentations are less than adequate. Rather, the textual problems and the questions of literary relationship and of editorial activity have come to be seen as much more complex. That the Hebrew Bible incorporates two such related and yet different works—alongside which the Priestly work may in some measure be placed as a third—is in itself an important witness to the liveliness with which questions of the nature and status of the religious community were under scrutiny and definition, particularly in the years from the sixth century B.C.E. onward. The shift in balance to this later period in the past generation and hence to a much more deserved appreciation of the importance of that period for a proper understanding of the biblical writings as they now exist, together with a better assessment of Jewish traditions that attempt to resolve the problems of religious and political continuity, is a change to be welcomed unreservedly. It marks one of the changes in the climate of scholarship gradually brought about by individual studies of the works concerned.

BIBLIOGRAPHY

Ackroyd, Peter Runham

1967 "History and Theology in the Writings of the Chronicler." *CTM* 38: 501–15.

1968a *Exile and Restoration.* OTL. London: SCM; Philadelphia: Westminster.

1068b "Historians and Prophets." *SEÅ* 33: 18–54.

1970 *The Age of the Chronicler.* Supplement to *Colloquium: The Australian and New Zealand Theological Review.* Auckland.

1974 "An Interpretation of the Babylonian Exile: A Study of 2 Kings 20, Isaiah 38–39." *SJT* 27: 329–52.

1976a "Chronicles, Books of." Pp. 156–58 in *IDBSup.*

1976b "God and People in the Chronicler's Presentation of Ezra." Pp. 145–62 in *La notion biblique de Dieu.* Ed. J. Coppens. BETL 41. Gembloux: Duculot; Leuven: Leuven University.

1978 "Isaiah i–xii: Presentation of a Prophet." Pp. 16–48 in *Congress Volume: Göttingen, 1977.* VTSup 29. Leiden: E. J. Brill.

1981a "Isaiah 36–39: Structure and Function." In *Von Kanaan bis Kerala: Festschrift J. P. M. van der Ploeg.* Ed. W. C. Delsman et al. AOAT 211. Kevelaer: Butzon & Bercker; Neukirchen-Vluyn: Neukirchener Verlag.

1981b   "The Succession Narrative (so called)." *Int* 35.

Allen, Leslie C.

1974   *The Greek Chronicles: The Relation of the Septuagint of I and II Chronicles to the Masoretic Text.* Parts I, II. VTSup 25, 27. Leiden: E. J. Brill.

Auld, A. Graeme

1980   *Joshua, Moses and the Land: Tetrateuch-Pentateuch-Hexateuch in a Generation since 1938.* Edinburgh: T. & T. Clark. (For a brief summary, see *ExpTim* 91 [1979–80] 301).

Beyerlin, Walter

1963   "Gattung und Herkunft des Rahmens im Richterbuch." Pp. 1–30 in *Tradition und Situation.* Ed. E. Würthwein and O. Kaiser. Göttingen: Vandenhoeck & Ruprecht.

Birch, Bruce C.

1976   *The Rise of Israelite Monarchy: The Growth and Development of 1 Samuel 7–15.* SBLDS 27. Missoula, MT: Scholars Press.

Blenkinsopp, Joseph

1965   "Theme and Motif in the Succession History (2 Sam. XI 2ff.) and the Yahwist Corpus." Pp. 44–57 in *Volume du Congrès: Genève, 1965.* VTSup 15. Leiden: E. J. Brill.

1980   "Tanakh and the New Testament: A Christian Perspective." Pp. 96–119 in *Biblical Studies: Meeting Ground of Jews and Christians.* Ed. L. Boadt, H. Croner, and L. Klenicki. New York: Paulist.

Boecker, Hans Jochen

1969   *Die Beurteilung der Anfänge des Königtums in den deuteronomistischen Abschnitten des I. Samuelbuches: Ein Beitrag zum Problem des deuteronomistischen Geschichtswerks.* WMANT 31. Neukirchen-Vluyn: Neukirchener Verlag.

Boling, Robert G.

1975   *Judges.* AB 6A. Garden City, NY: Doubleday.

Bowman, Raymond A.

1954   "The Book of Ezra and the Book of Nehemiah." *IB* 3: 551–819.

Braun, Roddy L.

1973   "Solomonic Apologetic in Chronicles." *JBL* 92: 503–16.

1976   "Solomon, the Chosen Temple Builder: The Significance of 1 Chronicles." *JBL* 95: 581–90.

1977   "A Reconsideration of the Chronicler's Attitude to the North." *JBL* 96: 59–62.

1979   "Chronicles, Ezra and Nehemiah: Theology and Literary
                             History." Pp. 52–64 in *Studies in the Historical Books
                             of the Old Testament*. VTSup 30. Leiden: E. J. Brill.

Brockington, Leonard Herbert
1969   *Ezra, Nehemiah and Esther*. NCB. London: Nelson.

Brueggemann, Walter
1968   "David and his Theologian." *CBQ* 30: 156–81.

Brunet, Adrien-M.
1953, 1954   "Le Chroniste et ses sources." *RB* 60: 481–508; 61:
                             349–86.

Butler, T.
1978   "A Forgotten Passage from a Forgotten Era (1 Chr. xvi
                             8–36)." *VT* 28: 142–50.

Campbell, Antony F.
1975   *The Ark Narrative (1 Sam 4–6; 2 Sam 6): A Form-
                             Critical and Traditio-Historical Study*. SBLDS 16. Mis-
                             soula, MT: Scholars Press.

Caquot, André
1966   "Peut-on parler de messianisme dans l'oeuvre du Chro-
                             niste?" *RTP* 99: 110–20.

Carlson, R. A.
1964   *David, the Chosen King: A Traditio-Historical Ap-
                             proach to the Second Book of Samuel*. Stockholm:
                             Almqvist & Wicksell.

Cazelles, Henri S.
1955   "David's Monarchy and the Gibeonite Claim." *PEQ* 87:
                             165–75.
1979   Review of Williamson, 1977. *VT* 29: 375–80

Childs, Brevard S.
1967   *Isaiah and the Assyrian Crisis*. SBT 2/3. London: SCM;
                             Naperville, IL: Allenson.
1979   *An Introduction to the Old Testament as Scripture*.
                             London: SCM; Philadelphia: Fortress.

Clements, Ronald E.
1974   "The Deuteronomistic Interpretation of the Founding of
                             the Monarchy in 1 Sam. VIII." *VT* 24: 398–410.
1980   *Isaiah and the Deliverance of Jerusalem: A Study of
                             the Interpretation of Prophecy in the Old Testament*.
                             JSOTSup 13. Sheffield: JSOT.
Forthcoming   "The Isaiah Narrative of 2 Kings 20, 12–19 and the Date
                             of the Deuteronomic History." (To appear in *Studies in
                             Ancient Narrative and Historiography: I. I. Seelig-
                             mann Anniversary Volume*. Ed. A. Rofé and Y. Zako-
                             vitch. Jerusalem.)

Conrad, J.
1972 "Zum geschichtlichen Hintergrund der Darstellung von Davids Aufstieg." *TLZ* 97: 321–32.

Conroy, C.
1978 *Absalom Absalom! Narrative and Language in 2 Sam. 13–20.* AnBib 81. Rome: Biblical Institute Press.

Cross, Frank Moore
1973 "The Structure of the Deuteronomic History." Pp. 274–89 in *Canaanite Myth and Hebrew Epic.* Cambridge, MA: Harvard University Press.
1975 "A Reconstruction of the Judean Restoration." *JBL* 94: 4–18 = *Int* 29: 187–201.

Delekat, Lienhard
1967 "Tendenz und Theologie der David–Salomo–Erzählung." Pp. 26–36 in *Das ferne und nahe Wort: Festschrift L. Rost.* Ed. F. Maass. BZAW 105. Berlin: de Gruyter.

Diepold, Peter
1972 *Israels Land.* BWANT 95. Stuttgart: W. Kohlhammer.

Dietrich, Walter
1972 *Prophetie und Geschichte: Eine redaktionsgeschichtliche Untersuchung zum deuteronomistischen Geschichtswerk.* FRLANT 108. Göttingen: Vandenhoeck & Ruprecht.

Eissfeldt, Otto
1947 "Die Geschichtsschreibung im Alten Testament." *TLZ* 72: 71–6 = *Kl.Schr.* III. 1966: 19–26.
1948 *Geschichtsschreibung im Alten Testament.* Berlin: Evangelische Verlagsanstalt.
1965 *The Old Testament: An Introduction.* Oxford: Blackwell; New York: Harper & Row.

Elmslie, William Alexander Leslie
1954 "The First and Second Books of Chronicles." *IB* 3: 341–548.

Engnell, Ivan
1945 *Gamla Testamentet: En traditionshistorisk inledning.* I. Stockholm: Svenska Kyrkans Diakonistyrelses Bokförlag, 1945. (Summary in C. R. North, "Pentateuchal Criticism" in Rowley: 63–70.)
1970 *Critical Essays on the Old Testament.* London: SPCK (Nashville: Vanderbilt University, 1969 under the title *A Rigid Scrutiny*). Original Swedish articles in Svenskt Bibliskt Uppslagsverk. Stockholm: Norstedt. 1962.

Fitzmyer, Joseph A., S.J.
1977   *The Dead Sea Scrolls: Major Publications and Tools for Study.* SBLSBS 8. Missoula, MT: Scholars Press.

Flanagan, James W.
1972   "Court History or Succession Document? A Study of 2 Samuel 9–20 and 1 Kings 1–2." *JBL* 91: 172–81.

Fohrer, Georg
1957   *Elia.* ATANT 31. Rev. ed., 1968. Zurich: Zwingli.
1970   *Introduction to the Old Testament.* London: SPCK. (Nashville, Abingdon, 1968.)

Freedman, David Noel
1961   "The Chronicler's Purpose." *CBQ* 23: 436–42.
1976   "The Deuteronomistic History." Pp. 226–28 in *IDBSup.*

Galling, Kurt
1954   *Die Bucher der Chronik, Esra, Nehemia.* ATD 12. Göttingen: Vandenhoeck & Ruprecht.

Gerleman, Gillis
1946   *Studies in the Septuagint. II. Chronicles.* LUÅ 44/5. Lund: Gleerup.
1948   *Synoptic Studies in the Old Testament.* LUÅ 44/5. Lund: Gleerup.

Goulder, Michael D.
1974   *Midrash and Lection in Matthew.* London: SPCK.
1978   *The Evangelists' Calendar: A Lectionary Explanation of the Development of Scripture.* London: SPCK.

Gray, John
1967   *Joshua, Judges and Ruth.* NCB. London: Nelson.
1970   *I and II Kings.* London: SCM; Philadelphia: Westminster. (3d rev. ed., 1977.)

Grønbæk, J. H.
1971   *Die Geschichte vom Aufstieg Davids (1 Sam. 15–2 Sam. 5): Tradition und Komposition.* ATDan 10. Copenhagen: Munksgaard.

Gunn, David M.
1978   *The Story of King David: Genre and Interpretation.* JSOTSup 6. Sheffield: JSOT.
1980   *The Fate of King Saul: An Interpretation of a Biblical Story.* JSOTSup 14. Sheffield: JSOT.

Hanson, Paul D.
1975   *The Dawn of Apocalyptic: The Historical and Sociological Roots of Jewish Apocalyptic Eschatology.* Philadelphia: Fortress.

Harrison, Roland Kenneth
1969   *Introduction to the Old Testament.* Grand Rapids: Eerdmans; London: Tyndale.

Hayes, John H., and J. Maxwell Miller, eds.
1977   *Israelite and Judaean History*. OTL. London: SCM;
                Philadelphia: Westminster.

Hölscher, Gustav
1941–42   *Die Anfänge der hebräischen Geschichtsschreibung*.
                Sitzungsberichte der Heidelberger Akademie der Wis-
                senschaften, Phil.-hist. Klasse, Abh. 3. Heidelberg:
                Akademie der Wissenschaft.
1952   *Geschichtsschreibung in Israel: Untersuchungen zum
                Jahwisten und Elohisten*. SHVL. Lund: Gleerup.

In der Smitten, W. T.
1972   "Die Gründe für die Aufnahme der Nehemiaschrift in
                das chronistische Geschichtswerk." *BZ* NF 16: 207–21.
1973   *Esra: Quellen, Überlieferung und Geschichte*. SSN 15.
                Assen: Van Gorcum.

Janssen, Enno
1956   *Juda in der Exilszeit: Ein Beitrag zur Frage der Ent-
                stehung des Judentums*. FRLANT 51. Göttingen: Van-
                denhoeck & Ruprecht.

Japhet, Sara
1968   "The Supposed Common Authorship of Chronicles and
                Ezra-Nehemiah Investigated Anew." *VT* 18: 330–71.
1971   "Chronicles, Book of." *EncJud* 5: 517–34.
1973   *Ideology of the Book of Chronicles and its Place in Bib-
                lical Thought*. Jerusalem: Hebrew University.
1977   *The Ideology of the Book of Chronicles and its Place in
                Biblical Thought* (Hebrew). Jerusalem: Bialik Institute.

Jellicoe, Sidney
1968   *The Septuagint and Modern Study*. Oxford: Clarendon.
                (Continuing bibliography in *Bulletin* of IOSCS.)

Jenni, Ernst
1961   "Zwei Jahrzehnte Forschung an den Büchern Josua bis
                Könige." *TRu* 27: 1–32, 97–146.

Jepsen, Alfred
1953   *Die Quellen des Königsbuches*. Halle: Niemeyer.

Jobling, David
1978   *The Sense of Biblical Narrative: Three Structural
                Analyses in the Old Testament*. JSOTSup 7. Sheffield:
                JSOT.

Johnson, Marshall D.
1969   *The Purpose of the Biblical Genealogies*. SNTSMS 8.
                Cambridge: University Press.

Kaiser, Otto
1975   *Introduction to the Old Testament: A Presentation of
                its Results and Problems*. Oxford: Blackwell.

Kellermann, Ulrich
 1967   *Nehemia: Quellen, Überlieferung und Geschichte.*
      BZAW 102. Berlin: A. Töpelmann.

Klein, Ralph W.
 1976   "Ezra and Nehemiah in Recent Studies." Pp. 361–76 in
      Magnalia Dei: The Mighty Acts of God. In Memoriam
      G. Ernest Wright. Ed. F. M. Cross, W. E. Lemke, and
      P. D. Miller. Garden City, NY: Doubleday.

Langlamet, F.
 1969   *Gilgal et les récits de la traversée du Jordain.* CRB II.
      Paris: Gabalda.
 1971   "Josué, II, et les traditions de l'Héxateuque." *RB* 78:
      5–17, 161–83, 321–54.

Lemche, Neils Peter
 1978   "David's Rise." *JSOT* 10: 2–25.

Lemke, W. E.
 1965   "The Synoptic Problem in the Chronicler's History."
      HTR 58: 349–63.

Loader, J. A.
 1976   "Redaction and Function of the Chronistic 'Psalm of
      David.'" Pp. 69–75 in *Studies in the Chronicler.* Ed.
      W. C. van Wyk. *OTWSA* 19. University of Stellenbosch.

Lohfink, Norbert
 1967   "Bilanz nach der Katastrophe: Das deuteronomische
      Geschichtswerk." Pp. 196–208 in *Wort und Botschaft.*
      Ed. J. Schreiner. Würzburg: Echter-Verlag.
 1978   "Die Gattung der 'Historischen Kurzgeschichte' in den
      letzten Jahren von Juda und in der Zeit des Baby-
      lonischen Exils." *ZAW* 90: 319–47.

Long, Burke O.
 1973   "2 Kings iii and Genres of Prophetic Narrative." *VT* 23:
      337–48.

McCarter, P. Kyle
 1980   *I Samuel.* AB 8. Garden City, NY: Doubleday.

McCarthy, Dennis J.
 1965   "II Samuel 7 and the Structure of the Deuteronomic
      History." *JBL* 84: 131–38.

Mettinger, Trygve N. D.
 1976   *King and Messiah: The Civil and Sacral Legitimation*
      of the Israelite Kings. ConBOT 8. Lund: Gleerup.

Michaeli, Frank
 1967   *Les Livres des Chroniques, d'Esdras et de Néhémie.*
      CAT XVI. Neuchâtel: Delachaux et Niestlé.

Miller, Patrick D., and J. J. M. Roberts
1977   *The Hand of the Lord: A Reassessment of the "Ark Narrative" of 1 Samuel.* Baltimore: Johns Hopkins University Press.

Mittmann, Siegfried
1975   *Deuteronomium 1.1–6.3 literarkritisch und traditionsgeschichtlich untersucht.* BZAW 139. Berlin: Walter de Gruyter.

Montgomery, James A., and Henry Snyder Gehman
1951   *The Books of Kings.* ICC. Edinburgh: T. & T. Clark.

Mosis, Rudolph
1973   *Untersuchungen zur Theologie des chronistischen Geschichtswerkes.* Freiburger TS 92. Freiburg: Herder.

Mowinckel, Sigmund
1964   *Studien zu dem Buche Ezra-Nehemia.* I, II, III. SNVAO II. Hist.-Filos. Klasse. 3, 5, 7. Oslo: Universitetsforlaget.

Murray, Donald F.
1979   "Narrative Structure and Technique in the Deborah–Barak Story, Judges iv 4–22." Pp. 155–89 in *Studies in the Historical Books of the Old Testament.* VTSup 30. Leiden: E. J. Brill.

Myers, Jacob M.
1965   *I Chronicles, II Chronicles, Ezra, Nehemiah.* AB 12, 13, 14. Garden City, NY: Doubleday.
1974   *I and II Esdras.* AB 42. Garden City, NY: Doubleday.

Newsome, James D., Jr.
1975   "Toward a New Understanding of the Chronicler and his Purposes." *JBL* 94: 201–17.

Nicholson, E. W.
1967   *Deuteronomy and Tradition.* Philadelphia: Fortress.

North, Robert
1974   "Does Archaeology Prove Chronicles' Sources?" Pp. 375–401 in *A Light unto my Path: Studies in Honor of J. M. Meyers.* Ed. H. N. Bream. Gettysburg Theological Studies, 4. Philadelphia: Temple University Press.

Noth, Martin
1943   *Überlieferungsgeschichtliche Studien.* Tübingen: Niemeyer. (Unchanged 2d ed., 1957.)
1968   *Könige.* BKAT 9/1. Neukirchen-Vluyn: Neukirchener Verlag.

Plöger, Otto
1968   *Theocracy and Eschatology.* Oxford: Blackwell.

Pohlmann, Karl-Friedrich
1970   *Studien zum dritten Esra: Ein Beitrag zur Frage nach dem ursprünglichen Schluss des chronistischen Geschichtswerkes.* FRLANT 104. Göttingen: Vandenhoeck & Ruprecht.

1978   *Studien zum Jeremiabuch: Ein Beitrag zur Frage nach der Entstehung des Jeremiabuchs.* FRLANT 118. Göttingen: Vandenhoeck & Ruprecht.

Polzin, Robert
1976   *Late Biblical Hebrew: Toward an Historical Typology of Biblical Hebrew Prose.* HSM 12. Missoula, MT: Scholars Press.

1980   *Moses and the Deuteronomist.* New York: Seabury.

Porter, J. Roy
1979   "Old Testament Historiography." Pp. 125–62 in *Tradition and Interpretation.* Ed. G. W. Anderson. Oxford: Oxford University Press.

Rad, Gerhard von
1953   *Studies in Deuteronomy.* SBT 9. London: SCM. (Originally published 1947.)

1965a   "The Beginnings of Historical Writing in Ancient Israel." Pp. 166–204 in *The Problem of the Hexateuch and Other Essays.* Edinburgh: Oliver and Boyd. (Originally published 1944.)

1965b   *Theology of the Old Testament* I. Rev. ed. London: SCM. (Originally published 1957; original English trans. 1962.)

Radjawane, Arnold Nicolaas
1973–74   "Das deuteronomische Geschichtswerk: Ein Forschungsbericht." *TRu* 38: 177–216.

Rehm, Martin
1956   *Die Bücher der Chronik.* 2d ed. Würzburg: Echter Verlag.

Rendtorff, Rolf
1971   "Beobachtungen zur altisraelitischen Geschichtsschreibung anhand der Geschichte vom Aufstieg Davids." Pp. 428–39 in *Probleme biblischer Theologie: Gerhard von Rad zum 70. Geburtstag.* Ed. H. W. Wolff. Munich: Chr. Kaiser.

Richards, Kent H.
No date   *Bibliography of Chronicles.* (Typescript obtainable from the compiler at Iliff School of Theology, Denver, CO, U.S.A.)

Richter, Wolfgang
1963   *Traditionsgeschichtliche Untersuchungen zum Richter-buch.* BBB 18. Bonn: Peter Hanstein.
1964   *Die Bearbeitungen des "Retterbuchs" in der deutero-nomischen Epoche.* BBB 21. Bonn: Peter Hanstein.

Rossum, J. van
1966   *Die Praedeuteronomistische Bestanddelen van het Boek der Richters en hun betekenis voor onze kennis van de geschiedenis van het volk Israel en zijn godsdienst.* Winterswijk: van Amstel.

Rost, Leonhard
1926   *Die Überlieferung von der Thronnachfolge Davids.* BWANT III, 6. Stuttgart: W. Kohlhammer. Reprinted pp. 119–253 in *Das kleine Credo und andere Studien zum Alten Testament.* Heidelberg: Quelle und Meyer.

Rowley, Harold Henry, ed.
1951   *The Old Testament and Modern Study.* London: Oxford University Press.

Rudolph, Wilhelm
1949   *Esra und Nehemia samt 3. Esra.* HAT 20. Tübingen: Mohr.
1954   "Problems of the Books of Chronicles." *VT* 4: 401–9.
1955   *Chronikbücher.* HAT 21. Tübingen: Mohr.

Sanders, J. A.
1975   "Palestinian Manuscripts 1947–72." Pp. 401–13 in *Qumran and the History of the Biblical Text.* Ed. F. M. Cross and S. Talmon. Cambridge/London: Harvard University Press.

Schicklberger, Franz
1973   *Die Ladeerzählungen des ersten Samuel-Buches: Eine literaturwissenschaftliche und theologiegeschichtliche Untersuchung.* Forschung zur Bibel 7. Würzburg: Echter Verlag.

Schmitt, H.-C.
1972   *Elisa: Traditionsgeschichtliche Untersuchungen zur vorklassischen nordisraelitischen Prophetie.* Gütersloh: Mohn.

Schulte, Hannelis
1972   *Die Entstehung der Geschichtsschreibung im Alten Israel.* BZAW 128. Berlin: Walter de Gruyter.

Simpson, Cuthbert Aikman
1957   *Composition of the Book of Judges.* Oxford: Blackwell.

Smend, Rudolf
1971   "Das Gesetz und die Völker: Ein Beitrag zur deutero-nomistischen Redaktionsgeschichte." Pp. 494–509 in

Probleme biblischer Theologie: Gerhard von Rad zum 70. Geburtstag. Ed. H. W. Wolff. Munich: Chr. Kaiser.

Snaith, Norman Henry
1951 "The Historical Books" in Rowley: 84–114.

Soggin, Juan Alberto
1967 "Deuteronomistische Geschichtsauslegung während des babylonischen Exils." Pp. 11–17 in *Oikonomia: Heilsgeschichte als Thema der Theologie.* Ed. F. Christ. Hamburg-Bergstedt: H. Reich.
1970 *Joshua: A Commentary.* OTL. London: SCM; Philadelphia: Westminster.
1976 *Introduction to the Old Testament.* OTL. London: SCM; Philadelphia: Westminster. (Rev. ed., 1980.)
1981 *Judges: A Commentary.* OTL. London: SCM; Philadelphia: Westminster.

Steck, Odil Hannes
1968 *Überlieferung und Zeitgeschichte in den Elia-Erzahlungen.* WMANT 26. Neukirchen-Vluyn: Neukirchener Verlag.

Stinespring, William Franklin
1961 "Eschatology in Chronicles." *JBL* 80: 209–19.

Stoebe, Hans Joachim
1973 *Das erste Buch Samuelis.* KAT 8/1. Gütersloh: Mohn.

Talmon, Shemaryahu
1970 "The Old Testament Text." Pp. 1–41 in *Cambridge History of the Bible*, I. Ed. P. R. Ackroyd and C. F. Evans. Cambridge: University Press.
1976 "Ezra and Nehemiah. Books and Men." Pp. 317–28 in *IDBSup.*
1978 "The Presentation of Synchroneity and Simultaneity in Biblical Narrative." Pp. 9–26 in *Studies in Hebrew Narrative Art throughout the Ages.* Ed. J. Heinemann and S. Werses. Scripta hierosolymitana, 27. Jerusalem: Magnes.

Ulrich, Eugene Charles
1978 *The Qumran Text of Samuel and Josephus.* HSM 19. Missoula, MT: Scholars Press.

Van Seters, John
1976 "Problems in the Literary Analysis of the Court History of David." *JSOT* 1: 22–28.
1981 "Histories and Historians of the Ancient Near East: The Israelites." *Or* 50: 137–95.

Vaux, Roland de
1978 *The Early History of Israel.* 2 vols. London: Darton, Longman and Todd; Philadelphia: Westminster.

Veijola, Timo
    1975   *Die Ewige Dynastie: David und die Entstehung seiner Dynastie nach der deuteronomistischen Darstellung.* AASF Ser. B. 193. Helsinki: Academia Scientiarum Fennica.
    1977   *Das Königtum in der Beurteilung der deuteronomistischen Historiographie: Eine redaktionsgeschichtliche Untersuchung.* AASF Ser. B. 198. Helsinki: Academia Scientiarum Fennica.

Weinfeld, Moshe
    1972   *Deuteronomy and the Deuteronomic School.* Oxford: Clarendon.

Weippert, Manfred
    1973   "Fragen des israelitischen Geschichtsbewusstseins." *VT* 23: 415–42.

Weiser, Artur
    1961   *Introduction to the Old Testament.* London: Darton, Longman and Todd.

Welch, Adam Cleghorn
    1935   *Post-Exilic Judaism.* London and Edinburgh: William Blackwood and Sons.

Welten, Peter
    1973   *Geschichte und Geschichtsdarstellung in den Chronikbüchern.* WMANT 42. Neukirchen-Vluyn: Neukirchener Verlag.

Whybray, R. Norman
    1968   *The Succession Narrative.* SBT 2/9. London: SCM.

Willi, Thomas
    1972   *Die Chronik als Auslegung: Untersuchungen zur literarischen Gestaltung der historischen Überlieferung Israels.* FRLANT 106. Göttingen: Vandenhoeck & Ruprecht.

Williamson, Hugh G. M.
    1977   *Israel in the Books of Chronicles.* Cambridge: University Press.
    1979a   "Eschatology in Chronicles." *TynBul* 28: 115–54.
    1979b   "The Origins of the Twenty-Four Priestly Courses: A Study of 1 Chronicles xxiii–xxvii." VTSup 30: 251–68.
    Forthcoming   *1 and 2 Chronicles.* NCB. London: Oliphants.

Wolff, Hans Walter
    1961   "Das Kerygma des deuteronomistischen Geschichtswerks." *ZAW* 73: 171–86. Reprinted pp. 308–24 in *Gesammelte Studien zum Alten Testament.* TBü 22. Munich: Chr. Kaiser, 1964.

Würthwein, Ernst

1974   *Die Erzählung von der Thronfolge. Davidstheologische oder politische Geschichtsschreibung?* TS 115. Zurich: Theologischer Verlag.

1977   *Die Bücher der Könige: 1 Könige 1–16.* ATD 11,1. Göttingen: Vandenhoeck & Ruprecht.

Wyatt, Nicholas

1979   "The Old Testament Historiography of the Exilic Period." *ST* 33: 45–68.

Young, Edward Joseph

1960 (1964)   *An Introduction to the Old Testament.* London: Tyndale.

10
Prophecy and the Prophetic Literature
Gene M. Tucker

The era under review has witnessed a dramatic increase in scholarly work on the prophets and the prophetic literature. While there have always been scholars concerned with the prophets, at the beginning of the era and in the preceding one there was relatively little interest in the prophets in comparison with, e.g., the Pentateuch, the history of Israel, and ancient Near Eastern backgrounds of the Hebrew Bible. That this was the case, especially in North American scholarship, was due in large measure to the dominance of the Albright school with its interest in archaeology and history and in biblical literature that could be related to the results of archaeological work. But since World War II there has been a veritable explosion of research and publication concerning the prophets and the prophetic literature.

It is not possible to take account here of all the research on the prophets since 1945. In fact, the space allotted for this chapter could hardly contain a list of even the significant works published in the last thirty-five years. (For extensive bibliography for most of the period, organized according to research topics and including evaluative comments, see Fohrer, 1951–52, 1962, and 1975–76.) Our goal is rather to delineate the major themes and advances in research over the past three and one-half decades, to assess successes and failures, and to identify the issues that call for attention in the future.

If there has been a dominant note in the study of the prophets and the prophetic literature, it has been the one identified by Wolff in 1955. He argued (446) that the present principal problems in the investigation of the prophets could be reduced to a simple formula: What is old here and what is new? What have the prophets in common with similar figures, and what is theirs in particular? Under this theme he identified six issues in current prophetic research: the religio-historical question of the roots of Israelite prophecy in the ancient Near East; the psychology of the prophets; traditio-historical questions; cultic prophecy; prophecy and politics; and the problem of false prophecy. Not all of these issues have continued to be as significant as they appeared to Wolff in 1955, and new ones have emerged. Interest in the psychology of prophecy and concern with the prophet and politics have receded in recent years, and new approaches to the role of the prophet have begun to emerge. Nevertheless, in a variety of ways the question of what is old and what is new in the prophets has been a leitmotiv in a considerable amount of research.

I. THE OLD AND THE NEW IN THE PROPHETS

The Law and the Prophets

Up to the beginning of the period under review the source-critical method and the reconstruction of the history of the religion of Israel that emerged from it continued to dominate the interpretation of the prophetic literature. However, with the application of form-critical, traditio-historical and redaction-critical approaches to the prophetic literature that is no longer the case. The loss of sway by source criticism has entailed important changes in the understanding of the origin and development of the prophetic literature and the interpretation of the role of the prophet. Among these changes is a different perception of the relationship between the law and the prophets; here the rudiments of a new consensus have begun to appear.

The traditional understanding of the relationship between the law and the prophets—whether conceived as bodies of literature, religious ideas, or institutions—continued in both synagogue and church until well into the era of critical scholarship. According to this view, the law, given through Moses, came before the prophets, who were seen as interpreters of that primary revelation of the divine will. In this understanding, "the Law" could represent the legislation attributed to the era of Moses and the events at Mt. Sinai or the entire Pentateuch. During the first two centuries of critical biblical scholarship (1670s to 1870s) the traditional view of this relationship continued to prevail. Long after the presence of several sources had been recognized in the Pentateuch it was still taken for granted that the most extensive strand and the one most dominated by divine law (present-day P) was the earliest layer. Consequently, the traditional understanding of the prophets as interpreters of the law remained basically unchanged.

It was the Graf-Wellhausen hypothesis and above all the publication of Wellhausen's *Prolegomena to the History of Ancient Israel* (1878) that quickly laid the traditional view to rest. That work did not directly address the question of the relationship between the law and the prophets but set out to establish the chronology of the sources of the Pentateuch as the foundation for a proper history of Israel, especially Israel's religious development. By demonstrating that the Priestly document and the final written form of the Pentateuch were quite late, Wellhausen could show that "the law is not the starting point for ancient Israel but for Judaism."

A new consensus concerning the relationship between the law and the prophets quickly emerged in the four or five decades following publication of the *Prolegomena*. The prophets, coming before the law, were now seen as great creative individuals, the ones who put the national religion of Israel on a high moral plain, the founders of "ethical monotheism." A line from J. Meinhold's *Einführung* (1919) is typical: "One can completely understand the prophets without the law, but not the law without the prophets" (cited by Bach, 1957:23).

It was seldom recognized that this new consensus was bought at the price of ignoring some of the results of Wellhausen's own detailed analysis of the evidence. It was the law in the form of the Priestly document and the final written form of the Pentateuch that were later than the prophets, but Wellhausen also concluded that J and E preceded or paralleled the rise of classical prophecy. Moreover, while he did not stress the point, he knew that the Pentateuchal sources, including P, were based on older written and oral traditions.

So the prophetic morality, even for Wellhausen, did not appear out of thin air. Rather, it was based on the ancient idea of the covenant, which the early prophets placed "'at the centre of their faith, and with it the corresponding concept of law.' . . . The statutory law, on the other hand, only emerges later" (Zimmerli, 1965:25). Thus for Wellhausen the relationship between law and prophets was not so simple as it became for his successors.

In spite of these qualifications expressed in Wellhausen's *Prolegomena* and although the seeds for a new and different reconstruction had already been planted by the turn of the century, the source-critical view of the relationship between the law and the prophets would reign well into the twentieth century. The groundwork for the demise of that view was laid where the consensus had been founded in the first place, in research on the Pentateuch. Such works as Gunkel's commentary on Genesis, Gressmann's *Mose und seine Zeit*, Alt's "Die Ursprünge des israelitischen Rechts," von Rad's "Das formgeschichtliche Problem des Hexateuch," and Noth's *Überlieferungsgeschichte des Pentateuch*, not to mention the results of archaeology, laid the foundation for a new understanding. By the middle of the twentieth century scholars were agreed that, when the so-called classical prophets began to emerge in the eighth century B.C.E., many if not most of the narrative and legal traditions that constitute the Pentateuch already had taken shape.

Were the new conclusions concerning the antiquity of the Pentateuchal materials to signal a return to the precritical understanding that the prophets were later than and interpreters of the law? Almost, but not quite. If the traditional view is seen as the thesis and the source-critical perspective as the antithesis, then what has appeared in recent decades is a synthesis, drawing valid features from both viewpoints.

There have been remarkably few detailed investigations of the use
of laws and legal materials in the prophetic literature. To be sure, there
have been numerous investigations of individual genres with possible
roots in legal and/or cultic-legal institutions, including the prophetic
judgment speech (Westermann, 1967), the priestly torah (Begrich, 1936;
Würthwein, 1963), and the so-called covenant lawsuit (Huffmon, 1959;
Harvey, 1962, 1967; see below). However, concerning the specific question of the relationship of the prophets to the law, general presentations
of the new synthesis began to appear without the benefit of the detailed
exegetical studies of prophetic texts that would make such a reconstruction reasonable.

The most important and influential work in this regard—as in some
others—was Gerhard von Rad's *Old Testament Theology*, Vol. II: *The
Theology of Israel's Prophetic Traditions* (1960; Eng. trans. 1965). This
work more than any other popularized the view that the prophets
depend heavily on older traditions, including the law: "As we now see,
they [the prophets] were in greater or lesser degree conditioned by old
traditions which they re-interpreted and applied to their own times" (4).
That sentence sounds not unlike the traditional, precritical view. But for
von Rad the relationship of the prophets to previous traditions is by no
means simple. He began his work by pointing out, "The fact that the
present *Old Testament Theology* is divided into two volumes suggests
that there is a definite break between the message of the prophets and
the ideas held by earlier Jahwism" (3). That sentence sounds not unlike
the views of Wellhausen and his successors.

According to von Rad, the prophetic message is found at the intersection of three major lines: the particular old election tradition in which
the prophet stands, the current social and political situation, and the new
word of Yahweh concerning the future (see 130). His treatment of the
relationship of the prophets to the law must be viewed in the light of this
understanding. He recognized that the prophets on occasion make the
old commandments the basis for their announcements, but he insisted
that in every instance they go further: "The point is not simply that in
this case there is a breach of one commandment of the old law given by
God, and in that the breach of another: the point is Israel's total failure
vis-à-vis Jahweh" (396). His summary virtually concluded that, in spite
of the recognition of old traditions and old laws in the prophets, what is
new predominates: ". . . confronted with the eschatological situation, the
prophets were set the task of taking the old regulations and making them
the basis of an entirely new interpretation of Jahweh's current demands
on Israel" (400).

In fact, von Rad continually subordinated the prophets' interest in
the old law to their concern with the election traditions and the
announcement of the future. "They did not reproach their fellows with

not living their lives in obedience to law: their reproach was rather this, that as Jahweh's own people they had continually transgressed the commandments and not put their confidence in the offer of divine protection" (186). In effect, Israel's failure was the refusal to accept and live out her election. Consequently, "the law" was not a very important theme in von Rad's interpretation of the prophetic role or message.

Zimmerli's *The Law and the Prophets: A Study of the Meaning of the Old Testament* (1965) includes two chapters (V and VI) which addressed directly the issue of the relationship between the law and the prophets. Like von Rad, he was reluctant to abandon the idea that with the classical prophets something truly new emerged. Zimmerli took it for granted that in Israel law was part of covenant. He noted that in this sense Amos and Hosea in particular view themselves and their contemporaries as bound to the revealed law of God (67ff.; 69ff.). Still, he stressed the distance between the law and the prophets: ". . . behind these concrete accusations lies a deeper interpretation of God's law, which does not demand individual acts of obedience from men, but the obedience of the heart which expresses itself in every separate outward action" (70). And finally, "'The Law and the Prophets' not only designate two forms of Old Testament thinking, but they also represent two successive stages of a development" (93). In effect, he stressed the interpretation of prophets as a dramatic new stage in the history of Israel's religion (see also Zimmerli, 1977). Zimmerli's synthesis, therefore, stands much closer to the position of the late nineteenth century than to the traditional viewpoint.

Some of the more narrowly focused studies, however, suggest a synthesis that emphasizes the dependence of the prophets on the law. Among these Bach's investigation of law in the message of Amos stands out (1957). While his exegetical work concentrated on the book of Amos, Bach's primary concern was the history of Israelite law and the relation of the prophets to the law. He assumed the conclusions of Alt concerning apodictic and casuistic law and turned to the earliest prophetic book to determine whether or not the two forms had come together by the middle of the eighth century B.C.E. He confirmed the conclusions of Würthwein (1950) that in many instances the "reasons" for judgment in Amos depend on laws known elsewhere in the Hebrew scriptures. He argued that a legal background is visible in the following texts: 3:9ff.; 4:1; 8:4; 5:7, 10, 11, 12; 6:12; 8:5; 2:6–8. He concluded that in every case where parallels can be discovered Amos depends entirely upon apodictic law and even turns against casuistic law. Therefore, the old dualism between the two types of law had not been overcome by the time of Amos (33). With regard to the message of Amos, this dependence upon apodictic law shows that his proclamation of judgment was founded on the covenant of Yahweh with Israel (34). In some respects Bach has pressed the evidence too far. It should be emphasized that in not a single

instance does Amos quote previous laws directly; consequently, in order
to conclude that the prophet depends strictly upon apodictic laws—
which Alt related to the covenant—one must reconstruct the law from
the description of wrong behavior. The conclusions concerning Amos
2:6–8 in particular are dubious. However, what Bach has demonstrated
is that Amos clearly assumes and depends upon old legal traditions and
does not invent new laws.

Beyerlin's study of the cultic background of Micah, which has
broader traditio-historical implications as well, arrived at similar conclusions concerning the relation of the prophets to the law. He examined
the message of Micah for the presence and use of traditions concerning
the meaning of "Israel," the Sinai covenant (including both the theophany tradition and the "tradition of the amphictyonic law"), the exodus
and the taking of the land, and the covenant with David. Beyerlin,
whose work at points rests on questionable redaction-critical foundations,
concluded that in Micah's message the three great streams of tradition
concerning Sinai, exodus/conquest, and the covenant with David come
together. Moreover, the tradition of the amphictyonic law is the presupposition, the standard, and the leitmotiv of the prophetic complaint and
criticism (87). Whoever asks about God's will must be referred to this old
amphictyonic legal tradition, which is linked to the covenant (87–88).
Beyerlin examined a series of texts to establish that point, showing the
connections between many of them and laws cited elsewhere in the OT,
virtually all of which turn out to be apodictic laws. He concluded further that there is not a trace of fundamental criticism of the covenant
cult and its traditions in Micah (96).

Brueggemann's study of Hosea included an investigation of the traditions employed by the prophet, including older laws. In language that
approaches the traditional explanation of the relationship between the
prophets and the law he asserted, "the prophets have as their primary
function the reassertion and application of the old traditions in ways
which are relevant and compelling for the present community of faith"
(13). While this generalization concerning the prophetic role and message is not necessarily valid, Brueggemann has added to the evidence
that Hosea, at least, depends upon old legal and other traditions. Moreover, he has assembled, with very little comment, an impressive series of
texts that allude to laws known elsewhere in the Hebrew Bible, especially in Deuteronomy (38ff.). Like Bach, Beyerlin, and others he saw
this legal tradition as integral to the covenant.

A particular interpretation of the relation of the prophets to the law
was developed by H.-J. Kraus, based primarily on some Pentateuchal
texts, especially Deut 18:15 (see also Muilenburg). He argued that there
had been in premonarchical Israel an office of covenant-mediator, which
was passed on in prophetic circles and influenced the classical prophets.

While the evidence for such an office is insufficient (Clements, 1975:13), his conclusion concerning the relation of the prophets to the law is sound: "Dass die Propheten nicht im Sinne der Erklärungen Wellhausens als evolutionischer Aufbruch eines neuen Ethos zu verstehen sind, sondern dass sie vom altisraelitischen Recht und seiner Verkündigung herkommen" (29).

It seems clear from recent research that the prophets, at least from the eighth century on, knew and alluded to laws long known and accepted in Israel (see Bergren). However, with the possible exception of Hos 4:1–2 and Jer 7:9, which refer to part of the Decalogue, there are few if any actual quotations of law by prophets. The prophets are to be understood neither as preachers of the law nor as originators of a new morality in Israel. With regard to the former, one need only compare the prophetic speeches with the sermons on the law in Deuteronomy. With regard to the latter, the dependence of the prophets on older traditions—including traditions of law—has now become obvious. Legal traditions were employed by the prophets primarily to establish that Yahweh's punishment of Israel was reasonable: Yahweh's expectations are assumed to have been communicated long before.

Theological Traditions

"Tradition" has been a central theme in OT studies especially since World War II, including in the study of the prophets (McKane: 180ff.). However, the term and the related expressions "history of tradition," "Überlieferungsgeschichte," and "traditio-historical research" have been used in diverse and often confusing ways (see Kniorim's comments in chapter 4 of this volume and the useful discussion of terms and methods by Steck). For our purposes here we may identify two major ways in which the study of tradition has been pursued with regard to the prophetic literature. The first concerns the history of the growth and composition of the prophetic books, traced from their final written forms back through every discernible written or oral stage, including the question of the institutional roots of the genres in the literature. This question will be taken up later. At this point we are concerned with a second perspective on tradition, the attempt to identify and analyze the particular streams of theological tradition in which each prophet stood.

Again it is Gerhard von Rad who has brought the interest in the theological traditions of the prophets to the forefront by making such traditions central features in his understanding of the theology of the prophets. (If OT scholarship in general has used "traditio-historical" in vague and confusing ways, von Rad's use was particularly imprecise; see Rendtorff, 1973:284–87). One fact concerning von Rad's volume on "the theology of Israel's prophetic traditions" should be noted: in contrast to the first volume this one was not preceded by a long series of technical and detailed studies of the subject matter. (He was, however, able at points to depend upon the work of E. Rohland.) Consequently, it should be viewed as a programmatic work. In this respect it has been especially important, and its major and distinctive contribution was the attempt—for the most part successful—to relate the prophets to prior theological traditions.

As noted above, von Rad stressed that the prophetic message was located at the intersection of three lines: the old election traditions in which they and their hearers stood, the particular historical circumstances, and the new word of Yahweh concerning the future. The prophets, to be sure, called into question the words of the tradition and changed them into a new form of prediction (130); they addressed the traditions that survived in their day, submitted them to criticism, and made them relevant for their own generation (138).

Von Rad concentrated his attention on two major circles of tradition, those of the exodus/conquest and those of David and Zion. Since Amos was a Judean, von Rad expected to find in his message the theology of David and Zion and was able to do so in Amos 9:11ff. Von Rad brushed aside without serious consideration the widely held view that this reference to the "booth" of David occurs in a late exilic or postexilic addition to the book (138). He acknowledged that there are allusions to the exodus traditions in the book, but he took them as the prophet's use of the theology of his hearers against them. The evidence suggests, on the contrary, that Amos knew and used the exodus-election tradition and not that of David and Zion. The texts that support the latter are later additions (9:11ff., and perhaps the doxologies in 4:13; 5:8–9; and 9:5–6), with the possible exception of 1:2. The texts that reflect the exodus circle of traditions (especially 2:9–10; 3:1–2; and 9:7–8a) on the other hand are integral to the message of the prophet.

Both Hosea and Jeremiah are deeply rooted in the history of salvation traditions that recall the exodus and related events. This is not surprising in the case of the northern prophet Hosea, and von Rad is able to assemble a long list of texts that allude to and build upon this history of salvation (140). But Jeremiah, active throughout his career in and around Jerusalem, knows nothing of the distinctively Judean traditions; rather, what we find here are exodus, covenant, and conquest (192). Von Rad explained this fact by pointing out that Jeremiah was, after all, from a village that belonged to the tribe of Benjamin and assumed those specifically Israelite traditions valued by Benjamin and Ephraim (192). Moreover, Jeremiah's dependence upon Hosea is obvious, and in his early years he must have come in contact with disciples of his predecessor (192).

It was primarily Isaiah—and to a lesser extent his contemporary Micah—who lived out of and passed on to us the Zion and David traditions. Von Rad found in Isaiah not a bit of the exodus traditions, although he expounds and interprets the law to the people of Jerusalem (140). The tradition concerning Zion is reflected in a number of passages that suggest the belief that the holy city was inviolable, a view von Rad related to the songs of Zion in the psalms (156–57). Micah knew of this tradition but rejected it, expecting the total destruction of Jerusalem (Mic 3:12) (170–71). Isaiah, on the other hand, based several important emphases, including the summons to faith, on the expectation that Zion would be delivered (159). Equally important to Isaiah, according to von Rad, was the tradition concerning Yahweh's anointed one, the promise concerning David's succession as reflected in 2 Samuel 7. This promise was the basis for Isaiah's "eschatological" hope—that in the immediate future a new anointed one would be enthroned and the city of Jerusalem restored (171).

The traditions were used with remarkable freedom by two other prophets, Ezekiel and Second Isaiah. Von Rad observed that Ezekiel depended at several points on old saving traditions, including that of Israel's history, which he reinterpreted in a highly individual fashion (225ff.). He was deeply rooted, however, in the tradition of the covenant at Sinai; his vision of the future was indebted to the David tradition, but he rejected the Zion tradition. "But the Sinai tradition dominates his thought—under the new David, Israel will obey the commandments (Ezek. xxxvii.24)" (236). Second Isaiah took up all the major traditions of exodus, David, and Zion. His vision of the future was patterned after and indebted to the old story of the exodus, which leads not to a promised land but to Zion (239). Deutero-Isaiah mentions the David tradition only once directly, but he applied the promises concerning the throne of David to the people as a whole (240). In addition, Second Isaiah drew upon a tradition not used by other prophets, that of creation, which he combined with the salvation traditions (240ff.).

In the years immediately preceding and following the appearance of von Rad's volume on the prophets a number of works appeared that supported the view that the prophets depended upon older traditions. Few went further than Beyerlin's treatment of Micah (1959), mentioned above. He argued that, in addition to depending upon old covenantal laws, Micah brought together the traditions of Sinai, exodus/conquest, and the promise to David. Such a conclusion, quite different from von Rad's brief notes concerning Micah, is possible only on shaky redaction-critical foundations. Wolff had argued (1956) that Hosea's rich use of the history of salvation and legal traditions showed that the prophet was rooted quite specifically in Levitical-prophetic circles which were the predecessors of Deuteronomy. Some features of this view have been successfully challenged by Rendtorff (1962b), but the identification of the traditions—if not the specific institutional roots—stands. Similarly, Brueggemann's study of Hosea interpreted the prophet in the context of covenantal traditions (legal and historical), forms of speech, and institutions. Clements (1965) also stressed the importance of tradition in the classical prophets, asserting that "the covenant tradition formed the heart of their religion" (18). Clements used the term "covenant tradition" in a rather comprehensive sense to encompass the exodus, wilderness, and conquest traditions as a "Sinai covenant tradition" which "was subsumed by a new covenant ideology centering in the divine election of David and of Mount Zion" (121).

Some of the individual traditions that influenced the prophets have been studied in detail. John Hayes (1963) investigated the history of the Zion tradition and its use by Isaiah. He saw the Zion tradition, which—with the David tradition—came into existence with the establishment of Jerusalem as a royal city, as based on the bringing of the Ark into the city (421). The Zion tradition was "joined to and expanded by pre-Israelite traditions. It is in these traditions rather than in the prophetical work of Isaiah that the origin of the tradition of Zion's inviolability must be found" (422). Isaiah used the common tradition to support the people and to proclaim the message of Yahweh, but he altered it in two ways: by calling for faith in Yahweh as a condition for salvation (7:9; 31:4-9) and by placing the enemy attacks on the city "within the arena of God's activity and work" as indicated in Isa 10:5-6 and 29:1-8 (423). Chr. Jeremias (1977b) investigated the prophetic use of the patriarchal traditions, usually subsumed under the exodus or covenantal traditions. He observed that Abraham is mentioned above all in Second Isaiah, Jacob in prophets from Hosea to Malachi, and of Isaac there is hardly a word. In addition there are numerous references to the patriarchal tradition as a whole or elements of it such as the promise of numerous descendants. The prophetic use concerns not so much the past as the present, and the negative use of the Jacob tradition (e.g., for indictment) dominates in the earlier prophets and the positive use of the Abraham tradition (often in reference to his call) coming to the fore in Second Isaiah. In addition to these the David tradition has been investigated by Seybold, the tradition of the election of Israel—including its appearance in the prophets—has been examined by Wildberger, and the dependence of the prophets upon tradition has been taken up by Schmidt. Moreover, the issue of theological traditions and their institutional roots has arisen in numerous studies of particular genres used by the prophets (see below).

Not all scholars, of course, have accepted the view that the prophets depend heavily upon older theological traditions. Two examples may be mentioned here, one a treatment of a specific issue and the other a work on prophecy in general. The first is Marie-Louise Henry's study of the prophetic vocation reports. Entitling her work *Prophet und Tradition,* she responded directly to the emphasis upon the traditional in the prophets by looking on the other hand for what was new and distinctive. On the basis of the vocation reports she argued that being overcome by God was the new and individual element in prophecy. Although she recognized that even the vocation reports incorporated traditional and stereotyped features, she stressed the individuality of each prophet and its importance: nothing is finally bound to tradition or to institution (76–77). The second is C. F. Whitley's *The Prophetic Achievement*, in many ways a reaction against the traditio-historical perspective: ". . . the extent to which the prophets were indebted to tradition remains a doubtful issue" (27). Whitley called one chapter "The Originality of the Prophets," in which he rejected the idea of covenantal traditions in the prophets—or even the view that a Sinai tradition was a dominant element in Israelite tradition (32–33)—and argued that the prophets based their authority entirely on the inspiration of their messages (44). These views, it is safe to say, have not characterized the dominant perspective of OT scholarship in our era.

An excellent summary and evaluation of the present state of the question was presented by R. E. Clements in *Prophecy and Tradition* (1975). He took up not only the question of theological themes as discussed here but also the broad issue of the relationship between originality and tradition in the prophets, accepting a broad and diverse understanding of "tradition." He has retreated somewhat from his earlier conclusions (1965), pointing out that covenantal and cultic traditions were more diverse in Israel than he had acknowledged. Clements argued against treating each tradition as though it were a doctrine and against using a particular motif, e.g., "Zion," to identify a particular theology (87). If he erred it was in the direction of caution about the impact of tradition upon the prophets.

There is work yet to be done on the relationship between the messages of the individual prophets and the theological traditions of ancient Israel and not only concerning the major "election" traditions they knew and used. The work needs to be carried out with the sort of methodological precision suggested by Steck, in which the terminology would be used with care and the theological themes identified on the basis of literary evidence.

II. FROM ORAL TRADITION TO PROPHETIC BOOKS

The Genres of Prophetic Speech and Literature

Major advances have been made in the last three and one-half decades in understanding the genres of prophetic speech and literature. Form-critical work has been considerable, contributing to other developments such as traditio-historical research, the question of the background and origin of prophecy, and the issue of the prophetic role. Since such work has been reported, summarized, and evaluated more than once in recent years (Koch, 1969; March; Tucker, 1978; Westermann, 1967;

Wilson, 1973), we may be relatively brief here, in view of the amount of research that has been done.

Since it is obvious that the prophets were first and foremost speakers—although we have only the written words of those speeches—it is not surprising that considerable attention has been given to understanding the nature and background of prophetic speech and to determining the "basic form of prophetic speech." Before World War II there had been little progress beyond the work of Gunkel, who took the earliest form of prophetic utterance to be short, oracular predictions of the future, either promises or threats. Later, he concluded, other genres developed, such as reproaches, which he took to be the word of the prophet in contrast to the threat and promise, which were given as the actual words of Yahweh (for the literature see Tucker, 1978:32, 38; and Hayes, 1973).

For the most part Gunkel's terminology and its implications prevailed until Westermann's *Grundformen prophetischer Rede* appeared in 1960 (translation 1967). Building upon a particular—and at points slanted—history of research, Westermann developed a different terminology for and interpretation of prophetic speech. He successfully argued that "threat" and "reproach" were inadequate categories for the speeches in question. Less successful but highly influential was Westermann's identification of prophetic speech in general as "messenger speech," based primarily upon the common appearance of the "messenger formula," "Thus says Yahweh" (98–128; see also Holladay). This identification has been challenged by Rendtorff (1962a) on the grounds that the formula occurs not only with "messages" but also with a wide variety of material, that messages do not always begin or end with the formula, and that there is such variability in content that the "message" cannot be considered a distinct genre (see esp. 247–52).

Westermann devoted most of his attention to what he called the prophetic judgment speech, Gunkel's threatening speech with a reproach. He distinguished between such speeches addressed to individuals—which he considered to be the original form—and those addressed to the nation. The address to the nation includes reasons for judgment (accusation and its development), followed by a messenger formula as a transition into the second major part, the announcement of judgment (including the intervention of God and the results of that intervention). He saw the judgment speech against the individual as rooted in patterns of expression and ideas at home in juridical procedure. The prophets were not considered to be acting in some kind of legal capacity but to be announcing Yahweh's judgment in language borrowed ultimately from the law court. Many of his observations are valid, including the identification of the speeches as announcement of the future instead of as its prediction, and his conclusion that what Gunkel had called "reproach" often functions as reasons for that announcement. Many of the morphological data on which some conclusions were based, however, do not stand up under close scrutiny, and the connection of prophecy with the law court remains open to debate.

It was Klaus Koch (1969:210–20) who questioned the legal language and its implications. What Westermann had called the prophecy of judgment he called—more neutrally with regard to background—the prophecy of disaster. Its counterpart was the prophecy of salvation. He saw the background of these genres to be in the prophet's "private oracle," which preceded the public address. His understanding of the relation of the speeches to the prophetic experiences—if not his terminology—is similar to that of Gunkel. Koch is presently engaged in a long-range and extensive form-critical analysis of the prophetic books, and the results of the analysis of Amos have already been published (Koch und Mitarbeiter).

My own investigation of prophetic speech (1978) in general supported Koch's terminology; it recognized that, while often the structure of prophecy includes the elements identified by Westermann (namely, reasons followed by announcement), the structure is quite variable. Prophetic address is not necessarily rooted in juridical practices, and the consistent features that define the genre are the presentation of a communication from God announcing future events.

Various genres in the prophetic literature have been identified as stemming from different spheres of Israelite life. Some genres are cultic and have been used by some scholars to support the view that the prophets were officials of the cult (see below). Others are similar to the genres found in wisdom literature. One of the first to recognize wisdom genres—and wisdom influence—in the prophets was J. Fichtner, who saw such language in Isaiah, concluding that the prophet depended upon scribal wisdom traditions but was ambivalent about the wise men. J. Lindblom's broader study of the question (1955) concluded that prophecy and wisdom were distinct but that the style of the prophets was influenced by wisdom instruction (e.g., parables, allegories, similes, metaphors, proverbial expressions, rhetorical questions, etc.), and that some late additions to prophetic books came from wisdom circles (204). S. Terrien, mainly on the basis of style and themes, argued for a close relationship between Amos and wisdom circles. Perhaps the most extensive use of "wisdom" genres to argue for the background of particular prophets has been in the works of H. W. Wolff. Primarily on the basis of genres considered to be wisdom, Wolff concluded that the background of Amos was in tribal wisdom (1973). He has recently (1978a) drawn similar conclusions concerning Micah. Finally, J. W. Whedbee included in his study of Isaiah and wisdom a treatment of the didactic genres in the book. He concluded that at many points Isaiah was dependent upon, although he quarreled with, the wisdom circles of Jerusalem.

Quite apart from the possible legal background of the so-called basic form of prophetic speech, other forms of expression have been related to juridical (or possibly cultic-juridical) situations. Most important in this regard is the *rîb* or covenant lawsuit. The discussion of this genre was advanced by Huffmon (1959), who identified two distinct "types" with different backgrounds; one he connected with the divine council and the other with the covenant between Yahweh and Israel (295). The background was not the ordinary law court, but the cultic, covenantal context. Harvey (1962, 1967) reached similar conclusions, but especially in his later work he saw the prophetic expressions more directly dependent upon certain political correspondence in which a suzerain accused a vassal of violating a treaty; he thereby tended to minimize the connection between the prophetic genre and the covenantal cult. Würthwein (1952) argued that the prophetic judgment speeches depended upon covenantal traditions and cultic practices; Limburg (1969) rejected the direct links with the cult, saw a variety of settings for the texts in question but favored the conclusion that the background of the genre is international law. The most recent treatment of this problem is the work of K. Nielsen, who summarized the history of the investigation (5–26), analyzed the relevant texts (Isa 1:2–3; 3:13–15; Hos 4:1–3; 2:2–15 [H2:4–17]; Psalm 50), and considered the question of the Sitz im Leben of the genre. Her own conclusions were quite close to those of H. E. von Waldow, who argued that the formal aspects of the prophetic lawsuit have their roots in secular—not cultic—juridical practice, while their content is dependent upon the traditions of the covenant between Yahweh and Israel (Nielsen: 20, 55–61).

An important dimension of Nielsen's work is the attempt to clarify a problem that has continued to plague some form-critical work on the prophets, the question of the relationship between genre and Sitz im Leben (2–4). Especially concerning the "nonprophetic" genres in the prophetic literature, one must be careful to distinguish between the formal and the actual Sitz im Leben of the genres. When Gunkel, e.g., suggested that the setting of the lawsuit speeches was secular law, he assumed that the prophets had borrowed language from juridical practice. Some discussions of the prophetic lawsuits—as of other genres—have tended to ignore such a distinction, concluding that if the genre came from the covenantal cult of international law that was its Sitz im Leben. Certainly the original or formal setting will have influenced the way the language was used and heard in actual prophetic address, but the two must be distinguished in exegetical work. This point is not unlike the one made by Wolff in 1955 with reference to cultic genres in the prophets: it has become important to ask of each form concerning both its prehistory and its actual use (223).

Genres that appear to be distinctly related to the prophetic office have received considerable attention in the last few decades. One question concerns the existence of calls to repentance and similar admonishing or exhorting genres, some of which Gunkel called reproaches. Westermann (1967) considered the reproach to be part of the prophetic judgment speech, functioning to give the reasons for judgment. Wolff (1951) had gone even further, concluding that there was not an independent admonition genre and that the motif of repentance, which was unusual in the early prophets, was a part of the judgment and salvation speeches. However, T. Raitt argued for the existence of a separate genre, the prophetic summons to repentance. He cited twenty-nine examples which include both threat of judgment and promise of salvation (33). The structure (cf. Jer 3:12–13) includes two main parts, each with three elements: appeal (including messenger formula, vocative, and admonition) and motivation (including promise, accusation, and threat) (33–35). He located the genre in law and covenant. Two recent works, although focused somewhat differently, appear to call some of Raitt's conclusions into question. Warmuth's study of the *Mahnwort* ("exhortation"?) in the preexilic prophets concluded that there is not an independent genre, but the *Mahnwort* functions in the context of both judgment and salvation speeches to announce the future as Yahweh will bring it about. In the judgment speeches it functions as reasons; in the announcements of salvation it does not present a condition for Yahweh's saving activity. Redactors, however, often reinterpreted the *Mahnwort*, turning it into a call for decision. Markert's investigation of the *Scheltwort* ("invective"?) reached similar conclusions. the genre, which comes from the teaching situation in the family, is found only once (6:12) in the (authentic) words of Amos and plays no significant role in prophetic speech, although the prophets occasionally employed invectives. The discussion of these genres and of their place in prophetic address is important because of its implications concerning the prophetic message and role. Most of the evidence supports the conclusion (noted above) that the prophets functioned primarily to announce the future as the word of God; they were not first of all preachers of repentance.

Another genre that has been intensively studied is the so-called woe oracle. Much of the current debate was set into motion by Gerstenberger, who reacted against Westermann's view (1967) that the woe speeches were variations of the prophetic judgment speech. Gerstenberger saw the introductory הוי related to אשרי and located the genre originally in the "popular ethos," serving a didactic function. Wanke argued that Gerstenberger and others had incorrectly identified אוי and הוי; the former is a cry of dread and expression of peril while the latter comes from lamentations over the dead. Clifford likewise argued that the origin of הוי was in the funeral lament and that the expression was taken over by the prophets as an "automatic reaction of the prophet upon hearing the word of God's punishment" (460). This view was carried forward in Janzen's detailed study. He demonstrated that the use of the cry in funeral songs was not limited to Israel but was found throughout the ancient Near East. Consequently, he rejected Gerstenberger's view that the woe came into prophetic speech through didactic circles, in favor of its direct derivation from the funeral lament (24ff.). However, as in the case of the funeral for one who had been murdered, the lament could become invective and accusation. Janzen has made a good case for the funerary background of the "woe," but Gerstenberger's analysis of the structure of the units that follow the cry is still sound. For the most part, what follows the introductory "woe" is the description of the addressees in terms of their deeds which evoke the cry (251). Moreover, almost without exception the speeches are not given as the word of Yahweh concerning the future and they therefore should not be identified as "oracles."

In spite of their ubiquity in the prophetic books, the oracles against foreign nations have received relatively little scholarly attention, but two studies should be mentioned. John Hayes (1968) investigated the oracles as a whole and concluded that they reflect a long tradition in Israel and that they include a variety of genres from various contexts in Israel— although warfare was the dominant original Sitz im Leben. He noted also that such oracles were used within cultic services of lamentation, often functioning as a salvation oracle within the songs of lamentation (87–88), and that the element of judgment in the oracles was "not the special creation of a 'prophetical perspective'" (92). D. L. Christensen interpreted the oracles against the nations from the perspective of F. M. Cross and his students: as part of the holy war and divine warrior tradition. The "war oracle" includes summons to battle, summons to flight (see also Bach, 1962), summons to mourn, battle curses, announcements of victory or defeat, and victory and taunt songs (15). He traced the background and history of the war oracle, arguing that Amos 1–2 and Jeremiah 46–51 represent two major turning points in its development. With Amos the oracle from warfare was turned into a prophetic judgment speech against Israel's enemies and Israel herself. With Jeremiah the focus becomes the preservation of the people in exile and the restoration of Zion; the foundation was laid for further developments of the oracle in apocalyptic literature and thought. As Christensen suggested, there is work yet to be done before the oracles against the nations are adequately understood.

The first extensive form-critical study of the prophetic (and other) vocation reports was published by Habel in 1965. He demonstrated that there were a great many consistent elements in the structure of the reports (divine confrontation, introductory word, objection, reassurance, and sign), suggested that the genre arose from the need for ambassadors or messengers to present their credentials (cf. Gen 24:35–48), and concluded that the purpose of the reports was to announce publicly that Yahweh had commissioned his representative. Baltzer's analysis of the structure of the reports is somewhat different. His understanding of their general background and purpose is not unlike that of Habel, but he goes much too far when he sees the prophet as parallel to the Egyptian vizier (1968; see also 1975). Zimmerli (1979:97–100) showed that there were two basic types of the genre. One type was structured in terms as the report of a vision in the divine court, similar to other vision reports (Isa 6:1–13; Ezekiel 1–3; 1 Kgs 22:19–23), while the other emphasized the coming of the word of God—an audition—to the prophet or other divine representative (Jer 1:4–10; Exodus 3–4; Judg 6:11–14). Long (1972) argued that both of Zimmerli's types went back to a single ancient Near Eastern tradition. It should be emphasized that none of these reports is biographical or autobiographical in anything like the modern sense (see Tucker, 1973, 1978). Their purpose is rather the authentication of the prophet's authority and message. The reports were shaped according to traditional patterns long after the events they report, either by the prophets themselves or by later tradents as arguments for the authority of the prophet (Long stressed the work of later generations, 1977).

Although a few general treatments have appeared and many of the individual texts have been analyzed, the prophetic vision reports likewise deserve more attention than they have received. F. Horst's article may be considered the programmatic form-critical analysis. He ordered the reports into three categories: (1) the presence-vision in which the experience of Yahweh dominates (1 Kgs 22:19ff.; Isa 6:1ff.; Ezek 1:4ff.), often involving a dialogue between prophet and deity (1 Sam 3:10–14; Jer 1:4–10); (2) the word symbol or word-assonance vision, in which what is seen leads to the perception of a word of God (Jer 1:13–15; Amos 8:1–3); and (3) the event-vision in which the prophet gives a detailed description of what he has seen as a revelation of the future (Isa 13:4–5; 21:1–9; Jer 4:19–20, 23–36; Nah 3:1–3). Long (1976a) sought to refine Horst's analysis by locating the vision reports more explicitly in the history of tradition and redaction. He observed that most visions are in autobiographical style and include three basic elements: announcement, transition, and vision sequence. He proposed a typology somewhat different from that of Horst: (1) oracle-vision, a short report dominated by question and answer (Amos 8:1–2); (2) dramatic word-vision, describing a heavenly scene, a supramundane situation or drama (1 Kgs 22:17; Amos 7:1–6); and (3) revelatory-mysteries-vision, which conveys in veiled form secrets of divine action and events of the future (Zech 2:1–2, 3–4; 4:1–6a). Long saw question-and-answer patterns in most of the types. He suggested that an important—but not the only—Sitz im Leben (we should say original or formal) of the vision reports would have been in prophetic acts of divination, or responses to requests for oracles (see 1 Kgs 22:13–23), but that most of the vision reports appear to be literary devices that developed as the words of the prophets were edited. The work of Chr. Jeremias on the night visions of Zechariah (1977a) should also be noted. In the process of developing a typology of vision reports he noted the dialogical features of the reports in Zechariah, which reports he saw as occupying a mediating position between prophetic and apocalyptic visions.

Another important prophetic genre is the symbolic action. Fohrer, who has made the only extensive study (1952, 1953) of the reports, found thirty-two of them in the OT, most in first person style, although some are narratives about prophetic activity. In their most extensive form, the reports include Yahweh's command to perform the action, the report of its performance, and its interpretation, often as the word of Yahweh (2 Kgs 13:14–19; Hos 1:2–9). However, one also finds only two of these elements (command and interpretation, Isa 8:1–4; Jer 16:2–4; or report and interpretation, 1 Kgs 11:29–31; Jer 28:10–11), and sometimes only one element (command, Isa 7:3; report, 1 Kgs 19:19–21; explanation, Isa 20:1–6) (1953:18). Fohrer took the original Sitz im Leben of the reports to be magical activities. It has become clear that such reports are part and parcel of the prophetic message—either originally or as interpreted by later tradents—and that they, like the prophetic words, were believed to set Yahweh's future into motion (cf. 2 Kgs 13:14–19).

The Growth and Composition of Prophetic Books

As indicated above, the term "traditio-historical" has been used in at least two different senses in the study of the prophetic literature. One use, the analysis of traditional theological themes, has been considered. The other, and perhaps more common, form of traditio-historical research is the inquiry into the history of the transmission and eventual composition of the prophetic books, including what has also been called redaction criticism.

The most important general treatment of the question of the development of the prophetic literature to appear in our era was published at its very beginning: Mowinckel's *Prophecy and Tradition: The Prophetic Books in the Light of the Study of the Growth and History of the Tradition* (1946). Mowinckel's monograph was to a great extent a reaction against the views of, for the most part, other Scandinavian scholars (for the literature see Gunneweg) who, according to Mowinckel, had made the mistakes of rejecting the results of literary-critical research, had exaggerated the role of oral tradition, and had in effect refused to investigate the *history* of the tradition in favor of accepting the final written forms of the books as the commitment of the oral tradition directly to writing. Engnell and others whom Mowinckel opposed considered it virtually impossible to distinguish in the books between the original prophetic words and the voice of later tradents. (For a somewhat more cautious statement of the Scandinavian "oral tradition" perspective, see Engnell.) Mowinckel argued, on the contrary, for the sort of combination of careful source-critical, form-critical, and traditio-historical research that came to be characteristic of the last few decades in the study of the prophetic literature. Both written and oral tradition must be taken into account, "both with the work of the transmitting process and of consciously working 'authors' on the collection, arrangement and shaping of the tradition" (33).

Mowinckel's general picture of the development of the prophetic books was typical of the dominant perspective on the question. The original form of the prophetic "speech" was the relatively brief and independent saying. Separate sayings were transmitted by oral tradition in prophetic circles, sometimes unchanged but sometimes adapted to new circumstances; at any rate they had a life in tradition because they served religious purposes for the circles who passed them on. Eventually "tradition complexes" and collections developed as sayings were combined with one another. Finally the complexes became books, although the process of writing down the tradition would have begun earlier and continued side by side with oral tradition (60). Consequently, Mowinckel argued that each stage in this process should be analyzed and that it was not out of the question to search for the *ipsissima verba* of the prophets:

> "Behind the tradition" there loom, after all, the powerful figures of the prophets, who have created that very tradition, and in a number of cases their "own words" speak to us so clearly that we cannot take amiss. We are not going to allow anybody to deprive us of the right to attempt to let them speak as clearly as possible. (88; see also Clements, 1976:64–70)

Many of Mowinckel's views were carried forward by Gunneweg, who tested many of the claims of the Scandinavian oral tradition school and found them wanting. While he agreed that in the preexilic period oral tradition was the usual means of transmission, he showed that writing was important as well and that both oral and written tradition contributed to the final forms of the books. Some prophets, including Isaiah, Jeremiah, and Ezekiel, had a part in the initiation of the written tradition. In no sense, then, should literary-critical work be abandoned. Gerhardsson found unacceptable Gunneweg's conclusions that the oral tradition was passed on in the everyday life ("the father's house") and that the written tradition had its Sitz im Leben in the sanctuary (219). He also challenged the view that it was the written tradition that was dominant and normative. (See also Eissfeldt's 1948 article, which is mainly a review of Mowinckel's book.)

Zimmerli, whose article on the subject (1979) was conceived as a response to Gunneweg, was optimistic about the possibility of recovering the original prophetic words from the books. He pointed to the texts (such as Isa 8:1ff. and 30:8) that refer to recording the prophetic words as evidence that the written tradition began in their own lifetimes. On the other hand, Zimmerli was also concerned about the final form of the prophetic books and the theological perspectives of their redactors. Regarding the late additions to Amos (e.g., 9:11ff.), he insisted that they do not deny the judgmental words of the prophet but rather place them into a broader context and interpret them in the light of an understanding of the will of God for his people (491). The Deuteronomistic redaction of the book of Jeremiah, for example, did not destroy the primary prophetic message; rather, in the context of the exile, when the realities of Jeremiah's words had been experienced, it affirmed the validity of those words and considered their implications for the future (see 493–94).

Only very recently have redaction-critical concerns come to the fore, at least in the sense of interest in the theological perspectives as well as the editorial activities of the final redactors of the prophetic books. Works have appeared which investigate the canonical form of the books and emphasize the importance of that form (Childs), which seek the patterns within the prophetic canon (judgment/salvation) and stress the eschatological meaning of the final shape (Clements, 1977), or which consider the function of the superscriptions of the books in their interpretation and eventual canonization (Tucker, 1977). These examples represent only the tip of an iceberg; no longer can the final stage in the prophetic tradition be ignored or relegated to secondary importance. Very important in these and similar developments is the tendency to reject the value judgments—both explicit and implicit—of source criticism that the "original" prophetic utterances were more authoritative than the additions of redactors and other later interpreters. However, it would be unfortunate if the preference of source criticism—and early form criticism—for the earliest stages of the tradition were simply transferred to the final, "canonical" form of the text.

It is perhaps in the recent commentaries on the prophetic books that the changed situation from a source-critical to a traditio-historical and redaction-critical perspective is most obvious. Only a few examples can be mentioned. Whereas an earlier generation had considered large sections of Ezekiel to be late and had struggled to find original poetry in much of the prose of the book, Zimmerli (1969) accepts most of the book as coming from the prophet, whose mark is evident on the whole; there is a continuity between prophet and his school. In general there is greater reluctance to consider material to be the work of later editors simply because it announces salvation instead of judgment (contrast Wolff, 1965, and Rudolph, 1966, on Hosea with earlier commentaries).

But at the same time the work of later annotators and redactors is not ignored; on the contrary, detailed and precise accounts of the history of the transmission and redactions of the books are presented. While Wolff and Rudolph do not agree concerning the history of the book of Hosea, both saw several distinct redactional stages, from original oral traditions and tradition complexes through a Judean redaction or two to the final form of the book. Wolff (1969:106ff.) found some six distinct redactional stages in the little book of Amos. While many have objected that such analysis cuts too sharply, and although not every step will have occurred as reconstructed, it must be recognized that the actual process of growth, development, and composition will have been even more complicated.

III. THE BACKGROUNDS AND ORIGINS
OF ISRAELITE PROPHECY

Prophecy in the Mari Texts

Before the discovery and publication of the Mari texts, ancient Near Eastern evidence for prophetic phenomena comparable to that in ancient Israel was quite limited. The best known and most widely used account was the Egyptian story of Wen-Amon, who says he witnessed in the court of the Prince of Byblos a youth who was possessed by the god and then delivered an oracle. However, in recent decades more and more Mari texts with references to various "prophetic" figures and their messages have appeared, and along with them a steady stream of studies on the subject.

When only a few of the texts had been published, Westermann (1964, 1967) rushed to some unjustified conclusions, including the judgment that the formulas and the form of address in the texts supported the identification of prophetic speech as messenger speech. Ellermeier, whose study is among the most extensive and careful, vigorously opposed many of Westermann's conclusions. He pointed out that Westermann had misinterpreted an account of a dream or vision in one of the texts as an actual event, and he marshaled evidence that the prophecies were not messenger speech: in some thirty oracles there are only three cases of the god's sending the "prophet," and all of them came in writing, many with the specific instructions that they be conveyed in written form. Ellermeier analyzed the structure, form, and content of the oracles, concluding that some were long and some short and that oracles appeared with reports of dreams or visions. Moreover, in the Mari "prophecies" the basic form is not the judgment speech, but various forms appear, most of them with the goal of establishing good relations with the deity. Ellermeier's analysis of the Mari texts is basically sound, but problematic is his assumption that "what was true of prophecy at Mari was also true of prophecy at Israel" (Walters: 80). Significant differences are apparent.

Major disagreements concerning the interpretation of these texts, and in particular their relation to Israelite prophecy, turn on how broadly one defines "prophecy" and, consequently, how many of the texts actually refer to something comparable to the Israelite phenomenon. Orlinsky (1965) objected to the comparison on the grounds that the Mari texts referred to divination and not prophecy. Moran, on the other hand, included more texts than most scholars in his investigation because of a broad and somewhat loose understanding of prophecy. He presented translations and interpretations of some fourteen letters from ARM X because they "cite prophecies, dreams or other channels of revelation . . ." (16). Malamat was more specific in his definition of the Mari "diviner-prophets," and more cautious about the parallels with the OT. He saw them as parallel to the prophets of the OT in their consciousness of mission and their willingness to speak uninvited to the authorities in the name of the god, but "the all-too obvious gap is apparent in the essence of the prophetic message and in the destiny assigned to the prophet's mission" (208). The Mari oracles address the ruler or his representatives—and not the nation as a whole—and express material concerns or local patriotism (208).

H. Huffmon (1968, 1976a, 1976b) has been particularly helpful in delineating the terminology for the prophetic figures at Mari and in working with a clear definition of prophecy, especially in contrast with divination: the prophet is "an inspired speaker, under divine constraint or commission, who publicly announces an immediate revelation" (1976b: 697). He distinguished between speakers with or without titles; the latter were private persons rather than cult personnel. Three titles appear with some frequency. The āpilu/āpiltu, understood as "answerer," could be male or female, usually was related to a specific deity, and could operate in a group. The title assinnu, in later times applied to cultic officials of the goddess Ishtar, at Mari was connected with Annunitum, a form of Ishtar. The designation muḫḫū/muḫḫūtu, "ecstatic," was applied to both men and women who served official cultic functions. Huffmon has also shown that some oracles were given in response to an inquiry or in response to a sacrificial offering and that they could be presented in the temple or elsewhere. Huffmon identified most of the communications as oracles of assurance (1976b:699). Although he was careful not to exaggerate the connections, Huffmon viewed these texts as important for understanding the background of Israelite prophecy (see also Hayes, 1967).

The most recent major treatment of the Mari texts, and also one of the most careful, is that of Noort, who is not at all convinced that the Mari "prophets" were the predecessors of those known from the OT or even that the two were related. In at least the last point he certainly goes too far, for the two are phenomenologically if not historically related. Whether or not one accepts his conclusion that the Mari oracles are basically unlike OT prophecy, he has presented a very useful analysis of the various means of revelation at Mari and of the roles of both the speakers and their addressees. The messages are quite diverse, but they have in common the communication of a word of a god in a situation of crisis.

Apart from the Mari texts there are not a great many other ancient Near Eastern "prophetic" documents to consider (for a summary see Huffmon, 1976b). What Grayson and Lambert (as others before them) called Akkadian "prophecies" were texts that describe the reigns of unnamed kings cast in the form of predictions, sometimes evaluating the reign as a good or bad time by using formulas from omen texts. They noted certain similarities to expressions in the book of Daniel (10). The Egyptian genre identified as "prophecy" predicts the future but not in the form of a communication of the deity (Huffmon, 1976b:697). Herrmann, however, argued that the comparison of Israelite and Egyptian texts is fruitful, revealing some parallels (1963). Concerning other Northwest Semitic material and the possibility of not just phenomenological but also historical connections with Israel, Ross analyzed the inscription of Zakir of Lu'ash and Hamath (ninth–eighth century B.C.E.). His attention was drawn to the account of Zakir's prayer and the response by means of seers and by means of messengers. "Both in general content and in specific terminology the closest parallels to this portion of the Zakir stele are to be found in the Old Testament" (3). He was not satisfied that either Israel or Hamath borrowed from one another; he looked for a common origin. This he found in the Mari texts. Through a number of complicated—and not altogether convincing—steps he attempted to show that Hamath (and Israel) can be linked with Mari.

The Origins of Prophecy

The appearance of the Mari texts and the renewed interest in some of the older ones such as the Neo-Assyrian prophecies (Huffmon, 1976a:175), as well as form-critical and traditio-historical work, have brought new perspectives on the question of the origin and development of early Israelite prophecy. Huffmon has suggested that to ask about the "origins" of prophecy may actually be the wrong question since the phenomenon is known in most cultures (1976a:171). In the past, the prevailing view was that Israelite prophecy emerged in the time of Samuel and out of Canaanite backgrounds, as suggested by OT reports of prophets of both Baal and Yahweh. The new materials show that, while "prophecy" was not everywhere the same and while in Mesopotamia it was never a central part of the religious institutions, prophecy did not in fact arise either in Israel or in Canaanite culture without significant antecedents (cf. Herrmann, 1976).

The OT sources for the early history of prophecy in Israel are difficult since no writings of the first prophets have been preserved; virtually all reports of their activities are retained in the Deuteronomistic history (Wilson, 1978:4). However, there is a growing awareness that early prophecy was diverse and its history complex. Some early prophets were related directly to the cult but others were not; some were ecstatics. However, "all of them delivered messages based on their understanding of Israel's covenant traditions" (Wilson, 1978:16). Rendtorff's important study of the early history of prophecy (1962b) stressed the connections with these traditions and the institutions which passed them on. Without serious recourse to the nonbiblical sources, he looked for the roots of prophecy by examining the traditions about it. In spite of the diversity, he conceived of the phenomenon of prophecy in Israel as a unified whole (16), which he tended to define in terms of charismatic activity. He stressed the roots of prophecy in the amphictyonic traditions and then looked for its prehistory, which he suggested would be found in the nomadic life of the tribes before the conquest.

IV. THE ROLE AND SOCIAL LOCATION OF THE PROPHET

In recent decades there has been a noticeable shift from a preoccupation with the individuality of the prophets—in some ways the remnants of romanticism and idealism—to a concern with the role of the prophet and prophecy as an institution. It is taken for granted now and has been for some time that there was an institution—or institutions—of prophecy in Israel. However, its nature, whether it was one or several, and by what means and evidence it is to be defined are far from settled. With regard to these general questions there has been movement since the end of World War II from concentration on the question of cultic prophecy and on ecstatic experience to the sociological and anthropological issues.

Cultic Prophecy

In 1951 O. Eissfeldt identified one of the central themes of recent research as the linking of the prophets more closely to the cult (119ff.; cf. also Neumann: 28ff.). The impetus for the view that there were cultic prophets in ancient Israel goes back to Mowinckel's *Psalmenstudien* III (1923) and even before that to Hölscher's *Die Profeten* (1914). One early work was Haldar's study of prophecy in the context of Mesopotamian evidence. He virtually equated the OT prophets with guilds of diviners known from Babylonian texts. He considered the OT seer to be the equivalent of the Babylonian *bārû*, diviner, and the prophet parallel to the *maḫḫû*, an ecstatic who gives oracles. He saw no difference between the preclassical and the classical prophets concerning their relationship to the cult: seers and prophets, both early and late, were organized into groups related to the cult. Even Amos, he said, was a cultic official (79). Few scholars have rallied around Haldar's banner. A more enduring early monograph was Johnson's *The Cultic Prophet in Ancient Israel*. Johnson examined the biblical evidence carefully and built up a persuasive case that there were cultic prophets with definite functions in worship. He discerned that prophecy was by no means a single institution or function in Israel. He explicitly did not commit himself on the question of the relation of the classical prophets to the cult (29–30) but showed that in any case ritual activity was an important background for them (see also Kapelrud).

Since these early works, views have ranged from the cautious judgment of Rowley to the almost thoroughgoing cultic interpretation of Reventlow. Rowley was persuaded that the radical distinction between priest and prophet had been exaggerated in the past; while he was willing to accept the possibility that there were cultic prophets, he did not consider the major canonical prophets members of such guilds (1956:359; see also Hesse and Wolff, 1956:225). Hentschke, whose monograph included a somewhat negative assessment of the cult in Israel, challenged the view that prophecy was originally cultic, recognized that prophecy was a complex phenomenon, knew there were some cultic prophets, but insisted that the main "oppositional" (classical) prophets were not part of the cult. However, some scholars recognized in quite a number of prophetic texts, especially Habakkuk and Joel, liturgical and ritual materials (see Clements, 1976:69ff.). Few have taken such form-critical indications further than Reventlow, whose various works have related many of the classical prophets to one or another cultic function. Reventlow has often been criticized (Gross; Rendtorff, 1962b:148), and not without reason: more often than the evidence will bear, he concludes that use of traditions or genres proves cultic function.

J. Jeremias's study of cultic prophecy in the late monarchy, on the other hand, is a model of the careful use of form-critical, traditio-historical, and redaction-critical methods to determine the social location of the prophets in question. He rejected the view that all prophets were cultic personnel, but he acknowledges there were cultic prophets, organized into guilds, part of the royal service in the temple, and active especially in services of lamentation and rituals of fasting. In many cases priestly and prophetic functions could overlap. He pointed out that the interpretation of Nahum as a cultic prophet depends upon the conclusion that the book is a unity and upon a particular understanding of his words of judgment (12). After a detailed analysis, Jeremias concluded that a great many individual units, as well as the final structure of the book (a prophetic liturgy), are late. Nahum, therefore, was not himself a cultic prophet, but the cult claimed—and cultic prophets used—the Nahum tradition. Habakkuk, on the other hand, is the foremost canonical

instance of the cultic prophet, although additions to the book have made
it even more suitable for liturgical use in the late exilic period. Evidence
from Habakkuk as well as certain psalms (12; 14; 75; 82; 50; 81; 95) shows
that cultic prophets proclaimed the word of God to the people and
interceded with God on their behalf. They identified sin and announced
judgment and operated mainly in rituals of lamentation during times of
trouble.

Ecstatic Phenomena

Given the rise of psychology in the late nineteenth century and the
history-of-religions perspective in OT scholarship early in the twentieth,
it was perhaps inevitable that attention would turn to the psychology of
the prophets. Gunkel, and especially Hölscher (*Die Profeten*, 1914),
focused attention in particular on the ecstatic experiences of the prophets. Early in the era under review the question of the nature of the prophetic experiences seemed to be a central one (Rowley, 1945:91; Wolff,
1956a), but remarkably little attention has been devoted to the question
recently.

One work on this question, however, deserves special attention. Perhaps in part because his interpretation of prophetic ecstasy is part of an
outstanding introduction to the prophets as a whole, Lindblom's view
(1962) has survived those of most of his critics. Approaching the question
of the prophetic experiences from a phenomenological perspective, he
distinguished between two forms of ecstasy. When the term is applied to
the state in which the ego loses consciousness of itself and becomes
absorbed in the divine, it does not apply to the OT prophets. It is the
other form, "concentration ecstasy," which applies to the prophets: a
mental state in which consciousness is so concentrated on a particular
idea or feeling "that the normal current of thoughts and perceptions is
broken off and the senses temporarily cease to function in a normal way"
(106). Lindblom then defined prophecy, whether in Israel or elsewhere,
primarily but not exclusively in terms of such experiences. The prophet
is "*a person who, because he is conscious of having been specially chosen and called, feels forced to perform actions and proclaim ideas
which, in a mental state of intense inspiration or real ecstasy, have
been indicated to him in the form of divine revelations*" (46).

Most of those who disagreed with Lindblom's position (e.g., Seierstad) did so on the grounds that emphasis on supranormal experiences
would minimize the personal and the rational in the prophetic messages.
Rowley insisted that "the true prophets are Yahweh's spokesmen, not His
ravers" (1945:21), and that "the prophet's message always bore the mark
of the personality of the man through whom it came" (1945:36). Lindblom's careful definitions of inspiration and ecstasy, however, rendered

most such criticisms impotent (Lindblom, 1962:423–24). Many of Lindblom's early critics accused him of minimizing the personal and the individual in the prophets. But that was not the case; if he erred it was in the direction of emphasizing individual experience at the expense of the social context of prophecy. Consequently, although he had sophisticated ideas about the importance of tradition, his summary of the theology of the prophets did not adequately resolve the question of the old and the new in their messages; it tended to stress the new.

The Social Location of Prophecy

There is a sense in which the question of the place of the prophets in the institutions of ancient Israel has been a persistent issue for the past several decades. Insofar as form-critical studies attempted to relate literature to a Sitz im Leben, it focused on the social location—or background—of that literature and hence of those who produced and/or preserved it. Various genres were linked with the cult, with legal institutions, with "wisdom" practitioners, and others. Moreover, there have been investigations of the relation between the prophets and political or military institutions, some studies primarily concerned with genres and their settings (Bach, 1962; Hillers; Dion), but others more broadly focused (Gottwald; Donner, 1963, 1964; Jenni). Some progress was made, but with the form-critical works progress more often concerned the "original" or "formal" setting than the social location of prophecy itself. However, recently several scholars have addressed that question more directly, some of them by drawing upon data or theory from anthropology, folklore studies, or sociology.

One important study was that of the sociologist Peter Berger. Berger's goal was to reconsider Max Weber's view of the importance of charismatic individuals in social change on the basis of the new understanding of Israelite prophecy. Weber had depended upon the best OT scholarship of his time, which saw the prophets as innovative, charismatic individuals, the originators of, among other things, "ethical monotheism." That interpretation in turn provided support for his explanation of social change in general. Berger correctly recognized that the late nineteenth-century view of prophecy had undergone significant changes. He stressed the connection of the prophets with the cult and proposed that Weber's theory of charisma and its importance in social change would then need to be modified to deemphasize the noninstitutional character of charisma. James G. Williams responded directly to Berger, challenging his interpretation of the scholarly work on Israelite prophecy, disagreeing that the classical prophets were cultic personnel, and insisting that they were charismatic figures "not subject to the institutional forms governed by the ruling groups of society . . ." (159). At least certain prophets—Amos, Isaiah, Jeremiah, and Hosea—"were completely alienated from cultic observance . . ." (164). Berger had actually been more cautious than Williams indicates, stating only that the canonical prophets "were closely associated with the cult" (948). Still, it is accurate to say that Berger overemphasized the cultic interpretation of prophecy. Nevertheless, his analysis is fundamentally sound and is consistent with a considerable amount of recent research: the Israelite prophets, early and late, were not solitary, isolated individuals but were part of social institutions and related to other institutional structures in Israel. It was the nature of those institutional relationships which remained to be defined more explicitly.

Several recent works have made explicit use of anthropological data and/or theories to explicate one or another problem in understanding prophecy. Simon Parker used a theoretical framework from anthropological studies of "altered states of consciousness" and their relationship to social change to address the issue of ecstatic experience in Israel. He concluded that "possession trance" and prophecy were distinct phenomena and that the former was not an element of the latter. Thomas Overholt has brought anthropological data to bear on the question of the institutional relation between the prophets and their audiences (1974, 1977, 1979). His concerns were the interaction among the parties and the dynamics of the process. He showed that the communication that took place both in Jeremiah's "relevatory experiences" and in his messages did not move in just one direction: "Without the god and the people there can be no prophet" (1977:144). Overholt addressed the question of the authority of Amos (1979) by using this same theory together with some specific data on parallel phenomena in native American cultures and New Guinea cargo cults. If prophets held a regular office in, e.g., the cult or the court, they were under the control and authority of superiors in the institution. Regardless of the official institutional authorization, there was also "process-specific" authority: "The hearers assume that they know how real prophets ought to function, and they accept or reject a given prophet on the basis of these preconceptions. . . . This authorizing process is the social reality that lies behind Amos 2:11–13 and 7:10–17" (532). Burke Long (1977) used similar evidence and sociological theory to address the question of prophetic authority, focusing upon the vocation accounts. Whereas Overholt examined the location of prophetic activity itself, Long concluded that the reports of the calls (as well as Amos 7:10–17) relate most directly to problems of authority among the tradents, as they looked back on the departed prophet (13). Concerning the prophets themselves, his view was similar to that of Overholt: "Legitimacy, and hence authority, can be accorded one who conforms to a consensual notion of piety, ethics, or demeanor" (18). Long has also used field studies by anthropologists and folklorists to shed light on the general question of oral tradition (1976b), the issue of Sitz im Leben (1976c), and the setting of prophetic miracle stories (1975).

The only comprehensive investigation of the social location of Israelite prophecy in our time is Robert Wilson's recent book (1980). The volume is a major contribution in terms of both method and substance. Without ignoring the contributions of prior research on the social location of prophecy, Wilson set a new course, which he identified as a "cross-disciplinary approach." He used field studies by anthropologists and sociologists of prophecy in modern societies in order to understand the social dimensions of the phenomenon in Israel (14). Because he was aware that comparative data can easily be misused, Wilson established a series of guidelines for its application (15–16). The introduction of the comparative data begins with a useful discussion of the major terms used for prophetic and related figures. Wilson accepted the term "intermediary" as a neutral, general title that applies to several of the specialists: "Prophet, shaman, medium, and diviner are all characterized by the fact that in some way they serve as intermediaries between the human and divine worlds . . ." (28). In analyzing the social functions of the modern intermediaries as well as those in the ancient Near East and in Israel, Wilson distinguished between "peripheral" and "central" intermediaries. The former generally advance the views of the spirits and of their own support groups while the latter are concerned with maintaining the established order and regulating the pace of change (88). The investigation of the OT figures distinguishes between the Ephraimite and the Judean traditions. Those in the early Ephraimite tradition, using stereotypical speech patterns and standard behavior, were considered central figures, the "only legitimate means of communication between God and the people" (251). They performed important social maintenance functions, including those of the cult. After the rise of the monarchy, however, they became peripheral, spokesmen for the views of their support groups, attempting to change the social structure (251–52). The picture from the Judean traditions is more complicated, with little evidence for stereotypical behavior. Although there were exceptions, for the most part the Judean tradition sees the intermediaries functioning within the central social structure "to assure orderly change and the preservation of the old traditions" (294). There were some peripheral Judean prophets, and some, like Isaiah, may have oscillated between peripheral and central (295). While his treatment of specific prophets certainly can be challenged here and there, it is clear that Wilson has been judicious and careful in his use of the comparative data, has brought precision to the terminology for prophecy and society, and has shown how sociological theory can deepen our understanding of prophets in relation to Israelite society.

One other work should be mentioned briefly, Utzschneider's dissertation on Hosea. The importance of this work is its attempt to bring the sociology of knowledge—as in Berger and Luckmann, *The Social Construction of Reality*—to bear on the question of prophecy as an institution, using the book of Hosea as an example. The sociology of knowledge provides a useful definition of institution—reciprocal typification of habitualized actions by types of actors—which Utzschneider used to advantage in interpreting Hosea's perceptions in relation to the historical realities.

V. TRUE AND FALSE PROPHECY

The problem of distinguishing between true and false prophecy—not unrelated to the issue of the role of the prophets—has been a persistent, if not overwhelming, theme in OT studies throughout the period under review (see Crenshaw, 1971:13–22, 1976; Neumann: 33–39). While the problem has by no means been resolved, it appears that some clarity has been achieved in the statement of the issues. Unfortunately, particularly early in the era, there was too often the tendency to equate false prophecy with cultic prophecy (Rowley, 1956:349) or with salvation prophecy (Rowley, 1945:125; von Rad).

Various means of distinguishing true from false prophecy have been proposed. Harms suggested that they should be separated on the basis of the motivation of the individual: the true prophet knows only the divine command and commission (29). G. Quell insisted that there was no rational, controllable criterion for determining who was the true or the false prophet; only another prophet could resolve the question (cf. 1952:230). He advanced the discussion by showing that the question could not be resolved on the basis of motivation or even appearance, since Hananiah (Jeremiah 28) used the same traditions, forms of speech, and symbolic actions as Jeremiah (1952:65ff.). E. Osswald insisted that the particular historical situation was decisive, that each case and text had to be analyzed in its own terms, and that recognizing true prophecy is a decision of faith since no text serves every case.

Three of the most important studies focused on the explicit and implicit conflicts between prophets. Overholt's work (1970) was limited to the book of Jeremiah and addressed the concept of falsehood in that book. Three chapters analyzed Jeremiah's conflict with his prophetic opponents and his oracles against them (24–85). He considered the various suggestions in the book as to what makes a prophet false (37ff.) and eventually concluded that, according to the book, false prophecy was viewed primarily in terms of the message of the figure in question: the wrong message for a particular historical situation would be not only ineffective but also destructive, leading the people astray (71, 85). Hossfeld and Meyer surveyed all of the OT texts on the theme with the goal of discerning criteria for true prophecy and with some concern for the systematic and practical theological implications. They concluded that in the last analysis the true prophet was the one whose words were effective and were received canonically, that in their own time they were the outsiders, that neither the court prophet nor the cult prophet nor the salvation prophet was false per se, that the Hebrew Bible provides no practical criterion to distinguish true from false prophecy, but that the accounts of the arguments provide a model for dealing with the issue (161–63). Crenshaw (1971) likewise concentrated on the conflicts between prophets and especially on the prophets' quotation of the words of the opponents. He succeeded in looking at the issue from the perspective of those who were considered to be false prophets, leading to an appreciation of the difficulty of the issue and of the views of both sides. It was his opinion that false prophecy—and prophetic conflict concerning truth—was inevitable since there were no clear and sure criteria for true prophecy. "Human limitation and divine sovereignty combined to create prophetic conflict" (110). Prophecy declined and eventually gave way to wisdom and apocalyptic because of its own inner contradictions and inflexibility (111).

The problem of true and false prophecy is, quite simply, as difficult as determining what is and is not the word of God, or ultimate "truth." It is no wonder the Hebrew scriptures report so many different attempts to resolve the question. Nor should it be surprising that even the most careful critical investigations of the texts in question should find it difficult to keep the descriptive-historical distinct from the normative-theological in the discussion. It is difficult but not impossible to analyze, describe, and classify ancient Israel's attempts to answer this question. However, it is even more difficult to establish grounds for choosing among those answers in order to face the question: But how can one recognize true prophecy? One attempt to face that question and to bridge the gap between the descriptive and the normative is the work of Sanders. He finally introduced a theological-hermeneutical criterion, but one which he believed to be grounded in the OT understanding and resolution of the issue. While no single criterion can be applied to discern false prophecy, "surely to polytheize (Deut 13:2; 18:20) in any form whatever (including particularizing God without affirming his ontological *and* ethical integrity) is in canonical terms falsehood" (40). Sanders's hermeneutic of "monotheizing," or of moving in that direction, is a defensible, if not inevitable, position, but it should be recognized that the theological criterion—monotheism—is coupled with a distinctly historical hermeneutic.

Critical works on the prophets and the prophetic literature have been many and diverse in the last thirty-five years, but several leading themes can be recognized: the relation of the prophets to tradition, their use of traditional forms of expression, the concern with the links of Israelite prophecy to similar ancient Near Eastern phenomena, and the interest in the social location of the prophets. As the discussion of false prophecy—as well as examination of earlier works such as this one—has shown, announcing or predicting the future can be hazardous. Nevertheless, it seems safe to expect research on the prophets and the prophetic literature to be as lively in the future as it has been in the recent past. Surely the application of sociological and anthropological questions to the prophets is only just beginning. And one may expect more attention to be concentrated on the final forms of the prophetic books. Such interests are visible in the concern with the canon, in the application of form-critical questions to large (written) units, and in recent developments in literature and linguistics (see, e.g., Smalley). Such future research will be productive to the degree that it is based on the solid foundation of careful exegetical work on the actual texts that have come down to us.

BIBLIOGRAPHY

Anderson, Bernhard W., and Walter Harrelson, eds.
1962   *Israel's Prophetic Heritage: Essays in Honor of James Muilenburg*. New York: Harper & Row.

Bach, Robert
1957   "Gottesrecht und weltliches Recht in der Verkündigung des Propheten Amos." Pp. 23–34 in *Festschrift für Günther Dehn*. Ed. Wilhelm Schneemelcher. Neukirchen: Neukirchener Verlag.
1962   *Die Aufforderungen zur Flucht und zum Kampf im alttestamentlichen Prophetenspruch*. WMANT 9. Neukirchen: Neukirchener Verlag.

Baltzer, Klaus
1968   "Considerations Regarding the Office and Calling of the Prophet." *HTR* 61: 567–81.
1975   *Die Biographie der Propheten*. Neukirchen: Neukirchener Verlag.

Begrich, Joachim
1936   "Die priesterliche Tora." Pp. 63–88 in BZAW 66. Berlin: A. Töpelmann. Reprinted pp. 232–60 in *Gesammelte Studien zum Alten Testament*. TBü 21. Munich: Chr. Kaiser, 1964.

Berger, Peter L.
1963   "Charisma and Religious Innovation: The Social Location of Israelite Prophecy." *American Sociological Review* 28: 940–50.

Bergren, Richard V.
1974   *The Prophets and the Law*. HUCM 4. Cincinnati, OH:
                Hebrew Union College–Jewish Institute of Religion.

Beyerlin, Walter
1959   *Die Kulttraditionen Israels in der Verkündigung des
                Propheten Micha*. FRLANT 72. Göttingen: Vanden-
                hoeck & Ruprecht.

Blenkinsopp, Joseph
1977   *Prophecy and Canon: A Contribution to the Study of
                Jewish Origins*. Notre Dame Center for the Study of
                Judaism and Christianity in Antiquity, 3. Notre Dame:
                University of Notre Dame Press.

Brueggemann, Walter
1968   *Tradition for Crisis: A Study in Hosea*. Richmond: John
                Knox.

Buss, Martin J.
1976   "Prophecy in Ancient Israel." Pp. 694–97 in *IDBSup*.

Carroll, Robert P.
1979   *When Prophecy Failed: Cognitive Dissonance in the
                Prophetic Traditions of the Old Testament*. New York:
                Seabury.

Childs, Brevard S.
1978   "The Canonical Shape of the Prophetic Literature." *Int*
                32: 46–55.

Christensen, Duane L.
1975   *Transformation of the War Oracle in Old Testament
                Prophecy: Studies in the Oracles Against the Nations*.
                HDR 3. Missoula, MT: Scholars Press.

Clements, R. E.
1965   *Prophecy and Covenant*. SBT 43. London: SCM.
1975   *Prophecy and Tradition*. Atlanta: John Knox.
1976   *One Hundred Years of Old Testament Interpretation*.
                Philadelphia: Westminster.
1977   "Patterns in the Prophetic Canon." Pp. 42–55 in *Canon
                and Authority: Essays in Old Testament Religion and
                Theology*. Ed. Burke O. Long and George W. Coats.
                Philadelphia: Fortress.

Clifford, Richard J.
1966   "The Use of HOY in the Prophets." *CBQ* 28: 458–64.

Crenshaw, James L.
1971   *Prophetic Conflict: Its Effect upon Israelite Religion*.
                BZAW 124. Berlin: Walter de Gruyter.
1976   "Prophecy, false." Pp. 201–2 in *IDBSup*.

Dietrich, M.
1972   *Prophetie und Geschichte*. Göttingen: Vandenhoeck & Ruprecht.

Dion, Paul-Eugene (H.-M.)
1970   "The 'Fear Not' Formula and Holy War." *CBQ* 32: 565–70.

Donner, Herbert
1963   "Die soziale Botschaft der Propheten im Lichte der Gesellschaftsordnung in Israel." *OrAnt* 2: 220–45.
1964   *Israel unter den Völkern: Die Stellung der klass. Propheten des 8. Jh.v.Chr. zur Aussenpolitik der Könige von Israel u. Juda*. VTSup 11. Leiden: E. J. Brill.

Eissfeldt, Otto
1948   "Zur Überlieferungsgeschichte der Prophetenbücher des Alten Testaments." *TLZ* 73: 529–34. Reprinted pp. 55–60 in *Kleine Schriften* III. Ed. R. Sellheim and Fritz Maass. Tübingen: J. C. B. Mohr, 1966.
1951   "The Prophetic Literature." Pp. 114–61 in *The Old Testament and Modern Study*. Ed. H. H. Rowley. Oxford: Clarendon.

Ellermeier, Friedrich
1968   *Prophetie in Mari und Israel*. Theologische und Orientalische Arbeiten, 1. Herzberg: Erwin Jungfer.

Engnell, Ivan
1969   "Prophets and Prophetism in the Old Testament." Pp. 123–79 in *A Rigid Scrutiny: Critical Essays on the Old Testament*. Ed. and trans. John T. Willis. Nashville: Vanderbilt University Press. Swedish original, 2d ed. in 1962.

Fichtner, Johannes
1949   "Jesaja unter den Weisen." *TLZ* 74: 75–80.

Fohrer, Georg
1951–52   "Neuere Literatur zur alttestamentlichen Prophetie." *TRu* N.F. 19: 277–346; 20: 193–271, 295–361.
1952   "Die Gattung der Berichte über symbolische Handlungen der Propheten." ZAW 64: 101–20.
1953   *Die symbolischen Handlungen der Propheten*. ATANT 25. Zürich: Zwingli.
1961   "Remarks on Modern Interpretation of the Prophets." *JBL* 80: 309–19.
1962   "Zehn Jahre Literatur zur alttestamentlichen Prophetie (1951–1960)." *TRu* N.F. 28: 1–75, 235–97, 301–74.
1967   *Studien zur alttestamentlichen Prophetie (1949–1965)*. BZAW 99. Berlin: A. Töpelmann.
1975–76   "Neue Literatur zur alttestamentlichen Prophetie (1961–1970)." *TRu* N.F. 40: 193–209, 337–77; 41: 1–12.

Gerhardsson, Birger
1961   "Mündliche und schriftliche Tradition der Propheten-
                    bücher." *TZ* 17: 216–20.

Gerstenberger, Erhard
1962   "The Woe-Oracles of the Prophets." *JBL* 81: 249–63.

Gottwald, Norman K.
1964   *All the Kingdoms of the Earth.* New York: Harper &
                    Row.

Gouders, Klaus
1971   "Zu einer Theologie der prophetischen Berufung."
                    BibLeb 12: 79–93.

Grayson, A. K., and W. G. Lambert
1964   "Akkadian Prophecies." *JCS* 18: 7–30.

Gross, H.
1964   "Gab es in Israel ein 'prophetisches Amt'?" *TTZ* 73:
                    336–49.

Gunneweg, Antonius H. J.
1959   *Mündliche und schriftliche Tradition der vorexilischen
                    Prophetenbücher als Problem der neueren Propheten-
                    forschung.* FRLANT 73. Göttingen: Vandenhoeck &
                    Ruprecht.

Habel, Norman
1965   "The Form and Significance of the Call Narratives."
                    ZAW 77: 297–323.

Haldar, Alfred
1945   *Associations of Cult Prophets among the Ancient
                    Semites.* Uppsala: Almqvist & Wiksell.

Hardmeier, Christof
1978   *Texttheorie und biblische Exegese: Zur rhetorischen
                    Funktion der Trauermetaphorik in der Prophetie.*
                    BEvT 79. Munich: Chr. Kaiser.

Harms, Klaus
1947   *Die falschen Propheten: Eine biblische Untersuchung.*
                    Göttingen: Vandenhoeck & Ruprecht.

Harvey, Julien
1962   "Le 'Rîb-Pattern,' réquisitoire prophétique sur la rupture
                    de l'alliance." *Bib* 43: 172–96.
1967   *Le plaidoyer prophétique contre Israël après la rupture
                    de l'alliance.* Studia 22. Montreal: Les Editions Bellar-
                    min.

Hayes, John H.
1963   "The Tradition of Zion's Inviolability." *JBL* 82: 419–26.
1967   "Prophetism at Mari and Old Testament Parallels." *ATR*
                    49: 397–409.

1968	"The Usage of Oracles Against Foreign Nations in Ancient Israel." *JBL* 87: 81–92.
1973	"The History of the Form-Critical Study of Prophecy." Pp. 60–99 in *SBL 1973 Seminar Papers*. Ed. George W. MacRae. Vol. 1. Cambridge, MA: Society of Biblical Literature.

Henry, Marie-Louise
1969   *Prophet und Tradition: Versuch einer Problemstellung.* BZAW 116. Berlin: Walter de Gruyter.

Hentschke, Richard
1957   *Die Stellung der vorexilischen Schriftpropheten zum Kultus.* BZAW 75. Berlin: A. Töpelmann.

Herrmann, Siegfried
1963   "Prophetie in Israel und Ägypten. Recht und Grenze eines Vergleichs." Pp. 47–65 in *Congress Volume: Bonn, 1962.* VTSup 9. Leiden: E. J. Brill.
1976   *Ursprung und Funktion der Prophetie im altern Israel.* Opladen: Westdeutscher Verlag.

Heschel, Abraham
1962   *The Prophets.* New York: Harper & Row.

Hesse, Franz
1953   "Wurzelt die prophetische Gerichtsrede im israelitischen Kult?" *ZAW* 65: 45–53.

Hillers, Delbert R.
1964   *Treaty-Curses and the Old Testament Prophets.* BibOr 16. Rome: Pontifical Biblical Institute.

Holladay, John S., Jr.
1970   "Assyrian Statecraft and the Prophets of Israel." *HTR* 63: 29–51.

Horst, Friedrich
1960   "Die Visionsschilderungen der alttestamentlichen Propheten." *EvT* 20: 193–205.

Hossfeld, Frank Lothar, and Ivo Meyer
1973   *Prophet gegen Prophet. Eine Analyse der alttestamentlichen Texte zum Thema: Wahre und falsche Propheten.* BibB 9. Fribourg: Schweizerisches Katholisches Bibelwerk.

Huffmon, Herbert B.
1959   "The Covenant Lawsuit in the Prophets." *JBL* 78: 285–95.
1968   "Prophecy in the Mari Letters." *BA* 31: 101–24. Reprinted pp. 199–224 in *The Biblical Archaeologist Reader*, 3. Ed. E. F. Campbell, Jr., and D. N. Freedman. Garden City, NY: Doubleday, 1970.

1976a   "The Origins of Prophecy." Pp. 171–86 in *Magnalia Dei, The Mighty Acts of God: Essays on the Bible and Archaeology in Memory of G. Ernest Wright*. Ed. Frank Moore Cross, Werner E. Lemke, and Patrick D. Miller. Garden City, NY: Doubleday.

1976b   "Prophecy in the Ancient Near East." Pp. 697–700 in *IDBSup*.

Janzen, Waldemar

1972   *Mourning Cry and Woe Oracle*. BZAW 125. Berlin: Walter de Gruyter.

Jenni, Ernst S.

1956   *Die politischen Voraussagen der Propheten*. Zürich: Zwingli.

Jeremias, Christian

1977a   *Die Nachtgesichte des Sacharja: Untersuchungen zu ihrer Stellung im Zusammenhang der Visionsberichte im Alten Testament und zu ihrem Bildmaterial*. FRLANT 117. Göttingen: Vandenhoeck & Ruprecht.

1977b   "Die Erzväter in der Verkündigung der Propheten." Pp. 206–22 in *Beiträge zur alttestamentlichen Theologie: Festschrift für Walther Zimmerli zum 70. Geburtstag*. Ed. Herbert Donner, Robert Hanhart, Rudolf Smend. Göttingen: Vandenhoeck & Ruprecht.

Jeremias, Jörg

1970   *Kultprophetie und Geschichtsverkündigung in der späten Königszeit Israels*. WMANT 35. Neukirchen: Neukirchener Verlag.

Johnson, Aubrey R.

1944   *The Cultic Prophet in Ancient Israel*. Cardiff: University of Wales Press. (2d ed., 1962.)

Kapelrud, Arvid S.

1951   "Cult and Prophetic Words." *ST* 4: 5–12.

Koch, Klaus

1969   *The Growth of the Biblical Tradition: The Form Critical Method*. Trans. S. M. Cupitt. New York: Scribner. German original, 2d ed. in 1967.

1971   "Die Entstehung der sozialen Kritik bei den Profeten." Pp. 236–57 in *Probleme biblischer Theologie: Gerhard von Rad zum 70. Geburtstag*. Ed. Hans W. Wolff. Munich: Chr. Kaiser.

Koch, Klaus, und Mitarbeiter

1976   *Amos: Untersucht mit den Methoden einer strukturalen Formgeschichte*. 3 Parts. AOAT 30. Kevelaer: Butzon & Bercker; Neukirchen-Vluyn: Neukirchener Verlag.

Kraus, Hans-Joachim
1957   *Die prophetische Verkündigung des Rechts in Israel.*
        Theologische Studien, 51. Zurich: Evangelischer Verlag.

Limburg, James
1969   "The Root ריב and the Prophetic Lawsuit Speeches."
        JBL 88: 291–304.
1978   "The Prophets in Recent Study: 1967–77." *Int* 32: 56–68.

Lindblom, Johannes
1955   "Wisdom in the Old Testament Prophets." Pp. 192–204
        in *Wisdom in the Old Testament and in the Ancient
        Near East.* VTSup 3. Leiden: E. J. Brill.
1962   *Prophecy in Ancient Israel.* Philadelphia: Muhlenberg.

Long, Burke O.
1972   "Prophetic Call Traditions and Reports of Visions."
        ZAW 84: 494–500.
1975   "The Social Setting for Prophetic Miracle Stories."
        Semeia 3: 46–63.
1976a   "Reports of Visions Among the Prophets." *JBL* 95:
        353–65.
1976b   "Recent Field Studies in Oral Literature and their Bear-
        ing on OT Criticism." *VT* 26: 187–98.
1976c   "Recent Field Studies in Oral Literature and the Ques-
        tion of *Sitz im Leben.*" *Semeia* 5: 35–49.
1976d   "Divination as Model for Literary Form." Pp. 84–100 in
        Language in Religious Practice. Ed. W. J. Samarin.
        Rowley, MA: Newbury House.
1977   "Prophetic Authority as Social Reality." Pp. 3–20 in
        *Canon and Authority: Essays in Old Testament Reli-
        gion and Theology.* Ed. Burke O. Long and George W.
        Coats. Philadelphia: Fortress.

McKane, William
1979   "Prophecy and the Prophetic Literature." Pp. 163–88 in
        *Tradition and Interpretation: Essays by Members of
        the Society for Old Testament Study.* Ed. G. W. Ander-
        son. Oxford: Clarendon.

Malamat, Abraham
1966   "Prophetic Revelations in New Documents from Mari
        and the Bible." Pp. 207–27 in *Volume du Congrès:
        Genève, 1965.* VTSup 15. Leiden: E. J. Brill.

March, W. E.
1974   "Prophecy." Pp. 141–77 in *Old Testament Form Criti-
        cism.* Ed. John H. Hayes. San Antonio: Trinity University.

Markert, Ludwig
1977   *Struktur und Bezeichnung des Scheltworts: Eine gat-
        tungskritische Studie anhand des Amosbuches.* BZAW
        140. Berlin: Walter de Gruyter.

Moran, William L.
1969 "New Evidence from Mari on the History of Prophecy."
Bib 50: 15–56.

Mowinckel, Sigmund
1946 *Prophecy and Tradition: The Prophetic Books in the Light of the Study of the Growth and History of the Tradition.* Oslo: Jacob Dybwad.

Muilenburg, James
1965 "The 'Office' of the Prophet in Ancient Israel." Pp. 74–97 in *The Bible in Modern Scholarship.* Ed. J. P. Hyatt. Nashville: Abingdon.

Neumann, Peter H. A.
1979 "Prophetenforschung seit Heinrich Ewald." Pp. 1–51 in *Das Prophetenverständnis in der deutschsprachigen Forschung seit Heinrich Ewald.* Ed. P. H. A. Neumann. Wege der Forschung, 307. Darmstadt: Wissenschaftliche Buchgesellschaft.

Nielsen, Kirsten
1979 *Yahweh as Prosecutor and Judge: An Investigation of the Prophetic Lawsuit (Rîb-Pattern).* JSOTSup 9. Sheffield: JSOT.

Noort, Edward
1977 *Untersuchungen zum Gottesbescheid in Mari: Die 'Mari-prophetie' in der alttestamentlichen Forschung.* AOAT 202. Kevelaer: Butzon & Bercker; Neukirchen-Vluyn: Neukirchener Verlag.

Orlinsky, Harry M.
1965 "The Seer in Ancient Israel." *OrAnt* 4: 153–74.
1969, ed. *Interpreting the Prophetic Tradition: The Goldenson Lectures 1955–66.* New York: Ktav.

Osswald, Eva
1962 *Falsche Prophetie im Alten Testament.* Tübingen: J. C. B. Mohr.

Overholt, Thomas W.
1970 *The Threat of Falsehood: A Study in the Theology of the Book of Jeremiah.* SBT 2/15. Naperville, IL: Alec R. Allenson.
1974 "The Ghost Dance of 1890 and the Nature of the Prophetic Process." *Ethnohistory* 21: 37–63.
1977 "Jeremiah and the Nature of the Prophetic Process." Pp. 129–50 in *Scripture in History and Theology: Essays in Honor of J. Coert Rylaarsdam.* Ed. Arthur L. Merrill and Thomas W. Overholt. PTMS 17. Pittsburg: Pickwick.
1979 "Commanding the Prophets: Amos and the Problem of Prophetic Authority." *CBQ* 41: 517–32.

Parker, Simon B.
1978   "Possession Trance and Prophecy in Pre-exilic Israel."
                VT 28: 271–85.

Quell, Gottfried
1952   *Wahre und falsche Propheten.* Gütersloh: Bertelsmann.
1956   "Der Kultprophet." *TLZ* 81: 402–3.

Rad, Gerhard von
1965   *Old Testament Theology, Vol. II: The Theology of
                Israel's Prophetic Traditions.* Trans. D. M. G. Stalker.
                New York: Harper & Row. Original, 1960.

Raitt, Thomas M.
1971   "The Prophetic Summons to Repentance." *ZAW* 83:
                30–49.

Rendtorff, Rolf
1954   "Zum Gebrauch der Formel ne'um jahwe im Jeremia-
                buch." *ZAW* 66: 27–37. Reprinted pp. 256–66 in *Gesam-
                melte Studien zum Alten Testament.* TBü 57. Münich:
                Chr. Kaiser, 1975.
1956   "Priesterliche Kulttheologie und prophetische Kultpo-
                lemik." *TLZ* 81: 339–52.
1962a   "Botenformel und Botenspruch." *ZAW* 74: 165–77.
                Reprinted pp. 243–55 in *Gesammelte Studien zum
                Alten Testament.*
1962b   "Erwägungen zur Frühgeschichte des Prophetentums in
                Israel." *ZTK* 59: 145–67. Reprinted pp. 220–42 in
                Gesammelte Studien zum Alten Testament. English
                translation pp. 14–34 in *History and Hermeneutic.* Ed.
                Robert W. Funk. *JTC* 4. New York: Harper & Row,
                1967.
1973   "Die alttestamentlichen Überlieferungen als Grund-
                thema der Lebensarbeit Gerhard von Rads." Pp. 21–35
                in *Gerhard von Rad. Seine Bedeutung für Theologie.*
                Munich: Chr. Kaiser. Reprinted pp. 281–95 in *Gesam-
                melte Studien zum Alten Testament.*

Reventlow, Henning Graf
1961   "Prophetenamt und Mittleramt." *ZTK* 58: 269–84.
1962a   *Das Amt des Propheten bei Amos.* FRLANT 80. Göt-
                tingen: Vandenhoeck & Ruprecht.
1962b   *Wächter über Israel: Ezechiel und seine Tradition.*
                BZAW 82. Berlin: A. Töpelmann.
1963   *Liturgie und prophetisches Ich bei Jeremia.* Gütersloh:
                Mohn.

Rohland, Edzard
1956   *Die Bedeutung der Erwählungstraditionen Israels für
                die Eschatologie der alttestamentlichen Propheten.*
                Diss. Heidelberg. Munich.

Ross, James F.
1970   "Prophecy in Hamath, Israel and Mari." *HTR* 63: 1–28.

Rowley, H. H.
1945   "The Nature of Old Testament Prophecy in the Light of Recent Study." *HTR* 38: 1–38. Reprinted pp. 95–134 in *The Servant of the Lord and other Essays on the Old Testament*. London: Lutterworth, 1952.
1956   "Ritual and the Hebrew Prophets." *JSS* 1: 338–60.

Rudolph, Wilhelm
1966   *Hosea*. KAT 13/1. Gütersloh: Mohn.

Sanders, James A.
1977   "Hermeneutics in True and False Prophecy." Pp. 21–41 in *Canon and Authority: Essays in Old Testament Religion and Theology*. Ed. Burke O. Long and George W. Coats. Philadelphia: Fortress.

Schmidt, Werner H.
1973   *Zukunftsgewissheit und Gegenwartskritik: Grundzüge prophetischer Verkündigung*. BibS (N) 64. Neukirchen: Neukirchener Verlag.

Seierstad, Ivar P.
1946   *Die Offenbarungserlebnisse der Propheten Amos, Jesaja und Jeremia: Eine Untersuchung der Erlebnisvorgänge unter besonderer Berücksichtigung ihrer religiös-sittlichen Art und Auswirkung*. Oslo: Universitetsforlaget. (2d ed., 1965.)

Seybold, Klaus
1972   *Das davidische Königtum im Zeugnis der Propheten*. FRLANT 107. Göttingen: Vandenhoeck & Ruprecht.

Smalley, William A.
1979   "Recursion Patterns and the Sectioning of Amos." *BT* 30: 118–27.

Steck, Odil H.
1977   "Theological Streams of Tradition." Pp. 183–214 in *Tradition and Theology in the Old Testament*. Ed. Douglas A. Knight. Philadelphia: Fortress.

Terrien, Samuel
1962   "Amos and Wisdom." Pp. 108–15 in *Israel's Prophetic Heritage: Essays in Honor of James Muilenburg*. Ed. Bernhard Anderson and Walter Harrelson. New York: Harper & Row.

Tucker, Gene M.
1973   "Prophetic Authenticity: A Form Critical Study of Amos 7: 10–17." *Int* 27: 423–34.

1977 "Prophetic Superscriptions and the Growth of a Canon." Pp. 56–70 in *Canon and Authority: Essays in Old Testament Religion and Theology.* Ed. Burke O. Long and George W. Coats. Philadelphia: Fortress.

1978 "Prophetic Speech." *Int* 32: 31–45.

Utzschneider, Helmut
1980 *Hosea, Prophet vor dem Ende: Zum Verhältnis von Geschichte und Institution in der alttestamentlichen Prophetie.* OBO 31. Göttingen: Vandenhoeck & Ruprecht; Freiburg, Schweiz: Universitätsverlag.

Waldow, H. Eberhard von
1963 *Der traditionsgeschichtliche Hintergrund der prophetischen Gerichtsreden.* BZAW 85. Berlin: A. Töpelmann.

Walters, Stanley D.
1970 "Prophecy in Mari and Israel." *JBL* 89: 78–81.

Wanke, Gunther
1966 "אוי und הוי." *ZAW* 78: 215–18.

Warmuth, Georg
1976 *Das Mahnwort. Seine Bedeutung für die Verkündigung der vorexilischen Propheten Amos, Hosea, Micha, Jesaja und Jeremia.* Beiträge zur biblischen Exegese und Theologie, 1. Frankfurt: Peter Lang.

Westermann, Claus
1964 "Die Mari-Briefe und die Prophetie in Israel." Pp. 171–88 in *Forschung am Alten Testament.* TBü 24. Munich: Chr. Kaiser.

1967 *Basic Forms of Prophetic Speech.* Trans. H. C. White. Philadelphia: Westminster. German original in 1960.

Whedbee, J. William
1971 *Isaiah and Wisdom.* Nashville: Abingdon.

Whitley, Charles F.
1963 *The Prophetic Achievement.* Leiden: E. J. Brill.

Widengren, Geo
1948 *Literary and Psychological Aspects of the Hebrew Prophets.* Uppsala: Lundequist.

Wildberger, Hans
1960 *Jahwes Eigentumsvolk: Eine Studie zur Traditionsgeschichte und Theologie des Erwählungsgedankens.* ATANT 37. Zurich: Zwingli.

Williams, James G.
1969 "The Social Location of Israelite Prophecy." *JAAR* 37: 153–65.

Wilson, Robert R.
1973 "Form-critical Investigation of the Prophetic Literature:

The Present Situation." Pp. 100–21 in *SBL 1973 Seminar Papers*. Ed. George W. MacRae. Vol. 1. Cambridge, MA: Society of Biblical Literature.

1978   "Early Israelite Prophecy." *Int* 32: 3–16.

1980   *Prophecy and Society in Ancient Israel*. Philadelphia: Fortress.

Wolff, Hans Walter

1951   "Das Thema 'Umkehr' in der alttestamentlichen Prophetie." *ZTK* 48: 129–48. Reprinted pp. 130–50 in *Gesammelte Studien zum Alten Testament*. TBü 22. Munich: Chr. Kaiser, 1964.

1955   "Hauptprobleme alttestamentlicher Prophetie." *EvT* 16: 446–68. Reprinted pp. 206–31 in *Gesammelte Studien*.

1956   "Hoseas geistige Heimat." *TLZ* 81: 83–94. Reprinted pp. 232–50 in *Gesammelte Studien*.

1960   "Das Gerichtsverständnis der alttestamentlichen Prophetie." *EvT* 20: 218–35. Reprinted pp. 289–307 in *Gesammelte Studien*.

1964   *Amos' goistige Heimat*. WMANT 18. Neukirchen: Neukirchener Verlag. English trans., 1973.

1965   *Dodekapropheton 1, Hosea*. BKAT 14/1. 2d ed. Neukirchen: Neukirchener Verlag. English trans., 1977.

1969   *Dodekapropheton 2, Joel und Amos*. BKAT 14/2. 2d ed. Neukirchen: Neukirchener Verlag. English trans., 1977.

1973   *Amos the Prophet: The Man and his Background*. Trans. Foster R. McCurley. Philadelphia: Fortress. German original in 1964.

1978a   "Wie verstand Micha von Moreschet sein prophetisches Amt?" Pp. 403–17 in *Congress Volume: Göttingen, 1977*. VTSup 29. Leiden: E. J. Brill.

1978b   "Prophecy from the Eighth through the Fifth Century." *Int* 32: 17–30.

Würthwein, Ernst

1950   "Amos-studien." *ZAW* 62: 10–52.

1952   "Der Ursprung der prophetischen Gerichtsrede." *ZTK* 49: 1–16.

1963   "Kultpolemik oder Kultbescheid? Beobachtungen zum Thema 'Prophetie und Kult.'" Pp. 115–31 in *Tradition und Situation: Studien zur alttestamentlichen Prophetie*. Ed. E. Würthwein and O. Kaiser. Göttingen: Vandenhoeck & Ruprecht.

Zimmerli, Walther

1965   *The Law and the Prophets: A Study of the Meaning of the Old Testament*. Trans. R. E. Clements. New York: Harper & Row. German original in 1963.

1969   *Ezechiel 1, I. Teilband.* BKAT 13/1. Neukirchen: Neu-
        kirchener Verlag. English trans., 1979.
1977   "Prophetic Proclamation and Reinterpretation." Pp. 69–
        100 in *Tradition and Theology in the Old Testament.*
        Ed. Douglas A. Knight. Philadelphia: Fortress.
1979   "Vom Prophetenwort zum Prophetenbuch." *TLZ* 104:
        481–96.

11

The Wisdom Literature

James L. Crenshaw

I. THE ELUSIVE QUEST

Identification

Reflection upon wisdom's inaccessibility prompted Ben Sira to utter an enigmatic truism that, *like her name*, חכמה is not accessible to many (6:22). For ancient sages like Ben Sira, Job (chap. 28), and Qoheleth, wisdom remained an elusive creature. Modern lovers of wisdom have also found her to be a slippery word (Whybray, 1978). One by one, they pronounce her name, only to have her essence slip away like oil through one's fingers. "She is humanistic, international, nonhistorical, eudaemonistic," they have claimed, but each term has required qualification. The eudaemonism has a theological foundation, for God created an orderly universe that rewards virtue and punishes vice. The sayings have their own history and are altered according to new social realities. The teachings of sages represent a special tradition that is known to a limited group, and their language constitutes "in-house" speech. Face to face with ultimate mystery, humanism acknowledges its own limits arising from finitude itself.

In the same way, increasing qualification characterizes all attempts to define wisdom: the art of steering one's life successfully into harbor; practical knowledge of laws governing the world, based on experience; the total experience transmitted as a spiritual testament by a father to his son; the right deed or word for the moment; an intellectual tradition; a body of literature, a way of thinking, and a tradition. Each definition captures a significant feature of wisdom, but none of them succeeds in isolating the total phenomenon that gave birth to wisdom literature (Crenshaw, 1976a:3–5).

Extrabiblical Parallels

Israel's wisdom belonged to a larger context; her teachers seem drawn to acknowledge familiarity with truth as it had been grasped by foreign sages (the sayings of Agur; the teachings of Lemuel's mother; Job). Such openness led to actual borrowing (eleven sayings from *The Instruction of Amenemopet*) without directly identifying the Egyptian source (Bryce, 1979). This reliance upon foreign wisdom, together with great similarity of the literature in general, has encouraged current scholars to search for a definition of Israelite wisdom in terms of Egyptian and Mesopotamian parallels.

The central feature of Egyptian wisdom, the principle of *Maat* (Volten; Gese, 1958:11–21; Schmid, 1966:17–22), has influenced Israel's understanding of Dame Wisdom, particularly the cosmological speculation in Proverbs 8 (Gilbert, 1979; Kayatz), and provides the underlying presupposition of all sapiential texts. That assumption of a harmonious universe explains the optimism that characterizes early wisdom. In time, historical events brought this belief into question, and a serious crisis exploded throughout the ancient world (Schmid, 1966). In Egypt, the failure of nerve gave rise to discussion literature (in which sages expostulated with deities) and stimulated reflection upon life's futility (Otto). Noteworthy shifts within the thinking of the sages occurred: reward and punishment ceased to be automatic, and the gods interceded in the nexus of cause and effect. As a result, piety came to characterize sages, and the former optimism faded. Israel's share of Egyptian wisdom represents, for the most part, the commingling of piety and old wisdom: the weighing of the heart, righteousness as the foundation of the royal throne, the satire of professions, the royal confession, and possibly the garland of honor (Kayatz). Decisive differences between Egyptian and Israelite wisdom exist despite these resemblances. The essential distinction concerns the setting: Egyptian wisdom literature arose in connection with the royal court and its particular goals (Kalugila). That is, sapiential literature functioned in Pharaoh's palace to ensure a successful political regime (Brunner, 1952).

Mesopotamian wisdom also belonged to an entirely different social milieu from the Israelite corollary (Lambert; van Dijk; Buccellati). Both Sumerian and Akkadian wisdom arose in schools and served as texts for scholarly instruction, particularly with regard to correct ritual and proper divinatory technique. In essence, wisdom meant mastery of magical arts in connection with the cult. Lacking an assumption of an orderly cosmos, Mesopotamian sages endeavored to determine the fate of their affluent clients by enabling them to act in accord with heavenly bodies and natural signs. Here too a crisis emerged quite early, and sages composed powerful dialogues about innocent suffering, divine injustice, and suicide's attraction. Israel's sages virtually ignored encyclopedic lists and omen wisdom, despite claims to the contrary by two critics (von Rad, 1960; Bryce, 1975), but joined their Eastern neighbors in asking about human misery and in challenging God's justice.

Canaanite wisdom (Albright; Khanjian) undoubtedly thrived alongside the Israelite, Egyptian, and Mesopotamian. Like the Edomite, which OT texts acknowledge, it has not survived—except in the form of some fatherly advice to a son who is about to leave on a journey, which symbolizes life itself (Nougayrol: 47–50). Other features of Canaanite thought are hardly wisdom's exclusive domain: myths about primal human beings, royal terminology concerning obligations to ensure justice for all, and divine epithets that allude to wisdom. Ebla's contribution in this regard has not yet been determined, although sapiential texts are said to exist in this recent discovery (Pettinato: 45).

Comparisons between Israelite wisdom and that of her neighbors rely upon the labor of specialists in those disciplines. An immense wealth of information has poured forth from these circles. Reliable translations of relevant texts (*ANET*; Simpson; Lambert; Lichtheim), explanatory commentaries (Zaba; Brunner, 1944), interpretative clarification of the literary corpus in toto (Lambert; van Dijk; Brunner, 1952), and specific monographs on particular problems have greatly enriched our knowledge and opened up these texts to biblical scholars. Rare indeed are the biblical critics who make themselves at home in this alien world (Gemser, 1960; Gese, 1958; Cazelles). Occasional congresses devoted to comparisons among the several sapiential collections have fostered further insight at the expense of some oversimplification (Wendel; Kraeling and Adams).

Perhaps more debate has raged over divine freedom than over any other topic. Some biblical scholars insist that Yahweh exercised control over the ordering principle of the universe (Gese, 1958), while others claim that a given human action sets a force into motion that works itself out for good or ill apart from divine intervention (Koch, 1955). Varying attempts to understand retribution in ancient sapiential thought have therefore arisen, many of which now appear in a single volume (Koch, 1972). Such endeavors assist in clarifying a world view and suggest that belief in retribution scarcely belongs to wisdom's distinctive characteristic, since all ancient peoples shared this conception of reality (Schmid, 1974).

Intracanonical Relationship

For the most part, caution has characterized recent search for ancient Near Eastern parallels to canonical wisdom. This cannot be said for attempts to ascertain wisdom influence in the Hebrew Bible. The effort to broaden the Israelite sapiential impact threatens to sweep a substantial portion of the Bible into its path. The result may render the term wisdom so diffuse as to be utterly worthless in scholarly discussion. At the same time, this desire to relate wisdom to other traditions in the Hebrew scriptures arises from a correct intuition: the sages did not operate in complete isolation. Ironically, the case for sapiential influence often rests upon an assumption of exclusive vocabulary employed only by the sages. More often than not these words belong to the semantic field of universal discourse (good and bad, wise and foolish, knowledge, understanding, and the like).

Prophetic literature was the first to come under the sweeping claim of wisdom influence. Isaiah first (Fichtner; Whedbee, 1971; Jensen) and then Amos (Terrien, 1962; Wolff, 1964) were viewed as former sages or students of the teachers. Then came Habakkuk (Gowan), Jonah (Trible; Fretheim), and Micah (Wolff, 1978) as well as scattered passages throughout the prophetic canon. Narrative texts were viewed in the same fashion, especially the Joseph story (von Rad, 1953), the succession narrative (Whybray, 1968), Esther (Talmon), the primeval history (McKenzie; Alonso-Schökel, 1962), the lost "Acts of Solomon" (Liver), and the wooing of Rebekah (Roth). Even the book of Deuteronomy succumbed to this bold endeavor (Weinfeld), and similarities between Deutero-Isaiah and hymnic texts in Job called forth a thesis of direct relationship (Terrien, 1965). To be sure, earlier scholars had perceived many of these affinities between wisdom literature and the remaining portions of the Hebrew Bible, but they explained them as later glosses or anthological composition, largely because of an assumption that wisdom represented, for the most part, a late development.

In the light of this trend toward transforming wisdom into a kind of insatiable "Sheol figure" who swallows the rest of the Hebrew canon, a call for self-conscious methodological reflection was issued (Crenshaw, 1969). This summons included three test cases (the Joseph story, the succession narrative, and Esther) and registered a negative judgment in each instance. Another treatment of this problem focused upon the circular reasoning required in such efforts to establish influence, especially linguistic studies, although reaching more positive conclusions (Whybray, 1974). Some subsequent research has indicated an awareness of the issues (Coats), but reluctance to abandon the effort altogether seems to prevail (Morgan).

Certain assumptions have become problematic as a result of this restless search for wisdom influence. Possibly the single most important issue concerns the development of wisdom thinking in ancient Israel (Cazelles). The crucial stage is the middle one—court wisdom (Humphreys). Did clan wisdom evolve into court instruction, and did a virtual enlightenment occur during Solomon's era (von Rad, 1953; Galling, 1952)? If this putative fresh burst of humanism stands between all subsequent scholars and early wisdom, how has that new world view affected older texts? Several attempts to trace a theologization of older secular wisdom have arisen, with modest success (Whybray, 1965; McKane). As yet, no compelling description of wisdom's evolution has appeared. Three distinct stages seem likely: clan, court, and scribal wisdom (Lemaire). Even though the canonical proverbs probably derive from the first of these, a definitive analysis of clan wisdom is lacking. Its kinship with apodictic legal texts has been emphasized (Gerstenberger, 1965).

The most disconcerting feature of this drive to discern wisdom's presence outside Proverbs, Job, and Qoheleth is the assumption that certain words constitute technical vocabulary. Naturally, חכם in its various forms does yeoman's service for such a theory, despite the ambiguity of the evidence (Whybray, 1974). A single example suffices, since it has led to considerable speculation. The adjective "wise," which describes the woman of Tekoa (2 Sam 14:2), may simply mean intelligent; if so, it would provide no support for elaborate theories about Tekoa as a center for sapiential instruction and the role of women in Israelite wisdom (Camp). One additional difficulty merits comment. Sometimes technical vocabulary may function differently in Israel from the way it functions in its Egyptian counterpart. David's two counselors (יועצים) in 2 Sam 16:20–17:23 may have nothing to do with the wisdom enterprise as it manifested itself in Israel.

Distinctive Tradition

It follows that the goal of wisdom research is to understand what was distinctive about Israelite wisdom with regard to ancient Near Eastern parallels and other canonical material. Israel's sages thought in different categories; as a result, they developed a unique tradition. In a word, they believed in the sufficiency of human virtue to achieve well-being in this life, apart from divine assistance. That unbridled optimism was grounded in a theological conviction about the goodness of creation. The pathos of the wisdom literature arose from a consuming passion to maintain this belief in human sufficiency in the face of unjust suffering and divine despotism. Little by little this distinctive viewpoint collapsed—first with the emergence of a heavenly messenger, Dame Wisdom, then with theophany as the resolution of a grievous spiritual problem, and finally with Ben Sira's wholesale embracing of sacral traditions which breathed the atmosphere of God's gracious dealings with a chosen race (Rylaarsdam).

Appropriation by Modern Interpreters

Ethics and Theology

Considerable attention has centered upon religious pragmatism, both in Egypt and Israel, as the singular ingredient of sapiential ethics. The adjective that modifies pragmatism has become increasingly significant as clarification of the underlying premise of all wisdom is achieved. This cosmostatic quality inherent in every human deed bestows immense gravity upon ethical action (Schmid, 1966:22–24) and justifies hostile language which was directed at hotheaded fools who undermined the universe itself. Since divine action took place at the moment of creation rather than in the living present, the sages in Israel concentrated upon the implications of creation for human conduct. Naturally, their theology presupposed the existence of one deity, the universal creator (Zimmerli, 1963; Hermisson,

1978). Even when the special name Yahweh occurs, it connotes the Lord of heaven and earth.

Aesthetics

In the area of sapiential aesthetics, virtual neglect has prevailed until now. We do not know what ancient sages thought about beauty, either visual or auditory. Certain clues have survived, nonetheless, that may enable sensitive critics to grasp this important aspect of sapiential thought (von Rad, 1972). These include, among other things, the exquisite poetic images (especially in Job and Sirach) that sear the imagination of contemporary readers and the polished rhetoric that demonstrates profound understanding concerning the art of persuasion (Crenshaw, 1981b, 1981c).

II. THE BOOK OF PROVERBS

Growth of Individual Collections

"Nuclear" Sayings and "Brief Essays"

A decisive shift has taken place in the theory concerning an evolutionary development from the short, one-line saying to longer essays, and with this change came a tendency to view the initial collection (Proverbs 1–9) as much earlier than had otherwise been thought possible (Skladny; Kayatz). The Egyptian *Instruction of Onchsheshonqy* has played a decisive role in this shift, for that relatively late demotic text resembles the putative early collections in that it uses short, pithy sayings (Gemser, 1960). The formal evidence for a developing complexity of sayings was thereby negated, and this new insight corresponded to a growing conservative trend in dating ancient texts. Older attempts (Schmidt) to show how brief sayings later took on motivation and result clauses and became increasingly theological were questioned. This rejection of earlier hypotheses also applied to the assumption that stylistic niceties arose at a later stage when sages became much more self-consciously literate (Hermisson, 1968).

As a result, the entire proverbial collection is thought to have arisen before or during the monarchical period, and emphasis falls upon different contexts within which the separate units developed. This trend appears to be on target, provided that it does not sacrifice the gains that have accrued to various attempts to show how simple proverbs achieved complexity in form. One can retain these insights while accepting the view that brief essays existed simultaneously with succinct sayings. Besides, the evidence for gradual adaptation of originally "secular" sayings, even within collections that use the short form altogether, seems conclusive. Furthermore, some of the short essays are actually constructed around a simple proverb, which they quote as the decisive argument supporting the point of the essay (Crenshaw, 1979).

The Sociological Context

If the several collections arose in different contexts, what characterized each one? On the assumption that sages expressed their special interests, interpreters have searched for evidence pointing to the sociological milieu in which individual sayings arose (Kovacs). Two opposing views have arisen: the proverbs reflect a clan ethos (Gerstenberger, 1965), particularly in the negative employed, or they point to a school setting (Hermisson, 1968). The special kind of negative has led one critic to argue for a group ethos (W. Richter). The existence of folk proverbs has been denied (Hermisson, 1968), largely because conscious literary artistry appears in nearly all Israelite sayings. The dubious assumption that only schools prized stylistic artistry renders this argument tenuous and strengthens the position of those who endorse popular proverbs (Scott, 1972) and traditional sayings (Fontaine).

Most scholars have assumed that the intellectual tradition depended upon ample leisure to permit reflection (Gordis, 1943/44; Whybray, 1974), a view that finds support in *The Satire of the Trades* and in Sirach, as well as in the scribal tradition in postcanonical Jewish circles (Urbach). Thus, a theory that sages were wealthy landowners has experienced general acceptance, and confirmation has seemed to come above all from Qoheleth, who writes like one lacking power to redress human grievances while escaping those ills that characteristically befall the poor.

Structural Unity

Although some signs of editorial intention manifest themselves, particularly in the introduction to the book (1:1–7), the general structure of Proverbs has defied analysis. Various theories have arisen to explain the structural unity of important segments within the book. One approach relies upon numerical equivalents for the Hebrew characters in the superscriptions and envisions the entire work in the shape of a house built upon seven columns (Skehan: 9–45). Another perspective distinguishes four main sections in the "Solomonic" proverbs which manifest an architectonic unity. These include (1) chaps. 10–15, the contrast between righteousness and wickedness; (2) 16:1–22:16, Yahweh and the king; (3) chaps. 25–27, nature and agriculture; and (4) chaps. 28–29, the king or potential rulers (Skladny). The third approach focuses upon the entire book and divides it into two basic forms: (1) the sentence (Prov 10:1–22:16; 24:23–34; 25–29); and (2) instruction (Prov 1–9; 22:17–24:22; 31:1–9) (McKane). If in fact a single editor was responsible for the final form of the book, the teacher's openness to diverse viewpoints has allowed remarkable diversity to characterize the collected sayings. Precisely what principle governed the clustering of proverbs remains an unresolved issue even if a single editor is granted (Plöger; Conrad), for only a few small units seem to be joined on the basis of similar consonants, a common word, or the same sounds.

Ancient Near Eastern Parallels

Proverb collections existed in Egypt and Mesopotamia (*ANET*; Lambert; Gemser, 1960); in addition, a few isolated proverbs or proverb-like sayings have been discovered at Mari (Marzal), in the Amarna letters (Albright), and in Ahiqar (*ANET*, 427–30). Sumerian proverbs (Alster; Gordon) and Babylonian sentences and instructions (Lambert) differ greatly in content from those preserved in the Hebrew canon, whereas striking similarities between Israelite and Egyptian proverbs occur (Gemser, 1960), even apart from the actual adaptation of one instruction in Prov 22:17–24:22 (Bryce, 1979; Würthwein). Apparent differences often vanish upon closer examination. For example, the opposites "wise/fool" appear in Egypt under "silent one/hotheaded one." Affinities become especially close with regard to language about hearing, although Egyptian sages were more likely to coin technical terms than their Israelite colleagues.

Theological Analysis

Themes

The lion's share of attention has gone to the theological meaning of a single phrase—"the fear of Yahweh." Its use approximates the contemporary word "religion," in all its richness. According to one modern exegete, this awareness that faith frees the intellect for maximum achievement offers a cogent corrective to twentieth-century scientific dogmatism (von Rad, 1972:53–73). Precisely what is implied by the motto, "The fear of Yahweh is the ראשית of knowledge," remains unclear, but both "essence" and "beginning" have their champions.

Equally ambiguous is the referent for the foreign woman who posed such a threat to Israel's youth. The older theory that she represented a cultic fertility goddess (Boström) has been found wanting, for the most part, and explanations from closer to home have prevailed. Accordingly, the foreign woman is usually viewed as an adulteress, although her enticement has certainly been enhanced by use of elements from fertility worship (Whybray, 1965; McKane). The personification of Dames Wisdom and Folly has also made free use of that cultic language (Lang; Bonnard).

In one sense, it is hardly accurate to speak of theological analysis of Proverbs, since most observations in this regard belong to the category of ethics. Some attention has fallen upon the "kerygma" in Proverbs (Murphy, 1966), as well as the place such a work must have occupied in Israel's total theological scheme. Such discussions have emphasized an openness to the world (Murphy, 1970), fundamental trust in men and women (Brueggemann), and symbolic language (Habel, 1972). The conservative nature of wisdom produced an appeal to ancient tradition (Habel, 1973), resulting in remarkable continuity with the past. For at least one scholar, wisdom's lack of sacred traditions places sapiential texts alongside pagan materials as devoid of revelatory content or redemptive power (Preuss, 1970).

Authority

One reason for this denial of revelatory authority grows out of the sages' way of expressing themselves. On the surface, "Listen, my son, to your dad's advice," hardly compares with the prophetic oracular formula, "Thus hath Yahweh spoken." Once this mode of expression is examined (Bühlmann), it becomes clear that sapiential sayings carried considerable authority beyond their own internal logic. Behind each bit of advice stood the weight of tradition, the authority of parents, the accumulated ethos, and the divine intention as it had penetrated reality at creation (Crenshaw, 1971:116–23; Gemser, 1968).

III. QOHELETH

The Composition of the Book

Literary Forms

Reflection upon the composition of Qoheleth arose already within those circles which endeavored to understand the work during the author's own lifetime or shortly afterward. According to this editorial gloss (12:9–14), Qoheleth sought earnestly to combine truth with literary artistry. If the result baffled his contemporaries, how much more puzzled must modern interpreters be. Obscurity reigns in the effort to determine the precise form of the book, whether a collection of sentences, a tract (Zimmerli, 1974), or even a diary. Consensus seems to have formed on the actual pedagogic use of these pleasing—yet trying—observations about life's emptiness (Gordis, 1951; Kroeber; Lauha, 1978; Scott, 1965).

As ancient rabbis surmised, the fiction of Solomonic authorship seems to be an effort to reinforce the weight of the claim that life had no real advantage over death. The Egyptian royal testament (instructions in the name of the pharaoh) lies behind the section in which Qoheleth reports the conclusions he drew from careful experimentation (1:12–2:26). Making generous use of autobiographical language, he shows a decided preference for stereotypical expressions (Wright; Loretz) and polar structures (Loader). Other literary forms (Crenshaw, 1974a) Qoheleth uses with considerable power include proverb and allegory, the latter of which characterizes the ravages of old age in a manner reminiscent of the opening lines in Ptahhotep's Maxims and a recently discovered Sumerian text (Alster, 1975:93). Although several kinds of proverbs occur, a preference for "excluding" ones is apparent, largely because they reinforced the negative impact of Qoheleth's thought (Müller, 1968). At least two didactic poems emphasize the monotony of existence under the sun and assert that everything belongs to its own particular moment (1:4–9; 3:1–9). The special character of the work derives in part from the strong emphasis upon deductions from experience, which form the basis for personal advice. Therefore, exhortation appears as the mode of address when positive counsel breaks free from the shadow cast by death's ominous presence (Crenshaw, 1978b).

Integrity

The inconsistency that stands out within the book does not necessarily indicate multiple authorship. The element of contradiction has been exaggerated, although attempts to deny it altogether (Kidner) have proved unsuccessful. The possibly complementary explanations for those opposing viewpoints have been brought forward. The first assumes that Qoheleth quoted generally acknowledged truisms as a foil for his opposing message (Gordis, 1951; Whybray, 1981). Considerable supporting evidence from ancient Near Eastern texts strengthens the case greatly. This thesis is further bolstered by awareness that Qoheleth had a tendency to juxtapose a *bonum* and a *malum* (Müller, 1968); the good is stated so as to demonstrate its basic falsity. When God is the subject, this exposure of real truth achieves intense pathos. The other solution to the presence of contradiction has its basis in psychology: Qoheleth lacked consistency because he recognized the impossibility of being dogmatic when discussing matters like punishment for sin and reward for virtue. The complexity of such issues forced him to view them from several different perspectives (J. Williams, 1981).

While both arguments carry a certain amount of persuasive power, they do not rule out the likelihood that a few actual glosses have been added to the text, especially to counter the impact of Qoheleth's denial that God rewarded and punished individuals according to their actions. This thesis of editorial additions grows stronger when one takes into account the undeniable fact that the final section of the book (12:9–14) comes from a sage other than Qoheleth (Sheppard, 1977). Furthermore, the author of this epilogue launches a mild attack against the book, while acknowledging its essential truth. The attempt to sum up Qoheleth's teaching in 12:13–14 misses the point entirely, and this bold piety hardly grew out of inability to understand what the gentle cynic had written. Instead, the epilogist offered advice that was intended to replace Qoheleth's counsel.

Thematic Unity

To be sure, one theme runs through the entire book: "Vanity of vanities, all is vanity." The word הבל may occur here in the sense of "profitless," as the word was used in daily commerce. It would seem to refer to a ledger on which life's credits and debits appear, the latter naturally prevailing. But the word must surely carry its original meaning as well; everything is as empty as breath itself, which remains outside our control. Like all God's gifts, it comes and goes according to divine time schedules (Galling, 1961) and thus constantly reminds creatures of their finitude (Gese, 1963).

Another theme which unites much of the book also points to the limits imposed upon human knowledge. This emphasis upon an inability to find out desired data or to know everything presses beyond mere denial of ultimate knowledge to outright attack on anyone who thinks otherwise. Dissent from traditional teachings assumes many forms: explicit rejection, implicit correction, alteration of language, and omission (Crenshaw, 1977b). One example demonstrates Qoheleth's skill in dealing with school tradition. In 3:11 he alludes to the Priestly creation narrative's refrain that every created thing was especially good, but Qoheleth varies the language appreciably and turns the original affirmation into an expression that approaches despair. Shunning the pregnant words ברא or טוב, he used instead עשה and יפה and thus divested the text of rich theological meaning. Not satisfied with this neutralization of heavily laden vocabulary, Qoheleth further qualifies the divine gift, bestowed at creation, and turns it into a burden. He very nearly accuses God of teasing human beings by giving them a valuable yearning for the hidden realities of life but rendering men and women incapable of discovering precious truth (Crenshaw, 1974b).

These two refrains ("Vanity of vanities, all is vanity" and "He cannot find it out") seem to provide structural unity to the book (Wright). In addition, several other formulas mark transitional points within the larger units. Among others, these include the concluding summary that encouraged the enjoyment of life during youthful vigor, the "contemplative" observations that referred to self-examination and the resulting personal action, and the allusions to chasing after the wind, toil, and lot. Qoheleth shows decided preference for certain words and phrases that seem to catch the monotony characterizing life under the sun (Loretz). In addition, he seems to use words in a double sense, almost playfully. This richness of meaning may explain the unusual form בוראיך, which alludes to one's *bonum* (his wife) and *malum* (the grave).

Thematic unity is achieved by other means as well, chief of which are mood and idea. A single atmosphere almost suppresses the written word itself; that oppressive mood arose from awareness that death cancels all supposed gain under heaven. No relief from this burden presented itself as an acceptable response to the aching cry for permanence—not even the hope of life beyond the grave. Alongside this ominous atmosphere exists a central conception that signifies an awareness of being alone in the universe (von Rad, 1972:232–33). The crisis of the spirit prevented Qoheleth from deciding whether God was a despot or not, although the sage comes perilously close to answering in the affirmative.

Foreign Influence

Older theories of pervasive Greek influence upon Qoheleth's thought have given way to alternative claims, particularly the attempt to demonstrate affinities with Phoenician (Dahood) and Mesopotamian literature (Loretz: 90–134). One interpreter has gone further afield in an effort to compare Qoheleth's concept of opposites with Taoist views (Horton). The pendulum has begun to swing back once again to its earlier position, although this time the thesis of Greek influence depends, for the most part, upon similarities with the teachings of popular Hellenistic philosophers (Braun; Whitley). This analysis of the environment within which Qoheleth worked has made significant advance toward clarifying the transition within wisdom thinking that a Hellenistic context must have precipitated (Marböck; Hengel; Middendorp). Nevertheless, attempts to show that Aramaic was the original language of Qoheleth continue (Zimmermann).

The Appropriation of Meaning

Pre-Christian and Early Christian Endeavors

The controversial views of Qoheleth and the dissent from established opinions could hardly be ignored, especially when such thinking supplied the justification for immoral behavior. The author of Wisdom of Solomon almost certainly has Qoheleth in mind when attacking conduct that seems to have arisen from a thorough misunderstanding of Qoheleth's counsel regarding enjoyment while one can still taste life's nectar (contra Skehan: 172–236). Rabbinic debate about books that defile the hands indicates further alarm over Qoheleth's teaching but bears strong witness to the power of tradition in the canonization process. Christian response differed little from the Jewish; the process of neutralizing Qoheleth's language, which began in the translation activity behind the LXX rendering of the book, gained impetus until grand claims surfaced (Holm-Nielsen). Qoheleth was understood as a splendid example of a person without Christ or of one caught in law's bondage. The Church Fathers seem never to have tired of comparing the Christian's promise of resurrection with the dismal fate facing this OT sage. In this sense, Qoheleth was viewed as a messianic prophecy (Hertzberg: 238).

Contemporary Theological Approaches

Perhaps the most appropriate word to characterize Qoheleth's thought is crisis (Gese, 1963). For him, the givens of human existence no longer compelled assent; the result amounted to discovery of human existence *in tormentis* (Galling, 1961:1). Dialogue with eternity as it occurred in the world had vanished, and in its place sprang up a self-centered monologue (von Rad, 1972:233, 237). The personal pronouns throw the spotlight on Qoheleth alone; the sense of isolation from God and other humans mounts as again and again the author exposes human misery and obtains momentary relief in awareness that a companion assists during danger and keeps one warm. Obviously, even here Qoheleth has not escaped self-centeredness, since others exist for his sake. The heart of the spiritual crisis concerns God's justice; for Qoheleth, arbitrariness characterizes divine action. It follows that the fundamental presupposition of wisdom collapses, since one cannot be sure what will greet a given act.

This recognition of God's freedom has been seen as a restoration of authentic Yahwism rather than as a departure from genuine wisdom (Zimmerli, 1963:135). To be sure, Israel's sages had always perceived an element of mystery beyond which they could not pass, but such limits did not become oppressive because both Yahweh and the world were thought to be trustworthy. Neither God nor the universe gave comfort to Qoheleth, who resented having to rely upon another for gifts dispensed in God's own good time. Naturally, the thesis that Qoheleth functioned as a guardian of authentic Yahwism depends upon an assumption that wisdom thinking hardened into a dogma of retribution. At least one interpreter rejects that hypothesis entirely (von Rad, 1972).

Since both Qoheleth and Job wrestle with existential concerns, comparison between the two thinkers is inevitable. In these assessments of two radical positions, Qoheleth invariably loses. One critic has labeled him an example of a secular individual as opposed to Job, a *homo religiosus* (Lauha, 1960). Perhaps the scales tipped against Qoheleth because of his unrelieved skepticism, although not all critics think Qoheleth's message lacked vigorous optimism (Whybray, 1982). After all, he did observe that light is sweet to behold (Miskotte: 450–60; J. G. Williams, 1971a; Witzenrath).

The emergence of skepticism in ancient Israel (Klopfenstein; Priest) owes much to a combination of factors: the crisis of tradition and ancient pedagogy (Crenshaw, 1980). In short, historical circumstances alone fail to offer an adequate explanation for the rise of skepticism. Alongside the element of a collapsing ethos stood an emphasis upon imponderables within the teaching enterprise. Certain things lay outside the scope of human knowledge, and these "intellectual teasers" assumed the form of riddle and impossible question (Crenshaw, 1978a, 1979). In Qoheleth, rhetorical questions achieved this end, especially the haunting "Who knows?"

Such skepticism tempers traditional affirmation and hallowed language. For example, the fear of God functions in Qoheleth as sheer terror in the presence of divine tyranny (Pfeiffer). Of course, the phrase occurs in its normal sense of religious devotion as well, but evidence seems to suggest that this traditional use belongs to the epilogist or represents school teaching which Qoheleth proceeds to attack (Murphy, 1979).

Current Non-Theological Interpretations

The powerful influence of Freudian psychology upon contemporary thought has led one critic to undertake a thoroughgoing analysis of Qoheleth from this particular perspective (Zimmermann). Seizing clues in their most fragile form, Zimmermann thinks Qoheleth suffered from all the classical symptoms that Freud exposed so tellingly: impotency, incest, Oedipus complex, inferiority complex, and so forth. Such flights of fantasy possess more entertainment value than truth. Scholars have often admired Qoheleth for the timeless quality of his message. Comparisons with existential philosophy have acknowledged this unusual modernity while recognizing essential differences (Gordis, 1951:112–21). Naturally, many philosophers have found in Qoheleth a kindred spirit.

IV. THE BOOK OF JOB

The Emergence of the Book

Prose and Poetry

Whereas older critics usually viewed the framing narrative and the poetry in isolation, the current trend is to link the two more closely. An old popular story with an epic substratum (Sarna) about a faithful just man who suffers without complaining seems to have been adapted for pedagogic ends by the author of the dialogue, but tensions remain nevertheless between the prose and the poetry (Fohrer, 1963). One way to neutralize the different viewpoints is to understand the divine commendation of Job as irony. One could even view Job's response in the same way; repentance would then be simple manipulation of a deity (J. G. Williams, 1971b). Regardless, the story moves in an entirely different environment from the poetry. As a result, many critics ignore the story altogether when interpreting the dialogue.

Within the dialogue, the poem on wisdom's inaccessibility (chap. 28) (Zerafa) and the Elihu speeches (32–37) present special problems. Sufficient stylistic similarities between these texts and the rest of the dialogue give some weight to theories about common authorship, especially when coupled with a thesis that several years separate them. Thus at least one interpreter thinks the same author who had earlier written the poem on wisdom later tried his hand at another answer to the problem of innocent suffering. The result was the Elihu speeches, which reflect the subsequent scribal solution (Gordis, 1978). The third cycle of speeches has suffered disarrangement; some think the poem in chap. 28 is also out of place since it anticipates the divine response in the theophany. Naturally, attempts to relocate 24–27 rely upon an assumption of logical consistency (Tournay). One could imagine other reasons for Job's contradictory remarks, especially in the light of his extraordinary psychological and physical state.

Literary Form

On one claim most scholars can agree: Job is sui generis. Beyond that consensus, considerable diversity in viewpoint prevails, largely because no single genre suffices in describing such a complex composition, which contains elements borrowed from prophecy (Bardtke), wisdom (Fohrer, 1963), and psalms (Westermann). The most appropriate category would seem to be disputation, if one takes into account the prose and poetry. Accordingly, one can distinguish a mythological prologue and epilogue, a debate, and the divine resolution of the dispute. Disregarding the prose, the category of lament seems apt, either a lament proper (Westermann) or a paradigm of an answered lament (Gese, 1958). Legal terminology certainly occurs, justifying attempts to distinguish a pre-judicial stage, a judicial process, and a verdict from the divine judge (H. Richter, 1959). The purification oath in chap. 31 strengthens this argument (Fohrer, 1974), although one need not see this act as forcing God's hand (contra Robertson; Good). Perhaps dialogue is the one term that comes closest to characterizing the poetry, but this word may assume more amicability between Job and the friends than is actually present. In any case, neither Elihu's observations nor God's speeches move beyond monologue, since both speak past Job.

Extrabiblical Sources

The Egyptian Book of the Dead offers a striking parallel to the negative confession in chap. 31 (Murtagh), but most parallels for Job are Mesopotamian in origin. Several studies of innocent suffering in Babylonian and Sumerian texts have called attention to similarities between Job and these earlier texts, even to the combination of prose and poetry (von Soden; Müller, 1978). Research into the problem of theodicy has also pointed to the Sumerian and Babylonian literature as the closest link with Job, although Egypt also wrestled with this issue (R. J. Williams). In the land of the Nile the seriousness of divine injustice was tempered by belief in life after death and by the conviction that justice was a gift of God rather than one's right. The remarkable affinity between Job and

Mesopotamian texts is broken at one point; only the former understands suffering as God's way of educating a person.

Although formal connections between Job and Mesopotamia can hardly be denied, certain links with Ugaritic texts have also been postulated (Irwin). The putative parallels with Dan'el lack cogency, and the explanation of the divine vindicator as Baal seems superfluous, given the Israelite concept of blood revenge. Still, numerous linguistic affinities between Job and Northwest Semitic are powerful testimony to the influence Canaanite culture exercised upon the author of Job (Pope). One need not assume a line of traditional wisdom at Canaanite city states (Gray) to explain this similarity in language and motifs, but some explanation for such common ideas seems called for (Cazelles).

Postcanonical Tradition

Discovery at Qumran of a variant tradition to Job (Fitzmyer; van der Ploeg and van der Woude) has illuminated the early postcanonical understanding of the book. That information has now been extended in two directions: (1) Job in Arabic and early Jewish tradition (Müller, 1970), and (2) Job in Jewish interpretation from the Middle Ages to the present (Glatzer, 1966). Such motif analyses have greatly enriched our sense of the presuppositions that control what we see in a particular text. A recent study of Job in French literature shows how intellectual moods change, and with each shift comes another way of viewing religious problems (Hausen). The profundity of the book of Job may be measured partly by the fascination it holds for intellectuals in many different disciplines, as exemplified by two recent anthologies on twentieth-century interpretations of Job (P. Sanders; Glatzer, 1969).

Theological Mystification

The Problem of Suffering

The suffering of innocent victims constitutes the fundamental problem addressed by the book of Job. It offers several explanations for undeserved suffering (J. Sanders) but fails to reach an adequate justification for it. Nevertheless, the author does not flinch from placing the blame upon God, although the divine speeches qualify that concession by drawing attention to the vast universe that lies under God's control. In ordinary human experience one cannot discover proof of God's justice; instead, an act of faith is called for despite the absence of convincing demonstration that God acts justly (Tsevat). Suffering may be disciplinary, educative, retributive, or redemptive. It follows that God may use innocent suffering to build character; hence, the way an individual reacts to discipline demonstrates true character. For this reason, one could even say that conduct during suffering is the real theme of the book (Fohrer, 1063). Thus the existential problem of suffering and the moral issue of correct response to innocent suffering comprise the basic themes of the book. The many answers to proper conduct range from outright Titanism to abject humility, and it is difficult to tell which one the author endorses.

Theodicy

A strong desire to justify God's ways (von Soden) occupies the thoughts of Job's erstwhile comforters and underlies the divine speeches, although in an oblique manner. Several features of Israelite and Mesopotamian religion exacerbated the issue of theodicy. The moral understanding of God and its correlate, a high degree of ethical demand placed on individuals, contributed most in this struggle to defend God's ways, since divine conduct did not always appear to accord with belief in an ethical deity. Conviction that reward and punishment accrued during this life made the problem of inappropriate fruits for conduct especially painful. So, too, did an individualizing of religious devotion and a suspicion of the cult, which received its share of criticism. The Babylonian Theodicy and Ludlul offer close parallels to Job in language and form, but a theory of direct literary dependence remains problematic.

Evidence seems to support the thesis of considerable popular wrestling with the problem of theodicy in Israelite texts other than the book of Job (Crenshaw, 1970, 1971, 1976b, 1983). While this struggle in Job and elsewhere may be illuminated through terms drawn from Thomas Aquinas (Scaltriti) or even Kantian philosophy (Faur), these discussions bear eloquent testimony to the persistence of the problem of divine injustice in modern times. That debate between two opposing sides in ancient Israel gave rise to a formula which can be found in Qoheleth and Sirach ("Do not say . . .") and shows how serious the dissenters understood the problem to be. The furor that typifies "imagined speech" issuing from the mouths of those who challenged God's justice can hardly be missed; in this respect, Job's literary heirs retained an authentic element of his speech (Crenshaw, 1975).

Theophany

It seems likely that the divine speeches offer the poet's real solution to the problems of innocent suffering and divine injustice. In God's presence, all previous understandings explode, paving the way for genuine knowledge. One achievement of the theophany is the crushing of the illusion that men and women occupy the central position (Neiman), a delusion that permits them to assume that the universe exists for their sakes alone. God's speeches, which seem to ignore the aching questions

Job has raised, force the accuser to glance backward in time to the beginning when no humans roamed the earth (Sekine) and far enough in space to perceive the habitat of wild animals whose ways are wholly unknown to people. Once Job focuses his thoughts on others, he has opened the way for a new vision of God. In truth the divine speeches necessitate the three fundamental intellectual stances: *Ignoramus, Ignorabimus*, and *Gaudeamus* (Gordis, 1965:134). The positive function of nature wisdom in shaping religious views, particularly the divine speeches in Job, emerges as the divine speeches become better understood (H. Richter, 1958; Keel; Kubina).

Naturally, Job's difficulty in the face of a blustering deity has prompted considerable contempt for the God described in the book. The speeches from the whirlwind have been labeled sublime irrelevance, and categories like humor, comedy, and irony have been applied freely to these passages (Robertson; Miles; Whedbee, 1977; J. G. Williams, 1977). The two divine speeches and human repentances still puzzle scholars, although most retain them while conceding that minor additions have occurred (the descriptions of the wild ostrich, horse, and hippopotamus).

Existential categories have illuminated the problem of Job's response to the theophany (Terrien, 1957; Cox). Job represents a person in dialectical tension between hopeless suffering and trust regardless of the circumstances. His suffering leads him into alienation so that he confronts God as enemy, only to discover at last that he is redeemer as well (Pope: LXXXIII). Others apply the categories of faith and grace, arguing that faith awakens through God's action and assures Job that suffering belongs to the divine economy. Whatever else the theophany accomplishes, it forces Job to acknowledge his creatureliness. Presumably, forgiveness and comfort accompany submission to God's will. In this case, a true dialogue of love and silence finally occurs (Leveque: 532).

Non-Theological Interpretations

Psychological

From the leader of one branch of modern psychology has come a particularly stringent critique of God for the answer given to Job (Jung). This provocative outburst of emotion has been criticized from different perspectives (Hedinger; J. G. Williams, 1971b), but the causes for the outrage are too substantial to ignore. Two other ventures to understand Job in the light of psychological studies have concluded that the biblical hero needed therapy above all else (Taylor) and that Job passed through the various stages of loss, grief, and integration (Kahn).

Literary

Of course, the modernization of Job in the play *J.B.* deserves special recognition (MacLeish), particularly because of its impact upon many intellectuals. This play, which had quite a long run on Broadway and stimulated lively discussion, succeeds remarkably well in showing how Job stands for everyone. Nevertheless, it departs from the biblical book in significant ways (Terrien, 1959) and ultimately opts for unrelieved humanism. A god who does not love but "is" cannot be the biblical deity, even if this passage actually refers to the revelation to Moses that God is appropriately identified as "I Am that I Am." Still, *J.B.* represents a powerful resurgence of an ancient message concerning divine injustice. In this regard, it towers high above the latest attempt to take up the Joban theme once again. The ironic title of that work, *God's Favorite* (Simon), and the tone capture the blasphemous mood of Job's speeches, although they hardly participate in the spirit of the biblical work.

Two recent attempts to capture the literary merit in the book of Job deserve some attention, particularly since historical norms still dominate much discussion of wisdom literature, where such a category is surely out of place (Roberts). The first, written by a specialist in comparative literature (Cook), applies standards of classical literary criticism (Barr) in a fruitful manner. The second endeavor in this realm consists of a number of essays by several scholars which have been published in a single issue of *Semeia*. The articles concentrate on the genre of comedy as the correct way of viewing the book of Job (Whedbee, 1977; Robertson), offer an analysis of the book in terms of drama (Alonso-Schökel, 1977; Cronshaw, 1077a), and treat humor and irony as they apply to Job (Miles; J. G. Williams, 1977). Perhaps one should include under this heading the comparison of Job and Faust (Zhitlowsky), which offers numerous insights into the meaning of the biblical figure as well as discussions of William Blake's artistic representations of the book of Job (Damon).

Political

The revolutionary mood of much contemporary political thought has led one critic to analyze Job in terms of the political struggle to overcome the strong tendency to maintain the status quo (Bloch). In this interpretation, Job abandons the status quo in the defiant appeal to another God. Reaction to this view has insisted that Job cannot be understood properly apart from faith in Yahweh, which gave birth to the book in the first place (Gerbracht).

V. THE WIDER QUEST

The means of determining precisely which psalms belong to the category of wisdom is by no means clear (Murphy, 1962; Gerstenberger, 1974; Crenshaw, 1974a). The basic criteria fall into one of three categories: (1) vocabulary (wise and foolish, understanding, knowledge); (2) themes (fear of God, innocent suffering); and (3) rhetorical devices ('ašre sayings, better speeches, ascending numbers). At best, such features only permit a conjecture of wisdom influence, inasmuch as they could also derive from other sources. Certain Psalms (49, 73) wrestle with the problem of innocent suffering, and this kinship with Job naturally draws attention to them (Perdue, 1974; Ross; Luyten). Conscious didactic intention has also prompted a claim that sages composed Psalm 34 (Kuntz).

The problem of theodicy elicited untraditional answers from Ben Sira as he endeavored to draw upon Hellenistic resources in addition to Hebraic ones (von Rad, 1972; Crenshaw, 1975; Prato). Naturally, this new combination of intellectual streams gave pride of place to the Israelite but allowed considerable Greek influence to infiltrate Ben Sira's teaching (Middendorp; Hengel). Furthermore, his openness to new theological traditions resulted in a remarkable combination of sapiential and sacral themes, so much so that wisdom entered a transitional stage (Marböck, 1971; Sheppard, 1980). The Yahwistic traditions threatened to subsume the wisdom ones, if the emphasis upon the fear of God provides a proper clue (Haspecker; contra von Rad, 1972). Still, Ben Sira emphasized the special profession of sages (Marböck, 1979) and reflected upon the dignity of human beings in a manner reminiscent of traditional wisdom thinking (Alonso-Schökel, 1978). New discoveries with regard to the text of Sirach (Yadin; Rüger; Rickenbacher) may enrich attempts to assess Ben Sira's thought (Jacob).

The Hellenistic background of the Wisdom of Solomon is firmly established (Reese, 1970), although the exact date of this work may be considerably later than earlier assumed, if the first century C.E. date recently postulated holds up (Winston). Similarities to Philo's thought are striking (Mack; Sandmel), and the Greek rhetoric employed by both suggests that their ideas, even when Hebraic, are clothed in Hellenistic forms. Even the lengthy critique of idolatry, which draws heavily upon biblical material, differs little from comparable Greek texts (Gilbert, 1973). Since Wisdom of Solomon is written in language that derives from Greek thought, perhaps a biblical hermeneutic based on contemporary philosophy (specifically, Paul Ricoeur's) offers a helpful way to interpret the ancient text (Reese, 1979).

VI. CONCLUSION: THE UNFINISHED TASK

Trends in Research

The preceding discussion, which carries on the work of earlier interpreters (Scott, 1970, 1971a; Kegler; Clements; Emerton; R. J. Williams, 1981; Murphy, 1981a, 1981b), calls attention to numerous unresolved issues that await satisfactory answers, but it also celebrates many significant responses to difficult questions. So far in this essay, little attention has fallen upon recent comprehensive attempts to interpret ancient wisdom, the impact of which is by no means negligible. The central thrust of each current analysis would seem to be that:

(1) Wisdom is a primordial revelation which God implanted in the universe and which actively woos men and women. Faith therefore makes knowledge possible, for wisdom is essentially another form of Yahwism (von Rad, 1972; Scott, 1971b).

(2) Biblical wisdom provides a valuable corrective to the modern Protestant burden of guilt, which arises from excessive emphasis upon the law and God's grace. That ancient literary corpus announces the joyous news that God trusts men and women to steer their lives successfully without fear of consequences. The creation narrative and Davidic history function as normative for Israelite wisdom in this analysis (Brueggemann).

(3) Nothing demands a theory of sages as an institution in ancient Israel; instead, the canonical texts suggest that an intellectual tradition existed among upper classes. These elite thinkers composed and treasured the wisdom corpus, which has its own distinctive vocabulary, but use of חכם in its various forms does not constitute a technical term (Whybray, 1974).

(4) Beginning with the Egyptian principle of *Maat*, this analysis focuses upon the world view of sages and postulates an evolution from genuine belief in an order governing the universe to a crisis in that belief and resultant frozen dogma. According to this approach, creation functions as the central theological concept in the entire Hebrew scriptures (Schmid).

(5) The stylistic niceties that characterize biblical proverbs imply self-conscious literary artistry, which invalidates the hypothesis of popular composition. Israelite wisdom had its center, origin, and places of cultivation in a school (Hermisson, 1968).

(6) Early wisdom possessed strong self-confidence, thereby lacking any sense of divine grace. In time, that optimism faded and grace came to play an increasing role in sapiential thought (Rylaarsdam).

(7) Research into wisdom literature has advanced along the lines of affinities with related texts, form, and structure. The importance of creation theology derives from the fact that it undergirds belief in divine justice, the presupposition of old wisdom (Crenshaw, 1976a, 1981a).

(8) Close examination of wisdom texts in which the cult is mentioned or implied shows a positive attitude, for the most part, despite the usual assumption that Israel's sages had little interest in cultic matters (Perdue, 1977).

(9) The literary dimensions of aphoristic thinking (the establishing of order by counterorder, orientation by disorientation, especially in Qoheleth and in Jesus' brief sayings) are clarified in the light of the Western gnomic tradition (J. G. Williams, 1981).

To be sure, space does not permit discussion of many significant monographs in the area of sapiential studies, particularly commentaries. Two recent collections of essays (*Israelite Wisdom: Theological and Literary Essays in Honor of Samuel Terrien*, and *La Sagesse de l'Ancien Testament*) and the forthcoming monographs by Donn F. Morgan (*Wisdom in the Old Testament Traditions*) and Roland E. Murphy (*Wisdom Literature*) demonstrate the vigor that characterizes the study of wisdom today.

Fruitful Avenues for Investigation

Since research has a certain cumulative character, it might be possible to predict the general direction in which the scholarly enterprise will move, but such conjecture would serve no real purpose. Instead, this survey of recent trends in wisdom scholarship will close by noting some significant areas that will reward further study.

(1) The current interest in aesthetics—that is, literary artistry—throughout the Hebrew scriptures will naturally extend to wisdom literature. Some progress has already occurred in this area, but much remains to be done. There is no more appropriate endeavor, since such analysis takes its cue from ancient sages who labored to master the art of speaking and writing. Perhaps we shall soon understand, among other things, the dynamics of sapiential dialogue.

(2) This study of the art of persuasion will inevitably encounter the problem of authority. Precisely what constituted the ground upon which sages stood when offering their valuable counsel? Previous responses to this important question stand in need of revision.

(3) The book of Job shows that the obvious authority that prophets and priests assumed tempted certain sages as they searched for means to legitimate their words. This conscious use of prophetic and psalmic motifs raises the issue of influence, which has as yet defied adequate resolution for the entire wisdom corpus.

(4) In the light of the sages' fondness for correct speech and artful composition, one can assume that collections of proverbs and wise sayings were not thrown together haphazardly. It follows that further research in the area of structure in Job, Proverbs, and Qoheleth cannot be off target.

(5) Current research outside the wisdom corpus threatens operative assumptions concerning the dating of various literary complexes. Reassessment of the entire Hebrew scriptures will become necessary, and fresh thinking will have to be given to the wisdom texts in particular. In this endeavor, we shall have occasion to discard some dominant hypotheses regarding the evolution of sapiential thought. In doing so, we may come closer to understanding the social milieu within which sages moved.

BIBLIOGRAPHY*

Albright, William F.
1960   "Some Canaanite-Phoenician Sources of Hebrew Wisdom." Pp. 1–15 in *Wisdom in Israel and in the Ancient Near East*. VTSup 3. Leiden: E. J. Brill.

Alonso-Schökel, Luis
1962   "Motivos sapienciales y de alianza en Gn. 2–3." *Bib* 43: 295–316. English, *TD* 13 (1965) 3–10. Reprinted in Crenshaw, 1976a: 468–80.
1977   "Toward a Dramatic Reading of the Book of Job." *Semeia* 7: 45–61.
1978   "The Vision of Man in Sirach 16:24–17:14." Pp. 235–45 in *Israelite Wisdom*. Ed. J. G. Gammie et al. Missoula, MT: Scholars Press.

Alster, Bendt
1974   *The Instructions of Šuruppak: A Sumerian Proverb Collection*. Mesopotamia, 2. Copenhagen: Akademisk Forlag.
1975   *Studies in Sumerian Proverbs*. Mesopotamia, 3. Copenhagen: Akademisk Forlag.

Bardtke, Hans
1967   "Prophetische Züge im Buche Hiob." Pp. 1–10 in *Das Ferne und Nahe Wort: Festschrift Leonhard Rost zur Vollendung seines 70 Lebensjahres am 30. November 1966 gewidmet*. BZAW 105. Berlin: A. Töpelmann.

Barr, James
1971   "The Book of Job and its Modern Interpreters." *BJRL* 54: 28–46.

* The *JAOS* volume on Oriental Wisdom (101, 1, 1981) arrived too late to be consulted in this essay. The articles on Egyptian wisdom (R. J. Williams), Israelite (Murphy), and Mesopotamian (G. Buccellati) are complemented by discussions of Arabic (D. Gutas), Asian (R. Dankoff), and Indian wisdom (L. Sternbach).

Bloch, Ernst
1972   *Atheism in Christianity*. New York: Herder and Herder.

Bonnard, P. E.
1979   "De la Sagesse personifiée dans l'Ancien Testament à la Sagesse en personne dans le Nouveau." Pp. 117–49 in *La Sagesse de l'Ancien Testament*. Ed. M. Gilbert. BETL 51. Gembloux: J. Duculot.

Boström, Gustav
1935   *Proverbiastudien. Die Weisheit und das fremde Weib in Spr. 1–9*. LUÅ 30:3. Lund: C. W. K. Gleerup.

Braun, Rainer
1973   *Kohelet und die fruhhellenistische Popularphilosophie*. BZAW 130. Berlin and New York: Walter de Gruyter.

Brueggemann, Walter A.
1972   *In Man We Trust*. Richmond: John Knox.

Brunner, Hellmut
1944   "Die Lehre des Cheti, Sohnes des Duauf." *Aegyptische Forschungen*, 13.
1952   "Weisheitsliteratur." *HO* 1, Aegyptologie, II: 90–110.

Bryce, Glendon E.
1975   "Omen-Wisdom in Ancient Israel." *JBL* 94: 19–37.
1979   *A Legacy of Wisdom: The Egyptian Contribution to the Wisdom of Israel*. Lewisburg and London: Bucknell University and Associated University Presses.

Buccellati, Giorgio
1981   "Wisdom and Not: The Case of Mesopotamia." *JAOS* 101: 35–47.

Bühlmann, Walter
1976   *Vom Rechten Reden und Schweigen*. OBO 12. Göttingen: Vandenhoeck & Ruprecht.

Camp, Claudia V.
1981   "The Wise Women of 2 Samuel: A Role Model for Women in Early Israel." *CBQ* 43: 14–29.

Cazelles, Henri
1963   "Les debuts de la sagesse en Israël." Pp. 27–39 in *Les sagesses du Proche-Orient ancien*. Paris: Presses Universitaires de France.

Clements, Ronald E.
1976   *One Hundred Years of Old Testament Interpretation*. Philadelphia: Westminster.

Coats, George W.
1973   "The Joseph Story and Ancient Wisdom: A Reappraisal." *CBQ* 35: 285–97.

1976	*From Canaan to Egypt.* CBQMS 4. Washington: The Catholic Biblical Association of America.

Conrad, Joachim
1967	"Die innere Gliederung der Proverbien." ZAW 79: 67–76.

Cook, Albert
1968	*The Root of the Thing.* Bloomington: Indiana University Press.

Cox, Dermot
1978	*The Triumph of Impotence: Job and the Tradition of the Absurd.* Analecta Gregoriana, 212. Rome: Universita Gregoriana Editrice.

Crenshaw, James L.
1969	"Method in Determining Wisdom Influence upon 'Historical' Literature." *JBL* 88: 129–42. Reprinted in Crenshaw 1976a: 481–94.
1970	"Popular Questioning of the Justice of God in Ancient Israel." ZAW 82: 380–95. Reprinted in Crenshaw 1976a: 289–304.
1971	*Prophetic Conflict.* BZAW 124. Berlin and New York: Walter de Gruyter.
1974a	"Wisdom." Pp. 226–64 in *Old Testament Form Criticism.* Ed. John H. Hayes. San Antonio: Trinity University Press.
1974b	"The Eternal Gospel (Eccl. 3:11)." Pp. 23–55 in *Essays in Old Testament Ethics.* Ed. J. L. Crenshaw and J. T. Willis. New York: Ktav.
1975	"The Problem of Theodicy in Sirach." *JBL* 94: 47–64.
1976a, ed.	*Studies in Ancient Israelite Wisdom.* New York: Ktav.
1976b	"Theodicy." Pp. 895–96 in *IDBSup.*
1977a	"The Twofold Search: A Response to Luis Alonso-Schökel." *Semeia* 7: 63–69.
1977b	"The Human Dilemma and Literature of Dissent." Pp. 235–58 in *Tradition and Theology in the Old Testament.* Ed. Douglas A. Knight. Philadelphia: Fortress.
1978a	*Samson: A Secret Betrayed, a Vow Ignored.* Atlanta: John Knox; London: S.P.C.K.
1978b	"The Shadow of Death in Qoheleth." Pp. 105–16 in *Israelite Wisdom.* Ed. John G. Gammie et al. Missoula, MT: Scholars Press.
1979	"Questions, dictons et épreuves impossibles." Pp. 96–111 in *La Sagesse de l'Ancien Testament.* Ed. M. Gilbert. BETL 51. Gembloux: J. Duculot.
1980	"The Birth of Skepticism in Ancient Israel." Pp. 1–19 in *The Divine Helmsman: Studies on God's Control of*

Human Events, Presented to Lou H. Silberman. Ed. J. L. Crenshaw and Samuel Sandmel. New York: Ktav.

1981a   *Old Testament Wisdom, an Introduction*. Atlanta: John Knox.

1981b   "The Conquest of Darius' Guards." Pp. 74–88 in *Images of Man and God*. Ed. Burke O. Long. Sheffield: Almond.

1981c   "Wisdom and Authority: Sapiential Rhetoric and its Warrants." Pp. 10–29 in *Congress Volume: Vienna, 1980*. VTSup 32. Leiden: E. J. Brill.

1983   *Theodicy in the Old Testament*. Philadelphia: Fortress.

Dahood, Mitchell
1952   "Canaanite-Phoenician Influence in Qoheleth." *Bib* 33: 30–52, 191–221.

Damon, S. Foster
1969   *Blake's Job*. New York: E. P. Dutton.

Dijk, J. J. A. van
1953   *La sagesse sumero-accadienne*. Leiden: E. J. Brill.

Emerton, J. A.
1979   "Wisdom." Pp. 214–37 in *Tradition and Interpretation*. Ed. G. W. Anderson. Oxford: Clarendon.

Faur, Jose
1970   "Reflections on Job and Situation-Morality." *Judaism* 19: 219–25.

Fichtner, Johannes
1949   "Jesaja unter den Weisen." *TLZ* 74: 75–80. = Pp. 18–26 in *Gottes Weisheit*. Stuttgart: Calwer, 1965. English trans. in Crenshaw 1976a: 429–38.

Fitzmyer, Joseph A.
1979   "The First-Century Targum of Job from Qumran Cave XI." Pp. 161–82 in *A Wandering Aramean*. SBLMS 25. Missoula, MT: Scholars Press.

Fohrer, Georg
1963   *Das Buch Hiob*. KAT 16. Gütersloh: Gerd Mohn.
1974   "The Righteous Man in Job 31." Pp. 1–22 in *Essays in Old Testament Ethics*. Ed. J. L. Crenshaw and J. T. Willis. New York: Ktav.

Fontaine, Carol Rader
1979   "The Use of the Traditional Saying in the Old Testament." Ph.D. dissertation, Duke.

Fretheim, Terence E.
1977   *The Message of Jonah: A Theological Commentary*. Minneapolis: Augsburg.

Galling, Kurt
1952   *Die Krise der Aufklärung in Israel*. Mainz: Johannes
Gutenberg-Buchhandlung.
1961   "Die Rätsel der Zeit im Urteil Kohelets (Koh 3:1–15)."
ZTK 58: 1–15.

Gemser, Berend
1960   "The Instructions of 'Onchsheshonqy and Biblical Wisdom Literature." Pp. 102–28 in *Congress Volume: Oxford, 1959*. VTSup 7. Leiden: E. J. Brill. Reprinted in Crenshaw 1976a: 102–28.
1968   "The Spiritual Structure of Biblical Aphoristic Wisdom." Pp. 138–49 in *Adhuc Loquitur. Collected Essays of Dr. B. Gemser*. Ed. A. van Selms and A. S. van der Woude. Leiden: E. J. Brill. Reprinted in Crenshaw 1976a: 208–19.

Gerbracht, Diether
1975   "Aufbruch zu sittlichen Atheismus. Die Hiob-Deutung Ernst Blochs." *EvT* 35: 223–37.

Gerstenberger, Erhard
1965   *Wesen und Herkunft des "apodiktischen Rechts."* WMANT 20. Neukirchen: Neukirchener Verlag.
1974   "Psalms." Pp. 179–223 in *Old Testament Form Criticism*. Ed. J. H. Hayes. San Antonio: Trinity University.

Gese, Hartmut
1958   *Lehre und Wirklichkeit in der alten Weisheit*. Tübingen: J. C. B. Mohr (Paul Siebeck).
1963   "Die Krisis der Weisheit bei Koheleth." Pp. 139–51 in *Les Sagesses du Proche-Orient ancien*. Paris: Presses Universitaires de France.

Gilbert, Maurice
1973   *La critique des dieux dans le Livre de la Sagesse (Sg 13–15)*. AnBib 53. Rome: Pontifical Biblical Institute.
1979   "Le discours de la Sagesse en Proverbes, 8. Structure et coherence." Pp. 202–18 in *La Sagesse de l'Ancien Testament*. Ed. M. Gilbert. BETL 51. Gembloux: Duculot.

Glatzer, Nahum N.
1966   "The Book of Job and its Interpreters." Pp. 197–220 in *Biblical Motifs*. Ed. A. Altmann. Cambridge, MA: Harvard University Press.
1969   *The Dimensions of Job*. New York: Schocken Books.

Good, Edwin M.
1973   "Job and the Literary Task: A Response." *Soundings* 56: 470–84.

Gordis, Robert
1943/44   "The Social Background of Wisdom Literature." *HUCA* 18: 77–118.

1951	*Koheleth—the Man and his World*. New York: Schocken Books.
1965	*The Book of God and Man*. Chicago and London: University of Chicago Press.
1978	*The Book of Job: Commentary, New Translation and Special Studies*. New York: The Jewish Theological Seminary of America.

Gordon, Edmund I.

1957	"Sumerian Proverbs: Collection Four." *JAOS* 77: 67–79.
1958	"Sumerian Proverbs and Fables." *JCS* 12: 1–21, 43–75.
1959	*Sumerian Proverbs. Glimpses of Every Day Life in Ancient Mesopotamia*. Philadelphia: Westminster.
1960	"A New Look at the Wisdom of Sumer and Akkad." *BO* 17: 122–52.

Gowan, Donald

1968	"Habakkuk and Wisdom." *Perspective* 9: 157–66.

Gray, John

1970	"The Book of Job in the Context of Near Eastern Literature." *ZAW* 82: 251–69.

Habel, Norman

1972	"The Symbolism of Wisdom in Proverbs 1–9." *Int* 26: 131–56.
1973	"Appeal to Ancient Tradition as a Literary Form." Pp. 34–54 in *Society of Biblical Literature 1973 Seminar Papers*. Ed. George W. MacRae. Cambridge, MA: Society of Biblical Literature. Vol. 1.

Haspecker, Josef

1967	*Gottesfurcht bei Jesus Sirach*. AnBib 30. Rome: Pontifical Biblical Institute.

Hausen, Adelheid

1972	*Hiob in der französischen Literatur*. Bern and Frankfurt: Herbert and Peter Lang.

Hedinger, Ulrich

1967	"Reflexion über C. G. Jungs Hiobinterpretation." *TZ* 23: 340–52.

Hengel, Martin

1974	*Judaism and Hellenism: Studies in Their Encounter in Palestine during the Early Hellenistic Period*. 2 vols. Philadelphia: Fortress.

Hermisson, Hans-Jürgen

1968	*Studien zur israelitischen Spruchweisheit*. WMANT 28. Neukirchen: Neukirchener Verlag.
1978	"Observations on the Creation Theology in Wisdom." Pp. 43–57 in *Israelite Wisdom*. Ed. J. G. Gammie et al. Missoula, MT: Scholars Press.

Hertzberg, Hans Wilhelm
    1963   *Der Prediger*. KAT 17. Gütersloh: Mohn.

Holm-Nielsen, Svend
    1974   "On the Interpretation of Qoheleth in Early Christianity." *VT* 24: 168–77.

Horton, Ernest, Jr.
    1972   "Koheleth's Concept of Opposites." *Numen* 19: 1–21.

Humphreys, W. Lee
    1978   "The Motif of the Wise Courtier in the Book of Proverbs." Pp. 161–75 in *Israelite Wisdom*. Ed. J. G. Gammie et al. Missoula, MT: Scholars Press.

Irwin, William A.
    1962   "Job's Redeemer." *JBL* 81: 217–29.

Jacob, Edmond
    1978   "Wisdom and Religion in Sirach." Pp. 247–60 in *Israelite Wisdom*. Ed. J. G. Gammie et al. Missoula, MT: Scholars Press.

Jensen, Joseph
    1973   *The Use of Torah by Isaiah*. CBQMS 3. Washington: Catholic Biblical Association of America.

Journal of the American Oriental Society. 101/1. 1981

Jung, Carl G.
    1970   *Answer to Job*. Cleveland and New York: World.

Kahn, Jack H.
    1975   *Job's Illness: Loss, Grief and Integration*. Oxford and New York: Pergamon.

Kalugila, Leonidas
    1980   *The Wise King*. ConBOT 15. Lund: Gleerup.

Kayatz, Christa
    1966   *Studien zu Proverbien 1–9*. WMANT 22. Neukirchen-Vluyn: Neukirchener Verlag.

Keel, Othmar
    1978   *Jahwes Entgegnung an Hiob*. FRLANT 121. Göttingen: Vandenhoeck & Ruprecht.

Kegler, Jürgen
    1977   "Hauptlinien der Hiobforschung seit 1956." Pp. 9–25 in C. Westermann, *Der Aufbau des Buches Hiob*. Stuttgart: Calwer.

Khanjian, J.
    1975   "Wisdom." Pp. 371–400 in *Ras Shamra Parallels*, II. AnOr 50. Rome: Pontifical Biblical Institute.

Kidner, Derek
    1964   *Proverbs*. Downers Grove: InterVarsity.

Klopfenstein, Martin
1972 "Die Skepsis des Qohelet." *TZ* 28: 97–109.

Koch, Klaus
1955 "Gibt es ein Vergeltungsdogma im Alten Testament?" *ZTK* 52:1–42.
1972 *Um das Prinzip der Vergeltung in Religion und Recht des Alten Testaments.* Wege der Forschung, 125. Darmstadt: Wissenschaftliche Buchgesellschaft.

Kovacs, Brian W.
1974 "Is There a Class-Ethic in Proverbs?" Pp. 171–89 in *Essays in Old Testament Ethics.* Ed. J. L. Crenshaw and J. T. Willis. New York: Ktav.
1978 "Sociological-Structural Constraints upon Wisdom: The Spatial and Temporal Matrix of Proverbs 15:28–22:16." Ph.D. dissertation, Vanderbilt.

Kraeling, Carl H., and Robert Adams, eds.
1960 *City Invincible: A Symposium on Urbanization and Cultural Development in the Ancient Near East.* Chicago: University of Chicago Press.

Kroeber, Rudi
1963 *Der Prediger.* SPAW 13. Berlin: Akademie-Verlag.

Kubina, Veronika
1979 *Die Gottesreden im Buche Hiob.* Freiburger TS 115. Freiburg/Basel/Vienna: Herder.

Kuntz, J. Kenneth
1974 "The Canonical Wisdom Psalms of Ancient Israel— Their Rhetorical, Thematic, and Formal Dimensions." Pp. 186–222 in *Rhetorical Criticism.* Ed. Jared Jackson and Martin Kessler. Pittsburg: Pickwick.

Lambert, William G.
1960 *Babylonian Wisdom Literature.* Oxford: Clarendon.

Lang, Bernhard
1975 *Frau Weisheit: Deutung einer biblischen Gestalt.* Düsseldorf: Patmos.

Lauha, Aarre
1960 "Die Krise des religiösen Glaubens bei Kohelet." Pp. 183–91 in *Wisdom in Israel and the Ancient Near East.* VTSup 3. Leiden: E. J. Brill.
1978 *Kohelet.* BKAT 19. Neukirchen-Vluyn: Neukirchener Verlag.

Lemaire, André
1981 *Les écoles et la formation de la Bible dans l'ancien Israel.* OBO 39. Göttingen: Vandenhoeck & Ruprecht.

Leveque, Jean
1970 *Job et son Dieu.* Paris: Gabalda.

Lichtheim, Miriam
1973, 1976, 1980 *Ancient Egyptian Literature*, I–III. Berkeley: University of California Press.

Liver, J.
1967 "The Book of the Acts of Solomon." *Bib* 48: 75–101.

Loader, J. A.
1979 *Polar Structures in the Book of Qohelet*. BZAW 152. Berlin and New York: Walter de Gruyter.

Lohfink, Norbert
1980 *Kohelet*. Neue EB. Würzburg: Echter Verlag.

Loretz, Oswald
1964 *Kohelet und der Alte Orient*. Freiburg/Basel/Vienna: Herder.

Luyten, J.
1979 "Psalm 73 and Wisdom." Pp. 59–81 in *La Sagesse de l'Ancien Testament*. Ed. M. Gilbert. BETL 51. Gembloux: Duculot.

Mack, Burton L.
1973 *Logos und Sophia: Untersuchungen zur Weisheitstheologie im hellenistischen Judentum*. SUNT 10. Göttingen: Vandenhoeck & Ruprecht.

McKane, William
1970 *Proverbs*. Philadelphia: Westminster.

McKenzie, J. L.
1967 "Reflections on Wisdom." *JBL* 86: 1–9.

MacLeish, Archibald
1956 *J.B.* Boston: Houghton Mifflin.

Marböck, Johann
1971 *Weisheit im Wandel: Untersuchungen zur Weisheitstheologie bei Ben Sira*. BBB 37. Bonn: Peter Hanstein.
1979 "Sir., 38:24—39:11: Der Schrift-gelehrte Weise. Ein Beitrag zu Gestalt und Werk Ben Siras." Pp. 293–316 in *La Sagesse de l'Ancien Testament*. Ed. M. Gilbert. BETL 51. Gembloux: Duculot.

Marzal, Angel
1976 *Gleanings from the Wisdom of Mari*. Studia Pohl 11. Rome: Pontifical Biblical Institute.

Middendorp, Th.
1973 *Die Stellung Jesu ben Siras zwischen Judentum und Hellenismus*. Leiden: E. J. Brill.

Miles, John A.
1977 "Gagging on Job, or The Comedy of Religious Exhaustion." *Semeia* 7: 71–126.

Miskotte, Kornelis H.
1967   *When the Gods Are Silent*. New York and Evanston: Harper & Row.

Morgan, Donn F.
1981   *Wisdom in the Old Testament Traditions*. Atlanta: John Knox.

Müller, Hans Peter
1968   "Wie Sprach Qohälät von Gott?" *VT* 18: 507–21.
1970   *Hiob und seine Freunde*. Theologische Studien, 103. Zurich: EVZ Verlag.
1978   *Das Hiobproblem*. EdF 84. Darmstadt: Wissenschaftliche Buchgesellschaft.

Murphy, Roland E.
1962   "A Consideration of the Classification 'Wisdom Psalms.'" Pp. 156–67 in *Congress Volume: Bonn, 1962*. VTSup 9. Leiden: E. J. Brill. Reprinted in Crenshaw 1976a: 456–67.
1966   "The Kerygma of the Book of Proverbs." *Int* 20: 3–14.
1970   "The Hebrew Sage and Openness to the World." Pp. 219–44 in *Christian Action and Openness to the World* (Villanova University Symposium II, III). Villanova, PA: Villanova University Press.
1979   "Qohelet's 'Quarrel' with the Fathers." Pp. 235–45 in *From Faith to Faith*. Pittsburgh: Pickwick.
1981a   "Hebrew Wisdom." *JAOS* 101: 21–34.
1981b   *Wisdom Literature: Job, Proverbs, Ruth, Canticles, Ecclesiastes, Esther*. Grand Rapids: Eerdmans.

Murtagh, J.
1968   "The Book of Job and the Book of Dead." *ITQ* 35: 166–73.

Neiman, David
1972   *The Book of Job*. Jerusalem: Massada.

Nougayrol, Jean
1963   "Les sagesses babyloniennes. Études recentes et textes inédits." Pp. 41–50 in *Les sagesses du Proche-Orient ancien*. Paris: Presses Universitaires de France.

Otto, Eberhard
1951   *Der Vorwurf an Gott: Zur Entstehung der ägyptischen Auseinandersetzungsliteratur*. Vorträge der orientalistischen Tagung in Marburg 1950. Hildesheim: n.p.

Perdue, Leo G.
1974   "The Riddles of Psalm 49." *JBL* 93: 533–42.
1977   *Wisdom and Cult*. SBLDS 30. Missoula, MT: Scholars Press.

Pettinato, Giovanni
1976 "The Royal Archives of Tell Mardikh, Ebla." *BA* 39: 44–52.

Pfeiffer, Egon
1965 "Die Gottesfurcht im Buche Kohelet." Pp. 133–58 in *Gottes Wort und Gottes Land: Hans-Wilhelm Hertzberg. Zum 70. Geburtstag.* Ed. H. G. Reventlow. Göttingen: Vandenhoeck & Ruprecht.

Ploeg, J. P. M. van der, and A. S. van der Woude, eds.
1972 *Le Targum de Job de la Grotte XI de Qumran.* Leiden: E. J. Brill.

Plöger, Otto
1971 "Zur Auslegung der Sentenzen-sammlungen des Proverbienbuches." Pp. 402–16 in *Probleme biblischer Theologie.* Ed. H. W. Wolff. Munich: Kaiser.

Pope, Marvin H.
1973 *Job.* AB 15. Garden City, NY: Doubleday.

Prato, Gian Luig
1975 *Il problema della teodicea in Ben Sira. Composizione dei contrari e richiamo alle origini.* AnBib 65. Rome: Pontifical Biblical Institute.

Preuss, Horst Dietrich
1970 "Erwägungen zum theologischen Ort alttestamentlicher Weisheitsliteratur." *EvT* 30: 393–417.
1972 "Das Gottesbild der älteren Weisheit Israels." Pp. 117–45 in *Studies in the Religion of Ancient Israel.* VTSup 23. Leiden: E. J. Brill.

Priest, John F.
1968 "Humanism, Skepticism, and Pessimism in Israel." *JAAR* 36: 311–26.

Pritchard, James B., ed.
1969 *Ancient Near Eastern Texts Relating to the Old Testament.* 3d ed. Princeton: Princeton University Press.

Rad, Gerhard von
1953 "Josephsgeschichte und ältere Chokma." Pp. 120–27 in *Congress Volume: Copenhagen, 1953.* Leiden: E. J. Brill. Eng. trans. in Crenshaw 1976a: 439–47.
1960 "Hiob XXXVIII und die altägyptische Weisheit." Pp. 293–301 in *Wisdom in Israel and the Ancient Near East.* VTSup 3. Leiden: E. J. Brill. English trans. in Crenshaw 1976a: 267–77.
1972 *Wisdom in Israel.* Nashville and New York: Abingdon.

Reese, J. M.
1970 *Hellenistic Influence on the Book of Wisdom and its Consequences.* Rome: Pontifical Biblical Institute.

1979   "Can Paul Ricoeur's Method Contribute to Interpreting
                        the Book of Wisdom?" Pp. 384–96 in *La Sagesse de
                        l'Ancien Testament*. Ed. M. Gilbert. BETL 51. Gem-
                        bloux: Duculot.

Richter, Heinz
1958   "Die Naturweisheit des Alten Testaments im Buch
                        Hiob." *ZAW* 70: 1–20.
1959   *Studien zu Hiob*. Theologische Arbeiten, 11. Berlin:
                        Evangelische Verlagsanstalt.

Richter, Wolfgang
1966   *Recht und Ethos: Versuch einer Ortung des weisheit-
                        lichen Mahnspruches*. SANT 15. Munich: Kösel.

Rickenbacher, Otto
1973   *Weisheits Perikopen bei Ben Sira*. OBO V. 1. Göttingen:
                        Vandenhoeck & Ruprecht; Freiburg/Schweiz: Universi-
                        tätsverlag.

Roberts, J. J. M.
1977   "Job and the Israelite Religious Tradition." *ZAW* 89:
                        107–14.

Robertson, David
1973   "The Book of Job: A Literary Study." *Soundings* 56:
                        446–69.
1977   "The Comedy of Job: A Response." *Semeia* 7: 41–44.

Ross, James F.
1978   "Psalm 73." Pp. 161–75 in *Israelite Wisdom*. Ed. J. G.
                        Gammie et al. Missoula, MT: Scholars Press.

Roth, Wolfgang M. W.
1972   "The Wooing of Rebekah: A Tradition-Critical Study of
                        Genesis 24." *CBQ* 34: 177–87.

Rüger, H. P.
1970   *Text und Textform im hebräischen Sirach*. BZAW 112.
                        Berlin and New York: Walter de Gruyter.

Rylaarsdam, J. Coert
1946   *Revelation in Jewish Wisdom Literature*. Chicago: Uni-
                        versity of Chicago Press.

Sanders, Jim Alvin
1955   *Suffering as Divine Discipline in the Old Testament
                        and Post-Biblical Judaism*. Rochester: Colgate Rochester
                        Divinity School.

Sanders, Paul S.
1955   *Twentieth Century Interpretations of the Book of Job*.
                        Englewood Cliffs: Prentice Hall.

Sandmel, Samuel
1070 *Philo of Alexandria*. New York and Oxford: Oxford
University Press.

Sarna, Nahum M.
1957 "Epic Substratum in the Prose of Job." *JBL* 76: 13–25.

Scaltriti, G.
1955 "Ciobbe tra Cristo e Zaratustra." *Palestra del Clero* 34:
673–82, 721–28.

Schmid, Hans Heinrich
1966 *Wesen und Geschichte der Weisheit*. BZAW 101. Berlin: A. Töpelmann.
1974 *Altorientalische Welt in der alttestamentlichen Theologie*. Zurich: Theologischer Verlag.

Schmidt, Johannes
1936 *Studien zur Stilistik der alttestamentlichen Spruchlite-
rature*. ATAbh 13/1. Münster: Aschendorffsche Verlags-
buchhandlung.

Scott, R. B. Y.
1961 "Folk Proverbs of the Ancient Near East." Pp. 447–56 in
Transactions of the Royal Society of Canada, 15. Re
printed in Crenshaw 1976a: 417–26.
1965 *Proverbs. Ecclesiastes*. AB 18. Garden City: Doubleday.
1970 "The Study of Wisdom Literature." *Int* 24:20–45.
1971a "Wisdom. Wisdom Literature." Pp. 557–63 in *EncJud*,
Vol. 16.
1971b *The Way of Wisdom in the Old Testament*. New York:
Macmillan.
1972 "Wise and Foolish, Righteous and Wicked." Pp. 146–65
in *Studies in the Religion of Ancient Israel*. VTSup 23.
Leiden: E. J. Brill.

Sekine, Masao
1958 "Schöpfung und Erlösung im Buche Hiob." Pp. 213–23
in *Von Ugarit nach Qumran*. BZAW 77. Berlin:
A. Töpelmann.

Sheppard, Gerry T.
1977 "The Epilogue to Qohelet as Theological Commentary."
CBQ 39: 182–89.
1980 *Wisdom as a Hermeneutical Construct*. BZAW 151.
Berlin and New York: Walter de Gruyter.

Simon, Neil
1975 *God's Favorite, a Comedy by Neil Simon*. New York:
Random House.

Simpson, William Kelly, ed.
1973 *The Literature of Ancient Egypt*. New Haven and London: Yale University Press.

Skehan, Patrick W.
1971   *Studies in Israelite Poetry and Wisdom.* CBQMS 1. Washington: Catholic Biblical Association of America.

Skladny, Udo
1962   *Die ältesten Spruchsammlungen in Israel.* Göttingen: Vandenhoeck & Ruprecht.

Smith, D. E.
1975   "Wisdom." Pp. 215–47 in *Ras Shamra Parallels, II.* Ed. Loren Fisher. AnOr 50. Rome: Pontifical Biblical Institute.

Soden, W. von
1955   "Die Frage nach der Gerechtigkeit Gottes im Alten Orient." MDOG 96: 41–59.

Talmon, Shemaryahu
1963   "'Wisdom' in the Book of Esther." *VT* 13: 419–55.

Taylor, W. S.
1956   "Theology and Therapy in Job." *TToday* 12: 451–62.

Terrien, Samuel
1957   *Job: Poet of Existence.* New York: Bobbs Merrill.
1959   "J.B. and Job." *The Christian Century* 76, 1 (January 7): 9–11.
1962   "Amos and Wisdom." Pp. 108–15 in *Israel's Prophetic Heritage.* Ed. B. W. Anderson and W. Harrelson. New York: Harper & Row. Reprinted in Crenshaw 1976a: 448–55.
1965   "Quelques remarques sur les affinites de Job avec la Deutëro-Ésaïe." Pp. 295–310 in *Volume du Congrès: Genève, 1965.* VTSup 15. Leiden: E. J. Brill.

Tournay, R.
1957   "L'ordre primitif des chapitres XXIV–XXVIII du livre de Job." *RB* 64: 321–34.

Trible, Phyllis
1963   "Studies in the Book of Jonah." Ph.D. dissertation, Columbia University.

Tsevat, Matitiahu
1966   "The Meaning of the Book of Job." *HUCA* 37: 73–106. Reprinted in Crenshaw 1976a: 341–74.

Urbach, Ephraim E.
1975   *The Sages: Their Concepts and Beliefs.* I–II. Jerusalem: Magnes.

Vawter, Bruce
1980   "Prov. 8:22: Wisdom and Creation." *JBL* 99: 205–16.

Volten, Aksel
    1963   "Der Begriff der Maat in den Ägyptischen Weisheits-
                        texten." Pp. 73–99 in *Les sagesses du Proche-Orient
                        ancien*. Paris: Presses Universitaires de France.

Weinfeld, Moshe
    1960   "The Dependence of Deuteronomy upon the Wisdom
                        Literature." Pp. 89–108 in *Yehezkel Kaufmann Jubilee
                        Volume*. Jerusalem: Magnes.
    1967   "The Origin of Humanism in Deuteronomy." *JBL* 80:
                        241–47.
    1972   *Deuteronomy and the Deuteronomic School*. Oxford:
                        Oxford University Press.

Wendel, François
    1963   *Les Sagesses du Proche-Orient ancien*. Paris: Presses
                        Universitaires de France.

Westermann, Claus
    1977   *Der Aufbau des Buches Hiob*. Stuttgart: Calwer (origi-
                        nal edition, 1956).

Whedbee, J. William
    1971   *Isaiah and Wisdom*. Nashville: Abingdon.
    1977   "The Comedy of Job." *Semeia* 7: 1–39.

Whitley, Charles
    1979   *Koheleth*. BZAW 148. Berlin and New York: Walter
                        de Gruyter.

Whybray, Roger N.
    1965   *Wisdom in Proverbs*. SBT 45. London: SCM.
    1968   *The Succession Narrative*. SBT 9. London: SCM.
    1974   *The Intellectual Tradition in the Old Testament*.
                        BZAW 135. Berlin and New York: Walter de Gruyter.
    1978   "Slippery Words. IV. Wisdom." *ExpTim* 89: 359–62.
    1981   "The Identification and Use of Quotations in Ecclesi-
                        astes." Pp. 435–51 in *Congress Volume: Vienna, 1980*.
                        VTSup 32. Leiden: E. J. Brill.

Williams, James G.
    1971a   "What Does It Profit a Man?: The Wisdom of Koheleth."
                        Judaism 20: 179–93. Reprinted in Crenshaw 1976a:
                        379–89.
    1971b   "'You Have not Spoken Truth of Me': Mystery and Irony
                        in Job." *ZAW* 83: 231–55.
    1977   "Comedy, Irony, Intercession: A Few Notes in Re-
                        sponse." *Semeia* 7: 135–45.
    1981   *Those Who Ponder Proverbs: Aphoristic Thinking and
                        Biblical Literature*. Sheffield: Almond.

Williams, R. J.
    1956   "Theodicy in the Ancient Near East." *CJT* 2: 14–26.

1981   "The Sages of Ancient Egypt in the Light of Recent Scholarship." *JAOS* 101: 1–19.

Winston, David
1979   *The Wisdom of Solomon*. AB 43. Garden City, NY: Doubleday.

Witzenrath, Hagia
1979   *Süss is das Licht.* . . . ArzTu Sprache, 11. St. Ottilien: Eos Verlag.

Wolff, Hans Walter
1964   *Amos' geistige Heimat*. WMANT 18. Neukirchen-Vluyn: Neukirchener Verlag. English trans., *Amos the Prophet*. Philadelphia: Fortress, 1973.
1978   "Micha the Moreshite—The Prophet and his Background." Pp. 77–84 in *Israelite Wisdom*. Ed. J. G. Gammie et al. Missoula, MT: Scholars Press.

Wright, Addison D. G.
1968   "The Riddle of the Sphinx: The Structure of the Book of Qoheleth." *CBQ* 30: 313–34. Reprinted in Crenshaw 1976a: 245–66.

Würthwein, Ernst
1970   "Die Weisheit Ägyptens und das Alte Testament." Pp. 197–216 in *Wort und Existenz, Studien zum Alten Testament*. Göttingen: Vandenhoeck & Ruprecht. English trans. in Crenshaw 1976a: 113–33.

Yadin, Yigael
1965   *The Ben Sira Scroll from Masada*. Jerusalem: Israel Exploration Society and Shrine of the Book.

Zaba, Z.
1956   *Les Maximes de Ptahhotep*. Prague: Ed. de l'Academie tchecoslovaque des Ceiences.

Zerafa, Peter Paul
1978   *The Wisdom of God in the Book of Job*. Rome: Herder.

Zhitlowsky, Chaim
1968   "Job and Faust." Pp. 90–162 in *Two Studies in Yiddish Culture*. Ed. P. Matendo. Leiden: E. J. Brill.

Zimmerli, Walther
1963   "Ort und Grenze der Weisheit im Rahmen der Alttestamentlichen Theologie." Pp. 121–36 in *Les sagesses du Proche-Orient ancien*. Paris: Presses Universitaires de France. English trans. "The Place and Limit of the Wisdom in the Framework of the Old Testament Theology." *SJT* 17 (1964) 146–58. Reprinted in Crenshaw 1976a: 314–26.
1974   "Das Buch Kohelet—Traktat oder Sentenzensammlung?" *VT* 24: 221–30.

1976   "Concerning the Structure of Old Testament Wisdom."
        ZAW 51: 177–204. Reprinted in Crenshaw 1976a:
        175–207.
1978   *Old Testament Theology in Outline*. Atlanta: John
        Knox.

Zimmermann, Frank
1973   *The Inner World of Qohelet*. New York: Ktav.

12

The Lyrical Literature

Erhard S. Gerstenberger

I. LYRICS IN THE HEBREW SCRIPTURES

Is it appropriate to employ a Greek term to identify a complex body of literature in the Hebrew scriptures? Lyric/lyrical is derived from "lyre" or "harp," and for many it brings to mind images of romantic individualism and sentimentality. However, that part of the Hebrew scriptures under discussion here is all but void of such romanticizing features. Lyrics in this case, even though implying poetry set to music and accompanied by stringed and other instruments, designates compositions deeply rooted in the life and work, war and cult of the Israelite people. No matter how varied such "lyrical" manifestations may appear, they have in common just this social, festive, and ritual dimension. Thus, if the Greek concept is understood in this extended sense, it can legitimately be applied to this body of Hebrew materials.

The lyrical literature of the Hebrew scriptures is found primarily in the books of Psalms, Lamentations, and the Song of Songs. It is generally recognized, however, that lyrical materials have also been combined with other literary genres in the Hebrew Bible—most notably with narrative, prophecy, and wisdom. Thus, Judges 5 (victory song), Isaiah 12 (thanksgiving hymn), and Job 30 (personal lament), although representing different categories of lyrical literature, are illustrative of the way in which this type of material has been incorporated into a number of different literary contexts. In addition, poetic oratory has influenced the style of a number of other genres in the Hebrew scriptures, although we cannot disregard the differences between the poetic styles of prophecy and wisdom, epic and lyric. However, in spite of obvious points of contact and interrelationship with other literary genres, we must remember that the lyrical materials of the Hebrew Bible constitute a separate body of literature that is distinguishable by particular characteristics. The distinctive linguistic structure of the lyrical literature, its musical qualities, and its ritualistic setting, all serve to identify it as a separate literary genre and consequently call for a method of analysis responsive to the particular characteristics and needs of the Hebrew poetic materials.

In addition to providing a general knowledge of the content and

form of the Hebrew lyrical literature, the study of this material is significant in view of its influence on our own culture and faith. The Psalms
have inspired liturgy, songs, and prayer in both the Jewish and Christian
communities. The theological affirmations of this literature have profoundly molded the thinking of many religious figures in the past and
continue to play a vital role in modern theological movements, especially
in the Third World (see Cardenal). Moreover, the ongoing spiritual
power of Israel's poetry transcends its ecclesiastical communities; its
influence is discernible not only in the religious sphere but also in modern literature, poetry, and art (see Kurz).

Research since 1945 on Israel's lyrical material reflects this widespread influence. Studies with a direct bearing on lyrical literature range
from archaeological reports to essays deeply rooted in philosophy and
theology, from anthropological observations to historical and literary
scrutinies. The great variety of methods and perspectives represented by
these studies, as well as the sheer mass of relevant publications, prohibits
extensive discussion of all items. The aim of this study, then, is to provide an overview of the research done on the lyrical material of the
Hebrew Bible since 1945 and to serve as an introduction to the most
significant issues and findings of that research.

II. TEXT CRITICISM

The foundation of any exegetical endeavor is the painstaking work
of recovering the oldest possible wording of the text. Unfortunately,
because of its very nature and its widespread use throughout its history,
the lyrical material in the Hebrew Bible has suffered considerable alteration and corruption. As a result, on almost every page the text poses
more problems than the interpreter may be able to solve. In two new
areas of research, the Dead Sea Scrolls and the Ugaritic materials, scholars are attempting to deal with these problems. By looking at their work,
we can gain a representative picture of the state of modern text criticism
of the lyrical literature.

When the discovery of the Dead Sea Scrolls was announced in 1947,
hope was immediately kindled in the scholarly world that this could
advance the knowledge of archaic forms of Hebrew writings. However,
the edition of the Qumran Psalms scroll (Sanders, 1967) and its comparison
with the MT (Sanders, 1966; Bardtke; Homan) showed a surprising degree
of agreement between these manuscripts, which originated centuries
apart. While the Qumran community took great liberty in arranging the
psalms and even in including noncanonical psalms, textual variants are at a
minimum. Apart from the Psalms scroll, virtually no canonical material of
the lyrical type has been found. The only other lyrical texts discovered at
Qumran are the *Hodayot*. These thanksgiving songs, however, represent a

later stage of psalmody and allow for inference back to the MT only in exceptional cases (see Sukenik; Mansoor).

The materials found at Ugarit proved to be an extraordinary stimulus to text-critical work. Excavation began at Ugarit in 1929 and in subsequent years yielded hundreds of tablets containing poetic texts. Analysis of these texts revealed that the Ugaritic language was closely related to Hebrew and that Ugaritic poetic style was quite similar to that of Israelite poetry. Consequently, numerous scholars began to draw on this newly recovered vocabulary and poetic structure in order to solve textual enigmas in the MT, and many emendations and new meanings of difficult terms and passages in the Hebrew scriptures were proposed. The use of Ugaritic materials thus touches not only the establishment of the text but matters of philology as well. A host of specialists from many countries dedicated themselves to this study of the Ugaritic literature: C. Virolleaud, C. H. Gordon, J. Gray, G. R. Driver, R. Dussaud, W. F. Albright, F. M. Cross, M. H. Pope, O. Loretz, L. R. Fisher, J. C. de Moor, A. S. Kapelrud, H. Gese, U. Cassuto, S. E. Loewenstamm, L. Delekat, and many others.

However, none of these scholars has been more prolific than Mitchell Dahood, who has published numerous articles as well as a three-volume commentary on Psalms. Throughout his studies the working premise is that analogies established between the Ugaritic and Hebrew literature warrant direct inference from Ugaritic to Hebrew poetry and vocabulary; consequently, Dahood is largely concerned to emend the Hebrew text on the basis of Ugaritic parallels. To cite but one example: Ps 22:30 reads in Dahood's translation (1965:138):

> Indeed to him shall bow down
>   all those who sleep in the nether world;
> Before him shall bend the knee
>   all who have gone down to the mud.
> For the Victor himself restores to life.

Two principal emendations lead to this reading. The difficult *dsny* is held to be composed of the "relative pronoun *dī* as in Ugaritic and Aramaic, and *šēnē* < *yᵉšēnē*, from *yāšēn*, 'to sleep.'" The "Victor," on the other hand, emerges from an audacious new interpretation of the lexeme *l'*, which now becomes a "stative participle . . . from *l'y*, a root frequently attested in Ugaritic and Phoenician" (1965:143–44).

Many scholars have protested Dahood's basic assumption and practice, however, as an unjustified and uncontrolled use of cognate material (see Loretz), and it is unlikely that many of Dahood's proposals will in the final analysis prove satisfactory. Yet he has made a significant contribution through provoking debate concerning the value and applicability of the Ugaritic materials to the Hebrew Bible in particular and the value of comparative vocabulary and literature studies in general.

Although the Dead Sea Scrolls and Ugaritic tablets have at times clarified difficult Masoretic wording, textual criticism of the Hebrew lyrical literature has basically been proceeding at a slow pace and without spectacular changes. Undoubtedly, scholars will continue to use information derived from such extra-biblical documents, including the newly discovered Ebla texts. Primary emphasis for text-critical studies, however, will continue to be on the Masoretic tradition, with secondary emphasis on the LXX and other ancient versions. Representative examples of this continuing approach in text-critical studies are those of Leveen and Schmuttermayr (see Gerstenberger, 1974b:23–26) in Psalms; Albrektson, Bergler, Dahood (1978), Gottlieb, and Hillers in Lamentations; and Pope and Schneekloth in the Song of Songs.

III. LYRICAL/POETIC LANGUAGE

Language is the basic material with which modern interpreters of ancient texts must work. The question in our case, then, is this: Do we find a particular poetic or lyrical language and linguistic structure in the Hebrew Bible? This issue has increasingly entered scholarly consciousness and debate, and much study has been done on the way in which lexicographical and syntactical units are structured in Israel's poetic literature. This section will discuss these overall cultural patterns of lyrical language. The more individual stylistic elements will be considered in the following section.

As early as 1753, Bishop Lowth described in considerable detail the outstanding characteristic of Hebrew and other Oriental poetry—the parallelism of words and ideas in a given poetic unit. Scholars have studied and reevaluated this phenomenon ever since, but the accuracy of Lowth's observation is still accepted (see G. B. Gray; Robinson, 1953; Boling). As Norman Gottwald observes, "Parallelism of thought, and corresponding word-mass, is the substance and mode of Hebrew poetic expression" (1962b:835). The continuing study of parallelism has isolated three or four principal types: synonymous, antithetic, synthetic, and climactic (Alonso-Schökel, 1963; Ridderbos, 1972; Kosmala). For the most part, there has been little alteration or modification of this basic schema. Although further types of parallelism have been proposed (e.g., the "coordinating" and "summarizing" parallelism of Horst), they have not been generally accepted. Proposals of this type do not, of course, in any way alter the overall significance of parallel stichoi (or cola) as being the most characteristic elements of the Hebrew poetic line.

The intricate problems of Hebrew meter are, however, the more difficult to resolve. The modern urge to investigate questions of meter and rhythm in Hebrew poetry seems to derive less from the Hebrew scriptures themselves than from our classical forebears. After all, if the

Greeks and the Romans knew and used a quantifying and accentuating verse melody, why should the Hebrews not have employed it also? Assuming, then, that the Israelites did seek to achieve metrical equilibrium in their poetry, the issue is whether they attained this by counting syllables or by counting stresses.

Experts are divided on this question. Continuing the work done by G. W. H. Bickell in the last century, Mowinckel and others have defended an alternating system, a regular sequence of stressed and unstressed syllables. Most scholars, however, including Robinson (1947), Kraus, and Feuillet, and going back to J. Ley and E. Sievers, prefer to see a system of accentuation more in line with the present Masoretic punctuation. Thus, for them the number of stressed syllables, usually separated by some number of unstressed ones, determines the balance of the line. The difficulty with both these interpretations is that these scholars must presuppose more than a millennium of linguistic history with no major changes in speech habits and grammar. This would be most unlikely. Between the time of the judges and that of the Masoretes profound shifts in spoken and written Hebrew occurred, not to mention the transition that took place in the very beginning of Israel's history from Aramaic to the language of Canaan. Given this historical perspective, it is little wonder that there is growing dissatisfaction in the scholarly world with any ironclad or exclusive theory regarding the meter and rhythm of Hebrew poetry (see Alonso-Schökel, 1963; Freedman, 1977).

Indeed, Segert has revised and elaborated an older hypothesis allowing for change and development in Hebrew poetry. In the beginning, he argues, Hebrew meter depended on verbal units, without regard to quantity or quality of syllables. Only later did Israelite poets adopt an accentuating beat as a schema for their compositions. While such hypotheses as these help in clarifying the issues regarding meter in Hebrew poetry, the material condition of our sources and the lack of any reliable information make it altogether inadvisable to hope for clear-cut solutions. As Freedman observes, no "magic key has ever been found, or is likely to be" (1977:10).

Inspired both by metrical and structural considerations, Fohrer challenged the hegemony of parallelism in Hebrew poetry. He describes a poetic system based on autonomous semi-stichs ("Kurzverse"—short lines). His evidence includes, besides some acrostic psalms (Psalms 111, 112, etc.), parts of prophetic speeches such as Isa 63:10. Mowinckel (1957), on the other hand, contests this interpretation, which in his opinion relies on exceptional and unusual passages. So far, then, this theory has found little support from other scholars, although Piatti comes to similar conclusions and some other exegetes will admit, rather reluctantly, the existence of verses that do not obey the rule of parallelism (Rudolph: 122, 124, 125; Ridderbos, 1972:12–13).

The use of a strophic structure in Hebrew poetry also remains a more or less open question. Those who claim that such structuring devices were used can point to Isa 5:1–7, which falls neatly into four strophes (Willis), or to the refrains of Psalm 42/43 and also to the Song of Songs generally. However, such examples of carefully structured strophic poetry appear to be the exception rather than the rule. Ridderbos, a dedicated scholar of all kinds of poetic phenomena, rightly observes that "only in relatively few cases can we detect a formal regularity" (1972:67). Somewhat more optimism regarding the possible organization of Hebrew poetry in stanzas is shown by Mowinckel, Montgomery, Baumann, Skehan, Kunz, Cross, Freedman, and many others. Further, we may suspect that if the occidental predilection for seeing strophic order prevails, analysis could degenerate into the construction of artificial strophic arrangements.

A significant innovation occurred in postwar studies when researchers identified nearly self-sufficient poetic elements smaller than the colon or line. This discovery bears a certain resemblance to the isolation of those components which make up atomic nuclei. Like subatomic particles, these self-sufficient elements in Hebrew poetry have been seen as the basic structural elements, as the kernels of Hebrew poetry, the building blocks used in the constructions. Consequently, a good number of scholars, beginning with H. L. Ginsberg, have dedicated themselves to this research. While some investigations, notably the recent monograph by Watters, have been criticized because of questionable methodology (Good: 274–75), on the whole scholars agree that fixed formulaic expressions of various kinds do constitute important poetic devices.

The use of such fixed formulas extends far beyond the cultures of the ancient Near East. As anthropologists and experts on compositional techniques have noted, standard phrases are part of the stock of creative elements used by all poets. Their use is especially prevalent, however, in the oral phase of poetic literature. Scholars of the Hebrew Bible have drawn on these general observations and have applied them to the questions of the setting and structure of Hebrew poetry. Thus, in the light of the general trend toward oral composition through the use of fixed formulas, Culley argued that the formulaic elements used in the psalms clearly demonstrate their oral origin. Gevirtz followed Ginsberg in analyzing traditional word pairs in Israel's poetry, and Dahood furthered this work significantly by considering Ugaritic parallels. Whallon, after an extensive study of classical Greek, Old English, and Hebrew poetic compositions, explicitly linked word pairs with the wider phenomenon of parallelism: "The word pairs became formulaic because they assisted the poet in *composing*" (141), and the act of composing in Hebrew poetry is tantamount to "creating parallelism" (154). We need to recognize, then, that societies create and provide, among other linguistic instruments for poetic work, fixed formulaic expressions which in some cultures, including Israel, included word pairs to be used in parallel lines. The conscious breakup or alteration of such fixed combinations is a matter of individual style, the significance and character of which will be discussed below.

In taking up other poetic devices we approach the realm of individual style, but since these linguistic features can be systematically identified they are at least partially collective in origin and function. While they may be distinctively altered and nuanced by individual poets, they are not the exclusive property of those poets or their times. From this perspective we may mention here further phenomena associated with Israelite poetry. Alonso-Schökel's work (1963) will serve as a guide because his book on Hebrew poetry is the most comprehensive treatment written since 1945.

According to Alonso-Schökel, the first task of prosody should be a verification of the "sound material" (*material sonoro*) of a given language (1963:71–117). In the case of biblical Hebrew the difficulties of recovering sound values should not be overemphasized. After all, phonological investigations have revealed that the Hebrew script is phonetic in character and that "we can sufficiently trust in the extant text as far as consonants are concerned. In many cases this is true also for the vowels, and in general for the accents as well" (1963:80). A second observation, based on specific texts, undergirds this optimistic conclusion. Certain sound-effects are universally known in all languages, and others we can extrapolate from semantic or symbolic values of the word or phrase concerned. Alonso-Schökel observes that "Hebrew writers kept alive the predilection for sound-effects much more so than our modern writers do" (1963:83). There must have been, then, an abundance of auditory devices at their disposal for use in both poetic and prose compositions.

In his analysis of selected texts in Isaiah, Alonso-Schökel systematically examines the sound qualities of poetic language, drawing on previous work done by Boström, Saydon, Cross and Freedman, and others on such devices as alliteration and assonance. But Alonso-Schökel consistently places his research in the wider context of literary theory and stresses the importance of the general use of sound duplication—an "effective phonetic means of establishing the unity of two members, without however destroying their duality" (1963:110). Repeated sounds function effectively in a variety of word combinations and stylistic settings. A second feature of Hebrew poetic language is the presence of "predominant sounds," that is, phonemes or clusters of phonemes which repeat themselves in a given poetic unit in order to underline the affirmation made. A good example of this phenomenon is Isa 17:12:

הוי המון עמים רבים כהמות ימים יהמיון

ושאון לאמים כשאון מים כבירים ישאון

Alonso-Schökel further distinguishes particular uses of the application of sound dominance, notably onomatopoeic, metaphoric, and symbolic (1963:113ff.).

The use in poetry of the linguistic "raw material" dealt with above (III) leads to various structural techniques and devices. Sound harmony can embellish all kinds of word arrangements within a poem: chiasm, antithesis, synonymy, etc. Sound dominance serves equally to enhance word play (paronomasia) and figurative meanings. To cite but one example, the repeated use of the consonants ל and כ in Isa 18:2 will, according to Alonso-Schökel, effectively evoke the idea of הלך, "to walk, to go" (1963:114f.). While Alonso-Schökel takes his examples for the most part from Isaiah, those researchers who have studied other poetic compositions in the Hebrew scriptures arrive at similar conclusions (Boström, Christian, Saydon, Díez Macho).

The use of synonymy and antithesis is also a phenomenon that seems to belong to the realm of personal style. But inasmuch as they represent linguistic opportunities provided by existing speech patterns and vocabulary, they certainly belong to the general mass of poetic "raw material" which we are discussing here. Alonso-Schökel sets these features apart from parallelism, justifying such treatment by asserting that "synonymy is a peculiar phenomenon which may exist with or without parallelism" (1963:231). The same would hold true, of course, for antithesis. According to Staiger, to whom Alonso-Schökel refers (1963:235), lyrical composition is based in a very special way on repetition, and repetition of emotional affirmations calls for synonymic expressions: "What keeps lyrical poetry from dissolution is, and exclusively so, repetition" (Staiger: 31). We should add that the evident overlapping of the phenomena of synonymy and antithesis with that of word pairs does not preclude their separate discussion. This is so because their construction and application constitute more than the simple use of conventionally predetermined formulas.

A weakness in Alonso-Schökel's analysis must be noted, however. He tends to deal with stylistic antithesis principally under the rubric of antithetic *thinking*, a position now questioned by linguistic theorists. Consequently, his general conclusion—"In Hebrew literature synonymy or repetition is predominant; in Western literature it is antithesis or juxtaposition" (1963:267)—should be received with caution.

Metaphors and symbols are widely used in all poetic language, and biblical poetry is no exception. Evidently, this preference for "nondirect" formulation has to do with the very nature of creative and inspired speech. The true poet of old was a powerful person, one who knew well how to synthesize reality in such a way as to give access to transcendental being (see Weiss; Freedman; Alonso-Schökel). Poetic language breaks through the confines of rationalistic world views, intuitively approaching the essence of things. Therefore, the use of comparative, inductive, indirect language is imperative for the poet. Every language possesses, from the very beginning, metaphors and symbols. Idioms are replete with them, and everyone who learns to speak a language at a given time learns to understand and handle their subtle meanings. Figurative speech, in this respect, is part of any given cultural heritage.

The importance of metaphors and symbols in Israel's poetry can hardly be overestimated. Unfortunately however, as Alonso-Schökel observes, relatively little attention has been paid to these phenomena. Luckily, through the work of Goodenough and of Keel (1978) a good part of Hebrew symbolism has become visible, enabling us to avoid the excessive rationalism and materialism that have often characterized our approach.

The sheer number of poetic linguistic devices quite naturally leads to the question of whether there existed anything like a genuine lyrical language in Israel. Those specialists whose work we have been discussing are by and large aware of this problem, although most commentaries on the biblical poetic books ignore it. A few basic differences between poetry and prose, in fact, have long been noted. Thus, the accusative particle rarely appears in poetic texts; a relative clause often remains formally unrelated to the main clause; the copulative *wĕ* is sometimes missing (Freedman, 1977). Poetic language in the Hebrew scriptures, furthermore, tends at times to archaisms (Robertson), exquisite vocabulary, and inverted word order. But all these are minor divergences that do not constitute sufficient reason to speak of a separate lyrical dialect, in contrast to the situation found in Sumerian literature.

One specific point in question, however, could be the verbal system employed in Hebrew poetry. As can be expected, the narrating forms of the verb occur only in historical psalms and similar texts (see Psalms 78; 105). Typical for most lyrical materials are simple perfects and imperfects, which occasionally pose problems if viewed with reference to the traditional schema of time sequence. The thorough study of Michel (1960), departing from earlier work done by E. Kuhr, H. S. Nyberg, J. Begrich, and L. Köhler, demonstrates a distinctive use of verbal tempora and word order (position of subject and predicate) in poetic language. Finite verbs, according to Michel (1960:177ff.), do not indicate a fixed spot in a simple schema of past, present, or future time. Rather, they relate to the beginning, duration, and modalities of the action involved. Michel further insists that the usual classification of sentence structure into nominal and verbal sentences does not apply to poetic language. Instead, the basic sentence forms need to be redefined, and their functions in composite sentence clusters must be investigated.

An example of the importance of the clarification of these grammatical issues is the thorny problem of divine enthronement psalms. How should we translate *yhwh mālāk* (Ps 93:1) and related expressions?

Michel applies his general rules concerning word sequence and type of phrase: verbal clauses "do not predicate a subject, but indicate an action"; a nominal clause "makes a statement about a subject. . . . Normally its sentence is subject-predicate" (1960:178; see also 1956). Therefore, Michel concludes, the affirmation *yhwh mālāk* "does not indicate how Yahweh became king, but rather how he acted as king" (1956:395).

It is not surprising that it was Dahood who hinted at more far-reaching conclusions regarding a grammar of poetic language. At the end of his commentary on Psalms he summarizes (in more than eighty pages, divided into nine chapters) his linguistic observations on the poems. After dealing with orthography and phonetics (1970:370–74) he presents poetic peculiarities according to the different word classes—pronouns, nouns, verbs, prepositions, particles—and uncovers in each a variety of hitherto unknown expressions and meanings (1970:374–410). The longest chapter is "Syntax and Poetic Devices" (1970:410–44). Among the newly discovered phenomena discussed in this chapter are the precative perfect (1970:414–17) and a good number of double-duty lexemes (1970:429–39).

However, as has been stated before, Dahood's suggestions are still in the experimental phase and are being hotly contested by other scholars. The grammatical appendix to his Psalms commentary, therefore, is not the final word on poetic language in the Hebrew scriptures. Consisting primarily of lists of passages, without discussion of the evidence or answers to opposing views such as the one just cited, this "Grammar of the Psalter" still lacks the plausibility it wishes to attain.

The idiosyncrasies of Hebrew poetic language also lead to the question of possible foreign influences on the language. Albright and his followers have long pointed out the affinities between Hebrew poetry and the Ugaritic literature. Kramer (1961) goes much further, insinuating that early Sumerian poetic practices established the patterns for poetic expression later to be employed throughout the ancient Near East. Other scholars have noted the above-average stock of Aramaic loanwords in Hebrew poetry. These and other observations leave us with the question of whether there was anything like an international poetic tradition in the ancient world (see below, VIII).

A summary description of all the research done on and the features discovered in Hebrew poetry could yield not only a "handbook" of poetic grammar but also a kind of semantic synthesis, a dictionary of lyrical terms and usage. In fact, such a work, *A Lexicon of Accadian Prayers* by C. J. Mullo Weir, was published in 1934. Initial steps in this direction have also been taken in regard to the Hebrew poetic literature. The various lexical studies of the special terminology of the psalms (see Mowinckel, 1962, 2:207–17; Delekat, 1964a, 1964b) demonstrate the necessity for further research in this field. In addition, given the basic importance the poetic materials in the Hebrew scriptures have for theology and for the message of the church and synagogue today, we might even speak of an urgent need for an independent dictionary of poetry. N. D. Williams's *A Lexicon for the Poetic Books* is a sign that this need is being recognized.

IV. STYLISTIC FEATURES

The Western concept of literary style is ambiguous. On the one hand, it usually assumes that there are figures and patterns of speech that are characteristic of a given cultural context. On the other hand, it reckons with the numerous varieties of individual articulations that result in an unmistakable profile of literary expression. This oscillation between social and individual traits is by no means arbitrary. On the contrary, it has its roots in the problem of language itself. Language has always been a prefabricated instrument handed over to be used (and abused) by individuals. In other words, the poets of all times have created their poetic realities in the midst of—not outside of—that conditioning network of social relations and linguistic structures which is their physical and spiritual home. In turning to the aspect of individual creativity in the Hebrew scriptures, it should be clear then that all the linguistic features discussed above may and do serve as vehicles of personal expression. If there were room enough to do so, we would treat them again in this section. Under the circumstances, however, we shall limit ourselves to a discussion of personal authorship in Israelite lyrical literature and of typical elements of lyrical style frequently considered in research on the Hebrew scriptures.

The question of authorship is a central issue in the discussion of lyrical poetry. Nineteenth-century criticism emphasized individual authorship to the extent of virtually equating the poet and the product; thus it tended to ignore the significance and influence of social and communal factors. However, with the rise of new areas of research (history of religions, cultic history, mythological research, folklore studies, form criticism, tradition history, etc.) attention became focused on the popular, anonymous, and collective origin of many ancient literary genres. It seems that in our times the pendulum is starting to swing back toward assuming individual authorship of Israel's poetry. One should expect, however, a better solution to the enigmatic problem of the individual/collective interplay in forming poems and lyrical literature. A wide variety of opinion still remains on this issue.

The Song of Songs, though occasionally still considered an authentic work of King Solomon (Thieberger), is for the most part interpreted in terms of folkloristic or royal religious ideology. Pope's surprising, but by no means absurd, localization of this cycle of love songs in funeral celebrations suggests a popular and religious background for them. On the whole, modern exegetes tend to stress the ritual character (in its broadest sense) of the book rather than to insist on its origin as a piece of individual artistry (Audet; Bentzen; Dubarle; Feuillet; Kramer, 1969; Schmökel; Widengren, 1948). The same interpretation also applies to the book of Lamentations. Modern research rarely attributes this book to Jeremiah, as did the LXX. Instead, the origin of these "communal dirges" is traced back to public laments after the fall of Jerusalem in 587 B.C.E. (Albrektson; Kraus, 1956; Hillers). Suggestions concerning the real poets behind these texts remain extremely tenuous.

With Psalms the situation is more complicated. Biblical tradition seeks to identify historical figures as the authors of various poems: David, Asaph, Korah, and others are mentioned in the superscriptions. Modern theological interest often unconsciously follows the same path and so tries to secure the testimony of faith in a psalm by assigning it to one particular witness. Small wonder, then, that conservative scholars still cling to Davidic authorship, while other critics, although abandoning the literal interpretation of the titles, opt for anonymous but still well-defined individual artists. Given this orientation, there seem to be two alternatives regarding the quest for the authors of the psalms: either our extant psalms are to be seen as private compositions, even though they are indebted to older liturgical poetry (Beyerlin, 1970; Kraus, 1978; Sabourin; Delekat, 1967; Weiss; and others) or they are the more professional compositions of temple singers and were destined for cultic use (Mowinckel, 1962; Ridderbos, 1976; Ringgren; Keel, 1972; Johnson; and others). Behind this controversy, however, there still lies the unresolved problem of how to evaluate justly the relative proportions of individual creativity and social convention in the process of poetic composition.

Lyrical poetry in the Hebrew scriptures outside of the poetic books is obviously subject to the same kind of uncertainty. A good illustration of this is the discussion that centers on the so-called Confessions of Jeremiah (Jer 11:18–12:6; 15:10–21; 17:12–18; 18:18–23; 20:7–18), lyrical compositions akin to the individual laments in the Psalter. The vast majority of experts insist on the personal authorship of these laments by the prophet. However, if the history of compilation and transmission of prophetic books is taken into consideration, their autobiographical character and intention must be doubted. Thus Reventlow and this writer (1963) have contested the private character of Jeremiah's laments, postulating instead a cultic and liturgical background. This latter interpretation has so far found little sympathy in scholarly circles but rather has provoked vehement protests from, among others, J. Bright, J. M. Berridge, and W. L. Holladay.

Similarly, other lyrical compositions in the Hebrew scriptures are, with varying degrees of probability, seen as the work of individual authors. They are attributed variously to particular historical figures (Judges

5 to Deborah; Exod 15:21 to Miriam; Deuteronomy 32 to Moses; 2 Sam 1:19–24 to David), are left to the anonymity of preliterary history (Gen 4:23–24; Genesis 49; Num 23:7–10), or are treated as interpolations by later editors or redactors (2 Sam 2:1–10; Isa 5:1–7; 38:9–20; cf. also the citation of biblical psalms in 2 Samuel 22 and 1 Chronicles 16). With regard to this issue, the Servant Songs in Deutero-Isaiah pose very specific problems (Seybold, 1977).

Unfortunately, there has been little discussion of the problem of how to recognize the personal involvement of poets in the emotions expressed in ancient texts. Are observations of style and content really sufficient to address this issue? The hidden presupposition behind studies of this kind seems to be that the emotional participation of the author is directly reflected in the surface or depth structure of the poem. But the results of intensive studies on this subject are, at best, ambiguous. As with the Confessions of Jeremiah, all the emotions expressed in ancient poetry can be understood in terms of individual emotional involvement, but these emotions are perhaps better understood as stylized liturgical language. Scholars almost unanimously emphasize the virtual absence of historical and biographical references in Psalms, the Song of Songs, and Lamentations. They readily admit a certain vagueness and generality of expression in the lyrical literature of the Hebrew scriptures (see Ridderbos, 1976:265ff.). How can we verify, then, any "real" emotional involvement by the authors with the feelings communicated by their poetry?

The same question arises in regard to all stylistic devices employed by ancient poets. In order to be able to distinguish personal style from general usage we need a far more thorough knowledge of Hebrew literature than we can ever hope to attain. The Hebrew scriptures, after all, preserve only a tiny percentage of the lyrical poetry actually used in Israel; note, for example, the lost collections mentioned in Num 21:14 or 2 Sam 1:18. In this connection modern observers like to point to the bold individualistic use of metaphors and symbols, comparisons and parables in the prophetic books. There is some justification for such statements, as a parallel study of Amos and Hosea or Isaiah and Jeremiah demonstrates. Nevertheless, can we be so certain of their individual styles? Not knowing much of the language of their immediate environment, it is extremely difficult for us to risk a final conclusion. Lyrical language, on the other hand, is not less bold in its imagery and structure. Yet it is, according to all experts, much more dependent on conventional patterns of speech and expression. What is the significance of this divergent evaluation regarding the role of "literary creativity" in prophetic as opposed to lyrical compositions? Is it justified, or has the appeal of the prophets as bold and innovative messengers of the word of God unduly influenced our perceptions and opinions?

We must be aware of all these difficulties posed by ancient poetic

texts. Proceeding with caution, however, we can detect certain "individualizing" features in Israel's lyrical materials, if it is understood that by
"individualizing" we do not here mean individual in the modern solip-
sistic sense. Rather, throughout Israel's history, stylistic traits were in all
likelihood the property of temple schools, groups of prophets or sages,
and guilds of singers, as well as of particular regions, social classes, and
historical periods. With this in mind, we may point out a few modes of
lyrical expression on which research has focused its attention and which
complement the observations made above.

The simple repetition of words or phrases within one poem is a stylistic
device known in all literatures. This form of expression in Hebrew lyrical
literature has been studied by Muilenburg, Alonso-Schökel, Ridderbos, and
others. M. Buber and F. Rosenzweig have also frequently called attention
to biblical repetitious styles. Albright, looking at the historical development
of Israelite poetry, has stressed the fact that the Canaanite style of literal
repetition of expressions and lines in a poem soon gave way in Israel to
more sophisticated and varying types of restatements. Functionally, all the
phenomena related to parallelism, alliteration, assonance, paronomasia,
etc. can be seen as nothing more than specialized versions of the simple
reiteration of words. Further, by these means of simple repetition, the
ancient poet readily found innumerable possibilities for driving home a
particular point of view, concern, or aspiration. Thus, Ps 13:2–3 repeats
reproachful questions; Ps 29:1–2 sounds like a jubilant call to praise; Ps
29:3–5 uniformly describes the "voice of the Lord"; and Ps 136:1–26 shows,
in the second colon of each verse, a type of antiphonal repetition apparently sung by the congregation.

Probably very early in the history of ancient Near Eastern poetry
the widely used repetitious style began to employ an antithetic or chiastic structure. That is, poets learned to juxtapose, within a given poetic
unit, words, ideas, and phrases in order to heighten expectation and
suspense in the listener or reader. There is an infinite variety of chiastic
arrangement in the lyrical materials of the Hebrew scriptures (see G. B.
Gray; Kosmala; Ridderbos; Weiss: 425ff.). Psalm 1 is structured in terms
of polar ideas (blessed—wicked; tree—chaff; prosper—perish; etc.), and
the whole poem is construed accordingly. In Isa 6:10 there are, altogether, seven cola. The first three speak about "heart," "ear," "eye"—a
sequence exactly inverted in the following three units. And similarly, but
on the level of entire lines, Ps 9:12–15 "shows chiastic structure. V. 12
corresponds to v. 15, v. 13 to v. 14; this correspondence applies to contents as well as to vocabulary . . ." (Ridderbos, 1972:143).

Another artistic feature sometimes imitated in our own hymns is the
acrostic structuring of a poem. In this arrangement, each line or group
of lines begins with another letter of the alphabet, or even with one
special word which forms part of a phrase. Psalms 25, 34, 37, 111, 112,

and 119, as well as Lamentations 3, are examples of alphabetic acrostics in the OT. It is doubtful that there are word acrostics in the Bible, although they are definitely to be found in the cuneiform materials. Acrostic arrangement is often considered artificial by modern exegetes. To us it looks contrived, it is true; we must remember, however, that our use of end rhyme in poetry would undoubtedly appear just as forced to the ancient Israelites (see Gottwald, 1962b; Freedman, 1972; Bergler).

Inclusio is the term used to identify an arrangement of complete units of poetry in which the beginning and end correspond to each other (see Psalms 8, 12, 20, etc.). In its most sophisticated form, thoughts and words ascend and descend to and from a climax that is reached in the middle of the poem. For more details regarding this literary device, see Liebreich and Ridderbos (1972).

The so-called break-up of composite phrases or word units has been studied only recently (Melamed; Dahood, 1973) The theory underlying such inquiry is that, if we can find parts of standard formulations separated by alien words or grammatical elements, we can assume that the author of the poem must have consciously broken up the traditional unit in order to achieve a special effect. For Dahood, typical examples of this device are such expressions as רוח עצה ("spirit of counsel") in Isa 11:2, which is dismembered in Isa 19:3, and כסא קדשו ("his holy throne") in Ps 47:9, which is taken apart in Ps 11:4. Taken by itself, the search for such dismembered standard expressions would seem to be an optimal means of identifying individual creativity in poetry. After all, does it not require unusual courage to counteract common linguistic usage? The whole theory, however, rests on shaky foundations, for the combination of two words does not necessarily make them a standard phrase, nor does the use of any word within a fixed expression preclude its further employment either individually or in combination with other words.

The list of stylistic features given above remains incomplete. There are more phenomena presently under discussion, as a study of the literature cited demonstrates. Moreover, continuing research will discover even more characteristics of the Hebrew lyrical materials. We must stop here, however, and draw an interim conclusion. On the one hand, we can be extremely grateful for the wealth of insights won so far in postwar research. Israel's lyrical literature is today far better known than it was before 1945. That knowledge has enhanced sympathetic understanding of these ancient texts, with the result that the poetic and lyric portions of the Hebrew scriptures have entered a new cycle of use and acceptance as valid expressions of faith and life experience (see below).

On the other hand, there certainly remain problems and uncertainties with regard to these ancient materials. Many formal, cultural, and religious traits of Hebrew prayers, hymns, laments, love-songs, incantations, and so forth are not easily accessible to modern investigations. Therefore, all our interpretive efforts are subject to the very natural temptation to ignore that which is alien or offensive in the texts and to impose on them exegetical schemes that produce the answers subconsciously desired by the interpreter. This danger is the motive for undertaking (below) a brief self-critical reflection on the different standpoints or perspectives of modern research.

V. OPINIONS AND SCHOOLS OF INTERPRETATION

The old positivistic, historically oriented school of thought is all but extinct in our time. Previously, B. Duhm had sought that historical and religious objectivity which the past century was hopeful and proud to conquer. H. Gunkel, however, in his commentary on Psalms rejected this orientation and sought to uncover the innermost religious sentiments of Israel's psalmists. In our day, objectivity is still a cherished working premise in technical and scientific studies, whereas in the humanities its role has gradually been deemphasized. Spiritually speaking, we are living in an age of growing concern for the state of humanity. Our thinking is inner-directed and overshadowed by great uncertainties regarding our true calling. So far as research in the Hebrew scriptures is concerned, historical objectivity lingers on only in our unintentional efforts to create a purely academic world of scientific facts and prestige. In other words, the continuing temptation, always present in scholarly undertakings, to rely excessively on external data—philological, historical, archaeological, or stylistic—is a leftover of that earlier positivistic age.

H. Gunkel and S. Mowinckel, working within an intellectual tradition that valued the emotional and mythical dimensions of being, were, as noted above, able to overcome the historical and literary positivism of their age. Their pioneering work in the field of Hebrew poetry is still very much alive, and their method continues to produce new fruits in terms of modified approaches to the texts of the Hebrew scriptures. It seems that, after a period which focused on analyses of poetic surface structures, a greater concern for the life situations that gave birth to the texts is now again coming to the fore. Gunkel's triad of methodological avenues—observation of literary form, situation in life, and religious sentiments—still offers ample room for further investigation. Form-critical work, in this sense, is just beginning (Gerstenberger, 1974a).

Notable shifts of emphases have also occurred in the so-called archaeological school of interpretation so closely aligned with the name of W. F. Albright. Its roots lie both in Christian concepts of salvation history and in liberal theology's concern for human progress. The Bible is seen as God's revelation, and the poetic strata within the OT constitute, because of their age and authenticity, the very fundamentals of Israel's faith. The task of modern research according to this school is clear: to reconstruct, as fully as possible, the literary history of Israel's poetry by assigning each individual poem to its appropriate historical situation. It is impressive to see the amount of work put to this task—and the optimism expressed concerning its final results. But, within this school, there has been an increasing openness to other approaches to biblical poetry (see Cross; Freedman).

Another methodology that has arisen in the last decades and has rapidly won adherents among researchers of the poetic literature of Israel is often called "New Literary Criticism." It is based on recent developments in literary science represented, for example, by the work of W. Kayser and R. Wellek and A. Warren. Each poem, for these scholars, is an independent work of art that speaks for itself. Not even the life of the poet may serve as a guideline for interpretation, much less all the accidental facts of history or general social background. Therefore, researchers following this line of thinking, notably Weiss and Alonso-Schökel, challenge traditional exegesis of Israel's poetry as being distractive. The modern exegete, they insist, has to pay attention to that poetic reality which the author created in the poem—and to nothing else. Among the questions that should be raised concerning this interpretation, two are especially significant. First, can we assume that these poems were the conscious work of gifted individuals as we visualize it today? Second, with regard to those charismatic creations of modern poets, might we not be missing something of their value and intent unless we set them in the context of the cultural patterns and social relations of their respective times?

Although the following methods of biblical interpretation have so far shown little concern for Hebrew poetry in particular, they should be watched. The first is that exegetical method which grows out of philosophical structuralism. In this approach, each text is taken as a linguistic expression of depth-structures of the mind, i.e., of being itself. Interest, therefore, does not rest with the poetic forms at all but rather with the underlying patterns of life, which we can readily compare with our own experiences and thus elucidate further our existence. The second method, the psychological, works basically with the same frame of reference as structuralism, so far as surface- and depth-structures of the text are concerned. But it goes further by applying the theories of Freud, Jung, Fromm, and others to the analysis of those depth-structures. And finally, there is a growing awareness among OT scholars that biblical texts in general and lyrical poetry in particular (because of its ritualistic character) have to a large extent been conditioned by the social and environmental factors of Israelite life. This last method is, of course, diametrically opposed to the new literary criticism summarized above (see Gottwald, 1962b; Albertz; Gerstenberger, 1980).

VI. MUSIC, INSTRUMENTS, AND RITUAL

In addition to all the problems discussed above, scholars are facing considerable difficulties in attempting to verify the musical and ritual accompaniment of Israel's poetic materials. That there was a great number of activities accompanying poetic "recitations" is clear from allusions within the poems themselves. There are also passing references to this effect in narrative and prophetic books. However, there is not a single complete ritual preserved in the Hebrew scriptures that would indicate exactly the place and kind of accompaniment of prayer or song. The sacrificial texts of Leviticus and the well-known ordeal ceremony in Num 5:11–31, both of which are common genres in the ancient Near East, are closest to this type of description. "Prophetic liturgies" preserve mainly the spoken parts (see Isa 63:7–64:11; Jer 14:1–22; Joel 1–2). However, painstaking scrutiny of the available evidence, deriving to a large extent from wider studies of the ancient Near East, has yielded valuable information regarding probable musical and ritual accompaniment in Israel.

Lyrical poems have from time immemorial been accompanied by musical instruments. The name of the Psalter (from the Greek ψαλτήριον, "harp," "lyre," from ψάλλω, "to tug") is a witness to this fact. It attests that stringed instruments often were a favorite means of accompaniment; many such have, in fact, been recovered from tombs and other archaeological sites (Kolari; Werner; Stauder). In addition, numerous other types of instruments were also used in musical and ritual settings. Hand drums accompanied the songs of victory (Exod 15:20); horns and trumpets apparently had their place in larger temple rituals (see Num 10:1ff.; Isa 27:13; Zech 9:14). Ps 150:3–5 gives the impression of a fully orchestrated hymn. Of course, the music produced by these instruments has been lost. Quite recently, however, the first piece of music written on a clay tablet has come to light (Draffkorn-Kilmer), a Ugaritic hymn with musical notes. Working with these various clues we can now reconstruct, at least approximately, the sound of a recital. Musical instruments served to reinforce and embellish the voices of singers and choirs. Noise instruments were used probably because the music also had an apotropaic (exorcistic) and charming function in ritual. We can assume also that wedding songs had their own special instrumentation (see Jer 7:34; 16:8–9; Ezek 33:32).

If instrumentation played an important part in ritual, vocal articulation of lyrical poems was indispensable to any correct performance. A recent attempt has been made by S. Vantoura to reconstruct the ritual songs and melodies used in Israel on the basis of the Masoretic accentuation. In the book of Chronicles especially, temple functionaries such as singers and choirs are mentioned as playing an important role in the vocal portions of the worship services. Modern research has revealed that very probably there never was anything like communal song during worship. Rather, the people would respond by refrains and shouts, leaving the presentation of the texts and the leading of chants to the experts (see Exod 32:18; 2 Sam 18:7, 10; see also Werner; Draffkorn-Kilmer). The same pattern was very likely followed in profane ceremonies.

In speaking about musical accompaniment and vocal expression we must not overlook all the rites that were, in one way or another, integral parts of ritual performances, sacred and profane. For Israel's various festivities our sources refer to dance, processions, gestures, and mime (2 Sam 6:14; Pss 26:6; 48:13; 68:26; etc.). There have been many efforts in postwar research to describe in more detail various great annual feasts in order to achieve a plausible background for one or the other group of lyrical poems. Thus, Mowinckel elaborated the ritual of the New Year festival with its royal ascension ceremonies. Weiser concentrated on a great renewal of the covenant between Yahweh and Israel, which could have provided the setting for the majority of the psalms. Beyerlin (1970) investigated the judgment before a temple court of those unjustly accused. Seybold (1973) explained the psalms of the sick as a part of the praxis of rehabilitation. Gerstenberger (1971, 1980) has tried to place individual laments in the context of a prayer service of the primary group. Kramer (1969) and Schmökel interpreted the Song of Songs against the background of Mesopotamian sacred marriage rites.

In view of the diversity of such proposals, how can we understand and identify the settings and genres of the poetic materials in the Hebrew scriptures?

VII. SETTINGS AND GENRES

The quest for genre definitions has been very intense in postwar research. It is motivated not only by form-critical methodology but also by new literary considerations. We may correctly say that genre classification of Israelite poetry has for the most part become commonplace, replacing the older identification of material on the basis of content or sentiment. Obviously, this does not mean that scholars are unanimous in applying categories or in evaluating the classification of individual texts. Nevertheless, even widely diverging opinions have a common denominator: everyone wishes to recognize the genre affiliation of a given lyrical text. Assuming this concern, we may now discuss briefly profane and then sacred poetry, knowing well that in Israel this distinction was not an absolute one.

The first group of poems are work songs, chanteys, harvest songs, and the like. Examples of this type of poetry are the song celebrating the construction of a well (Num 21:13–14) and a watchman's call, possibly preserved in Isa 21:11-12. Although such compositions are poorly represented in the Hebrew scriptures, all researchers and commentators pay at least passing attention to them. There has not, however, been any extensive study done on this topic.

Without doubt there were songs for all kinds of social gatherings in Israel. Even if such gatherings were possibly connected with a religious ceremony (the sacrifice in 1 Sam 9:12, 19-20), emphasis could be placed on the noncultic aspects and activities. From rare allusions in the texts (Judg 21:11; Isa 5:11-12; 24:8-9; etc.) we may surmise that there was a variety of chants connected with festivities of the family, clan, or neighborhood. Considering the Israelites' predilection for their own history, it would be legitimate to think also of more epical poems which might have been recited at such occasions (see Psalm 78; Deuteronomy 32; Habakkuk 3). The larger introductions to the OT, such as those of O. Eissfeldt and Sellin/Fohrer, give more information on this matter.

A well-known genre in secular lyrics is the wedding song. Extant examples are Psalm 45 and the Song of Songs; these poems should be put into life settings such as those indicated by Genesis 24 or Judges 14 and 16. Moreover, the comparative Egyptian and Mesopotamian material has to be taken into account. The work done so far (Rudolph; Kramer; Schmökel; Pope; Murphy, 1977; White) shows similar poetic practice all over the ancient Near East concerning the profane (and sacred!) setting of love poetry, the possible involvement of the king, and the social significance of such poetry. Exegesis of the Song of Songs has by now abandoned its doctrinal, messianic, and allegorical outlook (Würthwein). Yet there are still some differences of opinion regarding its interpretation—most notably between those who advance secular and those who propose cultic interpretations. Thus the picture is far from uniform. There are also laudable and creative efforts being made to compare these ancient love songs with corresponding situations in our own time (Lys; Müller; Segal; Dubarle; Dryburgh).

The dirge is the other lyrical type we can study directly in the OT. Examples preserved include 2 Sam 1:19-27; 3:33-34, and some prophetic imitations (see Amos 5:1-3; Isa 14:4-21). Ever since K. Budde and H. Jahnow did the pioneering work that identified this genre, there has been near agreement among scholars about its form and setting. Therefore, fundamentally new developments are not to be expected. Future research will tend to refine observations already made (Gevirtz), to discuss the function and transfer of the genre (Long), and most of all to compare more ancient and modern material (Littmann).

As can be expected from the nature of biblical writings, the sacred lyrical poetry is far better represented than the secular and has received much more attention in research. This writer has previously discussed the situation of scholarship in this particular field (1974a, 1974b). Therefore, we will limit ourselves here to the most essential observations.

Laments and thanksgivings, both of the individual and communal types, form a block of genres interrelated by analogous and corresponding life situations. They have been under careful scrutiny in the past decades, and there are numerous relevant publications. The purely literary and noncultic interpretations have found some support (Tur-Sinai; Becker: 75, "laments are pious literature; they do not have a life-setting but are rooted in literature"). The vast majority of scholars, however, still accepts the cultic or semicultic interpretation of Gunkel and Mowinckel.

The analysis of linguistic forms and structures within the four genres has been greatly refined (Westermann, 1961; Crüsemann; Ridderbos). Occasionally, someone wants to rename lamentation "supplication" (Beyerlin, 1970; Gese, 1968) or to eliminate the communal thanksgiving for formal and theological reasons (Crüsemann contra Mand). However, on the whole the genre picture is quite stable, even if attribution of some psalms to a determined category is controversial.

It is regarding the imagined and reconstructed life situations that most debate occurs. What was, after all, the ritual setting of the complaint prayer of the individual? Where should we locate public lament? To the first question there are at least four types of answers. The sufferer took the prayer to the great temple service (Mowinckel; Weiser; etc.), as apparently Elkanah did in 1 Samuel 1. Others insist that it must have been a special tribunal at the temple that tried and rehabilitated the falsely accused (Delekat, 1967; Beyerlin, 1970). Still others deny the existence of an appeal to divine justice, suggesting that the laments are really thanksgivings; they complain of past misery in order to celebrate recovery (Weiser; Gese, 1968; Seybold, 1973). Finally, those who defend the royal interpretation declare all individual and communal prayers the work of the monarch acting in the name of the people (Bentzen; Engnell; Soggin; Widengren, 1955; Mowinckel in his later works). In opposition to all these hypotheses, Gerstenberger advances his own, reconstructing on the basis of Mesopotamian rituals a healing ceremony in the family circle, independent of the temple and official cult. Whatever other settings are identified, however, communal laments would obviously have their place within rituals of public fasting and mourning (Kraus, 1956; Gottwald, 1962a; Hillers; Wolff).

The setting of the thanksgiving song seems to be less disputed. Thanksgiving songs, at least those for the individual, are clearly attested in special worship services after a decisive salvation event had been experienced.

The hymns of praise form a second large and diversified group of sacral poems. Again, the groundwork of structural analysis and identification of genre and setting was laid by Gunkel and Mowinckel. Since 1945 their theories have been amplified but seldom challenged. Modifications of hymnic attributes such as those proposed by Westermann

(1961, "narrating" vs. "affirming" praise) or Crüsemann ("imperative" vs. "participle" hymn) did not have much impact on the scholarly world.

It also remains a common opinion that Israel's hymns grew out of larger community festivities. For the most part these were cultic celebrations. As noted above, the Chronicler is essentially correct in making families of temple singers responsible for hymn singing. In this regard scholarly attention is especially captured by the figures of Asaph and Korah, Levitical (?) singers known both from Psalms and from Chronicles (see Mowinckel; Buss; Gese, 1962; Wanke).

Modern scholarship singles out several main types of hymns associated with the different feasts and festivals in Israel. The first of these is the victory song. These songs were part of the celebrations after military victories and are marked by the significant participation of women (Judges 5; Exod 15:21; Psalm 68; see Globe; J. Gray; Soggin). The second type, royal hymns, adorned those festivities in which the king played a significant role. Some experts, especially from northern European countries, attribute to these festivals a formative influence on virtually all psalmic genres (Mowinckel; Engnell; Widengren; Bentzen; Birkeland). The idea of a royal ideology was repudiated, however, by Bernhardt. The third type is the Zion songs, hymns about the holy city of Jerusalem (Psalms 46; 48; 76; 87; 132). There must have existed, during Israel's long history, various festive occasions to commemorate Yahweh's presence on Mount Zion (see Psalms 24 and 122). The Yahweh-kingship hymns, celebrating the supreme power of Israel's deity (Kraus; Asensio; Coppens; Lipinski, 1965; Moor; Widengren, 1955) certainly belong in this context also (Psalms 47; 93; 96–99). Most of the hymns, notably those which glorify Yahweh's creative and salvific power, probably belong to the seasonal cycle of feasts (Halbe). Unfortunately, we can no longer say where exactly they would have been used in the liturgy of these events (see Weiser; Kraus; Leslie; van der Ploeg; Podechard).

The last comprehensive group of lyrical poems contained in the Psalter apparently is not cultic in origin, but it nevertheless shows a marked theological orientation. Sapiential psalms (see Psalms 1; 19B; 37; 49; 73; 119) derive from circles of sages, which may in some instances be identified with priestly or levitical groups. Wisdom psalms focus on ethical problems. They try to define the position of humanity in this world and wrestle with Yahweh's apparent injustice. One of the main critical questions to be clarified is the identity and function of the sages in relation to the cult and religious education (Perdue). For now, we cannot go much beyond the affirmations of Mowinckel (1955), who considered some of these psalms to be authentic prayers, although free from cultic functions (see Murphy, 1963; Skehan, 1971; Trible; Crenshaw; Gemser).

VIII. PARALLELS FROM OUTSIDE ISRAEL

We have repeatedly referred to literary, cultural, and religious analogies taken from Israel's neighbors. These references were neither accidental nor arbitrary. They reveal the historical truth that Israel's lyrical poetry, although a cultural and theological phenomenon in its own right, still remained part of the larger ancient Near Eastern civilization. There are too many cross-connections and correspondences between the poetry of the OT and that of Israel's neighbors to allow them to be ignored by modern scholarship. In fact, research since 1945 has widely accepted this, utilizing with caution and prudence that vast material available in the relevant disciplines.

Where can we expect to find contributions to research on Israel's lyrical poetry? Relevant ancient Near Eastern texts normally come from archaeological excavations. It is impossible to enumerate all the important sites or, for that matter, to mention only the most important text publications. Suffice it to say that all of the four large regions that make up the arena of ancient Near Eastern history—Egypt, Syria-Palestine, Asia Minor, and Mesopotamia—have already yielded valuable comparative material and will continue to do so. In fact, every year the avalanche of relevant texts is increasing, and the next substantial amount of material will likely come from the clay tablets found at Ebla in Syria.

What types of texts (genres) are available for comparative study? The answer is simple. All the poetic genres found in the Hebrew Bible are also known from the neighboring cultures, from love song to individual prayer, from blessing to hymn, from thanksgiving to pun, from lament and dirge to incantation. To mention but a few examples from literally hundreds of important publications of comparative material, we can point to the new collection of Babylonian and Assyrian hymns and prayers edited by M.-J. Seux and the more recent monograph on Babylonian prayer formulations by W. Mayer. A widely used collection of translated hymns and prayers is that of A. Falkenstein and W. von Soden.

How can we legitimately compare Israelite poetry with extant texts from elsewhere in the ancient Near East? We should admit that grave errors have been committed in the past. The attempt at schematic comparison in order to demonstrate the superiority of one culture over the other (Israelite vs. Babylonian vs. Egyptian, etc.) is certainly not adequate. Each culture, in spite of all affinities, has its own character and value. Nevertheless, we are able to juxtapose carefully the texts of one culture with the corresponding texts of another, to compare life situations, genre profiles, intentions, social conditions and so forth, and to come to valid internal conclusions, using the insights gained on one side as leads to discover inherent traits in the other. It should be added that this writer has the firm conviction that this same cautious method of comparison is also applicable to texts from cultures other than those of the ancient Near East, be they ancient or modern.

IX. DATING LYRICAL TEXTS

Our historically minded age has been bent on dating the texts of antiquity, and there is some good reason for this. Fixation in a particular epoch can be a useful instrument in determining the message of a document. Lyrical texts, however, by definition lack historical and biographical references and therefore are very hard to date. Further, if one views the "point of origin" in terms of a transmission process, dating is again problematic. For these reasons Gunkel and his followers substituted references to genre and setting for specific historical dates. Yet as Gunkel's commentary on Psalms clearly shows, even if this is done there still remains a certain tendency to look for historical points of fixation.

The late dating of the psalms and other lyrical poetry so characteristic of the Wellhausen school (see B. Duhm) has been practically abandoned in research since World War II. In general, the date of poems has been pushed backward, and preexilic dates for Israel's poems today are the rule not the exception. The most interesting recent attempt in research is that of sequence-dating, inaugurated by Albright and used extensively by Cross, Freedman, and others. The assumption underlying this approach is that linguistic and stylistic features give clues to the formative epoch for a given poem. After establishing a sequence from archaic to more "modern" poems, one can then try to tie the whole network to historical events, thus gaining a reliable chronological order for the development of Hebrew poetry.

In addition to studying the dates of individual poems, scholars have also invested much energy in seeking to illuminate the complex processes that resulted in the present shape and collection of lyrical materials in the Hebrew Bible. This has involved the study of their transmission, the efforts that led to the compilation of biblical books, and the developments that brought about their final canonization (Gese, 1972).

X. ANTHROPOLOGY, THEOLOGY, AND INFLUENCE

There is growing awareness that Israel's poetry bears direct witness to human suffering and joy, faith and hope. This anthropological dimension is becoming ever more important in OT exegesis. Furthermore, small-group relations and to a certain extent also secondary social organization are reflected in our texts (see Turner). Of course, the poems in question do not contain treatises on social subjects. Yet their informal and unintentional information is therefore all the more valid, especially with regard to the life and cult of the small group (see Westermann, 1961; Albertz; Gerstenberger, 1980; Muntingh; Anderson; Gottwald, 1962b; Trible, 1978).

The lyrical poems do not speak only about human beings; rather, they speak primarily to and about God. They do so on many levels—implicitly in much of the "profane" poetry, explicitly and with audacity in cultic and liturgical compositions. Depending on the life situation, affirmations about God can be extremely scathing and desperate or highly exuberant and almost ecstatic with happiness. There are in many of these poems marvelous manifestations of confidence and admiration; indeed, quite often they make statements about God so sublime that we are immediately impressed by their truth and depth (e.g., Ps 139:1–12). A good theology of lyrical poetry would have to distinguish, therefore, among the different human situations and recreate for each one of them that freedom of communication with God that we encounter throughout the Hebrew scriptures. Von Rad, in his *Theology of the Old Testament*, gave a sensible exposition of the psalmists' faith; research should pursue this direction further (see also Ringgren; Albertz; Vorländer; Westermann, 1961). Most recently Kraus, in the newest edition of his commentary, devotes extensive treatment to the theology of the psalms.

Any text that is preserved and used has an "after-life." In a very deep sense, this process of being utilized and interpreted is an integral part of the text. Therefore, research in the Hebrew Bible must not overlook the interpretive history of the texts. In the case of the lyrical literature we see three main areas in which research is occurring and where it should be strengthened even further. In the first place, each poem has to be followed through its interpretive history *within* a community of faith, be it Jewish, Christian, or other (see Knuth; Arens; Cohen; Fischer; Schneekloth). Second, we are witnessing today, especially in the Third World, the birth of a new singing by the often oppressed communities of faith, and this "new song" is greatly indebted to the old poems of Israel (Cardenal; Sciadini). Finally, throughout the course of cultural history the lyrics of the Hebrew scriptures have spread their influence far beyond the confines of organized religion. The art and literature of many nations reveal the impact of these poems (see Kurz). Quite often the recognition of such unexpected aftereffects will deepen and enhance our understanding of the ancient texts.

BIBLIOGRAPHY

Albertz, Rainer
    1978   *Persönliche Frömmigkeit und offizielle Religion.* Stuttgart: Calwer.

Albrektson, Bertil
    1963   *Studies in the Text and Theology of the Book of Lamentations.* Lund: Gleerup.

Albright, William F.
1968   *Yahweh and the Gods of Canaan.* Garden City, NY: Doubleday.

Alonso-Schökel, Luis
1963   *Estudios de poética hebrea.* Barcelona: Juan Flors.
1976   "The Poetic Structure of Psalms 42–43." *JSOT* 2: 4–11.

Anderson, Bernhard W.
1974   *Out of the Depths: The Psalms Speak for Us Today.* Philadelphia: Westminster.

Arens, Anton
1961   *Die Psalmen im Gottesdienst des Alten Bundes.* Trier: Paulinus.

Asensio, Félix
1966   "El Yahweh Malak de los 'Salmos del Reino' en la historia de la 'Salvación.'" *EstBib* 25: 299–315.

Audet, Jean-Paul
1955   "Le sens du Cantique des Cantiques." *RB* 62: 197–221.

Bardtke, Hans
1969   *Liber Psalmorum.* BHS 11. Stuttgart: Württembergische Bibelanstalt.

Baumann, Eberhard
1949/50   "Strukturuntersuchungen im Psalter." *ZAW* 61: 114–76; 62: 115–52.

Becker, Joachim
1975   *Wege der Psalmenexegese.* Stuttgart: Katholisches Bibelwerk.

Bentzen, Aage
1948   *Messias, Moses redivivus, Menschensohn.* Zurich: Zwingli.

Bergler, Siegfried
1977   "Threni V." *VT* 27: 304–20.

Bernhardt, Karl-Heinz
1961   *Das Problem der altorientalischen Königsideologie im Alten Testament.* Leiden: E. J. Brill.

Berridge, John M.
1970   *Prophet, People and the Word of Yahweh: An Examination of Form and Content in the Proclamation of the Prophet Jeremiah.* Zurich: EVZ.

Beyerlin, Walter
1970   *Die Rettung der Bedrängten.* Göttingen: Vandenhoeck & Ruprecht.
1979   *Werden und Wesen des 107. Psalms.* Berlin: Walter de Gruyter.

Birkeland, Harris
1955   The Evildoers in the Book of Psalms. Oslo: Jacob
                    Dybwad.

Boling, Robert G.
1960   "'Synonymous' Parallelism in the Psalms." JSS 5:
                    221–55.

Boström, Gustav
1928   Paronomasi i den äldre hebreiska maschal-literaturen.
                    Lund: C. W. K. Gleerup.

Bright, John
1970   "Jeremiah's Complaints—Liturgy or Expressions of Per-
                    sonal Distress?" Pp. 189–214 in Proclamation and Pres-
                    ence: Old Testament Essays in Honor of Gwynne
                    Henton Davies. Ed. J. I. Durham and J. R. Porter. Rich-
                    mond: John Knox.

Buber, Martin, and Franz Rosenzweig
1975   Die Schrift. 4 vols. 8th ed. Heidelberg: Lambert
                    Schneider.

Buss, Martin J.
1963   "The Psalms of Asaph and Korah." JBL 82: 382–92.

Cardenal, Ernesto
1967   Zerschneide den Stacheldraht. Wuppertal: Jugenddienst.

Christian, Viktor
1953   Untersuchungen zur Laut- und Formenlehre des
                    Hebräischen. Vienna: Österreichische Akademie der
                    Wissenschaften

Cohen, Gerson D.
1962/1974   "The Song of Songs and the Jewish Religious Mentality."
                    Pp. 262–82 in The Canon and Masorah of the Hebrew
                    Bible. Ed. S. Z. Leiman. New York: Ktav.

Coppens, Joseph
1977/1978   "La royauté de Yahvé dans le Psautier." ETL 53:
                    297–362; 54: 1–59.

Crenshaw, James L.
1975   Hymnic Affirmation of Divine Justice. SBLDS 24. Mis-
                    soula, MT: Scholars Press.

Cross, Frank M.
1974   "Prose and Poetry in the Mythic and Epic Texts from
                    Ugarit." HTR 67: 1–15.

Cross, Frank M., Jr., and David N. Freedman
1975   Studies in Ancient Yahwistic Poetry. SBLDS 21. Mis-
                    soula, MT: Scholars Press.

Crüsemann, Frank
1969 *Studien zur Formgeschichte von Hymnus und Danklied in Israel*. Neukirchen-Vluyn: Neukirchener Verlag.

Culley, Robert C.
1967 *Oral Formulaic Language in the Biblical Psalms*. Toronto: University of Toronto Press.

Dahood, Mitchell
1965, 1968, 1970 *Psalms*. 3 vols. AB 16, 17, 17A. Garden City, NY: Doubleday.
1973 "The Breakup of Stereotyped Phrases." *JANESCU* 5: 83–89.
1978 "New Readings in Lamentations." *Bib* 59: 174–97.

Delekat, Lienhard
1964a "Zum hebräischen Wörterbuch." *VT* 14: 7–66.
1964b "Probleme der Psalmenüberschriften." *ZAW* 76: 280–97.
1967 *Asylie und Schutzorakel am Zionheiligtum*. Leiden: E. J. Brill.

Díez Macho, Alejandro
1948/1949 "La homonimia o Paronomasia." *Sef* 8: 293–321; 9: 269–309.

Draffkorn-Kilmer, Anne
1974 "The Cult Song with Music from Ancient Ugarit." *RA* 68: 69–82.

Dryburgh, B.
1975 *Lessons for Lovers in the Song of Solomon*. New Canaan: Keats.

Dubarle, André M.
1954 "L'amour humain dans le Cantique des Cantiques." *RB* 61: 67–86.

Engnell, Ivan
1967 *Studies in Divine Kingship*. 2d ed. Oxford: Blackwell.

Falkenstein, Adam, and Wolfram von Soden
1953 *Sumerische und akkadische Hymnen und Gebete*. Zurich: Artemis.

Feuillet, André
1953 *Le Cantique des Cantiques*. Paris: Editions du Cerf.

Fischer, Balthasar
1962 "Christliches Psalmenverständnis im 2. Jahrhundert." *BibLeb* 3: 111–19.

Fohrer, Georg
1954 "Über den Kurzvers." *ZAW* 66: 199–236.

Freedman, David N.
1972 "Acrostics and Metrics in Hebrew Poetry." *HTR* 65: 367–92.

1977   "Pottery, Poetry and Prophecy." *JBL* 96: 5–26.

Gemser, Berend
1963   "Gesinnungsethik im Psalter." *OTS* 13: 1–20.

Gerstenberger, Erhard S.
1963   "Jeremiah's Complaints. Observations on Jer 14:10–21."
                       JBL 82: 393–408.
1971   *Der bittende Mensch.* Heidelberg (Habilitation).
1972   "Literatur zu den Psalmen." *VF* 17: 82–99.
1974a   "Psalms." Pp. 179–223 in *Old Testament Form Criti-
                       cism.* Ed. J. H. Hayes. San Antonio: Trinity University
                       Press.
1974b   "Zur Interpretation der Psalmen." *VF* 19: 22–45.
1980   *Der bittende Mensch.* Neukirchen-Vluyn: Neukirchener
                       Verlag.

Gese, Hartmut
1963   "Zur Geschichte der Kultsänger am zweiten Tempel."
                       Pp. 222–34 in *Abraham unser Vater. Festschrift für
                       Otto Michel.* Ed. O. Betz, M. Hengel, and P. Schmidt.
                       Leiden: E. J. Brill. Reprinted pp. 147–58 in *Vom Sinai
                       zum Zion.* BEvT 64. Munich: Chr. Kaiser, 1974.
1968   "Psalm 22 und das Neue Testament." *ZTK* N.F. 65:
                       1–22. Reprinted pp. 180–201 in *Vom Sinai zum Zion.*
1972   "Die Entstehung der Büchereinleitung des Psalters." Pp.
                       57–64 in *Wort, Lied, und Gottesspruch. Festschrift für
                       Joseph Ziegler.* Ed. J. Schreiner. Würzburg: Echter-
                       Verlag. Reprinted pp. 159–67 in *Vom Sinai zum Zion.*

Gevirtz, Stanley
1963   *Patterns in the Early Poetry of Israel.* Chicago: Univer-
                       sity of Chicago Press. 2d ed. 1973.

Ginsberg, Harold L.
1950/1951   "Some Emendations in Psalms." *HUCA* 23: Pt. 1.
                       97–104.

Globe, Alexander
1974   "The Literary Structure and Unity of the Song of Deb-
                       orah." *JBL* 93: 493–512.

Goldingay, J.
1977/1978   "Repetition and Variation in the Psalms." *JQR* 68:
                       146–51.

Good, E. M.
1978   "Review of *Formula Criticism and the Poetry of the
                       Old Testament* by Wm. R. Walters." *JBL* 97: 274–75.

Goodenough, Erwin R.
1953–   *Jewish Symbols in the Greco-Roman Period.* 13 vols.
                       Princeton: Princeton University Press.

Gottlieb, Hans
1978   A Study on the Text of Lamentation. Aarhus: Aarhus
               University Press.

Gottwald, Norman K.
1954   Studies in the Book of Lamentations. SBT 37. Chicago:
               Alec R. Allenson.
1962a   Studies in the Book of Lamentations. 2d ed. London:
               SCM.
1962b   "Poetry, Hebrew." Pp. 829–38 in IDB, Vol. 3.

Gray, George B.
1972   The Forms of Hebrew Poetry. 2d ed. New York: Ktav.

Gray, John
1977   "A Cantata of the Autumn Festival: Psalm LXVIII." JSS
               22: 2–26.

Halbe, Jörn
1975   "Passa-Massot im deuteronomischen Festkalender."
               ZAW 87: 147–68.

Hillers, Delbert R.
1972   Lamentations. AB 7A. Garden City, NY: Doubleday.

Holladay, William L.
1974   Jeremiah: Spokesman out of Time. Philadelphia: United
               Church.

Homan, M. J.
1977/78   "A Comparative Study of the Psalter in the Light of
               11 QPs[a]." WTJ 40: 116–29.

Horst, Friedrich
1953   "Die Konnzeichen der hebräischen Poesie." TRu 21:
               97–121.

Johnson, Aubrey R.
1979   The Cultic Prophet and Israel's Psalmody. Cardiff: Uni-
               versity of Wales.

Kayser, Wolfgang
1960   Das sprachliche Kunstwerk. 6th ed. Bonn: Franche Ver-
               lag.

Keel, Othmar
1969   Feinde und Gottesleugner. Stuttgart: Katholisches
               Bibelwerk.
1978   The Symbolism of the Biblical World. New York: Sea-
               bury. German original in 1972.

Knuth, Hans Chr.
1971   Zur Auslegungsgeschichte von Psalm 6. Tübingen:
               Mohr.

Kolari, E.
1947   *Musikinstrumente und ihre Verwendung im Alten Testament*. Helsinki: Suomalaisen Kirjallisuuden Seuran Kirjapainon Oy.

Kosmala, Hans
1964/1966   "Form and Structure in Ancient Hebrew Poetry." *VT* 14: 423–45; 16: 152–80.

Kramer, Samuel N.
1961   "Sumerian Literature." Pp. 249–66 in *The Bible and the Ancient Near East*. Ed. G. E. Wright. Garden City, NY: Doubleday.
1969   *The Sacred Marriage Rite*. Bloomington: Indiana University Press.

Kraus, Hans-Joachim
1956   *Klagelieder*. BKAT 20. Neukirchen-Vluyn: Neukirchener Verlag.
1978   *Psalmen*. BKAT 15. 5th ed. Neukirchen: Neukirchener Verlag.

Kunz, L.
1963   "Zur Liedgestalt der ersten fünf Psalmen." *BZ* 7: 261–70.

Kurz, Paul K.
1978   *Psalmen vom Expressionismus bis zur Gegenwart*. Freiburg: Herder.

Leslie, Elmer A.
1949   *The Psalms*. Nashville: Abingdon.

Leveen, Jacob
1971   "Textual Problems in the Psalms." *VT* 21: 48–58.

Liebreich, Leon J.
1956   "Psalm 34 and 145 in the Light of their Key Words." *HUCA* 27: 181–92.

Lipinski, Edouard
1965   *La royauté de Yahwé dans la poésie et le cult de l'ancien Israel*. Brussels: Paleis der Academiën.
1969   *La liturgie pénitentielle dans la Bible*. Paris: Editions du Cerf.

Littmann, Enno
1949   *Abessinische Klagelieder*. Tübingen: Mohr.

Long, Burke O.
1966   "The Divine Funeral Lament." *JBL* 85: 85–86.

Loretz, Oswald
1979   *Die Psalmen*. Teil II. Kevelaer: Butzon & Bercker; Neukirchen-Vluyn: Neukirchener Verlag.

Lys, Daniel
1976   "Une histoire d'amour." *Foi et Vie* 75: 48–61.

Mand, Fritzlothar
1958   "Die Eigenständigkeit des Danklieder des Psalters als Bekenntnislieder." *ZAW* 70: 185–99.

Mansoor, Menahem
1961   *The Thanksgiving Hymns*. Grand Rapids: Eerdmans.

Mayer, Werner
1976   *Untersuchung zur Formensprache der babylonischen "Gebetsbeschwörungen."* Rome: Pontifical Biblical Institute.

Melamad, Ezra Z.
1961   "Break-up of Stereotype Phrases as an Artistic Device in Biblical Poetry." Pp. 115–53 in *Studies in the Bible*. Ed. Chaim Rabin. Scripta hierosolymitana 8. Jerusalem: Magnes.

Michel, Diethelm
1956   "Studien zu den sogenannten Thronbesteigungspsalmen." *VT* 6: 40–68.
1960   *Tempora und Satzstellung in den Psalmen*. Bonn: Bouvier.

Montgomery, James A.
1945   "Stanza Formation in Hebrew Poetry." *JBL* 64: 379–84.

Moor, Johannes C. de
1972   *New Year with Canaanites and Israelites*. 2 vols. Kampen: J. H. Kok.

Mowinckel, Sigmund
1955   "Psalms and Wisdom." Pp. 205–24 in *Wisdom in Israel and the Ancient Near East*. VTSup 3. Leiden: E. J. Brill.
1957   *Real and Apparent Tricola in Hebrew Psalm Poetry*. Oslo: Norske Videnskaps Akademi.
1962   *The Psalms in Israel's Worship*. 2 vols. Nashville: Abingdon.

Muilenburg, James
1953   "A Study in Hebrew Rhetoric." Pp. 97–111 in *Congress Volume: Copenhagen, 1953*. VTSup 1. Leiden: E. J. Brill.

Müller, Hans-Peter
1976   "Die lyrische Reproduktion des Mythischen im Hohenlied." *ZTK* 73: 23–41.

Muntingh, L. M.
1963   "A Few Social Concepts in the Psalms and Their Relation to the Canaanite Residential Area." *OTWSA* 6: 48–57.

Murphy, Roland E.
1963   "A Consideration of the Classification of Wisdom
            Psalms." Pp. 156–67 in *Congress Volume: Bonn, 1962.*
            VTSup 9. Leiden: E. J. Brill.
1977   "Towards a Commentary on the Song of Songs." *CBQ*
            39: 482–96.

Perdue, Leo G.
1977   *Wisdom and Cult.* SBLDS 30. Missoula, MT: Scholars
            Press.

Piatti, P. T.
1950   "I carmi alfabetici della Bibbia: chiave della metrica
            ebraica?" *Bib* 31: 281–315, 427–58.

Ploeg, Johannes P. M. van der
1971–   *Psalmen.* Roermond: J. J. Romen.

Podechard, E.
1949–   *Le Psautier.* Lyon: Facultés Catholiques.

Pope, Marvin H.
1977   *Song of Songs.* AB 7C. Garden City, NY. Doubleday.

Rad, Gerhard von
1962   *Old Testament Theology*, vol. I. New York: Harper &
            Row.

Reventlow, Henning Graf
1963   *Liturgie und prophetisches Ich bei Jeremia.* Gütersloh:
            Mohn.

Ridderbos, Nicolaus H.
1972   *Die Psalmen.* Berlin: Walter de Gruyter.
1976   "Psalmen und Kult." Pp. 234–79 in *Zur neueren
            Psalmenforschung.* Ed. P. Neumann. Darmstadt: Wis-
            senschaftliche Buchgesellschaft. Dutch original, 1950.

Ringgren, Helmer
1974   *The Faith of the Psalmists.* Philadelphia: Fortress.
            Swedish original, 1957.

Robertson, David A.
1972   *Linguistic Evidence in Dating Early Hebrew Poetry.*
            SBLDS 3. Missoula, MT: Scholars Press.

Robinson, Theodore H.
1947   *The Poetry of the Old Testament.* London: Duckworth.
1953   "Hebrew Poetic Form." Pp. 128–49 in *Congress Vol-
            ume: Copenhagen, 1953.* VTSup 1. Leiden: E. J. Brill.

Rudolph, Wilhelm
1962   *Das Buch Ruth. Das Hohelied. Die Klagelieder.* Güters-
            loh: Mohn.

Sabourin, Leopold
1969   *The Psalms, their Origin and Meaning.* 2 vols. Staten
             Island: Alba House.

Sanders, James A.
1966   "Variorum in the Psalms Scroll (11 QPs[a])." *HTR* 59:
             83–94.
1967   *The Dead Sea Psalms Scroll.* Ithaca: Cornell University
             Press.

Saydon, Pierre P.
1955   "Assonance in Hebrew as a Means of Expressing Empha-
             sis." *Bib* 36: 36–50, 287–304.

Schmökel, Hartmut
1956   *Heilige Hochzeit und Hoheslied.* Wiesbaden: Franz
             Steiner.

Schmuttermayr, Georg
1971   *Psalm 18 und II Sam 22.* Munich: Kösel.

Schneekloth, I. G.
1977   *The Targum of the Song of Songs.* Dissertation, Univer-
             sity of Wisconsin—Madison.

Sciadini, Patrício
1978   *Salmos do homem contemporâneo.* Rio de Janeiro: Civ-
             ilizaqão Brasileira.

Segal, Moses H.
1962   "The Song of Songs." *VT* 12: 470–90.

Segert, Stanislav
1960   "Problems of Hebrew Prosody." Pp. 283–91 in *Congress
             Volume: Oxford, 1959.* VTSup 7. Leiden: E. J. Brill.

Seux, M.-J.
1976   *Hymnes et prières aux dieux de Babylonie et d'Assyrie.*
             Paris: Editions du Cerf.

Seybold, Klaus
1973   *Das Gebet des Kranken im Alten Testament.* Stuttgart:
             W. Kohlhammer.
1977   "Thesen zur Entstehung der Lieder vom Gottesknecht."
             Biblische Notizen 3: 33–34.

Skehan, Patrick W.
1959   "Strophic Structure in Ps 72 (71)." *Bib* 40: 302–8.
1971   *Studies in Israelite Poetry and Wisdom.* Washington,
             DC: Catholic Biblical Association.
1976   "Again the Syriac Apocryphal Psalms." *CBQ* 38: 143–58.

Soggin, J. A.
1977   "Il canto di Débora." *Rendiconto dell' Academia
             nazionale die Lincei* VIII/32: 97–112.

Staiger, Emil
   1051   *Grundbegriffe der Poetik.* Zurich: Atlantis.

Stauder, Wilhelm
   1961   *Die Harfen und Leiern Vorderasiens in babylonischer und assyrischer Zeit.* Frankfurt am Main: Bildstelle d. J. W. Goethe-Universität.

Sukenik, Eleazer L.
   1955   *The Dead Sea Scrolls of the Hebrew University.* Oxford: Oxford University Press.

Thieberger, Frederic
   1947   *King Solomon.* Oxford: East and West Library.

Trible, Phyllis
   1975   "Wisdom Builds a Poem." *JBL* 94: 509–18.
   1978   *God and the Rhetoric of Sexuality.* Philadelphia: Fortress.

Turner, Victor W.
   1969   *The Ritual Process.* Chicago: Aldine.

Tur-Sinai, Naftali H.
   1976   "Zum literarischen Charakter des Psalmen." Pp. 217–33 in *Zur neueren Psalmenforschung.* Ed. P. Neumann. Darmstadt: Wissenschaftliche Buchgesellschaft.

Vantoura, Suzanne H.
   1976   *La musique de la bible révélée.* Paris: R. Dumas.

Vorländer, Hermann
   1975   *Mein Gott.* Kevelaer: Butzon & Bercker.

Wanke, Gunther
   1966   *Die Zionstheologie der Korachiten.* Berlin: A. Töpelmann.

Watters, William R.
   1976   *Formula Criticism and the Poetry of the Old Testament.* Berlin: Walter de Gruyter.

Weir, C. J. Mullo
   1934   *A Lexicon of Accadian Prayers in the Ritual of Expiation.* London: Oxford University Press.

Weiser, Artur
   1950   *Die Psalmen.* Göttingen: Vandenhoeck & Ruprecht.

Weiss, Meir
   1961   "Wege der neuen Dichtungswissenschaft in ihrer Anwendung auf die Psalmenforschung." *Bib* 42: 255–302. Reprinted pp. 400–451 in *Zur neueren Psalmenforschung.* Ed. P. Neumann. Darmstadt: Wissenschaftliche Buchgesellschaft, 1976.

Wellek, Rene, and Austin Warren
1975   *Theory of Literature*. 3d ed. New York: Harcourt Brace Jovanovich.

Werner, Eric
1962   "Music" and "Musical Instruments." Pp. 457–76 in *IDB*, Vol. 3.

Westermann, Claus
1961   *Das Loben Gottes in den Psalmen*. 2d ed. Göttingen: Vandenhoeck & Ruprecht. English trans., 1965.
1980   *The Psalms: Structure, Content and Message*. Trans. R. D. Gehrke. Minneapolis: Augsburg (Originally published, 1967).

Whallon, William
1969   *Formula, Character, and Context*. Washington: Center for Hellenic Studies.

White, John B.
1978   *A Study of the Language of Love in the Song of Songs and Ancient Egyptian Poetry*. SBLDS 38. Missoula, MT: Scholars Press.

Widengren, Geo
1948   "Hieros gamos och underjordsvistelse." *RoB* 7: 17–46.
1955   *Sakrales Königtum im Alten Testament und im Judentum*. Stuttgart: W. Kohlhammer.

Williams, N. D.
1977   *A Lexicon for the Poetical Books*. Irving: Williams & Waltrous.

Willis, John T.
1977   "The Genre of Isaiah 5:1–7." *JBL* 96: 337–62.

Wolff, Hans Walter
1964   "Der Aufruf zur Volksklage." *ZAW* 76: 48–56.

Würthwein, Ernst
1967   "Zum Verständnis des Hohenliedes." *TRu* 32: 177–212.

13
Legends of Wise Heroes and Heroines
Susan Niditch

A review of scholarship on Esther, Ruth, and Daniel 1–6 necessarily touches on subjects found elsewhere in this volume. Discussions of wisdom literature and historical literature emerge in the scholarship on all three works, while studies of Daniel 1–6 lead to the discussion of prophetic and apocalyptic genres. Most innovative, however, in recent approaches to Esther, Ruth, and Daniel 1–6 is the application of literary-critical methods employed by disciplines related to our own. Increasingly scholars are asking how techniques employed by structuralists and by students of oral literature and folklore can help us better to understand biblical literature and especially biblical narrative. The brief tales in Esther, Ruth, and Daniel 1–6, in a sense, are serving as an exciting testing ground.

In this chapter, our primary focus is on Esther and Ruth. The third brief section deals with the significant corpus of scholarship that specifically compares the tales found in Daniel 1–6 with narratives such as Esther and Ruth.

1. ESTHER

Research on the book of Esther has centered on questions of date, historicity, redaction history, and genre, but there are no clear trends or easily identifiable clusters of opinions. Those who agree on date often disagree about the work's historicity, its genre, and so on.

Date: Maccabean, Hellenistic, Persian

In the 1950s, Ruth Stiehl attempted to prove that the rise of the Maccabees was the sociological background of Esther. Her dating, 167–140 B.C.E., rests on rather weak arguments: (1) the fact the Esther or references to it appear neither in the Qumran corpus nor in Ben Sira; (2) an uncomfortable identification of Esther's genre with that of the Hellenistic romance. George A. Knight (1955:23) and Robert H. Pfeiffer (742) share Stiehl's Maccabean dating, but suggestions of such a late date are seen less and less in recent scholarship. In favor of earlier Hellenistic dates for Esther are Ernst Würthwein (172) and Hans Bardtke (1963:254), who rely on Hans Striedl's linguistic analysis but place Esther in the third century B.C.E.

Many scholars place Esther in the Persian period (e.g., Moore, 1971: LIV–LX), arguing from the author's seeming knowledge of Persian court customs, the presence in Esther of Persian names and loanwords, the absence of hints of Greek language in the work, and the lack of strongly negative sentiment toward the Gentile king. Specific dates suggested include the beginning of the Persian period (Talmon: 453); the reign of Xerxes I, 486–465 B.C.E. (Horn: 14–18); the reign of Artaxerxes II, 404–358 B.C.E. (Ringgren, 1958:114); and the mid-fourth century B.C.E. (Eissfeldt: 510).

Historicity

It is easy to point to historical impossibilities and improbabilities in Esther; if, for example, Mordecai had been deported in the time of Nebuchadnezzar (Esth 2:5), he would be about 150 years old in the time of Ahasuerus = Xerxes (Anderson: 826; Barucq: 80–81; Gaster: 4; Moore, 1971:XLV–XLVI). The strongest recent defender of historicity in Esther, C. Schedl, attempts unsuccessfully to explain away such problems (85–90).

Those scholars who regard Esther as Maccabean propaganda (Stiehl; Pfeiffer) find no significant references to the Persian period. Those who, like Gaster (35) and Bickerman (199–200), treat Esther as Jewish folklore, which in its current form is an etiology for the celebration of Purim, likewise discount the allusions to the Persian period.

While acknowledging the historical "errors" in Esther, many recent scholars note the importance of A. Ungnad's publication of a cuneiform text that mentions a certain Mardukâ who was a high official of the Susa court during the reign of Xerxes I. Ungnad identifies this official with the Mordecai of Esther and considers the reference to him to be evidence of genuine historicity in the work. Horn (20) agrees with Ungnad and brings to bear other epigraphic evidence that proves that Jews were in positions of prominence around the period in which the Esther narrative is set (22–24). Scholars also employ archaeological information from the excavations of Susa to support the historicity of certain details in the work (Moore, 1971:XLI; Anderson: 827–28) and note that the word *pur* (3:7) is a genuine Babylonian word meaning "lot," "fate" (Lewy; Cazelles: 21–23; Gordis, 1972:6). None of the above points is compelling. Any author of legend can include genuine "local color" in a work. The majority of scholars agree, however, that the book does have a historical kernel in the persecution theme (Ringgren, 1955:24; Knight, 1955:19; Anderson: 827; Moore, 1971:LII–LIII).

Genre: Historical Novel, Festal Legend, Midrash

The question of historicity leads to that of genre. Most scholars treat Esther as a historical novel/romance, but the definitions of historical novel/romance differ considerably. For Stiehl (8) historical romance implies a comparison with the so-called erotic romances of the Hellenistic period such as the Ninosroman. Stiehl approaches the book of Judith from the same direction. Cazelles (19–20) argues successfully against Stiehl's approach and would be supported by B. Edwin Perry's analysis of the romance genre; the term "romance" simply does not apply to a brief work such as Esther. B. W. Anderson applies the term "historical novel" to Esther and Judith, but his invocation of Sir Walter Scott is not very helpful were one seriously to compare the structure, content, style, and message of Esther with, for example, those of *Ivanhoe* (827). For Anderson (824) and Moore (1971:53) a historical novel is a work with a historical core that has been interwoven with the fictive motifs of legend.

S. Talmon calls Esther a "historical wisdom-tale," emphasizing the courtly wisdom features of the work in a comparison with the structure, content, and concerns of the Joseph story, Daniel 1–6, Judith, and Ahiqar (see also Dubarle: 164). In this context should also be mentioned A. Meinhold's term "Diasporanovelle." Meinhold is interested in a pattern of content shared by Esther and the Joseph story (see also Gan, Berg: 128, 136), each of which is grounded in the social situation of exile. E. Würthwein calls Esther simply a novel, accepting Goethe's definition, "the unexpected event" (166–67). Thus the novel/romance approach to Esther admits of different directions and concerns.

While Anderson (824), Moore (1971:XX, LIII), and Bardtke (1963: 251–52) describe Esther as a historical novel, each writes that a chief motivation of its author is to justify the celebration of Purim (also see Berg: 40, 47, 123). In this way, they overlap with Gaster, Ringgren, Bickerman, and others who consider Esther to be a "Festlegende." W. Dommershausen regards the Festlegende as the factor that organizes the many smaller literary units he isolates in Esther (1968:156). Most scholars consider Purim to be originally a non-Jewish festival that came to be observed by the Jews and was then associated with their own legends (Gaster: 4; Moore, 1971:XLIX; Lebram: 211–12; Anderson: 825; cf. Berg: 41). Barucq suggests that Purim came to be associated with a native holiday, the Day of Mordecai (2 Macc 15:36), and its explanatory legend (89). In addition to the designations historical novel and festal legend, there is a less popular description of the genre of Esther— haggadic midrash (Barucq: 80–81; Lusseau: 692). Yet this approach implies a loose definition of midrash that ignores the exegetical implications of that term (Wright: 45–48).

The most successful work on the genre of Esther is that which describes it comparatively in relation to other appropriate works. When Stiehl traces the savior-heroine pattern shared by Esther and Judith, she is on firm ground. An important contribution is made also by the many scholars who trace the "exile's rise-at-court" pattern found in Esther, the

Joseph story, Daniel 2, and elsewhere. Terms such as historical novel/ romance and midrash are confusing and lead to forced comparisons with inappropriate literatures. The term "festal legend" implies unity between narrative and etiological portions of Esther, a viewpoint not shared by all scholars.

Sources, Redaction History

Scholars point to three narrative threads in Esther: (1) the story of Vashti, the disobedient wife; (2) the story of Esther, the beautiful maiden who outwits those more powerful in order to save her people; (3) the Mordecai-Haman story, a version of the court contest found also in the Joseph story and in Daniel 1–6. Gaster discusses the first two (20), and Bickerman emphasizes the latter two (172–81). Bardtke posits the existence of one written source that contained a variety of Persian narratives including the three threads mentioned above. He suggests that the author of Esther drew on sections of this source and combined them with other materials to form one story (248–51). Gaster and Bickerman note, however, that the narrative threads of Esther are so skillfully combined as to defy precise disentanglement. Berg finds in Esther a symmetrical arrangement of key recurring motifs, such as the banquet and kingship, which give the work a balanced unity of structure (31–35, 72). The evidence suggests that Esther results from the efforts of one author, who drew in a natural way from folk traditions common in the culture, and not from an artificial process of selecting, copying, and combining (see Fuerst: 34).

More traditional source-critical approaches are suggested by Cazelles (28) and Lebram (214–16), who look for doublets, repetitions, and seeming inconsistencies in Esther: the two banquets (1:3, 5), the two lists of seven names (1:10, 14), and so on (see also Schedl: 90). Cazelles posits one source centering on Esther, liturgical in bent and oriented toward the provinces, and another source centering on the Mordecai-Haman conflict, more political and oriented toward Susa. However, the fact remains that the Esther narrative (at least through the defeat of Haman and the rescue of the Jews) fits together very well; repetitions may be better explained as characteristic of the traditional narrative style of the author.

Another issue is where the book of Esther originally ended. This question poses fewer problems to scholars who view the work as a festal legend. To them the final two chapters, dealing in large part with the justification for and the establishment of the feast of Purim, are integral to the work, which is essentially a unit (Bardtke, 1965/66:526). Berg argues similarly from literary symmetry (82, 168). Loewenstamm does not deal with the larger issues of unity, but he argues convincingly that

9:29–32, Queen Esther's Purim decree, is a late addition. Knight regards chap. 10 as an addition (47), and Barucq points to the "strongly composite" quality of 9:20ff. (130). Barucq (89) and Würthwein (171–72) suggest that the narrative originally ended at 9:19 and that 9:20–10:3 and the etymology of Purim in 3:7 were added later (see also Gordis, 1972:44 n. 14). C. C. Torrey goes further than Barucq and Würthwein, suggesting that the original work ended with the hanging of Haman, the elevation of Mordecai, the annulment of the order to kill the Jews, and the rejoicing feast (13–14). While Torrey's theory of an Aramaic *Vorlage* to Esther has not been accepted, his sense of where the original story ended may well be correct (see Cook: 374). One hesitates to delineate between specific original and nonoriginal materials in chap. 8. The motifs of conversion (8:17) and the right to self-defense (8:11), however, strike one as Maccabean in tone and concern. Herein may lie some support for the suggestion of Schneider (207–8), Lebram (219–22), and others that Esther was revised in the Maccabean period.

Greek Versions

Scholars note that the Greek translations have an almost targumic quality (Barucq: 79–80). They expand the account of Esther's audience with the king (5:1–2), create the "actual" texts of decrees mentioned in 3:13 and 8:11–12, and most important of all make Esther and Mordecai appear more pious by having them pray and by having Mordecai dream God-sent visions. In trying to improve Esther, the Greek translators show themselves sensitive to its supposed theological weaknesses. The A-text of Esther is much shorter than the versions of the LXX or the MT. Moore's suggestion that the A-text—the so-called Lucianic recension—reflects a Hebrew *Vorlage* different from that of the LXX and the MT is gaining general acceptance (1967, 1971:LXIII; Cook: 369). A complete discussion of the additions and the versions is provided by Moore (1977:153–250).

Theology

Research on the book of Esther reflects two main theological concerns: (1) Esther has too little reference to God and religion for a biblical work; (2) Esther has too much violence and vengeance for a religious work. Some scholars take comfort in the one possible reference to divine providence in 4:14 or claim that, if not mentioned directly, God's guiding hand lies behind the events of the narrative (Ackroyd: 82; Ringgren, 1958:116, 131; Barucq: 87; Würthwein: 170; Cohen). Gerleman claims to find in Esther the history-of-redemption pattern that characterizes the Exodus narrative (1966:10–28, 1973:11–23). The seeming lack of religious bent in Esther has been adequately explained by Talmon, who points to the "cosmopolitan nature" of Esther, a wisdom work whose author is primarily concerned with human situations "irrespective of religio-nationalistic allegiances" (430; Moore, 1971:XXXIII–XXXIV). One might add to Talmon's observations those of Jones (177) and Sandmel (497–98), who emphasize the humorous, nontheological stance of the work. Moreover, Esther presents themes and motifs that are typical of folktales. It is an ethnic legend, popular among Jews because it shows that they, the underdogs, defeat adversaries who are stronger and of higher status. The exilic, underdog mentality of the work has been underlined by Meinhold and Humphreys.

The issue of the vengeance and violence in the work is more disturbing, because it has led to unfortunate generalizations about Judaism, "the Jewish mentality," Jewish ethnocentricity, and so on (Knight, 1955:17; Barucq: 130; Anderson: 828, 830; Eissfeldt: 511–12; Weiser, 312). This results from misunderstanding the genre of the work. The book of Esther should not be viewed as a serious reflection of Jewish theology but as an ethnic wisdom legend. Moreover, if Gordis's syntactic analysis is correct, then 8:11 does not say that the Jews were about to "slaughter children and women" but that they were about to defend themselves against those who wished to slaughter Jewish children and women according to the edict in 3:13 (1976:49–53). When one adds to Gordis's suggestion an emphasis on the folktale quality of the work, the vengefulness comes into perspective. It is not a specifically Jewish phenomenon; nor does it reflect the holy war and divine retribution. It shows how the downtrodden turn the tables on would-be oppressors—a common wish-fulfilling message of traditional narrative.

Style

The folklorist's approach also helps to explain supposed weaknesses in Esther's style. Esther's use of repetition, criticized by Moore (1971:LVI), is a technique of traditional narrative. The flat, undeveloped characters in Esther (Anderson: 831) should be viewed in the same light. The stupid king, the clever court official, the beautiful wise queen are all common folktale motifs, nuanced with the special ethnic concerns of the writer. Dommershausen provides a recent analysis of the language of Esther with attention to the role of key terms in the work, and Berg analyzes motifs to show that Esther is a beautifully balanced literary structure built on repetition with chiastic content which Berg calls "a pattern of reversals" (108–9). In general, scholars describe Esther as a fine entertaining literary work that uses irony to good effect.

New Directions

Thinking of Esther in terms of traditional literature sheds light on its form, its possible historicity, its style, and its world view. While Esther is not precisely a folktale—no one would suggest, for example, that it was orally composed—it shares much with folk literature in terms of narrative patterns, character types, and style. A comparative analysis of Esther from the folklorist's vantage point might lead to a better understanding of its genre and to a proper placement of Esther in the context of world literature.

II. RUTH

Date

A clear trend emerges regarding the date of Ruth. Until recently modern scholarship has preferred an exilic or postexilic date (Joüon: 12–13; Gray: 399), a position reflected in many of the major OT introductions (Eissfeldt: 483; Pfeiffer: 718; Fohrer: 252; Sandmel: 489). Increasingly, however, this trend has been reversed. Campbell (1975:28), Gerleman (1965:8, 10), Hals (73), and Beattie (252) date Ruth to the tenth century B.C.E., Hertzberg (259) to the middle of the period of the monarchy, Rudolph (29) to 1000–700 B.C.E., preferring the latter portion of that time span, and Würthwein (6) less specifically to the preexilic period.

Nevertheless, the case is far from closed, as shown by recent studies by Vesco, Gordis (1974), and Lacocque (1979), who retain a late date. A number of scholars leave the question of date open (Bentzen, 1957, 2:185; Rowley: 180; Fuerst: 7), while Glanzman and Myers suggest stages of development for Ruth, the earliest preexilic, the latest postexilic.

Arguments in dating are based on linguistic, theological, and legal criteria. In this way the issue of date provides the context for several of the major areas of discussion about the book of Ruth.

Language

Scholars now discount the presence of a few Aramaisms in Ruth as evidence of a late date. Instead, following S. R. Driver (454), most point to the classical quality of Ruth's prose and to the presence of some early linguistic features such as the paragogic *nun* in the second person singular (תדבקין, 2:8, 21; תעשׂין, 3:4; תדעין, 3:18) and the second person feminine of the perfect with *yod* (וירדתי, 3:3; ושכבתי, 3:4); see Beattie (253), Campbell (1975:26), and Myers (20). But that which for Campbell and others is genuinely archaic style for Gordis (1974:245) and others is successful archaizing. In fact, noting the exact correspondence between phrases in Ruth 1:1 and Gen 12:10 and in Ruth 2:20 and Gen 24:27, Vesco suggests that the author of Ruth intentionally quotes Genesis in the anthological style typical of the postexilic period (246–47; Gray: 400). By the same token, late Hebrew usages in 1:4 (וישׂאו להם נשׁים, "they took wives"), 1:13 (תעגנה, "you will be chained"), and 2:19 (עשתה עשיתי, "spent time") are genuinely late features to Gordis but mere dialectal aberrations to Campbell (1975:26).

Thus, at present, linguistic evidence for the date of Ruth is inconclusive. A model for a fresh approach to the problem might be provided by Polzin's statistical syntactic analysis of the writings of the Chronicler and P. Although Myers includes a brief discussion of syntax in his work, it is not the detailed comparative analysis presented by Polzin. Such an approach might lead to more convincing results about the relative chronology of language in Ruth.

Legal Information

Many recent articles on Ruth have dealt with the pandora's box of legal problems presented by the narrative (Burrows; Rowley; Beattie; Thompson and Thompson). All note that the customs of levirate marriage, land redemption, and inheritance presented in Ruth differ significantly from the laws presented in Deut 25:5ff., Lev 25:25ff., and Num 27:8–11 respectively. For example, in Ruth the supposed levir is not a brother-in-law; the marriage itself is optional rather than obligatory; and so on. For Burrows (1940b:454) and others who consider Ruth to be preexilic, the book reflects a legal situation earlier than the legal corpora—a time when the clan rather than the immediate family was responsible for the welfare of young widows. For Gordis (1964) and others who consider the book to be postexilic, Ruth reflects a relaxation, a broadening, or even a deterioration of the old laws (Vesco: 242–43; Lacocque, 1979; Gray: 399; Eissfeldt: 483). Once again date remains elusive.

Problems presented by legal allusions in Ruth are too complex to detail here. We shall point to areas of agreement among scholars, to problems that remain, and to certain new focuses that have been proposed.

(1) Most scholars agree that, in spite of Num 27:8–11, Ruth shows that, in custom, a wife could inherit the property of her husband (Rowley: 184; Burrows, 1940b:448; Beattie: 256, 266; Thompson and Thompson: 97–98; contrast Gordis, 1974:258–59). There remain, of course, unexplained narrative problems: (a) Why is Naomi, a landowner, so destitute? (b) More important, why is the issue of land never mentioned until the scene at the gate? What does this contribute to the narrative? Gerleman, who views Ruth as an archive of Davidic family history, suggests that the author wishes to show historic Davidic claims to Judahite land despite his Moabite ancestry (1965:9)—an interesting suggestion but one that rests upon acceptance of Gerleman's view of the raison d'être of the work.

(2) While reaching their conclusions from several directions, most scholars agree that Ruth refers to some kind of levirate marriage (contrast

Beattie: 265; Gordis, 1974:252). Land redemption and levirate duties are viewed as complementary and interrelated; acceptance of the one responsibility meant acceptance of the other—one became the dead man's redeemer on all levels (contrast Beattie: 262). Naomi and Ruth's closer kinsman would agree to redeem Elimelech's field, but could not, for his own family reasons, agree to marry Ruth and raise children in the line of Elimelech. Boaz accepts both responsibilities (Thompson and Thompson: 98–99; Campbell, 1975:156; Rowley: 186–87; Hertzberg: 278).

(3) Current scholarship is in general agreement that the removal of the shoe in Ruth 4 is not to be identified with the ritual of Deut 25:9, the young widow's public denouncement of the recalcitrant levir. Ruth 4:8 employs the verb שלף, not חלץ, and describes a common ancient Near Eastern commercial practice involving transfer of rights to land (Carmichael: 324, 334; Gordis, 1974:451; Rudolph: 68; Hertzberg: 281; Burrows, 1940b:451) and also perhaps rights to Ruth (Carmichael; Hertzberg). In criticism of Burrows (1940a, 1940b), Thompson and Thompson rightly show that comparisons between ancient Near Eastern non-Israelite law and Israelite law should be careful and controlled. They also note that when one seeks to explain the date of certain laws and customs one should keep in mind important differences in genre between legal collections in Exodus, Leviticus, and Deuteronomy and narratives such as Ruth and Genesis 38. Rauber wisely notes that scholarship has spent an enormous amount of time on the legal aspects of Ruth to the exclusion of the more important literary features of the work. More attention to the literary quality of the book may even help in dealing with legal complexities presented by Ruth.

Theology and Purpose

Certain constants emerge in theological discussions of Ruth: (1) the providence of God (Gray: 401; Campbell, 1975:29); (2) the notion of *ḥesed* (Würthwein: 5–6; Campbell, 1975:29–30; Trible: 184); (3) the fact that God appears not in flashy miracles in Ruth but in subtle, everyday ways (Hals: 16; Gerleman, 1965:10; Campbell, 1975:28–29). God is continuously behind the events in the book, ultimately rewarding the good and deserving women (Hertzberg: 259; Rudolph: 32–33).

Talmon (451) and Gordis (1974:243) emphasize a wisdom quality in Ruth and in this way point more to the self-reliance of the characters (e.g., Naomi's wise womanly advice to Ruth on how to approach Boaz and Ruth's own initiative in seeking him at the threshing floor). Trible goes further, suggesting that Ruth presents "a theological interpretation of feminism," as the women find themselves in "a man's world" (166, 195–96).

One should note briefly that Hals (57) and several following him (Gerleman: 10; Campbell, 1975:28–29; Beattie: 252) consider the theology of God's "hidden all-causality" as a specific outgrowth of the "Solomonic Enlightenment." Hals views the tenth century as a period displaying a new humanism, a new interest in people. Thus God appears more in the background, behind events, as humans fend for themselves. Hals finds this theology also in the Davidic court history and the narratives preserved by the Yahwist. Yet such a theology is often attributed to Esther (see most recently Berg: 178–79) and could as well be used to support a date in the Persian period. Ruth's theology cannot be used to settle the question of date.

In addition to pointing to the theological and edifying purposes of Ruth, scholars have suggested several other possibilities: (1) support for the institution of levirate marriage (see the section on legal information above; Carmichael writes that Ruth shows the problems that existed in enforcing the levirate responsibility [336]); (2) the recording of a family history of David (Gerleman, 1965; the importance one places on the genealogical theme and on the attendant theme of the Moabite ancestry of David depends on viewing 4:17b–22 as original to the work [see below]); (3) universalist, pro-conversion propaganda against the Ezra-Nehemiah reforms banning intermarriage (Weiser: 304; increasingly scholars play down this theme, noting that Ruth simply is not polemical in tone, e.g., Gordis [1974:247] and Pfeiffer [719], who date Ruth to the fifth century B.C.E., but Lacocque [1979] makes a strong case for the presence of this message in Ruth); (4) Gordis (1974) and Pfeiffer emphasize appreciation of the story for its own sake, and D. F. Rauber points to the multiplicity of purpose in Ruth, which is a subtle and complex literary creation. He insists that one should not oversimplify the work but seek in Ruth many levels of meaning (36).

Unity

Scholars agree about the essential unity of Ruth. Most, however, consider the genealogy in 4:18–22 to be an appendix to the original work (Campbell, 1975:172; Würthwein: 2–3; Joüon: 96; Rudolph: 71–72), although Bertman and Rauber note that this genealogy may form an inclusio with the family history recounted at 1:1–5. Eissfeldt (479), Würthwein (2–3), and Gray (414) doubt the authenticity of 4:17b as well, a position increasingly unpopular among scholars. Claiming that no biblical writer would dare to create and add such a Moabite genealogy for David, most scholars consider 4:17b to be historical (Gerleman, 1965:7–8; Joüon: 7–8; Hals: 72). Gerleman is especially interested in 17b–22, since he views Ruth as a chronicle of Davidic family history. Campbell and Hals go one step further. They write that the notion of Moabite ancestry for David would have been especially unthinkable by the time of the Deuteronomistic historian in view of his hatred of Moabites (Deut 23:4, Eng. 23:3) and his veneration of David. Thus they claim that Ruth must at least predate the Deuteronomist. But their line of reasoning suits Vesco's postexilic date just as well, for he states that the universalism implied by a Moabite ancestor must be postexilic.

Redaction History

Suggestions that Ruth is based on an ancient fertility myth (Sheehan) are rejected by most scholars. Myers's hypothesis that the present Ruth is based on an original poetic core has not won general acceptance, nor has Glanzman's suggestion of three stages of development.

Style and Genre

It is agreed that Ruth's prose has a beautifully poetic quality. Dommershausen (1968) traces key terms employed by the author to create emphasis and structure in each of the four main sections of the narrative (also Campbell, 1975:13; Trible). Bertman, Rauber, and Trible point to Ruth's careful symmetry of plot and theme.

Goethe's genre description of Ruth as "idyll" has been replaced by "short story," a term that indicates the actual complexity of the work. Ruth as a short story has been compared with the court history of David, the Joseph cycle, Genesis 24, 38, and other examples of Hebrew narrative (Hals; Campbell, 1974). Campbell points out literary traits shared by these works, such as vividness of color, the technique of repetition, and the use of foreshadowing. These are universal narrative techniques; yet Hals and Campbell cite them as evidence that the Hebrew short story was a distinctive new genre that suddenly made its appearance in the tenth century B.C.E.! In his work with haggadic midrash, Dan Ben-Amos has noted that when the structure of a narrative changes, the genre changes (59). One should keep this in mind when comparing Ruth with other OT narratives. A detailed comparison of Ruth with Genesis 38, a narrative that shares Ruth's essential structure in a clear and meaningful way, would seem to hold more promise than Campbell's generalized approach. Gunkel's *RGG* study is a beginning in this direction, although he reaches some rather untenable redaction-critical conclusions. In any event, again, conclusions about Ruth's genre cannot be used as proof of its date.

We should cite two new directions among analyses of Ruth's genre. Invoking the work of A. B. Lord, Campbell suggests that Ruth was an oral composition produced by a "Hebrew singer of tales" (1975:18–23). Careful reading of Lord's work shows that Ruth has neither the usual percentage of formulaic language found in truly oral works (Lord: 47) nor the expected formulism of story pattern (Lord: 68–98). It is a poetic, symmetrically elegant story that does contain a traditional happy ending—a muted rags-to-riches theme. Yet these features do not qualify

Ruth as an oral composition. More helpful and interesting is Jack Sasson's application of V. Propp's *Morphology of the Folktale* to an analysis of the story pattern of Ruth. Yet this formalist approach runs the risk of forcing the complex story of Ruth into a framework abstracted from one hundred Russian folktales. For example, Sasson declares Ruth's "acceptance within Boaz's clan" to be a Proppian function, "hero acquires the use of a magical agent" (205). Yet Propp clearly uses this designation to refer to the hero's obtaining a special sword, a flying horse, or the like (Propp: 43). Such forced efforts call into question the legitimacy of Sasson's approach to Ruth.

Summary

Work on the style, structure, and literary qualities of Ruth in general has been excellent, although we need to be careful of loose genre comparisons between Ruth and other OT narratives. Problems remain in fully understanding the legal allusions in Ruth and their relationship to laws as found in OT legal corpora. Theological analyses of Ruth have successfully described its world view in relation to other Hebrew literature. The author of Ruth may have had many purposes—both conscious and unconscious—in writing the story. Neither style, legal information, nor theology can be definitely used to date Ruth. Further analysis of the language and syntax of Ruth in relation to other examples of Hebrew prose may provide a solution.

III. DANIEL 1–6

Daniel 1–6 is a collection of tales about the exiled Jew Daniel and his colleagues, prefaced by a chapter that sets the scene and presents the characters. Much of the scholarship on Daniel 1–6 concerns the unity of this corpus, the dates of the various chapters, and their roles in the larger book of Daniel (see Collins: 7–21). This brief review is concerned not with redaction history but with the boundary where studies on Esther, Ruth, and Daniel 1–6 meet. The common issue is that of genre.

Lacocque (1976:18) and Hartman/Di Lella (55) loosely invoke the term midrash as a description of the tales in Daniel 1–6 (see above in the discussion of Esther). Equally unsatisfying is the designation "popular romance" (Heaton: 37–40; Hartman/Di Lella: 55–61). Somewhat more specific are descriptions of Daniel 1–6 as tales about a wise courtier (Eissfeldt: 508; Hartman/Di Lella: 57–61). This wisdom focus has been considerably sharpened by S. Talmon's description of "the historicized wisdom tale." Talmon points to specific motifs of event and character, patterns of content, and themes of exile shared by the stories of Esther, Joseph, Ahiqar, and Daniel. Talmon avoids using the term "wisdom" loosely by showing that these tales are all "an enactment" of courtly wisdom as preserved and collected in Proverbs and Aḥiqar.

Humphreys approaches the genre of Esther and the Daniel tales from a sociological perspective, viewing them as expressions of life in the Diaspora, a means of encouraging the Jews in exile. He points to motifs shared by Daniel 1–6 and Esther (e.g., endangering of the hero, irrevocable laws, court feasts) and finds a literary form—"the tale of the courtier" (211, 220).

While the descriptions "historicized wisdom tale" and "tale of the courtier" point accurately to traits shared by Daniel 1–6 and the other works, such designations are general and can lead one to ignore important differences between the various wisdom tales. Recent studies by Hans-Peter Müller and John J. Collins distinguish more clearly between the "tales of contest" in Daniel 2, 4, and 5 and the "tales of conflict" in chaps. 3 and 6 (Müller: 338–39; Collins: 35–50; see also Heaton: 17). The former are more concerned with the wisdom of the hero, while the latter present a drama of danger averted through divine intervention (Collins: 49–50).

Robert Doran and the present writer go one step further in the effort to define and understand the biblical tales of wise heroes. Concentrating on Daniel 2, Genesis 41, and the Book of Aḥiqar, we note that these tales fit a long-established folktale type as outlined in the Aarne-Thompson Folktale Index—type 922. Each of these narratives involving the solution of seemingly impossible problems shares a specific motif pattern with a plentiful array of non-Israelite, non-Near Eastern tales. Use of the type index thus allows one to examine biblical narrative in the context of world literature. More important, the general tale type provides a foil that underlines the special ways in which biblical writers tell their versions of type 922. The most important nuances appear in Daniel 2. Unlike typical traditional versions of the tale in which the hero solves the problem through his own wisdom, Daniel appeals to a divine helper. It is only through God that Nebuchadnezzar's dream is told and interpreted. Here enters the writer's theology. Moreover, in Daniel 2 the impossible problem involves a dream that eschatologically traces the passage of kingdoms on earth. The lengthy dream and its interpretation differ from the typical trick questions posed to the sage and lend a special dimension to Daniel's version of the type. Knowledge of the traditional type makes one more sensitive to the biblical writer's own special cosmology. Folklore methodology thus becomes a tool of biblical criticism.

Using another comparative, crosscultural approach, Collins explores the use of dreams in Daniel 2 as well as other nuances in the tales of Daniel 1–6. Discussing these narratives in the light of Babylonian and Hellenistic mantic wisdom, Collins emphasizes that Daniel is portrayed not merely as a wise man but also as a mantic practitioner—as one who decodes dreams and interprets divinely sent signs. In this approach Collins's work overlaps with that of Müller, although the two scholars define "mantic wisdom" somewhat differently. While Collins's suggestion that Babylonian mantic wisdom directly influenced the author(s) of Daniel is not entirely convincing, the comparison itself is useful. In discussing Daniel in terms of divination or mantic wisdom, Collins points to the boundary where prophecy and wisdom meet, which in turn leads to the discussion of apocalyptic.

BIBLIOGRAPHY

Aarne, Antti, and Thompson, Stith
1973   *The Types of the Folktale*. Folklore Fellows Communications 184. Helsinki: Suomalainen tiedeakatemia.

Ackroyd, Peter R.
1967   "Two Hebrew Notes." *ASTI* 5: 82–85.

Anderson, Bernhard W.
1954   *Esther. IB* 3.

Bardtke, Hans
1963   *Das Buch Esther*. KAT 17/5. Gütersloh: G. Mohn.
1965/66   "Neuere Arbeiten zum Estherbuch: Eine kritische Würdigung." *Ex oriente lux* 19: 519–49.

Barucq, A.
1959   *Judith, Esther*. La Sainte Bible. Paris: Editions du Cerf.

Beattie, D. R. G.
1974   "The Book of Ruth as Evidence for Israelite Legal Practice." *VT* 24: 251–67.

Ben-Amos, Dan
1967   "Narrative Forms in the Haggadah: Structural Analysis." Doctoral dissertation, Indiana University.

Bentzen, Aage
1957   *Introduction to the Old Testament*. 2 vols. Copenhagen: Gad.

Berg, Sandra Beth
1979   *The Book of Esther: Motifs, Themes and Structure*. SBLDS 44. Missoula, MT: Scholars Press.

Bertman, Stephen
1965   "Symmetrical Design in the Book of Ruth." *JBL* 84: 165–68.

Bickerman, Elias
1967   *Four Strange Books of the Bible*. New York: Schocken Books.

Botterweck, G. Johannes
1964   "Die Gattung des Buches Esther in Spektrum neuerer Publikationen." *BibLeb* 5: 274–92.

Bruno, D. Arvid
1955   *Die Bücher Josua, Richter, Ruth: Eine rhythmische Untersuchung.* Stockholm: Almqvist & Wiksell.

Burrows, Millar
1940a   "The Ancient Oriental Background of Hebrew Levirate Marriage." *BASOR* 77: 2–15.
1940b   "The Marriage of Boaz and Ruth." *JBL* 69: 445–54.

Campbell, Edward F., Jr.
1974   "The Hebrew Short Story: A Study of Ruth." Pp. 83–101 in *A Light unto My Path: Old Testament Studies in Honor of Jacob M. Myers.* Ed. Howard N. Bream, Ralph D. Heim, and Carey A. Moore. Gettysburg Theological Studies, 4. Philadelphia: Temple University Press.
1975   *Ruth.* AB 7. Garden City, NY: Doubleday.

Carmichael, Calum C.
1977   "A Ceremonial Crux: Removing a Man's Sandal as a Female Gesture of Contempt." *JBL* 96: 321–36.

Cazelles, Henri
1961   "Notes sur la composition du rouleau d'Esther." Pp. 17–29 in *Lex tua veritas: Festschrift für Hubert Junker.* Ed. Heinrich Gross and Franz Mussner. Trier: Paulinus.

Cohen, Abraham D.
1974   "'Hu Ha-goral': The Religious Significance of Esther." *Judaism* 23: 87–94.

Collins, John J.
1977   *The Apocalyptic Vision of the Book of Daniel.* HSM 16. Missoula, MT: Scholars Press

Cook, Herbert J.
1969   "The *A* Text of the Greek Versions of the Book of Esther." *ZAW* 81: 369–76.

Dommershausen, Werner
1967   "Leitwortstil in der Ruthrolle." Pp. 394–412 in *In Theologie im Wandel: Festschrift zum 150 jährigen Bestehen der Katholischtheologischen Fakultät an der Universität Tübingen 1817–1967.* Munich and Freiburg: Wewel.
1968   *Die Estherrolle.* Stuttgart: Katholisches Bibelwerk.

Driver, S. R.
1913   *Introduction to the Literature of the Old Testament.* Edinburgh: T. & T. Clark.

Dubarle, A. M.
1966   *Judith: Formes et sens des diverses traditions.* Rome: Pontifical Biblical Institute.

Eissfeldt, Otto
1965   *The Old Testament: An Introduction.* New York: Harper & Row.

Fohrer, Georg
1968   *Introduction to the Old Testament*. New York: Abingdon.

Fuerst, Wesley J.
1975   *The Books of Ruth, Esther, Ecclesiastes, The Song of Songs, Lamentations*. Cambridge: University Press.

Gan, Moshe
1961–1962   "The Book of Esther in the Light of the Story of Joseph in Egypt." *Tarbiz* 31: 144–49 (Hebrew).

Gaster, Theodor H.
1950   *Purim and Hanukkah in Custom and Tradition*. New York: Schuman.

Gerleman, Gillis
1965   *Ruth, Das Hohelied*. BKAT 18. Neukirchen-Vluyn: Neukirchener Verlag.
1966   *Studien zu Esther: Stoff—Struktur—Stil—Sinn*. BibS(N) 48. Neukirchen-Vluyn: Neukirchener Verlag.
1973   *Esther*. BKAT 21. Neukirchen-Vluyn: Neukirchener Verlag.

Glanzman, George S.
1959   "Origin and Date of the Book of Ruth." *CBQ* 21: 201–7.

Gordis, Robert
1972   *Megillat Esther*. New York: Rabbinical Assembly.
1974   "Love, Marriage, and Business in the Book of Ruth: A Chapter in Hebrew Customary Law." Pp. 241–64 in *A Light unto My Path: Old Testament Studies in Honor of Jacob M. Myers*. Ed. Howard N. Bream, Ralph D. Heim, and Carey A. Moore. Gettysburg Theological Studies, 4. Philadelphia: Temple University Press.
1976   "Studies in the Esther Narrative." *JBL* 95: 43–58.

Gray, John
1967   *Joshua, Judges and Ruth*. NCB. London: Nelson and Sons.

Gunkel, Hermann
1930   "Ruth." Cols. 2180–82 in *RGG*. 2d ed. Vol. 4.

Hals, Ronald M.
1969   *The Theology of the Book of Ruth*. Philadelphia: Fortress.

Hartman, Louis F., and Alexander A. Di Lella
1978   *The Book of Daniel*. AB 23. Garden City, NY: Doubleday.

Heaton, E. W.
1956   *The Book of Daniel: Introduction and Commentary*. London: SCM.

Hertzberg, Wilhelm
1960   *Die Bücher Josua, Richter, Ruth.* ATD 9. Göttingen: Vandenhoeck & Ruprecht.

Horn, Siegfried H.
1964   "Mordecai, A Historical Problem." *BR* 9: 14–25.

Humphreys, W. Lee
1973   "A Life-style for Diaspora: A Study of the Tales of Esther and Daniel." *JBL* 92: 211–23.

Jones, Bruce William
1977   "Two Misconceptions about the Book of Esther." *CBQ* 39: 171–81.

Joüon, Paul
1953   *Ruth, Commentaire philologique et exégétique.* Rome: Pontifical Biblical Institute.

Knight, George A.
1955   *Esther, Song of Songs, Lamentations.* London: SCM.
1966   *Ruth and Jonah.* London: SCM.

Lacocque, André
1976   *Le Livre de Daniel.* CAT 15b. Neuchâtel: Delachaux et Niestlé.
1979   "Date et milieu du Livre de Ruth." *Melanges Edmond Jacob. RHPR* 59: 583–93.

Lebram, J. C. H.
1972   "Purimfest und Estherbuch." *VT* 22: 208–22.

Lewy, J.
1938   "Old Assyrian puru'um and pūrum." *RHA* 36: 117–24.

Loewenstamm, Samuel E.
1971   "Esther 9: 29–32: The Genesis of a Late Addition." *HUCA* 42: 117–24.

Lord, Albert B.
1968   *The Singer of Tales.* New York: Atheneum.

Lusseau, H.
1959   "Esther." Pp. 688–94 in *Introduction à la Bible*, 2d ed. Vol. 1. Ed. A. Robert and A. Feuillet. Tournai: Desclée & Cie.

Meinhold, Arndt
1975   "Die Gattung der Josephsgeschichte und des Estherbuches. Diasporanovelle I." *ZAW* 87: 306–24.
1976   "Die Gattung der Josephsgeschichte und des Estherbuches: Diasporanovelle II." *ZAW* 88: 72–93.

Moore, Carey A.
1967   "A Greek Witness to a Different Hebrew Text of Esther." *ZAW* 79: 351–58.
1971   *Esther.* AB 7B. Garden City, NY: Doubleday.

1977   *Daniel, Esther and Jeremiah: The Additions.* AB 44. Garden City, NY: Doubleday.

Müller, Hans-Peter
1976   "Märchen, Legende und Enderwartung." *ZAW* 26: 338–50.

Myers, Jacob M.
1955   *The Linguistic and Literary Form of the Book of Ruth.* Leiden: Brill.

Niditch, Susan, and Robert Doran
1977   "The Success Story of the Wise Courtier: A Formal Approach." *JBL* 96: 179–93.

Perry, Ben Edwin
1967   *The Ancient Romances: A Literary-Historical Account of Their Origins.* Berkeley: University of California Press.

Pfeiffer, Robert H.
1948   *Introduction to the Old Testament.* New York: Harper and Brothers.

Polzin, Robert
1976   *Late Biblical Hebrew: Toward an Historical Typology of Biblical Hebrew Prose.* HSM 12. Missoula, MT: Scholars Press.

Propp, Vladimir
1968   *Morphology of the Folktale.* Austin: University of Texas Press.

Rauber, D. F.
1970   "Literary Values in the Bible: The Book of Ruth." *JBL* 89: 27–37.

Ringgren, Helmer
1955   "Esther and Purim." *SEÅ* 20: 5–24.
1958   *Des Hohe Lied, Klagelieder, Das Buch Esther.* ATD 16. Göttingen: Vandenhoeck & Ruprecht.

Rowley, Harold H.
1965   "The Marriage of Ruth." Pp. 171–94 in *The Servant of the Lord and other Essays on the Old Testament.* Oxford: Blackwell.

Rudolph, Wilhelm
1962   *Das Buch Ruth. Das Hohe Lied. Die Klagelieder.* KAT 17/1. Gütersloh: Mohn.

Sandmel, Samuel
1978   *The Hebrew Scriptures: An Introduction to their Literature and Religious Ideas.* New York: Oxford University Press.

Sasson, Jack M.
1979   *Ruth: A New Translation with a Philological Commentary and a Formalist Interpretation*. Baltimore. Johns Hopkins University Press.

Schedl, Claus
1964   "Das Buch Esther." *Theologie der Gegenwart* 7: 85–93.

Schneider, B.
1962–1963   "Esther Revised According to the Maccabees." *SBFLA* 12: 190–218.

Sheehan, John F. X.
1973   "The Word of God as Myth: The Book of Ruth." Pp. 35–43 in *Essays in Honor of Frederick L. Moriarty, S.J.: The Word in the World*. Ed. Richard J. Clifford and George W. MacRae. Cambridge: Weston College.

Stiehl, Ruth
1956   "Das Buch Esther." *WZKM* 53: 4–22.

Striedl, Hans
1937   "Untersuchung zur Syntax und Stilistik des hebräischen Buches Esther." *ZAW* 55: 73–108.

Talmon, Shemaryahu
1963   "'Wisdom' in the Book of Esther." *VT* 13: 419–55.

Thompson, Dorothy, and Thomas Thompson
1968   "Some Legal Problems in the Book of Ruth." *VT* 18: 79–99.

Torrey, Charles Cutler
1944   "The Older Book of Esther." *HTR* 37. 1–40.

Trible, Phyllis
1978   *God and the Rhetoric of Sexuality*. Philadelphia: Fortress.

Ungnad, Arthur
1940–1941   "Keilinschriftliche Beiträge zum Buch Ezra und Esther." *ZAW* 58: 240–44.

Vesco, Jean-Luc
1967   "La date du livre de Ruth." *RB* 74: 235–47.

Weiser, Artur
1964   *The Old Testament: Its Formation and Development*. New York: Association.

Wright, Addison G.
1967   *The Literary Genre: Midrash*. New York: Alba House.

Würthwein, Ernst
1969   *Die fünf Megilloth. Ruth, Das Hohelied. Esther*. HAT 18/1–3. Tübingen: Mohr.

14

Apocalyptic Literature*

Paul D. Hanson

When one takes a comprehensive view of the scholarly publications devoted to apocalyptic literature from World War II to the present, one is struck by the intense theological interest that has motivated much of the work.[1] In the century preceding this period, studies on the subject were rare, and those that were produced tended to treat matters of a textual and literary nature. While exceptions like H. Gunkel's *Schöpfung und Chaos* must not be forgotten, the subject was one that was more the source of theological embarrassment than of genuine concern.

With theologians like W. Pannenberg and J. Moltmann placing the spotlight on apocalypticism as a phenomenon of profound importance for Christian theology, a new chapter in the history of the subject was opened. Biblical scholars were not lacking who caught the enthusiasm for the subject. The trend was abetted by factors as diverse as the discovery of the Dead Sea Scrolls and the "apocalyptic" mood of the Nuclear Age. Needless to say, when systematic theologians, historians, and biblical scholars are all actively writing on the subject from their diverse perspectives and when, moreover, they are joined by ecologists, futurologists, and fundamentalist preachers, definitions and issues become blurred and confused. An investigation such as this can best contribute to the subject by clarifying definitions, sorting out issues, and pointing to conclusions that have been established and to problems where further inquiry is urgently needed. This study will proceed first by discussing the attempts that have been made to define apocalyptic, next by considering the equally debated question of the time of origin of this phenomenon, and then in turn by considering the problems of the sources of apocalyptic, the writings within the OT that fit into this category (with special attention to Daniel), and finally the theological significance of this literature.

* Research and writing of this paper were supported by Grant Number RO–32371–78–1495 from the National Endowment for the Humanities.

1 Since this chapter will cover only those writings on apocalyptic literature appearing in the post-World War II period, the reader is referred to two works by J. Schmidt and P. D. Hanson (1976c) which deal with earlier scholarship.

I. THE QUESTION OF DEFINITIONS

In 1895 Gunkel struggled with the problem of accounting for two aspects of apocalyptic, namely, form and content. After having posed an important question, however, he did not go on to resolve the problem of definitions. This was due in part to the fact that he did not persist in his earlier inquiry into apocalyptic texts. In the period we treat, most scholars seem to ignore even Gunkel's basic awareness of the distinction between form and content. Consequently, they have continued to define apocalyptic by compiling lists of characteristics that indiscriminately mix formal, conceptual, and even sociological categories. Thus D. S. Russell lists the following: transcendentalism, mythology, a cosmological orientation, a pessimistic historical view, dualism, the division of time into eras, teaching of two eras, numerology, pseudo-ecstasy, artificial claims of inspiration, pseudonymity, esoterism, unity of history, a conception of cosmic history that treats of earth and heaven, a notion of primordiality, speculation on the source of evil in the world, conflict between light and darkness, good and evil, God and Satan, Son of Man, life after death, individualism (1964:105). How can a list like this lead to an understanding of apocalyptic? If a given work contains nine of them, does it qualify? Or is it sufficient if it manifests the literary traits? Or the conceptual features? There is no doubting the fact that most of the items listed play an important part in certain apocalyptic writings, but since such a random list fails to identify a definable center, it contributes little to a clear definition. Russell is not to be singled out in this criticism. Not only was he drawing on the work of J. Lindblom,[2] but a similar (if not as exhaustive!) approach was taken by J. Schreiner, H. Ringgren (464), and P. Vielhauer (582–94). The most recent author to address the problem, F. Dexinger, acknowledges the validity of the present writer's criticism of the list approach and then in his own treatment follows the approach of P. Vielhauer by differentiating between concepts and literary characteristics (60–91). The result is a greater degree of clarity than found in earlier treatments. Even in Dexinger, however, one looks in vain for a definition of apocalyptic that will solve the problem he acknowledges at the beginning of his chapter on motifs (58). It seems likely that the problem which continues to plague scholarship is of twofold origin: (1) Apocalyptic continues to be treated as if it were a homogeneous system of thought. This tendency is illustrated clearly by W. Schmithal's recent treatment of apocalyptic as a "movement" that spans the centuries without substantial change.[3] (2) There is a woeful lack of attention to the

---

[2] Of Lindblom's "marks of apocalyptic," Rowley (13) correctly observes, "some of these are rather the accidents than the essence of apocalyptic."

[3] The English title of Schmithal's book betrays this monolithic view. Treating apocalyptic as one unified movement, he gleans characteristics from a wide range of diverse writings,

social and historical matrix behind each apocalyptic work. Only if these two areas of scholarly neglect are redressed can a more accurate and nuanced picture of apocalyptic emerge. A starting point in such an effort is the attempt to replace the older static definitions with new ones that have sufficient flexibility and clarity to account both for the multifaceted nature of the phenomenon and for its various stages of development amidst changing political and social conditions.

J. Barr observes, "scholars have been divided over one question in particular, namely whether they should use the term apocalyptic as the designation for a literary form, a type or genre of literature, or for a mode of thinking, a religious current" (14–15). He pursues a promising tack by further refining the differentiation into four levels: language use, structure, the sort of thing that is told, and doctrine. While a move in the right direction, his categories do not yet adequately locate the central perspective that allows us to recognize apocalyptic as an identifiable phenomenon despite much diversity and a long history of development. Furthermore, his categories are not sensitive to the sociopolitical dimension of apocalypticism. Nevertheless, with Barr (and we can add K. Koch [1972] and two authors already mentioned, P. Vielhauer and F. Dexinger), we can accept as an initial assumption that a clear distinction between apocalyptic as a literary designation and as a religious current is essential to conceptual clarity.

In the attempt here advanced to distinguish between three levels in an adequate definition of apocalyptic, it is necessary first to recognize as the first level of definition the literary genre of the "apocalypse." Some years ago K. Koch took preliminary steps toward such a definition. The present writer added to this effort several years later (1976a). While further research will undoubtedly lead to refinements, the essential features of this genre have now been identified and explained.

Unfortunately, far less clarity prevails in the ordering of the remaining aspects of the apocalyptic phenomenon: What sort of religious current do we intend to name with the adjective apocalyptic? When does it begin? What sources does it utilize? What central quality can one identify in order to differentiate it from other phenomena? One of the underlying reasons for the confusion is located in the inability of scholars to agree on a definition of another term, "eschatology." Unclarity in defining this latter term immediately spills over into definitions of apocalyptic as well. Therefore the attempt to clarify the second level of definition must be prefaced with some attention to the concept "eschatology."

obscuring important differences and overlooking the complexities of historical development, differences in sociopolitical matters, and diversity in the types of material incorporated in the various writings. In a word, his treatment, due to generalizations detached from the specifics of the writings themselves, overlooks the presence of different movements underlying the apocalyptic writings.

The difficulty becomes apparent when one contrasts H. Gressmann's insistence that eschatology is already to be found in the myths of the ancient, second-millennium kingdoms of the Near East with S. Mowinckel's argument that eschatology developed only in the postexilic period (125–33).[4] The most useful definition lies between these extremes. Gressmann is correct in recognizing the source of many motifs of both prophecy and apocalyptic in myth, but he overlooks the significant transformation that these motifs underwent in being absorbed into Yahwism: Once transferred from their cyclic matrix in a mythopoeic cult into Israelite worship, they served to portray not a recurrent recapitulation of primordial realities but an awaited one-time denouement in the future. Since only the latter is true eschatology, we can maintain that eschatology originated with Yahwism, and especially with prophetic Yahwism. Mowinckel, on the other hand, draws an exaggerated distinction between the "future hope" of the preexilic prophets and the eschatology of the postexilic period. In his view an ontological dualism is essential to eschatology, which implies that fulfillment can occur only as the result of the total destruction of the present evil order. An element common to both is thereby obscured, namely, the perspective that views reality as directed toward a decisive (i.e., fulfilling) final (i.e., eschatological) act of God. This is not to obscure differences, for such are found especially in relation to the role and status of human agents and mundane structures in this eschatological event. But it does clarify eschatology as a basic religious perspective that developed in Israel from the early prophetic period through postexilic times. K. D. Schunck's definition captures this essential perspective when he defines eschatology as "the new and the entirely other [occurring] after a break with that which has gone before" (120),[5] although the elaboration of his definition perhaps goes beyond biblical prophecy in the direction of modern existentialism when he speaks of "ein neues Sein." B. Vawter correctly observes that this eschatological perspective was well developed by the time of Amos and is at the heart of classical prophecy (38–41).

This clarification of the term "eschatology" clears the way for defining the second level of apocalyptic, namely, that which identifies the central religious perspective of the phenomenon. In the debate arising in opposition to the theory that apocalyptic is a late outgrowth of wisdom,

---

[4] Mowinckel (125–33) thus argues that a basic dualism is essential to eschatology, which presupposes that the fulfillment can occur only with the total destruction of the present evil order.

[5] F. Dingermann argues a similar position and summarizes his view of the tie between prophecy and apocalyptic thus: "Viele der Merkmale, die der apokalyptischen Schau ihr besonderes Gepräge verheihen, erwuchsen aus einer Weiterführung prophetischer Denk- und Aussageweise. Die *gemeinsame eschatologische Ausrichtung* bildet das eigentliche und stärkste Bindeglied" (332).

it has grown increasingly clear that at the heart of apocalyptic is its eschatological orientation (Osten-Sacken). This orientation was inherited from prophecy, yet it is not identical to the perspective of prophecy. The best conceptual means of preserving both the line of continuity from prophecy to apocalyptic and the distinction between them seems to be that of designating the central perspective of prophecy as "prophetic eschatology," and that of apocalyptic as "apocalyptic eschatology." Both turn to a vision of divine activity for the key to the meaning and direction of human history. Both maintain that all reality moves toward a divinely ordained goal. But beyond this lies an important difference. This eschatological orientation in the prophets incorporates mundane realities and human agents in the interpretation of how God's purposes unfold. In apocalyptic, for sociopolitical and religious reasons (Hanson, 1971a), that unfolding becomes increasingly detached from the realities of this world.

This difference between prophetic and apocalyptic eschatology has been addressed from another angle by scholars seeking to clarify prophecy's and apocalyptic's different attitudes toward history. The discussion is complicated, however, by scholars using the same evidence and coming to opposite conclusions. G. von Rad denies apocalyptic any roots in prophecy, partly because of "the impossibility of reconciling its view of history with that of the prophets" (272). K. Koch, on the other hand, sees a direct line of continuity, with apocalyptic enlarging the earlier prophetic perspective to encompass universal history. Once again, there is truth in both positions; that is to say, both continuity *and* new departures characterize the relationship, as the contrast prophetic eschatology/ apocalyptic eschatology in fact suggests. M. Noth, for example, is therefore on the mark in seeing the emphasis in Daniel 7 not on the *details* of history but on "the mutual confrontation of world history as a whole and the kingdom of God" (213). In a similar vein R. North contrasts the interpretation of the concrete events of history in the classical prophets with "history as pattern" in apocalypticism. These scholars are correct in observing that history is drawn into a more cosmic interpretive framework in apocalyptic. As J. Collins observes, a lively interaction occurs between the horizontal axis or historical chronology and the vertical antithesis between heaven and earth, an interaction experienced by a growing fascination with a mythical way of viewing reality (158–62). But the role that the chronological framework continues to play in apocalyptic eschatology safeguards against its being cut off entirely from its prophetic roots. Once that occurs, we speak no longer of apocalypticism, but of gnosticism.

The tension between an abiding concern with history on the one hand and a tendency to lift attention from the concrete to the universal on the other can best be understood by paying attention to the social and political history of the groups that kept the apocalyptic spirit alive. Unfortunately, inadequate attention has been paid to this dimension of the apocalyptic phenomena, a lack which several recent works lead one to hope may be redressed in the future (Steck; Petersen; Hanson, 1971a). Such studies, by being attentive to the changing social conditions within which groups tried to keep hope and faith alive, are sensitive to the continuity in eschatological perspective all the way from Amos to Daniel, which perspective, however, adopts new modes of expression in response to changing conditions. Throughout this sweep of time, God was believed to be guiding history toward a fulfillment of divine purpose. But whereas normal times encouraged interpretation of that purpose within the categories of human events, times of severe hardship encouraged a view that thought in terms of epochal patterns in disregard of concrete historical detail.

Our discussion of the second level thereby introduces a third by drawing attention to the social carriers of apocalyptic eschatology. Apocalyptic is not confined to the literary genre of the apocalypse, nor is it circumscribed by the religious perspective we call apocalyptic eschatology. It is also to be recognized as a socioreligious phenomenon, or what we can call an apocalyptic movement. For this dimension one can best reserve the term "apocalypticism." That is to say, "apocalypticism" is the thought world (or "symbolic universe") of a particular apocalyptic movement. During the period when neo-orthodoxy was regnant, little attention was paid to the sociopolitical dimensions of apocalypticism. God's word was what counted, and it broke into human experience in a manner quite detached from the social and political structures of a people. For this reason one must look to works before the time of Barth for explorations of this dimension. But it is encouraging as well to detect a gradual renewal of interest in the social roots of apocalypticism over the decade. In the time intervening, contributions were made primarily by those (like anthropologists) working outside of the sphere of influence of theological or biblical studies.

Since attention is focused here on the period after World War II, we only mention in passing the several classics of the sociology-of-knowledge school which analyzed movements and experimented with typologies that laid the groundwork for subsequent study of the sociology of apocalypticism. In carefully analyzing and contrasting the characteristics of "church" and "sect," Ernst Troeltsch paved the way for further research. This approach bore fruit in application to Judaism in Max Weber's classics, which breathed life into categories like "charismatic leader," "priest," and "pariah" (1922, 1946). Karl Mannheim introduced an important dichotomy in his contrast between "utopia" and "ideology" (1929). The most notable example of the recent reapplication of this approach to the study of religious groups is P. Berger and T. Luckmann. As noted, there is an encouraging renewal of interest among certain biblical scholars in this dimension of apocalyptic movements (Steck; Petersen; Hanson, 1971a). This is in no small measure due to the shift away from an abstract "word theology" toward an understanding of theology as deeply involved in the political and social struggles of a community.

From outside of the biblical field have come works contributing to our understanding of the social dimension of apocalypticism (Burridge; Stanner; Thrupp; Worsley; Cohn; Talmon). It is much to be hoped that future research in this area will be carried on in dialogue with the broader fields of sociology, social psychology, and sociology of religion.

An approach to the study of Jewish apocalypticism that includes alongside literary and historical methods of research the sociological sensitivity that is an indispensable part of form criticism's search for Sitz im Leben can contribute much to a deeper understanding of the complexity of the apocalyptic phenomenon. Eschewing the imposition of simplistic, rigid conceptual, or literary definitions that ignore historical, literary, and sociopolitical detail, such an approach can identify the central perspective of apocalyptic movements while at the same time taking into full account the vast array of materials drawn into specific apocalyptic writings. Recognition of the eschatological dimension in the apocalyptic writings is now almost universal. Such recognition is not surprising when one realizes that the perspective of apocalyptic eschatology (described above as the second level of definition) is the perspective that forms the heart of apocalyptic. But it is not a static heart nor a bed of Procrustes that cuts or stretches all materials to fit one form. As a perspective it provides only the starting point for any specific apocalyptic writing. The exact form of expression to emerge is determined by much more, including the antecedent traditions used, contemporary (including foreign) influences, as well as social and political conditions (especially the status of the protagonists vis-à-vis opponents). In relation to the second level of definition we can observe that apocalyptic eschatology, as a religious perspective, can exist alongside other perspectives (e.g., hierocratic, sapiential, "scientific") without producing an apocalyptic movement (in fact, this is the usual case in ordinary times), but it is ever present in late biblical religion as a latent source of apocalypticism. And apocalypticism takes shape when a group, experiencing a profound sense of alienation from the dominant social system, embraces the perspective of apocalyptic eschatology as an ideology upon which to build an alternative symbolic universe. Sociological analysis therefore does not at all deny the uniqueness of a given apocalyptic work. Indeed, it insists that adequate study of each such work of necessity involves penetration to the specific political and social circumstances within which that work arose. But it is also able to recognize a perspective common to all ancient apocalyptic works (the perspective of apocalyptic eschatology) and a basic experience in response to which apocalyptic movements are born (the group experience of alienation). In a generalized way the study of apocalyptic can describe also a function common to all such movements, that of reconstituting the identity of a disfranchised group in relation to God and in opposition to the dominant social system and its leaders. This function relates directly to the central perspective of all ancient apocalyptic movements, for it is exercised through the elevation of the perspective of apocalyptic eschatology to the ideology of the protagonist group.

With the application of this set of definitions one may hope that a greater degree of clarity might come to characterize the study of apocalyptic than has obtained in the past. It should allow scholars to do the following: to identify clearly to themselves and for their readers the level of the phenomenon they are treating; to distinguish between random characteristics (what H. H. Rowley called "rather the accidents than the essence of apocalyptic" [23 n. 3]) and the perspective, basic experience, and function common to all ancient apocalyptic movements; and to remain sensitive to the high degree of diversity and change in relation both to the sources utilized by apocalyptic writers and to the history of development through which the various apocalyptic movements passed. Beyond the definitions suggested above for "apocalypse," "apocalyptic eschatology," and "apocalypticism," the further suggestion might be added that the nominal sense of the word "apocalyptic" be used when one wishes to designate the phenomenon in general without specifying one of the three particular levels of definition.

II. TIME OF ORIGIN

The question of the time of origin of apocalyptic has been closely related to the question of definitions. Here too it is necessary to distinguish between the three levels of the apocalyptic phenomenon, for while interrelated, they are not identical. In addressing each level, one must be content with examples illustrating the range of theories found in the recent literature.

H. Gese, on the basis of a careful examination of Zechariah 1–6, concluded that "the nocturnal visions of Zechariah are the oldest and best-known apocalypses" (24). On the other hand, many scholars argue that the oldest apocalypse is Daniel and that from that starting point the genre spread through other Jewish and then Christian writings (Flusser). F. Dexinger, in the course of a detailed study of the Ten Weeks Apocalypse of *1 Enoch*, argues that it was a leaflet of those supporting the struggle of the Maccabees and draws the conclusion that the composition has prior claim over Daniel as being the first apocalypse (187–89). Other writers argue the case for the so-called Isaiah apocalypse (Isaiah 24–27),

Joel, Ezekiel 38–39, or Zechariah 1–8. The reason for this wide range of opinions is primarily that scholars have been misguided by a static, idealistic definition of genre, a definition plaguing form-critical research in general (Hanson, 1973; Vawter: 33–34). If the literary category of genre is understood not in terms of ideal types impervious to change but organically in terms of mutation and development, all of the works mentioned above will be seen as fitting into the history of development of the genre of the apocalypse. The further tendency among continental form critics to assume the existence of one original pure exemplar of a genre at the earliest stage of its history, with all subsequent manifestations representing a degeneration of the original,[6] must also be rejected in favor of an approach that is sensitive to the qualities of each apocalypse, regardless of its position in the history of that genre's development. Such an approach will lead inevitably even behind the nocturnal visions of Zechariah to antecedents among visions found in earlier prophets. This is not to argue that the visions of Ezekiel (aside from chapters 38–39), Jeremiah, or Amos are apocalypses but rather that the genre of the apocalypse grew organically from such antecedents.[7] The exact determination of which apocalypse is actually the first pales in significance before the more important task of understanding that genre's history and dynamic.

When we move to the question of when the perspective of apocalyptic eschatology originates, one is aided by an organic approach analogous to that described above in relation to the genre question. Only here, instead of dealing with the development of a literary type, one is dealing with a typology tracing the development of a religious perspective. The present author has argued that the development from prophetic eschatology to apocalyptic eschatology can be traced within materials belonging to a school of Second Isaiah (Isaiah 34–35, 40–55, 24–27 and 56–66), which development can be dated roughly to the years 538–500 (Hanson, 1971a). On the other hand, there are still scholars who ascribe to Persian influence the major impetus for apocalyptic eschatology, placing the time of origin several centuries later (Murdock; cf. Vielhauer: 594–95). This position is weakened by the impossibility of either dating the Persian documents or demonstrating actual lines of influence on Jewish writings (Frye). S. B. Frost has made an important contribution to this problem by analyzing earlier and later forms of eschatology in the Bible, concluding that apocalyptic writings manifest the mythologization of

---

[6] This is a tendency flawing even as basic a study as C. Westermann's *Basic Forms of Prophetic Speech*.

[7] H. Gese is sensitive to this diachronic dimension in the genre of the apocalypse (22). In the course of his discussion, however, the distinction between apocalypse and apocalypticism gets blurred (23–24).

eschatology, a process that can be traced back to the time of the exile. F. M. Cross has added an important element of control and specificity by tracing this process in relation to the motif of the divine warrior (1966, 1973:91–111). To be discussed below is the theory, most recently popularized by G. von Rad, that apocalyptic has its origins in wisdom, a theory diverging sharply from the reconstruction favored by the present writer that the central current of Jewish apocalyptic is to be seen in the development of apocalyptic eschatology out of prophetic roots in the sixth and fifth centuries B.C.E.[8]

Finally, what is the time of origin of apocalypticism, that is to say, of the complex of thought evolved by an apocalyptic movement? W. Millar, on the basis of a study of Isaiah 24–27 and in consideration of the work done by the present writer on Isaiah 56–66 and Zechariah 9–14, concludes, "It was in the years of exile and shortly thereafter that the [sic] apocalyptic movement was born" (Millar: 120). K. Müller on the other hand has drawn attention to similarities between the Oracle of Hystaspes, the Potter's Oracle, and Daniel 2, concluding that all stem from the same historical, political situation, namely, the destruction of national optimism stemming from the triumphs and efforts at Hellenizing the conquered peoples by Antiochus IV Epiphanes. That is to say, a widespread apocalyptic movement arose in the first half of the second century B.C.E., which prompted a transference of historical hope to an apocalyptic vision. Important in this connection is the study of O. Plöger, in which apocalypticism is seen to originate in conventicles of the period 400–200 B.C.E., which drew on prophecy, were open to Persian ideas, and stood in opposition to the theocratic structures of the Zadokites. A major flaw in Plöger's study is his failure to discern the major shift away from prophetic eschatology that occurred during the period 538–500. Thus he situates the rise of apocalypticism in the relatively calm years 400–200 and overlooks the significance of the controversies centering on the rebuilding of the temple, which gave rise to the earliest apocalyptic movement in Jewish history (Hammerton-Kelly). There is also too strong a tendency in Plöger to tie apocalypticism to one party rather than to study it as the outgrowth of a religious perspective available to different parties at different times. Nevertheless, the strength of Plöger's approach remains, namely, his emphasis on examining the historical and social setting within which apocalypticism arose.

The time is ripe for much more refined study of apocalyptic movements in ancient Israel. The plural is emphasized, for much study has been misdirected by the false notion that Jewish apocalyptic is one

---

[8] On the question of the time of origin of apocalyptic eschatology, see further B. Vawter (33–34).

homogeneous system and that it was produced by one continuous movement. There will be no need to argue that one particular movement is *the* authentic apocalyptic movement in Israel if apocalypticism is seen in proper relation to the perspective of apocalyptic eschatology. The latter was a perspective available to all Jewish parties from the late sixth century B.C.E. on. It appealed to groups suffering oppression and experiencing alienation from the dominant social system. When those groups elevated it to their group ideology and built their ideas and their identity around it, an apocalyptic movement was born. This did not occur only once, nor once having occurred did it flow within a single channel. Apocalyptic movements arose and disappeared in Israel, and they were sponsored by different parties at different times. New research must study these *different* movements in their uniqueness and not blur lines of distinction. This can be done only if literary study goes hand in hand with historical and sociological reconstruction. To be sure, common features will be recognized between, say, the apocalyptic movement of the visionaries of the sixth century and that of the Covenanters of Qumran, for both based their efforts on the perspective of apocalyptic eschatology, were responding to the experience of alienation, and produced writings that functioned to establish a symbolic universe that defined their relationship to God and to their antagonists. But beyond this, careful study will give full account of differences as well. For example, in the sixth century the antagonists were Zadokites; in the second century the tables had turned, and the Zadokites were the apocalypticists! Also, the types of native and foreign materials utilized by different movements differ vastly, as do the literary forms they adopt and develop.[9]

On this level, then, we conclude that apocalypticism first arose in Israel within a sixth-century movement but that later stressful periods gave rise to other apocalyptic movements. An exciting challenge stands before biblical scholars to study each of these movements, sensitive both to the properties unique to each and to the relationships between them.

---

[9] For guidelines for this type of restudy of apocalypticism, cf. P. D. Hanson (1976b: 401–8). Generally speaking, the lack of careful attention to the social matrix of apocalypticism has led to a narrow literary interpretation of a supposed rectilinear development of apocalyptic. For example, those who regard Daniel as the first fully developed apocalyptic writing tend to seek antecedents only in the late third and the early second century B.C.E. If proper attention is paid to the social and political dimensions of apocalypticism, it will be seen that apocalyptic movements flourished at different times, and while betraying certain resemblances, they cannot be regarded as expressions of the same movement. A good example of the careful tracing of the roots of Hellenistic apocalypticism back to biblical antecedents that does not blur the distinctiveness of the works of different periods is found in G. Nickelsburg.

III. SOURCES OF APOCALYPTIC

Where one locates the sources of Jewish apocalyptic thought is not just a matter of historical interest, for any theory of origins influences one's understanding of the phenomenon itself. In this section apocalyptic eschatology and apocalypticism will be considered together, since their linkage in the scholarly literature makes it difficult to maintain a clear distinction between them in relation to the question of sources. The different sources that have been considered in the scholarly literature will be surveyed, in full recognition of the fact that individual scholars often blend more than one of these sources into their overall theory of origins. It is noteworthy that the sources discussed since World War II are basically the same ones cited by scholars over the preceding century and a half, namely, prophecy, royal cult, ancient Semitic myth, wisdom, Persian dualism, and Hellenistic syncretism (Schmidt: 98–276).

H. H. Rowley published a study covering the entire phenomenon of Jewish and Christian apocalypticism in which he defended the theory of prophetic roots. He makes reference to prophets like Amos, Isaiah, Zechariah, and Joel in the following manner: "To all these writers history was moving swiftly towards a great climax, and the birth of a new age which should belong to the faithful Remnant of Israel." From this it was but a short step to note the following contrast: "Speaking generally, the prophets foretold the future that should break into the present" (38). A similar position was developed by G. Ladd, who found that "the basic elements of an apocalyptic eschatology are present in the Old Testament prophets and are essential to their view of history" (197). P. von der Osten-Sacken set out to locate the roots of apocalyptic by focusing on what he identified as the central theme of Daniel, namely, that history is determined by a divine plan. The antecedents of this theme he finds to be definitely prophetic. In preexilic prophecy Yahweh gives promises and leads history according to his plan (15). After the crisis of 587 this theme persists, but through the inclusion of hymnic materials Second Isaiah draws into a unified whole God's directing all from creation to the eschaton, a view close to the determinism of Daniel 2. As far as foreign schemata like the four-kingdom theory are concerned, they are subservient to the purpose of announcing the eschaton and thus merely develop the two-period idea found already in Second Isaiah (23–28).

In addition to such comprehensive overviews, there have appeared studies that seek to analyze the way in which a specific prophetic corpus is transitional from prophecy to apocalyptic. Chr. Jeremias concludes his study of the nocturnal visions of the book of Zechariah with the argument that Zechariah is best understood as such a transitional link rather than as "the first apocalypticist" as H. Gese had maintained (Jeremias). H.-P. Müller argues that the eschatological hope expressed in Joel

1:5–2:27 did not materialize, leading to the apocalyptic interpretation of 1:2–4 and chaps. 3–4. This interpretation removed the drama from a concrete historical situation, universalized it to include all nations, and substituted for the battle a legal trial. In this transition can be detected nothing less than a new understanding of reality, according to Müller. The call to free decision is replaced by a trans-mundane gnosis, "which accomplishes an inner emigration out of the present in anticipatory enjoyment of that which is to come" (250).

Various scholars have attempted to trace the development of apocalyptic out of prophecy within the writings collected in the book of Isaiah. The present author has concentrated on Isaiah 56–66, to which he related Zechariah 9–14 (Hanson, 1971a). W. Millar takes a similar approach to Isaiah 24–27. D. Petersen studies Isaiah 40–66, in addition to Joel, Malachi, and Jer 23:34–40. For P. von der Osten-Sacken, the Second Isaiah corpus plays a very important role.

For many scholars, Ezekiel contributed much to the development of apocalyptic, although few would go as far as did L. Dürr in calling Ezekiel the "father of apocalyptic." S. B. Frost, however, has argued for a secondary level in the book of Ezekiel written in Babylon during the exile in which the prophecies of Ezekiel are reinterpreted in an apocalyptic vein: "It is this Unknown, this Babylonian-Ezekiel, who is the father, if any one man can claim that title, of the apocalyptic genre of thought and writing" (84–85). C. Stuhlmueller places much emphasis on the role played by Ezekiel, in whom "the formative elements of the apocalyptic style combined and produced the standard 'model' for centuries to come" (339). In addition to Ezekiel, Stuhlmueller discusses the cosmic and universal orientation discernible in Jeremiah as well as three characteristics of the Deuteronomistic movement that reappear among the apocalypticists—"a theology of history; an actualization of the past; an hostility to the Jerusalem Zadokite priests" (339).

Another source discussed in the literature is the royal cult of Jerusalem. Here connection is made with a long line of scholars, including notables like Gunkel, Gressmann, Hooke, Engnell, and Mowinckel. Mowinckel's contribution in this regard stands out, for he combines the recognition that the ultimate source of many motifs used by apocalyptic writers is in ancient myth with the important observation that these materials were not derived directly from the foreign cults but were mediated by the royal cult of Jerusalem (56, 102–24). A. Bentzen pursues a line of inquiry similar to Mowinckel's in application to the book of Daniel. Finding in the Ugaritic corpus many of the mythical motifs cropping up in Daniel, he views as the native carrier of these materials the royal cult. Fresh treatment has been given to this theory by F. M. Cross who has traced specific motifs from ancient Canaanite myth, through the literature of the league, and on down into the royal cult of the Judean monarchy. He has further pointed out that the cessation of the worship of the Jerusalem temple released ritual materials for adaption to new settings in the exilic and postexilic period (1969, 1973:343–46).

Inseparably connected with the theory that looks to the royal cult as a source of origin for apocalyptic is the theory invoking a connection with ancient Semitic mythology. Gunkel's theory of a Babylonian source has largely been replaced with a Canaanite theory as a result of the discovery of the Ras Shamra library. A weighty theological question has arisen in this connection: Is the borrowing of mythical material to be construed merely in terms of literary embellishment (Hartman/Di Lella), or does it exercise important influence on the essential theological meaning of the literature (Emerton; Collins)? This is a question that is sure to continue to evoke lively discussion in the future.

In 1919 G. Hölscher published the theory that apocalyptic developed not out of prophecy but out of wisdom. This theory was taken up anew by G. von Rad, who argued that the determinism and pessimism of apocalyptic as well as the titles it applies to its heroes (sages and scribes) pointed not to prophecy but to wisdom as its source. Von Rad has won few followers to his position, and for good reason. For one, the eschatological perspective that is basic to apocalyptic is not to be found in wisdom, and this alone is a crippling flaw in the wisdom theory. Moreover, the determinism that plays such a central role in von Rad's argument must be examined more closely. In wisdom, it is nature and the individual who stand under the canopy of a determinist universe. In apocalyptic, it is human history, a view, moreover, that can be traced all the way back to Second Isaiah, thus betraying roots in prophecy, not wisdom. What has happened is this: von Rad began with collections like *1 Enoch*, which indeed contain sapiential materials, and made these central in his search for antecedents. When the center of apocalyptic is located in its eschatological perspective, however, the primary line of derivation from prophecy becomes unmistakable (Vielhauer: 596–98; Barr: 24–25; North: 58–61). But this view must not fail to account for the undeniable wisdom materials that are conspicuously present in apocalyptic writings like *1 Enoch*. P. von der Osten-Sacken has argued plausibly in the following manner: In view of the eschatological point of view at the center of apocalyptic, the sapiential material (like foreign) is secondary and subservient (substantially speaking). However, with Second Isaiah there entered Israel's eschatological tradition a point of connection with wisdom, this occurring when creation was coupled with history as the unity determined by God. Apocalyptic, a child of prophecy, thus later opened up to wisdom traditions. A tension was thereby introduced into the apocalyptic writings between the static orientation of wisdom and the eschatological orientation at the heart of apocalyptic (Osten-Sacken: 59–63). This explanation fits nicely the view expressed above, namely, that apocalyptic movements build upon the foundation of the perspective of apocalyptic eschatology but draw widely from diverse sources in amplifying and applying that perspective. Since apocalyptic writings arise within contexts of extreme hardship, disallowing the luxury of careful synthesis, tensions such as the one arising between sapiential and eschatological orientations are not surprising.

Within the history-of-religions approach, an explanation came to replace Gunkel's Babylonian source theory in the first decades of this century. This was the view that traced the main teachings of apocalyptic to Persian dualism (Böklen; Reitzenstein). It has grown more brittle with repetition, for no new evidence has been advanced in its support, although neither has any arisen to eliminate it outright. The problem lies in the lateness of the extant Persian sources and in the impossibility of proving direct lines of connection between specific Persian teachings and elements found in apocalyptic writings. Nevertheless, scholars continue to cite Persian dualism in their discussion of origins, either as a major influence accounting for teachings central to the apocalyptic writings (Murdock) or as a secondary and less important source of influence (Ringgren; Rowley: 42–43; Frost: 77; Schmithals: 115–24).

Passing reference should be made to two other theories of origin. W. Schmithals takes the position that while "apocalyptic cannot be derived from gnosis, . . . individual mythologoumena in apocalyptic writings betray a gnostic influence" (126). The examples of this influence cited by Schmithals are best explained in other ways. For example, the motif of the fall of the angels can be explained as derivative of native Semitic traditions (Hanson, 1977). Finally, H. D. Betz, after noting the high degree of diversity characterizing the various apocalyptic writings of the Hellenistic era and the failure of most scholars to explain or even acknowledge that fact, proposes that "we can study and describe this phenomenon adequately only within the larger context of the Hellenistic-oriented syncretism of the time" (198). Betz's proposal is correct, even as any document must be studied within the context of the broad cultural milieu of its time. But methodological controls must be strictly applied to ensure that similarities in fact result from a borrowing from non-Jewish sources rather than from influence in the reverse direction or from mere coincidence.

The various theories of origin have done little to dislodge the oldest theory of them all, that the taproot of apocalyptic is embedded solidly in biblical prophecy. Nevertheless, they have drawn attention to an important fact that many studies operating too simplistically with the prophetic-derivation theory tend to overlook: In the course of their development, apocalyptic movements have drawn very freely from their environment; indeed, almost anything that was useful in developing the ideological perspective of apocalyptic eschatology was fair game. Scholars therefore should be trained to recognize a wide range of possible influences, e.g., from ancient Semitic myth (normally mediated through the league and

royal cults), native and foreign wisdom, neo-Babylonian astrological speculation, Persian dualism, or the eclectic cultural phenomenon Betz refers to
as "Hellenistic-oriented syncretism." But scholars must exercise extreme
caution not to invent instances of influence or borrowing or even to over-
emphasize them. Such caution will best be maintained if each apocalyptic
writing and each apocalyptic movement is understood within its broadest
diachronic and synchronic context. Only then will the complexity of each
be understood from the heart to which the rich and often bewildering
diversity of themes and sources relate.

IV. THE OLD TESTAMENT APOCALYPTIC CORPUS

Each collection of writings that has been treated by some individual or
group of scholars as apocalyptic cannot be discussed here. Reference has
been made, in various contexts above, to most of these writings. By some
they have been treated as transitional to apocalyptic, by others as examples
of genuine apocalyptic. It is perhaps convenient to group such writings
according to the point at which they would fall along a typological
sequence, which sequence would take into consideration both the prophetic eschatology/apocalyptic eschatology continuum and evidence that
the perspective of apocalyptic eschatology was being drawn into the service of an apocalyptic movement (apocalypticism). In such a sequence, for
example, Ezekiel and Second Isaiah could be considered proto-apocalyptic,
Isaiah 55–66, Isaiah 24–27, Joel (in its final edition), and Malachi early
apocalyptic, Zechariah 12 and 14 middle apocalyptic, *1 Enoch* 6–11, Daniel 7–12, and subsequent compositions late apocalyptic.

Obviously, the book of Daniel occupies a preeminent position among
OT apocalyptic writings, whether or not one considers it the first true
example of the genre apocalypse or of apocalypticism. Although S. Niditch
is also treating Daniel (especially chaps. 1–6) in this volume, as is J. Collins
(especially as it relates to apocalyptic writings outside the Hebrew canon)
in a companion volume, several works that illustrate trends in research on
Daniel since World War II should be mentioned here.

In 1948 H. L. Ginsberg published his *Studies in Daniel*. Although
not purporting to cover the whole range of literary, historical, and theological problems raised by the book, this study broke new ground in
special areas, such as the question of the original language of the book,
Aramaisms, overall literary structure, genres used, and the background
of the four-kingdom theory. The historical importance of Ginsberg's
studies recently has been underscored by the extent of the dependence
of Hartman and Di Lella on Ginsberg's theories.

A new direction was pursued in research on Daniel by A. Bentzen,
whose commentary appeared in its second edition in 1952. Although thin
from the point of view of text and literary criticism when compared

with Montgomery's commentary in the ICC series, it integrates for the first time the newly discovered materials from ancient Ugarit into a critical commentary on Daniel (see also Emerton). Because of this aspect of Bentzen's work, its value outlasts, in the present writer's opinion, the more recent commentary of N. Porteous. A stimulating study has recently been published by J. Collins, who follows Bentzen's example in paying careful attention to the materials derived both from Jewish and non-Jewish (especially) Canaanite sources. Collins is careful in evaluating how borrowed materials take on new meanings within the thought world of the Jewish authors.

The Anchor Bible commentary by L. Hartman and A. Di Lella represents a retreat from the history-of-religions emphasis found in the works of Bentzen and Collins. The impact of mythopoeic thought is played down, and images like the "Son of Man" are interpreted unireferentially. However, the commentary reinstates textual criticism as a matter of importance in Daniel studies, even as it betrays a real sensitivity to the theological meaning of that book. Finally, mention should be made of the most recent commentary to appear, A. Lacocque's, a work noted for its sensitivity both to the position of Daniel in the history of religions and to the need to interpret each text within its own social and historical setting.

Even though this brief description has left unmentioned several other recent works on Daniel (Steinmann; Heaton; de Menasce; Hammer; Delcor), those cited indicate that considerable scholarly interest continues to be devoted to the book. Although certain theories now seem to be well established (e.g., the *hasidic* background of the book and the historical setting of the final recension in the Antiochian persecution), other questions remain hotly debated (e.g., the source and meaning of mythic allusions, the provenance of the tales in chaps. 1–6 and their relation to chaps. 7–12, the source and significance of the dual language of the book). While further research must continue on Daniel, it is to be hoped that some of the liveliness that characterizes the research will spill over into renewed study of the many neglected apocalyptic writings that fall outside the Hebrew canon.

V. THEOLOGICAL SIGNIFICANCE

The first book dedicated to the subject of apocalyptic published during the period covered by this essay addressed the problem of theological significance directly, as the title of Rowley's well-known book indicates: *The Relevance of Apocalyptic* (168–93). Rowley attacked what he considered an illegitimate and abusive literalism which drew correspondences between predictions in apocalyptic writings and contemporary events. Striving to identify lasting spiritual truths amidst much that was time-conditioned and ephemeral, Rowley listed the following teachings: (1) God guides history toward a final goal; (2) the reality of evil; (3) the kingdom of God can come only as an act of God, and of humans it requires loyalty to God; (4) hope in the hereafter. For a modern world bent on achieving its own paradise, apocalyptic admonishes: Confuse not what humans can accomplish with the kingdom of God, for it can be established by God alone (Rowley: 181–82).

Apocalyptic writings of Jewish and Christian antiquity became the center of theological debate as a result of the work of a group of German theologians, especially W. Pannenberg and E. Käsemann. Pannenberg gave the concept of universal history central position in his theology, and in apocalypticism he found this concept well developed, for there it was viewed as alone it can be, from the perspective of the consummation of history. In 1960 E. Käsemann published his article "Die Anfänge christlicher Theologie," in which he maintained that apocalyptic was "the mother of all Christian theology." The debate touched off by that thesis continues (Funk). New impetus to the study of apocalypticism, finally, has come from J. Moltmann's writings, where it is argued that if Christian eschatology is to avoid the snares of ethnic human history or existentialistic individual history, it must draw deeply from the universal and cosmic perspective of apocalyptic.

The theological literature dealing with apocalypticism has grown enormously and cannot be treated further here (see Russell, 1978). It is clear, however, that a renewed appreciation of the theological significance of apocalyptic was made possible by understanding it as the manifestation of divine activity amidst the struggles of historical communities in their specific sociopolitical settings. Thus even in the interests of theological research a historical-critical approach to the study of apocalyptic that is sensitive to the concrete settings of the writings is urgently called for. This is especially necessary at a time when systematic theologians have joined the ranks of those intensely interested in this material, for by training they usually are not able to be as attentive to the particularities of philology and the whole dimension of Sitz im Leben as is necessary for accurate interpretation.

VI. CONCLUDING OBSERVATIONS

Although scholarship since 1945 has opened new paths of understanding the apocalyptic phenomenon, it provides only a beginning for research in the years ahead. Several desiderata should be noted: (1) The touchstone of all future work must be detailed study of individual writings with careful attention to all available textual evidence in the effort to produce reliable critical editions, and interpretation should be controlled by the application of up-to-date critical methods. (2) Needed are thorough studies of the history of the genres used by apocalyptic writers (the apocalypse, of course, being one of them), studies that will trace each from roots in the preexilic period down through the period of the Jewish and Christian apocalyptic movements. (3) Research is also needed that will continue recent efforts to trace the history of apocalyptic and other religious movements throughout the Second Temple Period.

Apocalyptic is a complex and many-faceted phenomenon, and matters are not simplified by the restless development that characterizes its passage through time. Therefore, further research must be carried out on the scales of a double sensitivity—on the one hand to the central perspective that allows us to speak of apocalyptic as a phenomenon in the first place and on the other hand to the broad diversity of sources and materials that were drawn into the service of that central perspective.

BIBLIOGRAPHY

Barr, James
1975   "Jewish Apocalyptic in Recent Scholarly Study." *BJRL* 58: 9–25.

Bentzen, Aage
1952   *Daniel*. HAT 19. Tübingen: Mohr (Paul Siebeck).
1955   *King and Messiah*. London: Lutterworth.

Berger, Peter, and Thomas Luckmann
1966   *The Social Construction of Reality: A Treatise in the Sociology of Knowledge*. Garden City, NY: Doubleday.

Betz, Hans Dieter
1966   "The Concept of Apocalyptic in the Theology of the Pannenberg Group." *JTC* 6: 192–207.

Böklen, Ernst
1902   *Die Verwandschaft der jüdisch-christlichen mit der persischen Eschatologie*. Göttingen: Vandenhoeck & Ruprecht.

Burridge, Kenelm
1969   *New Heaven, New Earth: A Study of Millenarian Activities*. Oxford: Blackwell.

Cohn, Norman
1957   *The Pursuit of the Millennium*. London: Secker and Warburg.

Collins, John J.
1977   *The Apocalyptic Vision of the Book of Daniel*. HSM 16. Missoula, MT: Scholars Press.

Cross, Frank Moore
1966   "The Divine Warrior in Israel's Early Cult." Pp. 11–30 in *Studies and Texts III: Biblical Motifs*. Ed. A. Altmann. Cambridge, MA: Harvard University Press.
1969   "New Directions in the Study of Apocalyptic." *JTC* 6: 157–65.
1973   *Canaanite Myth and Hebrew Epic*. Cambridge, MA: Harvard University Press.

Delcor, Mathias
1971   *Le livre de Daniel*. SB. Paris: Gabalda.

Dexinger, Ferdinand
1977   *Henochs Zehnwochenapokalypse und offene Probleme der Apokalyptikforschung*. Leiden: E. J. Brill.

Dingermann, Friedrich
1967   "Die Botschaft vom Vergehen dieser Welt und von den Geheimnissen der Endzeit. Beginnende Apokalyptik im Alten Testament." Pp. 329–42 in *Wort und Botschaft*. Ed. J. Schreiner. Würzburg: Echter Verlag.

Dürr, Lorenz
1923   *Die Stellung des Propheten Ezekiel in der israelitisch-jüdischen Apokalyptik*. Münster: Aschendorff.

Emerton, John A.
1958   "The Origin of the Son of Man Imagery." *JTS* 9: 225–42.

Flusser, David
1971   "Apocalypse." *Encyclopaedia Judaica* 3: 179–81.

Frost, S. B.
1952a   "Eschatology and Myth." *VT* 2: 70–80.
1952b   *Old Testament Apocalyptic: Its Origins and Growth*. London: Epworth.

Frye, Richard N.
1962   "Reitzenstein and Qumran Revisited by an Iranian." *HTR* 85: 261–68.

Funk, Robert W., ed.
1969   *JTC* 6: *Apocalypticism*.

Gese, Hartmut
1973   "Anfang und Ende der Apokalyptik, dargestellt am Sacharjabuch." *ZTK* 70: 20–49.

Ginsberg, H. L.
1948   *Studies in Daniel*. New York: Jewish Theological Seminary.

Gressmann, Hugo
1905   *Der Ursprung der israelitisch-jüdischen Eschatologie*. Göttingen: Vandenhoeck & Ruprecht.

Gunkel, Hermann
1895   *Schöpfung und Chaos in Urzeit und Endzeit.* Göttin-
               gen: Vandenhoeck & Ruprecht.

Hammer, Raymond
1976   *The Book of Daniel.* CBC. Cambridge: University Press.

Hammerton-Kelly, R. G.
1970   "The Temple and the Origins of Jewish Apocalyptic."
               VT 20: 1–20.

Hanson, Paul D.
1971a   "Jewish Apocalyptic against its Near Eastern Environ-
               ment." *RB* 78: 31–58.
1971b   "Old Testament Apocalyptic Reexamined." *Int* 30:
               454–79.
1973   "Zechariah 9 and the Recapitulation of an Ancient Rit-
               ual Pattern." *JBL* 92: 37–59.
1976a   "Apocalypse, Genre." Pp. 27–28 in *IDBSup.*
1976b   "Apocalypticism." Pp. 28–34 in *IDBSup.*
1976c   "Prolegomena to the Study of Jewish Apocalyptic." Pp.
               389–413 in *Magnalia Dei: The Mighty Acts of God:
               Essays on the Bible and Archaeology in Memory of
               G. Ernest Wright.* Ed. F. M. Cross, Jr., W. E. Lemke,
               and P. D. Miller, Jr. Garden City, NY: Doubleday.
1977   "Rebellion in Heaven, Azazel, and Euhemeristic Heroes
               in I Enoch 6–11." *JBL* 96: 195–233.

Hartman, Louis, and Alexander Di Lella
1978   *The Book of Daniel.* AB 23. Garden City, NY: Doubleday.

Heaton, E. W.
1956   *Daniel.* London: SCM.

Hölscher, Gustav
1919   "Die Entstehung des Buches Daniel." *TSK* 92: 113–39.

Jeremias, Christian
1977   *Die Nachtgesichte des Sacharja.* Göttingen: Vanden-
               hoeck & Ruprecht.

Käsemann, Ernst
1960   "Die Anfänge christlicher Theologie." *ZTK* 57: 160–85.

Koch, Klaus
1961   "Spätisraelitisches Geschichtsenden am Beispiel des
               Buches Daniel." *Historische Zeitschrift* 193: 1–32.
1972   *The Rediscovery of Apocalyptic.* Trans. M. Kohl. Lon-
               don: SCM.

Lacocque, André
1979   *The Book of Daniel.* Trans. D. Pellauer. Atlanta: John
               Knox.

Ladd, George E.
1957   "Why Not Prophetic Apocalyptic?" *JBL* 76: 192–200.

Lindblom, Johannes
1938   *Die Jesaja-Apokalypse*. Lund: Gleerup.

Mannheim, Karl
1936   *Ideology and Utopia: An Introduction to the Sociology of Knowledge*. Trans. L. Wirth and E. Shils. New York: Harcourt, Brace. First German edition, 1929.

Menasee, J. de
1958   *Daniel*. Paris: Cerf.

Millar, William R.
1976   *Isaiah 24–27 and the Origin of Apocalyptic*. HSM 11. Missoula, MT: Scholars Press.

Moltmann, Jürgen
1967   *Theology of Hope*. Trans. James W. Keitch. London: SCM. First German edition, 1964.

Montgomery, James A.
1927   *The Book of Daniel*. ICC. Edinburgh: T & T Clark.

Mowinckel, Sigmund
1954   *He That Cometh*. Trans. G. W. Anderson. Nashville: Abingdon.

Müller, Hans-Peter
1966   "Prophetie und Apokalyptik bei Joel." Pp. 231–52 in *Theologia Viatorum* 19. Berlin: Walter de Gruyter.

Müller, Karlheinz
1973   "Die Ansätze der Apokalyptik." Pp. 31–42 in *Literatur und Religion des Frühjudentums*. Ed. J. Schreiner and J. Maier. Würzburg: Echter Verlag.

Murdock, William R.
1967   "History and Revelation in Jewish Apocalypticism." *Int* 21: 167–87.

Nickelsburg, George W. E.
1972   *Resurrection, Immortality, and Eternal Life in Inter-testamental Judaism*. Cambridge, MA: Harvard University Press. Esp. 11–42.

North, Robert
1972   "Prophecy to Apocalyptic via Zechariah." Pp. 47–72 in *Congress Volume: Uppsala, 1971*. VTSup 22. Leiden: E. J. Brill.

Noth, Martin
1967   "History in Old Testament Apocalyptic." Pp. 194–214 in *The Laws in the Pentateuch and other Studies*. Trans. D. Ap-Thomas. Philadelphia: Fortress.

Osten-Sacken, Peter von der
1969   *Die Apokalyptik in ihrem Verhältnis zu Prophetie und Weisheit*. Munich: Chr. Kaiser.

Pannenberg, Wolfhart
1959 "Heilsgeschehen und Geschichte." *KD* 5: 218–22.

Petersen, David L.
1977 *Late Israelite Prophecy: Studies in Deutero-Prophetic Literature and in Chronicles.* SBLMS 23. Missoula, MT: Scholars Press.

Plöger, Otto
1968 *Theocracy and Eschatology.* Trans. S. Rudman. Richmond: John Knox.

Porteous, Norman W.
1965 *Daniel.* OTL. Philadelphia: Westminster. Original German edition, 1962.

Rad, Gerhard von
1965 *The Message of the Prophets.* Trans. D. Stalker. New York: Harper & Row.

Reitzenstein, Richard
1921 *Das iranische Erlösungsmysterium.* Bonn: A. Marcus & E. Weber.

Ringgren, Helmer
1957 "Jüdische Apokalyptic." Pp. 464–66 in *RGG.* 3d ed. Vol. 1. Tübingen: Mohr (Paul Siebeck).

Rowley, H. H.
1947 *The Relevance of Apocalyptic.* 2d ed. London: Lutterworth.

Russell, D. S.
1964 *The Method and Message of Jewish Apocalyptic.* Philadelphia: Westminster.
1978 *Apocalyptic: Ancient and Modern.* Philadelphia: Fortress.

Schmidt, Johann M.
1969 *Die jüdische Apokalyptik. Die Geschichte ihrer Erforschung von den Anfängen bis zu den Textfunden von Qumran.* Neukirchen-Vluyn: Neukirchener Verlag.

Schmithals, Walter
1973 *The Apocalyptic Movement: Introduction and Interpretation.* Trans. J. Steely. Nashville: Abingdon.

Schreiner, Josef
1969 *Alttestamentlich-jüdische Apokalyptik.* Munich: Kösel.

Schunck, Klaus-Dietrich
1974 "Die Eschatologie der Propheten des Alten Testaments und ihre Wandlung in exilisch-nachexilischer Zeit." Pp. 116–32 in *Studies in Prophecy: A Collection of Twelve Papers.* VTSup 26. Leiden: E. J. Brill.

Stanner, W. E. H.
1959   "On the Interpretation of Cargo Cults." *Oceania* 29: 1–25.

Steck, Odil Hannes
1968   "Das Problem theologischer Strömungen in nachexilischer Zeit." *EvT* 28: 445–58.

Steinmann, Jean
1950   *Daniel*. Paris: Editions du Cerf.

Stuhlmueller, Carroll
1968   "Post-exilic Period: Spirit, Apocalyptic." Pp. 337–43 in *The Jerome Biblical Commentary*. Ed. Raymond E. Brown, S.S., Joseph A. Fitzmyer, S.J., and Roland E. Murphy, O. Carm. Englewood Cliffs, NJ: Prentice-Hall.

Talmon, Yonina
1962   "The Pursuit of the Millennium: The Relation between Religion and Social Change." *European Journal of Sociology* 3: 125–48.

Thrupp, Sylvia L., ed.
1970   *Millennial Dreams in Action*. New York: Schocken Books.

Troeltsch, Ernst
1916   *The Social Teaching of the Christian Churches*. 2 vols. Trans. O. Wyon. New York: Harper & Row. First German edition, 1911.

Vawter, Bruce
1960   "Apocalyptic: Its Relation to Prophecy." *CBQ* 22: 33–46.

Vielhauer, Philipp
1964   "Apocalyptic." Pp. 581–600 in *New Testament Apocrypha*. Ed. W. Schneemelcher. Eng. trans. edited by R. McL. Wilson. Philadelphia: Westminster. Vol. 2.

Weber, Max
1946   "Religious Rejections of the World and Their Directions." From *Max Weber: Essays in Sociology*. Ed. H. H. Gerth and C. W. Mills. New York: Oxford University Press.
1963   *The Sociology of Religion*. Trans. E. Fischoff. Boston: Beacon. First German edition, 1922.

Westermann, Claus
1967   *Basic Forms of Prophetic Speech*. Trans. Hugh Clayton White. Philadelphia: Westminster.

Worsley, Peter
1968   *The Trumpet Shall Sound*. London: Macgibbon and Kee.

15

The Hebrew Bible
and Modern Culture

Walter Harrelson

I. THE POSTWAR YEARS

The Holocaust

When volumes of the *Altes Testament Deutsch* began to appear after the Second World War had ended—volumes such as the Twelve Prophets commentary by Artur Weiser—scholars in North America were able to see the extent to which the Holocaust and the events preceding and accompanying it had cut deeply into the soul of German colleagues. The period prior to and during the war had been used to good effect by some German scholars. Literary-critical, form-critical, and traditio-historical studies of great import had been completed during those years, and some major theological works were being brought to completion. But much of the work done by Christian scholars of the period salvaged the Hebrew Bible for the Christian community either by a new form of typology or by showing its value over against the New Testament and Christianity. Some of the work simply accepted the Nazi line.

Prophetic judgments upon a faithless people of God struck home to many survivors of the war years, often living in poverty themselves and seeing church and scholarly life slowly emerge from the ruins. In North America, these testimonies from German colleagues had much weight, for many on this side of the Atlantic recognized the extent to which they also had been silent or acquiescent as the news had come concerning the fate of the Jewish people in Europe. Modern culture impinged upon the study of the Hebrew Bible for the decade from 1945 to 1955 in considerable measure on the basis of the war's aftermath: the fate of the Jewish people and the establishment of the state of Israel; East-West relations and a reassessment of the Church's attitude toward the Soviet Union in particular and toward socialism in general; the development of a "hard-line" international policy on the part of the United States, with mixed reactions on the part of the churches and synagogues.

Other factors also were coming into prominence. Chief among them was the attitude of the government and the society to the continuation of racial discrimination and segregation. Blacks in the United States were no longer willing to tolerate segregation in large sections of the country, nor were they willing to return from wartime pursuits to take up positions either menial or less well compensated than similar or identical jobs held by whites. The impetus toward ecumenism was very considerable and would not long be ignored within the church bureaucracies. The question of an English-language Bible that was in line with the heritage of the Authorized Version but was both accurate and in contemporary English was recognized to be an important, if not urgent, matter. The appearance of the entire RSV Old and New Testaments by 1952 and the subsequent sale of millions of copies within weeks indicated the extraordinary interest in the Bible on the part of the populace at large. The public was captivated by the news of the manuscript discoveries at Qumran and at Nag Hammadi.

The Bible and Political Conservatism

Another issue of great importance actually had considerable overlap with the publication of the Revised Standard Version. What came to be called "McCarthyism" appeared on the scene. Anticommunism became a way of life for Senator Joseph R. McCarthy of Wisconsin and for many who rallied behind him. The churches, the Bible's translation committee, professors and prominent clergy, as well as actors, artists, columnists, and many writers, were singled out for harassment by McCarthy and many other committees and movements bent upon stamping out "un-Americanism." The cry that there were "communists in the State Department" got many headlines, until finally McCarthy was repudiated by the Senate's own investigation of him, but the harm done to many thousands of artists, writers, actors, directors, producers, clergy, and professors is beyond calculation.

The remarkable fact was the almost unselfconscious way in which seminarians and graduate students of theology and Bible found it possible to turn to the Hebrew Bible and to the New Testament for immediate and direct help. They recognized fully that the biblical message had to be approached with critical faculties intact and that the world of the Bible was in many ways quite different from their own world. The approach of Karl Barth was the one most widely accepted and used, but it was rather the realistic way in which Reinhold Niebuhr related contemporary issues of war and peace, of social and racial justice, to the heritage of biblical faith that enabled this widespread drawing upon the biblical message to take place.

Reinhold Niebuhr was extraordinarily sensitive to both the possibilities and the dangers of relying upon the biblical message in determining an appropriate Jewish or Christian critique of culture. H. Richard

Niebuhr's *Christ and Culture* was to provide a marvelous typology, but his brother's essays, sermons, letters to the editor of the *New York Times*, and the soirees in his apartment provided for generations of students the best guide for relating biblical religion and contemporary political and cultural issues. His wife Ursula, a biblical theologian of great discernment, contributed much to these evenings in the Niebuhr apartment.

A fund-raising campaign launched by Auburn Seminary quoted from John Foster Dulles under the rubric of "What Great Christian Thinkers Are Saying in Our Time," or something of the sort. Niebuhr came to the rescue of students who attacked this use of Dulles in a way held by the students to be blasphemous. Niebuhr had inspired the protest, but he also chided the protesters for their ideological position and their ad hominem response. Niebuhr also chided but came to the aid of some of the same students when they had sought to organize the employees at Union—most of them West Indian blacks and quite poorly paid—for the same lack of realism in providing concrete help. The paternalism of the seminary, he pointed out, was probably actually more in the interest of the staff than would be their being swallowed up into a catchall union of the United Mine Workers.

It was this "biblical realism" that went so far to transform, for a time, the character of North American Christianity, inviting clergy and laity alike to find the points of connection between the "strange world of the Bible" (Barth) and the equally strange world of twentieth-century Western society. Instead of focusing on the class war and on the exploitation of the poor, many of the sermons pointed to the ironies of our contemporary life, in which what the prophet Amos said about religious revivals that ignored the social realities seemed written for our time, or in which the biblical picture of sin as having its seat both in the human heart and in the fabric of social existence was as vividly accurate a picture of a life in sin as one could find anywhere. It was the time of the rehabilitation of biblical religion. Paul Tillich was considered by a number of the newer biblical theologians, both professional biblical scholars and systematic theologians, as too speculative, though he considered himself also to be an expositor of biblical religion.

Issues of war and peace were being weighed once more. As the massive writings of Karl Barth began to be translated into English and more widely studied, fresh emphases on biblical pacifism began to appear. Barth's exegesis of the commandment not to kill and his other studies of violence, especially in the volumes devoted to ethics, caused many who had accepted Reinhold Niebuhr's views on the impossibility any longer of holding to Christian pacifism to think anew about pacifism. More important, after the McCarthy era, there was a renewed interest in Christian socialism, not of a doctrinaire sort, but as a closer approximation of what biblical social ethics apparently entailed. The Fellowship of

Socialist Christians changed its name to the Frontier Fellowship, but
some of its members continued, especially through the publication *Christianity and Crisis*, to keep open the debate on Christian pacifism and on
the relations of East and West.

Desegregation and the Bible

The emergence of the black church in the United States into
national prominence greatly affected the reading of the Hebrew Bible in
much of North American society. The identification of the eleven o'clock
hour on Sundays as the "most segregated hour in America" and the
unbearable hypocrisy of a church that segregated on the basis of race
prompted many white clergy and theologians and, above all, theological
students to join in the effort to bring the segregation of public institutions to an end. Within the black church, where the power of this movement lay, critical biblical scholarship was little in evidence, even though
many of the black clergy who were leaders in the civil rights movement
of the late 1950s and the 1960s were themselves highly educated men
and women. What was present, without critical scholarly support, was an
understanding of the pervasiveness of the biblical message of divine
concern for poor and oppressed people. The retelling of the biblical story
of God's deliverance of oppressed people from bondage furthered an
already well-developed sense of human dignity and worth that would no
longer acquiesce in mistreatment. Marxist and other forms of critical
evaluation of colonialism, economic exploitation, and social inequality
made common cause with a Jewish and Christian understanding of the
worth and dignity of human beings as created in the divine image and
destined for a wholesome social existence on earth.

Some works on the Bible and segregation took up this theme directly,
making it evident that the biblical materials not only corresponded well
with the aims and hungers of exploited peoples and individuals but, in
central ways, affirmed these aims. Again, the approach of certain of the
neo-orthodox biblical theologians turned out to be of very great help. These
writings gave a sense of realism to the efforts of individuals, groups, and
nations to seek ways of reform while always continuing, in greater or lesser
degree, to serve their own social, economic, and political ends. These
writings—by the Niebuhr brothers, Paul Tillich, Karl Barth, Emil
Brunner, Will Herberg, and Abraham Heschel, to name a few—offered
the sort of summaries of biblical themes, critically reviewed, that enabled
white and black students of the Bible to join forces in the struggle against
segregation, recognizing that the institution of segregation had to be
destroyed but that in the process other forms of oppression of one group by
another would almost certainly appear. Political realism, the ability to
keep struggling to eliminate segregation while fully aware that Jeremiah

was right in describing the human heart as "deceitful above all things, and desperately corrupt" (Jer 17:9) and that therefore one had to be prepared for the next stage in the struggle for human dignity, was of immense importance for the battle against segregation and the exploitation of blacks by whites. It enabled religious leaders to affirm the importance of legislation and executive and judicial action, while granting that morality cannot adequately be legislated.

Sociological and Literary Studies

This political realism was being explored in monographs and special studies of the prophets of Israel, of the Torah, of the historical writings, of the cult and wisdom. Here we have perhaps the most important source of the influence of the Hebrew Bible upon modern culture: the exegetical explorations of the political, economic, social, and cultural realities of the world of ancient Israel. Many of the aspects of biblical scholarship contributed to this purpose. Form criticism required that the forms of the literature be set in their social and cultural contexts, to the extent possible. Studies of ancient Israelite law did that and in the process enabled students to see the extent to which the fundamental commitment to a God who abhorred political and social oppression was implicit in the forms of categorical law that had been preserved. Comparative work on ancient Near Eastern treaties in relation to the covenant between God and people again showed a setting for the covenant in both the worship of the people and in their adaptation of political and economic structures of the ancient world to serve the ends of a people bound inescapably to a sovereign God. Studies of the place of the king in the cult of ancient Israel make it evident both that the king had enormous power as the divine representative on earth and that this earthly king was bound to live within the limits of a relationship between God and people, the chief model for which was not kingship but rather family and tribal life—the relation of parent to child, of clan to clan, of tribe to tribe. Studies of the relations of prophets to the ancient Near Eastern cultic life made it clear that Israel's prophets had a distinctive concern with the life and fate of all the people and greater boldness in addressing the political leaders in God's name than was usually in evidence in Mesopotamia, Canaan, or Egypt.

It was similar with the newer approaches to the literature of the Hebrew Bible. The power of the story to break open the surface dimensions of life and provide first disorientation and then reorientation for individual, group, and community enabled the sort of social protest that was brought by desegregation efforts to find analogies in ancient Israel for what happened in the black pastor's retelling of the biblical story. Structural analyses of the literature sought such depth-dimensions in the story and sought also to let the story disclose its own way of positioning the dramatis personae of the story. Rhetorical studies were devoted to discerning the balance and imbalances within a story, how the story developed its thought, how it framed particular unities in the midst of larger entities. These approaches that laid great weight on the aesthetic dimensions of biblical poetry and narrative also made common cause with the efforts to place the biblical literature more fully in the service of proclamation, social and political critique, and the rallying of a community for action against injustice and oppression.

The Bible and Women

The movement for women's rights also influenced the reading and interpretation of the Hebrew Bible. The influence went in two opposite directions. There were some who from the start saw much in the Hebrew Bible that was positive in its treatment of women and its exposé of the mistreatment of women in biblical times. For these interpreters, especially Phyllis Trible of Andover Newton Theological School and now on the faculty of Union Theological Seminary in New York and Letty Russell of the East Harlem Protestant Parish and now on the faculty of the Yale University Divinity School, the biblical heritage had many breakthroughs in understanding the equality of women and men under God, which had been overlaid by the male-dominated tradition of interpretation from biblical times to the present. Searching out these treasures was a fascinating new stage of biblical exegetical work that is still under way with the help of male interpreters as well as female scholars.

Others, however, thought that the biblical materials were hopelessly deficient in their portrayals of the place and value of women; the choices seemed to be either to abandon biblical religion entirely for some new form of Judaism or Christianity not wedded to these no longer usable or bearable texts, or to abandon Judaism and Christianity for some alternative position in the world, religious or nonreligious. The debate over which alternative should be followed is far from over, but its continuation has been one of the enlivening elements in the discussion of the relation of the Hebrew Bible to modern culture.

In Reform Judaism, and to a lesser extent in other Jewish groupings in North America, the material in the Hebrew Bible concerning women and the oral tradition embodied in Mishnah and Gemara were approached from the same two angles just mentioned. Some felt that it is better not to seek—in the male-dominated Tanak or rabbinical texts— themes or perspectives that give a just and fair interpretation of the place of women in society. But there were those who chose the other course and discovered in the earlier and the later texts a much more positive view of women and their place in the world than had been supposed. This work too has been joined by numbers of scholars, men as well as women, who find in the Jewish texts of the period between the close of the Hebrew Bible and the period of the Mishnah much that is of significance for the place of women in ancient Jewish society and in Jewish religion and theology.

War and Peace

Issues of war and peace and of economic exploitation continue to be as vital for the relating of the Hebrew Bible to modern culture as they have been in earlier decades, although the numbers involved in addressing these matters have considerably shifted. The new engagement with issues of the exploitation of the resources of earth—the skies and waters and forests and fauna and air—is deeply rooted in a fresh understanding of the place of the natural world in the religion of the people of Israel and the place of the creation. Furthermore, the concern for the study of chunks of literature in nondiachronic ways also has led to an increased readiness to appreciate portions of the biblical materials that long had been neglected.

II. THE IRONIES
OF THE BIBLE'S INFLUENCES

The irony of the relation of biblical scholarship to contemporary cultural developments that has been sketched above is evident. The society's own changing self-understanding reflects itself in what is emphasized in biblical studies. Scholars work today on Jewish apocalyptic materials because they are much less convinced than they once were that the prophetic effort to offer a reasoned and cogent restatement of the divine revelation suffices to present the actual biblical heritage of our forebears, or perhaps what the present generation most needs from that heritage. It is difficult indeed to trace progress in history from the earlier to the later materials, and the result is that interpreters are much more content to trace not developments that evolve to higher understandings from lower but rather patterns of self-understanding that emerge, are transformed, subside, and are reshaped in new ways under ever-changing circumstances. Modern believers find their own patterns of cult and worship often thin, if not threadbare, and look with longing to those of ancient and different times. Those who are made nauseous with the corruptions of contemporary life are much more ready than before to suppose that the moral commitments of the ancient Hebrews or their aesthetic approaches to reality or their social arrangements and economic practices deserve commendation if not outright imitation. Thus, there seems to be a thorough cultural relativity in the "scientific" study of the Hebrew Bible and its ancient literature: biblical interpreters look for what they need, exploit it to the full, and leave the rest aside.

The irony is deeper, however. There seems to be no denying that the same biblical material that has helped to demonstrate the demand for public justice to the poor and the oppressed has been taken to support those with power in their continuing exploitation of the powerless. The same texts that have spoken of humankind, male and female, as an entity before God, charged to live together with one another in harmony, each contributing to the fulfillment of the life of the other, have been used (with other selected texts) to show how the male dominates the female, at God's direction, and to show how the hierarchy of one class or caste or race over another has warrants in biblical texts and should therefore continue to be supported and affirmed. The same Bible that demands a society free for its members to interpret the heritage for themselves, individually and collectively, not tied to the views of some dominant priestly class, has become an instrument for enforcing conformity of thought. The same biblical heritage that narrates that God sees the plight of the poor and oppressed folk and comes to their aid is used to support systems of economic life that seem designed to assure that the wealthy get wealthier yet, resisting all initiatives that might provide some redistribution of the goods of earth.

Indeed, if we look back over the past thirty-five years of Western biblical scholarship and examine the application of its results, we have no difficulty in seeing that every breakthrough toward human liberation in Western society has been both *affirmed* and *denounced* on the basis of appeals to biblical religion, biblical thought, and biblical practice. Is it not prudent, therefore, to follow the counsel of our forebears in the Society of Biblical Literature and refuse to raise questions about the import of the Hebrew Bible for modern cultural developments?

III. CENTRAL BIBLICAL THEMES

The new situation may make it impossible for us to do so. The resurgence of the radical religious right into contemporary political life in North America is probably not just a passing phenomenon. It would seem that the time has come when biblical scholars will need to help their colleagues in attempting to specify what seem to be the main lines of an anthropology and a sociology present in the Hebrew Bible (and in other great religious traditions as well, such as the New Testament, the Talmud, the Qur'an). Such statements of the "main lines" will of course have to be rather general in order that they not be too subjective. They also will have to be capable of statement into language useful for theology as well as for general discourse outside the structures of theology, if that is possible.

Can one discern in the religion of ancient Israel certain fundamental notions bearing on human values, on human rights and obligations, that might be accepted as central by most interpreters of the Hebrew scriptures? Any such list will be tentative, of course, and cannot expect to find universal acceptance. But despite the fact that scholars may be in continuing disagreement about details, the situation may not be hopeless. Persons are not equally right and equally wrong in claiming that their particular political, cultural, and ethical commitments are faithful renderings of the thought of the Hebrew Bible.

The Themes Stated

The Hebrew Bible's outlook on the general cultural realities of ancient Israel and its neighbors seems to include the following elements, despite all the differences in detail that could be indicated:

(1) Israel begins as a community of kinship groups committed to a way of life in the world that does not depend upon allegiance to the then existing social and political hierarchies. Whether or not the Israelites arose as an oppressed people committed to equality and to the avoidance of kingship or other oppressive modes of government, it seems evident that they recognized themselves to be a people committed to their Lord in a radical way and to no other lords at all.

(2) Central to Israel's self-understanding is their Lord's special concern for the oppressed and suffering of earth and the commitment to intervene in the historical processes of life to ease the suffering of the oppressed and lead them to liberation.

(3) The community is bound to God in covenant and charged to hold fast to the covenant law. Summaries of the law, such as the Ten Commandments, specify God's exclusive claim upon the people of the covenant and the kinds of conduct that are ruled out in principle.

(4) At the same time, the suspicion is widely expressed that God's people Israel will fail, and perhaps fail miserably, in embodying and keeping vividly alive this way of life to which they are committed. The prophetic element in Israelite religion focuses upon this likely failure, warning against mistreatment of the poor and the weak, against presumption in claiming God's authority and stamp of approval, and against any tendency to separate religious life from public life. Prophets do not simply castigate the people for their failures, however; they plead with them not to continue on the path that leads to ruin.

(5) Prophets also insist that God's purposes are on the way to realization in the world, even though the realization may (and probably will) cost the people of God dearly—because of their failures. Prophetic eschatology contains both a confirmation of the coming judgment of God upon the faithless and an insistence that *God* will not fail. The variety of ways of portraying the consummation of God's work on earth is great,

but prophetic eschatology is never bolder than in its insistence that public justice, peace, and wholeness of life are to come to God's earth in a "day" close at hand.

(6) This "day" never dawns, but its import for every time and generation was probably immense. Indeed, it is difficult to understand the dynamism of biblical ethics, in Jewish, Christian, or Muslim traditions, apart from the continuing impact of this prophetic eschatological hope. One assumes that the import of this hope and confidence in God's coming triumph lies especially in the way in which it combines both judgment and promise, never leaving room for complacency in current achievements and never permitting utter despair regarding the course of the world's history.

(7) Israelite religion also offers support for communities, families, and individuals in its insistence on the nearness of the divine Presence. This nearness was by no means experienced always as a comforting reality; frequently it was threatening (Psalm 139) or even oppressive (Job 7). The struggles of the people to make their way in God's world were struggles marked by this accompanying Presence. The Presence frequently did not prove helpful or responsive to prayers of petition. Yet rarely was there any radical sense of the absence of this holy Presence. Absence of meaning, of any indication of personal readiness to help, of any continuing bond of affection or commitment—yes, these could all be experienced as absent, but not the Presence itself.

(8) This Presence was not capable of being caught up into the religious story, or its cultic practices, confessions, creeds. The very name of God was a name that both hid and revealed the divine being and purposes for the world. The name YHWH was not to be used to bend persons to one's own way or will. Images were not to be fashioned of this elusive One. Nothing in all the creation could quite serve to focus the being or power of God. Biblical religion is thus aniconic at its heart.

The Cultural Impact of the Hebrew Bible

On the basis of these summary statements we may now attempt to sketch the impact of the Hebrew Bible upon modern culture in a way that—though it remains debatable—may be claimed to be defensible. If the summary is approximately right, then the sketch of the continuing impact of biblical religion upon culture may be not arbitrary but—at the least—suggestive and useful. We shall offer only a sketch, seeking to register only the central points that seem most likely to find assent among students of the Bible and of Jewish and Christian theology and ethics.

The Foundation of Modern Culture

Biblical religion unmistakably grounds the totality of the creation in God and in the divine intentions and purposes for the creation. The hypothesis of some underlying purpose to historical and natural existence can certainly be maintained in a pluralistic and secular world, at least in the sense of a Pascal-like wager. It seems evident that religious communities can and should talk about this grounding of purpose in God in two ways: within the circle of faith the traditional affirmations belong, though of course they require explanation, critique, and challenge in the light of contemporary thought; and in the public arena one can best indicate that this presumed divine purpose was and is weighty for the religious community but that its import for the public world is found in its actual *content*.

The Purpose of Modern Culture

This content, as found in the Hebrew Bible and summarized above, has to do with the life of human beings in community. It should be noted that, while the Hebrew Bible begins with the story of the creation of heaven and earth, a creation declared to be good—indeed, very good—the purpose of life on the earth, or of the earth, is not presented as a "return" to that primordial time. The images of fulfillment are social and political for the most part. Natural gifts of earth will abound, as "the plowman overtakes the reaper," to use an image of the book of Amos (9:13), but these will be for the sake of living beings—the animals and humankind. The dominant images are of a new exodus and a new entrance into the land of the promise (Hosea, Jeremiah, Ezekiel, and Second Isaiah in particular), a new and glorious city that is the focal point of blessing for all the nations of earth (Isaiah, Micah, Second Isaiah), or a new leader of the people, whose reign means peace with righteousness the world over (Isaiah, Micah, Zechariah).

The Hebrew Bible's vision of the purpose toward which the nations move is perhaps its most powerful influence upon contemporary culture. These visions hold all cultural realities under judgment, for they indicate what it would be like for the social existence of humankind to be what people sense that it should be. Such visions also sustain hope in the community, for they are presented not as utopian notions but as images portraying a process under way that has fixed contours already finding realization, however imperfectly. These visions beckon; they evoke commitment and a dynamism in the direction of their realization. They serve as the lure for moral action in the society.

It is worth noting that these images of a purpose for human social existence that is finding realization can be talked about without direct reference to the presence of Israel's deity or of any God. They are something less than a political philosophy of the Marxist sort, which specified a historical necessity in the movement toward this certain goal. The biblical imagery is presented by prophets confident of the reality of this coming day of consummation, but they are equally confident that God may defer the day for reasons that humanity may or may not comprehend. No one but God alone knows the day of consummation.

The images of a purpose-laden history of humanity are also of a quite different character from that of the claims made by Enlightenment thought or the deism of the American or the French Revolution. There is nothing self-evident about this divine purpose for humankind. The appeal is not to human reason but to the mystery of the divine concern and care for the whole of creation and in particular for the people of God through whom the blessing is to reach to earth's ends.

The Trials of Social Existence

The Hebrew Bible was produced by a people more often than not undergoing severe testing, as it was explained to them by their leaders, for failing God and their fellow Israelites. Rarely is their situation one in which they can praise God for the richness and meaningfulness of their life. There are much praising and giving thanks, but these are frequently tinged with the complaint or the petition. Petition and lament far outnumber praise and thanksgiving in the Hebrew Psalter.

The relation of people and God is a relationship in the midst of Israel's struggles for life, security, fulfillment of the divine promise. It is a relationship in which Israel fails and, in quite practical terms, God also fails. What the relation of people and God is designed to produce—peace with righteousness, economic and social health, a sense of confidence in the open future—is elusive, continuingly failing of realization, and never at hand. In this sense, the Babylonian exile is just the culmination of a long and frustrating history of the people in association with God, a history marked by rich promise, but promise always deferred and delayed. It is not surprising that the return from exile continues the sense of a life unfulfilled for the people of God.

Not enough attention has been given in theological treatises to the positive import of these portrayals of incompleteness, failure, and frustrated hopes. A religious community that portrays its own history as almost unmitigated disappointment and failure, sharing the blame for the failure between a good, just, loving God on the one hand and a people who do not keep covenant with God on the other hand, is a strange religious community. The severity of the questionings of this good, just, and loving God and the blunt insistences now and again that Israel is not in fact faithless to the covenant only deepen the vigor and power of this religious community's outlook.

The import of this understanding for contemporary culture is considerable. This element in the biblical heritage is a reminder that biblical religion is the farthest thing from a success story. The relation of people and God is one of struggle for life and blessing, where the presence of God with the people is unmistakable but often without material benefit. God does not leave the people alone in their failings but keeps challenging, demanding, and sometimes comforting and offering reassurance. The sense of loss, frustration, and anger over promises too long deferred of realization is deep in this literature, but the sense of a divine Presence that at the least does not leave Israel utterly alone in a meaningless and heartless world is a powerful element, holding despair at a distance.

In all likelihood this sense of a Presence that seems rarely to change the situation of misery or of oppression but which is nonetheless an undeniably holy Presence is probably one of the reasons why the Hebrew scriptures have been of such value in the lives of those living with little or no hope—prisoners in the Nazi camps awaiting death and black slaves being systematically dehumanized by the vicious institution of slavery, for example. It is also the kind of sustenance that comes to those who struggle against militarism or racism or sexist practices, who struggle for an easing of the plight of prisoners, who live out their lives seeking to mitigate one or more of the pervasive forms of unrelenting injustice in our world. They can identify with this heritage of a divine Presence that sustains even when it does not bring about radical change, a Presence that is quite simply there, unmistakably there.

The Value of Commandment

The Hebrew Bible also offers one special treasure for contemporary culture that is very difficult to accept because it is so difficult for contemporary thinkers to believe in its soundness. It is the heritage of moral guidance, especially in the form of the prohibition that flatly specifies that certain courses of human behavior are not acceptable, not to be engaged in. Such prohibitions, as for example in the Ten Commandments, set limits to human freedom in light of what are understood to be the divine demands and the kinds of human action that make for life in community. Put negatively, they require communal reflection on *how* the prohibition can be made effectual and on what the positive import of the negation actually is. Such communal reflection becomes part of the ethos, the tradition of a people, changing over time, while the stark prohibition stands there, much as the Bill of Rights of the U.S. Constitution (negatively put) requires a continuing communal preoccupation with interpreting what the specifications actually mean.

Few elements of the heritage of the Hebrew Bible could be said to be of greater positive guidance for the community today in its struggle to see how this biblical heritage continues to offer moral guidance. All of the major issues confronting our contemporary society find illumination in relation to these ancient biblical specifications of what God demands, what God will not under any circumstances allow.

The Basic Modesty of the Hebrew Bible's Theological Claims

The last item in our sketch is of very great importance for contemporary application of the biblical message. Not too much is claimed for biblical religion by our literature. The community of ancient Israel recognized that it did not know all that it would like to know about God, about the way of Israel in the world, about the day of consummation, or about the inner workings of the creation. This essential modesty becomes outright agnosticism on particular points: the inner meaning of the name YHWH (Exod 3:14); where wisdom is to be found (Job 28); whether the meaning of life can be found at all (Ecclesiastes).

The psalmists make it evident that the worship of God carries no guarantees of blessing, though blessing was certainly realized more often than not in the cult, we may suppose. The prophets were able to trace the divine action in the people's history, but God always remained free over decisions taken or planned, even when the decisions might be already in the process of being realized. The holy city, Zion, with its temple was a special meeting place for God, but the meeting between God and people was not dependent upon Zion's continuing existence.

The sacred history revealed the divine will, but it also hid God's purposes. God's strange work, God's alien acts, were no less God's work because of their strangeness. Knowledge of God was always imperfect, incomplete. The presence of God was not fully plumbed with regard to its purpose or even with regard to its character (see Psalm 139).

It is hard, therefore, for biblical religion to claim too much, to become a comfortable interpretive scheme or a comfortable cultic practice. Too little is known; so much must be searched out, questioned, pondered, resolved in community debate. For this reason, we can conclude our all too subjective and partial essay on the Hebrew Bible and modern culture by saying that the Bible offers a modest contribution to the critical reassessment of contemporary cultural existence in the light of the biblical heritage. It is modest because there is no approved cultural form that receives the stamp of approval of biblical thought or of biblical eschatology.

In one respect, however, the claim of the biblical heritage is entirely otherwise than modest. Its vision is of a creation made just and whole, nothing less than a new heaven and a new earth. In the face of that glorious vision, all cultural achievements are modest indeed.

BIBLIOGRAPHY

Barr, James
1973   *The Bible in the Modern World*. New York: Harper &
                     Row.

Barth, Karl
1944   *The Church and War*. New York: Macmillan.

Berger, Peter L.
1969   *A Rumor of Angels*. Garden City, NY: Doubleday.

Brueggemann, Walter
1972   *In Man We Trust*. Richmond: John Knox.
1977   *The Land*. Philadelphia: Fortress.

Burkhardt, Frederick, ed.
1960   *Five Essays on the Bible*. New York: American Council
                     of Learned Societies.

Cone, James A.
1969   *Black Theology and Black Power*. New York: Seabury.

Conway, James F.
1973   *Marx and Jesus: Liberation Theology in Latin America*.
                     New York: Carlton.

Craato, J. Severino
1981   *Exodus: A Hermeneutics of Freedom*. Maryknoll, NY:
                     Orbis Books.

Drinan, Robert F.
1970   *Vietnam and Armageddon: Peace, War, and the Chris-
                     tian Conscience*. New York: Sheed and Ward.

Gottwald, Norman K.
1979   *The Tribes of Yahweh*. Maryknoll, NY: Orbis Books.

Harrelson, Walter
1980   *The Ten Commandments and Human Rights*. Philadel-
                     phia: Fortress.

Haseldon, Kyle
1959   *The Racial Problem in Christian Perspective*. New
                     York: Harper & Row.

Herberg, Will
1960   *Protestant, Catholic, Jew: An Essay in American Reli-
                     gious Sociology*. Rev. ed. Garden City, NY: Doubleday.

Heschel, Abraham
1962   *The Prophets*. New York: Harper & Row.

Lincoln, C. Eric., ed.
1974   *The Black Experience in Religion*. Garden City, NY:
                     Doubleday.

Lucas, George R., Jr., and Thomas W. Ogletree, eds.
1976   *Lifeboat Ethics: The Moral Dilemmas of World Hunger.* New York: Harper & Row.

Miranda, José P.
1974   *Marx and the Bible: A Critique of the Philosophy of Oppression.* Maryknoll, NY: Orbis Books.

Neher, André
1981   *The Exile of the Word: From the Silence of the Bible to the Silence of Auschwitz.* Philadelphia: Jewish Publication Society of America.

Niebuhr, H. Richard
1951   *Christ and Culture.* New York: Harper.

Niebuhr, Reinhold
1939   *The Nature and Destiny of Man.* New York: Charles Scribner's Sons.

Paris, Peter J.
1978   *Black Leaders in Conflict.* New York: Pilgrim.

Ricoeur, Paul
1967   *The Symbolism of Evil.* Trans. Emerson Buchanan. Boston: Beacon.

Ruether, Rosemary R.
1974   *Religion and Sexism: Images of Women in the Jewish and Christian Traditions.* New York: Simon & Schuster.

Russell, Letty M.
1974   *Human Liberation in a Feminist Perspective.* Philadelphia: Westminster.

Sandeen, Ernest R., ed.
1982   *The Bible and Social Reform.* Society of Biblical Literature Centennial Publications: The Bible in American Culture, 6. Philadelphia: Fortress; Chico, CA: Scholars Press.

Shannon, Thomas, ed.
1980   *War or Peace: The Search for New Answers.* Maryknoll, NY: Orbis Books.

Sleeper, C. Freeman
1968   *Black Power and Christian Responsibility: Some Biblical Foundations for Social Ethics.* Nashville: Abingdon.

Topel, L. John
1979   *The Way to Peace: Liberation Through the Bible.* Maryknoll, NY: Orbis Books.

Trible, Phyllis
1978   *God and the Rhetoric of Sexuality.* Philadelphia: Fortress.

Weiser, Artur
   1949   *Die Propheten: Hosea, Joel, Amos, Obadja, Jona,*
                        Micha. ATD 24. Göttingen: Vandenhoeck & Ruprecht.

Wright, G. Ernest, ed.
   1954   *The Biblical Doctrine of Man in Society.* London: SCM.

Yoder, John Harold
   1964   *The Christian Witness to the State.* Newton, KS: Faith
                        and Life Press.

Zimmerli, Walther
   1968   *Der Mensch und seine Hoffnung im Alten Testament.*
                        Göttingen: Vandenhoeck & Ruprecht.

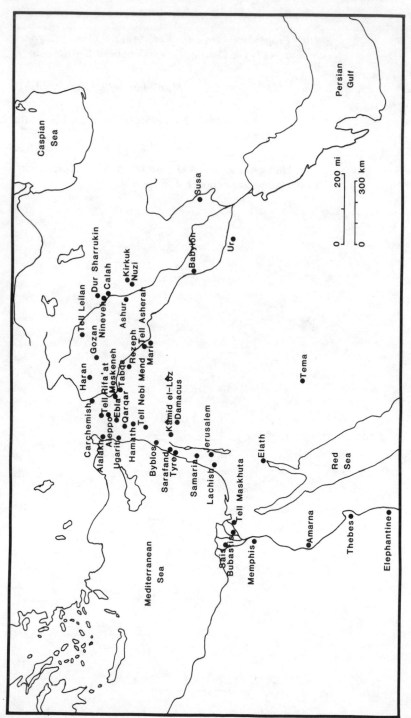

The Fertile Crescent

Persian Gulf

Caspian Sea

Susa

200 mi
300 km

Dur Sharrukin
Tell Leilan
Gozan
Nineveh
Calah
Kirkuk
Nuzi
Ashur
Babylon
Ur
Reseph
Tell Asherah
Mari
Haran
Carchemish
Tell Rifa'at
Meskeneh
Aleppo
Ebla
Qarqar
Tabqa
Tema
Alalah
Ugarit
Hamath
Tell Nebi Mend
Kamid el-Loz
Damacus
Byblos
Sarafand
Tyre
Jerusalem
Samaria
Lachish
Elath
Tell Maskhuta
Sais
Bubastis
Memphis
Amarna
Red Sea
Thebes
Elephantine

Mediterranean Sea

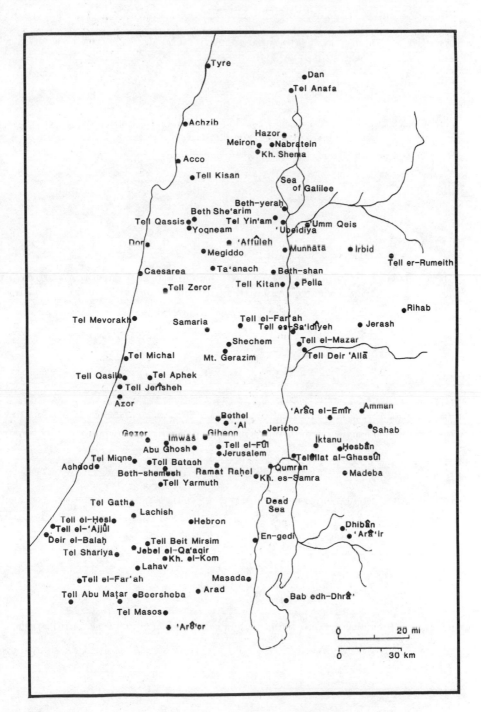

Archaeological Sites in Palestine-Transjordan

INDEX OF MODERN AUTHORS

Aarne, Antti, 457-58
Ackroyd, Peter R., 298-99, 301-5, 309-11, 449, 458
Adams, Robert, 371, 398
Al-A'dami, Khalid Ahmad, 83, 97
Aharoni, Yohanan, 3, 5, 23, 35, 37, 41-42, 63, 67, 227-28
Ahlström, Gösta, 218, 228
Aistleitner, Joseph, 78, 97
Albertz, R., 216-17, 228, 425, 432-33
Albrektson, Bertil, 88, 97, 212n, 228, 240, 258, 412, 420, 433
Albright, William Foxwell, 4-6, 8-9, 11, 15, 19, 20-23, 31, 33-34, 36, 40-41, 53-56, 58-61, 65, 67-68, 75-80, 87, 92, 97, 184, 191, 202, 210, 213, 226-229, 302, 370, 376, 391, 411, 413, 418, 422, 424, 432, 434
Allen, Leslie C., 298, 312
Alonso-Schökel, Luis, 135, 158, 169, 191, 372, 387, 388, 391, 412, 415-17, 422, 425, 434
Alster, Bendt, 90, 94, 97, 376, 378, 391
Alt, Albrecht, 10, 13-14, 19-24, 93, 97, 207, 210, 222, 268-269, 327, 330
Amiran, Ruth, 37, 41-42, 63, 68
Andersen, Francis I., 167, 169, 191
Anderson, Bernhard W., 9, 24, 135, 158, 356, 432, 434, 446-47, 450, 458
Anderson, George W., 13, 24
Archi, Alfonso, 86n, 97
Arens, Anton, 434
Asensio, Félix, 430, 434
Assmann, Jan, 90, 98
Audet, Jean-Paul, 420, 434
Auld, A. Graeme, 301, 312
Austin, J. L., 178
Avigad, Nahman, 32, 37, 41, 227, 229
Avi-Yonah, Michael, 41, 63, 67

Bach, Robert, 327, 329-30, 340, 351, 356
Bahnassi, A., 46
Baltzer, Klaus, 222, 229, 285, 288, 341, 356
Baly, Denis, 63, 68
Bar-Adon, P., 37
Bardtke, Hans, 383, 391, 410, 434, 445, 447-48, 458

Barghouti, Assam, 44, 45
Barr, James, 57, 68, 78-79, 98, 201, 206, 229, 240, 253-54, 258, 270, 288, 387, 391, 467, 478, 483, 503
Barré, M. L., 92, 98
Barrick, W. Boyd, 228-29
Barth, Hermann, 124, 129, 131, 133, 137, 139, 140, 146-47, 150-55, 158
Barth, Karl, 202, 204, 470, 490-92, 503
Barthes, Roland, 175, 178
Barton, John, 258
Barucq, André, 90, 98, 446-47, 449-50, 458
Bar-Yosef, O., 42
Bauer, Theodor, 81, 98
Baumann, Eberhard, 414, 434
Baumgärtel, Friedrich, 124, 129, 131, 136, 158, 207n, 229
Baumgartner, Walter I., 78, 109, 212
Beattie, D. R. G., 451-53, 458
Beauchamp, Paul, 173, 191
Beck, Pirhiya, 42
Becker, Joachim, 429, 434
Beegle, Dewey M., 253, 258
Beek, G. van, 31, 41, 68
Begrich, Joachim, 16, 24, 328, 356, 417
Ben-Amos, Dan, 458
Bennett, Crystal-M., 34, 37, 44
Ben-Tor, A., 43
Bentzen, Aage, 278, 288, 420, 429-30, 434, 451, 458, 477, 480-81, 483
Benveniste, E., 178
Berg, Sandra Beth, 447, 448, 450, 454, 458
Berger, Peter L., 187, 191, 351-52, 354, 356, 470, 483, 503
Bergerhof, K., 77, 98
Bergler, Siegfried, 412, 423, 434
Bergren, Richard V., 331, 357
Bermant, Chaim, 84, 98
Bernhardt, Karl-Heinz, 219, 229, 430, 434
Berridge, John M., 420, 434
Bertman, Stephen, 454-55, 458
Betz, Hans Dieter, 479-80, 483
Beyerlin, Walter, 95, 98, 226, 229, 269, 288, 301, 312, 330, 333, 357, 420, 427, 429, 434
Bickell, G. W. H., 413
Bickerman, Elias, 446-48, 458
Biggs, Robert D., 45, 68, 86n, 98

Bikai, Patricia, 46
Bimson, John J., 11, 22, 24
Binford, Lewis Roberts, 53n, 68
Binford, Sally R., 53n, 68
Biran, Avraham, 37, 41-42
Birch, Bruce C., 254-55, 258, 302, 312
Birkeland, Harris, 430, 435
Blenkinsopp, Joseph, 287-88, 302, 310, 312, 357
Bloch, Ernst, 387, 392
Boecker, Hans Jochen, 129, 158, 300, 302, 312
Böklen, Ernst, 479, 483
Boling, Robert G., 80, 98, 301, 312, 412, 435
Bonnard, P. E., 376, 392
Bordreuil, Pierro, 77, 98
Borger, Riekele, 88, 92, 98
Boström, Gustav, 376, 392, 415-16, 435
Bottéro, Jean, 87, 92, 99
Botterweck, G. J., 458
Bouni, A., 46
Bousset, Wilhelm, 263
Bowman, Raymond A., 306, 312
Braun, Rainer, 380, 392
Braun, Roddy L., 306, 309-10, 312
Briend, J., 44
Bright, John, 8-9, 18-19, 24, 56, 68, 76, 88, 93, 99, 226, 229, 258, 269, 288, 420, 435
Brinkman, A. J., 88, 99
Brockington, Leonard Herbert, 306, 313
Broshi, M., 37
Brothwell, Don, 52, 68
Brueggemann, Walter, 248, 251, 256, 258, 270, 279, 288, 302, 313, 330, 333, 357, 377, 389, 392, 503
Brunet, Adrien-M., 308, 313
Brunner, Emil, 492
Brunner, Hellmut, 370-71, 392
Bruno, D. Arvid, 459
Bryce, Glendon E., 173, 178, 191, 370, 376, 392
Buber, Martin, 205n, 422, 435
Buccellati, Giorgio, 14, 24, 46, 81, 86, 99, 190, 192, 370, 392
Budde, Karl, 428
Bühlmann, Walter, 377, 392
Bull, Robert J., 36, 41
Bultmann, Rudolf, 203, 249, 259
Burkhardt, Frederick, 503
Burridge, Kenelm, 471, 483
Burrows, Millar, 452-53, 459

Buss, Martin J., 167, 187, 191–92, 357, 430, 435
Butler, T., 307, 313

Cagni, Luigi, 90, 99
Callaway, Joseph A., 11, 24, 34, 36
Calloud, Jean, 174–75, 178, 192
Camp, Claudia V., 373, 392
Campbell, Antony F., 137, 158, 302, 313
Campbell, Edward F., Jr., 87, 99, 451–55, 459
Cancik, Hubert, 88, 99
Caquot, André, 77–78, 99, 310, 313
Cardascia, Guillaume, 92, 99
Cardenal, Ernesto, 410, 433, 435
Carlson, R. A., 302, 304, 313
Carmichael, Calum C., 453–54, 459
Carroll, Robert P., 187, 192, 357
Carter, Theresa H., 45
Casalis, Mathieu, 174–75, 192
Cassuto, Umberto, 78, 99, 205, 229, 278, 288, 411
Cauvin, J., 45
Cazelles, Henri S., 19, 124n, 127, 129, 153, 158, 278, 288, 301, 306, 309, 313, 371–72, 384, 392, 446–48, 459
Charpentier, Etienne, 174, 192
Chehab, Emir Maurice, 47
Childs, Brevard S., 57, 68, 77, 96, 100, 202, 206, 213, 229, 240, 249, 251–52, 254–55, 259, 268–70, 287–88, 298, 301, 304–5, 308, 313, 344, 357
Christensen, Duane L., 340, 357
Christian, Viktor, 416, 435
Clark, W. Malcolm, 148, 159
Clements, Ronald E., 245–46, 253, 259, 289, 297, 300, 302–3, 313, 331, 334–35, 343–44, 349, 357, 389, 392
Clifford, Richard J., 78, 100, 226, 230, 339, 357
Clines, D. J. A., 287, 289
Coats, George W., 148, 158, 372, 392
Cogan, Morton, 224, 230
Cohen, Abraham D., 449, 459
Cohen, Gerson D., 433, 435
Cohen, Mark E., 100
Cohen, Rudolph, 41–42, 48, 50n, 68
Cohn, Norman, 471, 483
Cole, D. P., 41
Collins, John J., 184, 192, 456–57, 459, 469, 478, 480–81, 483
Cone, James A., 503
Conrad, D., 38
Conrad, Joachim, 302, 314, 375, 393
Conroy, C., 304, 314

Conway, James F., 503
Coogan, Michael David, 78, 100
Cook, Albert, 387, 393
Cook, Herbert J., 449, 459
Cooper, Jerrold S., 90, 95, 100
Coote, Robert B., 158, 181, 183, 192
Coppens, Joseph, 89, 100, 430, 435
Couroyer, B., 94, 100
Cox, Dermot, 386, 393
Craato, J. Severino, 503
Craigie, P. C., 284, 289
Craigie, P. E., 78, 100
Crenshaw, James L., 216, 230, 289, 354–55, 357, 369, 372, 374, 377–79, 381, 385, 387–89, 393–94, 430, 435
Crim, Keith, 63
Cross, Frank Moore, 3, 18–19, 25, 78–80, 100–101, 131, 136, 148, 159, 208–10, 213–14, 220, 222, 226, 230, 271, 285, 287, 289, 303, 306–7, 314, 340, 411, 414–15, 425, 432, 435, 474, 477, 484
Crossan, John Dominic, 173, 180, 190, 193
Crüsemann, Frank, 429–30, 436
Culley, Robert C., 135n, 144, 171–72, 174, 178, 181, 183, 193, 272, 274, 289, 414, 436

Dahood, Mitchell J., 78–79, 85, 89, 101, 380, 394, 411–12, 414, 418, 423, 436
Dajani, R., 38, 41
Dalglish, Edward R., 89, 101
Damon, S. Foster, 387, 394
Davies, G. Henton, 226, 230
Delcor, M., 481, 484
Delekat, Lienhard, 302, 314, 411, 418, 420, 429, 436
Dentan, Robert C., 204, 230, 241, 259
Detweiler, Robert, 173–74, 179, 193
Dever, William G., 6, 22–23, 25, 31, 35n, 36, 38n, 41–42, 48–51, 53n, 54n, 56, 60, 63, 68–69, 82–83, 101, 148, 159
De Vries, B., 42
De Vries, Simon J., 125, 159
Dexinger, Ferdinand, 466–67, 472, 484
Diepold, Peter, 303, 314
Dietrich, Manfred, 76–77, 98, 101, 358
Dietrich, Walter, 303, 314
Díez Macho, Alejandro, 416, 436
Dijk, J. J. A. van, 92, 107, 370–71, 394
Di Lella, Alexander A., 456, 460, 478, 480–81, 485
Dingermann, Friedrich, 468n, 484

Dion, Paul-Eugene, 351, 358
Dommershausen, Werner, 447, 450, 455, 459
Donner, Herbert, 80, 88, 101, 351, 358
Doran, Robert, 184, 197, 457, 462
Dornemann, R. H., 45
Dossin, G., 82, 101
Dothan, M., 32, 37, 42
Dothan, Trude, 37, 41–43, 48
Douglas, Mary, 185–86, 193
Draffkorn-Kilmer, Anne E., 76, 91, 101, 426–27, 436
Dressler, Wolfgang U., 169, 193
Drinan, Robert F., 503
Drioton, Étienne, 94, 102
Driver, G. R.; 78, 102, 411
Driver, S. R., 451, 459
Dryburgh, B., 428, 436
Dubarle, André M., 420, 428, 436, 447, 459
Duhm, B., 424, 432
Dürr, Lorenz, 477, 484
Dussaud, R., 411

Eaton, John H., 219, 230
Ebeling, Erich, 89–90, 102
Edzard, Dietz Otto, 83, 86–87, 102
Eichhorn, Albert, 124, 149, 263
Eichler, Harry L., 76–77, 102
Eichrodt, Walther, 204, 222, 244–45, 247–48, 259
Eissfeldt, Otto, 9, 19, 25, 128–30, 150–51, 159, 230, 277, 289, 299, 300, 307, 314, 343, 348, 358, 428, 446, 450–52, 454, 456, 459
Eitan, A., 43
Ellermeier, Friedrich, 82, 102, 345, 358
Elliger, Karl, 55, 69, 134, 139, 159
Ellis, Peter F., 277–78, 289
Elmslie, William A. L., 306, 314
Emerton, John A., 389, 394, 478, 481, 484
Engnell, Ivan, 130, 159, 204, 218–19, 230, 271, 273, 278, 289, 300, 314, 343, 358, 429–30, 436, 477
Ewald, H., 12

Falkenstein, Adam, 89, 102, 431, 436
Farber-Flügge, Gertrud, 91, 102
Faur, Jose, 385, 394
Fensham, F. Charles, 223, 230
Ferrara, A. J., 90, 102
Feuillet, André, 413, 420, 436
Fichtner, Johannes, 124–25, 129–31, 153, 159, 337, 358, 372, 394
Finet, André, 46, 92, 103
Finkelstein, Jacob J., 56, 69, 83, 89, 92, 103, 106

Finnegan, Ruth, 181, 194
Fischer, Balthasar, 433, 436
Fisher, Loren R., 77, 80, 103, 411
Fitzmyer, Joseph A., 79, 103, 298, 315, 384, 394
Flanagan, James W., 189, 194, 302, 315
Floyd, Michael H., 145, 159
Flusser, David, 472, 484
Fohrer, Georg, 13, 25, 124n, 129, 131, 133-34, 137, 139-40, 146-50, 152-55, 157, 159, 208, 211, 214, 219, 231, 259, 270, 277, 289, 300, 303, 315, 325, 342, 358, 382-83, 385, 394, 413, 428, 436, 451, 460
Fontaine, Carol Rader, 375, 394
Fox, Michael, 214
Fraine, Jean de, 219, 231
Franken, Hendricus J., 35, 38, 45, 46, 69
Franken-Battershill, C. A., 35n, 69
Frankfort, Henri, 91, 103, 202-3, 210, 231
Fraser, James G., 181, 194
Freedman, David Noel, 10, 25, 31, 46, 70, 79-80, 84-85, 101, 103, 129, 136, 159-60, 213, 230-31, 303, 307, 310, 315, 413-17, 423-25, 432, 435-37
Freedman, Nadezhda, 103
Fretheim, Terence E., 129, 131, 153, 160, 372, 394
Freud, S., 382, 425
Freydank, Helmut, 93, 103
Frick, Frank S., 184, 189, 194
Friedrich, Johannes, 222
Fritz, Volkmar, 38, 226-27, 231
Fronzaroli, P., 86
Frost, S. B., 473, 477, 479, 484
Frye, Richard N., 473, 484
Frymer-Kensky, T., 91, 104
Fuerst, Wesley J., 448, 451, 460
Funk, Robert W., 482, 484
Fuss, Werner, 150, 160, 286, 290

Gaber, Pamela, 41
Galling, Kurt, 19, 95, 104, 306-7, 315, 372, 379, 381, 395
Gan, Moshe, 447, 460
Gardiner, Alan H., 94, 104
Garelli, P., 86
Gaster, T. H., 181, 183, 194, 446-48, 460
Gehman, H. S., 303, 318
Gelb, Ignace J., 45, 70, 81, 84-85, 104
Gemser, Berend, 94, 104, 371, 374, 376-77, 395, 430, 437
Geraty, L. T., 36, 41
Gerbracht, Dlether, 387, 395
Gerhardsson, Birger, 343, 359
Gerleman, Gillis, 95, 104, 298, 315, 449-54, 460

Gerstenberger, Erhard, 90, 93, 104, 144, 160, 216, 231, 339-40, 359, 372, 375, 388, 395, 412, 420, 424-25, 427, 429, 432, 437
Gese, Hartmut, 78, 88, 94, 104, 370-71, 379, 381, 383, 395, 411, 429-32, 437, 472-73, 476, 484
Geus, C. H. J., de, 82, 104, 226, 231
Gevirtz, Stanley, 181, 194, 414, 428, 437
Gibson, J. C. L., 78, 104
Gilbert, Maurice, 370, 388, 395
Gilkey, Langdon, 57, 70, 240, 259
Ginsberg, H. L., 19, 78, 80, 105, 205, 231, 414, 437, 480, 484
Gitin, S., 41-42, 48
Glanzman, George S., 451, 455, 460
Glatzer, Nahum N., 384, 395
Globe, Alexander, 430, 437
Glock, Albert E., 31, 60, 70
Glueck, Nelson, 3-6, 25, 56, 70
Goedicke, Hans, 91, 105
Goldingay, J., 437
Good, E. M., 383, 395, 414, 437
Goodenough, Erwin R., 417, 437
Goodwin, Donald Watson, 80, 105
Gordis, Robert, 79, 105, 375, 377, 378, 382-83, 386, 395, 446, 449-54, 460
Gordon, Cyrus H., 9, 25, 76-79, 105, 205, 376, 411
Gordon, Edmund I., 94, 105, 396
Görg, Manfred, 88, 105, 226, 231
Gottlieb, Hans, 412, 438
Gottwald, Norman K., 11-12, 22, 25, 82, 83, 87, 105, 144, 160, 184, 188-89, 194, 215, 232, 270, 290, 351, 359, 412, 423, 425, 429, 432, 438, 503
Gouders, Klaus, 359
Goulder, Michael D., 305, 310, 315
Gowan, Donald, 372, 396
Graf, Karl Heinrich, 124, 275
Gray, George B., 412, 422, 438
Gray, John, 78, 94, 105, 219, 221, 225, 232, 301, 303, 315, 384, 396, 411, 430, 438, 451-54, 460
Grayson, Albert K., 88, 90, 106, 347, 359
Green, Margaret Whitney, 106
Greenberg, Moshe, 8, 25, 76, 87, 106
Greenfield, Jonas C., 70, 206
Greimas, A. J., 169, 173-78, 194
Gressmann, Hugo, 95, 106, 132, 201, 263, 327, 468, 477, 484

Grobel, Kendrick, 125, 129, 131, 136, 153, 160
Grønbaek, J. H., 302, 315
Cröndahl, Franke, 106
Gross, H., 349, 359
Gross, Walter, 170-71, 178, 194
Gülich, Elizabeth, 169, 194
Gunkel, Hermann, 127, 132-33, 136, 149, 183, 201-2, 209, 263-65, 269, 272-76, 290, 327, 336, 338-39, 350, 424, 429, 432, 455, 460, 465-66, 477-79, 485
Gunn, David M., 182, 195, 302, 304, 315
Gunneweg, Antonius H. J., 342-44, 351
Gurney, Oliver R., 89-90, 106
Güterbock, H. G., 90, 106

Habel, Norman, 106, 124n, 129, 131, 160, 340-41, 359, 377, 396
Hachmann, R., 47
Hadidi, Adnan, 38, 44
Hahn, Herbert F., 180, 184, 195
Halbe, Jörn, 430, 438
Haldar, Alfred, 348-49, 359
Hallo, William W., 89, 92, 106-7
Hals, Ronald M., 451, 453-55, 460
Hammer, Raymond, 481, 485
Hammerton-Kelly, R. G., 474, 485
Hammond, P. C., 36
Hanhart, Robert, 16, 26
Hanson, Paul D., 148, 160, 188, 195, 310, 315, 465n, 470-71, 473, 475n, 477, 485
Haran, Menahem, 226, 232
Harding, L., 32
Hardmeier, Christof, 131, 137, 139-40, 160, 359
Harms, Klaus, 354, 359
Harper, R. P., 45
Harrelson, Walter, 356, 503
Harrison, Roland Kenneth, 306, 315
Hartman, Louis F., 456, 460, 478, 480-81, 485
Harvey, Julien, 223, 232, 328, 338, 359
Hasel, Gerhard, 58, 70, 241, 245, 247, 259
Haseldon, Kyle, 503
Haspecker, Josef, 388, 396
Hausen, Adelheid, 384, 396
Hayes, John H., 7, 25, 60, 70, 125, 160, 316, 334, 336, 340, 346, 359
Heaton, E. W., 456-57, 460, 481, 485
Hecker, Karl, 90, 107
Hedinger, Ulrich, 386, 396
Heinrich, E., 45

Heintz, Jean-Georges, 82, 107
Helck, Wolfgang, 87, 107
Held, Moshe, 79-80, 107, 205
Helms, S. W., 44
Hempel, Johannes, 51, 132, 160
Hengel, Martin, 380, 388, 396
Hennessy, J. B., 37, 44
Henry, Marie-Louise, 279, 290,
    334, 360
Hentschke, Richard, 349, 360
Herberg, Will, 492, 503
Herbert, Sharon, 41
Herdner, A., 77-78, 99, 107
Hermann, Alfred, 88, 107
Hermisson, Hans-Jürgen, 373-
    75, 389, 396
Herrmann, Siegfried, 88, 107,
    347, 360
Hertzberg, Hans Wilhelm, 380,
    397, 451, 453, 461
Herzog, Z., 42
Heschel, Abraham, 360, 492, 503
Hesse, Franz, 160, 248, 257-59,
    270, 290, 349, 360
Higgs, E. S., 50n, 52, 68
Hillers, Delbert R., 92-93, 95,
    108, 223, 232, 351, 360, 412,
    420, 429, 438
Hoffner, H. A., Jr., 88, 91, 108
Hoftijzer, J., 108, 249, 259
Holladay, J. S., Jr., 41, 336, 360
Holladay, William L., 420, 438
Holland, T. A., 45
Holm-Nielsen, S., 44, 380, 397
Hölscher, Gustav, 128-29, 136,
    160, 278, 290, 300, 316, 348,
    350, 478, 485
Homan, M. J., 410, 438
Hooke, S. H., 204, 218, 232, 477
Hoonacker, van, A., 18
Horn, Siegfried H., 36, 446, 461
Horst, Friedrich, 125-29, 131,
    153, 160, 341, 360, 412, 438
Horton, Ernest, Jr., 380, 397
Hossfeld, Frank Lothar, 354, 360
Houtman, C., 276, 290
Houwink ten Cate, Ph. H. J., 90,
    108
Huffmon, H. B., 81, 93, 108,
    187, 195, 223, 232, 328, 338,
    346-47, 360
Hulin, P., 89, 106
Humbert, J. B., 44
Hummel, H. D., 79, 108
Humphreys, W. Lee, 372, 397,
    450, 457, 461
Hurvitz, A., 285, 290
Hvidberg, Flemming F., 204,
    232
Hyatt, J. Philip, 268, 290

Ibrahim, Moawiyah, 5, 25, 38,
    44, 45
Imschoot, Paul van, 259
In der Smitten, W. T., 305-6,
    309, 316

Irvin, Dorothy, 183, 195
Irwin, William A., 384, 397

Jackson, Jared J., 135, 160, 169,
    195
Jacob, Edmond, 240, 245, 260,
    388, 397
Jacobsen, Thorkild, 91-92, 108,
    202-3, 216, 233
Jahnow, H., 428
Janssen, Enno, 300, 304, 316
Janzen, Waldemar, 340, 361
Japhet, Sara, 304, 306, 309, 316
Jaroš, K., 283, 291
Jason, Heda, 169, 172, 195
Jellicoe, Sidney, 298, 316
Jenks, A. W., 283, 291
Jenni, Ernst S., 301, 316, 351,
    361
Jensen, Joseph, 372, 397
Jepsen, Alfred, 16-17, 19, 25-26,
    300, 316
Jeremias, Christian, 342, 361,
    476, 485
Jeremias, Jörg, 349, 361
Jobling, David, 177-78, 195,
    304, 316
Johnson, Aubrey R., 220, 233,
    349, 361, 420, 438
Johnson, Marshall D., 307, 316
Jolles, André, 180
Jones, Bruce William, 450, 461
Joüon, P., 451, 454, 461
Jung, Carl G., 386, 397, 425

Kahn, Jack H., 386, 397
Kaiser, Otto, 78, 108, 124n, 129,
    131, 147, 149, 153-54, 161,
    244, 260, 300-303, 316
Kalugila, Leonidas, 370, 397
Kapelrud, Arvid S., 19, 78, 108,
    204, 233, 349, 361, 411
Käsemann, Ernst, 482, 485
Kaufmann, Yehezkel, 19, 205,
    209, 215, 233, 285, 291
Kayatz, Christa, 370, 374, 397
Kayser, Wolfgang, 425, 438
Keck, Leander E., 129, 131, 136,
    153, 161
Keel, Othmar, 95, 109, 386, 397,
    417, 420, 438
Kegler, Jürgen, 389, 397
Keller, Werner, 56, 70
Kellermann, Ulrich, 18, 26,
    305-6, 309, 317
Kelley-Buccellati, M., 46
Kempinski, A., 39n, 42, 70
Kenyon, K. M., 32-35, 37-38,
    40-41, 44, 63, 70
Kessler, Martin, 135, 160, 169,
    195
Khairy, Nabil, 44
Khanjian, J., 370, 397
Kidner, Derek, 378, 397
Kilian, Rudolf, 132-33, 150, 161,
    285, 291

Kirkbride, Diana, 34, 37
Kitchen, Kenneth A., 87, 109
Kittel, R., 17
Klatt, Werner, 202, 233
Klein, Ralph W., 305, 317
Klengel, Evelyn, 87, 109
Klengel, Horst, 86, 109
Klopfenstein, Martin, 381, 398
Knierim, Rolf, 161, 169, 187,
    195, 260, 331
Knight, Douglas A., 146, 161,
    181, 187, 196, 272-73, 275-76,
    291
Knight, George A., 445-46,
    449-50, 461
Knudtzon, J.-A., 87, 109
Knuth, Hans Chr., 433, 438
Koch, Klaus, 124n, 127, 129,
    131-32, 136, 137-43, 146-48,
    150-51, 153-54, 156, 161,
    206-7, 233, 285, 291, 335, 337,
    361, 371, 398, 467, 469, 485
Kochavi, M., 42
Köhler, L., 78, 109, 161, 417
Kolari, E., 426, 439
Kooij, G. Van Der, 45, 108
Korošec, Victor, 222
Kosmala, Hans, 412, 422, 439
Kovacs, Brian Watson, 173, 189,
    191, 196, 375, 398
Kraeling, Carl H., 371, 398
Kramer, Samuel Noah, 90, 94,
    109, 418, 420, 427-28, 439
Kraus, Fritz R., 83, 110
Kraus, Hans-Joachim, 124-25,
    129, 131, 136, 140, 161, 220-
    22, 233, 241, 260, 276, 291,
    330, 362, 413, 420, 429-30,
    433, 439
Krentz, Edgar, 124n, 126, 161
Kroeber, Rudi, 377, 398
Kruger, E. W., 37, 44
Kubina, Veronika, 386, 398
Kuenen, A., 16-17
Kuhl, Curt, 94, 110, 124, 129,
    131, 148, 153, 162
Kühne, H., 46
Kuhr, E., 417
Kümmel, Hans Martin, 110
Kümmel, Werner Georg, 124n,
    129, 149, 161
Kunstmann, Walter G., 90, 110
Kuntz, J. Kenneth, 388, 398
Kunz, L., 414, 439
Kupper, Jean-Robert, 11, 26, 82,
    86, 110
Kurz, Paul K., 410, 433, 439
Kuschke, A., 46
Kutsch, E., 88, 94, 110
Kutscher, R., 90, 110

Labuschagne, C. J., 215, 233
Lack, Rémi, 178, 196
Lacocque, André, 451-52, 454,
    456, 461, 481, 485
Ladd, George E., 476, 485

La Fay, Howard, 84, 110
Lambert, W. G., 76, 88–90, 94–95, 110–11, 347, 359, 370–71, 376, 398
Lance, H. Darrell, 35–36, 63, 69, 71
Lang, Bernhard, 376, 398
Langhe, Robert de, 219, 233
Langlamet, F., 301, 317
Lapointe, Roger, 274, 291
Lapp, Paul W., 3, 11, 26, 31, 34–36, 41–42, 59, 71
Lauha, Aarre, 377, 381, 398
Leach, Edmund, 173–74, 184–86, 196
LeBlanc, Steven A., 72
Lebram, J. C. H., 447–49, 461
Legge, A. J., 50n
Lehmann, Johannes, 111
Lemaire, André, 372, 398
Lemche, Neils Peter, 302, 317
Lemke, W. E., 299, 317
Leonard, A. E., 41
Leslie, Elmer A., 430, 439
Leveen, Jacob, 412, 439
Leveque, Jean, 386, 398
Levine, Baruch, 205, 224–25, 233
Levine, Louis D., 2, 28
Levinson, Stephen, 170, 197
Lévi-Strauss, Claude, 169, 173–75, 177–78, 196
Lévy-Bruhl, Lucien, 184
Lewy, J., 446, 461
Ley, J., 413
Lichtheim, Miriam, 371, 399
Liebreich, Leon J., 423, 439
Liebwitz, H., 41
Limburg, James, 338, 362
Lincoln, C. Eric, 503
Lindblom, Johannes, 337, 350–51, 362, 466, 486
Lipiński, Edouard, 17, 26, 91, 111, 221, 234, 430, 439
Littmann, Enno, 428, 439
Liver, J., 372, 399
Liverani, M., 82, 111
Ljung, Inger, 182, 196
Loader, J. A., 307, 317, 377, 399
Loewenstamm, S. E., 411, 448, 461
Lohfink, Norbert, 129, 134–35, 162, 300, 303–4, 317, 399
Long, Burke O., 92, 111, 181, 187, 196, 269, 291, 317, 341, 352, 362, 428, 439
Longacre, Robert, 169, 170–71, 197
Lord, Albert B., 18–82, 197, 455, 461
Loretz, Oswald, 90, 98, 101, 111, 377, 379–80, 399, 411, 439
Lucas, George R., Jr., 504
Luckmann, Thomas, 354, 470, 483

Lugt, P. van der, 80, 111
Luke, John Tracy, 11, 26, 82–83, 111
Lundquist, John M., 46, 70
Lusseau, H., 447, 461
Lux, Ute, 37, 44
Luyten, J., 388, 399
Lys, Daniel, 428, 439

Maass, F., 38
Mabee, Charles, 145, 162
McCarter, P. Kyle, 302, 317
McCarthy, Dennis J., 93–94, 112, 139, 162, 223, 234, 304, 317
McCreery, D. W., 36
Macdonald, B., 42
McEvenue, Sean E., 285, 291
Machinist, P., 88, 112
Mack, Burton L., 388, 399
McKane, William, 94, 112, 331, 362, 372, 376, 399
McKay, John, 224, 234
McKenzie, John L., 244–45, 256, 260, 372, 399
McKnight, Edgar V., 173, 197
MacLeish, Archibald, 387, 399
Maier, Johann, 226, 234
Maisler, B., 32 (see also Mazar)
Malamat, Abraham, 81–83, 88, 112, 187, 197, 346, 362
Mand, Fritzlothar, 429, 440
Mann, T. W., 89, 112
Mannheim, Karl, 470, 486
Mansoor, Menahem, 411, 440
Marböck, Johann, 380, 388, 399
March, W. E., 335, 362
Margueron, J. Cl., 45
Markert, Ludwig, 339, 362
Martinez, Ernest R., 78, 112
Marzal, Angel, 112, 376, 399
Masson, Emilia, 77, 99
Matthers, J., 46
Matthews, Victor Harold, 82, 112
Matthiae, Paolo, 45, 71, 84, 86, 112
May, Herbert G., 63, 71
Mayer, Werner, 90, 111, 113, 431, 440
Mayes, A. D. H., 13, 26, 226, 234, 284, 291
Mays, James L., 204, 234
Mazar, A., 42, 43
Mazar, Benjamin, 9, 19, 26, 32, 35, 37, 41, 59, 71 (see also Maisler)
Meier, Gerhard, 92, 113
Meinhold, Arndt, 461
Meinhold, Johannes, 327, 447, 450
Melamed, Ezra Z., 80, 113, 423, 440
Melugin, Roy F., 135, 162
Menasee, J. de, 481, 486
Mendelsohn, I., 76, 113

Mendenhall, George E., 11–12, 22, 26, 82, 93, 113, 188, 197, 214–15, 222, 234, 268, 292
Merendino, R. P., 283–84, 292
Meshel, Ze'ev, 65, 71
Mettinger, Trygve, 220, 234, 302, 317
Meyer, Ivo, 354, 360
Meyers, Carol, 41, 66n
Meyers, Eric M., 41–42, 66n, 71
Michaeli, Frank, 306, 317
Michel, Diethelm, 417–18, 440
Middendorp, Th., 380, 388, 399
Miles, John A., 386–87, 399
Milgrom, Jacob, 92, 113, 224, 225, 234
Millar, William R., 474, 477, 486
Millard, Alan R., 90, 111
Miller, J. Maxwell, 4–5, 7, 14, 16–17, 26–27, 42, 60, 70, 125, 160, 227, 235, 270, 300–302, 316
Miller, Patrick D., Jr., 78, 89, 113, 201–2, 208, 213, 222–23, 235, 318
Miranda, José P., 504
Miroschedi, P. de, 44
Miscall, Peter, 175, 197
Miskotte, Kornelis H., 381, 400
Mittmann, Siegfried, 9, 27, 38, 132, 135, 150, 153n, 162, 284, 292, 303, 318
Moltmann, Jürgen, 465, 482, 486
Montgomery, James A., 303, 318, 114, 440, 481, 486
Moor, Johannes C. de, 78, 98, 114, 411, 430, 440
Moore, A. M. T., 45, 79
Moore, Carey A., 446–47, 449–50, 461–62
Moortgat, A., 45
Moran, William L., 81, 87, 91, 114, 223, 346, 363
Morgan, Donn F., 372, 390, 400
Mosis, Rudolph, 306, 310, 318
Mowinckel, Sigmund, 19, 201, 204, 219–21, 235, 273, 286, 292, 305–6, 318, 342–43, 348, 363, 413–14, 418, 420, 424, 427, 429–30, 440, 468, 477, 486
Muilenburg, James, 129, 134–35, 162, 169, 184, 197, 260, 330, 363, 422, 440
Müller, Hans-Peter, 94, 114, 278, 292, 378, 383–84, 400, 428, 440, 457–58, 462, 476–77, 486
Müller, Karlheinz, 474, 486
Muntingh, L. M., 432, 440
Murdock, William R., 473, 479, 486
Murphy, Roland E., 376–77, 382, 388–90, 400, 428, 430, 441
Murray, Donald F., 304, 318

Murtagh, J., 383, 400
Myers, Jacob M., 306–8, 318, 451–52, 455, 462

Na'aman, N., 2, 27
Neher, André, 504
Neiman, David, 385, 400
Neumann, Peter H. A., 348, 354, 363
Newman, B. M., 169, 197
Newmann, Murray, 14, 27
Newsome, James D., Jr., 307, 310, 318
Nicholson, E. W., 284, 292, 304, 318
Nickelsburg, G. W. E., 475n, 486
Niditch, Susan, 184, 197, 462, 480
Niebuhr, H. Richard, 490–92, 504
Niebuhr, Reinhold, 490–92, 504
Nielsen, E., 19, 93, 114
Nielsen, Kirsten, 338, 363
Noetscher, F., 79, 114
Noort, Edward, 82, 114, 346, 363
Norin, Stig I. L., 80, 115
North, Robert, 308, 318, 469, 478, 486
Noth, Martin, 1–2, 7–9, 10–11, 13, 19–23, 27, 41, 44, 55–56, 71, 81, 115, 124, 131, 146, 162, 207–9, 219, 225–26, 235, 265–79, 282–87, 292, 299–301, 303, 305–9, 318, 327, 469, 486
Nougayrol, Jean, 94, 115, 371, 400
Nyberg, H. S., 273, 292, 417

Ogletree, Thomas W., 504
Olávarri, E., 38
Oldenburg, U., 78, 115
Oren, E., 42
Orlinsky, Harry M., 13, 19, 21, 27, 270, 293, 346, 363
Orthmann, W., 46
Osswald, Eva, 354, 363
Osten-Sacken, Peter von der, 469, 476, 478, 486
Otto, Eberhard, 370, 400
Otto, Eckart, 148, 162
Overholt, Thomas W., 187, 197, 352, 354, 363

Page, Stephanie, 27, 88, 115
Pannenberg, Wolfhart, 465, 482, 487
Paris, Peter J., 504
Parker, Judson F., 177–78, 198
Parker, Simon B., 90, 93, 108, 111, 187, 198, 223, 232, 352, 304
Parr, P. J., 34, 44, 46
Parry, Milman, 181–84, 198
Patte, Aline, 198

Patte, Daniel, 174, 177–78, 198, 272, 293
Patton, John H., 89, 115
Paulsen, Henning, 149, 162
Perdue, Leo G., 388, 390, 400, 430, 441
Perlitt, Lothar, 94, 115, 132, 135, 139, 163, 223, 235, 268, 281, 293
Perrot, J., 35, 37, 44
Perry, Ben Edwin, 447, 462
Petersen, David L., 470–71, 477, 487
Petrie, W. M. F., 49
Petschow, H., 115
Pettinato, Giovanni, 83–86, 91, 115, 371, 401
Pfeiffer, Egon, 382, 401
Pfeiffer, Robert H., 445–46, 451, 454, 462
Piaget, Jean, 173, 198
Piatti, P. T., 413, 441
Pitt-Rivers, Julian, 174, 185–86, 198
Ploeg, J. P. M. van der, 384, 401, 430, 441
Plöger, Otto, 310, 318, 375, 401, 474, 487
Podechard, E., 430, 441
Pohlmann, Karl-Friedrich, 298–99, 307, 319
Polzin, Robert, 9, 28, 174–75, 198, 272, 293, 304, 306, 319, 452, 462
Pope, Marvin H., 78, 95, 116, 384, 386, 401, 411–12, 428, 441
Porteous, Norman W., 481, 487
Porter, J. Roy, 297, 300–301, 306, 310, 319
Posener, Georges, 91, 116
Prag, Kay, 44
Prato, Gian Luig, 388, 401
Preuss, Horst Dietrich, 377, 401
Priest, John F., 381, 401
Prignaud, P., 44
Pritchard, James B., 6, 28, 31–32, 34, 36, 46, 59, 71, 95, 116, 401
Propp, Vladimir, 169, 171–172, 174, 176–78, 198, 456, 462
Pury, Albert de, 171, 198

Quell, Gottfried, 354, 364

Rad, Gerhard von, 19–20, 28, 55–57, 71, 94, 116, 129, 136, 180, 204, 208–9, 222, 235, 246–51, 254, 260, 265–74, 276, 278–79, 281–82, 284–86, 293, 300, 302, 319, 327, 328–33, 354, 364, 370, 372, 374, 376, 380–81, 388–89, 401, 433, 441, 469, 474, 478, 487
Radjawane, Arnold Nicolaas, 300, 319

Raible, Wolfgang, 169, 194
Rainey, Anson F., 6, 28, 42, 87, 116, 219, 224, 236
Raitt, Thomas M., 339, 364
Rashid, F., 86
Rasmussen, Larry L., 254–55, 258
Rast, W. E., 41, 163
Rauber, D. F., 453–55, 462
Reagan, Charles, 198
Redman, Charles L., 53n, 72
Reese, J. M., 388, 401–2
Rehm, Martin, 308, 319
Reiner, Erica, 92, 116
Reitzenstein, Richard, 479, 487
Rendtorff, Rolf, 129–33, 136, 139, 153, 155, 163, 206–7, 225, 236, 249, 256, 260, 271, 274–75, 281, 285–87, 294, 302, 319, 331, 333, 336, 348–49, 364
Reuss, Eduard, 275
Reventlow, Henning Graf, 130, 163, 285, 294, 349, 364, 420, 441
Richards, Kent Harold, 305, 319
Richter, Heinz, 383, 386, 402
Richter, Wolfgang, 127–29, 131, 133, 137, 139–40, 146–47, 150–51, 153–56, 163, 168–70, 199, 268, 279, 294, 301, 320, 375, 402
Rickenbacher, Otto, 388, 402
Ricoeur, Paul, 168–69, 179–80, 189–90, 199, 388, 504
Ridderbos, Nicolaus H., 412–14, 420–23, 429, 441
Riemann, P. A., 94, 116
Rietzschel, Claus, 150, 163
Ringgren, Helmer, 208, 214, 220, 236, 420, 433, 441, 446–47, 449, 462, 466, 479, 487
Roberts, J. J. M., 88–89, 92, 94, 113, 116, 222, 235, 302, 318, 387, 402
Robertson, David A., 79, 117, 126–28, 131, 136, 163, 169, 199, 213, 236, 383, 386–87, 402, 417, 441
Robinson, Theodore H., 412–13, 441
Rogerson, J. W., 174, 179–80, 184, 199
Rohland, Edzard, 332, 364
Römer, Willem H. Ph., 117
Rose, G. L., 41
Rose, Martin, 216, 236
Rosenzweig, F., 422, 435
Ross, James F., 347, 365, 388, 402
Rossum, J. van, 301, 320
Rost, Leonhard, 268, 294, 302, 320
Roth, Wolfgang M. W., 178, 199, 372, 402
Rothenberg, Geno, 6, 28

Rowley, H. H., 18-19, 28, 75, 320, 349-50, 354, 365, 451-53, 462, 466n, 472, 476, 479, 481-82, 487
Rowton, M. B., 11, 28, 82-83, 117
Rudolph, Wilhelm, 280, 282-83, 294-95, 299, 305-6, 310, 320, 344, 345, 365, 413, 428, 441, 451, 453-54, 462
Ruether, Rosemary R., 504
Rüger, H. P., 388, 402
Russell, D. S., 466, 482, 487
Russell, Letty, 494, 504
Rylaarsdam, J. Coert, 373, 389, 402

Sabloff, Jeremy A., 49-50, 53, 73
Sabourin, Leopold, 420, 442
Saebø, Magne, 148, 163
Saggs, H. W. F., 96, 117
Saideh, Roger, 47
Sandeen, Ernest R., 504
Sanders, James A., 252, 260, 287, 294, 298, 320, 355, 364, 402, 410, 442
Sanders, Paul S., 384, 402
Sandmel, Samuel, 280, 294, 388, 403, 450-51, 462
Sarna, Nahum, 205, 382, 403
Sasson, Jack M., 83, 117, 171, 199, 456, 463
Sauer, James A., 5, 23, 28, 36, 42, 45, 48, 72, 365
Saydon, Pierre P., 415 16, 442
Scaltriti, G., 385, 403
Schaeffer, Claude F. A., 77, 117
Schaub, R. T., 41
Schedl, Claus, 446, 448, 463
Schicklberger, Franz, 302, 320
Schiffer, Michael B., 52-53, 72
Schmid, Hans H., 94, 117, 132, 163, 271, 274, 281, 287, 294, 370-71, 373, 389, 403
Schmidt, Johannes, 374, 403
Schmidt, Johann M., 465n, 476, 487
Schmidt, Ludwig, 279, 294
Schmidt, Werner H., 78, 117, 133, 163, 208, 212, 214, 236, 334, 365
Schmithals, Walter, 466-67n, 479, 487
Schmitt, Hans-Christoph, 283, 294, 303, 320
Schmitt, Rainer, 226, 236
Schmökel, Hartmut, 95, 117, 420, 427, 428, 442
Schmuttermayr, Georg, 412, 442
Schneekloth, I. G., 412, 433, 442
Schneider, B., 449, 463
Schramm, Wolfgang, 88, 118
Schreiner, Josef, 466, 487
Schulte, Hannelis, 129, 132, 134, 164, 269, 278, 294, 301, 320

Schunck, Klaus-Dietrich, 468, 487
Schweizer, Harald, 170, 199
Sciadini, Patrício, 433, 442
Scott, R. B. Y., 375-77, 389, 403
Searle, J. R., 178
Segal, Dimitri, 169, 195
Segal, Moses H., 428, 442
Seger, J. D., 22-23, 36, 41-42
Segert, Stanislav, 413, 442
Seierstad, Ivar P., 350, 365
Seitz, Gottfried, 151, 164, 283-84, 295
Sekine, Masao, 386, 403
Sellin, Ernst, 428
Seux, Marie-Joseph, 90, 118, 431, 442
Seybold, Klaus, 334, 365, 421, 427, 429, 442
Shanks, Hershel, 86, 118
Shannon, Thomas, 504
Sheehan, John F. X., 455, 463
Shenkel, James Donald, 16, 28
Sheppard, Gerry T., 378, 388, 403
Shiloh, Yigael, 5, 28, 43
Sievers, E., 413
Simon, Neil, 387, 403
Simpson, Cuthbert A., 277-78, 295, 301, 320
Simpson, William Kelly, 371, 403
Sjöberg, A. W., 94, 118
Skaftymov, A., 172
Skaist, A., 77, 118
Skehan, Patrick W., 375, 380, 404, 414, 430, 442
Skladny, Udo, 374-75, 404
Sleeper, C. Freeman, 504
Smalley, William A., 170, 199, 356, 365
Smend, Rudolf, 244, 280, 275, 277, 295, 303, 320
Smith, Clyde Curry, 123, 164
Smith, D. E., 404
Smith, Morton, 18, 29, 144, 164
Smith, R. H., 36, 44
Smith, Sidney, 75, 118
Smith, W. Robertson, 184
Snaith, Norman Henry, 297, 301, 321
Soden, Wolfram von, 89, 91, 102, 118, 279, 295, 383, 385, 404, 431, 436
Soggin, J. Alberto, 56, 72, 300-301, 304, 321, 429-30, 442
Sollberger, E., 86
Spalinger, A. J., 88, 95, 118
Speiser, E. A., 76-77, 118
Spriggs, D. G., 247, 261
Stager, L. E., 41
Stählin, W., 56, 72
Staiger, Emil, 416, 443
Stanner, W. E. H., 471, 488
Starkey, John L., 6, 29
Stauder, Wilhelm, 426, 443

Steck, Karl Gerhard, 164
Steck, Odil Hannes, 124, 129, 131, 130, 137, 130 40, 116 18, 150-55, 158, 164, 303, 321, 331, 335, 365, 470, 471, 488
Steinmann, Jean, 481, 488
Stekelis, M., 37
Stendahl, Krister, 57, 72, 203-4, 236, 241-42, 261
Stern, Ephraim, 43, 63, 68
Stewart, David, 198
Stiehl, Ruth, 445-47, 463
Stinespring, William Franklin, 310, 321
Stoebe, Hans Joachim, 302, 321
Strange, J. F., 41, 66n, 71
Striedl, Hans, 445, 463
Strommenger, Eva, 46
Stucky, R., 46
Stuhlmueller, Carroll, 477, 488
Sukenik, Eleazar L., 411, 443
Szlechter, Emile, 119
Sznycer, Maurice, 78, 99

Tadmor, Hayim, 19, 88, 119
Talmon, Shemaryahu, 299, 304-5, 321, 372, 404, 446-47, 449-50, 453, 456, 463
Talmon, Yonina, 471, 488
Taylor, W. S., 386, 404
Tell, Safwan, 44
Tengström, Sven, 287, 295
Terrien, Samuel, 245-46, 261, 337, 365, 372, 386-87, 404
Thieberger, Frederic, 419, 443
Thiel, Winfried, 150, 164
Thiele, Edwin R., 15-16, 29
Thomas, D. Winton, 63, 72, 95, 119
Thompson, Dorothy, 452-53, 463
Thompson, Stith, 183-84, 199, 457-58
Thompson, Thomas L., 9, 29, 58, 72, 76, 83, 119, 148, 164, 270, 280, 295, 452-53, 463
Thrupp, Sylvia L., 471, 488
Tillich, Paul, 491-92
Tocci, Franco Michelini, 119
Todorov, T., 175
Toombs, L. E., 34, 41
Topel, L. John, 504
Torrey, C. C., 309, 449, 463
Tournay, R., 383, 404
Trible, Phyllis, 372, 404, 430, 432, 443, 453, 455, 463, 494, 504
Troeltsch, Ernst, 263, 470, 488
Tsevat, Matitiahu, 88, 119, 205, 384, 404
Tucker, Gene M., 8, 29, 129, 131, 137, 153, 161, 164, 335-36, 341, 344, 365
Tufnell, Olga, 6, 29
Turner, Victor W., 432, 443
Tur-Sinai, Naftali H., 429, 443

Tushingham, A. D., 63, 68

Ullendorff, Edward, 85, 119
Ulrich, Eugene C., 298, 321
Ungnad, A., 446, 463
Urbach, Ephraim E., 375, 404
Urbrock, William J., 181-82, 199
Ussishkin, D., 42
Utzschneider, Helmut, 354, 366

Van Loon, M., 45, 46
Van Seters, John, 8, 10, 29, 77,
83, 119, 132, 148, 164, 183,
199, 213, 236, 269-74, 280-83,
286-87, 295, 302, 321
Vantoura, Suzanne H., 426, 443
Vatke, Wilhelm, 209
Vaught, Patrick, 228, 236
Vaux, Roland de, 8, 19, 29, 32,
35, 41, 44, 56, 59, 67, 72, 76,
81, 87, 120, 184, 200, 226,
236, 248, 261, 301, 321
Vawter, Bruce, 404, 468, 473-
74, 488
Veijola, Timo, 302-3, 322
Vesco, Jean-Luc, 451-52, 455,
463
Vielhauer, Philipp, 466-67, 473,
478, 488
Vink, J. G. 285, 295
Virolleaud, Charles, 77, 120, 411
Vita-Finzi, C., 50n
Vogel, Eleanor K., 63, 72
Volten, Aksel, 370, 405
Volz, Paul, 280, 282-83, 295
Vorländer, Hermann, 216, 237,
433, 443
Vriezen, Th. C., 208, 212, 237,
261

Wagner, Norman E., 167, 200,
280, 295
Waldow, H. Eberhard von, 338,
366
Walker, Anita, 41
Walters, Stanley D., 345, 366
Waltke, Bruce K., 11, 29
Wanke, Gunther, 150, 164, 339,
366, 430, 443
Warmuth, Georg, 339, 366
Warren, Austin, 135, 165, 425,
444
Watson, Patty J., 51, 53n, 72
Watters, William R., 181, 200,
414, 443
Weber, Max, 351, 470, 488
Webley, D., 50n
Weidner, E. F., 222
Weimar, Peter, 132, 151, 153n,
155, 164
Weinberg, S. S., 41

Weinfeld, Moshe, 94, 120, 284,
295, 304, 322, 372, 405
Weippert, Manfred, 4, 10, 29,
38, 58, 72, 83, 120, 304, 322
Weir, C. J. Mullo, 418, 443
Weiser, Artur, 220-22, 237, 300,
303, 322, 427, 429-30, 443,
450, 454, 463, 489, 505
Weiss, H., 46
Weiss, Meir, 135, 165, 416, 420,
422, 425, 443
Weitzman, Michael, 84, 98
Welch, Adam Cleghorn, 306,
322
Wellek, Rene, 135, 165, 425, 444
Wellhausen, Julius, 94, 124, 128,
130, 136n, 165, 208-10, 213,
215, 223, 264-65, 271, 275-76,
279, 282, 295, 326-28, 331,
432
Welten, Peter, 306-8, 310, 322
Wendel, François, 371, 405
Werner, Eric, 426-27, 444
Westenholz, A., 217, 237
Westermann, Claus, 141, 165,
207-8, 216, 237, 249, 250, 261,
328, 335-37, 339, 345, 383,
405, 429, 432-33, 444, 473n,
488
Wette, W. M. L. de, 284, 366
Whallon, William, 181, 200,
414, 444
Wharton, James A., 150, 165
Whedbee, J. William, 337, 366,
372, 386-87, 405
Wheeler, Robert E. M., 33-35,
38n, 73
Whitaker, Richard E., 77, 120
White, Hugh C., 178, 200
White, John B., 95, 120, 428, 444
Whitley, Charles F., 17, 30, 335,
366, 380, 405
Whybray, R. Norman, 281, 302,
322, 369, 372-73, 375-76, 378,
381, 389, 405
Widengren, Geo, 204, 218-19,
237, 366, 420, 429, 430, 444
Wifall, Walter R., 16, 30
Wildberger, Hans, 334, 366
Wilhelm, G., 87, 120
Willey, Gordon R., 49-50, 53, 73
Willi, Thomas, 299, 306, 310,
322
Williams, James G., 351-52,
366, 378, 381-82, 386-87, 390,
405
Williams, N. D., 419, 444
Williams, Ronald J., 94-95, 120,
383, 389, 405-6
Williamson, Hugh G. M.,
298-99, 306-7, 309-10, 322

Willis, John T., 414, 444
Wilson, Robert R., 83, 92, 120,
144, 165, 183-84, 186-87,
189-90, 200, 336, 348, 353,
366
Winnett, Frederick V., 32, 213,
274, 279-83, 286-87, 296
Winston, David, 388, 406
Wiseman, Donald J., 3, 30, 63,
73, 76, 87, 120
Wittig, Susan, 183, 200
Witzenrath, Hagia, 381, 406
Wolf, Herbert Marlin, 88, 121
Wolff, Hans Walter, 136, 165,
249-50, 261, 270, 279, 283,
288, 296, 300, 304, 322, 325,
333, 337, 338-39, 344-45,
349-50, 367, 372, 406, 429,
444
Wood, Leon James, 21, 30
Worrell, J., 41
Worsley, Peter, 471, 488
Woude, A. S. van der, 269, 296,
384, 401
Wrede, Wilhelm, 263
Wright, Addison D. G., 379,
406, 447, 463
Wright, G. Ernest, 19-20,
30-31, 34-36, 41, 53-54, 59-
61, 69, 73-74, 76, 202-5, 212,
222-23, 237, 242-43, 247, 262,
505
Wright, G. R. H., 34-35, 74
Würthwein, Ernst, 302-3, 323,
328-29, 338, 367, 376, 406,
428, 444-45, 447, 449, 451,
453-54, 463
Wyatt, Nicholas, 304, 323

Yadin, Yigael, 4, 5, 30, 35-37,
41, 388, 406
Yaron, Reuven, 92, 121
Yassine, Khair, 44-45
Yeivin, S., 35
Yoder, John Harold, 505
Yoder, P. B., 181, 200
Young, Edward Joseph, 306, 323

Zaba, Z., 371, 406
Zaborski, Andrzej, 168, 200
Zayidine, Fawzi, 38, 44
Zenger, Erich, 131-32, 151, 165
Zerafa, Peter Paul, 382, 406
Zhitlowsky, Chaim, 387, 406
Zijl, Peter J. van, 78, 121
Zimmerli, Walther, 218, 237,
245-46, 249, 262, 327, 329,
341, 344, 367, 373, 377, 381,
406-7, 505
Zimmermann, Frank, 380, 382,
407